Thomas Jefferson's Image
of New England

Thomas Jefferson's Image of New England

*Nationalism Versus Sectionalism
in the Young Republic*

ARTHUR SCHERR

McFarland & Company, Inc., Publishers
Jefferson, North Carolina

LIBRARY OF CONGRESS CATALOGUING-IN-PUBLICATION DATA

Names: Scherr, Arthur, 1951– author.
Title: Thomas Jefferson's image of New England : nationalism versus
sectionalism in the young republic / Arthur Scherr.
Description: Jefferson, North Carolina : McFarland & Company, Inc.,
Publishers, 2016. | Includes bibliographical references and index.
Identifiers: LCCN 2016029438 | ISBN 9780786475377 (softcover : acid
free paper) ∞
Subjects: LCSH: Jefferson, Thomas, 1743–1826—Political
and social views. | Jefferson, Thomas, 1743–1826—Philosophy. |
Nationalism—United States—History—19th century. | New England—
Relations—Southern States. | Southern States—Relations—New England. |
Political culture—United States—History. | New England—Civilization.
Classification: LCC E332.2 .S34 2016 | DDC 974/.03—dc23
LC record available at https://lccn.loc.gov/2016029438

BRITISH LIBRARY CATALOGUING DATA ARE AVAILABLE

ISBN (print) 978-0-7864-7537-7
ISBN (ebook) 978-1-4766-2621-5

Front cover image of Thomas Jefferson by Thomas Sully,
oil on canvas, 1856 (U.S. Senate)
background map of New England © 2016 iStock

Printed in the United States of America

McFarland & Company, Inc., Publishers
Box 611, Jefferson, North Carolina 28640
www.mcfarlandpub.com

Table of Contents

Preface

Throughout his political career, Thomas Jefferson confronted a paradox he could never resolve. He regarded the New England states (generally defined as present-day Maine, New Hampshire, Vermont, Massachusetts, Connecticut, and Rhode Island), especially Massachusetts and Connecticut, as epitomizing local democratic and republican government. Embodied in their town meetings, this was the political structure he most admired. If he could have had his way, he would have had it adopted by Virginia and all the other states in the Union. Moreover, during the 1760s, Massachusetts, guided by James Otis and Samuel and John Adams, took the lead in the resistance to British measures infringing on colonial rights of self-government and taxation that led to the American Revolution and independence from Great Britain, an outcome that created the first modern republic and the first formerly colonial nation-state.

At the same time, Jefferson perceived the New England states as the most fervent opponents of his political party, the Democratic-Republicans. Despite their steady democratic habits, their voters tended to select conservative political regimes that upheld restrictive suffrages, established churches, and limited the rights of minorities. Most appallingly, in Jefferson's view, politicians from these same states, including his old friend John Adams, as second president of the United States during the late 1790s, had favored policies of fiscal nationalism and a closer relationship with England than with the Revolutionary ally, France. As members of the Federalist Party, they threatened the constitutional guarantees of freedom of speech and press embodied in the First Amendment to the Constitution. And, when Jefferson and his colleague James Madison finally gained control of the national government in 1801, these same New England Federalists, especially in Massachusetts and Connecticut, pursued ultimately abortive measures designed to promote their states' secession from the Union, both in 1804 and 1808. Even worse, during the War of 1812, when the democratic republic to whose construction Jefferson had devoted his life, and which New England leaders had played a vital role in creating, was in danger of succumbing to British armed might and renewed control by the former mother country, the New England states not only refused to help the rest of the Union but once again planned for secession and a possible alliance with the British against their brothers.

In endorsing New England as a great component part of the Union, despite its people's failure to vote for him and their seeming attachment to "monarchical" (Federalist) elements, Jefferson revealed his own devotion to American nationhood and permanence. He invariably asserted that the vast majority of New Englanders, the masses of the people, actually favored republicanism and were committed to the Union. The problem was, they had been hood-winked by their "incurable" anti-democratic leaders, the Merchants, Planters, and River Gods of lore, to feel an affinity for the British Mother Country and a distrust for anarchical, "Jacobinical" France and the Democratic-Republicans, who were supposedly the subversive agents of French Revolutionary Terror.

Nonetheless, during his presidency and its aftermath, the War of 1812, Jefferson insisted that the people of New England, particularly Massachusetts, were devoted to the Union despite their failure to assist the war effort and some fugitive overtures their governments made toward a separate peace with Britain. He reaffirmed his nationalist vision, of which New England was an essential part, continuously in the years after the War of 1812, until his death. By that time, the crisis over slavery in the territories aroused his greatest fears. He was relieved that several New England politicians were willing to accept the Missouri Compromise, and happy when the old ideological contest of states' rights versus consolidation replaced the dispute over the extension of slavery, which he presciently regarded as more dangerous to the preservation of American nationhood.

Jefferson's religious sympathies and antipathies were best evoked by the divergent religious faiths that most vigorously sprouted in New England: Timothy Dwight and Lyman Beecher's Presbyterianism, and William Ellery Channing's Unitarianism. Jefferson's lifelong admiration for New England's town-meeting form of direct democracy, which he considered the ideal form of government, most convincingly demonstrated his love for the region. On a more personal note, Jefferson displayed his confidence in New Englanders' republicanism by his end-of-life friendship with John Adams, and perhaps even more so when he offered several young New England scholars professorships at his brainchild, the University of Virginia.

As a final testimony to his affection for New England and his admiration for its renunciation of human slavery, Jefferson enthusiastically endorsed his favorite grand-daughter Ellen's marriage to Joseph Coolidge, a Boston businessman. Jefferson sadly agreed with her opinion that the absence of the "hideous evil" of bondage from Massachusetts might make it a better place to bring up children than Virginia, despite his love for his home state's beauty and his "little mountain" Monticello's salubrious climate.

Brief portions of *Thomas Jefferson's Image of New England* have earlier appeared, and its argument is foreshadowed, in two of my articles in scholarly journals: "Thomas Jefferson's Nationalist Vision of New England and the War of 1812," in *The Historian: A Journal of History*, 69, no. 1 (Spring 2007): 1–35; and "'The Most Agreeable Country': New Light on Democratic-Republican Opinion of Massachusetts in the 1790s," in *Historical Journal of Massachusetts* 35, no. 2 (Summer 2007): 148–166. I would also like to thank the prominent, distinguished young historian David Waldstreicher for reading and commenting on an earlier version of the manuscript. I alone am responsible for any errors.

Except when specifically mentioned or when necessary to make quotations understandable, I have tried to retain the original spelling and punctuation of Jefferson and his correspondents, including Jefferson's habitual spelling of "its" as "it's." This structure was not unique to him in those days before *Webster's Dictionary* and the development of uniform orthography and calligraphy.

Introduction

For the better part of the past two centuries, Thomas Jefferson has stood for American nationalism. Even in the depths of the Civil War, Abraham Lincoln and his fledgling Republican Party enthusiastically recruited his memory and reputation to the cause of Union and slave emancipation.[1] However, in recent years the image of Jefferson the nationalist has been tarnished and the perception of him as a states' righter who put Southern, and particularly Virginian interests, first and national well-being second has gained increasing ascendancy among Jefferson scholars.[2]

At the head of this stream of books on Jefferson, one of the most prominent, Peter Onuf's *Jefferson's Empire: The Language of American Nationhood* (University of Virginia Press, 2000), examines the third president's torment surrounding issues of nationhood during his last years. Most reviewers praised the book as a valuable contribution to an understanding of Jefferson's political psychology.[3] Onuf, former Thomas Jefferson Foundation Professor of History at the University of Virginia, argues that, from his quest for the presidency in the 1790s until he died in 1826, Jefferson regarded his Federalist opponents, in their diverse guises, as traitors to America's federal republican union and his quest for "affection" between its different regions. Virtual "foreigners" whose goal was to sunder the nation and return to England's monarchical rule, these "consolidationists" sought to obliterate states' rights. Especially in the case of diehard Federalist New England, Jefferson dreaded that his opponents intended to "inevitably ... dissolve the union and so enable the 'Hartford nation' to enter into alliance with like-minded Europeans." In Jefferson's opinion, the section's leaders were guilty of attempting to prevent his rightful election to the presidency in 1801; smuggling in opposition to the Embargo Act (1807–1809); and conspiring at the Hartford Convention in December 1814 to secede from the Union, and later during the Missouri Controversy to prevent the admission of any future slave states.[4]

In Onuf's interpretation, Jefferson was convinced that the New England states, especially Massachusetts and Connecticut, plotted against his political future and thus the republic's survival. Especially during the War of 1812, he thought that the republic's self-defense dictated that the rest of the Union, led by Virginia, militarily obliterate—"destroy"—New England, thereby thwarting its royalist scheme for a servile return to the British Empire that would endanger the rest of the states. After suffering as colonies under the selfish dominion of the British transatlantic "metropolis," in Jefferson's projected, ethnocentric republican empire the states and their (white) citizens would be free to enjoy life, liberty, and the pursuit of happiness. As president, Onuf argues, Jefferson felt that his efforts to create such an amicable,

[handwritten marginal note: Jefferson nationalist vs. Jefferson state rights]

3

voluntary federal republic, with every state a contented, equal partner in a "republican empire" had been thwarted by Burrites (supporters of Aaron Burr's secessionist schemes, among whom were Federalists who favored his candidacy for governor of New York in 1804) and New England Federalist obstructionists. As Onuf depicts Jefferson's disingenuously benign guiding principle, "In sharp contrast to Old World regimes, the independence and prosperity of the new republican empire did not depend on the massive concentration of coercive force but rather on ties of affectionate union and harmonious interest."[5]

According to Onuf, Jefferson belied his ostensibly benevolent intentions by insisting that the states play by *his* rules. Only if they adopted Jeffersonian Republican political economy and foreign policy and elected Jefferson and his friends to public office could they consummate a fraternal egalitarian union. The ties between the American states would replace the link between the colonies and Great Britain. Emerging from the provincial, localist "periphery," Jefferson abhorred aristocrats and monarchist minions of the Mother Country's grasping, centralizing "metropolis" and was determined to prevent their return to power. He intended to distribute the pie of national prosperity among the states with his native Virginia as impresario and *primus inter pares*. As Onuf perceives Jefferson's mindset, the Virginian was confident that his state, in compensation for surrendering much of its colonial-charter territory to the new national government and sister states, deserved "boundless opportunity" as the natural leader of the new "republican empire" whose independence he proclaimed in 1776. Ostensibly, Jefferson regarded the expansive new nation as a field for Virginia's power, in essence Virginia writ large: "For Jefferson, Virginia's future and America's were inextricable, even indistinguishable…. Making Virginia smaller only made sense to the patriotic Jefferson to the extent that it could freely exploit its advantageous situation in an ever larger, more perfect republican union."[6]

Seeking "free trade in a more perfect republican empire" lacking an inimical "center, or dominant metropolis" like the old London-dominated colonial regime, Jefferson upheld an agrarian ideal. To him, cities were analogous to the British monarchical metropolis that had disdained American farmers' virtuous "independence." In Onuf's interpretation, Jefferson considered cities, in England or America, as cauldrons of corruption that engendered inferior, machine-like inhabitants, chained to monarchical servility and incapable of thinking like republicans: "His profound aversion to the old imperial regime and the degrading dependency and subordination that it supposedly entailed provided the animus for his assault on cities and celebration of agrarian virtue."[7] Foreign citizens and foreign agents who plotted to return the United States to the womb of the London-centered "metropolis" threatened the new republican empire's harmony.

With their commerce and industry and attempts to dominate the naive countryside, cities emulated Britain's "metropolitan" dominance, despised by Jefferson. He particularly hated relatively "urbanized" New England, Onuf asserts, which for him embodied the threatened renewed subjugation of the farmer to the merchants, financiers and industrialists of Old England. In the scenario depicted by Onuf, Jefferson (ignoring the fact that most New Englanders were farmers?) was pathologically convinced that, in choosing to follow the British example, "many nominal republicans seemed all too prepared to accommodate to and prosper from the insidious form of metropolitan power that threatened to subvert American independence and reverse the outcome of the Revolution."[8]

When men from other parties and other sections of the union disagreed with Jefferson and his party, Onuf observes, he automatically assumed they were malevolent representatives of the foreign, monarchical "metropolis," Great Britain. Particularly "in times of crisis Jefferson and his coadjutors could imagine that the revival of metropolitan influence and monarchical sentiment had led to the gangrenous corruption of a geographically defined portion of the Union": New England. Jefferson likely thought that the virtue of many Americans had declined as a result of insidious British "metropolitan" influence," a "possibility [that] cast a darkening shadow over the Republican opposition to the High Federalist ascendancy in the late 1790s," Onuf points out. However, he asserts that Jefferson had one part of the republic especially in mind—New England—and that section had to be *destroyed*. With its commercial economy, dominated by "alien" British merchants and financiers, the region was the antithesis of his homogeneous ideal of the freehold farmer. In addition, Onuf contends, the Jeffersonians— erstwhile "friends of the people"—wanted someone to blame for their political defeats: "Republicans attributed their eroding position in the 1790s to insidious alien influences that penetrated the countryside through systems of commerce and credit."[9] It therefore followed that Jefferson regarded the Federalist bastion of Connecticut as an especially dangerous "foreign country" that threatened Southern (and Jeffersonian) supremacy.[10]

After the victory of 1800, Onuf contends, Jefferson felt his view vindicated that the Federalists were "sectionalists who sought to destroy the union and forge an alliance with their secret British sponsors." By the end of his glorious first term, Jefferson was confident that the Federalist Party had been demolished. However, the unpopularity of the War of 1812 in New England "gave them a new lease on life," as Onuf puts it. "As a result, Jefferson began to imagine a more sanguinary, less principled sort of 'combat' against his old Federalist foes."[11]

Late in life, after witnessing New England Federalist obstructionism during the Embargo, War of 1812, and Missouri crises, Jefferson, Onuf asserts, abandoned his conviction that the majority of New Englanders were good citizens, who had merely been deluded by a few bad leaders. In Onuf's perspective, the elderly Jefferson truculently desired a war of extermination against innocent citizens that he perceived as his country's enemies—"sores" on the body politic. During both the War of 1812 and the Missouri crisis, Jefferson imagined, New England leaders expounded anti-republican and monarchical precepts, clamored for their section's secession, and favored "foreign alliances" with the British. Although lacking evidence, Onuf starkly asserts, after distorting some phrases in a few of Jefferson's letters, "In 1813 and 1814 he welcomed a war with the New England Federalists that he knew the loyal Republican states would easily win." He perceived national carnage as the inevitable solution to the threat of "monarchical corruption." Traumatized by the calling of the Hartford Convention during the nadir of American fortunes in the War of 1812 climaxed by the British army's burning of the White House, Jefferson feared the conference presaged a request by New England Federalists for European help to fulfill their secessionist goals. But Onuf fails to demonstrate that Jefferson believed the New England states would secede. He merely refers to an article by historian Robert Shalhope to verify "TJ's animus toward New England," but that work does not depict Jefferson as hostile to the people of the region.[12]

Melodramatically distorting the content of a letter from Jefferson to James Martin, dated 20 September 1813, Onuf claims that Jefferson warned that the "High Federalist" leaders intended to maneuver New England's withdrawal from the union. Consequently, the old man from Monticello hankered to obliterate a nest of rebellious monarchists: "Such men deserved to be destroyed, and Jefferson reveled in the prospect: a temporary Europeanization of American politics would lead to the Union's ultimate perfection–the elimination of all foreign influences." According to Onuf's perception of Jefferson's stance, after a civil war in which Virginia and her allies among the states, duplicating the "European" violence of wars of national unification, devastated New England's towns (many of whose citizens would flee to more "democratic" states), he predicted the wayward Puritans would return humbly to the Union.[13]

In the aftermath of the Treaty of Ghent and the national euphoria induced by military successes in the War of 1812, Jefferson temporarily calmed down, confident that domestic metropolitan monarchists had been obliterated. Soon enough, however, when the problem of slavery in the incoming state of Missouri in 1819–1820 arose, Jefferson again grew alarmed. Contrary to his earlier desire to "destroy" New England in order to convert it to his model, he now insisted that a state's neighbors had no right to dictate its internal affairs, particularly with respect to the institution of slavery.[14]

To a certain degree, Onuf emulated Leonard W. Levy's point of view in his classic, *Jefferson and Civil Liberties: The Darker Side* (1963). Onuf charged that Jefferson, with a trace of intolerance belying his reputation as a humanistic libertarian, perceived New England Federalists as "traitors" to the republic, mainly because they had criticized his policies, violated his Embargo Act, and failed to support the war effort after 1812. Jefferson even suspected that they were eager to request to become British colonies once again, especially during sessions of the abortive Hartford Convention in December 1814. A few years after the war's end, congressional Federalists (especially from New York and Pennsylvania, with substantial Republican support) tried to abolish slavery in the Louisiana Purchase during the debate over Missouri's admission to the Union in 1819–1820, reviving Jefferson's "boundless hatred for his northern enemies."[15] Obsessed with the voluntary nature of each state's participation in the union, a characteristic that distinguished it from monarchy, Jefferson, Onuf argues, now insisted that no state, including slave-holding Missouri, should be bullied in its internal concerns in any way by the evil "metropolitan" unit: the national government, which could legitimately conduct only foreign affairs. Amid the party arguments of the 1790s between national allegiance to France versus allegiance to Britain spanning the Wars of the French Revolution, the Embargo Crisis and the War of 1812 over a decade later, and finally the dispute over Missouri's admission as a slave state, Jefferson perceived anti-republican, "foreign influences" at work that intolerably challenged his will and would pervert America's happy Union into conflicting sectional fragments like the separate nations of Europe. Once more, Onuf notes, Jefferson felt "an irrepressible animus against his Yankee tormentors."[16]

As Onuf explains with regard to the final episode of Missouri, "Jefferson was convinced that securing the sovereignty and equality of the respective states–for him, the central issue of the Missouri controversy–was the essential condition for guaranteeing republican government and promoting a durable union."[17] Ironically, this is the exact opposite of Onuf's depiction of Jefferson's convictions only a few years earlier, when he was determined on the "destruction" of New England for failing to join the rest of the Union in fighting the British.

Despite the validity of some of Onuf's observations, such as his assertion that Jefferson suspected the loyalty to the Union of those New England Federalists who attended the Hartford Convention, for the most part Jefferson had confidence in the patriotism and integrity of the vast majority of New England's citizens. For most of his life, Jefferson regarded New Englanders as at least as much devoted to representative democracy as the citizens of the other states of the Union. He generally considered them potential recruits to his democratic ideology and his Democratic-Republican Party. However, most of Onuf's work distorts Jefferson's actual views and policies.

Onuf's thesis that Jefferson sought Virginia's hegemony within the Union and intended to quell New England opposition by force, convinced that it was a "foreign" entity, has received surprisingly little specific scholarly affirmation. It is incorporated into Joseph A. Fry's brief survey, *Dixie Looks Abroad: The South and U.S. Foreign Relations, 1789–1973* (Louisiana State University Press, 2002), and indirectly in Brian Steele's 2008 article in the *Journal of Southern History*. Another recent work, Elizabeth Varon's general survey, *Disunion!*, unquestioningly accepts Onuf's thesis that Jefferson hated New England. Unfortunately, Varon's discussion of Jefferson's view of sectionalism is based exclusively on Onuf's book, without delving into any other secondary sources and avoiding examination of Jefferson's own words and actions. Varon emphasizes the Missouri controversy as the reason for Jefferson's rage against New England, ignoring the fact that he discovered indispensable Massachusetts allies for Missouri's admission as a slave state in congressmen John Holmes, Jonathan Mason, and Mark Langdon Hill. Citing pages 113–114 of *Jefferson's Empire* as her only source, Varon summarizes and adheres to Onuf's interpretation. Transcending Onuf in exaggerating Jefferson's disgust with antislavery politicians, she writes: "In Jefferson's view, all the blame for this nightmarish scenario [of threatened disunion] lay on the Northern side of [Mason-Dixon] line—his hatred of Northern critics of slavery was now all consuming. The virulence of this hatred, Onuf observes, reveals how deeply complicit Jefferson was in betraying his own vision of a Union sustained by love. Jefferson so feared for the Union precisely because 'he could not stop himself from imagining its destruction.'" Varon is apparently quoting Onuf here.[18]

Sadly, neither Onuf nor Varon provides any evidence of Jefferson's detestation of the abolitionists, perhaps because none exists. On the contrary, the opposite of their claims is closer to the truth. At this time, increasingly alarmed by the threat to the Union posed by the controversy over slavery, Jefferson more feverishly than at any time in his life proposed the immediate emancipation of the South's slaves and their deportation to Haiti's black regime upon reaching adulthood.[19]

The *reductio ad absurdum* of Onuf's thesis in *Jefferson's Empire* is presented in a recent book by Francis D. Cogliano, *Emperor of Liberty: Thomas Jefferson's Foreign Policy* (Yale University Press, 2014), whose title and arguments in many ways reiterate those of Onuf's earlier book. Cogliano similarly makes the bizarre assertion that Jefferson insisted that members of the Federalist Party could not legitimately be citizens of the United States because they supposedly opposed Jefferson's agrarian values. (In fact, much of the Federalist press regularly published panegyrics to the farmer's way of life, and the party had a significant rural base.) As he puts it, "In Jefferson's view, his Federalist enemies, who sought to concentrate power in a strong federal government and to promote manufacturing, embraced policies which were antithetical to the long-term health of the republic."[20]

Such a statement denies basic facts about Jefferson: that he was the strongest president and exerted governmental authority to a greater degree than any chief executive before Lincoln, in such great ventures as the war on the Barbary Pirates (far more successful than our wars against Arabs in recent years), his extralegal purchase of Louisiana, his recommendations for specific legislation in his annual messages to Congress, and his Embargo Act. These measures concentrated power in the national government. Indeed, the Embargo Act was among the most extreme measures ever undertaken to promote domestic manufacturing (something

Jefferson reluctantly supported as early as the 1780s, despite his notorious comments in *Notes on the State of Virginia* and a few letters written at the same time that castigated "the mobs of the great cities").

Even during the 1780s, when Jefferson's rhetoric was most extremely anti-urban and anti-manufacturing, he supported the idea that the United States should aspire to independence from Europe in manufacturing. Writing to G. K. Van Hogendorp in 1785, he admitted his personal preference that the United States "practice neither commerce nor navigation," like "China," enabling it to "avoid all wars," and all its citizens to take up farming. However, accepting the fact that Americans preferred to undertake mercantile activities, he was aware that eventually the United States population would become so great that a large part of its citizenry would have to engage in manufacturing. He wrote, "Whenever indeed our numbers should so increase as that our produce would overstock the markets of those nations who should come to seek it, the farmers must either employ the surplus of their time in manufactures, or the surplus of our hands must be employed in manufactures, or in navigation. But the day would, I think, be distant, and we should long keep our workmen in Europe, while Europe should be drawing rough materials and even subsistence from America. But this is theory only, and a theory which the servants of America are not at liberty to follow."[21]

Taking Onuf's ideas to their logical conclusion, Cogliano, without presenting any evidence, concludes that Jefferson was "willing to use force to exterminate or exclude those who were a barrier to the success of the American republic."[22] Disputing such recent popular historical interpretations of Jefferson's attitudes, this book will examine his opinion of New England and New Englanders during his lifetime to determine whether his attitude reflected hostility and a states' rights ideology or a more pro–Union, nationalist outlook. It is hoped that such a study will extend our understanding of Jefferson's motivation as a political leader and statesman.

· · · · ·

The following study is based on the assumption that an accurate understanding of Jefferson's outlook on New England is significant in evaluating the predominance of nationalism or states' rights in his political thought. Since New England's orthodox Congregationalist-"Presbyterian" Federalists were his most bitter political enemies, one might expect him to view the people and politics of that region with a jaundiced eye. However, if his nationalist proclivities and tendency to exalt American progress as a democratic republic superseded his resentment of sectional discord, we might find him occasionally praising or condoning Massachusetts/New England conduct in his writings and during his tenure as president of the U.S.

Considering that such prominent Jefferson scholars as Peter Onuf place Jefferson's attitude toward New England in a prominent position in the course of evaluating his political and personal psychology, a closer look at Jefferson's thoughts and actions regarding New England during his lifetime is warranted. Such an examination will enhance our understanding of Jefferson's political attitudes and the extent of his democratic beliefs as well as contribute to our comprehension of the Early Republic's political culture. A byproduct of this examination may be the encouraging of further investigations of the substance of Jefferson's public life and political philosophy, in contrast to the majority of Jefferson studies over the past twenty years, which have concentrated on his family surroundings and sexual life: works often based on speculation as much as fact.

1

Jefferson's Early Opinions of New England

Jefferson was no stranger to New England, which he had first visited in May 1784, during the troubled years after the death of his wife. Before leaving on a mission to Europe to negotiate trade treaties with its various powers, in May 1784 he departed from Annapolis, where he sat in Congress, to tour New England. He desired to find out more about New Englanders' commercial and fishing needs for the purpose of his negotiations. Preparing for his journey several months earlier, he explained to his old friend Edmund Pendleton that national feeling moved him to embark on his trip. "It is very essential for us to obtain information of facts, of opinions, & of wishes from our own country," he said, meaning the whole Union rather than the "country" (state) of Virginia, in contrast to his use of the noun at various points in his *Notes* on his home state.[1] On May 25, 1784, he again asserted that his motive was to help all regions. "I mean to go thro' the Eastern States in hopes of deriving some knoledge [*sic*] of them from actual inspection and inquiry which may enable me to discharge my duty to them somewhat the better."[2]

He regarded New England as culturally and morally distinct from the South. As early as 1785, for instance, he listed his perceptions of the sections' contrasting qualities for the Marquis de Chastellux, a French officer who in 1782 had met Jefferson in Virginia, where he had fought during the American Revolution. They met again when Jefferson was in Paris as U.S. minister and he asked Jefferson to read his famous *Travels* describing his experiences in America. Objecting to Chastellux's charge that Virginians were greedy, Jefferson argued otherwise: that, because of "that warmth of their climate which unnerves and unmans both body and mind," they were "careless" in their business transactions, overly "generous" and "disinterested." He imputed selfishness instead to the Northern mercantile classes. Enumerating the various sectional traits, he wrote: "*In the North they are*: cool, sober, laborious, persevering, independant, jealous of their own liberties, but just to those of others, [self] interested, chicaning, superstitious and hypocritical in their religion. *In the South they are*: fiery, voluptuary, indolent, unsteady, independant, zealous for their own liberties, but trampling on those of others, generous, candid, without attachment or pretentions to any religion but that of the heart."[3] Jefferson was hardly impressed with his fellow Virginia planters' diligence and industriousness, perhaps because slavery was so entrenched among them that they relied on slaves to do all their work. As he wrote only half-jokingly about the failure of his friends to write him during his ministry to France, "I have no late news from our friends in Virginia. You know that indolence is one of the characteristics of that country. They write seldom and little."[4]

That Jefferson wrote candidly to Chastellux about the differences between the sections without mentioning New England's pervasive religious intolerance indicates either that he was so overwhelmed by guilt over the Southern institution of slavery, which in 1783 a Massachusetts judge had declared unconstitutional in that state, that he deliberately omitted what he considered a lesser crime; or that, as a ("states' rights") Virginian, he believed that, constituting part of Massachusetts' internal polity, its religious Establishment was none of his business. Nevertheless, in light of his fervent belief in freedom of thought and religion, it must have been difficult for him to abstain from criticizing New England's religious condition. In Massachusetts, the recently ratified Constitution of 1780, written in part by his friend John Adams, made the Congregational Church the established church. The state government continued to treat Quakers and Baptists unfairly during the Revolutionary period.

Indeed, Jefferson seemed to deny this fact to himself and to Chastellux when he said that the Northerners were "jealous of their own liberties, but just to those of others." Except that the Northern states had few slaves—in any case they treated free blacks in most cases in a discriminatory manner—this was not true.[5] As much as anyone, Jefferson was starkly aware that New England ("the North") denied freedom of religion to dissenters. It was to secure freedom of religion in Virginia that he had devoted much of the past ten years of his life, in his most arduous struggle. At the outset he took on this fight with great energy and seriousness, even though the religious establishment in Virginia was relatively weak compared to those in the New England states. When he left for Europe as minister to France, his political lieutenant James Madison renewed the struggle with perhaps even greater dedication. Jefferson's unflinching demand for religious freedom was the subject of the most eloquent passages of *Notes on Virginia*, and he considered his authorship of the Virginia Bill for Religious Freedom, along with writing the Declaration of Independence and founding the University of Virginia, one of the three most important achievements of his life, to be recorded on his tombstone. Paradoxically, it was not until the Protestant Federalist clergy abused his words and actions to brand him an atheist and an immoralist, in the presidential elections of 1796 and especially 1800, that Jefferson in private letters castigated the established churches.[6]

Always painfully conscious of slavery's perversion of Southern character, Jefferson strove to objectively evaluate his countrymen, Southerners and Northerners alike.[7] He was appalled by Southern planters' love for dueling (which he strongly opposed) and horse-racing, in addition to their devotion to slavery and the tendency of planters to sexually abuse their slaves. He must have had these odious habits in mind when he referred to Southerners as "fiery, voluptuary, indolent … zealous for their own liberties but trampling on those of others."[8] Since Jefferson considered religious freedom among the most important natural rights, it must have taken a great effort of will, prompted by awareness that New Englanders had abolished slavery, to moderate his criticism of their religious practices in his commentary to Chastellux.

During the 1780s, Jefferson informed other foreigners about the difference between North and South on the issue of slavery. He tended to adopt a posture more defensive of the South than one might expect from the author of *Notes on the State of Virginia*, with its castigation of slavery. After writing *Observations on the American Revolution* (1784), with its praise of the American Revolution and its hope that the United States would soon abolish slavery, the English Radical dissenting clergyman Richard Price sent Jefferson a copy in return for a copy of Jefferson's *Notes on Virginia*. Although Price's views on slavery were moderate, and he believed that once freed the slaves, who he thought would present a threat to social order, could not safely remain in the United States, he was alarmed and disillusioned by South Carolinians' reports that his book's support for abolition had angered Southern slaveholders.[9]

While acknowledging Jefferson's "wisdom and liberality" in urging slavery's abolition in *Notes*, Price, appalled by South Carolinians' protest against his work, now labeled his praise of the Revolution "ridiculous." "It will appear that the people who have been Struggling so earnestly to save *themselves* from Slavery are very ready to *enslave* others," he sarcastically commented. "The friends of liberty and humanity in Europe will be mortify'd, and an event which has raised their hopes will prove only an introduction to a new Scene of aristocratic tyranny and human debasement."[10]

Jefferson felt a need to defend at least Virginia from Price's imputations against the South. At the same time, he downplayed the magnanimity of the Northern states' abolition of slavery. Explaining to Price the sectional divergence over slavery, he said of Price's recommendations for abolition: "Southward of the Chesapeak [i.e., in South Carolina and Georgia] it will find but few readers concurring with it in sentiment on the subject of slavery." Claiming that a virtuous minority of Virginia slaveholders were ready to manumit their slaves, he continued, "From the mouth to the head of the Chesapeak [in North Carolina, Virginia, and Maryland], the bulk of the people will approve it in theory, and it will find a respectable minority ready to adopt it in practice, a minority which for weight and worth of character preponderates against the greater number, who have not the courage to divest their families of a property which however keeps their consciences inquiet."[11] Thus, Jefferson depicted Southerners as guilty and torn over slavery, and claimed that many slaveholders were ready to emancipate their slaves.

Jefferson remained deeply interested in the future of Virginia. He favored a more distinct separation of powers in the state's constitution, which had given virtually total control of the government to an undemocratically apportioned legislature. He advocated a state governor with veto powers, and in 1791 he informed a friend that he would be willing to attend a state constitutional convention, if one were called, despite his national responsibilities as Washington's secretary of state.[12]

Discussing the Northern states, which included New England, Jefferson acknowledged that they were engaged in the abolition of slavery. He did not mention that Pennsylvania was the only state up to that time that had actually passed laws abolishing slavery, in 1780 and 1788. In Massachusetts historians have not yet discovered by what legal means slavery was in fact abolished, although the chief justice of the state, William Cushing, declared in the famous *Quock Walker* decision in 1783 that in his interpretation the 1780 state constitution made slavery illegal.[13] Without going into details, and with a modicum of admiration, Jefferson wryly reported to Price: "Northward of the Chesapeak you may find here and there an opponent to your doctrine [abolition of slavery] as you may find here and there a robber and a murderer, but in no greater number. In that part of America, there being but few slaves, they can easily disencumber themselves of them, and emancipation is put into such a train that in a few years there will be no slaves Northward of Maryland."[14] Thus, like his friend John Adams, Jefferson was not inclined to romanticize the motives for Massachusetts or other

New England states' abolishing slavery; he ascribed it bluntly to (the lack of) Northern economic self-interest in the execrable institution.[15]

Eager to depict his home state as a benign and enlightened region, Jefferson asserted that Virginia's slaveholders, infused with natural rights' ideology and humanitarianism, were close to liberating their bondspersons *en masse*. He claimed that they were more zealous than their neighbors in Maryland in this regard, "where I do not find such a disposition to begin the redress of this enormity as in Virginia." Hardly attempting a defense of slavery as a benign institution, Jefferson insisted that it was unjust. He assured Price that Virginia would soon follow New England as "the next state to which we may turn our eyes for the interesting spectacle of justice in conflict with avarice and oppression: a conflict wherein the sacred side is gaining daily recruits." Viewing antislavery as a holy cause, Jefferson claimed that the younger generation of Virginians now taking over political office was infused with abolitionist ardor because they wanted to extend their fathers' achievement of liberty for whites from British oppression to their black brothers and sisters. "These have sucked in the principles of liberty as it were with their mother's milk," he explained in a strong metaphor (perhaps many of these young men were nursed by female slaves!), "and it is to them that I look with anxiety to turn the fate of this question."[16]

Withholding praise for New Englanders' abolitionist zeal, Jefferson preferred to acclaim his state's humane slaveholders and their manumission law passed in 1782. He claimed in his *Autobiography* to have unsuccessfully urged this measure as a member of the House of Burgesses, in which he served from 1769 to 1775. In that manuscript, written in his late seventies, he implied that the opposition of the royal governor and council and in the final analysis the king's Privy Council in Britain, thwarted his attempts. He wrote that he made "one effort in that body [the assembly] for the permission of the emancipation of slaves, which was rejected." While his fellow legislators had good intentions, royal officials intimidated them, so that "every hope of amelioration" for the slaves was blocked.[17]

In retrospect, Jefferson tended to blame the mother country for colonial Virginia's failures to curtail slavery's abuses. In addition to insisting that the thirteen colonies' declaration of independence had enabled his state to finally escape the grasp of British slave traders who had demanded that the King veto all bills in the House of Burgesses to prohibit the importation of slaves, his manuscript autobiography stated that he initiated the 1778 Virginia law that prohibited the importation of slaves. He reminisced, "This passed without opposition, and stopped the increase of the evil [slavery] by importation, leaving to future efforts its final eradication." In 1800, after hearing about rumors of his death propagated by his Federalist opponents during the presidential election campaign, Jefferson privately composed "A Memorandum of Services to My Country," an exercise in convincing himself that he had performed useful public services during his lifetime. One of the numerous accomplishments he listed, along with the Declaration of Independence and the bills for ending Virginia's Anglican religious establishment and for enacting religious freedom, was "the act prohibiting the importation of slaves."[18] He regarded his actions against slavery as an important aspect of his political career. Ostensibly with good reason, Jefferson considered himself in the forefront of American political leaders in the fight against slavery.

In 1785, believing that liberation from the mother country had opened up a new birth of freedom for the South, he encouraged Price to continue his attack on slavery, thinking that "it will do a great deal of good" in the South. Jefferson urged Price to send a personal address against slavery to the students at his alma mater, William and Mary College, Virginia's leading educational institution, where his friend the antislavery judge George Wythe was a professor. Believing that the "young men" would be receptive to such a message, Jefferson quixotically predicted "that its influence on the future decision of this important question would be great, perhaps decisive."[19]

In Paris, at nearly the same time in 1785 that he wrote this letter to Price, Jefferson expounded his views on slavery to young John Quincy Adams, who was sixteen years old and could do little but listen and admire. (John Quincy Adams was his father John's secretary at the time, and Papa John, U.S. minister to Great Britain, as well as his wife Abigail, were captivated by Jefferson's suavity and their friendship with him was at its height.) Since Jefferson's views were almost verbatim identical to his commentaries on slave population and the evils of tobacco-growing in *Notes on Virginia*, which he published in Paris at this time, it is likely that he wrote the section of *Notes* titled "Population," or Query VIII, in France and not in Virginia as is generally believed. According to Adams' diary for May 4, 1785, Jefferson abruptly began conversing about slavery. He took a defensive tone on the topic: "Mr. Jefferson spoke concerning Virginia, a State, which he knows very particularly, as it is his native Country. The blacks, he tells me, are very well treated there; and increase in population, more in proportion, than the whites. Before the War, he says the negroes, were to the whites, in the proportion of 3 to 4. Now they are as 10 to 11, which is a very material difference. He supposed about 500,000 souls in the State. He disapproves very much of the Cultivation of Tobacco, and wishes, it may be laid entirely aside. He thinks wheat would be much more advantageous, and profitable, much less Laborious, and less hurtful to the ground: he is a man of great judgment."[20]

In his later years, Jefferson preferred growing wheat rather than tobacco. In the 1790s, he ceased growing tobacco at Monticello for several years, although he continued to raise it at Poplar Forest, depending on it for his cash income. He engaged in wheat cultivation at Poplar Forest to an even greater extent than at Monticello. He made this choice not only because tobacco was becoming increasingly unprofitable, but because wheat-growing could be more easily performed by free labor than tobacco cultivation, which was considered too arduous for free white men. At the same time, he thought black slaves would not be as hard pressed growing wheat, especially female slaves, although he preferred that women not work in the fields but be confined to household occupations. (One-third of all of Jefferson's slaves worked in the fields.) Jefferson apparently did not confide to the teenager Adams his belief that slavery was evil and ought to be abolished; indeed, he condoned slavery and, perhaps for the young Yankee's edification, treated it as a legitimate institution that may have even been a "positive good" for the blacks, as it was called before the Civil War. In cultivating a harmonious relationship between Virginia and New England, Jefferson perhaps thought, it would be helpful for young, naïve Adams to believe that the Peculiar Institution was not so peculiar after all. For most of his active political career, John Quincy Adams remained publicly indifferent on the issue of slavery, and indeed usually supported the institution, until old age, when he made a name for himself as an antislavery agitator, albeit an elderly one.[21]

In the last years of Jefferson's life, he devised a scheme for emancipating all Southern slaves and deporting them to Haiti. He proposed to finance the project by selling the massive government lands his administration had bought in the Louisiana Purchase. Slave-holding

Virginia and Georgia ceded their public lands, a legacy of the colonial period, to the national government in 1784 and 1801, respectively, he reasoned; and they were among "the very States now needing this relief" from slavery. Emphasizing that the Northern states' congressional representatives, including those from New England, had demanded legislation to abolish slavery in the new states during the Missouri crisis, Jefferson expected them to eagerly grasp this remedy. "The object, though more important to the slave States, is highly so to the others also, if they were serious in their arguments on the Missouri question," he argued in 1824 in a letter to Jared Sparks, a Massachusetts magazine publisher, historian, and member of the American Colonization Society. As he had done in his correspondence with Price and others throughout his life, Jefferson continued to stress that the abolition of slavery had been far easier for the Northern states than Southern states. They had fewer slaveholders, far fewer slaves, and their economy did not depend on human bondage. "In the Northern States it [slavery] was merely superficial, and easily corrected," he observed to a Baptist preacher in 1815. "In the southern it is incorporated with the whole system, and requires time, patience, and perseverance in the curative process."[22] For Southerners who had arguably gained great profits from slavery, on which they had relied for hundreds of years, much self-sacrificing republican virtue was required to surrender their human property; while for New Englanders, Jefferson pointed out, little loss was entailed when their states abolished the peculiar institution.

Jefferson belittled the antislavery acts of New Englanders, perhaps because he doubted that they demonstrated much self-sacrificing "republican virtue." He was aware that New Englanders were far less dependent on slavery than Virginians and other Southerners were. On the other hand, he evinced no hostility toward Northerners, even though they were already, in the 1780s, beginning to attack Southerners for their immorality in keeping slaves. This was especially true of New Jersey and Pennsylvania Quakers like John Woolman and Anthony Benezet.[23] Jefferson showed himself staunchly against slavery in his letter to Price. Perhaps Jefferson, in France far away from his home country, felt homesick and was eager to discuss the attitudes of his countrymen and compare North and South to whoever would listen. He also wanted foreign friends of the United States like Price and Chastellux to know more about his country. That may explain his eagerness to write so frankly about slavery and sectional differences to these men.

Early in his career, Jefferson voiced admiration for New England's political culture. In 1788, residing in Paris as U.S. minister at the time the Constitution was under debate at home, he praised the Massachusetts ratifying convention's conduct. Jefferson had originally favored a second national convention to consider the amendments proposed by the various state ratifying conventions—especially the addition of a bill of rights—before the new government went officially into operation. He was especially enthusiastic about the Massachusetts convention's suggestion that the new government take effect after nine states had ratified the Constitution, while Congress was expected to discuss amendments later, saying, "the plan of Massachusetts is far preferable, and will I hope be followed by those [states] who are yet to decide" on the Constitution.[24]

As time passed, Jefferson's enthusiasm for the Massachusetts convention's proposal increased. Maintaining keen interest in the struggle for ratification of the Constitution, he observed in July 1788, "The first vessels will probably bring us news of the accession of S. Carolina and Virginia to the new Confederation. The glorious example of Massachusetts, of accepting unconditionally, and pressing for future amendment, will I hope reconcile all parties," he wrote. "The argument is unanswerable that it will be easier to obtain amendments from nine states under the new constitution, than from thirteen after rejecting it."[25]

One notoriously recalcitrant New England state, little Rhode Island, probably the most mercantile in the Union (although a majority of its inhabitants were small farmers), had refused even to call a ratifying convention. In 1786, Jefferson had analyzed its legislature's stubbornly consistent refusal to approve an amendment to the Articles of Confederation permitting Congress to tax imports. Replying to Jean Nicolas Démeunier's request for information in preparing an article about the United States for the prestigious *Encyclopédie Méthodique*, Jefferson, at this time United States minister to France, denounced Rhode Island's obstructionism.

At this juncture, Jefferson made his first attempt to distinguish different New England states, ascribing personality characteristics to them based on their citizens' occupations. From his perch in distant Paris, he seemed uninformed about Rhode Island's politics or class structure. His analysis was thus superficial. He recurred to his favorite distinction between urban and rural society and values. As he had already made clear in Query 19 of *Notes on Virginia*, he much preferred the latter. He argued that because of their differing topographies, Rhode Island's political character differed substantially from that of its neighbor Connecticut. As a state with a small land mass, mostly composed of seaports (Newport, Portsmouth, Warwick, and Providence), Jefferson asserted, Rhode Island's government was dominated by merchants. He seemed unaware of its rich southern farmlands, and that merchants, though extremely influential, were few in number. Moreover, there were numerous small debtor-farmers, who took control of the state legislature in the spring 1786 elections and passed notorious paper money and debtor stay laws. As historian Jackson Turner Main notes more accurately than Jefferson, comparing the state with its southern neighbor, Connecticut, "In the interior the farmers practiced a self-sufficient economy; there were many debtors and many poor—more, apparently, than in Connecticut," where the towns gave paper money bills almost no support.[26]

Jefferson was an ardent foe of government issuance of paper money. As early as 1788, he denounced it as a fiscally irresponsible procedure. Denouncing the Bank of England's policy of issuing paper money, he warned that it would lead to bankruptcies and "a general panic" because "paper is poverty ... only the ghost of money, and not money itself."[27]

Jefferson stressed that Connecticut possessed a comparatively larger "interior country" than Rhode Island, and therefore farmers were more numerous. And farming, according to Jefferson, was a less greedy, more "virtuous" occupation than the maritime trades conducted by merchants and seamen. Jefferson insisted that mercantile greed explained Rhode Island's refusal to accommodate the other states by agreeing to an "impost," as the tariff was then called.[28] Charles A. Miller, a serious student of Jefferson's thought, perhaps exaggerates the import of Jefferson's observations in this instance. He finds that Jefferson espoused a "sophisticated" form of "environmentalism," in which he applied his (proto-Madisonian) idea of an expansive land area's impact on political economy to explain diverse types of "social character."[29]

Ostensibly, Jefferson arbitrarily attributed superior "virtue" to one New England state over another, depending on whether it favored his program of a stronger Congress empowered to levy taxes. Since Rhode Island had most frequently opposed amending the Articles of

Confederation to permit Congress to levy a tariff from 1782 to 1787 (although other state legislatures, including Virginia, Pennsylvania, and New York vetoed the proposal on different occasions), Jefferson impugned the morals of its merchants, overlooking the consensus within the state against an impost. Rhode Island's legislature, both houses of which had always been directly elected by the voters, had rejected a congressional impost in 1782 by a unanimous vote. Simplistically explaining the state's opposition to reform as the result of the selfishness of its merchants, he observed that Rhode Island consisted mainly of "sea-ports," while Connecticut was mostly farmland ("interior country") and had "no good ports in it." He reiterated his Physiocratic view, already stated in *Notes*' Query 19 and elsewhere, that farming was the source of all physical productivity and moral virtue, in terms almost identical, in letters to John Jay and others: "The cultivators of the earth are the most virtuous citizens and possess most of the *amor patriae*. Merchants are the least virtuous, and possess the least of the *amor patriae*." Jefferson greatly exaggerated in claiming that "there is not a single man" in Rhode Island "who is not a merchant of some sort." This bogus statistic buttressed his argument that the primary reason for the state's refractoriness was its merchants' selfishness and apathy toward strengthening the common Union. Ironically, the small farmers had a greater fear of centralized power and more consistently opposed granting Congress the impost than did the creditor merchants. Fearing that the farmer-dominated state legislature would force public creditors to accept payment in paper money, merchants supported a tariff to pay the national debt in 1785 and 1786.[30]

At least in 1786, Jefferson based his analysis of New England politics more on his agrarian prejudices and wishful thinking than facts. Unlike the 1790s, the era of partisan conflict between Federalists and Republicans, he was not on the American political scene.

By 1788, Jefferson was perhaps more thoroughly informed about the political situation in Rhode Island, whose farmer/debtors took over the state legislature and nullified the famous pro-merchant *Trevett vs. Weeden* decision of the state supreme court. He seemed more sympathetic to its people's reputation for dilatoriness and obstruction, and its democratic, town meeting mode of government and direct legislative and gubernatorial elections. Several nationalists favored bullying Rhode Island into joining the new union by burdening it with discriminatory tariffs. However, Jefferson, demonstrating his belief in reason and persuasion in preference to any kind of coercion, opposed the use of force. Had he been as hostile to New England's commercial states as Onuf suggests, he would have seized this opportunity to destroy a (reputedly) excessively commercial region. Welcoming news of imminent ratification of the Constitution by nine states, the minimum required for it to take effect, he hoped that Virginia's convention, "now in session, may give the 9th vote of approbation." Although optimistic, he anxiously asked Virginia congressional representative Edward Carrington, "What do you propose to do with Rhode Island?" Despite his enthusiasm for the Constitution, he warned against forcing Rhode Island to adopt it. "As long as there is hope, we should give her time. I cannot conceive but that she will come to rights in the long run. Force, in whatever form, would be a dangerous precedent."[31]

Jefferson apparently rejected even economic sanctions against the state, since few politicians had ever seriously contemplated a military incursion. He must have sympathized with Rhode Island's reluctance to join a Union that had regarded it as a pariah throughout the 1780s, when small farmers took over the state legislature and passed notorious laws inflating the currency and forced merchants to accept it as legal tender. On the other hand, his motives may have been less benign. Although he never mentioned it at the time, the exclusion of "mercantile" Rhode Island from the Union strengthened the position of Virginia and the "agrarian" Southern states.[32]

Jefferson decided to take in the region of Hampshire and Berkshire Counties where Shays Rebellion had occurred in 1786–1787. As most scholars know, Jefferson's response to Shays Rebellion was to justify and exonerate the rebels and praise the idea of rebellions in general—"the tree of liberty must be refreshed from time to time with the blood of patriots and tyrants"—although the rebels did not kill any government officials or soldiers.[33] Jefferson appreciated the beauty of western New England's wooded countryside, encompassing Vermont and the Connecticut River Valley. Accompanied by his slave James Hemings and James Madison, he toured New York, Vermont, western Massachusetts (Berkshire and Hampshire counties, where Shays' Rebellion had occurred) and Connecticut from May 20 to June 16, 1791. Jefferson admired the lakes, mountains, and vegetation of the area. He said he had become so relaxed during the trip that he lost a migraine headache that had plagued him before. He and Madison wrote little about the politics of the people of New England during this period, although it marked the beginning of their organization of the Republican Party. It is possible that they visited New York's senator Aaron Burr and Governor George Clinton in New York City to plan their opposition to Hamilton, but no definite evidence of this exists. In New York City, Jefferson met the great poet and Republican editor, Philip Freneau, who was working for the moderately Federalist *New York Daily Advertiser*. A few weeks earlier, his Princeton classmate James Madison had offered him the chance to edit a major Republican newspaper that he and Jefferson had contemplated setting up in Philadelphia, the nation's new capital, and he had shown some interest. During the trip, Jefferson met Freneau for the first time, spoke to him at greater length about the job, and probably hinted that he could offer him simultaneous part-time employment as a translator in the State Department.[34]

Alexander Hamilton's friend Nathaniel Hazard, a New York City merchant and iron manufacturer, gave an account of Jefferson and Madison's alleged courtship of the western farmers. To Hamilton he relayed gossip he had heard from Aaron Burr's uncle, young Pierpont Edwards at a dinner in New Haven, where he sat with many Federalist political leaders. The youngest son of famed Berkshire (Northampton) theologian Jonathan Edwards, Pierpont, not yet a Jeffersonian, "ridicule[d] J——n & M——'s Tour; in which they scouted silently thro' the Country, shunning the Gentry, communing with & pitying the Shayites," and complaining about the quality of "the Eatables." With their ostensibly demagogic appeals to former rebels, Jefferson and Madison "are supremely contemned by the Gentlemen of Connecticut," Hazard noted, "which State I found on a Review right as to national Matters." Reporting that Hamilton's policies were very popular in New England, Hazard expected Jefferson and Madison to arouse little response, other than to "provoke ... [a] stinging Satire" by Federalist poet John Trumbull, a member of the Hartford Wits.[35]

As a premature assessment of Jefferson and Madison as radical agrarian democratic politicians, Hazard's report is interesting but probably not accurate. It seems that the New England portion of the trip was undertaken primarily for pleasure. They referred to it as a "botanizing expedition" to increase their knowledge of the region's plants and wildlife. (Indeed, Madison owned some land in the Genesee Valley of upstate New York.)[36]

It was during the 1790s that Jefferson first asserted his admiration, indeed envy, of New

England's democratic town meetings, and regretted that they supported the aristocratic Federalists rather than his own party, which he believed was more oriented toward the common man. He blamed the actions of the Massachusetts, New Hampshire, and Connecticut town meetings for his defeat by John Adams in the presidential election of 1796, in which he won 68 electoral votes to 71 for Adams. Many newspapers reprinted the *New York Herald*'s brief, not entirely complete description of the mode of voting in the states in 1796: "The electors in Virginia, Maryland, Massachusetts, and New-Hampshire are chosen by the people. The whole number of electors to be appointed is 138–58 of which are north, and 65 south of Pennsylvania. The number of each state is as follows–N. Hampshire 6, Massachusetts 16, R. Island, 4, Connecticut 9, Vermont, 4, New York 12, New-Jersey 7, Pennsylvania 15, Delaware 3, Maryland 10, Virginia 21, N. Carolina 12, S. Carolina 8, Georgia 4, Kentucky 4, Tennessee 3."[37]

Massachusetts and New Hampshire had particularly convoluted electoral systems. Massachusetts' fourteen electoral districts, identical to its congressional districts, were defined in "an act for dividing the Commonwealth into districts for the choice of Representatives in the Congress of the United States." A U.S. senator or representative, or a person holding office under the United States government, was not eligible to be a presidential elector. Under the law, fourteen electors were chosen by the voters in each of the congressional districts while the legislature picked two at-large electors, making up the state's total of sixteen. However, the legislature also had the power to choose electors for any election district that did not give a majority to any one electoral candidate. Unexpectedly, there was such strong competition between Republicans and Federalists in the state that, in the elections held on November 7, no elector received a majority of votes in seven of the fourteen electoral districts. This proved a boon for the Federalists, since the legislature (also called the General Court), which they controlled, thus picked nine electors, all of them Federalists, when it voted on November 18. Among the candidates they chose were moderate Federalists Elbridge Gerry and Dr. Samuel Holten. Both men were politically inactive in 1796. Though they had not at first supported the U.S. Constitution, they emerged as supporters of the Washington Administration's policies when they served in Congress during the early 1790s. Governor of Massachusetts Samuel Adams, running for Boston's presidential elector as a Jeffersonian Republican, was defeated by relatively unknown local politician Thomas Dawes, by a vote of 975 to 1428. This revealed the devotion of Boston voters to Sam's cousin John Adams.[38]

In Massachusetts, the state legislature chose nine of the state's sixteen electors because of the exceptional circumstance that no candidate secured a popular majority in seven of the fourteen electoral districts. New Hampshire's General Court faced a similar situation. In 1796, New Hampshire's six electors were chosen by statewide popular vote on a general ticket. But, as was the case with Massachusetts, except that New Hampshire conducted a statewide vote, if fewer than six candidates obtained a majority, the legislature would choose from the two with the highest numbers. Federalists made a clean sweep of the New Hampshire electoral contests. Five of their candidates obtained popular majorities on a general ticket, and the legislature chose the remaining elector from the two men who stood sixth and seventh on the statewide poll. Both men were Federalists. New Hampshire's six electors voted uniformly for John Adams and Oliver Ellsworth, Connecticut senator and chief justice of the United States Supreme Court. Ellsworth was not in the running for the office, and the votes for him were throwaway votes designed to prevent Hamilton's candidate, Thomas Pinckney, from surpassing Adams in electoral votes. Without New Hampshire's electoral votes for Adams, Jefferson would have won the presidency.[39]

Unique among the states, New Hampshire's voters chose congressmen directly at-large and instituted a run-off election if not all four candidates got a majority of the votes. (Massachusetts and Vermont had "trials," as the run-off elections were called, in districts.)[40] This method was more democratic than the state's mode of having the legislature pick a presidential elector from candidates with less than a majority, irrespective of their number of popular votes, if fewer than six electoral candidates obtained a majority. As the (Concord) *Courier of New Hampshire* reported in October 1796, "The town meetings for choosing the fourth Representative to Congress [what we call a run-off today] and also for the choice of Electors for President and Vice-President, are to be held on first Monday in November."[41]

It took some time for New Hampshire to count the statewide vote for president. On November 29, 1796, the *Courier of New Hampshire* finally reported that Federalist candidates Oliver Peabody, John Taylor Gilman (the state's governor), Benjamin Bellows, Timothy Farrar, Ebenezer Thompson, and Timothy Walker had the highest number of votes, but only five had a majority of votes. "The five first were elected by the People by a great majority," the newspaper observed. "Beza Woodward had about 2000 votes, and Timothy Walker about 800, the choice of one of these two devolving on the Legislature, the latter gentleman [Walker] received a very respectable majority of their [the assembly's] suffrages."[42]

There was a big difference in the vote for the two candidates, and the legislature selected the much less popular one, but it did not really matter to Democratic-Republicans because both men were Adams supporters. Ironically, in 1800, Walker, a Concord judge, favored legislative incorporation of the Republican-controlled Union Bank, a measure opposed by most Federalists, especially investors in Exeter's New Hampshire Bank. He ended up running for governor as a Democratic-Republican against Federalist John T. Gilman, losing a relatively close race.[43] A strange and colorful character, Beza (also known as Bezaliel or Bezaleel) Woodward of Lebanon, Connecticut, and Dresden, New Hampshire, graduated from Yale College in 1764. He taught at Moor's Charity School for Indians in Lebanon, Connecticut, where he met Eleazar Wheelock, founder and president of Dartmouth College. In 1772, after moving to Hanover, New Hampshire, he married Wheelock's daughter and became a Mathematics professor at Dartmouth and the college's librarian. Although after Wheelock's death, he was intermittently president of the College in 1779, 1782 and 1783, Woodward found time to fight in the Revolutionary War. Woodward briefly led a sporadic, abortive popular revolt of the western towns against the New Hampshire government that lasted from 1776 to 1782. In 1781, these Connecticut River Valley towns, under the leadership of Grafton County's delegate Woodward, sought to join the fledgling state of Vermont. They objected that New Hampshire's 1776 constitution concentrated too much power in the legislature, whose members used their power to elect themselves and their friends to most executive and judicial positions, creating a potentially corrupt oligarchy. The western towns also argued that they received inadequate legislative representation. Once some of the rebels' demands were satisfied, Woodward settled down in New Hampshire and was chosen for various judgeships.[44] Although one would expect an individual with such an anomalous career to be a Democratic-Republican rebel against the Establishment, Woodward was a Federalist, and apparently a popular politician.

Republican newspapers were aware of the significance of the electoral vote in New Hampshire for the contest's final outcome. As late as November 29, 1796, *Greenleaf's New-York*

Journal pessimistically reported, "No full return of ELECTORS from New Hampshire yet—and it is said, that those for Vermont and those for Georgia, will be lost."[45] A Concord, New Hampshire, newspaper reported that the state house and senate examined the returns for electors, and stopped after examining the entry for Rockingham County. The paper observed that they "met in convention," a radical-sounding term for such a conservative procedure. Governor Gilman, a leading Federalist, addressed the joint session. He asserted, "The time of our present meeting was regulated with a view that you might seasonably examine the votes given by the citizens of this State, for Electors of a President and Vice-President of the United States, and complete the choice, in case it has not been done by the people."[46]

New Hampshire newspapers reported on the election in detail. In Keene, New Hampshire, for example, where Timothy Walker was apparently not very popular, the votes for presidential elector were: John Taylor Gilman, 75; Ebenezer Thompson, 76; Oliver Peabody, 76; Benjamin Bellows, 76; Simeon Olcott, 76; Timothy Farrar, 76; and Timothy Walker, 1. The town's choice for congressional representative, Peleg Sprague, a Keene native, received eighty-six votes, but he was ultimately defeated in the congressional district by Jeremiah Smith, a more prestigious Federalist. All these candidates were denominated "Esquires," indicating that they were respectable and wealthy citizens.[47] Newspapers as far away as New York City and Philadelphia paid careful attention to New Hampshire's presidential election. On December 13, 1796, *Greenleaf's New York Journal* reported that Gilman, Peabody, Thompson, Farrar, Bellows, and Walker were chosen.[48] Rhode Island's legislature chose its four electors. Apparently the assembly was not composed of extreme Federalists. It chose the popular governor, Arthur Fenner, as one of the electors. Like most successful Rhode Island politicians, Fenner had been an Antifederalist but after the new national government went into operation he favored his state's joining the Union. He was perhaps the most popular and long-tenured governor Rhode Island ever had, holding office from 1790 to 1805; he died in office. Although historians have generally ignored Rhode Island's politics during the 1790s, it deserves further study. Even more than Massachusetts, it is an intriguing example of a state that desired to retain its autonomy to as great an extent as possible, while maintaining allegiance to its foremost Revolutionary War figures. Few newspapers reported Rhode Island's political activities in 1796, but two New York journals, one Federalist and one Republican, recorded the assembly's choices (albeit in very small print): "The Hon. General Assembly of the State of Rhode-Island elected Arthur Fenner, Samuel J. Potter, William Greene, and George Champlin, Esqrs., to serve as electors of President & Vice-President of the United States."[49] Connecticut's state legislature cast its nine electoral votes as well.[50]

Jefferson was angry at what he perceived as Federalist leaders' enforcement of party unity, believing they had stamped out pro–Jefferson dissent. "The event of the election has never been a matter of doubt in my mind," he told Madison. "I knew that the Eastern states were disciplined in the school of their town meetings to sacrifice differences of opinion to the great object of operating in phalanx, and that the more free and moral agency practised in the other states would always make up the supplement of their weight." Jefferson apparently reasoned that in New England the people chose the state legislatures, which picked presidential electors, none of whom voted for him.[51]

More bluntly, Jefferson wrote to Edward Rutledge of South Carolina, a wealthy planter and friend, who at the time was neutral between Federalists and Republicans. As a South Carolina elector, Rutledge cast a ballot for Jefferson and a ballot for South Carolina Federalist

Thomas Pinckney, his cousin. In 1796, South Carolina's electoral vote was divided equally between Jefferson and Pinckney. Writing to Rutledge at the end of December 1796, Jefferson said that he expected Adams to win: "I have never one moment doubted the result. I knew it was impossible Mr. Adams should lose a vote North of the Delaware, and that the free and moral agency of the South would furnish him an abundant supplement."[52] Thus, Jefferson was aware that Southern disunity would lead to his defeat, even though he was the "Southern" candidate.

From Jefferson's perspective, the town meetings had violated classical republican anti-party ideology by combining against his candidacy and denying his supporters a voice. On the other hand, as Jefferson viewed it, several Southern states which should have unanimously favored him, by their fair-minded "free and moral agency" had allowed a few Adams electors to creep in. This upheld freedom of opinion but cost him the election. Adams had obtained nine votes south of the Delaware, including seven of Maryland's electors (to Jefferson's four from that state), and one from Jefferson's Virginia.[53]

Seemingly optimistic despite his defeat, Jefferson claimed that "the vote comes much nearer an equality than I had expected."[54] However, Jefferson was probably more disappointed by his loss to Adams than he admitted. He wrote several of his friends that the Federalists, particularly in Pennsylvania, where Adams received only one electoral vote, had resorted to skullduggery. "I value the late vote highly," he explained to the French philosopher Constantin-François Volney, "but it is only as the index of the place I hold in the esteem of my fellow-citizens. In this point of view the difference between 68 and 71 votes is little sensible, and still less that between the real vote which was 69 and 70, because one real elector in Pennsylvania was excluded from voting by the miscarriage of the votes, and one who was not an elector was admitted to vote."[55]

Although during the 1790s Jefferson praised New England's democratic procedures, he apparently overlooked its restrictive suffrage, which probably hindered Republican success. In an era when most Anglo-American politicians argued that party organizations formed to win elections were an illegitimate, "factious" and demagogic kind of political activity, Jefferson blamed Federalists' "immoral" enforcement of party unity for his defeat by three electoral votes (68 to 71) for the presidency in 1796. He denounced the actions of the Massachusetts, New Hampshire, and Connecticut town meetings, whose electors had voted unanimously for John Adams. He objected that, while the New England electors operated in a disciplined and united "phalanx," "the more free and moral agency practised in the other states" led to his losing some of their electors, and consequently the election, because his party lacked cohesion. Jefferson deduced that political discipline was facilitated by the Federalist-dominated town meetings' direct democracy.[56]

In fact, in 1796 Connecticut and Rhode Island's legislatures picked their states' electors. In Massachusetts, they were chosen in each district by popular vote, with the legislature choosing two additional delegates (a total of sixteen), but possessing the added power of picking the electors in those districts where no candidate got a majority of votes. In New Hampshire, electors were chosen by statewide popular vote, but the legislature had the opportunity to choose an elector if only five rather than six obtained the requisite majority.[57] Despite his disappointment that the town meetings (whose role he may have exaggerated) had flouted nonpartisan "classical republican" ideology by denying him support, Jefferson professed relief that "the vote comes much nearer an equality than I had expected."[58]

Jefferson was acutely aware of New Englanders' contribution to American independence; their "unquestionable" republicanism; and democratic polity. Thus, he lamented that their support of Federalist belligerence toward revolutionary France negated republican ideals. "If a prospect could be once opened upon us of the penetration of truth into the Eastern states, if the people there, who are unquestionably republican, could discover that they have been duped into the support of measures calculated to sap the very foundations of republicanism, we might still hope for salvation, and that it would come, as of old, from the East," he wrote New York Republican politician Aaron Burr. "But will that region ever awake to the true state of things? Can the middle, Southern and Western states hold on till they awake?"[59] In a reversal of the situation in 1776, when "salvation" came from the Eastern states, led by John Adams and Massachusetts, who were in the forefront of the demand for independence from England, in 1797 it appeared to Jefferson that the common people of New England had allowed themselves to be duped by their lawyers, merchants, clergy, and Connecticut Valley land baron River Gods, into adopting a policy subservient to the former mother country and belligerent toward the Revolutionary War ally France.

2

Jefferson, New England and the Shadow of Slavery in the 1790s[1]

Jefferson was not the only Democratic-Republican who admired New England's political *mentalité*. Many years before Jefferson made the analogy between wards and New England towns as optimal modes of citizen participation, Benjamin Franklin Bache, editor of the most important Republican newspaper, the *Philadelphia General Advertiser/Aurora*, praised Bostonians' political astuteness and involvement, which he observed first-hand on his journey north in the summer of 1795 selling copies of Jay's Treaty. On July 1, 1795, shortly after the Senate ratified the treaty, he obtained its text from a Virginia senator, Stevens Thomson Mason, an episode constituting the first "scoop" in American journalism history. Traveling through New York, Hartford, and the Connecticut River Valley en route to Boston, Bache was impressed by New England's fertile landscape and its farmers' relative equality of economic condition. He wrote his wife, Margaret Markoe Bache, that the region was "the most agreeable country I think, I ever passed thro' in my life. But little of the land … appeared to be bad."[2]

Bache displayed humor rather than animus when he encountered that alleged Massachusetts monarchist, Vice President John Adams, on the road from Philadelphia to Boston. As a young boy during the American Revolution, Bache, grandson of U.S. minister to France Benjamin Franklin, had attended the Le Coeur boarding school in Paris with Adams's son John Quincy.[3] Now he irreverently had fun at Adams's expense. (Adams was apparently unaware of Bache's activities.) Bache neglected to tell him the reason for his trip and his recent coup in publishing Jay's Treaty. "At Worcester, a very pretty town of Massachusetts, I overtook the Vice President & breakfasted with him & Mrs. [Abigail] Adams," he wrote to Margaret. "He asked me whether the treaty had leaked out in Philadelphia: I told him a little. He assured me that the generality of the people would like it very well after a trial of a few months." On July 6, 1795, after vending copies of the Treaty in Boston, Bache attended a town meeting, which he estimated at fifteen hundred people, called to protest the pro–British instrument. He happily witnessed a unanimous vote against it. Unsurprisingly, he applauded the Bostonians' wisdom. "I watched the countenance of the citizens assembled on that occasion, when not one instance of that stupid gaze was to be seen, so often to be observed among a people less enlightened," he told his wife. "All appeared intelligent and to feel the force of every argument that was used." Showing concern for law and order, belying his reputation among Federalists (and recent historians) for callowness and impulsiveness, Bache was "highly delighted ... by the orderly and spirited manner in which the business was conducted."[4]

Like Jefferson himself, Bache viewed the Boston town meeting as epitomizing democracy at work. "I hope every city throughout the Union will follow their example," he admitted. "I wish Philadelphia particularly could be got together in a town meeting. This is a momentous crisis in our affairs," he said concerning the debate over ratification of Jay's Treaty, "and much depends on our exertions at this instant." He was also pleased by the amiability of Massachusetts Republican Governor, Revolutionary War legend Samuel Adams, Vice-President Adams' second cousin: "At Boston I thrice visited the Governor, the venerable [Samuel] Adams, twice by invitation," he observed. "He is a patriot according to my own heart."[5] Bache's valuable testimony gives us first-hand experience of Bostonian town meeting democracy. Rather than belaboring Massachusetts as an anti–Republican stronghold, Bache appreciated the direct democracy of its citizens' political activities.

Another witness to small town Massachusetts politics was the indefatigable merchant and revolutionary, Benjamin Vaughan (1751–1835), whose travels took him to London, Paris, Strasbourg (Germany), Cambridge, Massachusetts, and Hallowell, Massachusetts (later part of Maine). A radical British politician in the 1790s, Vaughan was born in Jamaica (West Indies), the son of Samuel Vaughan, an English merchant and planter, and Sarah Hallowell of Boston. A jack-of-all trades, he studied theology at Cambridge University, law at the Middle Temple, and medicine at Edinburgh, before ending up a merchant like his father. In London, he converted to Unitarianism and was befriended by Joseph Priestley, Jeremy Bentham, and Benjamin Franklin. In 1779 he issued the first collected edition of Franklin's works, and in 1806 he published Franklin's *Complete Works* in London. A supporter of American independence, friend of leading Whig politician Lord Shelburne and such English radicals as Richard Price, Joseph Priestley, and Thomas Paine, in 1782–1783 he served as an unofficial British negotiator, securing better peace terms for the thirteen independence-seeking colonies in the Treaty of Paris.

In 1790, Vaughan journeyed to Paris, where he briefly fomented revolutionary action. Elected to the British House of Commons in 1792, he returned to Paris when his radicalism aroused the suspicion of William Pitt's Tory government, which tried to implicate him in treasonable correspondence with France. Unluckily arriving at the beginning of war between France and Great Britain and the commencement of the Reign of Terror, when Englishmen and foreigners were likely to be guillotined as traitors, Vaughan immediately went into hiding. Despite Robespierre's efforts to protect him, he was eventually discovered and imprisoned for a month, after which he departed for Geneva. Indeed, on 9 Thermidor, the day of Robespierre's downfall, Jean Nicholas Billaud-Varenne, having discovered letters between Vaughan and Robespierre, denounced them to the National Convention as royalists conspiring with Pitt to overthrow the Republic. Actually, Vaughan's letters merely advised that Robespierre cease wars of conquest, and instead unite the territories of Belgium, Holland, and the German Rhineland into a great democratic federation that would serve as a buffer between France and its enemies. But Robespierre's rivals in the Committee of Public Safety slyly withheld its text from the Convention. They instead pretended that the correspondence proved Robespierre's intention to partition France between himself and his friends, and abandon Belgium and the Rhineland to the Austrians and Prussians. Despite the danger, Vaughan briefly returned to Paris in 1796, after writing a pamphlet praising France's new government, the Directory. In 1797 he finally returned to Massachusetts, spending the rest of his life in peaceful retirement at Hallowell with his mother, wife, and children.[6]

As this capsule biography amply reveals, Vaughan was atypical, even by the tempestuous standards of late eighteenth-century politics. This Old World radical's assessment of Boston political life, in a letter written in September 1797 from nearby Cambridge to his friend, Democratic-Republican ex-minister to France James Monroe, is refreshingly incisive. Indeed, Vaughan's hitherto unpublished letter deserves to be quoted at length:

> The mass of the people [in Boston] are sincere, but many of them are deceived. Very little is told to them but through the medium of the public papers, which in these parts preponderate for the moment in favor of aristocratical objects. The other [Democratic-Republican] side often manage their public papers [i.e., newspapers] ill, being too frequently personal, instead of offering principles & documents. But though many of the people are thus deceived, they neither forget their sufferings from the English, nor their attachment to liberty. They are sometimes angry with French depradations [*sic*]; but their great motive of action is a dread of *anti-federalism* as implying *a dissolution of their present government*, which they are told is the aim of many, especially to the Southward. The clergy also dread the principles of Jacobinism, from their supposed connection with infidelity, rather than from their aversion to a strong dose of liberty. The people seem more uneasy at the apprehension of war, than angry at the French. The hostilities on the side of the [European military] coalition, which have been projected by some of the federalists [*sic*] leaders, if carried into effect at present, would disgust the whole community. In short, the politics of the country [*sic*] are to a great degree personal, that is, consist of attachments or aversion to particular characters.[7]

Although Vaughan had only recently returned to New England, he had astutely observed its political life. He had kept up-to-date with the latest national political scandals, as is revealed by his acerbic comment to Monroe: "It seems a matter of regret, that some of the supposed friends to liberty, have neither been grave in their character nor correct in money matters."[8]

The ill-fated land speculation enterprises of Robert Morris and John Nicholson, and reckless investments by the Bank of Pennsylvania had recently caused the financial failure of those prominent individuals, precipitated the bankruptcy of Philadelphia merchant John Swanwick, a leading Republican congressman, and adversely affected Pennsylvania secretary of state Alexander James Dallas, Chief Justice Thomas McKean, and other Jeffersonians. These misadventures scandalized puritanical, anti–Bank New England Federalist John Adams.[9]

They also disturbed the newly-arrived Vaughan. But the scandals involved Pennsylvanians, not New Englanders, thus impelling Vaughan's encomia to New England's contrastingly pristine, democratic political habits. Notwithstanding the Federalist loyalties of many Massachusetts and Connecticut voters, Vaughan was "more & more convinced, that the New Englanders are in general not friends to aristocracy, though bearing respect to many aristocrats; that the clergy in particular are philanthropic and lovers of liberty; and that the cause of liberty will soon prevail here." Vaughan concluded that, once the French Directory stopped seizing American ships carrying British goods and negotiated in good faith with American envoys, the political tide would turn in favor of the Jeffersonians. "The late directory have behaved unwisely to America," he pointed out. "But a recantation of their impudence & injustice, far from strengthening their enemies here, will serve to *reconcile the Americans to France*; in which case the present triumph of aristocracy will but deceive them."[10] Apparently, Vaughan thought that New Englanders, including their clergy, would ultimately embrace the French Revolution and the Democratic-Republican Party.[11] Had he read the essays by "Pelham" that appeared in the Hartford *Connecticut Courant* during the presidential election of 1796, he would not have been so certain.

In the early republic, charges that the "three-fifths clause" of the Constitution was deliberately designed to benefit the South are at least as old as "Pelham," the writer in the Hartford *Connecticut Courant* who stigmatized the "three-fifths clause" for granting the slave-holding states an unfair advantage. He argued that such proslavery provisions justified Northern secession from the Union.[12] Jefferson read his articles. As he reported to the Massachusetts solon and political fence-straddler Elbridge Gerry, he was at least temporarily alarmed by their advocacy of the Northern states' secession from the Union.[13]

"Pelham" has not been identified by historians but he was probably Governor Oliver Wolcott, Sr., an orthodox Federalist who wrote his son, Secretary of the Treasury Oliver Wolcott, Jr., at this time recommending New England leave the Union if Jefferson won the presidential election of 1796. "Pelham" must have antagonized those Southerners who, like Jefferson, anticipated tumultuous slave revolts in the future and did not expect the Northern states to send military forces to assist Southern militias in suppressing them. Indeed, Jefferson, probably sarcastically, said he would be satisfied if the Northern states, which were controlled by anti-Southern Federalists in the late 1790s, did not *help* the rebels. When Virginia jurist St. George Tucker proposed a plan of gradual emancipation, which would simultaneously deprive the ex-slaves of most civil rights to encourage them to emigrate, Jefferson voiced his belief that the situation was too urgent for such measures. He advised that Virginia immediately pass an emancipation law before its slaves revolted as those in Haiti had done several years earlier, with catastrophic results for the white planters. "Every day's delay lessens the time we may take for emancipation," he warned. Perhaps having read "Pelham's" articles, Jefferson predicted that the Northern states would stand aloof if such a revolt took place. "Some people derive hope from the aid of the confederated states," he said. "But this is a delusion. There is but one state in the Union which will aid us sincerely if an insurrection begins," he predicted, cryptically alluding to the Carolinas or Georgia, "and that one may perhaps have it's [*sic*] own fire to quench at the same time."[14]

"Pelham's" letters must have fanned these worries. Pelham viewed the Constitution as a mistake, as surrender by the virtuous Puritans of the North to the violent slave-holders of the South, and believed the Northern states would be well-advised to secede from the Union. (He said that they should keep the form of the U.S. Constitution in their new, rump republic.) Despite all the assertions that the Constitution was the result of compromises between the sections, "Pelham" observed, "it will not be an easy task to discover any thing like an equivalent gained by the northern states, for the admission of the negroes into the mass of inhabitants in the southern states, in order to swell the size of their representation in the general congress." The Southern slaveholders were undoubtedly aware of the advantage they had gained, because they continued to treat their slaves like draught animals rather than human beings. "Negroes, are in all respects except in regard to life and death, the CATTLE of the citizens of the southern states," "Pelham" wrote. He was being inadvertently euphemistic; most Southern states had laws exempting owners from prosecution for murdering their slaves if they did so in the course of "correcting" them for misbehavior. "If they were good for food," he continued in a perversely cannibalistic vein, "the probability is, that even the power of destroying their lives would be enjoyed by their owners, as fully as it is over the lives of their cattle." Emphasizing his detestation of slavery, but not suggesting any congressional measures to fund gradual emancipation, "Pelham" described the plight of slaves: "They are bought and sold, they are fed or kept hungry, they are clothed or reduced to nakedness, they are beaten, turned out to the fury of the tempest, and torn from their dearest connexions, with as little remorse, as if they were beasts of the field." Belaboring the obvious, "Pelham" pointed out that masters only insisted that their slaves have congressional representation to advance their own political and economic self-interest, since slaves had "no interests to protect, no happiness to advance" (certainly not on the floor of Congress). Northern delegates at Philadelphia could as fairly have demanded representation for three-fifths of their horses and cattle, he argued. "But it was thought expedient, that the southern states should be indulged in a claim equally absurd and unfounded. Where the equivalent rests, I am ignorant."[15]

According to "Pelham," the Northern states had exaggerated the Constitution's benefits to their section in 1787. They were overwhelmed by fear: the country was in the grip of an economic depression, and Congress under the Articles of Confederation's weak central government, had failed to fund the public debt, raise adequate revenue, or gain respect for the U.S. abroad. Consequently, "the aid of the southern states, was considered by the northern, as of more importance than it was really worth." Rather quietly suggesting that the North leave the South behind, "Pelham" assured his readers that his recommendation of secession should not be dismissed as "depraved," but viewed rationally and objectively. He despised the political and social philosophy of those who called themselves "Democrats," although he was dubious that such a label fit Southern slaveholders. He regarded "Democrats" as radical revolutionary conspirators and evil social disorganizers. "Whoever shall execrate, let the tongues of the Democrats be sealed in silence; for the machinations of Pandemonium are outstripped in the course of guilt, by the plots of our Democratic fellow citizens."[16]

This pseudonymous Connecticut luminary and would-be secessionist implied that he was an important political figure in the confidence of President Washington, lending credence to the suspicion that he might be Governor Wolcott or his son, Secretary of the Treasury Oliver Wolcott, Jr. Insisting on the virtue of his secessionist proposals, "Pelham" wrote, "I am sensible that many excellent men (and among them the most highly revered of all, the great, the beloved Washington) contemplated the subject of this address with extreme anxiety." Admitting that he felt "anxiety also," "Pelham" overcame his fears, because it was "more interesting [i.e., important] to us all" that the North take the major step of leaving the Union because the North and South no longer possessed the same ideals. Convinced that the time for Northern secession had arrived, "Pelham" told his readers he would write additional articles urging them to leave the Union in the near future.[17]

"Pelham" bluntly expressed his conviction: "The northern states *can* subsist as a nation, a republic, without any connection with the southern." He believed that Southerners, because of their slave-holding and their "Jacobin" radicalism, were less virtuous than New Englanders; indeed, they were depraved. As he put it, "It cannot be contested, that if the southern states were possessed of the same political ideas, a union would still be more desirable than a separation." Because of Southern political extremism, and the "Democrats'" paradoxical slave-holding, the sections had little in common. To permit the election of the slave-holding "Democrat" Jefferson, "Pelham" warned, was tantamount to Northerners' "giving up our government." He preferred to "part with the states south of the Potowmack"; and he believed that "no man north of that river, whose heart is not thoroughly Democratic, can hesitate what decision to make. That the question is nearly ripe for decision, there can be but little doubt."

Thus, "Pelham" was averse to remaining in the union with any "Democrats," Northern or Southern; he probably hoped that the Federalists would bring the "Democratic" minority in New England under control once the Northern states seceded.[18]

Most imperative was that the Jeffersonian "Democrats" be kept from power. The "public mind" in Connecticut must "attentively" consider the question of secession, so that when it became necessary, "the decision may be made coolly, and with firmness." The author vaguely predicted "great events" that would make secession inevitable. He advised that the Northern states not abandon "their present constitution," whether the state or national one he did not make clear, "even at the expence of a separation." He intended to "prove the impossibility of a union for any long period in future, both from the moral, and political sentiments and habits of the citizens of the southern states."[19] In "Pelham's" view, the perverse political ideas and slaveholding culture of Southerners placed the onus for inevitable Northern secession on them.

As promised, a few weeks later "Pelham" produced another letter, more moderate in tone. With most of the election results in, it seemed likely that Adams had defeated Jefferson. Therefore, "Pelham" no longer stressed the need for Northern secession. On the contrary, the Southerners were to blame for preventing a united country because Southern Democrats labeled Northern statesmen, including Adams, "monarchists" and "aristocrats." The rise of reckless political parties was to blame for this abrasive language by the Democrats, "Pelham" asserted. "Is there any motive strong enough to overcome the spirit that reigns triumphant over political parties?" he lamented. "Danger fades before it, Virtue shrinks from the conflict, and Patriotism, calls on the rocks and mountains for a shelter from its wrath."[20]

In addition to supporting the "virtuous" Federalist Party, Northerners were more honest and industrious in their personal habits than Southerners were, "Pelham" argued. Unlike Southern "Democrats" of the Jeffersonian ilk, Northerners paid their debts and devoutly attended church. "Pelham" playfully speculated that, for the sections to remain united, they would have to become closer in their social psychologies. Southerners would need to become more virtuous and Northerners would need to become more depraved and debauched, so that both sides could adapt their personalities to a golden mean. Nevertheless, "Pelham" rejected the idea that New Englanders must become immoral to save the Union. He warned, "Which party [it is unclear here if he meant political or social groups] is to yield for the sake of union? Is there to be an accommodation from each? A partial reformation on their part and a partial depravation on ours? Doubtless there is little prospect of the first event, Heaven defend us from the latter."[21] Southern Democrats were irredeemably corrupt; it was dangerous to compromise with them, "Pelham" seemingly advised.

Slavery, with its invidious moral and political effects, was the worst aspect of Southern depravity and the leading cause of sectional divisions, according to "Pelham." Overlooking such slave-holding Southern Federalist leaders as Washington and Pinckney, "Pelham" insisted that, along with Southern degeneracy, "the instance of slavery may be viewed as one forcible cause of a final separation of the United States." He predicted that slave uprisings similar to those that had occurred in the French colonies, especially Haiti, would eventually erupt across the South. He did not want freedom-loving New Englanders to be forced to help suppress these uprisings, as they were obligated to do under the Constitution, a responsibility that their cowardly Southern neighbors would shirk and require them to fulfill. A vicious, disgusting, inherently unstable institution, slavery would eventually precipitate the dissolution of the Union when a situation like that of "France and her colonies" arose. The time of "confusion" (slave uprising) was "not far distant," "Pelham" warned; and the Northern states must refuse to participate in crushing slave uprisings. "A call for assistance (which will certainly be made, for our southern brethren are not calculated to fight their own battles)," he pointed out, "will plunge us into difficulty." If Northerners ignored Southern requests for help in putting down this "rebellion," as the Constitution might call it, they would violate the Constitution; if they helped them, they would disobey their consciences.[22]

The second installment of "Pelham," though less enthusiastic about Northern secession, was more powerful than its predecessor. It recommended policies, specifically advising Northern states to refuse assistance to the South in suppressing slave insurrections, that would provoke ill will in the South and might indeed lead Southerners to choose secession. Ironically, "Pelham" expected to achieve the Union's demise one way or the other.

In 1797, Jefferson wrote to Elbridge Gerry, who had begun a correspondence with him and Adams urging them to cooperate in a fusion government after his election to the vice-presidency. Jefferson admitted the fears of disunion that "Pelham" had aroused in him. He suspected that Pelham was the pseudonym for a British merchant residing in New England, who thought he would advance his government's interests by encouraging New England secession from the Union. Jefferson claimed that British merchants and bankers controlled the American economy, many of them in the guise of "false citizens" and naturalized traders. He insisted that, as secretary of state and in private life, he had shown no partiality for the French over the British despite Federalist charges, and that he "wish[ed] that we could take our stand on a ground perfectly neutral and independant towards all nations." He considered "Pelham's" writings as evidence of British influence in American politics. "They have wished a monopoly of commerce and influence with us," he asserted. "And they have in fact obtained it." British merchants and financiers used their money and influence in the seaports and the small towns to gain the Federalists political power, and, "advancing fast to a monopoly of our banks and public funds," they were "placing our public finances under their control." Emulating his more famous Mazzei letter, he wrote, perhaps alluding to Hamilton and Washington, if not Adams, that the British "have in their alliance the most influential characters in and out of office," and controlled the national government. He considered the United States government "under the bondage" of the British. With their control of the U.S. press, the British had even succeeded in convincing many Americans that the Republicans, who "wish merely to recover self-government," were guilty of "the charge of subserving one foreign influence, because they resist submission to another." Jefferson believed the British partisans aimed to involve the United States in the war against France; they changed their minds when the collapse of the Bank of England and recent military reverses caused the British government to seek a negotiated peace.[23]

Jefferson identified Pelham's secessionist, pro–British agitation, not with the average native New Englander, whom he still considered loyal to the Union and republicanism (if not to his Republican Party), but with a small group of British merchants and bankers and their upper-class elite Federalist associates. What Jefferson especially feared was that pro–British partisans would use American intervention in the European war to create violent dissension between North and South, and thereby split the Union into several hostile nations. He viewed the Pelham letters as symptomatic of this objective. "After plunging us in all the broils of the European nations, there would remain but one act to close our tragedy," he warned Gerry, "that is, to break up our union: and even this they [the pro–British faction] have ventured seriously and solemnly to propose and maintain by argument, in a Connecticut paper."[24]

"Pelham's" articles were republished in several newspapers, mainly in New York City and Philadelphia. They appeared in the Philadelphia *New-World* and Benjamin Franklin's Bache's Philadelphia *General Advertiser: Aurora*, the leading Republican newspaper. One Republican writer, "Greene," bluntly charged that Pelham represented the views of extremist New England Federalists who wanted to secure domination of a smaller Union without the Southern states. They were willing to precipitate civil war to secure their objectives, he asserted. According to "Greene," writers like Pelham sought "to set the *north* at war with the *south*, to make our *northern* fellow citizens hate their *southern* fellow citizens." He targeted the "host of 'exclusive federalists'" as the originators of Pelham's "unfortunate indiscretion."[25]

With a different, more nationalistic emphasis that was sympathetic to New England, Jefferson ascribed the disunionist screeds, not to a native of Connecticut or Massachusetts, but to "foreign and false citizens" who were natives of Britain but for convenience sake had become "factitious" American citizens in order to advance their mercantile careers. Unlike "Pelham," *real* Americans, even those native New Englanders who were inclined to follow Jefferson's political foes, the Federalists, unhesitatingly rejected "Pelham's" cry for disunion. Jefferson was relieved to find that their lack of enthusiasm had brought Pelham's articles to an abrupt close. As he optimistically put it, in words that would resound more strongly in his First Inaugural Address, "I have been happy however in believing, from the stifling of this effort that that dose [of pro-secession rhetoric] was found too strong, and excited as much repugnance there [among Connecticut Federalists] as it did horror in other parts of our country, and that whatever follies we may be led into as to foreign nations, we shall never give up our union, the last anchor of our hope, and that alone which is to prevent this heavenly country from becoming an arena of gladiators."[26]

Perhaps more than any of his contemporaries, even New Englanders like his friend John Adams, Jefferson admired the political structure and the political culture of the New England towns, though he was disappointed by the anti–Jeffersonian objectives they often pursued. Like Vaughan, at this time he was hopeful that New England would soon transfer its allegiance to the Republicans. In June 1797, he wrote Aaron Burr, who had spent several weeks campaigning in the New England states in the fall of 1796, congratulating him on his election to the New York assembly.[27]

As he would show even more decisively during the presidential election of 1800, Burr was a zealous and charming campaigner. He travelled throughout New England during the election of 1796, attempting to rouse Republican support. It was rumored that he asked Samuel Adams to run as a Jefferson/Burr elector in Massachusetts, which Adams did, although he lost. Burr reported to Massachusetts presidential elector Elbridge Gerry and others that Alexander Hamilton spread false reports that Vermont's electoral votes for Adams would be disqualified because the legislature did not employ the proper procedures, and therefore it was imperative that all New England electors vote for Hamilton's choice for president, Thomas Pinckney. Burr probably hoped that on the basis of this information, Gerry would cast an electoral vote for him or Jefferson to prevent Pinckney from gaining the presidency. In furtherance of this objective, he wrote Gerry that New York's Republicans "see with much pleasure your Name … in the list of Electors." He warned Gerry that Pinckney would receive all of South Carolina's electoral votes, and if he obtained all the electoral votes of Massachusetts he would become president, not Adams. Perhaps not entirely accurately, he assured Gerry, "The republican[s] here would prefer A. [to Pinckney] having confidence in his Talents and integrity." However, Gerry did not vote for Jefferson, but threw away his second ballot to ensure that Adams won the first office.[28]

Burr was more successful in winning the spring 1797 elections to the New York assembly, campaigning for peace with France and defending the rights of tallow chandlers (candle-makers) to pollute the atmosphere of lower New York City, than he was in the presidential contest of 1796. He received only thirty electoral votes. Still, this was a good showing for someone who was relatively unknown on the national level.[29]

Burr's assembly victory, Jefferson confessed, had surprised him, given his impression that New York was irredeemably aristocratic, "what with the English influence in the lower, and the Patroon influence in the upper parts of your state, I presume[d] little is to be hoped." In fact, he was more interested in learning Burr's opinion about the prospects that the "Eastern States" (New England) would turn to the Republicans. Hopeful that the New England farmers would perceive that their natural interests ought to prompt them to join the Jeffersonians, he asked, will "the people there, who are unquestionably republican," "ever awake to the true state of things?" He hoped that they would lead in the republican reform of the nation, as they had in conducting the resistance to Great Britain before the Revolution.[30]

Despite his confidence that New Englanders would eventually turn to him and his Republican Party for guidance rather than the "aristocratic" Federalists, Jefferson continued to link New Englanders with monarchy and reverence for established authority. Compared with some of them, he thought, even the conservative matriarch Martha Washington was democratic. He enjoyed telling a story about "a man from New England" who sought an interview with Washington after his election as president. According to the English visitor Joshua Brookes, Jefferson told him, "A man from New England called one time on George Washington when President, and [while] going up stairs, he met Mrs. Washington. The man asked her: 'Is His Majesty at home?' [to which she replied:] 'Sir, Is His Majesty at home! Mr. Washington is at home, Sir!'" In a *Memoir* now owned by the New-York Historical Society, Brookes mentioned this anecdote, which he heard from Jefferson during his visit to Monticello in August 1799. (According to Brookes' account, Jefferson also brazenly criticized Washington.)[31] However, Jefferson was confident that Federalist political maladroitness, together with the attractiveness of his Republican Party's low-tax, free speech and free press platform, would eventually convert New England's lukewarm Federalists, whom he thought composed the majority, to the Jeffersonian way of thinking.[32]

3

Jefferson and New England
The Crisis of the Late 1790s

Even during the desperate period of the Alien and Sedition Acts and the undeclared war with France, Jefferson had never desired the New England states' departure from the Union. Painfully aware that the president, two-thirds of the Senate, and half of the House of Representatives sided with the Federalists, in 1798 he felt "the most gloomy apprehensions." Although Jefferson considered it the most desperate juncture in the brief history of American freedom, he remained optimistic about New England's conversion from Federalism to Republicanism. Aside from the possibility that a Napoleonic victory in Europe might lead to a "republican revolution" in Great Britain (which would vitiate Federalist hopes for war as England's ally), something that Jefferson unrealistically continued to expect for much of his life, he took solace from the increase of Republican newspapers in New England. "There can be no doubt that a revolution of opinion in Massachusetts & Connecticut is working," he observed to Madison. "Two whig [i.e., Jeffersonian] presses have been set up in each of those States." He ascribed the "wonderful stir ... commencing in the Eastern States" to farmers' fear that Congress would impose national direct taxes on land to pay for military operations against France.[1]

Jefferson wrote to Edmund Pendleton that the attention of New Englanders had turned to national events as a result of the sensational brawl between Democratic-Republican Vermont congressman Matthew Lyon and Connecticut Federalist Roger Griswold, after which citizens became increasingly concerned about the mismanagement of government finance and foreign policy. Once Massachusetts voters became aware that "it is their members who are for war measures," Jefferson was confident they would vote against "these gentlemen" for re-election that summer: "We have, therefore, great reason to expect some favorable changes in the representatives from that quarter." Jefferson wrote Pendleton concerning the New Englanders, "They begin to open their eyes on this to the Eastward & to suspect they have been hoodwinked. Two or three whig presses have set up in Massachusetts, & as many more in Connecticut." Jefferson took solace from news that Adams's message to Congress of March 19, 1798, which Jefferson called a "war message," caused "new alarm," precipitating town meetings in Massachusetts and "petitions & remonstrances by great majorities, against war-measures, and these meetings are likely to spread." Jefferson did not disguise his joy at the prospect that Massachusetts and Connecticut would contribute to the Republican representation in the lower house of Congress. He also expected conversions to Jeffersonianism in

Pennsylvania, New Jersey, Maryland, and Virginia, which would give the "whigs … a very strong majority in the H of Representatives."[2]

Viewing the violent encounter on the floor of the House of Representatives between New Englanders Griswold and Lyon in a larger context, Jefferson predicted that the national legislature's boisterous demeanor would increase public respect for the state governments. As he wrote to Peregrine Fitzhugh, a young Maryland Republican from a prominent family, "Some very disagreeable differences have taken place in Congress. They cannot fail to lessen the respect of the public for the general government, and to replace their state governments in a greater degree of comparative respectability. I do not think it for the interest of the general government itself, & still less of the Union at large, that the state governments should be so little respected as they have been."[3]

Employing a solar system-analogy between the states and the federal government, Jefferson depicted the national government as the center and most important part ("sun") of the republic. He thus revealed his nationalism. "However I dare say that in time all these [state governments] as well as their central government, like the planets revolving round their common Sun," he said, "acting & acted upon according to their respective weights & distances, will produce that beautiful equilibrium on which our constitution is founded, and which I believe it will exhibit to the world in a degree of perfection unexampled but in the planetary system itself." Jefferson concluded with a summary of his moderate, "enlightened" nationalism: "The enlightened statesman therefore will endeavor to preserve the weight & influence of every part, as too much given to any member of it would destroy the general equilibrium."[4]

In 1798, Jefferson's anxiety over the possibility of war with France led him to extreme conclusions about the intentions of his political opponents. Evaluating events of the previous decade from the perspective of the current Federalist-Republican conflict, Jefferson accused several Eastern Federalists of being potential secessionists. Anger at the prospect that Federalists in Congress might provoke war with France distorted his retrospective view of Massachusetts' state legislators' rationale for opposing a stronger central government during the 1780s, which he misguidedly imputed to an alleged conspiracy to weaken the national government's powers sufficiently to make monarchy a palatable alternative.[5]

This was a common suspicion among Virginians about the "Eastern" states at the time of Shays' Rebellion in 1786–1787. Indeed, Jefferson may have originally picked it up from his friend James Madison years earlier. Prior to the calling of the Constitutional Convention in 1787, Madison, Washington, John Jay, Henry Knox, and others, predicted that the failure of the Confederation Congress, whose requests for funds most of the states ignored, might terminate in the Union's destruction. Madison predicted that if the Philadelphia Convention proved unable to institute a stronger national government, the result would be three separate regional confederations or monarchy. In February 1787, he wrote to Governor Edmund Randolph of Virginia and many others in this vein, particularly charging that New Englanders desired a king: "Our situation is becoming every day more and more critical…. No respect is paid to the federal authority; and people of reflection unanimously agree that the existing Confederacy is tottering to its foundation. Many individuals of weight particularly in the Eastern district are suspected of leaning towards Monarchy. Other individuals predict a partition of the States into two or more Confederacies." Madison thought that there was greater likelihood of what he called a "revolution" in the direction of a fragmented Confederation than monarchy, although he hoped Randolph, as governor of Virginia, would take action to prevent either outcome.[6]

Jefferson was dismayed by what he called President Adams's "insane message" after receiving the XYZ dispatches. Adams recommended increasing the army and navy and making other war preparations. Although ignorant of the details of the XYZ Affair, Jefferson anticipated that monarchists and New England secessionists would demand war with France to facilitate governmental centralization and a gradual transition to monarchy. In his opinion, he wrote James Madison, no "views either of interest or honour" justified a U.S. declaration of war against France. Going back in time, he reflected bitterly on the alleged monarchical quests of Hamilton and the New England delegates at the 1786 Annapolis Convention and the 1787 Constitutional Convention. Pondering the Federalist "views" for now seeking war, he suspected they wanted to break up the Union. He advised Madison, "Whatever then be our stock of charity or liberality we must resort to other views, and those so well known to have been entertained at Annapolis & afterwards at the grand convention [1787 Constitutional Convention] by a particular set of men [monarchists], present themselves as those alone which can account for so extraordinary a degree of impetuosity," as to seek a declaration of war. He recalled a recent conversation with two Republican congressmen, Thompson J. Skinner of Massachusetts and Abraham Baldwin of Georgia, the latter a delegate to the 1787 Philadelphia Convention, who suggested that New Englanders, hoping for the United States' eventual return to monarchy, had deliberately obstructed progress at the 1786–1787 Annapolis and Philadelphia conventions. He warned Madison, "Perhaps instead of what was then in contemplation [monarchy] a separation of the union, which has been so much the topic to the Eastward of late, may be the thing aimed at."[7] From Jefferson's point of view, the Federalists, their monarchical hopes thwarted, had shifted their designs to New England's secession, as "Pelham's" articles during the election of 1796 hinted.

In notes that he later organized for posthumous publication as the famous *Anas*, Jefferson described his January 1798 conversation with Skinner and Baldwin. They told him that in 1786, while he was abroad in Paris, an *entente* was formed between New Yorkers and Eastern state congressional delegates involving "people who were partly monarchical in principle or frightened with Shays' rebellion & the impotence of the old Congress" in confronting it. According to Jefferson's informants, these Easterners were plotting a *coup* to overthrow the government and asked Washington for help, but he angrily rejected them. These monarchical Easterners hoped for the Constitutional Convention's failure, an outcome that they thought would promote their objectives. Jefferson's nemesis Hamilton was "their leader," and when the Convention politely ignored Hamilton's extremist views at the Convention, his disillusioned "associates" sought to prevent the Convention from adopting any plan. Disappointed by the Constitution as finally adopted, they were prepared to use "force" to achieve their objectives, only awaiting their opportunity. For Jefferson, Skinner and Baldwin's seemingly reliable revelations, which Madison may have confirmed, explained the reluctance of several New England members to attend the Annapolis Convention and the Constitutional Convention. As he wrote, they shed "a blaze of light on the conduct of several members from NY & the Eastern states in the Convention of Annapolis & the Grand convention. At that of Annapolis several Eastern members most vehemently opposed Madison's proposition for a more General Convention with more general powers. They wished things to get more & more into confusion to justify the violent measure they proposed." Although not there to observe it,

Jefferson wrote that they "publicly ridiculed ... the idea of establishing a government by reasoning & agreement." Ironically, Jefferson's *a posteriori* observations vigorously denounced foes of the Constitution even though he was only a lukewarm advocate at his perch in Paris during 1787–1789.[8]

Whatever his hostility toward New England voters' rejection of his party during the 1790s, Jefferson could not help but admire the region's practice of direct democracy. Even at the height of his disgust over the Alien and Sedition Acts, Jefferson appraised the Federalist sanctuary's custom of directly electing jurors as eminently suitable for his state's emulation. He was painfully aware that in Virginia, where county sheriffs chosen by county courts picked state juries, and U.S. marshals analogously chosen by the president picked federal grand juries, Republican congressman Samuel J. Cabell was recently humiliated after Richmond's Federalist marshal selected a federal grand jury. After Federalist Supreme Court Justice James Iredell delivered an inflammatory "charge" to the jury, the jurors "presented" (denounced) Cabell for disseminating "unfounded calumnies" against the Adams Administration in a circular letter to his Albemarle County constituents over a year *before* passage of the Sedition Act.[9]

Jefferson's anxiety about the way his state chose federal and local jurors was greatly exacerbated by the trial of anti–Federalist violators of the Sedition Act. Conducted in a browbeating manner by Supreme Court Justice Samuel Chase in the state's federal circuit court, these trials were travesties of freedom of speech. All the defendants were convicted. Thus, in November 1798 Jefferson sent his old friend John Taylor of Caroline, then serving in the state assembly, a petition requesting passage of a law for the direct election of state and federal jurors. Deriding the presence of English and Scottish merchants (whom he assumed were pro-monarchical) on Virginia's juries as "the *jury of all nations*," he proposed that the state's voters choose its federal grand jurors, who should be confined to native-born Americans; or that they be picked by lot. His model for this radical proposal, he made clear, was the New England states. As he wrote Taylor, "The New England states have always had these [jurors] elected by their selectmen, who are elected by the people." Less enthusiastically describing the laws of other states, he said, "Several or most of the other states have a large number appointed (I do not know how) to attend, out of whom 12 for each cause are taken by lot."[10]

Jefferson was only vaguely conversant with existing laws regarding jury selection in the New England states. Despite being Federalist strongholds, Massachusetts, Vermont, and Connecticut employed the most democratic methods of jury selection. In Massachusetts, all juries were directly elected by town freeholders, although selectmen, themselves elected officials, first presented a list of those eligible to be petty jurors. Vermont and Connecticut stipulated that only substantial freeholders, selected at annual town meetings, might serve as jurors.[11]

Hoping his state's implementation of direct democracy would eventually surpass that of New England, Jefferson proposed that Virginia implement popular election of juries. Although the petition he sent Taylor to present in the legislature praised the New England states, which "have provided, with laudable foresight, for the appointment of jurors by select men [*sic*] chosen by the people themselves," he believed his state could surpass their democratic achievement. He proposed to utilize the "precincts" (wards) or "districts" into which the assembly had recently divided counties for setting up public schools, enabling the "inhabitants of every precinct [to] ... meet at a given time & place" to select grand and/or petit jurors by lot. Undoubtedly, Jefferson hoped by this means to secure more authentic democracy in his state, which he later proposed to further extend by the popular election of state

and federal judges. He also hoped to impede the Sedition Law's operation by a more egalitarian (and presumably more Republican) selection of jurors.[12]

The greatest obstacle to democracy in Virginia and most of the other Southern states
was not the undemocratic method of jury selection but the restriction of the suffrage to fifty-
acre freeholders and, most significantly, the overshadowing institution of slavery. In a searing
indictment in notes composed while writing his famous series of essays for the *National
Gazette* in 1792 (perhaps because he was writing for himself rather than for public consumption), Jefferson's friend Madison, after citing Aristotle and the well-known fact that the majority of the population in the ancient "democracies" of Athens and Rome were slaves, labeled
Virginia an aristocracy. Because of the existence of slavery, Madison considered Virginia an
aristocracy and viewed the Northern states as more democratic. Only one-fourth of the adult
white males in Virginia were freeholders entitled to vote, he pointed out. The rest were slaves
and propertyless whites. Showing a radical side that he confined to these notes and his anonymous essays of 1791–1793, Madison observed: "Were the slaves freed and the right of suffrage
extended to all, the operation of the government might be far different. The slavery of the
Southern States, throws the power much more into the hands of property, than in the Northern States. Hence the people of property in the former are much more contented with their
established Governments, than the people of property in the latter."[13]

Perhaps convinced by such events as Shays' Rebellion, which he hardly mentioned during the debates in the Constitutional Convention, Madison thought that the upper classes
in New England were less politically secure than Virginia's slaveholders, what a later generation
of historians would call "insecure versus secure elites." In this case, Madison's commentary
was less than astute with regard to the contests between Democratic-Republicans and Federalists. During the 1790s, the Federalist Party more securely controlled New England's governments and politics than the Democratic-Republicans did those of the slaveholding states.
They had a greater foothold in the Jeffersonian South than the Jeffersonians possessed in
New England; and the Federalists would continue to dominate the politics of the Northeast,
except for a few years during Jefferson's second term as president, until the 1830s.[14]

By the summer of 1798, Jefferson, feeling desperate at the bold steps the Federalist Congress was taking to prepare for war with France, seemed ready to forgive New England's ostensible deviations from the democratic faith of Democratic-Republicanism. By contrast, his
friend, Virginia planter and states' rights philosopher John Taylor of Caroline, appalled that
Virginia's interests were suffering in a Northern-dominated Union, hoped that Virginia and
North Carolina would secede and form an independent confederation. During 1797 and
1798, disillusioned by the presidential victory of John Adams, whom he considered a monarchist, and the rupture with France, Taylor contemplated "whether it will be better to submit
to an immovable fixation of our monarchy for the sake of union; or to break the union for
the sake of destroying our monarchy." He expected peaceful secession, rather than a violent
confrontation with the other states. Indeed, he was optimistic that they might experience a
revival of republicanism in response, precipitating "a renovation ... upon principles which
may generate the public good." If Virginia remained in a union dominated by New England
Federalists and Anglophiles, "the union will exist, but upon principles which will oppress
human nature," he warned.[15] Taylor anticipated a bitter fate for Virginia if she remained in
the Union. He feared that "the southern states must lose their capital and commerce–and
that America is destined to war–standing armies–and oppressive taxation, by which the power

of the few here, as in other countries, will be matured into an irresistible scourge of human happiness."[16]

Jefferson replied temperately, firmly stating his opposition to breaking up the Union merely to express irritation at New Englanders. "It is true that we are compleatly [*sic*] under the saddle of Massachusetts & Connecticut, and that they ride us very hard, cruelly insulting our feelings as well as exhausting our strength and substance," he agreed. "If to rid ourselves of the present rule of Massachusetts & Connecticut we break the Union, will the evil stop there?" he inquired. He believed political disputes were inherent in human nature, and would not be eliminated if the sister states, Virginia and North Carolina, formed their own nation. Envisaging the unlikely secession of Massachusetts and Connecticut, he observed, "Suppose the N. England States alone cut off, will our natures be changed? Are we not men still to the south of that, & with all the passions of men?" To Jefferson's knowledge, "an association of men who will not quarrel with one another is a thing which never yet existed, from the greatest confederacy of nations down to a town meeting or vestry." "In every free & deliberating society" it was natural that "there must, from the nature of man, be opposite parties & violent dissensions & discords; and one of these, for the most part, must prevail over the other for a longer or shorter time." Predicting that the existence of any federal government would be impossible if every disgruntled party chose to secede to escape from the "temporary superiority" of its opponent, he pointed out, "If we reduce our Union to Virginia & N. Carolina, immediately the conflict will be established between the representatives of these two States, and they will end by breaking into their simple units." In accord with this theory, he humorously advised, "Seeing that we must have somebody to quarrel with, I had rather keep our New England associates for that purpose than to see our bickerings transferred to others."[17]

Observing that New Englanders had a unique character of their own, as he had in his letter to Chastellux years earlier, Jefferson implied that the pressures of an increasing population on their meager, often scrabbly land supply would exacerbate New Englanders' naturally argumentative character, but at the same time make them natural foils for the more easygoing, freewheeling Southern farmers and slaveholders. Feeling relieved at the prospect that Southern Republicans would remain in the Union with cantankerous New Englanders as adversaries rather than join a fraternal confederacy with North Carolina and other Southern states, which would inevitably fall apart because of their own disagreements, Jefferson wrote, "They [New Englanders] are circumscribed within such narrow limits, & their population so full, that their numbers will ever be the minority, and they are marked, like the Jews, with such a peculiarity of character as to constitute from that circumstance the natural division of our parties." Thus, Jefferson had reached the conclusion that the puritanical New Englanders were natural antagonists to Virginians, and he believed that what was natural was good.[18]

Taylor was unpersuaded by Jefferson's reasoning. He refused to believe that political parties were inevitable. Ironically, despite his objections to New England's Federalist politics, Taylor rated Connecticut's consensual town meeting democracy the ideal form of government, a disconcerting admission in light of his proposal for Virginia's secession from Massachusetts and Connecticut. He wrote Jefferson at the end of June 1798: "That parties, sufficiently malignant to destroy the public good, are not naturally the issue of every popular government, seems to be evinced by the examples of the state governments, and particularly by the eminent example of Connecticut, which has for about two centuries enjoyed a compleat [*sic*] unanimity under a government; the most democratic of any representative form which ever existed."

As long as the people were happy under their government, Taylor prophesied, consensus would naturally emerge. He deplored political parties as "artificial" byproducts of constitutions, such as the British and American that institutionalized a deleterious "scheme of ballancing [sic] power against power." "Is it not possible," Taylor asked Jefferson, "that our great error has been imitation of the latter [British] precedent, by counterpoising power against power, instead of securing to liberty an ascendant over power, whether simple or complex."[19] Questioning the Anglo-American system of separation of powers, Taylor instead advocated the greatest possible degree of direct democracy. For this reason, he praised Connecticut, where, although suffrage was restricted to Congregationalist landholders, the people directly elected all officials, including the governor and the legislature.

Deriding Jefferson's optimism that the Federalist "reign of witches" would defeat itself by voting unpopular new taxes and war preparations, Taylor retorted "that parties ... are not natural to a republican government really dependent on national will and also that there is nothing supernatural in the party paroxysm which now exists." Since the crisis arose from the emergence of parties, "the cure must lie in the abolition of these causes," not in the ascendancy of a different party. Expounding a pessimistic view of human nature, Taylor found little consolation even in the prospect of a Republican victory. Although he ostensibly sought Southern secession from a union dominated by mercenary New Englanders, he preferred compromise. Warning that a "southern aristocracy oppressing the northern states, would be as detestable, as a northern, domineering over the southern states," Taylor hoped that state conventions would be called to demand a national constitutional convention. Unlike the Great Convention of 1787, he hoped this one would aim for greater democracy, passing constitutional amendments that provided for a vast extension of the suffrage and rotation in office. Such reforms, Taylor believed, would end popular "submission to anti-republican measures" and provide "for the people, a real influence over the government." Ironically, Taylor's demand for direct democracy had its closest parallel with the New England town meetings, which were controlled by Federalists. On the national level, Taylor despised the Federalist-run government, charging that it created a war atmosphere in order to increase the size of the army and government bureaucracies, to be financed by oppressive direct taxes that made feudal serfdom seem pleasant by comparison. As he wrote Jefferson, "Avarice and ambition, entrenched behind perpetual taxation, in a disciplined corps, have become the Lords paramount of the creation." In Taylor's view, the threat of unlimited national taxation was merely a type of slavery, a legerdemain by which the "rulers of man, have discovered that he may be turned to a greater account, by allowing him a nominal liberty, as an excitement to labor."[20]

Jefferson's feelings toward New England remained favorable, even at this dark period for the Republican Party, and in Jefferson's opinion, for America's representative democracy. He invariably depicted the New England political scene in a positive light, forecasting a favorable turn of events for the Democratic-Republican Party. For example, as early as February 1799, he reported in detail to his friend Madison that New Hampshire seemed less hostile to the Jeffersonians than in the past. "The opposition to Livermore were not republican," he remarked of the opponents of moderate Federalist congressman Samuel Livermore. He learned that popular opinion there was undecided, but no longer hostile to the Jeffersonians. The members of the state assembly wanted more information about what was actually going on in the government and in the Adams Administration's dealings with France. "I have however seen letters from New Hampshire from which it appears that the public sentiment there ...

at present it is dead water," he wrote. "That during the whole of their late session not a word has been heard of Jacobinism, disorganization &c no reproach of any kind cast on the republicans. That there has been a general complaint among the members that they could hear but one side of the question, and a great anxiety to possess a paper [newspaper] or papers which would put them in possession of both sides." Compared to earlier reports, Jefferson considered this state of inertia in New Hampshire encouraging. "From Massachusetts and R.I. I have no information," he regretfully continued. "Connecticut remains riveted in her political & religious bigotry."[21]

Even during the 1790s, when New England was the stronghold of his political opponents, Jefferson accepted its merchants' desire to reap profits from the "carrying trade." This was the term used for ships carrying the products of foreign countries, such as sugar and coffee from French or Spanish colonies, to their mother countries or to other parts of the world, rather than exporting products made in the U.S. At the same time, he regretted that the Government's protection of the carrying trade was a major cause of its friction with the French and especially the British, who said that such trade was illegal in both peace and war (the notorious Rule of 1756). Ideally, he would have preferred that American ships restrict themselves to exporting U.S. products alone, or even confine themselves to domestic trade to avoid wars over freedom of the seas. During the Quasi-War with France, this subject was on his mind. He was also painfully aware of the power of the Congregationalist clergy in Massachusetts, and the influence it exerted in state politics. He imputed the defeat of General William Heath, the Republican candidate, in the 1799 election for governor of Massachusetts, by Increase Sumner, the Adams Federalist incumbent, to religious orthodoxy's influence on the voters. Heath received a larger number of votes in Norfolk and Middlesex Counties, as well as Boston, than his Republican predecessors. "I observe in the election of governor of Massachusetts that the vote for Heath (out of Boston) is much strengthened," he wrote Virginia Judge Edmund Pendleton. "Could the people of that state emerge from the deceptions under which they are kept by their clergy, lawyers, and English presses, our salvation would be sure & easy. Without that, I believe it will be effected; but it will be uphill work."[22]

He thought that Massachusetts was on the verge of a breakthrough in favor of Democratic-Republicanism, but that the state's support for the Jeffersonians would always be tenuous and unreliable because the merchants dominated its politics and economic life; and they would always demand that their interests, particularly protection for the carrying trade, come before those of the nation's farming majority. "Nor can we expect ever their cordial co-operation, because they will not be satisfied longer than while we are sacrificing every thing to navigation and a navy," he bluntly informed Pendleton. He favored attempting to convince the New England merchants to engage in domestic trade alone. This would preserve peace with foreign countries and consequently lead to reductions in the size of the army and navy, for which there would be less need. But Jefferson was pessimistic that this would ever happen. He wrote, "What a glorious exchange would it be could we persuade our navigating fellow citizens to embark their capital in the internal commerce of our country, exclude foreigners from that, and let them [the foreign traders] take the carrying trade in exchange." He considered a policy of isolation the safest road to keeping out of wars, even quixotically proposing to "abolish the diplomatic establishments & never suffer an armed vessel [such as French minister 'Citizen' Edmund Genet's privateers in 1793] of any nation to enter our ports." Quickly returning to reality, he concluded, "But these things can be thought of only in times of wisdom, not of passion and folly."[23] Jefferson always recognized that any national leader, especially the president, would have to commit himself to protecting New England's right to the carrying trade and to neutral rights on the seas as a constituent part of representing *all* the people.[24]

Although the New England states had given him no electoral votes for the presidency in either 1796 or 1800, Jefferson remained optimistic that they would eventually turn to the Democratic-Republicans. In this hope he may have gained solace from an unexpected source: ex-president John Adams, who wrote him shortly after his return to Quincy in 1801, that Massachusetts was united behind him: "This part of the Union is in a state of perfect Tranquility and I See nothing to obscure your prospect of a quiet and prosperous Administration, which I heartily wish you."[25]

After election to the presidency in March 1801, Jefferson was confident that New Englanders would abandon their fanatical, conservative clergy and Federalist leaders and enter the Republican fold. He assured Massachusetts-born Moses Robinson (1742–1813), a member of a prominent Vermont family, one of that state's founding fathers, and a leading layman in the Bennington Congregational Church, of his optimistic expectations for the "eastern States." Unlike most New Englanders, Robinson was a zealous Jeffersonian. As one of Vermont's U.S. senators during the early 1790s, he had opposed Hamilton's financial program as well as the Jay Treaty, a critical test of party adherence. During Jefferson's administration, he stalwartly supported the Embargo Act as necessary to the growing pains of nationhood. In a letter to Jefferson the day before his inauguration, Robinson pledged his support. He analyzed the Federalist opposition in terms similar to those Jefferson often used.

As a leading political and religious figure of Vermont, Robinson's Republicanism and his devotion to Jefferson were anomalous. He had served in most of Vermont's important state offices, including the state legislature and the governorship, although Federalist Nathaniel Chittenden was probably more popular. In Robinson's opinion, it was regrettable that Adams rather than Jefferson had succeeded Washington. He believed that the majority actually preferred Jefferson. He thought that Adams' presidency had discredited the principles of the American Revolution. "The late Administration gave them [the voters] Greater Evidence of the importance of Placing one in the Executive branch of Government, whom they are Persuaided [sic] Possessed the Same Sentiments that Generally prevailed in 1776, who believes that a Republican form of Government is best Calculated to promote the happiness of mankind—to Such a person and to Such only Should the people of the United States Commit the Administration of the Government as the safe Guardian of their Constitutional Rights and priviledges," he asserted. Since most people were aware that Jefferson wrote the Declaration of Independence, the new president was undoubtedly pleased by Robinson's praise.[26]

Robinson concluded his analysis of the dangers of executive prerogative by cautiously hoping for institutional reform: "I hope however that the time may arrive when the Safety of our Civil and Religious Rights will not so much depend on the disposition of the person administering the Executive branch of Government, as at present it does."[27]

Jefferson must have appreciated Robinson's information on the political environment in Vermont, a region of the country he had not visited since his trip with Madison in 1791. His assessment bore much in common with Jefferson's evaluation. "This State have [sic] ever Since the XYZ business, been deceived Especially the Eastern part of it adjacent to the State of New hampshire [*sic*] and Massachusetts, they begin to have their Eyes open & Just at the last Session of the Legislature there was but a mere majority [for the Federalists]," Robinson reported. "I believe it will not Continue Long in the Same Sentiments; as in other parts of the union so in this State every Republican were [*sic*] Represented as Enemies to their Country and friends to France and many honest men truly believed it to be the case—it has in a measure Subsided—and the Republicans appear to be gaining Ground[,] at least they are bolder and the Federalists appear more down."

The new president learned that Bennington's Republicans intended to celebrate his inauguration day, which even "the most Sober men of the Republicans" considered "an auspicious Event in the Course of divine Providence." While zealously applauding a recent French victory over the Austrians, the peaceful Robinson lamented "the Great Carnage and Sheding [*sic*] of human blood in Europe." Nevertheless, he predicted, "there will doubtless come good from this partial Evil." Eccentrically equating the Jeffersonian and French "victories," he assured Jefferson, "I Rejoice to See the Republican Interest prevail in any Place or Country but more Especially in our native land."[28]

Jefferson was aware of Robinson's party loyalties as well as his religious devotion when he speedily and enthusiastically replied to him. "I entertain real hope that the whole body of your fellow citizens (many of whom had been carried away by the X.Y.Z. business) will shortly be consolidated in the same sentiments" as the majority of the electorate that chose him for the presidency, Jefferson confided to Robinson. In the warm glow of his election, he chose to minimize the differing ideologies of the two parties, and believed that the Federalist rank-and-file were devoted to "republicanism," if only with a small "r." "When they examine the real principles of both parties, I think they will find little to differ about," he observed.[29]

Jefferson revealed that, despite his contempt for the New England Federalist leadership, he was willing to forgive their opposition and allow them to enter the Republican fold. "I know, indeed, that there are some of their leaders who have so committed themselves, that pride, if no other passion, will prevent their coalescing" with the Republicans, he admitted. "We must be easy with them." He reserved his greatest hostility for the clergy of the "eastern States." He blamed their exaggerated attacks on his anticlericalism, which depicted him as a wild-eyed atheist contemptuous of Jesus and morality in general, for the widespread opposition to his election in New England. He conjectured that, in light of their hostility to the French Revolution and their support for the Sedition Act, which restricted freedom of speech and the press, they intolerantly hoped to establish the Christian religion as the national religion of the United States. He somberly predicted, "The eastern States will be the last to come over, on account of the dominion of the clergy; who had got a smell of union between Church and State, and began to indulge reveries which can never be realised [*sic*] in the present state of science."[30]

In his letter to Robinson and many others at this time, he compared the New England clergy to benighted medieval priests. He surmised that their opposition to progress, science, and rational enlightenment, qualities he embodied, was the basic reason for their fanatical opposition to his candidacy. "If, indeed, they could have prevailed on us to view all advances in science as dangerous innovations, and to look back to the opinions and practices of our forefathers, instead of looking forward, for improvement, a promising groundwork would have been laid" for their desire to create an "established religion" of neo-Puritanism in the United States. Jefferson credited the clergy with political pragmatism despite their religious extremism, which latter he considered an underhanded vehicle of their political ambitions. He thought they would eventually subscribe to the Jeffersonian political faith, in obedience to the maxim, if you can't beat 'em, join 'em. He hoped that they might acquiesce in his moderate administration, even if they did not see the superior merits of his secularized, rationalistic, anemic deism to their fervid religious orthodoxy and proselytism. Obviously resigned to the fact that the orthodox clergy would never get as excited over a big moose head as they were about persecuting those who blasphemed against Jesus and denied the Trinity, he hoped that they would recognize his adherence to the ethics and morality espoused by Jesus, if not to the idea of his divinity. Jefferson was sure that his deistic version of "the Christian religion" would indubitably advance the prosperity, freedom, and "science" of his countrymen. As he put it: "I am in hopes that their good sense will dictate to them [New England orthodox clergy], that since the mountain will not come to them, they had better go to the mountain: that they will find their interest in acquiescing in the liberty and science of their country, and that the Christian religion, when divested of the rags in which they have enveloped it, and brought to the original purity and simplicity of its benevolent institution, is a religion of all others most friendly to liberty, science, and the freest expansion of the human mind."[31]

Agreeing with Robinson that the executive enjoyed too much discretionary power under the Constitution, Jefferson thought that stringent laws were essential to safeguard the people from "bad men" elected to office. "I sincerely wish with you, we could see our government so secured as to depend less on the character of the person in whose hands it is trusted," he said, voicing a sentiment that was popular in the early republic, when the politically articulate thought political institutions ought to be designed to restrain arbitrary conduct. With the presidency particularly in mind, Jefferson argued, "Bad men will sometimes get in, and with such an immense patronage, may make great progress in corrupting the public mind and principles. This is a subject with which wisdom and patriotism should be occupied."[32] He poignantly appreciated the importance of New England and its sister states working together to make the national Union a success. He desired to assure Robinson and his friends that they need not worry that he would burn their bibles as president, as Federalist fear-mongers, advising them to hide their good books at the bottom of wells or under their beds, had warned during the election.[33] Jefferson did not consider himself a "bad man." But, despite the odium he knew it would incur from the Federalists, he was prepared to take on the dirty work of dismissing some of his opponents from office in an effort to equalize patronage between the parties. Washington and Adams had appointed few Republicans.[34]

4

President Jefferson, New England Politics and Patronage

First Years

At the outset of Jefferson's administration, when he began dismissing Federalist appointees in the customs service and replacing them with Republicans, some Federalist New England merchants took offense. Perhaps they feared that the allegedly anti-commercial Republicans would enforce the customs laws more stringently than their Federalist predecessors. In response, Jefferson made a famous address to the New Haven merchants, in which he stressed the fairness of his goal that eventually as many Republicans as Federalists hold office under the government; and since "few die, and none resign" of his predecessors' Federalist appointees, he was compelled to immediately fire a few.[1]

Attorney General Lincoln informed Jefferson that his address did not alienate Massachusetts' moderate Federalists. He said that, after Jefferson's conciliatory inaugural address, most Federalists adopted "a spirit of acquiescence, accomodation [sic] and attachment to the new order of things." He advised Jefferson that he would gain increased popular support if he persevered with "steadiness, firmness, and independence, in a strict adherence to those great republican principles, which you have so happily avowed." Firm adherence to Republican policies and ideals would eventually gain him Federalists' respect and allegiance, since "the knowing of the federalists ... see that the Executive must & will become popular, and attach to its measures the citizens, en masse; They consider the new order of things as established beyond the hope of any material alteration, and that it is their wisdom, their duty & their interest to make the best of it." The Federalists remained ready to work with him, in order to keep the government jobs they already possessed, while Republicans "admired" the address and were appeased by his promise that they would obtain government employment in the future, from which Adams and Washington had excluded them.[2]

The Federalists, Lincoln observed, were intimidated by Jefferson's firmness. "It is perceived by the papers that your answer to the N.H. remonstrance produced great excitements for the moment," he wrote him in August 1801. "The remarks on it were pitiful, the expressions of deep mortification & disappointment. They are dying away—and its beneficial effects discovering themselves, in more caution & prudence on the part of the federalists."[3]

Jefferson was relieved by this news. He wrote Lincoln, "I am glad to hear from you that the answer to Newhaven [sic] had a good effect in Massachusetts on the republicans, & no ill effect on the sincere federalists. I had foreseen, years ago, that the first republican president who should come into office after all the places in the government had become exclusively occupied by federalists, would have a dreadful operation to perform." Jefferson considered it his duty to appoint some of his followers to office, believing it "neither just nor politic" for his enemies to retain all the positions. Still, he was reluctant to serve as metaphorical "executioner" of the Federalist office-holders, and intended to proceed slowly in order to uphold his conciliatory reputation. Speaking for his leading advisers and Cabinet members, rather than for radicals in states like Pennsylvania and New York, who were eager to grab Federalist patronage plums, he reminded Lincoln, "You know the moderation of our views in this business, and that we all concurred in them. We determined to proceed with deliberation. This produced impatience in the republicans & a belief we meant to do nothing." He observed that he intended his reply to the "Newhaven remonstrance" more for the edification of the Jeffersonian radicals than for angry Federalists. As worried about retaining the support of his Republican allies as with gaining new adherents among the Massachusetts Federalists, he concluded that his reply had "the most wholsome [sic] effect" in placating Republicans "every where [sic]." Glad to have retained his Republican supporters, he exulted, "Appearances of schismatising [i.e., creating new Republican factions] from us have been entirely done away."[4]

Jefferson was confident that most people supported Congress and its Democratic-Republican majority. "The majority of the present legislature [Congress] are in unison with the agricultural part of our citizens," he wrote his French colleague Pierre Samuel Du Pont de Nemours. He thought that democratic reforms such as tax reduction, reductions in the army and navy, direct election of federal jurors, and repeal of the Federalist Naturalization and Judiciary acts which he recommended in his first annual message to Congress, were popular with the voters. "Some things may perhaps be left undone from motives of compromise for a time, and not to alarm by too sudden a reformation: but with a view to be resumed at another time." Believing that his popularity had suffered with his former opponents because he removed some Federalists from office, he decided temporarily to pursue a cautious course on appointments.[5] On the other hand, in matters concerning his ideological differences with the proto-aristocratic Federalist Party, he stood firm.

He believed that congressional legislation to enforce Republican principles would "consolidate the great body of well meaning citizens together, whether federal or republican, heretofore called." "I do not mean to include royalists or priests," he explained. "Their opposition is immoveable, but they will be … leaders without followers." He assumed that the diehard Federalists, erstwhile advocates of monarchy who denied the value or feasibility of republican government, would remain irreconcilable to his administration. He referred to *A Stroke at the Branch* (1801), a pamphlet by John Leland, whom he called "a plain country farmer." Leland argued that there was little difference between Massachusetts Federalists and Republicans, thus backing up Jefferson's prediction "that within one year from this time were an election to take place between two candidates, merely republican and federal, where no personal opposition existed against either, the federal candidate would not get the vote of a single elector." Reiterating his distrust of monarchical Federalist leaders and extremist Federalist "priests," he insisted, as he had in his inaugural address, that most voters genuinely favored Democratic-Republicanism. During the undeclared war with France, Federalist clergy and Anglophile Federalist leaders had misled the people into a paranoid belief that French Jacobins were sending an army to take over the United States. The Republicans soon disabused them of this conviction: "The body of our people, tho' divided for a short time by an artificial panic, and called by different names, have ever had the same object in view, to wit, the maintenance of a federal, republican government; & have never ceased to be all federalists, all republicans: still excepting the noisy band of royalists inhabiting cities chiefly, & priests both of city & country."[6]

Jefferson supposed that, having alienated numerous Federalists by removing a few members of their party from office, he would be less eligible as a candidate for re-election than a new Republican face who would arouse less partisan animosity. Styling himself a political martyr, he continued, "It was my destiny to come to the government when it had for several years been committed to a particular political sect [the Federalists], to the entire and absolute exclusion of those who were in sentiment with the body of the nation. I found the country entirely in the enemy's hands." As president, he considered it his duty to replace some Federalist "enemy" appointees with Republicans, but he said he had only replaced nine out of thousands of public officials for Federalist partisanship, and twelve others for suspicion of embezzlement. Although he had only fired about twenty Federalist officials, he charged, this was sufficient to incite Federalist rage. In language that indicated that he remained bitter at the Federalist mudslinging and dirty tricks during the recent election, he informed Du Pont, "The whole herd have squealed out, as if all their throats were cut. These acts of justice, few as they have been, have raised great personal objections to me, of which a new character would be clear."[7]

Although Jefferson was willing to risk alienating New England Federalists in order to retain his stalwart Republican supporters, he was pleased by Lincoln's report that the moderate Federalists still trusted him. As Jefferson put it, "I own I expected it [his appointment of Republicans] would check the current with which the republican federalists were returning to their brethren the republicans. I extremely lamented this effect." Claiming that he accepted the presidency only because he thought that he had the charm, rationality, and power to convert most of the Federalists to Republicanism, he said, "The moment which would convince me that a healing of the nation into one is impracticable would be the last moment of my wishing to remain where I am." Writing with hyperbolic wit, he said did not expect the extreme Federalists to join his party: "Of the monarchical federalists I have no expectations. They are incurables, to be taken care of in a mad-house if necessary & on motives of charity."[8]

Lincoln's letters had calmed Jefferson's fears. "I am much pleased therefore with your information that the republican federalists are still coming in to the desired union," the president replied, especially since "Eastern newspapers" and periodicals such as Joseph Dennie's Philadelphia *Port Folio*, Fisher Ames' *New England Palladium* and Benjamin Russell's *Columbian Centinel* continued to be hostile. "I supposed the printers knew the taste of their customers & cooked their dishes to their palates," Jefferson sarcastically observed. Demonstrating his continuing distrust of Federalist Episcopal, Dutch Reformed, and Congregational clergy, who had vehemently attacked his religious views during the election of 1800, he noted, "The palladium is understood to be the *Clerical* paper, & from the clergy I expect no mercy." With barely masked contempt for religious hypocrisy, he continued, "They crucified their Saviour [not *our* savior] who preached that their kingdom was not of this world, and all who practice on that precept [separation of church and state] must expect the extreme of their wrath." Employing heightened rhetoric, he claimed that the extremist Federalist clergy would have liked to employ the measures of the Roman Catholic Inquisition against their enemies, secular and spiritual. "The laws of the present day withhold their hands from blood, but lies and slander still remain to them," he warned. He considered the newspaper attacks on him Machiavellian efforts to provoke him to fire Federalist officials *en masse* and ruin any prospects of "amalgamation" of the Federalist moderates into the Jeffersonian party. As he put it, "I am satisfied that the heaping of abuse on me personally has been with the design & the hope of provoking me to make a general sweep of all federalists out of office. But as I have carried no passion into the execution of this disagreeable duty, I shall suffer none to be excited." He would not fall for the Federalist schemes. Revealing his political acumen, he said, "The clamour which has been raised will not provoke me to remove one more, nor deter me to remove one less than if not a word had been said on the subject." He intended to be particularly cautious respecting Massachusetts officials. "In Massachusetts you may be assured great moderation will be used," he wrote Lincoln. Perhaps sarcastically, he listed the states where his supporters clamored for lots of Federalist firings: "Indeed Connecticut, New York, New Jersey, Pennsylva & Delaware are the only states where any thing considerable is desired."[9]

Feeling little sympathy for his defeated Federalist foes, Lincoln portrayed them as unprincipled ogres: "Falsehood & violence is still the system, of the leaders of the opposition; they will lose their followers, the moment they can be made to understand the principles & the measures of the past & the present administrations." Implementing recommendations Jefferson had been making for over a decade, in December 1801, Lincoln set up a newspaper, the *Worcester Aegis* to combat Isaiah Thomas's popular Federalist sheet, the *Massachusetts Spy*. Lincoln's newspaper was the only Republican journal in Massachusetts between Boston and the Berkshire Mountains. Jefferson, Madison, and other Republicans subscribed to Jeffersonian journals in diverse parts of the country, to encourage their editors' perseverance. By the presidential election of 1804, Republicans had failed to catch up with Federalist newspapers, which still vastly outnumbered them. Nevertheless, Democratic-Republican sheets made up in enthusiasm for their lack in numbers. Except for Connecticut, whose "Stand Up" law during this period required *viva voce* voting, intimidating voters who owed money to wealthy Federalist creditors or landlords, by the end of Jefferson's presidency all the New England states elected Republican legislatures and governors. The total votes cast for Republican candidates as well as the number of people voting in New England rose greatly, a result of accelerated party competition and popular interest.[10]

Writing to Joel Barlow, a Connecticut poet, writer, and famed Hartford Wit who became a democratic radical after living in France for a few years during the 1790s and was returning to Paris, Jefferson showed even greater enthusiasm for New England's impending conversion to Republicanism. Jefferson assured Barlow that, once the people became fully aware of the reforms he proposed in his December 1801 annual message to Congress, such as the repeal of all internal taxes; reduction of the army and navy; and decrease in the number of federal judicial officers, most of which the Republican Congress soon passed, the permanent victory of his party in New England was guaranteed. Although admitting that recent reports indicated that the Jeffersonians had lost a few seats in the Massachusetts state senate, Jefferson pointed out that they had increased their strength in the rest of New England. "Everywhere else we are becoming one," he asserted. "In Rhode Island the late elections gave us two to one over the whole state. Vermont is decidedly with us. It is said and believed that New Hampshire has got a majority of republicans now in its Legislature, and wanted a few hundreds only of turning out their federal governor." He boasted that even Connecticut, a hotbed of Congregationalist power and extreme Federalism, was turning to the Republican cause. "Connecticut is supposed to have gained us about fifteen to twenty per cent, since her last election; but the exact issue is not yet known here," he reported to Barlow. He claimed that the Federalist Party was undone; only its diehard and extremist members remained in Congress, where they represented an insignificant minority of the people. Ironically, he hinted that the Federalists might serve a useful function in preserving Republicans' unity as "censors" of administration actions. "A respectable minority is useful as censors," he observed, quickly adding that the Federalists currently serving in Congress were far from respectable. Paradoxically, he warned that once the Federalist Party completely disappeared from politics, the Republicans would end up fighting and dividing among themselves, although all would avoid the odious, discredited party label "Federalist": "for freemen thinking differently, and speaking and acting as they think, will form into classes of sentiment" over political issues according to their individual characters and psyches.[11]

As Jefferson often said, most notoriously in the "Mazzei Letter" in 1796, and would argue even more stridently in old age, he expected that the upright, confident, altruistic person who respected and trusted the people would naturally be a Republican; while the weak, corruptly rich, cowardly person who felt he needed a strong "executive" to protect him from popular violence and caprice would prefer the Federalists. Framing the concept in yet another form, he said that the "natural" division of "mankind" was into "whig and tory, as in England formerly." The strong and virtuous, trusting "the many" to govern fairly, refused to yield more power to a strong "executive" than was necessary, while "the weakly and nervous, the rich and the corrupt" considered a strong national government necessary to protect their ill-gotten gains from popular contrivances. He believed that Democratic Republicanism was the true American's identity.[12]

5

Religion, Irreligion and Politics

Jefferson the President Views New England and the Danbury Baptist Association, 1801–1802

After his narrow victory in the presidential election of 1800–1801 without receiving any Massachusetts or Connecticut electoral votes, Jefferson felt less than charitable toward New England's Federalists. He resented Adams's "midnight appointments." He also thought that the Federalist editors who mercilessly attacked his political and personal reputation during the contest were, like the Salem witch-hunters of the 1690s, opportunists thriving on discontent and turmoil. "The aegis of government, & the temples of religion & of justice, have all been prostituted there to toll us back to the times when we burnt witches," he complained in March 1801 to the moderate Federalist Elbridge Gerry of Marblehead, recently defeated for governor of Massachusetts by Hamiltonian Caleb Strong. Hoping to foster the union of conflicting parties under Republican leadership, Jefferson decried the unbending stance of Federalist newspaper editors. "A coalition of sentiments is not for the interest of printers," he observed, aiming his hostility at the Federalist press: "They, like the clergy, live by the zeal they can kindle, and the schisms they can create. It is contest of opinion in politics as well as religion which makes us take great interest in them, and bestow our money liberally on those who furnish aliment to our appetite…. So the printers can never leave us in a state of perfect rest and union of opinion. They would be no longer useful, and would have to go to the plough."

Nevertheless, perhaps in an effort to convince Gerry to transfer his allegiance finally to the Republicans, Jefferson declared his confidence that New Englanders would return to the ardent libertarianism and opposition to governmental abuses that had impelled their revolt against Great Britain in 1775: "Your people will rise again. They will awake like Sampson from his sleep, & carry away the gates & posts of the city. You, my friend, are destined to rally them again under their former banner."[1]

Jefferson might not have felt so confident of Massachusetts citizens' stability and devotion to the Union if he were privy to John Quincy Adams' recent letters. After learning of Jefferson's election, Adams, though still in Europe as U.S. minister to Prussia, a position to which his father appointed him, felt disgruntled by the elder Adams' defeat. He claimed not to care whether the Union continued or broke apart, although he did not think that either Burr or Jefferson would advocate dismantling the republic if the other won the contest between them in the House of Representatives. Complaining that he personally did not benefit from the Union's continuation, he asserted, "If their object be to preserve it, the issue of the election will not prove materially hurtful. If otherwise, if they will break us up—in God's name, let the Union go. I love the Union as I love my wife. But if my wife ask and insist upon a separation, she should have it, though it broke my heart."[2]

Despite his familial metaphors, John Quincy Adams' bitterness at the likely end of his political career under a Jefferson Administration was evident. In April 1801, expressing anti–Jacobin views held since his early twenties (first manifested in his "Publicola" essays in 1791), young Adams perversely concluded that the country would be better off if France regained Louisiana. (This had in fact happened seven months earlier at the Convention of San Ildefonso.) Rumors of this event did not worry him. "I did not feel alarmed at finding that France was like to get her old footing on our continent," he explained. He looked forward to the likelihood that France and the U.S. would become perpetual enemies if France gained control of the Mississippi River; mutual enmity would insulate Americans from radical Jacobin ideas. He expected French occupation would raise clashing interests between the former allies, diminishing the likelihood of invidious French influence in the United States. He believed that France's revolutionary policy of abolishing slavery, adopted in 1794, would ultimately alienate Southern slaveholding Democratic-Republican partisans from the radical erstwhile republic. "With a system of liberating slaves and of shackling trade (for France cleaves to both), she will not be likely to employ many means of seduction to debauch our southern planters," he observed, "and it must be strange indeed if the mouth of the Mississippi and the natural antipathies of borderers [sic] should lose their power of kindling animosities under a French government. Let them take Louisiana."[3]

When the question of admitting Louisiana to the Union arose a few years later, Adams was in the U.S. Senate. He was the only Federalist who supported the territory's annexation, and even he recommended to Jefferson that only a constitutional amendment would make it legal. Thus, the volatile, unpredictable young philosopher-politician Adams may not have been the typical Massachusetts Federalist. Nonetheless, his frustrated, irrational lucubrations at the time of Jefferson's victory in 1801 amply reflected the disillusionment of the Federalist ruling class, who sensed that their days of power were permanently gone.[4]

Nevertheless, during the next few years Jefferson's exuberance proved justified. Massachusetts, New Hampshire, and Vermont elected Republican majorities.[5] He was buoyed by his party's enthusiasm over his election as president and his supporters' approval of the legislative program outlined in his first annual message to Congress in December 1801. With this address, the first in which a chief executive actually laid out the policies he wanted to achieve, Jefferson pledged army and navy reductions, repeal of the internal taxes imposed by the Federalists and their partisan Judiciary and Naturalization Acts, and suggested popular election of federal juries.[6]

During his presidency's first year, Jefferson for the first time specifically expressed his desire that Virginia emulate the town meeting (he called it "ward") system of Massachusetts local government. He experienced this revelation at the time of his immortal "wall of separation" address to the Danbury Baptist Association. On January 1, 1802, Jefferson responded to a eulogistic address sent him by a committee of the Danbury, Connecticut Baptist Association. Although they had composed the laudatory address in October 1801, their message did not reach Jefferson until December 30, 1801, conveyed personally by a leader of the Massachusetts

Baptists, Elder John Leland. He was accompanied by a pro–Jefferson crowd from distant Cheshire, Massachusetts, and most conspicuously, by a famous twelve-hundred-pound cheese as a gift for the Virginian. The Danbury Baptist Association was formed in 1790. Composed mainly of churches in areas of western Connecticut, such as Stratfield, Southington, Hartford and Farmington, along with a few eastern New York Baptist churches, it held advanced religious and political views. At its October 1800 meeting, it undertook a movement for freedom of religion, statewide repeal of oppressive compulsory religious laws, and disestablishment of the Congregational Church in Connecticut. In a petition campaign after Jefferson's election, the Baptist Association tried to attract support from liberal Congregationalists and Episcopalians. In October 1801, it appointed a committee composed of Elders Nehemiah Dodge, Deacon Ephraim Robbins, Elder Stephen S. Nelson, and others to compose an address to President Jefferson somewhat inappropriately asking his intervention in the struggle for disestablishment of the Congregational Church in their state. The address assured Jefferson of the Danbury Baptists' "rejoicing" and "great satisfaction" at his election, even though their expressions might be "less courtly and pompous" than those of some others. Like the Quakers whose dress and customs they tended to imitate, the Baptists bluntly declared their objectives: "Our Sentiments are uniformly on the side of Religious Liberty. That Religion is at all times and places a Matter between God and Individuals. That no man aught to suffer in Name, person or effects on account of his religious Opinions."[7]

This was what Jefferson had been saying for many years, most notably in his bill for religious freedom in Virginia, composed in 1779, and his Query XVII of *Notes on the State of Virginia*, written in the early 1780s. Indeed, the Baptists probably had the latter work in mind when they asserted, "That the legitimate [*sic*] Power of civil Government extends no further than to punish the man *who works ill to his neighbor.*" Turning to Connecticut's constitution, they lamented that it "is not specific" in protecting their rights of worship, a euphemism for their objection to the biased colonial charter's retention after the American Revolution. The state constitution, therefore, denied them free exercise of religion except as "favors granted, and not as inalienable rights: and these favors we receive at the expence of such degrading acknowledgements as are inconsistent [*sic*] with the rights of freemen." The Danbury Baptists firmly aligned with Jefferson, despite his disavowal of belief in any religious dogma. They agreed with the stand adopted in his letter to Benjamin Rush in September 1800: "I have sworn upon the altar of god, eternal hostility against every form of tyranny over the mind of man."[8]

Indeed, the Danbury Baptists were amateur theologians after the president's own heart. Their message continued, in terms that Jefferson obviously applauded as virtually identical to his unpublished letter to Rush and many of his other writings, "It is not to be wondred [*sic*] at therefore; if those, who seek after *power & gain* under the *pretence of government & Religion* should reproach their fellow men—should reproach their chief Magistrate, as an enemy of religion Law & good order because he will not, dares not assume the prerogative of Jehovah and make Laws to govern the Kingdom of Christ."[9]

Although they were grateful that Jefferson did not intend to interfere in the religious concerns of the several states, the Baptists incompatibly urged him to exert his personal influence and presidential prestige in local religious matters. They wanted him to persuade or coerce the New England states to repeal laws granting the Congregational Church a preferred status and encroaching on the rights of conscience and organizational practices of the Baptists and other evangelical denominations. Revealing less naïveté than at first appeared, the Baptists acknowledged that neither the president nor "the national government" was empowered to "destroy the Laws of each State." Still, they hoped that "our beloved President" and his "genial sentiments" for religious freedom would triumph, and "like the radiant beams of the Sun, will shine & prevail through all the States and all the world till Hierarchy and tyranny be destroyed from the Earth."[10]

After their daring request that Jefferson publicly recommend the disestablishment of state churches, the Danbury Baptists assured the scientifically-minded president that his election was the work of Divine Providence, "America's God," as they called it. As his "past services" and "glow of philanthropy and good will" during a period of "more than thirty years" demonstrated (they probably had his struggle for religious freedom in Virginia in mind, although that was in the late 1770s), it was clear to them "that America's God has raised you up to fill the chair of State out of that good will which he bears to the Millions which you preside over." Those who opposed Jefferson, they had "reason to believe," opposed God, but their existence was necessarily predestined ("predetermin'd" was the word they used) to arouse Jefferson to defeat them, like David against Goliath. "May God strengthen you for the arduous task which providence & the voice of the people have cal'd you to sustain and support you in your Administration against all the predermin'd opposition of those who wish to rise to wealth & importance on the poverty and subjection of the people," they exhorted him, decrying the centuries-long alliance of throne and altar that had brought parishioners slavery and degradation.[11]

Jefferson must have been pleased by this evidence of enthusiastic support for him in Connecticut, the land of steady habits and steadier Federalism. But he was already aware of the Baptists' adherence to his views. He must have enjoyed their vehement diatribes against the established Protestant clergy, whom he had little reason to venerate. He may have been less comfortable with their peroration, and its assurance that, as the Lord's Chosen, a seat in Heaven awaited him: "And may the Lord preserve you safe from every evil and bring you at last to his Heavenly Kingdom throug[h] Jesus Christ our Glorious Mediator."[12]

Jefferson was eager to rally his followers against the menace of extremist New England Federalist Congregationalism and fundamentalism. However, he wanted to be cautious how he went about it, so as not to alienate "moderate" Federalists he had always hoped to unite behind his Enlightenment credo. He was aware that many New Englanders were devout Congregationalists, and he did not want his response to the Baptists to offend latter-day Puritans. The new president felt his political position strengthened by such indications that many New Englanders supported his new regime of liberty and greater respect for the common man's natural rights. The committee of the Danbury, Connecticut Baptist Association praised him for protecting freedom of religion. Eager to clarify where he stood on such matters, for both friends and foes, he quickly composed, within a few hours, his famous reply applauding the "building [of] a wall of separation between church and state."[13] That he composed the letter to the Baptists so rapidly reveals the spontaneity and depth of his feelings.

The Danbury Baptist Association's paean provided him with an opportunity to declare his heartfelt belief in religious freedom and his conviction that governments must not interfere in their citizens' religious lives. At the same time, he hoped to satisfy his New England supporters among the Dissenters from Congregationalism and perhaps attract some new followers. Viewing his message as both a statement of his political philosophy and a political rallying cry for his partisans, he asked the advice of his attorney general, Levi Lincoln of Massachusetts, a Republican bulwark for the party, the same day he delivered the message, New Years' Day 1802. This was also the day that he addressed the Cheshire Baptist delegation from western Massachusetts' Berkshire County (home of Shays' Rebellion), headed by Elder John Leland. On December 30, Leland presented the "Mammoth Cheese," and simultaneously delivered the Danbury Baptists' address to Jefferson. (It is not clear how it got into his possession.[14])

Jefferson was eager to respond to the Danbury Baptists as quickly as possible. He told Lincoln that the question of freedom of religion was on his mind. He seized the opportunity to proclaim devotion to "eternal separation between church and state," as he strongly put it in the original draft of his address.[15] Jefferson was explicit to Lincoln about his motives in writing the brief but trenchant message. "Averse to receive addresses, yet unable to prevent them, I have generally endeavored to turn them to some account, by making them the occasion, by way of answer, of sowing useful truths & principles among the people, which might germinate and become rooted among their political tenets," he explained. Obviously, he hoped that respect for the religious opinions and religious freedom of others would "become rooted" among the "political tenets" of all Americans, rather than insistence upon any dogma or set of dogmas. He sent Lincoln, a leader among Massachusetts Democratic-Republican orthodox Congregationalists, a copy of the Baptists' address along with his brief reply, for his last-minute advice, fearing that he may have too stridently advocated religious freedom for conscientious New Englanders' taste. "The Baptist address now inclosed admits of a condemnation of the alliance between church and state, under the authority of the Constitution. It furnishes an occasion, too, which I have long wished to find, of saying why I do not proclaim fastings & thanksgivings, as my predecessors did." He acknowledged that he was belaboring the point, since the Baptist address did not request his opinion on this matter. "The address, to be sure, does not point at this, and its introduction is awkward, but I foresee no opportunity of doing it more pertinently."[16]

Jefferson's original draft of his letter to the Danbury Baptists mocked a venerable New England Puritan tradition, gubernatorial proclamations of days of fasting, thanksgiving, humiliation and prayer, and the like. Governors in most New England states continued to engage in this ceremony, establishing the holiday of Thanksgiving on November 26 around this time. Indeed, President John Adams zealously performed this ritual at the outset of hostilities with France in 1798. Seeking to strengthen support for government with the incentive of religious fervor, Adams proclaimed a day of fasting and prayer, secretly asking Ashbel Green, a prominent Philadelphia Presbyterian minister who had been chaplain of the U.S. House of Representatives for many years, to compose the proclamation. In this instance, Adams came close to violating the First Amendment, for which Democratic-Republican newspapers reproached him.[17]

Jefferson intended to avoid Adams' example. He believed his support for freedom of religion, governmental nonintervention, and a strict construction of the Constitution jibed in forbidding the president to issue public proclamations of thanksgiving, fasting, etc. As he put it in the original draft of his letter to the Danbury Baptists, in something of an *obiter dictum*, "Congress thus inhibited from acts respecting religion [by the First Amendment] and the Executive authorised [*sic*] only to execute their acts, I have refrained from prescribing even occasional performances of devotion prescribed indeed legally where the Executive is the legal head of a national church, but subject here, as religious exercises only to the voluntary regulations and discipline of each respective sect."[18]

Such language, conveyed with Jefferson's frequently-exercised underlying sarcasm, suggested that if he began delivering religious proclamations, he would become like the King of England, symbolic head of the national Anglican Church. This statement might hint that he favored adopting monarchical forms, a ridiculous idea; or it might imply derision of the governors of the New England states, where the Congregationalist Church was established (except in Rhode Island) and the governors emulated monarchies when they instituted days of fasting, thanksgiving, and prayer. In either case, Jefferson threatened to unnecessarily stir up indignant protests from conservative elements. His desire to get these feelings off his chest overruled his political acumen and good judgment. However, he prudently asked Lincoln for his opinion of the address.

An astute politician as well as a Massachusetts Congregationalist, Lincoln advised Jefferson to delete the sentence impugning executive proclamations of days of fasting and prayer. He warned that such ideas might anger not only Federalists, but offend "some of our republican friends in the eastern states where the proclamations of thanksgivings &c by their Executive is an antient habit, & is respected," as Jefferson summarized Lincoln's opinion in the margin of his draft of the address.[19] More precisely, Lincoln warned the president against aspersing "fasts and thanksgivings," whose observance following on gubernatorial directives was common in the New England states, with the exception of Baptist-controlled Rhode Island, he pointed out. "This custom is venerable being handed down from our ancestors," he said. "The Republicans of those States generally have a respect for it. They regreted [*sic*] very much the late conduct of the legislature of Rhode Island on this subject." (Unlike Massachusetts, Connecticut, and New Hampshire, the Rhode Island legislature did not officially celebrate November 26 as Thanksgiving Day in 1801.)[20]

At the same time that Jefferson wanted to declare his principles, he did not desire to further estrange the established Congregational clergy, even though most of them were his inveterate enemies. As he explained, "I know it will give great offence to the New England clergy. But the advocate of religious freedom is to expect neither peace nor forgiveness from them." Thus, Jefferson's first instinct was to use the message as vicarious revenge for the bitter attacks that the Protestant clergy had leveled against him as an amoral atheist during the recent presidential election. On the other hand, he respected Lincoln's familiarity with New England's political and religious climate, and hoped he would help him avoid making any new enemies among the rank-and-file voters. "Will you be so good as to examine the answer, and suggest any alterations which might prevent an ill effect, or promote a good one, among *the people*? You understand the temper of those in the North, and can weaken it, therefore, to their stomachs: it is at present seasoned to the Southern taste only."[21]

Suspecting that his free-thinking deistic hostility to presidential religious proclamations was suited solely to "the Southern taste," Jefferson recurred to the antinomy between Southern passion and irreligion and New Englanders' cold theological dogmatism he noted in his 1785 letter to Chastellux. In light of the Second Great Awakening's growing power in Virginia and other parts of the South, he had likely lost touch with his constituents. Within a few years, Jefferson would have reason to question the palatability of his deistic faith in absolute religious freedom for "the Southern taste." The evangelical Presbyterian leader John Holt Rice became one of Jefferson's most bitter enemies when Jefferson sought to set up the University of Virginia on a secular, nonsectarian basis. On the other hand, in general, Rice and other Virginia Presbyterians wanted, at least as a matter of public relations, to be considered as nationalistic and modern in their thinking. During the American Revolution, they changed the name of their religious school, Augusta Academy, to Liberty Hall. In the 1790s, they lobbied with President Washington to give them 100 shares of his stock in the James River Canal Company, which that corporation had recently bestowed upon him, to improve their school. When he gave the school the stock (under the misleading impression that they were a wholly secular, literary, and mathematics-oriented institution without religious leanings), they renamed their academy Washington Academy and later, in 1813, Washington College. Insisting that such contributions helped them to meet the secular standards of state and private institutions, they hoped thereby to influence the state legislature and convert students and politicians to Presbyterianism. "Methodists and Baptists would have to conform and learn," one historian comments, "and rationalist freethinkers like Jefferson could only wince and build their own schools in competition."[22]

Although Jefferson apparently regarded each section's religious views as partaking of their inhabitants' personalities and cultural differences, he sought to conciliate them with his message to the Danbury Baptists. He did not expect Levi Lincoln to need much time to offer suggestions regarding his brief reply, which has acquired greater importance than he ever anticipated. "I would ask the favor of you to return it, with the [Baptist] address, in the course of the day or evening," he requested.[23] Lincoln's politically pragmatic commentary caused him to water down the vigorous secularism of his message, and to abandon the idea of denouncing presidential proclamations of days of fasting and prayer.

Even more aptly, Jefferson asked Postmaster General Gideon Granger (probably in person), a Connecticut native, about the mindset of the people of Connecticut and how far the Danbury Baptist Association represented their views. Jefferson relied on Granger for political information about New England. When Granger briefly returned to Connecticut for his health in August 1802, Jefferson requested him to investigate the truth of rumors that Boston congressman William Eustis and leading Connecticut Republican Abraham Bishop, whom Jefferson intended to appoint customs collector for New Haven, had secretly joined a faction in support of Vice-President Aaron Burr. "I always expected the New York schism [between supporters of ex-Governor George Clinton and Burr] would produce a boisterous struggle," he wrote. He questioned the accuracy of reports that Eustis and Bishop were Burr's underlings. "I am sorry to see the freedoms taken to implicate ... some characters. The manner in which Dr. Eustis and Mr. Bishop have been spoken of is neither just nor judicious." Jefferson warned Republicans not to allow personal factions to deter them from following Jeffersonian "principle, and to play into the hands of the tories [Federalist leaders]." He relied on Granger for accurate reports on the political situation "in the New-England states."[24]

Unlike Lincoln, Granger thought that his Connecticut constituents would favorably receive a forthright and vigorous reply from Jefferson. Granger endorsed Jefferson's original draft, and its inclination to use the occasion to denounce presidential religious days of fasting, responding:

> G Granger presents his compliments to The Presidt. and assures him that he has carefully & attentively perused the inclosed Address & Answer—The answer will undoubtedly give great Offence to the established Clergy of New England while it will delight the Dissenters as they are called. It is but a declaration of Truths which are in fact felt by a great Majority of New England, & publicly acknowledged by near half of

the People of Connecticut; It may however occasion a temporary Spasm among the Established Religionists yet his mind approves of it, because it will "germinate among the People" and in time fix "their political Tenets"—He cannot therefore wish a Sentence changed, or a Sentiment expressed equivocally—A more fortunate time can never be expected.[25]

On January 1, 1802, in the now-famous dénouement, Jefferson assured the New England Baptists that he would uphold the First Amendment's protection of freedom of religion. "Adhering to this expression of the supreme will of the nation in behalf of the rights of conscience," he said, "I shall see with sincere satisfaction the progress of those sentiments which tend to restore to man all his natural rights, convinced he has no natural right in opposition to his social duties."[26]

Jefferson's surprising eagerness to denounce the idea of presidential proclamations of days of fasting and prayer, even when there was no pressing need for him to do so, reveals his desire, after a frustrating, perhaps humiliating presidential campaign, to throw down the gauntlet to his clerical enemies. It also indicates that such religious historians as Daniel Dreisbach severely misread Jefferson's beliefs when they claim that he actually favored presidential proclamations of a religious nature.[27]

Even more than Dreisbach, historian Johann Neem bizarrely distorts Jefferson's religious ideology. In a different manner than Dreisbach, Neem misreads Jefferson's Danbury Address as a covert malevolent attack on all revealed religions, including the Baptists. Its hidden message was to unveil Jefferson's plan to employ reason to eventually convert, perhaps by force, everyone to his rational brand of Christianity or "civil religion." Neem poses Jefferson's ideas, or rather his interpretation of Jefferson's ideas, in strange terms. For example, he writes, "Jefferson told the Baptists that the wall of separation may protect them from New England's Standing Order in the short run, but in the long run their ideas, like those of the Standing Order, were slated for extinction."[28]

Jefferson never said anything remotely as totalitarian as this in his writings. Far from hoping to force his disturbingly evangelical countrymen to adopt his free-wheeling, laidback deism, his only interest was in the "morality" of religion, which he thought well-embodied (at least ideally) in Jesus' Sermon on the Mount and other ethical discourses. More than the study or even practice of morality or ethics, Jefferson extolled the unlimited freedom of the human mind, considering its preservation the only way that individual homeostasis and meaningful scientific advance, progress, and ultimately maximum social happiness could occur. As he once said, "To preserve the freedom of the human mind then & freedom of the press, every spirit should be ready to devote itself to martyrdom; for as long as we may think as we will, & speak as we think, the condition of man will proceed in improvement."[29]

Throughout his life, Jefferson respected the individual's right to follow any religion or no religion, as long as no person or government interfered with the right of others to believe or not as they chose. He respected those who were devout, even though he might think their beliefs puerile, as long as they did not hinder anyone else's worship. This is clear as early as *Notes on the State of Virginia*, which he wrote when his wife was seriously ill and he was in a generally angry mood, following humiliating treatment by the Virginia legislature and the British army as governor of Virginia. In Query XVII, Jefferson, after harshly denouncing the Christian Church and its interminable persecutions and belittling religious belief generally, emphasized the value of "truth," a noun he privately considered relevant only to the exact sciences. Nonetheless, he stated (tongue-in-cheek), probably to assuage his readers' fears of his "infidelity," as it was called, that "reason" would discern "the true religion," although to him this was meaningless, since there was no "true" religion: all their dogmas were man-made.[30]

The only religious belief Jefferson professed was that one "god" existed. If not for the Christian Church's history of oppression and the abuse to which his political opponents and the established clergy subjected him during his election campaigns, he probably would have thought little about theology. This conclusion seems rather obvious, since before the election of 1800 his comments about religion, apart from advising anyone who asked him about it to confront it with a free mind, were few and far between.

Unfortunately, in the *Autobiography,* Jefferson provided few details about his role in dis-establishing the Anglican Church and instituting religious freedom in Virginia. He gave the impression that he merely responded to a public outcry from dissenters, who "crowded" the "first republican legislature which met in 76 with petitions to abolish this spiritual tyranny." Indeed, the brunt of the struggle for Jefferson's epochal Statute for Religious Freedom was undertaken by Madison during the 1780s, when Jefferson was U.S. minister to France. How-ever, Jefferson briefly recalled that the months from October to December 1776, when the Virginia assembly debated whether to abolish the Anglican Church's special privileges and the compulsory financial contributions of nonmembers such as Presbyterians and Baptists, "brought on the severest contests in which I have ever been engaged." (Unfortunately, scholars have not uncovered much information about these "contests.") Among the most determined enemies of Disestablishment, Jefferson reminisced, were his close friends, ardent Whigs Robert Carter Nicholas and Edmund Pendleton. Eschewing bitterness over their opposition to his libertarian aims, he said, "In justice to the two honest but zealous opponents.... I must add that although, from their natural temperaments, they were more disposed generally to acquiesce in things as they are, than to risk innovations, yet whenever the public will had once decided, none were more faithful or exact in their obedience to it."[31]

Jefferson did not regard differences over the merits of complete freedom of religion, fought out fairly in the public sphere, as reason to abandon friends or to express violent emo-tions. His most violent emotions about religion were aroused later, when he observed New England revivalists attempting to convert the world to their form of religion, and denying dissenters equal freedoms with themselves, particularly in Connecticut and Massachusetts.

A philosophical rationalist and materialistic "Epicurean," Jefferson never felt comfortable entering into alliances with religious fundamentalists like the Presbyterian, Baptist and Methodists evangelicals. After they won the fight for religious freedom in Virginia, he seldom if ever corresponded with them, and then only out of politeness. Such occasions occurred most often during his retirement, usually when an antislavery evangelical minister, knowing that he had recommended the abolition of slavery in his book, *Notes on the State of Virginia* (1787), quixotically asked him to make a public statement against slavery. This was the case with the antislavery Virginia and Kentucky Baptist, David Barrow, in 1815.[32]

As he continued to argue even more forcefully in old age, Jefferson insisted that members of the clerical hierarchy were generally corrupt, greedy, and power-seeking. Together with unscrupulous secular rulers, they grasped for riches and authority. It was not only Congre-gationalist and Presbyterian clergy who charged Jefferson with atheism; even more frequently it was his secular political opponents, such individuals as the august John Marshall and Samuel Chase, justices of the U.S. Supreme Court. During the election of 1800 and the years of his presidency, such venerable Federalist newspapers as the Philadelphia *Gazette of the United States* and the Boston *Columbian Centinel* were joined by the *Washington Federalist*, founded in 1800. As historian Constance B. Schulz writes, "Clearly the attacks were not confined to New England but were spread throughout the nation."[33]

The most virulent of his clerical denouncers during the election of 1800, the Reverends William Linn and John Mitchell Mason, were New Yorkers and members of the Dutch Reformed Church, although they later became Presbyterians.[34] Thus, Jefferson was not being entirely accurate in his famous letter to Rush in September 1800, when he wrote that his main religious opponents were "the Episcopalians & Congregationalists." Indeed, considering his role in overthrowing the Anglican Episcopal Church in Virginia, surprisingly few of his clerical enemies were Episcopalians.[35]

Ironically, in attacking their Federalist foes even Democratic-Republican newspapers in devout Congregationalist Massachusetts expressed offensively orthodox opinions, though they were likely tongue-in-cheek. The *Independent Chronicle*, Boston's foremost Jeffersonian paper, condemned Benjamin Russell's arch-Federalist *Columbian Centinel*, the newspaper with the largest circulation in the country, as anti–Christian, after the *Centinel* eulogized Philadelphia Federalist Judge Alexander Addison's speech defending the constitutionality of the Alien and Sedition Acts. Russell enthusiastically printed the document as a handbill, ordering parents to read it to their children because of its wisdom. When the *Centinel* promised the reward of a "GOLD MEDAL" to children who memorized the speech, the *Chronicle* denounced Russell's offer as evidence of his meretricious wealth and his "disregard of the Bible." Charging that the *Centinel*'s gold supply was "Tory Federal, or British Gold," the *Chronicle* urged "the People at Large to consider that if this deluding Editor shall go on to *offer His gold* to such as will not only learn but *repeat* all the Anti-Christian and Anti-Republican sentiment which disgraces the sheets of the *Centinel*—what damage may not be done to the cause of Christianity and Morals, Republican Freedom and good Government." Revealing an anti–Jewish bias, the *Chronicle* warned that the Federalists "covet" their "Tory" gold, and that some Federalist "Reverend Cockader" would "receive a *wedge* [of Gold, not 'Cheese and crackers'] and then hide it with the secrecy of a Jew."[36]

It was during the election of 1800 that Jefferson first took note of the religious attacks on him as an atheist and a generally irreverent individual. He was not a very introspective or religious person, apart from considering a moral life as a kind of religion. For him, "true" Christianity was merely adherence to Jesus' moral teachings of kindness, brotherhood, and asceticism, a commonplace doctrine in the eighteenth century. Dr. Benjamin Rush, despite being an orthodox Presbyterian, was Jefferson's friend as well as Adams.' He inclined to Republican rather than Federalist politics. In 1799 or 1800, Rush discussed religious matters with Jefferson, and hoped to convert Jefferson to standard Christian faith. Rush considered revealed Christianity synonymous with republicanism. "You promised when we parted, to read [William] Paley's last Work" (a testimony in favor of revealed religion), he wrote Jefferson in August 1800, "and to send me your religious Creed. I have always considered Christianity as the *strong ground* of Republicanism. Its spirit is opposed, not only to the Splendor, but even to the very *forms* of monarchy, and many of its precepts have for their Objects, republican liberty & equality, as well as simplicity, integrity & Oconomy [*sic*] in government. It is only necessary for Republicanism to ally itself to the Christian Religion, to overturn all the corrupted political and religious institutions in the World."[37]

Rush was probably disappointed when Jefferson's reply avoided agreement with such fervid Christian views. Instead of praising Christianity, he extolled secular freedoms and denounced the clergy, whom he considered companions of secular kings and aristocracies throughout history in depriving the people of their lives, liberties, and property. Indeed, especially after he retired from the presidency, Jefferson told those who asked him that he considered traditional Christianity a corrupt and irrational religion. He mocked the idea of the Trinity as fit for inhabitants of an insane asylum ("bedlam") and went so far as to stigmatize modern Christianity (which he charged had divorced itself from Jesus' humanitarian teachings) as incompatible with virtuous republicanism.[38]

Being involved in more mundane pursuits than religious thought (such as winning the presidency), Jefferson wrote Rush in 1800: "I promised you a letter on Christianity, which I have not forgotten. On the contrary it is because I have reflected on it, that I find much more time necessary for it than I can at present dispose of. I have a view of the subject which ought to displease neither the rational Christian or Deist; & would reconcile many to a character they have too hastily rejected. I do not know however that it would reconcile the genus irritabile vatum, who are all in arms against me. Their hostility is on too interesting ground to be softened."[39]

Thus, Jefferson doubted that his moderately deistic views and acceptance of Jesus' ethical teachings would win many votes from the "irritabile" orthodox clergy. He viewed the orthodox clergy as more dedicated to securing financial and political power than teaching their parishioners to love one another. He angrily insisted that they had taken advantage of the Federalist power-grab during the undeclared war with France from 1798 to 1800 to pursue advantages and ultimately an establishment of Protestant Christianity as the only legal religion in the United States, in violation of the First Amendment. As he put it: "The delusion into which the X.Y.Z. plot showed it possible to push the people; the successful experiment made under the prevalence of that delusion on the clause of the constitution, which, while it secured the freedom of the press, covered also the freedom of religion, has given to the clergy a very favorite hope of obtaining an establishment of a particular form of Christianity thro' the U.S.; and as every sect believes its own form the true one, every one perhaps hoped for his own, but especially the Episcopalians & Congregationalists."[40]

Jefferson was confident that President Adams' dispatch of a peace commission to France at the end of 1799, followed by the expiration of the Alien and Sedition Acts in June 1800 and March 1801, respectively, had squelched orthodox Protestants' ambitions for an established religion similar to Britain's Anglican Church, and burst the Federalists' bubble of achieving a one-party state. "The returning good sense of our country threatens abortion to their hopes, & they believe that any portion of power confided to me, will be exerted in opposition to their schemes," he wrote regarding the Federalist Protestant clergy's leaders. "And they believe rightly, for I have sworn upon the altar of god, eternal hostility against every form of tyranny over the mind of man. But this is all they have to fear from me: & enough too in their opinion, & this is the cause of their printing lying pamphlets against me."[41] Jefferson wanted Rush to know that impeding his political opponents' religious freedom or curtailing their religious observances was the farthest thing from his mind, despite reckless Federalist charges.

As a revivalist Presbyterian, member of a sect only lukewarmly in favor of Jefferson, which turned against him during his second term as president, Rush was not entirely convinced of his friend's religious sincerity. It was only after Jefferson sent him a summary of his religious views, titled "A Syllabus of an Estimate of the Merit of the Doctrines of Jesus, Compared with those of Others," in April 1803, which praised Jesus' teachings as a better system of morality than the ancient Jews and the Greeks and Romans offered, that Rush dismissed the idea that Jefferson was a closet atheist.[42] However, Jefferson denied adherence to the Trinity or even the immortality of the soul. Unlike Jefferson, Rush believed in Jesus' divinity and human immortality. After receiving Jefferson's testimony in the "Syllabus," he wrote him, "I have read your creed with great attention, and was much pleased to find you are by no means so heterodox as you have been supposed by your enemies."[43] Rush seemingly retained suspicions of the sincerity of Jefferson's belief in God. Perhaps sensing his friend's skepticism on this score, the sensitive Jefferson seldom corresponded with him for the next six years (and even then mainly to tell him he was not being chosen for government employment) until he retired from the presidency.[44]

6

The "Mammoth Cheese" and Jefferson's Loose Alliance with Massachusetts Baptists

On January 1, 1802, the same day that Jefferson replied to the Danbury Baptist Association's letter, he welcomed the delegation of New England Democratic-Republicans from Cheshire, Massachusetts, headed by a former Virginia clergyman, evangelical Baptist Elder John Leland. They arrived in Washington bearing the legendary twelve-hundred-pound "Mammoth Cheese," a product for which the town was famous. It took several months to transport the cheese from Cheshire to Washington, D.C. Its progress was reported in several newspapers, both Federalist and Republican (although the Federalists made fun of it). The first newspaper account of the making of the Cheshire Cheese appeared in the Providence, Rhode Island, *Impartial Observer* on August 8, 1801. Stating that the female members ("ladies") of Leland's Baptist church in Cheshire, many of whom were born in Rhode Island, agreed to make the cheese, it emphasized the role of the Cheshire women in creating the huge cheese in an article titled "The Cheshire Ladies' Respect to President Jefferson." The ladies, whose number and precise location were not given, somehow managed to milk 900 cows at a single sitting.[1]

Leland had been an itinerant Baptist minister in various parts of Virginia during the 1770s. He had finally settled down in Orange County, home of James Madison, and a neighboring county to Jefferson's Albemarle. Leland lived and preached in Orange County from 1778 to 1791. He supposedly influenced Madison's struggle to obtain a bill for religious freedom in Virginia, although there is no solid evidence that he was personally friendly with either Jefferson or Madison. Nevertheless, the idea for the "Mammoth Cheese" evidently originated with Leland, and he convinced his parishioners, who were mostly Democratic-Republicans, to go along with it. The motto imprinted on the cheese, "Rebellion to tyrants is obedience to God," was among Jefferson's favorite epigraphs. At the Continental Congress in 1776, Jefferson unsuccessfully recommended its appearance on the Great Seal of the United States. He embossed it on his personal Coat of Arms. Either Madison or Jefferson had probably mentioned this saying to John Leland at some time during his residence in Orange County.[2]

The moniker, "Mammoth Cheese," for the huge cheese originated in a western Massachusetts Federalist newspaper, the *Hampshire Gazette*, home of the wealthy Connecticut Valley "River Gods." When the Mammoth Cheese reached its destination, a brief notice appeared in the Baltimore *Federal Gazette* of Friday, January 1, 1802: "The Mammoth Cheese, made in Massachusetts, to be presented to the president, arrived at the city of Washington on Tuesday [December 29]."[3]

Jefferson took time out from government business to welcome the cheese-bearers. According to a Federalist newspaper, "The President stood in his door to receive it."[4] The arrival of the Berkshire County Republicans (home of Shays' Rebellion in 1786–1787), bearing their enormous cheese, was a less solemn moment than the Danbury Baptists' address, but Jefferson considered it an equally useful opportunity for him to proclaim his political ideology. According to contemporary sources, he delivered his brief reply to the Committee of Cheshire, Massachusetts, as a short speech. His equally brief but far more famous letter to the Danbury Baptists Association apparently was not delivered as a public address, was printed in few newspapers, and received less attention than the "Mammoth Cheese" at the time.[5]

Flattered that the "Ladies of Cheshire" had gone to so much trouble to make him this gigantic cheese during the summer, Jefferson, according to an eyewitness's testimony on New Years' Day, was "highly diverted" when Leland and his group presented it to him. "The great cheese arrived last night and this morning was presented to President Jefferson as a New Year's gift," Benjamin Robinson wrote. "It has received no injury on the way and appears in excellent state for its age. If I can judge from Mr. Jefferson's countenance he is highly diverted with the present curiosity, as all alive people are flocking in from all quarters to see the New England mammoth."[6]

Republican newspapers praised the cheese as an example of farmers' devotion to the president, and their republican fortitude and patriotism. Federalists derided it as an instance of Jeffersonian partisans' wastefulness and stupidity (although they lacked grounds to denounce it as a case of government bureaucracy and abuse, which would have been their angle in more recent eras). They considered it symptomatic of dangerous public adulation of Jefferson. Far from appreciating the cheese's huge size as a sign of American ingenuity and superiority to the Old World, as later generations of American "exceptionalists" might do, they jokingly predicted that Jefferson would soon receive mammoth pies, mammoth casks of cider, and other dubious delicacies.[7]

Two versions of the Cheshire Committee's address to Jefferson exist. One is a manuscript, preserved in the Williams College archives. The other, a more elaborate, doctored version, apparently revised for rhetorical effect by the foremost radical Democratic-Republican newspaper editor William Duane, appeared in his newspaper, the Philadelphia *Aurora*, on January 15, 1802, two weeks after the address. Duane's version included the headline, "The Greatest Cheese in America, For the Greatest Man in America," which some scholars have thought either the Cheshire Committee or Leland devised. Duane also added to the address the witticism that the twelve-hundred-pound cheese was "a pepper-corn of the esteem which we bear to our chief magistrate, and as a sacrifice to republicanism." The original address was amply eloquent testimony to the Cheshire Baptists' devotion to republicanism and their respect for the Bill of Rights and the Constitution. It also eulogized Jefferson for preserving the freedoms guaranteed by the Constitution against "Aristocracy," especially freedom of religion. As they examined the Constitution, most important to the Cheshire Baptists "among its beautiful features, [were]—The right of free suffrage, to correct all abuses—The prohibition of religious tests, to prevent all hierarchy—and the means of amendment which it contains within itself, to remove defects as fast as they are discovered."[8]

Jefferson may have winced at the committee's next statement, which emphasized that the cheese was the product of "the personal labor of freeborn farmers. Jefferson made a brief speech in response, which was highly unusual for him or any other politician in that era of low-key politics where the president was what one scholar labels a "mute tribune." Concurring with the Cheshire Baptists' constitutional interpretations, he borrowed their phraseology, grateful for their gift as "a mark of esteem from freeborn farmers, employed personally in the useful labors of life."[9]

Even the fanatically Federalist Philadelphia *Port Folio*, edited by Joseph Dennie and Thomas Boylston Adams, John Adams' youngest son, printed Duane's account of the Mammoth Cheese. It did not even omit the effusive headline (in pretty small print in those days), "The greatest Cheese in America, for the greatest Man in America," and Jefferson's brief reply, "I concur with you in the sentiments expressed in your kind address … on the Constitution." The witty snob Dennie added, "When one reflects upon the mummery of the Cheshire simpletons, over their Mammoth cheese, and the extreme weakness of the whole transaction, it forces one to remember a descriptive line of POPE, and to be confident that this political, or rather *Indian* gift, is 'A mere white curd of asses' milk.'" In an instance of news reporting rare for the times, Dennie added some wry comments about Vice-President Aaron Burr, who was absent from the cheesy festivities. He preferred to visit New York City and carouse with the ladies, Dennie reported. "The *vice* president of the United States seems to prefer pleasure at New-York, to politics at Washington," he noted, emphasizing the noun "vice." Alluding to Burr's reputation for amorality, which historians like Nancy Isenberg currently dispute, he continued, "Dear *liberty* is emphatically the motto of this gay officer, who, careless of his *little senate*, lingers, as long as he can, in the bower of delight, 'And makes *his* heaven in a lady's lap, And [be]witches women with his looks and words.'"[10] It would take a few months before Federalist editors, inspired by the renegade Republican James Callender, would shift to Jefferson's "affair" with his slave Sally Hemings as a topic for titillating their readers.

Replying to the Cheshire committee's address from his doorstep, Jefferson used the occasion to repeat basic Democratic-Republican principles with which all people could agree ("we are all republicans, we are all federalists," as he said in his memorable First Inaugural Address): the desire for freedom, prosperity, and low taxes. First, he made clear that he supported the Constitution the same way that they did, as a manifesto of "We the people," as the first sentence of the Constitution's preamble puts it. "I concur with you in the sentiments expressed in your kind address on behalf of the inhabitants of the town of Cheshire, that the constitution of the United States is a Charter of rights to it's officers; and that among it's most precious provisions are the right of suffrage, the prohibition of religious tests, and it's means of peaceable amendment," he began. He was probably aware that the Constitution did not guarantee voting rights, a field of legislation that the Founding Fathers left to the states; but he probably thought it could not hurt if the Cheshire farmers believed that the Constitution assured their voting rights, especially since he assumed they would always vote for his party.[11] He stressed his long-held belief that the people must keep vigilant over the actions of their government officials, who were responsible to them alone. "Nothing ensures the duration of this fair fabric of government so effectually as the due sense entertained by the body of our citizens, of the value of these principles, & their care to preserve them."[12]

Expressing his enduring loyalty to the farming majority and his respect for their wives and daughters (whose hands had made the mammoth cheese), Jefferson patriarchally continued, "I recieve, with particular pleasure, the testimony of good will with which your citizens have been pleased to charge you. It presents an extraordinary proof of the skill with which those domestic arts, which contribute so much to our daily comfort, are practiced by them, and particularly by that portion of them most interesting to the affections, the cares & the happiness of man."[13] The Cheshire Committee's address had emphasized that its members had made the cheese themselves, with the help of their wives and daughters. They inadvertently impugned Jefferson's slaveholding practices, when they asserted: "The Chees[e] was produced by the personal labor of *Freeborn Farmers*, with the voluntary and cheerful aid of their wives and daughters, without the assistance of a single slave."[14]

In general, the Cheshire Cheese committee's address was an exuberant testimonial to Jefferson's statesmanlike greatness. "The trust is great! The task is arduous!" they asserted. "But we console ourselves, that the Supreme Father of the Universe, who raised up men to achieve great events, has raised up a Jefferson for this critical day, to defend Republicanism and baffle all the arts of Aristocracy." The cheese-makers were neither lords nor serfs, and they did not seek to flatter a king or gain his favor, they pointed out (in a published version of their address, containing creative revisions by Duane, published in his *Philadelphia Aurora* as well as such journals as the Federalist Philadelphia *Port Folio*): "The Cheese was not made by his lordship for his sacred majesty, nor with a view to gain dignified titles or lucrative offices; but by the personal labor of free born farmers (WITHOUT A SINGLE SLAVE TO ASSIST) for an elective President of a free people, with the only view of casting a mite into the scale of democracy."[15]

Jefferson ignored the embarrassing mention of the institution of slavery, which he perhaps mentally qualified as an allusion to European serfs, since the Cheshire Committee said that God had "raised up *Jefferson* to defend *Republicanism,* and to baffle the arts of *Aristocracy.*" He assured the farmers that he would fight for their freedom and their right to the fruits of their labor. "To myself, this mark of esteem from freeborn farmers, employed personally in the useful labors of life, is peculiarly grateful," he said. Then, in words reminiscent of his Inaugural Address, in which he said he stood for "a wise and frugal government, which shall restrain men from injuring each other, and shall not take from the mouth of labor the bread it has earned," he concluded. "Having no wish but to preserve to them [the farmers] the fruits of their labour, their sense of this truth will be my highest reward."[16]

Further demonstrating his appreciation for the Democratic-Republican Cheshire Committee's effusions, the usually anticlerical Jefferson made sure to attend Leland's sermon in the House of Representatives two days later. One of the most entertaining and inadvertently humorous accounts of the Mammoth Cheshire Cheese's effects on a Massachusetts Federalist is contained in a letter by the Reverend Manasseh Cutler, a Federalist Congregationalist clergyman, land speculator, and representative of Essex County in Congress in 1802. As a member of the "Essex Junto," the land-speculator congressman, who as director of the Ohio Company in the 1780s bribed members of Congress to support a charter enabling his corporation to monopolize public land purchases in the Old Northwest, was about as secularized as a man of the cloth could get. Cutler's letter, dated January 4, 1802, displayed his hostility to Jefferson and evangelical Baptists. At 11 a.m. on New Years' Day, 1802, Cutler wrote, he and a few other Federalist congressmen, attempting to keep up "the old custom … of waiting on the President, with the compliments of the season," were greeted by Jefferson and "treated with cake and wine." (In those days, people drank wine the same way we drink tea and coffee today.) Jefferson invited them "into the mammoth room to see the mammoth cheese." The president was obviously proud of this gift from the constituents of Cutler's state, although Cutler was less impressed by it.[17]

Two days later, on Sunday, January 3, 1802, Cutler witnessed an event that left a far more profound impression on him than the deteriorating mammoth cheese. With unrepressed indignation he wrote to a friend, "Leland, the cheesemonger, a poor ignorant, illiterate, clownish creature (who was the conductor of this monument of weakness and folly [the Mammoth Cheese] to the place of its destination), was introduced as the preacher to both Houses of Congress, and a great number of gentlemen and ladies from I know not where. *The President, contrary to all former practice, made one of his audience.* Such a performance I never heard before, and I hope never shall again."[18]

Contrary to recent historians' emphasis on Jefferson's attendance at Leland's sermon as evidence that he was a religious, even Christian statesman, Cutler's testimony that the president had never previously attended sermons in the House suggests that he was motivated by devotion to Leland's political beliefs and gratitude for his cheese rather than adherence to his religious doctrines. James H. Hutson, Librarian of the Manuscript Division of the Library of Congress and a distinguished historian, seeking to prove his argument that Jefferson was a devout Christian, implausibly pointed to his attendance at Leland's sermon as having convinced Federalist doubters that he was a Believer, and uses Cutler for proof. However, Cutler did not seem persuaded that Jefferson demonstrated religious zeal by attending this radical Republican's evangelical discourse.[19]

The title and contents of Leland's sermon, which seemingly deified Jefferson, further outraged Cutler. Titled "And behold a greater than Solomon is here," Leland's homily glorified Jefferson rather than Jesus Christ. Cutler bitterly noted that this disgusting "farrago" [meaningless mixture] inspired "shame or laughter in every countenance. Such an outrage upon religion, the Sabbath, and common decency, was extremely painful to every sober, thinking person present. But it answered the much-wished for purpose of the Democrats, to see religion exhibited in the most ridiculous manner."[20] Ostensibly, Cutler thought that Jeffersonian "Democrats" in Congress actually mocked religion in hiring Leland to conduct his sermon. He may have considered them similar to the atheist radicals who briefly perpetuated the Cult of Reason during the French Revolution's Reign of Terror, and worshiped an actress as the Goddess of Reason at the Cathedral of Notre Dame.[21]

Unfortunately, Jefferson's attendance at Leland's sermon may have enhanced his reputation for political wiliness and contempt for organized religion. But Jefferson probably considered it unlikely that he would gain the votes of such "irreconcilables" as the Reverend Cutler anyway. Hutson misleadingly exaggerated the significance of Jefferson's attendance at Leland's sermon as evidence of his religious orthodoxy. Though a fine scholar of the colonial period and the diplomatic history of the American Revolution, Hutson is not known for expertise on Jefferson. In several studies, Hutson repeated nearly verbatim arguments he first made in 1998, when the FBI removed some palimpsests from Jefferson's letter to the Danbury Baptists in the Library of Congress. Hutson claimed that, although Jefferson's letter to the Baptists failed to exonerate him from Federalist charges of atheism, their orthodox clergy admired his attendance at John Leland's sermon before the House of Representatives, despite the Baptist preacher's reputation for fervid evangelical preaching and opposition to state support for religion. Hutson mentions an unnamed Federalist congressman (actually Manasseh Cutler) who said that Jefferson attended the sermon "contrary to all former practice." He does not quote the rest of the letter, in which Cutler mercilessly insulted Jefferson and Leland. Hutson continued, adding information that he perhaps invented or culled from later events or non-contemporary recollections, but that did not appear in contemporary accounts of Leland's sermon or in other historical narratives: "Jefferson ... attended an evangelical religious service and sang hymns, accompanied by the Marine Band, on public property two days after writing that the First Amendment erected a wall of separation between church and state." Indeed, Hutson's account of the Leland/Jefferson episode is starkly incomplete. That Hutson did not mention that Leland delivered the "Mammoth Cheese" along with the Danbury Baptists' letter to Jefferson, as well as his effusive praise of Jefferson in his embarrassing sermon, suggests that Hutson deliberately obscured the obvious: that Jefferson attended the congressional sermon as a political favor to a zealous Baptist admirer, rather than because of his religious enthusiasm.[22] The Baptist citizens of Cheshire, however, remained devoted Republicans, voting for Jefferson and his party throughout his presidency.[23]

Captivated by such palpable evidence of at least some New Englanders' devotion to the Republican Party (although much of the cheese rotted away during the trip from Cheshire to Washington, D.C.), Jefferson immediately and exuberantly wrote about this experience to his sons-in-law. To Thomas Mann Randolph, Jr., husband of his eldest daughter, Martha, he mentioned the cheese's exact dimensions. Jovially writing about its arrival, as if it were a momentous historical event, he said, "The Mammoth cheese is received here and is to be presented this day. It ... weighed in August 1230 lbs. They were offered 1000 D. in New York for the use of it 12 days as a shew [sic]," but refused the offer. After listing these impressive evidences of the cheese-makers' devotion to Republicanism, Jefferson somberly alluded to its larger political significance: "It is an ebullition of the passion of republicanism in a state where it has been under heavy persecution."[24] Regarding Massachusetts as the cradle of the Revolution and its town meeting form of government as the archetype of local democracy, Jefferson vaunted the cheese incident as evidence of increasing devotion to the Republican Party in New England. As he occasionally hinted, although he seldom explicitly asserted it, he considered the triumph of Republicanism in New England vital to the permanent ratification of a stable democratic/republican constitution in the nation.

Writing to another son-in-law, John Wayles Eppes, Jefferson elaborated the ramifications of New Englanders' increasing devotion to the Republican Party. Eppes lived with his wife, young, sickly Mary Jefferson in Chesterfield County, Virginia. Recently elected to the House of Delegates, Eppes was actively involved in state government, so Jefferson even more strongly emphasized to him this latest double proof of New England Baptists' emerging attachment to the new Republican regime. Excitedly telling him about the Cheshire Baptists' unique gift, and using some of the same words as in the letter to Randolph, he optimistically depicted it as evidence that Massachusetts was converting to Jeffersonian Republicanism. "The Mammoth cheese is arrived here, & is to be presented to-day," he said. "It is an ebullition of Republicanism in a state where it has been under heavy suppression. That state of things however is rapidly passing away, and there is a speedy prospect of seeing all the New England states come round to their antient principles; always excepting the real Monarchists & the Priests, who never can lose sight of the natural alliance between the crown & mitre."[25] Thus, he regarded the attitude of the New England extreme Federalists as a replay of the *Ancien Regime*'s reactionary politics and tyranny of church and king/state over the people, which the French Revolution's egalitarian principles had vanquished.

At this point, Jefferson abruptly changed the subject. He wanted to know if the democratic reform of Virginia's constitution, which he had advocated since he served in the state legislature during the American Revolution, was underway. "Are you laying off our counties into hundreds or captaincies?" he asked Eppes. There was no reason for him to inquire about this, since no one in the House of Delegates had recently introduced bills for constitutional amendment. It was the unanticipated manifestation of support from the Cheshire cheesemakers, which inadvertently reminded him of his early admiration for the New England town meeting mode of governance that precipitated his recommendation to Eppes. "There can be no other basis of republican energy," he continued. "Police, justice, elections, musters, schools, and many other essential things can have no other effectual bottom. There is not a single political measure for our state which I have so much at heart. The captain or headborough would be there what the serjeants are in an army; the finger of execution."[26]

Although his terminology evoked the Saxons of medieval England and their reputedly democratic assembly, the *Witan*, it is more likely that Jefferson had the Massachusetts town meeting in mind. The Cheshire cheese certainly had its effect on his mind as well as his stomach and his wallet. He paid Leland and Daniel Brown $200 out of his own pocket for the cheese, considerably more than it was worth. He desired to encourage the spread of Democratic-Republicanism in Massachusetts, and this was one way of doing it.[27]

A few months later, Jefferson reported at length on New England politics to Constantin Volney, a French latter-day Enlightenment *philosophe* who vented his hatred for the Roman Catholic Church in his famous autobiographical work, *Les Ruines, ou, Méditation sur les Révolutions des Empires* (1797), which Jefferson eagerly if imperfectly translated into English during 1801–1802. After the Federalist Congress passed the Alien Acts in 1798, Volney, who had visited Jefferson at Monticello in June 1796 and was busy touring the country, fled the United States, fearing that he would be imprisoned on trumped-up charges as a French spy. With the repressive recent history of the United States in mind, Jefferson in 1802 subtly compared the French Revolution's collapse in Napoleon Bonaparte's dictatorship at the end of 1799 with the New England states' rejection of his candidacy in the presidential election a year later.[28]

Like Volney, Jefferson felt disillusioned and betrayed by Bonaparte's "usurpation" of what was supposed to be a revolution for freedom and democracy. The new president concluded that the French, because of their heritage of monarchical absolutism, were not yet prepared to handle a republican form of government. Hiding his disappointment behind professions of ignorance, Jefferson opined. "I shall say nothing of your country, because I do not understand either its past or present state, nor foresee its future destiny. Those on the spot possess alone the facts on which a sound judgment can be formed." Implying that his countrymen demonstrated their superior virtue and intelligence by their adherence to republican government, which they had reasserted in electing him president, Jefferson proceeded to dissect France's debacle. "Believing that forms of government have been attempted to which the national character is not adapted, I expect something will finally be settled as free as their habits of thinking & acting will admit. My only prayer is that it may cost no more human suffering," he concluded, reiterating his antipathy to Robespierre and the violent Reign of

Terror.[29] After thus disposing of events in France, Jefferson turned his attention to the American scene.

Jefferson implied that Americans, because they were better educated, had a more equitable distribution of wealth, and were in general happier than Europeans, were naturally more law-abiding. He argued that happy people were less likely to commence revolutions. Nonetheless, he was bitter that Aaron Burr's complicity in Federalist machinations in the House of Representatives had nearly caused him to lose the presidency. At that point, he had contemplated calling a second constitutional convention to revise the electoral college procedures (as the Twelfth Amendment did in 1804) to declare him the winner, and even directed his friends Governors Monroe in Virginia and McKean in Pennsylvania to call out the militia if it seemed that Burr and the Federalists would block his inauguration. Relieved that the situation had not gotten that desperate, he now boasted, "In fact, my countrymen are so much in the habits of order, and feel it so much their interest, that they will never be wanting in the support of the existing government, tho' they may disapprove & mean to change it" when they disliked their current leaders. Assuring Volney that he had seen the U.S. government at its worst, when the Adams Administration implemented the Sedition Act and threatened to enforce the Alien Acts (but never did), Jefferson lamented that his countrymen, cajoled by Federalist propaganda, had almost abandoned their devotion to freedom of the press and the rights of minorities. "Principles & pursuits were then brought forward, the most adverse to those of the nation in its sound state of mind, and maintained for a short period by delusion, terror, corruption & every artifice which those who held the power & resources of the nation could put into exercise," he recalled, "yet the people soon corrected themselves, and brought things back to their course by the regular exercise of their elective franchise."[30]

Jefferson proudly listed the achievements of his first year as president: repealing all taxes except for the tariff; reducing the army and the navy; eliminating superfluous government offices that the Federalist Congress had created to aggrandize Executive patronage; balancing the budget and using the surplus to pay off the national debt ahead of schedule; and not pressing for renewal of the Sedition Act, which had expired the day before his inauguration, or the Alien Friends Act, which had expired in June 1800.

After listing these accomplishments, Jefferson claimed that his policies were supported by all sections of the country except for a few New England states. "The main body of our citizens are come back to one mind in all the states south of those of New England; and even of these Rhode Island and Vermont have joined us, and New Hampshire has been within a very small number of votes of manifesting the same in the choice of their governor," he reported. Jefferson remained eager to assess the political situation from a perspective favorable to his party. Nevertheless, he strove to be objective and not exaggerate Republican strength in the region. He believed that the Republican Party was less successful in Massachusetts and Connecticut than elsewhere because of the strength of their Established Church and clergy, who hated his struggle for religious freedom. "In Massachusetts the progress is slower. Federalism still triumphs there, and is yet more strong in Connecticut," he believed. "The empire of the priesthood over those states is the cause of their slow recovery from their delusions, but they advance, because they are essentially with their fellow citizens of the other states." He estimated that twelve of the sixteen state governors were Jeffersonian Republicans, while three affected to be "neutral" because their constituents were Republicans; and only one, the veteran Federalist Jonathan Trumbull, Jr., of Connecticut, "acted decidedly on his old principles."

Jefferson was convinced, as he would be throughout his life, that New Englanders were as devoted to republicanism as any other Americans, but that they had been deceived and "deluded" by their foremost opinion-molders, the clergy and the lawyer-politicians.[31]

Despite his confidence in the eventual triumph of his party, Jefferson could barely suppress his resentment of the harsh Federalist newspaper attacks, which he told Volney had only increased in abusiveness over the years. Unlike the fear and contempt he expressed in the letter to Gerry a year earlier, however, Jefferson now tried to joke about Federalist vindictiveness, ascribing it to their despair in the face of his mushrooming popularity. "The leaders of the quondam [Federalist] party however become more bitter as they are more impotent; they fill their newspapers with falsehoods, calumnies & audacities far beyond anything" that Volney had seen in 1797 and 1798, according to Jefferson. But he claimed that their libels did not bother him. Comparing the press to chimney flues in supplying "an innocent conveyance and discharge to smoke & vapours which might be dangerous if pent up in their bowels," he considered the deluge of newspaper abuse a peaceful substitute for more violent resistance to Republicanism.[32]

Jefferson assured Volney that he considered the defense of freedom of the press as one of the aims of his presidency. He viewed his presidency as an "experiment" to discover whether protecting "freedom of discussion" and permitting his opponents' lies and abuse would ultimately validate "an administration"—his—"pure and upright in its actions and views." Prematurely referring to his opponents as "ex-federalists," as if the party had totally collapsed, he said their hatred for him was a kind of mania, "and [they] exhibit against me such atrocities as no nation has ever before heard or endured." He stoically pledged to "protect them in the right of lying and calumniating, and [I] shall go on to merit the continuance of it," because, unlike these New England Federalists who denied that the people deserved self-government and freedom of speech, Jefferson would "pursue steadily my object of proving that a people, easy in their circumstances as ours are, are capable of conducting themselves under a government founded not in the fears & follies of man, but on his reason." Democratic-Republican government would vindicate the primacy of the moral sense, benevolence and sociability in human nature, prove "the predominance of his moral over his dissocial passions, so free as to restrain him in no moral right, and so firm as to protect him from every moral wrong, which shall leave him in short in possession of all his natural rights; nothing being more demonstrable than that he has no natural right in opposition to his social duties."[33]

Thus, Jefferson hoped during his presidency to attain a humanitarian utopia, in which all citizens would commit moral acts and help each other, or at least avoid deliberately hurting each other in pursuit of selfish gain. To an extent, he assumed that the selfish New England Federalist financiers, merchants, lawyers, and clergy opposed his aims of brotherhood and the victory of good over evil, which, in his opinion, would go hand in hand with the practice of republican government. Ironically, he seemed to place the upper-class Federalists in the same category as the amoral, unpredictable and untrustworthy ruler of France, Napoleon Bonaparte. Jefferson feared that Bonaparte might intervene in the Western Hemisphere's internal affairs, thereby blighting his New World Utopia. "An important means of giving free course to this experiment [in freedom of thought] is to keep Europe and its quarrels at a distance," he told Volney. "On this subject we are not without some uneasiness. But I hope that wise calculations on that side the Atlantic will dissipate our inquietudes and leave our relations with them in their present state." Although he preferred that the European powers would not impair the United States' political isolation, he was aware that Napoleon, who had recently invaded St. Domingo (Haiti) and re-annexed the massive Louisiana Territory in his plans for a New World empire, might upset the apple cart. With self-restraint he wrote Volney, who had Bonaparte's ear, "I count greatly on the wisdom of your chief. But on this subject it is not for me to speak."[34] If only Bonaparte and the New England High Federalists would listen to reason and do what was best for humankind, Jefferson perhaps mused, he could expect soon to retire from public life, "have the leisure to enjoy my family, my friends, my farm & books," and leave his country in peace and prosperity.[35]

7

Jefferson the Politician Courts the New England Federalists

Jefferson was not only a political philosopher but a practical politician and statesman. He was not above playing a counterfeit role if he thought it necessary to the nation's preservation. He performed such a role in his interactions with the New England Federalists in Congress during his first administration. By December 1802, he was forced to acknowledge that war between the U.S. and Napoleon's French Empire was likely as a result of France's impending repossession of its old, vast Louisiana territories. They encompassed most of the land west of the Mississippi up to the Rocky Mountains, including New Orleans and the mouth of the Mississippi River, vital to U.S. trade. He began making covert military preparations for such an eventuality, including the possibility of war with Great Britain if it decided to invade the Floridas during a Franco-American conflict.[1]

Recognizing that national unity, including the cooperation of his Federalist foes, was essential for conducting a successful war against the great powers, Jefferson began courting Federalist congressmen. Manasseh Cutler's letters and journals provide an excellent source for examining Jefferson's maneuvers. Cutler did not understand Jefferson's motives. He may not have recognized the significance of the impending crisis over Louisiana. However, he recorded in his diary for December 13, 1802, that the invited guests to the first presidential dinner of the congressional session were all Federalists, most of them from New England. "Dined with the President," he wrote: "We were the first company invited by billets sent into the Hall. Our billets were sent last Friday. Our company were: Messrs. Dana, Shepard, J.C. Smith, Davenport, Perkins, Van Rensselaer, Stanly, Read, Dennis, Woods, and myself. The President's two daughters, Mrs. Randolph and Mrs. Eppes, were at the table. They appeared well-accomplished women—very delicate and tolerably handsome. The President was very social. I presented him with a specimen of wadding for Ladies' cloaks and of bed-ticks from the Beverly [Massachusetts] Factory. We took coffee in the evening, and came away at eight. *It is a matter of curiosity that the first public dining company should be all federalists.*"[2]

Contrary to custom, Jefferson had not invited members of his own party to dine with him first at the outset of the short second session of the Seventh Congress from December 1802 to March 1803. Cutler's records provide additional proof that Jefferson was intensely interested in winning friends among the new Federalist members at this critical epoch in his presidency. Most of the congressmen with whom Cutler attended dinner at Jefferson's house were freshmen Federalists. The rest were moderate old-timers who had not disgracefully distinguished themselves by zeal to persecute Democratic-Republicans, make war on France, or insult Jefferson during the late 1790s, which journalist Claude G. Bowers called "The Reign of Terror in America."[3]

Although Samuel W. Dana of Connecticut and General William Shepard of Massachusetts were Federalist congressional veterans, they maintained a low profile in Congress and sometimes voted with the Jeffersonians. Josiah C. Smith of Massachusetts was a newcomer, as were Killian K. Van Rensselaer of New York, John Stanly of North Carolina, Elias Perkins of Connecticut, and Cutler of Massachusetts. A Massachusetts Federalist, Nathan Read, was initially elected to fill a vacancy caused by Samuel Sewall's resignation during the Sixth Congress in 1800, and served in the Seventh Congress, after which he left politics. John Dennis of Maryland served from the Fifth through the Eighth Congress, but he, like Henry Woods of Pennsylvania, who served in the Sixth and Seventh Congresses, was a nondescript Federalist who exerted little influence beyond his vote. Jefferson sought to influence, not Federalist powerhouses whom he probably considered "incurable," but by flattery and attention, persuade insignificant members and newcomers who had not aroused his wrath to support him. If possible, Jefferson wanted to convince new or uncommitted Federalist members of Congress to adopt reasonable, nonpartisan positions in vital national issues instead of automatically voting against every measure he advocated. This indicated Jefferson's political acumen.[4]

Jefferson was even willing to temporarily assume the unwonted role of church-goer. In the early days of Congress, religious services were held in the hall of Congress since no churches had yet been built. Jefferson, whose daughter Martha became increasingly religious with age, at the end of 1802 suddenly discovered an urge to attend religious services. In September 1802, the arrival of the notorious deist and great radical thinker and writer, Thomas Paine, in the United States at the president's invitation, to sit at Jefferson's dinner table, had revived the president's reputation for "infidelity" and increased the rage of devout Federalists toward his regime. Paine, the author of *Common Sense*, had become unpopular in the United States after writing his anti-biblical masterpiece *The Age of Reason* (1793–1794), and denouncing George Washington as a scoundrel in his *Letter to Washington* (1796), for not demanding his release from prison by the French government during the Reign of Terror. For Jefferson, who had dined with him at the President's House after his arrival in the United States, he was a political liability in a time of crisis. Jefferson thus found the need to take on the aura of a religious president and distance himself from Paine.[5]

On New Years' Day, January 1803 and for several months thereafter, Jefferson attended religious services in the House with his family. The astute Cutler, a man of the world as well as a clergyman, appreciated Jefferson's political showmanship. He reported that Jefferson joined his daughter Martha, his grandson Thomas Jefferson Randolph, and his secretary Meriwether Lewis, in attending House services. Cutler was convinced that this was merely a political ploy to dissociate himself from Paine. "The political necessity of paying some respect to the religion of the country is felt," he wrote his friend Joseph Torrey. Jefferson was taking special pains to be polite to the moderate Federalist faction. "Courting popularity is his darling object," Cutler commented, especially since his "caressing of Paine has excited his fears. He and his family have constantly attended public worship in the Hall." One Sunday in December 1803, Jefferson, an expert horseman, leaving his family at home, even went "through the rain and on horseback to the [Congress] Hall." As far as Cutler could tell, Jefferson had abandoned his pre-presidential ambition to "overturn our religious institutions," formerly his "favorite object."[6] Although Jefferson never had any such intention, he obviously thought that it was politically advisable for him to participate in the nation's "civil religion" of watered-down Christianity at this juncture, when even most "Democrats," according to Cutler, shunned Paine for fear that he would damage their reputations with their constituents.[7]

In courting the moderate Federalists, Jefferson temporarily became a church-goer. In any case, according to Margaret Bayard Smith's reminiscences, Sunday church service at the House of Representatives in Washington during the Adams and Jefferson administrations was more a social occasion, where young men and women flirted and dressed in their finest outfits, rather than one of somber religiosity. Few other public venues existed in the infant city.[8] As a recently elected congressman who had not participated in the burlesque House balloting in 1801 in which diehard Federalists sought to elect Burr president instead of Jefferson, Cutler early experienced Jefferson's hospitality. Surprised at his recent invitation to dine with Jefferson along with other New England Federalists, he wrote Torrey, "There has been an evident change in the conduct of Mr. Jefferson with respect to the Federal party in Congress. His first public attentions were paid to them. I happened myself to be one of the first party invited publicly to dine, and I believe most of the Federalists were invited before any of the Democrats." Notorious, at least among his political enemies, for his slovenliness, Jefferson was even beginning to wear more formal attire, Cutler reported. "His dress has been quite decent," he wrote, "and to me, he has appeared to exert himself in sociability." Perhaps Cutler did not perceive that it took a great effort for Jefferson to curry favor with an elitist Federalist land speculator like him.[9] But Jefferson had a strong stomach, at least for a vegetarian, at this point.

Presbyterian Reverend Samuel Taggart, another devoutly Federalist Massachusetts man of the cloth, who served in Congress from 1803 until 1817, also received Jefferson's attentions. Taggart was a firm Federalist, who voted against the Louisiana Purchase and the Twelfth Amendment to the Constitution at the outset of his term. Apparently this did not deter Jefferson, who met with him in October 1803. "I have had one short interview with the President," Taggart wrote his brother in October 1803. "He appears to be a gentleman of polite manners and had I been entirely free from prepossession I should have viewed him in a favourable point of light."[10]

As a revivalist clergyman, Taggart kept track of Jefferson's church attendance. He discovered that the president "attended public worship" more than he expected. When asked about Jefferson's church attendance, he reported, "He does occasionally; of six times which I have attended at Congress Hall he has been present four, and I have heard several times of his attending when I did not. I do not attend much at the Hall of Congress on the Sabbath. The Presbyterian meeting is nigher [nearer], and I am rather disgusted than otherwise with the Episcopal service."[11]

Nevertheless, Taggart was impressed with the independent spirit of one of Congress's Episcopalian preachers, Walter Dulaney Addison (1769–1848), who was appointed chaplain of the U.S. Senate in 1810. An opponent of slavery who later freed his slaves, Addison came from a wealthy Maryland planter family and lived at Oxon Hill plantation. Nephew of the famous Loyalist preacher, Jonathan Boucher, Addison was personally ordained as an Episcopal priest by the Reverend Thomas Claggett, the first Episcopal Bishop of Maryland. Taggart said that Jefferson also seemed to enjoy Addison's sermons. Addison "has preached two excellently well adapted sermons in Congress, in which he has plainly, and faithfully," warned against the adverse effects of religious "infidelity" on "rulers and Civil Government," Taggart observed. "The President has attended [Addison's sermons] both days. I wish both he, and all of us may get good by his labours."[12]

By early 1807, Taggart reported, the Republicans had gained ground in Massachusetts and become the majority party. He observed that the Massachusetts delegation to Congress was composed almost entirely of "Democrats, with one or two exceptions." He was relieved that the Massachusetts assembly had not joined the "multitude" of state legislatures in urging Jefferson to run for a third term, "but I find democracy goes on hopefully in the legislature…. I wonder by what clause in our state constitution or the Constitution of the United States, state legislatures are vested with the power of, in this way, attempting to controul the election of a President."[13] Although Taggart was a firm Federalist, Jefferson probably considered him relatively harmless compared with writers in the *Port Folio*, the *New England Palladium*, and the *Columbian Centinel* who trashed democracy and seemingly longed for a restoration of monarchy.

On the other hand, New England Jeffersonians were intent on getting rid of the Old School Federalists who had participated in the XYZ sessions of Congress from 1797 to 1799, in which the notorious Quasi-War legislation, high taxes, Army increases, and Stamp Act, Alien, Sedition, and Naturalization Acts were passed. Most notorious among the fanatical Federalists from that period who remained in Congress were Roger Griswold of Connecticut and John Rutledge, Jr., of South Carolina. "He [Jefferson] has shown a marked neglect to Mr. Griswold and Mr. Rutledge," Cutler observed. "It is a great object with the party to get them out of Congress; but Mr. Griswold will remain two years longer."[14]

One venerable New Englander who had maintained a friendship with both Jefferson and Adams, even though he was probably closer to the Federalist solon, was Elbridge Gerry. Still bitter about the way the leading Federalists had ostracized him when he returned from France in late 1798 and told President Adams that the sly Foreign Minister Talleyrand wanted peace with the United States, at the beginning of Jefferson's presidency Gerry was a political nonentity. In 1800, though claiming that Adams supported him, he lost the election for governor of Massachusetts to Caleb Strong, an ex-senator who would become a political powerhouse in the next decade. Gerry's political career seemed to be over. Although he would never regain the national prominence he held during the Revolution and the Washington Administration, he was a wealthy man, with investments in land, federal stocks and bonds, and mercantile enterprises. Nevertheless, he tended to adopt popular causes, such as favoring discrimination between original holders of the public debt and speculators in the 1790s. In Congress in 1793, he supported Revolutionary War veterans who demanded full interest payments on their war pensions instead of four percent. Thus, he had a certain affinity for the populist aspects of Jeffersonian Democracy. He was impressed by Jefferson's achievements as president. In any case, if he wanted to return to politics, he had no place to go but to the Democratic-Republicans. Thus, it is not surprising that he wrote Jefferson a friendly letter in October 1803, praising the Louisiana Purchase, a controversial measure that was unpopular with Massachusetts Federalists. Praising the stalwart republicanism of the Old Dominion and ignoring the stigma of Southern slaveholding while filling Jefferson in on current political trends in New England, the elderly Founding Father observed, "Three of the eastern states are still antirepublican; they had great merit in establishing their independence; but owe the preservation of it to the southern states."[15]

Blending reason and revelation in his praise of Jefferson, Gerry continued, "Pursue sir your just system of politics, it must be sanctioned by the sovereign of the universe, and infallibly raise the US to the acme of national wealth, security, & honor." Touting his nonpartisanship, as he had done throughout his career, he said, "This is my candid opinion, & with few exceptions, I believe the opinion of the impartial party of the community." Ostensibly regarding Jefferson as intrinsically nonpartisan, or at least as President of All the People, Gerry was worried that if the Twelfth Amendment to the Constitution, providing separate balloting for presidential and vice-presidential candidates were not ratified, the Federalists might attempt to create another snafu as they had in 1800, and elect Burr president. "Congress, I hope, will make effectual provision for preventing those election contentions, which had nearly involved us in a civil conflict," he reminded Jefferson.[16]

Undoubtedly aware that Gerry had little political clout in Massachusetts at this time, Jefferson took his time answering his letter. However, he considered Gerry a long-time friend and in the past had written important letters to him about his beliefs and policies, especially the famous letter of January 26, 1799, which constituted the "Republican platform" for the election of 1800, according to some historians.[17] Thus, when he finally replied in March 1804, his remarks were well-considered and revealing of his state of mind. He wanted Gerry to know that he considered New England essentially loyal to him and to republicanism, and regarded its Federalist voting habits as an aberration that would soon end. "In the middle and southern States, as great an union of sentiment has now taken place as is perhaps desirable," he said. Most of their voters were Republicans. As he had asserted in the past, he believed that his inveterate opponents favored monarchy. "For as there will always be an opposition, I believe it had better be from avowed monarchists than republicans." He contended that some partisan opposition to the Republicans was a good thing, since it would preserve unity in the party, which would otherwise dissolve into competing factions if it had no competitors to confront. Perhaps with the factions of Burr and Clinton in mind, he pointed out, "New York seems to be in danger of republican division." Of the New England states, he happily observed, "Vermont is solidly with us," as was Rhode Island, even though its adherence might be temporary, a consequence of moderate Republican governor Arthur Fenner's widespread popularity. Of the other New England states, he optimistically reported, "New Hampshire [was] on the verge of the republican shore; Connecticut advancing towards it very slowly, but with steady step." He was most pessimistic about Massachusetts, writing Gerry in the nautical metaphors he often used, "your State only [is] uncertain of making port at all." He mistakenly joined Massachusetts together with Delaware, "which will always be uncertain, from the divided character of her citizens," whose Quakers he generally considered Anglophile Federalists. In this instance, Jefferson's evaluation was incorrect. Massachusetts gave him its electoral votes in the election of 1804, while Connecticut and Delaware alone voted for the venerable South Carolina Federalist Charles Cotesworth Pinckney.[18]

Ostensibly sharing Gerry's concern that Burr might somehow weasel his way into the presidency, Jefferson observed, "If the amendment of the Constitution passes Rhode Island, (and we expect to hear in a day or two) the election for the ensuing four years seems to present nothing formidable." Perhaps thinking that Gerry, who endlessly insisted on his own lack of political ambition, might think him too interested in holding power, he assured him that he would have preferred to serve only one term as president. He claimed that the Federalist attacks on his character and his policies had forced him to prove his popularity and public acclaim for his measures by running for office a second time. As he put it, "I sincerely regret that the unbounded calumnies of the federal party have obliged me to throw myself on the verdict of my country for trial, my great desire having been to retire, at the end of the present term, to a life of tranquility; and it was my decided purpose when I entered office. They force my continuance." He made it clear to Gerry that he had no intention of serving more than two terms (which might make him seem like a would-be monarch or dictator): "If we can keep the vessel of State as steadily in her course for another four years, my earthly purposes will be accomplished, and I shall be free to enjoy, as you are doing, my family, my farm, and my books."[19] Regarding the upcoming presidential election, Jefferson relied on Connecticut's "steady step" toward the Democratic-Republicans to help him gain the victory over another Southerner, Pinckney.

More than Jefferson seemed to understand, at this juncture Connecticut, the Land of Steady Habits, was the land of steadier Federalism. By 1804, however, Jefferson thought that its citizens were coming around to see the Democratic-Republican light. His postmaster general, Gideon Granger, was on the ground reporting political activities there to him. Apparently, he had learned something about the Federalist scheme, promoted by Timothy Pickering in Massachusetts, Senator William Plumer of New Hampshire, and others in New York and Connecticut, to form a coalition of extreme Federalists and renegade Republicans into a new political party. This political party, which was ostensibly to be headed by Vice-President Aaron Burr, would attempt to gain control of Congress and if unsuccessful would attempt to incite the secession of the "seven eastern States." Granger had apparently discussed this conspiracy in a conversation with Jefferson in 1803 or early 1804.[20]

Writing to Granger, Jefferson, seemingly alarmed by the possibility of such a Third Force, brought up rumors about this would-be party. "In our last conversation you mentioned a federal scheme afloat, of forming a coalition between the federalists and republicans, of what they call the seven eastern States," he wrote.[21] Jefferson had not previously heard about this scheme, which he found repulsive. He considered it a Federalist Party attempt to trick or manipulate a disgruntled Republican "minority" into joining it, hoping thereby to control the sectional, and eventually the national, balance of power. He ostensibly disdained any attempt by Connecticut Federalists, aware of their rapid decline as a national force, to seduce would-be turncoat Republicans to join them in a third party. But his "reflections," inspiring in him a consciousness that his former enemies were intent on "return[ing] into power in some other form," actually caused him some anxiety. The Connecticut Federalists were aware that on the national level their party was finished ("gone forever"), he reasoned. They could only retake power by convincing a substantial minority of Republicans to abandon the party he had worked so hard to build, and instead join them in a bogus third party, which, even if they called it a "new" version of the Jeffersonians, would actually be a masked Federalist Party dominated by Federalists. Seemingly cynically, Jefferson professed confidence that "the majority of the republicans not needing them, will not buy them." Jefferson admitted that some Republicans were more interested in profits and office than in maintaining a virtuous government. He bluntly asserted, "The minority [of Republicans], having no other means of ruling the majority, will give a price for auxiliaries, and that price must be principle." (In other words, they would become "auxiliaries" or flunkies, of the new ersatz third party, led by Federalists.) In order to gain these new adherents, Jefferson argued, the Federalists would also have to pretend to compromise on matters of "principle." Sounding a grim note, as if this new party, based on crass opportunism, threatened the foundations of the republic, Jefferson warned, "Thus a bastard system of federo-republicanism will rise on the ruins of the true principles of our revolution."[22]

Such a party would obviously be controlled by extremist Federalists, who would "dictate" policy to the renegade Republicans, Jefferson pointed out. The Federalists would comprise the "majority," and any turncoat Republicans who thought otherwise were fools, he said. Alluding to an obscure proposal the famous compromiser Roger Sherman may have made at the Constitutional Convention, he drolly asserted, "Thus their proposition of putting themselves into gear with the republican minority, is exactly like Roger Sherman's proposition to add Connecticut to Rhode Island." He assumed that most of the Republicans who joined such an ersatz party were unprincipled opportunists, demagogues seeking political power and disappointed office-seekers. Such partisans were not truly devoted members of his party, he was sure. The mercenary Republicans who joined the third party at the outset would stay with it after it gained power, Jefferson's hypothetical scenario continued, while those "principled" Republicans who had been temporarily deceived about the disinterestedness of the founders of this new party would eventually leave. But it would be too late, because the bogus Federalist-Jeffersonian party would already have taken over the New England governments: "They [the genuine Republicans] may quit them, indeed, but, in the meantime, all the venal will have become associated with them, and will give them a majority sufficient to keep them in place."[23]

In this unlikely, extremely pessimistic outline of the future, Jefferson foresaw the corruption and downfall of republican governments by those obsessed with their own avarice and ambition, in accordance with the classical theory of government decline expounded by the ancient Greeks and Romans. Perhaps learning from other sources that Pickering and Griswold actually were plotting to create their own New England-led republic, he perceived that the Federalists intended their states to leave the Union: "The idea of forming seven eastern States is moreover clearly to form the basis of a separation of the Union," he warned. "Is it possible that real republicans can be gulled by such a bait?"[24] Those Republicans, even those who grumbled at certain aspects of Jefferson's policies, like the Quids in Pennsylvania, but were devoted to the party from principle should easily see through the Federalist scheme. "Can any one deny, that in all important questions of principle, republicanism prevails?" Those power-hungry Republicans who desired "that their individual will shall govern the majority," an "unjust wish" in any case, would soon learn that the Federalist majority of the new party would tell *them* what to do.[25]

With his pessimistic view of human nature (to Jefferson, it often seemed that everyone wanted authority for selfish reasons but himself), he had no doubt that the Federalists did not intend to share power once they got hold of it: "The federalists must not have the passions of other men, if, after getting thus into the seat of power, they suffer themselves to be governed by their [Republican] minority. This minority may say, that whenever they relapse into their own [Federalist] principles, they will quit them, and draw the seat from under them." Such expectations were naïve, he argued, because the "venal" ex-Republicans would stay with the Federalists for their own ambitious reasons, "and will give them a majority sufficient to keep them in place, and to enable them to eject the heterogeneous friends by whose aid they get again into power."[26]

Jefferson did not seem entirely logical here. Where would this incongruous mix of disloyal Republicans and excessively principled party members (perhaps "Old Republicans" of whom John Randolph of Virginia would soon become the leader) come from? And, if one of these groups abandoned the ersatz third party, how would the party be able to make up for their loss? Wouldn't it then lose its majority? But, Jefferson was being melodramatic rather than logical. He believed that the voters of New England were essentially republicans. They would not follow a bogus, suspect third party combining motley, suspicious elements, disgruntled Republicans and parochial-minded Federalists, especially once it declared its intention to leave the Union and form its own country.

Indeed, when he returned to the real political world, Jefferson felt reassured that there was nothing to fear. As far as he was concerned, the mass of the rank-and-file Federalists of New England were turning more and more to the Democratic-Republican Party. The people would never tolerate an ersatz third party, and few Republicans would consider joining it. His brief nightmare of party corruption, Federalist domination, and the republic's demise ended in a happy daydream of absolute Jeffersonian triumph. As he more soberly put it: "I cannot believe any portion of real republicans will enter into this trap; and if they do, I do not believe they can carry with them the mass of their States, advancing so steadily as we see them, to an union of principle with their brethren. It will be found in this, as in all other similar cases, that crooked schemes will end by overwhelming their authors and coadjutors in disgrace, and that he alone who walks strict and upright, and who, in matters of opinion, will be contented that others should be as free as himself, and acquiesce when his opinion is fairly overruled, will attain his object in the end."[27]

Jefferson was convinced that republican virtue, embodied in himself and his supporters, would ultimately triumph, even should the Federalists by legerdemain briefly regain power in New England and the "eastern states." Still, Jefferson would not have employed military force against them, even if they seceded from the Union. Such a response contradicted his principles of voluntarism and self-determination, most fully expounded during the crises precipitated by the Alien and Sedition Acts and the Kentucky and Virginia Resolutions. At that time, he pondered the possibility that it would be better for Virginia to secede from the Union than for its citizens to suffer the denial of their civil liberties, and the states of their rights and concurrent powers under the Constitution.[28]

Less urgently, Jefferson confided to Granger that he believed that his prediction that New Hampshire's elections would all favor Republican candidates was doubtful. "I wish your information as to the N. H. election may be verified," he wrote. "But the last accounts give reason to apprehend a small majority against [John] Langdon," the Republican candidate for governor. "However his success [in] another year will be certain, & there is hope of a republican legislature this year."[29]

Jefferson's prediction proved more accurate than Granger's, even though Granger was in New Hampshire and the president was not. The Republicans won the state legislature, but Langdon lost the election for governor by a small margin. He won the governorship in 1805. The New Hampshire legislature elected in 1804 was the first Republican assembly in the state's history. When it met in June 1804, it endorsed Jefferson's reelection, blighting Federalist hopes. Indeed, any interest New Hampshire Federalists showed in the secession schemes presided over by New Englanders Roger Griswold, Timothy Pickering, and (to a lesser extent) William Plumer were dashed by the Republican victories in the state's legislative elections. However, New Hampshire was closer to secession than Jefferson perhaps comprehended. Senator Plumer and his colleague Simeon Olcott, as well as New Hampshire congressman

Samuel Hunt, an influential Connecticut Valley politician and nephew of Massachusetts governor Caleb Strong, were involved in Pickering's secession plot during the winter of 1803–1804. The results of the elections of 1804 in New England made the failure of secessionist schemes inevitable. Since Rhode Island and Vermont were Republican enclaves, and Connecticut and Massachusetts were Federalist but with a resourceful Republican minority, New Hampshire gained inordinate significance as a kind of balance wheel whose political fate determined secession's future. According to an expert on the topic, the state's switch to Jefferson in 1804 and 1805 made secession a "hopeless" dream for the High Federalists.[30]

Republicans' upset victory dismayed John Taylor Gilman, New Hampshire's leading Federalist, who was annually elected governor from 1794 to 1804. Not taking the defeat lightly, Gilman often angrily vetoed measures passed by the Republican legislature, decreasing his popularity and making him appear irrational. By contrast, John Langdon, whom the Republicans elected speaker of the state house of representatives, adopted a temperate, high-minded attitude.[31] Hoping to retain Federalist seats in Congress after the recent fiasco on the state legislative level, Plumer chaired a secret meeting in Concord on July 4 to create a strong party organization. In August 1804, he composed an *Address to the Electors of New Hampshire* to inspire voters to choose Federalists.[32]

Travelling through New England to exhort Republicans, Postmaster General Granger was shocked by the "astonishing exertions" of the Federalists. In September 1804, he sent Jefferson "a few words as to Politics." He believed that New Hampshire was safely in Republican hands, although the results of the congressional elections were still "unknown." He had spoken with John Taylor Gilman's brother Nicholas Gilman, "who is perfectly confident of Our success both in members of Congress and Electors." Nicholas Gilman had served in Congress as a Federalist from New Hampshire from 1789 to 1797, but had changed his party affiliation to the Democratic-Republicans in 1802. After he was defeated for the U.S. Senate in 1802, Jefferson appointed him a federal bankruptcy commissioner to encourage his party loyalty. Granger was doubtful of Gilman's optimistic predictions (however, Gilman would finally win his U.S. Senate seat in the upcoming elections): "I must observe the returns which I have seen appear to me a little alarming." Granger was more optimistic about the Massachusetts vote, writing: "Our friends in Massachusetts are in the highest Spirits, for once well united and organized, they move in a solid Phalanx." "There are at least some hopes of Success in our electoral Ticket" there, he believed.[33]

Of particular concern to Granger was the fate of Connecticut, which he believed was firmly in Federalist hands. As a former Federalist who joined the Republicans in 1800, Granger had some powerful Federalist friends, among them former Chief Justice Oliver Ellsworth, who had served in the U.S. Senate from 1789 to 1796 before being appointed to the High Court by Washington. Despite his strident Federalism, Ellsworth was rumored to be among those New England Federalists who espoused disunion both in 1794 and, more seriously in 1804. Granger wrote Jefferson that Connecticut remained impervious to Republicans, but they were fighting back: "In Connecticut the Republicans are more severely treated than any where else, and on their part strike bolder Strokes." They had organized public meetings and printed dozens of pamphlets "with a view to prostrate the faction," he reported. He observed that the formerly aloof Ellsworth, who had contracted a severe illness when he went to Europe as minister extraordinary to France under Adams in 1800, was now campaigning for the Federalists: "My former friend Mr. Ellsworth has taken *open* and *active* ground," he noted. He was writing articles for the Hartford *Courant* and spreading copies of the newspaper all over the state. "He must abide by the Consequences, a part of which I presume will be unpleasant. He has even descended to be the Instrument of party to circulate the *Courant* under *feigned* pretences."[34]

At least in New Hampshire, the Federalist state organization was successful in winning Congress. Their glee in this triumph was dampened by Jefferson's capture of the electoral votes of all the New England states but Connecticut, in sharp contrast to his failure to gain any of the section's electors in 1800. Nonetheless, there will still some rumblings of secession, even in the Massachusetts legislature despite elderly John Adams' support for Jefferson. At the end of 1804, it passed the Ely Amendment, a proposal to repeal the "three-fifths clause" of the Constitution. The state's Democratic-Republicans protested that passage of the measure would result in Southern secession, leaving the remainder of the Union, including Massachusetts, to pay their individual state debts, which under the Funding Act of 1790 were "assumed" (adopted) by the national government, and employing an onerous land tax on their citizens. Throughout the Union, Southern newspapers warned that such an amendment would violate the terms on which the South had come into the Union in 1787. These sentiments brought smiles to Pickering and his friends, who hoped that the Southern states would leave the Union so that the Federalists might retain control of what was left. The Massachusetts legislature instructed Governor Strong to send copies of the Ely Resolution to the other states. New Hampshire's Governor Gilman contended that repealing the "three-fifths clause" would be good for the state, which did not benefit from its provisions. He admitted that, when direct taxes on land and slaves were passed by Congress, the state benefited from the clause. But this had only occurred once so far, during the undeclared war with France in 1798. He anticipated that the national government would seldom impose direct taxes, and would generally rely on tariffs and excises. The Democratic-Republicans countered that, in the inevitable event of war, Congress would resort to direct taxes, and the existence of the "three-fifths clause" would benefit New Hampshire and other slaveless states.[35]

None of the states voted to submit the Ely Amendment to Congress. The New Hampshire Assembly, dominated by Republicans defeated it by a vote of 87 to 70, but even legislatures controlled by Federalists rejected it, including Connecticut and Delaware.[36] When this provocative measure failed to receive substantial approval, the would-be secessionist Federalists in Congress, led by senators Pickering, Uriah Tracy of Connecticut, and Plumer of New Hampshire abandoned any other disruptive schemes. The state legislatures that considered the amendment uniformly observed that the Southern states would regard repeal of the "three-fifths clause" as a betrayal of promises the Northern states made at the Constitutional Convention.

Unfortunately, among the repercussions of the Jeffersonian victory in 1800 was Congress's impeachment of the harmless, albeit senile and alcoholic New Hampshire District Judge John Pickering, a Federalist, which was conducted during most of 1803, ending with his conviction by the Senate in January 1804. Pickering (no relative of Timothy Pickering) had been among the leading lawyers and local political figures of revolutionary New Hampshire. He served in the state constitutional conventions of 1781 and 1791–92, and was a member of the state ratifying convention that approved the United States Constitution in 1788. Although he was not a prominent Federalist, Washington appointed him district judge of Connecticut in 1792. Shortly after his appointment, Pickering began to drink heavily and seemingly suffered from dementia.[37]

When several people reported that Pickering was unable to perform the simplest judicial duties, mainly because he was often drunk, and he summarily dismissed a customs violation case in a state of inebriation, Secretary of the Treasury Gallatin informed Senator Plumer that if Pickering did not resign, he would be impeached. When Plumer and other Federalists opposed his resigning, knowing that Jefferson would fill his place with a Republican, Jefferson followed Gallatin's advice and recommended his impeachment in a letter to Congress. He overlooked Pickering's evident insanity, preferring to emphasize his "criminal drunkenness," although this habit was hardly a "high crime and misdemeanor" deserving impeachment. In any case, Jefferson was eager to fill a few judicial posts with Democratic-Republicans, who were unrepresented in that department as a result of the exclusionist policies of the Washington and Adams administrations. Still, at the time Plumer was offended and outraged by the callous treatment of Pickering, his mentor and friend, although in later years, after he had become a Jeffersonian, he condoned the Republicans' actions.[38]

Despite the pragmatic leadership of politicians like Plumer, New Hampshire's Federalist Party was intrinsically weak. Most of the state's small farmers (the vast majority of the population), grain and saw millers, and small merchants favored the Republicans.[39] In addition, Federalist leaders were snobbish, picayune, and inattentive to their constituents. Plumer himself, despite his political skills, was an "insecure" Federalist elitist from the Granite State. He distrusted popular rule, and was devoted to law, order, and respected tradition. A self-made lawyer and political opportunist, he eventually turned from an extreme Federalist and advocate of New England secession to an ardent nationalist and Jefferson's friendly correspondent during the latter's retirement.[40]

In certain ways, Plumer deviated from the New England Federalist norm. As a young man, he underwent multiple religious conversions, from Puritan Congregationalism to Baptism, even serving as a lay preacher and zealously attempting to convert his friends to the revivalist faith. However, within a few years, he became a devout deist and was drummed out of the Baptist meeting. Although he supported freedom of religion from his youth, as a practical politician in later life he virulently denounced Jefferson's deism as virtual atheism, particularly in newspaper attacks he composed as "Impartialis" and "Cato" during the presidential election of 1804. In stressing Jefferson's religious infidelity, as well as urging New Hampshire to secede from the Union if the "three-fifths clause" of the Constitution were not repealed, Plumer publicly contributed to the abortive Pickering-Griswold plan to form an independent New England-New York republic nominally headed by Aaron Burr.[41]

Whatever his reputation in later years, during his lifetime Aaron Burr was surprisingly respected, especially by conservative Federalists. Plumer was among his admirers. After meeting him, he favorably compared him to Jefferson. Arguing that Vice-President Burr was far more refined and intelligent than Jefferson and deserved to be president instead, he wrote, "If Aaron Burr had the reputation of as much integrity and virtue as his good sense actually imposes on him, we should not live under the feeble, nerveless administration of a dry-dock & indissoluble salt mountain philosopher."[42] The plot to form a republic headed by Burr was abandoned after Burr lost the election for governor of New York, famously, albeit temporarily relieving his frustration by killing his nemesis Hamilton in July 1804. To make matters worse for the schemers, a few months later Jefferson was overwhelmingly reelected president.

As a New Hampshire senator, Plumer tended to vote with the rest of the Federalist delegates. Historians remain grateful for his habit of recording congressional activities in his journals and memoranda, which have been published. One of the reasons for Plumer's distaste for the Republican Party was his disgust with Jefferson's renowned poor grooming habits and boorish etiquette as president, specifically in several famous (or infamous) Washington dinners in 1803 and 1804, attended by British Minister Anthony Merry and his wife. The Britons and Plumer (who did not attend these notorious dinners, but learned about them through an "informant") were enraged at the discourteous treatment Mrs. Merry received at "the philosopher's table," as Plumer mockingly labeled Jefferson. Among the numerous *faux-pas* Jefferson committed, according to Plumer, were inviting Merry and the French *chargé d'affaires*, Louis-André Pichon, to dinner at the same time, even though the countries were bitter enemies currently at war. Moreover, Pichon was only a minor official, while Merry was a minister plenipotentiary. Compounding the insult, Jefferson escorted Dolly Madison, the secretary of state's wife, to the dinner table when traditional etiquette dictated that he take Mrs. Merry's hand. Plumer felt contempt for the whole Cabinet, as well as Jefferson.[43]

In an ostensible attempt to make amends, Madison gave a dinner for the diplomatic corps a few days later at his home. Even Jefferson attended the festivities, though "he never dines abroad," Plumer observed. Plumer learned that the wives of the notables debated beforehand (before Mrs. Merry arrived) which of them should hold "first rank." Each agreed that priority belonged to herself, although Plumer believed that Mrs. Merry should certainly have had preference. Dolly Madison, wife of the secretary of state, although merely "the daughter of a woman who only kept a boarding-house in Philadelphia at the time of her marriage," thought President Jefferson should take her hand, as he had done at the President's House. To his disgust, Plumer learned that Mrs. Merry was ultimately ignored. The President did not take her hand, and her husband had to escort her to the table, while Madison took Dolly. Such conduct was horrendously improper, Plumer was well aware. It is not clear from Plumer's record how Jefferson conducted himself on this occasion, except that he showed he did not deserve to be president: "Whoever has seen Mr. Jefferson, to all his other failures, must add, that his manners are not only unpolished but awkward & clownish."[44]

Plumer had reached this conclusion following several experiences of Presidential hospitality. In 1802, graphically describing his first meeting with Jefferson at the White House in the company of a Democratic-Republican senator from Massachusetts, Joseph B. Varnum, the freshman New Hampshire senator wrote his friend, New Hampshire judge Jeremiah Smith: "In a few minutes, a tall highboned man came into the room; he was drest, or rather undrest, with an old brown coat, red waistcoat, old corduroy smallclothes, much soild—woolen hose—& slippers without heels. I thought this man was a servant; but Genl Varnum surprised me by announcing that it was the President. Never, never rally me again upon my inattention to dress—I certainly dress as well as the first officer of the nation. I tarried about twenty minutes. He is easy of access, & conversed with great ease & freedom."[45]

Jefferson's ostensible candor and naiveté were merely additional reasons to distrust this slovenly, demagogic, states' rights Virginian who did not care about New England, Plumer concluded at the time. The conviction that New Hampshire was ill-served by this "clown" was among the reasons that Plumer advocated his state's secession from the Union and its membership in an "Eastern confederacy." During his tenure as a senator, he opposed most of Jefferson's policies. He voted against the Louisiana Purchase, the Twelfth Amendment to the Constitution, and the repeal of the Judiciary Act of 1801. Like John Quincy Adams (although Adams supported the Purchase), Plumer considered the Louisiana Purchase unconstitutional.

He was appeased to an extent when Jefferson confided to him his intention to propose a constitutional amendment permitting the purchase of foreign territory for addition to the Union. (As is well-known, Jefferson's friends easily convinced him that such an amendment was superfluous and would only cause trouble with France and political ammunition for the Federalists; he soon abandoned the idea.) Plumer remained suspicious of Jefferson's character and repulsed by his often sloppy attire, even though he eventually concluded that he was charming and liked the taste of the president's fine French wines.[46]

Plumer's opinion of Jefferson became more favorable after he learned that the president did not intend to run for a third term. At that point, he assessed Jefferson as a man of "integrity," but not a "practical man." Underestimating Jefferson's political skill, he called him "a closet politician—but not a practical statesman." Perhaps deceived by Jefferson's adroit performance at his political dinners, Plumer considered him excessively "credulous." Indicating his conflicting feelings about Jefferson, Plumer contradicted himself, labeling Jefferson as "cunning" but also "indecisive," "too timid," "too irresolute, too fickle, he wants nerve—he wants firmness & resolution."[47] For the psychoanalyst, such contrasting depictions suggest unconscious envy of a would-be father figure.[48]

Seeking to discover all he could about the personality of this inscrutable genius, Plumer attended several of Jefferson's dinners. He regularly drank wine with the president. "Even two glasses of wine oftimes [sic] renders a temperate man communicate [sic]," he confided to his diary. Ostensibly, Plumer plied him with wine because that made him more "communicative," although Jefferson, a veteran wine-drinker, was probably only pretending to be intoxicated.[49] He must have told Plumer what he thought he wanted to hear, in order to gain his support for Jeffersonian programs.

When Plumer informed Jefferson that he intended to write a history of his own times containing autobiographical fragments, and thought that conversations with the president would increase the work's value, Jefferson became alarmed. Perhaps he thought that the New Hampshire Federalist intended to emulate the example of Chief Justice John Marshall, whose recently-published *Life of Washington* was a poorly-veiled attack on the Democratic-Republicans and their devious leader, Jefferson. Plumer and his fellow New Englander, John Quincy Adams, distrusted Jefferson and thought that he would not want posterity to know the truth about him. Ironically, both men became advocates of Jeffersonian policies. At least in the beginning, their political careers suffered for it.

It is difficult to discern how Plumer evolved from would-be secessionist to ardent nationalist. He was perhaps shocked into Republicanism by disgust at the *Chesapeake* Incident in June 1807. After this insult to American honor, Plumer favored anti–British measures extending from the Embargo to all-out war. In 1808, his former Federalist colleagues let him know that his pro–Jefferson sentiments were not welcome, and he was virtually read out of the party.[50]

After several years of political quiescence, with Republican help Plumer succeeded John Langdon as governor of New Hampshire in 1812. In 1813, unlike his Connecticut and Massachusetts counterparts, Plumer consented to dispatching militia across state borders to fight in the War of 1812, leading to his defeat for reelection. Following the relative success of the American war effort and the disgrace of would-be Federalist secessionists at the Hartford Convention (this time Plumer was not in on the act), Plumer regained popularity. He was reelected governor from 1816 to 1819, during which time he developed a substantial correspondence with Jefferson. In one letter, Jefferson elucidated for Plumer his philosophy that "the earth belongs to the living generation." He wrote, "The idea that institutions established for the use of the nation cannot be touched nor modified, even to make them answer their end, because of rights gratuitously supposed in those employed to manage them in trust for the public, may perhaps be a salutary provision against the abuses of a monarch, but is most absurd against the nation itself."[51] It is hard to imagine Jefferson confiding these thoughts to a former Federalist chieftain, as Plumer had been earlier in his political career. But, like many former New England Federalists after the War of 1812, Plumer was now a Republican whom the superannuated third president felt he could trust.

And Plumer had become Jefferson's admirer and would-be imitator. Inspired by one of the ex-president's greatest achievements, the establishment of the University of Virginia, Plumer supported converting Dartmouth College into a state university, a project that Daniel Webster famously thwarted in the Supreme Court case, *Dartmouth College v. Woodward* (1819).[52]

8

Jefferson, Freedom of the Press and Federalist "Sedition" in Connecticut

Jefferson's career as an advocate of liberty of the press was not one flawless demand for unlimited freedom of expression, especially where personal slander against *him* was concerned. He endlessly protested that he had no hard feelings against those Federalists, secular and clerical, who labeled him an atheist, anarchist, slave-breeder, drunkard, and other negative attributes. They subjected him to this calumny regularly after 1792, especially during the presidential elections of 1796 and 1800. For the latter year, even though he was vice-president, the Federalist Congress had deliberately written the Sedition Act in 1798 to exclude his office from its protection. He was perhaps seething with a desire for revenge. In 1805, much of his bizarre Second Inaugural Address was devoted to mocking his Federalist abusers for failing to unseat him. He was re-elected by the enormous electoral majority of 162 to 14, and only Connecticut and Delaware voted against him. He concluded this major speech, however, by reassuring his enemies that he would protect their freedom of expression.[1]

Making little effort to mask his anger behind a veneer of objectivity, Jefferson, in the official (or at least semi-official) guise of his second inaugural address revealed his disgust with New England pamphleteers, who even more often abused his personal character than his public acts. Regretting that the "artillery of the press," still controlled by Federalists, targeted an administration overwhelmingly endorsed by the voters, he implied that their freewheeling calumnies were an illegitimate exercise of freedom of speech. "These abuses of an institution so important to freedom and science, are deeply to be regretted, inasmuch as they tend to lessen its usefulness, and to sap its safety," he warned. "They might, indeed, have been corrected by the wholesome punishments reserved and provided by the laws of the several States against falsehood and defamation; but public duties more urgent press on the time of public servants, and the offenders have therefore been left to find their punishment in the public indignation."[2]

Implying that state courts would be justified in prosecuting such licentiousness, which was outside the purview of federal lawsuits, he maintained that the "truth" embodied in his presidency's devotion to the public weal had thus far successfully combatted seditious statements and "false facts" without the necessity of pursuing legal action. "Since truth and reason have maintained their ground against false opinions in league with false facts," he told his audience, "the press, confined to truth, needs no other legal restraint; the public judgment will correct false reasonings and opinions, on a full hearing of all parties; and no other definite line can be drawn between the inestimable liberty of the press and its demoralizing licentiousness." Maintaining his confidence that the voters would sagely separate facts from lies by continuing to elect his party to office, he stressed his faith in "public opinion." "If there be still improprieties which this rule [of the public being able to tell newspapers' truth from lies] would not restrain," he said, "its supplement must be sought in the censorship of public opinion."[3] By this, Jefferson probably meant that an intelligent people, which he assumed Americans were, would not buy newspapers that often printed lies ("false facts"), putting them out of business.

However, Jefferson must have been aware that Federalist newspapers generally outnumbered Republican sheets, although the disparity nationally decreased from two to one to three to two between the 1790s and the end of Jefferson's presidency; meaning that Republicans ran about one-third of the newspapers in the 1790s and forty percent by 1809. Historian Donald H. Stewart argued that many estimates of the partisanship of early national newspapers are inaccurate, because the smallest newspapers did not consistently maintain a party identification. Agreeing with leading journalism historian Frank L. Mott, during the presidential election of 1800, he stated, the ratio of Federalist to Republican newspapers was 2:1. Leading historian David Hackett Fischer agreed with the 2:1 ratio, and tended to support Stewart's view that many past historians had underestimated the salience of Republican newspapers. According to Fischer's detailed examination, in the election of 1800, judging by their commentaries, forty-eight "strongly Republican" newspapers were being published in the United States, and nineteen "strongly Federalist" papers, with eighty-four "moderately Federalist" and sixteen "moderately Republican" sheets also coming out. Fischer claimed that in 1800, a total of 103 Federalist newspapers and sixty-four Republican papers appeared.[4]

Although these calculations allot the Republicans more clout than previous studies, it is still obvious that they controlled fewer newspapers than their opponents, especially in New England. Because of greater access to capital, Federalists invariably controlled more newspapers than Republicans. In 1810, newspaper and magazine publisher Isaiah Thomas estimated that there were twenty-three Republican and sixty-six Federalist newspapers in New England.[5] This factor may have tended to diminish Jefferson's zeal for preserving unlimited freedom of the press during his presidency.

$$\bullet \quad \bullet \quad \bullet \quad \bullet \quad \bullet$$

Leonard W. Levy's classic critique of Jefferson, *Jefferson and Civil Liberties: The Darker Side* (1963), asserted that Jefferson generally favored a federal law against seditious libel and opposed unrestricted freedom of speech and the press until 1823, in a private letter he wrote to Adamantios Coray (1748–1833), a Greek philosopher and expert on Aristotle.[6] Contrary to Levy's charges, Jefferson actually advocated unlimited freedom of the press as a young Virginia politician. One of the provisions of the state constitution he composed in 1776, which he was unable to submit for consideration because he was in Philadelphia writing the Declaration of Independence (by the time George Wythe finally brought it, the Convention was almost over and they ignored it), allowed full scope for seditious behavior. In the first of his three drafts of a constitution, he buried restrictions on violent behavior in a declaration of religious freedom, implying that he wished to restrain religions whose adherents attempted to murder unbelievers, perhaps including the Christian faith, which was historically intolerant.

He wrote, "All persons shall have full & free liberty of religious opinion, nor shall any be compelled to frequent or maintain any religious service or institution (but seditious behavior to be punishable by civil magistrate according to the laws already made or hereafter to be made)."[7] This section imposed no restraints on freedom of speech.

While this statement certainly established religious freedom, from its wording it appears that Jefferson was reluctant to allow freedom to commit violent political acts or act out "seditious behavior." This libertarian qualification seemingly included the political and civil religious spheres. Apparently, he would thwart fanatical Christian, proto-Nazi or Radical Right religious groups that attacked Jews, abortion clinics, or African Americans in the streets today, since his strictures applied only to "behavior," not speech or writing. Indeed, Jefferson's concept of freedom of speech was probably *too* broad. Julian P. Boyd, the editor of Jefferson's works, commented, "This highly interesting passage about seditious behavior was bracketed by TJ in the First Draft, indicating that he regarded it as optional or possibly open to question; he copied it in the Second Draft, then struck it out; it was omitted entirely from the Third Draft."[8]

At least in 1776, Jefferson desired the state constitution to endorse complete freedom of speech on public affairs. However, he was prepared to legalize lawsuits by individuals for personal defamation. For his first, second and third drafts of a constitution, he included the statement, "Printing presses shall be free, except where by commission of private injury they shall give cause of private action." He deleted a more awkward phrase, "except so far as they or their managers shall be subject themselves to the private action of any individual." Thus, in Jefferson's view, private libel or slander suits *by private individuals* were permissible.[9] His third, final draft maintained full freedom of the press, but once more permitted private civil suits for slander: "Printing presses shall be free, except so far as by commission of private injury cause may be given of private action."[10] Thus, contrary to Levy's accusations, from the beginning of his political career Jefferson advocated complete freedom of the press with regard to expressions of political opinion.

In *Jefferson and Civil Liberties*, Levy's efforts to make Jefferson appear a foe of absolute freedom of the press, particularly in his youth, fell flat. In one glaring instance, he mentioned that in 1783 Jefferson proposed adding an amendment to the Virginia constitution of 1776, which lacked specific provisions protecting freedom of the press other than section twelve of the bill of rights, which merely observed that it was "one of the great bulwarks of liberty, and can never be restrained but by despotic governments." Jefferson's 1783 amendment asserted that newspapers should be exempt from prosecution for any statements except for suits by individuals for printing (oxymoronic) "false facts." Levy quoted part of an Albemarle County resolve supposedly designed to advise Jefferson at this time. However, the resolutions were proposed in late 1776, not 1783 as Levy asserted, and it is doubtful that Jefferson had access to them, even though Julian P. Boyd considered it possible. In any case the resolutions were actually far more restrictive of freedom of the press than anything Jefferson proposed. The Albemarle County citizens recommended subjecting newspaper *authors*, not editors, to prosecution (without limiting the kinds of cases eligible). They wanted to forbid newspaper publishers to print anything without attaching the author's name, although almost all essays and statements of opinion employed pseudonyms. The Albemarle residents thus proposed a uniquely drastic form of censorship, which would eliminate most of the articles published in newspapers at this time. This sweeping permission to governments and individuals to sue writers, rather than editors, for seditious or libelous materials Levy ludicrously labels the "more liberal recommendation" that Jefferson rejected.[11]

Indeed, a portion of the Albemarle petitioners' resolution that Levy omitted made clear that they wished to severely punish slander or libel of the gentry. Urging widespread prosecutions, they asserted, "Many good people have been lately mislead [*sic*] by the artifices of ingenious, but malicious, interested and corrupt writers. Had their names been published, their Characters would have been the antidote to their own poison. We are convinced that by such a regulation many inconveniences may be avoided."[12] By gagging would-be troublemakers, they would reduce the amount of litigation and effectively end freedom of the press.

By contrast, Jefferson's draft of a constitution in 1783 upheld complete freedom of opinion. He rejected coercion of authors or editors of controversial pieces: "Printing presses shall be subject to no other restraint than liableness to legal prosecution for false facts printed and published."[13] Judging from Jefferson's earlier intentions, he meant that only false statements concerning the personal conduct and character of individuals would be subject to private lawsuits ("private action," as he called it in his 1776 draft of a constitution).

Rather oddly, Levy admires Jefferson's 1823 letter to Coray, claiming that it "catapulted Jefferson into the ranks of the most advanced libertarians, for no one had ever advocated a wider freedom than that which was restrained only by liability for 'personal injuries.'" In the letter to Coray, Jefferson said that the ideal constitution should uphold "freedom of the press, subject only to liability for personal injuries. This formidable censor of the public functionaries, by arraigning them at the tribunal of public opinion, produces reform peaceably, which must otherwise be done by revolution. It is also the best instrument for enlightening the mind of man, and improving him as a rational, moral, and social being."[14] However, Jefferson said exactly the same thing in 1776. Levy distorted Jefferson's earlier views on freedom of the press in order to support his thesis that Jefferson was slow to embrace complete freedom of thought and covertly persecuted his Federalist political enemies in Connecticut in 1807 in the case of *United States v. Hudson and Goodwin.*

Inconsistently, *Jefferson and Civil Liberties* praises the "Jeffersonian" followers of Thomas Jefferson, especially James Madison and George Hay, James Monroe's son-in-law, for fearlessly expounding absolute freedom of speech and the press during the crisis of 1798–1800. The "libertarian" Jeffersonians pointed out that, because the truth of opinions could not be proven, they could not be subjected to punishment; something that Jefferson had been saying ever since *Notes on Virginia* and his bill for religious freedom over twenty years earlier. In Levy's view, the Jeffersonian radicals were the first to reject the idea there was "such a thing as seditious libel."[15] "The new libertarianism was genuinely radical because it broke sharply with the past and advocated absolute freedom of political expression," Levy asserted. The radical Jeffersonians contended that, *prima facie*, a free government could not be criminally attacked or endangered by the opinions of its citizens. Freedom of the press must be absolute, like virginity, George Hay said, or it did not exist. The radicals insisted that only "injurious conduct," dangerous acts, not words, ought to be considered criminal. "They did not refine this proposition except to recognize that the law of libel should continue to protect private reputations against malicious falsehoods," according to Levy. "They would not even recognize that under certain circumstances words might immediately and directly incite criminal acts."[16] In this, although Levy deliberately denied it, Jefferson was their prototype, inspiration, and mentor.

· · · · ·

Although the second inaugural address seemingly emphasized Jefferson's devotion to free speech, he implied that his great reelection victory entitled him to punish his enemies. He argued that his administration had conducted itself with such precise obedience to the Constitution, and pursued such upright and popular measures that Federalist newspapers' "falsehood and defamation" could hardly influence public opinion. Insinuating that the extreme Federalists who libeled him were monarchists whose plans to overthrow the republic had been thwarted by his overwhelming public endorsement in the election of 1804, he declared: "The experiment [in unlimited press freedom] has been tried; you have witnessed the scene; our fellow citizens have looked on, cool and collected; they saw the latent source from which these outrages proceeded; they gathered around their public functionaries, and when the constitution called them to the decision by suffrage, they pronounced their verdict, honorable to those who had served them, and consolatory to the friend of man, who believes he may be intrusted with his own affairs."[17]

Jefferson boasted of his administration's protection of freedom of the press and his belief that the educated and intelligent condition of American public opinion (manifested, he implied, by his great popularity) was the only restraint the press required. He concluded that his administration's "experiment" in the press's total immunity from federal prosecution was a success. On a more discordant note, he warned: "No inference is here intended, that the laws, provided by the states against false and defamatory publications, should not be enforced; he who has time, renders a service to public morals and public tranquillity, in reforming these abuses by the salutary coercions of the law; but the experiment is noted, to prove that, since truth and reason have maintained their ground against false opinions in league with false facts, the press, confined to truth, needs no other legal restraint."[18] Although Jefferson claimed to be too busy as president to police the press, he seemed to be egging on those state officials who wanted to prosecute pamphleteers who calumniated his private (and especially his sexual) activities.

Despite aggressive Federalist persecution of Connecticut's Republican newspapers, the Federalist Party's control of the state government, and virulent Federalist newspaper attacks on Jefferson, he was optimistic that the state's citizens would soon elect Republican majorities. Paying careful attention to the results of its local elections, he convinced himself that the voters were beginning to see the Republican light. He minimized the Republicans' loss of fifteen seats in the state legislature's fall 1802 elections. In 1803, learning that the Republican gubernatorial candidate had been defeated by a smaller majority than the year before, Jefferson considered it cause for celebration. Upon receiving the news from Gideon Granger, he requested Samuel Harrison Smith, editor of the Washington, D.C., *National Intelligencer*, the closest thing to an official government newspaper, to publicize the information. "Mr. Granger informs me that the election in Connecticut in 1802 gave [Jonathan] Trumbull 11,000 some odd votes & [Ephraim] Kirby 4,523," he wrote, "and that of the present year has given Trumbull 14,300 & Kirby 7848. Then in 1802 of every 100 votes the federalists had 71 & the republicans 29 & in 1803 of every 100 votes the federalists had 65 & the republicans 35, so that the latter have advanced from 29 to 35 and the former sunk from 71 to 65 in the hundred." He thought that as many people as possible, even in Washington, D.C., should know about this ostensible Republican upsurge in Connecticut. "Would it not be worth presenting to the public in this concise view, to let them see that tho' from causes we do not understand, we have lost ground in their H. of Representatives, yet we have unquestionably gained in the mass of the people?" he argued. "And that Connecticut is advancing slowly to a reunion of sentiment with her sister states."[19]

Feeling supremely confident after consummating the Louisiana Purchase, Jefferson took to writing pseudonymous articles for the newspapers defending his policies, something he had never done before. He took aim at recent charges in Hamilton's newspaper, the *New-York Evening Post*, nominally edited by William Coleman, that he was engaged in wholesale removal of his predecessors' appointees to office, almost all Federalists, replacing them with Democratic-Republicans. In his rebuttal, Jefferson concentrated on his appointment and removal policies in Massachusetts and Connecticut. He was aware that many Republicans thought he should get rid of all Federalist hold-overs from the Washington and Adams administrations. He was reluctant to adopt this stance because, in the first years of his presidency, he hoped to unite Federalists with Jeffersonians in a single political party. At the same time, he had "a great desire to reconcile the parties among the republicans," both moderates and radicals, on the question, while refuting the *New York Post*'s accusations of his unbridled partisanship. Employing the pseudonym "Fair Play," Jefferson pretended to be a Republican resident of Boston. Emphasizing that he had retained veteran Federalists Benjamin Lincoln in the prestigious and lucrative offices of Collector of the Port of Boston and Samuel Bradford in the powerful position of U.S. marshal for the district of Massachusetts, Jefferson attempted to prove that his administration intended merely to achieve a fifty-fifty division of offices between the parties, even though, had the allocation of jobs been according to their national popularity, the Republicans would have been entitled to two-thirds or three-fourths of the offices.[20]

Alluding to the Adams Administration's persecution of Republicans during the undeclared war with France, "Fair Play" asserted, that even moderate, "real federalists," whom he was ready to "take ... to my bosom as brothers," were willing to deny their opponents' civil rights. In ostensible pursuit of national security, Federalist leaders from 1798 to 1800 insisted that "we should pass alien & sedition laws, punishing men with exile without trial by jury, & usurping the regulation of the press, exclusively belonging to the state governments."[21]

For the most part, Jefferson's article was dry and matter-of-fact, lacking the eloquence he was generally capable of. As he often did, he distinguished between the genuinely partisan Federalists, who adhered to the republican form of government while favoring legislation more favorable to the upper classes and the big merchants and financiers, and pseudo-Federalists who were really disguised "monarchists." He bitingly observed: "Under that name [Federalists] lurks the heretical sect of monarchists. Afraid to wear their own name, they creep under the mantle of federalism, & the federalists, like sheep, permit the fox to take shelter among them, when pursued by the dogs. These men have no right to office. If a monarchist be in office any where, & it be known to the President, the oath he has taken to support the constitution, imperiously requires the instantaneous dismission of such officer; & I should hold the President highly criminal if he permitted such to remain."[22]

After thus making his proverbial distinction between the Anglophile, Hamiltonian Federalists who he believed ready to discard the republic in favor of monarchy, and the majority of conservative republican Federalists, "Fair Play" could not help but add an anticlerical gibe. "To appoint a monarchist to conduct the affairs of a republic," he pointed out, "is like appointing an Atheist to the priesthood."[23] Undoubtedly aware that any harsher satires on the clergy would alienate New Englanders, Jefferson ceased his witticisms at that point. He sent the article to Attorney General Levi Lincoln, asking him to have it placed in the Democratic-Republican *Boston Independent Chronicle*, but to keep his authorship secret in "religious silence." The article appeared in the *Independent Chronicle* of June 27, 1803, largely unchanged.[24]

He maintained his optimism about the state even after he lost its electoral votes in the election of 1804. Writing to his foreign confidant Volney, a French radical who fled from anticipated prosecution under the Alien Friends Act in 1798, he assured him that the future of liberalism and democracy in the United States was bright, like its climate. In a letter devoted mainly to discussing Volney's most recent works on American geography, geology, and natural history, Jefferson compared the climate of the United States (probably with his home state of Virginia primarily in mind) with that of Europe. He admitted that thinking about the prevalence of cold weather in Canada and Europe gave him "the shivers." Overlooking the generally cold and damp weather of Massachusetts and Connecticut, he observed that the U.S. climate was "more cheerful" than Europe's because there were usually fewer clouds in the sky. Revealing a surprising if *noir* sense of humor, Jefferson said, "I prefer much the climate of the United States to that of Europe. I think it a more cheerful one. It is our cloudless sky which has eradicated from our constitutions all disposition to hang ourselves, which we might otherwise have inherited from our English ancestors." He claimed that during his residence of nearly seven years in Paris as U.S. minister, almost every day was cloudy.[25]

Jefferson was more interested in discussing the political situation than in elucidating the climate and respective dispositions to yellow fever in Europe and America. He remarked that Volney's new book, *View of the Soil and Climate of the United States of America*, which developed Volney's deistic religious ideas, earlier expounded in his more famous study, *The Ruins of Empires* (which Jefferson had translated into English) was under attack by the orthodox New England clergy. Disparagingly referring to these "holy calumniators" as the "*genus irritabile vatum*," he regretted that New England's ministry, repulsed by Volney's advocacy of religious freedom and the separation of church and state, misrepresented his books to make them appear atheistic. Such distortions "displeased" some of his "American readers" with the work even before they read it. Publishing their critiques in New England's Federalist newspapers, the clergy "excited a disapprobation even in friendly minds, which nothing but the reading of the book will cure," Jefferson lamented. "But time and truth will at length correct error."[26]

On a brighter note, Jefferson displaced his "cheerful" mindset from America's weather to its political climate. Informing Volney of his landslide reelection, he boasted that even the New England states except for Connecticut voted for him. He expected to face little meaningful opposition in the future. The "people" of Connecticut were really on his side, he was sure, but their religious and secular leaders had temporarily deluded them. Indeed, he predicted that soon even Connecticut would join the Jeffersonian bandwagon. His observations to Volney substantially reiterated his words to Christoph Daniel Ebeling ten years earlier, in 1795:

> A word now on our political state. The two parties which prevailed with so much violence when you were here, are almost wholly melted into one. At the late Presidential election I have received one hundred and sixty-two votes against fourteen only. Connecticut is still federal by a small majority; and Delaware on a

poise, as she has been since 1775, and will be till Anglomany with her yields to Americanism. Connecticut will be with us in a short time. Though the people in mass have joined us, their leaders had committed themselves too far to retract. Pride keeps them hostile; they brood over their angry passions, and give them vent in the newspapers which they maintain. They still make as much noise as if they were the whole nation. Unfortunately, these being the mercantile papers, published chiefly in the sea ports, are the only ones which find their way to Europe, and make very false impressions there.[27]

Analyzing the attacks on him in New England's Federalist press, Jefferson made an effort to distinguish between public criticism of government policies, which he believed should be free from prosecution, and newspaper attacks on the personal character or private conduct of government officials. He considered the latter out of bounds if irrelevant to government legislation or administration; and subject to legal prosecution if the publications contained lies or gross distortions. As Dumas Malone put it, "he [Jefferson] made a sharp distinction between public and private matters and regarded the latter as an improper subject of public discussion."[28] Regarding his overwhelming victory in 1804 as a referendum on his personal virtue and public sagacity, he considered himself relatively inviolable. Martyr-like, he perceived renewed Federalist attacks on his youthful sexual indiscretions as a "fiery ordeal" to which he must submit, sacrificing his personal honor "on the altar of the public good," as he wrote a Pittsfield clergyman.[29]

Concerning federal judicial prosecution of slanders directed at him, Jefferson never publicly denied the existence of a federal "common law" of seditious libel, even though he believed Congress could not pass such a law. He contended that the individual states had the power to validate the common law through their legislatures and constitutions, as Virginia had done in 1776, when it reinstated many previous British precedents in force during the colonial period. Jefferson had participated in this process as a member of the assembly's committee of revisal. In *Notes on the State of Virginia*, he alluded to common law, asserting that the dictum that the will of the majority (*lex majoris partis*) should rule was "founded in common law as well as common right. It is the natural law of every assembly of men."[30] During the crisis provoked by the Quasi-War with France in 1798, Jefferson was shocked to find that some Federalist Supreme Court justices and other Federalists recommended that the federal government arrogate the right to implement the common law. He took for granted that this power did not belong to the national government; if exercised, it would nullify the Bill of Rights.

Observing the Federalists' biased enforcement of the Sedition Act in 1798 and 1799, Jefferson became alarmed that federal courts might institute a common law of seditious libel that prohibited truth as a defense against charges of defaming federal officials. "Of all the doctrines which have ever been broached by the federal government the novel one, of the common law being in force &cognizable as an existing law in their courts, is to me the most formidable," he wrote Edmund Randolph, an expert on constitutional law. The idea that the federal courts would implement the "audacious, bare-faced, and sweeping pretension to a system of law for the US, without the adoption of their legislature, and so infinitively beyond their power to adopt," was the most shocking thing he ever heard. In addition to threatening individual civil liberties, such a concept would eviscerate the state governments.[31]

Jefferson acknowledged that in representative governments the legislature embodied the nation's will, just as the emperor of Russia represented the will of the nation in an absolutist regime. Recalling his famous letter to Gouverneur Morris in 1793 on the validity of the

Franco-American treaties of 1778, even though France had since become a republic and guillotined its king, Jefferson observed that, unless explicitly repealed, a nation's laws remained in force even though it changed its form of government. Before the American Revolution, "the nation of Virginia," as he called it, enforced three types of law: common law, statute law, and chancery law. Since Virginia's 1776 constitution had not repealed the common law, but incorporated portions of it into the positive (statute) laws, Jefferson said that the common law was comprised within the state's ordinances: "The common law, therefore, which was not in force when we landed here [in 1607], nor till we had formed ourselves into a nation [i.e., the state of Virginia] and had manifested by the organs we constituted that the common law was to be our law, continued to be our law, because the nation continued in being."[32]

Unlike Virginia's action in laws passed from 1776 to 1779, Jefferson pointed out, the U.S. government had never incorporated or "adopted" the common law. Indeed, he said, it could not legally do so. The U.S. government was created during the Revolution by the Articles of Confederation to conduct the war and administer foreign affairs, and had no business considering whether the common law applied to the individual states. Obviously, Jefferson observed, the state governments had never intended or permitted the national government to enact a common law. The delegates to the Philadelphia Convention in 1787 had not discussed the possibility, and it had certainly not become part of the U.S. Constitution. Therefore, the "new doctrine that the common law is the law of the US & that their courts have, of course, a jurisdiction co-extensive with that law, that is to say, general over all cases & persons," had no basis in law or fact. With combined mockery and anxiety, Jefferson ended this letter, "But, great heavens! Who could have thought in 1789 that within ten years we should have to combat such windmills."[33]

Jefferson regarded Connecticut, where seven years later he condoned Democratic-Republican courts' violation of freedom of the press under a federal common law of seditious libels, as the stronghold of Federalist advocacy of a national common law and other centralizing, quasi-monarchical credos. During the election of 1800 contest, he wrote his party lieutenant in Connecticut, Gideon Granger of Suffield, that he was grateful for news that the Republican cause was gaining strength in the state, although it was still a weak minority. He denounced the Federalist view that there was a national common law, which the citizens of the individual states must obey. He thought that such an opinion would lead to rampant governmental fraud and bureaucratic corruption, and an omnipotent, all-encroaching national government that obliterated the states' powers.[34]

Although confident that the Federalists' unpopular measures during the Quasi-War with France guaranteed the Republicans a majority in the incoming Congress, Jefferson wanted "the whole body of New England" to approve his party platform. Jefferson's manifestos to Gerry and Granger endorsed civil liberties, "freedom of religion, freedom of the press, trial by jury"; national government frugality, and the confinement of its powers to foreign affairs; and states' rights. He hoped that Connecticut in particular rejected unitary government and ultimately monarchy, and rather embraced the federal system of divided powers. The national government could survive only if the New England states supported the libertarian policies of the incoming Republicans, he insisted. He was confident that the people of Connecticut would return to their Revolutionary War-era beliefs in republicanism, and eventually become Democratic-Republicans. As he put it, "I rejoice, therefore, in every appearance of their returning to those principles which I had always imagined to be almost innate in them."[35]

Informing Granger that in his state, the few Virginians "deluded by the XYZ duperies" had returned to Jeffersonianism, he hoped that something similar would occur in New England. He recommended an obscure, pro–Jefferson article by "Don Quixote" printed in the Hartford *American Mercury* designed to "introduce the real truth to the minds even of the most prejudiced."[36]

At the beginning of his presidency, Jefferson was relatively tolerant of Federalist abuse. In March 1802, after reading some particularly vituperative Federalist newspapers, he briefly considered prosecuting the offenders, or at least implied that Attorney General Lincoln might want to take action. Appalled that such trash could attract a sufficient number of subscribers to survive, he sent Lincoln the newspapers, commenting, "I had no conception there were persons enough to support a paper whose stomachs could bear such aliment as the inclosed papers contain. They are far beyond even the *Washington Federalist* [a new Federalist newspaper in the nation's capital]." However, he was reluctant to commence prosecutions for libel against Federalist printers in their state courts, in part because he thought that local officials would impanel mainly anti–Jeffersonian jurors, likely to decide in favor of Federalist abusers and against Republican plaintiffs. He decided that it would be best not to institute lawsuits against the publishers. He tersely concluded, "To punish however is impracticable until the body of the people, from whom juries are to be taken, get their minds to rights; and even then I doubt its expediency."[37] If he expected Lincoln to consider instituting proceedings on the federal level as attorney general, apparently he had not dismissed the idea of a federal common law of libel; but he gave Lincoln no specific instructions.

Throughout his career, Jefferson had maintained that individual citizens could sue for defamation of character. Emphasizing that individuals (ostensibly including himself) had the option of prosecuting offenders for libel and slander, he continued, "While a full range is proper for actions by individuals either private or public for slanders affecting them, I would wish much to see the experiment tried of getting along without public prosecutions for *libels*. I believe we can do it. Patience and well-doing, instead of punishment, if it can be found sufficiently efficacious, would be a happy change in the instruments of government."[38]

In 1804, he replied to a letter from Abigail Adams, who had chided him for subsidizing James T. Callender's calumnies against her husband during the presidential campaign of 1800; then, as president, pardoning him and reimbursing the fine he paid under the Sedition Act. Afterwards, Callender attacked Jefferson more viciously than he had slandered any of his other political enemies. Beginning in September 1802, he disclosed Jefferson's secret subsidies to him and publicized the story of Jefferson's attempt as a young man to cuckold one of his closest friends, John Walker, and seduce his wife Elizabeth. He provided some details of Jefferson's slave mistress, "Sally," by whom he allegedly fathered several children. Although Callender had died by drowning in 1803 under mysterious circumstances, neither Jefferson nor Abigail Adams had much regard for his memory. Explaining that he had pardoned Callender and reimbursed his fine because he considered the Sedition Act an unconstitutional "nullity," he insisted that the state legislatures possessed "full" power to restrain "the overwhelming torrent of slander which is confounding all vice and virtue, all truth and falsehood in the US." "It was reserved to them, and was denied to the general government, by the constitution according to our construction of it," he said. "While we deny that Congress have a right to control the freedom of the press, we have ever asserted the right of the states, and their exclusive right, to do so. They [the states] have accordingly, all of them, made provisions for punishing slander, which those who have time and inclination resort to for the vindication of their characters."

Therefore, Jefferson did not deny that defamation suits could be prosecuted; but he thought that the proper place to do so was in the state courts. He insisted on permitting defendants to use truth as a defense in libel and slander cases. Such a qualification was absent from English common law, which defined freedom of the press as freedom from prior governmental restraints on publication. "In general the state laws appear to have made the presses responsible for slander as far as is consistent with their useful freedom," he concluded. "In those states where they do not admit even the truth of allegations to protect the printer, they have gone too far."[39] Although Jefferson thought that Congress could not pass laws against libel, he was silent on the possibility that the executive branch might prosecute libel and slander under the common law. He favored freedom of the press sufficiently to permit truth as a defense in such cases, which Federalist prosecutions under the Sedition Act for all practical purposes had prohibited.[40]

What conditions changed Jefferson's mind, making him willing to condone federal prosecutions for seditious libels against him on the state level, as happened in Connecticut in 1807? As his inaugural address in 1805 revealed, he had become obsessed by the personal abuse thrown at him by Federalist pamphleteers and newspaper editors. Many of these attacks emanated from Massachusetts and Connecticut. Not only in his second inaugural address, but in letters in March 1805 to Reverend Thomas Allen of Pittsfield, a small Massachusetts town with a growing Republican minority, and James Sullivan, a wealthy leading Republican politician in the state in May, he agonized over Federalist clergymen and newspaper hacks' insults to his personal and public morals. (He seemed especially embarrassed by the revival of the incident of his youthful lust for his friend's wife Elizabeth Moore Walker.)[41]

By contrast, during the Republican fight against Federalist persecution in the form of Congress' 1798 Sedition Act, Jefferson denied that congressional suppression of partisan polemics was tolerable or constitutional. To give his party a chance to survive in the electoral arena and safeguard it from annihilation, he insisted in his renowned Kentucky Resolutions that only the individual states could pass laws concerning sedition and slander. "The States ... retain to themselves the right of judging how far the licentiousness of speech and of the press may be abridged without lessening their useful freedom, and how far those abuses which cannot be separated from their use should be tolerated, rather than the use be destroyed," he asserted. Even in this testament in defense of freedom of the press, Jefferson included a warning that the right was not unlimited, but could be regulated by the state governments to protect individual reputations from "abuses."[42]

In March 1802, Jefferson seemed calm and comparatively benevolent when writing to Levi Lincoln. However, a few months later, in September 1802, Callender, writing in the *Richmond Recorder*, exposed his "affair" with Sally Hemings and his attempt to seduce his friend John Walker's wife. These embarrassingly personal matters were revived by Massachusetts and Virginia Federalists in 1805 as a result of the agitation of Thomas Turner, a Virginia Federalist planter.[43]

Jefferson was ready to explode from these renewed assertions of his "moral turpitude," as it was called. He blamed the revived witch-hunt against him on the Federalist newspapers of the cities. Perhaps hoping to forewarn a Geneva scientist and astronomer who intended to visit the United States of the calumny he was subjected to as president, he wrote him, "The abuses of the freedom of the press here have been carried to a length never before known or borne by any civilized nation." Nonetheless, he assured him that freedom of the press in the United States was virtually unlimited, which he favored, though he regretted that the wealthy commercial sections of the country hostile to his democratic-minded administration controlled most of the newspapers. In any case, he said, he enjoyed nearly unanimous popular support because "the great mass of our people are agricultural; and the commercial cities, though, by the command of newspapers they make a great deal of noise, have little effect in the direction of the government." Juxtaposing the cities against the farms, he asserted, "They [city folk] are as different in sentiment & character from the country people as any two distinct nations, and are clamorous against the order of things established by the agricultural interest."[44]

As he had declared most fervently in *Notes on Virginia*, in a passage (Query XIX) written as he viewed the slums of London and Paris as U.S. minister to France, Jefferson identified with the farmers. Under the "order" maintained by the "agricultural interest," with himself as its guardian, "our citizens generally are enjoying a very great degree of liberty and security in the most temperate manner. Every man being at his ease, feels an interest in the preservation of order, and comes forth to preserve it at the first call of the magistrate."[45]

Impelled by the renewed attacks of Federalists who mimicked Callender, he sharply distinguished between the urban and rural sections of the country, linking the former with his enemies and the latter with his supporters. Although the New England states were hardly uniformly one or the other, Jefferson regarded them as commercial and financial centers by comparison with the agrarian South. To some extent, therefore, during his first term as president, the renewed newspaper attacks on him inspired him with negative feelings toward New England. Several years later, a group of his Republican supporters in Connecticut belatedly offered him an opportunity for revenge. Though hardly enthusiastic, Jefferson's ambivalent response revealed that he did not automatically put his theoretical defense of unlimited freedom of speech into practice in the real, political world, and that he did not always bar his feelings from consideration.

Jefferson was not enthusiastic about automatically applying English common law—the statutes, traditions, court decisions, usages, and customs of the Mother Country before 1776—to legal cases in the now independent U.S. state and national governments. Several times in his life, he had stated his conviction that Christianity was not part of the common law, although historically many English judges and lawyers, including Lord Coke, had asserted or implied that it was part of England's common law.[46]

After the Constitution's ratification by the states, Jefferson avoided making a similar categorical statement prohibiting federal common law prosecutions for libel and slander. However, his commentaries from Europe during the debate over the U.S. Constitution incessantly lamented the absence of a Bill of Rights. He insisted that such a declaration of the citizens' freedoms must contain complete liberty of speech and the press. In a letter to Madison in July 1788, in which he applauded the news that nine states had ratified the Constitution, making it national law, Jefferson voiced nearly anarchical views relating to the desirability of protections for individual liberty. Proposing that Congress adopt a bill of rights to "establish trials by Jury, the right of Habeas corpus, freedom of the press & freedom of religion in all cases," he demanded an unlimited right to habeas corpus, which was not protected in the Constitution. "Why suspend the Habeas corpus in insurrections &

rebellions?" he asked the Father of the Constitution, who had neglected to advocate the right at the Constitutional Convention. "The parties who may be arrested may be charged instantly with a well defined crime." Warming to his task, paradoxically feeling the most radical urges of his lifetime in monarchical Paris, surrounded by left-wing *philosophes* and ideologues, Jefferson now sought to convince Madison that freedom of the press should be unrestricted. Seeking to assuage his friend's doubts, he assured him, "A declaration that the federal government will never restrain the presses from printing any thing they please, will not take away the liability of printers for false facts printed." Insisting that absolute freedom of religious thought and peaceful religious practice did not pose a threat to social order, he asserted, "The declaration that religious faith shall be unpunished, does not give impunity to criminal acts dictated by religious errors."[47] On the other hand, he always thought that Congress had no constitutional right to abridge freedom of speech by law, and he invariably declared that the Sedition Act of 1798 was unconstitutional.[48]

Most Republican Party members never insisted that freedom of speech and the press should be unlimited, but they denied the national government powers over it because of First Amendment prohibitions. Meanwhile, the Connecticut state courts persecuted Republican editors, and Federalist preachers unreservedly denounced Jefferson from their pulpits. Connecticut Jeffersonians considered themselves justified in seeking revenge. They also resented the Federalists for hindering the formation of a state constitutional convention to devise a new constitution. The old one, which preserved the Congregational Church as the established church and restricted the suffrage, had been in existence since 1662. However, when five Republican justices of the peace signed a petition for a convention at New Haven in August 1804, the Federalist-controlled General Court (state legislature) dismissed them from office.[49]

Jefferson was painfully aware that Connecticut retained its Federalism. It was the only state besides Delaware that had not given its electoral vote for him in the election of 1804. In December 1805, he attempted to strengthen its Republican Party organization by reappointing Alexander D. Wolcott the collector of customs for Middletown. At least according to Federalists who sought to stigmatize Republicans as selfish political hacks, Wolcott then became the state party manager. In February 1806, Jefferson chose Pierpont Edwards, a diehard Republican and son of the great revivalist leader and theologian Reverend Jonathan Edwards, Connecticut district court judge. In December 1805, he reappointed Joseph Wilcox (who spelled his name "Willcox"), whom he chose marshal of Connecticut in October 1801 on the recommendation of Pierpont Edwards, Ephraim Kirby, and other leading Republicans, and appointed Hezekiah Huntington district attorney for the state.[50] These actions put Republicans in full control of the state's federal courts.

According to local Federalists, the Connecticut "state party manager" (selected by a party caucus) who appointed "county managers," who in their turn chose loyal, "active influential, republican manager[s]" for each town, constituted the apex of Republican party centralization in New England. Charging that these party oligarchs decided who the candidates for elective office in the state would be, the Hartford *Courant* exploded in righteous indignation, "What is it but taking the affairs of the government entirely from the many, and placing them in the hands of the few?"[51]

It is likely that the Federalists deliberately exaggerated the efficiency of the Republican Party machine to embarrass their opponents. Vigorous party organization was still considered rather disreputable; it violated the alleged tradition that good public officials invariably exhibited uncorrupted virtue, independence of judgment, and lacked personal ambition. Republican newspapers were soon making similar charges against the Federalists. However, in the spring 1806 state elections, Republicans made their best showing to date in Connecticut. Further strengthening Republicans in the federal judiciary, several months earlier Jefferson appointed Joseph Willcox as marshal and Hezekiah Huntington as district attorney in Connecticut. Republicans controlled Connecticut's federal courts, but the Federalists still held sway in the more important state courts, where they continued to prosecute Republican editors, among other things, for advocating a constitutional convention. Elisha Babcock, editor of the Hartford *American Mercury*, which he had started up as early as 1784 with Republican radical Joel Barlow, was fined $1000 for such statements, and he wanted retribution. Republican editors convicted of sedition, like Selleck Osborne, editor of the *Litchfield Witness*, complained that they were thrown into prison with violent offenders. Osborne was jailed when he refused to pay the fine for seditious libel in the town that was home of Judge Tapping Reeve, the Oliver Wolcott family, and other venerable Federalists. Thomas Collier, editor of a Federalist newspaper, the *Litchfield Monitor*, to which Judge Reeve contributed numerous articles denouncing the libertine Jefferson, resented Osborne's encroachment on his turf.[52]

In April 1806, Connecticut Republicans, led by District Judge Pierpont Edwards, moved to prosecute leading Federalist writers and anti–Jefferson agitators for seditious libel, not in the Federalist-dominated state court, but in federal district court. This strategy violated the states' rights ethos of Jefferson and his followers, adopted in the Kentucky and Virginia resolutions and in the battle against the Federalist Sedition Act of 1798, a law that targeted Democratic-Republicans. At the time, most Jeffersonians contended that prosecutions for politically-oriented cases of seditious libel or slander could only be undertaken in the state courts, because the first amendment to the Constitution prohibited federal action. (However, most Republicans, emulating Benjamin Franklin in his famous final publication, "An Account of the Supremest Court of Judicature in Pennsylvania," would agree that personal libel or slander should be prosecuted in the courts, if the accusations were blatant lies.) Steven Hochman, one of the most astute writers on the subject, observes, "Merely because Jefferson and the Republican party had opposed the [Sedition] act in 1798, it did not follow that they therefore favored an unlimited press. To be sure, no Republican ever said he opposed liberty of the press, but then neither had any Federalist. The definition of the concept was still murky."[53] With the Supreme Court's resolution of the case of *U.S. v. Hudson and Goodwin* in 1812, the mists would substantially clear.

The Connecticut prosecutions had not begun on an elevated plane. It is unclear who started them, but it was probably the town's Democratic-Republican leaders, Alexander Wolcott, a Yale graduate and Jefferson's appointee as collector of customs at Middletown, who was so loyal to the president that he later supported the Embargo Act; and Connecticut Republican Judge Thomas Seymour. They may have persuaded the federal marshal, Democratic-Republican General Joseph Willcox, to empanel a grand jury to decide whether to indict these Federalist agitators. Edwards was the Connecticut district court judge who presided over the case. Since one of the defendants, Tapping Reeve, was his niece's husband, he dismissed that indictment; therefore, he probably did not initiate it. The court cases began at New Haven in April 1806, with grand jury indictments for sedition of Federalist preachers and pamphleteers Reeve, Osgood, and Collier. The following month, a Hartford grand jury likewise indicted newspaper publishers Barzillai Hudson and George Goodwin of the Hartford

Connecticut Courant and Congregationalist preacher Azel Backus. Jefferson had appointed Edwards a district judge only a few weeks earlier. The Hartford *Connecticut Courant,* one of the foremost Federalist newspapers, whose publishers were under indictment, reported regularly on the case.[54] Only Federalists took much interest in it. Jefferson seemed unaware of it. He had more important things to do. Nonetheless, even Dumas Malone, who took pains to defend Jefferson's every action, admitted that his failure to immediately dismiss the Connecticut libel cases was the greatest stain on his reputation as the guarantor of human freedom.[55]

9

Jefferson and the Opéra Bouffe Prosecution of "Savage" Connecticut Federalists, 1806–1809

Jefferson did not order the prosecution of Federalist preachers and writers, most notably Tapping Reeve and the Reverend Azel Backus, in Connecticut's federal courts. However, he made no effort to quash it when first informed of it in December 1806 by Thomas Seymour, a Republican stalwart. Jefferson was not unduly alarmed that his states' rights principles were being flouted by his ally Edwards' initial conduct of the case. Edwards acted as the lone circuit judge, because Federalist Supreme Court Justice William Paterson was ill. At least at the outset, Jefferson was reluctant to discourage his ardent supporters, Thomas Seymour and other Hartford Democratic-Republicans, from vindicating him.[1]

· · · · ·

Born in Norwich, Connecticut, in 1765, Azel Backus (no relation to the Massachusetts Baptist Isaac Backus) was the son of Congregationalists. He was briefly attracted to deism after his graduation from Yale in 1787. He started out as a schoolteacher in Wethersfield, but his uncle, the Reverend Charles Backus, convinced him of the virtues of Congregational orthodoxy and he became an ordained Congregational minister in 1789. In 1791, he succeeded Dr. Joseph Bellamy as a minister in Bethlehem, Connecticut, simultaneously running a school. Known for his strait-laced Federalist politics and his religious orthodoxy, Backus published numerous anti–Jeffersonian sermons from 1797 to 1813. He delivered the annual election sermon before the Connecticut legislature in 1798, after composing a famous eulogy honoring hard-bitten Federalist governor Oliver Wolcott when he died in 1797. He preached at Bethlehem, Connecticut, churches until 1812, when he was elected the first president of Hamilton College in upstate Clinton, New York.[2]

Tapping Reeve (1744–1823) was the leading attorney and judge of Connecticut and one of the foremost Federalist legal authorities in the country. In 1798, Reeve was appointed a judge of the Connecticut Superior Court and turned over most of his teaching responsibilities to his former student and legal associate, James Gould. In May 1814, Reeve rose to the position of chief judge of the Connecticut Superior Court, a position that he held for only one year, having reached the mandatory retirement age of seventy. In his final years he joined the great Presbyterian revivalist and conservative foe of Jefferson, Lyman Beecher, in propagating religious education and alcoholic temperance.[3]

Of perhaps greater significance in Reeve's contempt for Jefferson, he was married to Sally Burr, Aaron Burr's sister. She died in 1797, and a year later he married his housekeeper, Elizabeth Thompson, thirty years his junior. Reeve was probably aware that after 1801, when Burr silently attempted to steal the election from Jefferson, his former brother-in-law and the president hated each other. Reeve, who founded Litchfield Law School, the first private law school in the United States, in 1784, was Burr's law teacher. Reeve had a permanent influence on the history of American law in other ways. His text, *The Law of Baron and Feme* (1816), promulgated the law of coverture, by which a wife became merely the legal extension of her husband during his lifetime and could own no property, although after her husband died she had dower rights to one-third of his real and personal estate (and one-half of the latter if he had no living children). A prolific writer and staunch opponent of Jefferson, Reeve later wrote a pamphlet discussing the Connecticut federal court cases in which he, Backus, and a few other Federalist agitators were indicted by a federal grand jury and threatened with prosecution by Connecticut's federal district attorney in 1806 for libeling the president. He took for granted that Jefferson had instigated the lawsuits. Since district court Judge Pierpont Edwards, who conducted the Connecticut trials, was Burr's uncle and therefore related to Reeve, he refused to prosecute him. (Indeed, in his pamphlet Reeve admitted that, because of his prestige in Connecticut and his close association with the Republican federal district court judge, Pierpont Edwards, his prosecution was immediately cancelled.)[4]

Like Yale College, Litchfield Law School was a cradle of Congregationalism, Federalism, and conservative thoughts and habits. Students were even expected to wear old-fashioned, pre–Revolutionary style clothing. Occasionally, rebellious students from the Southern states, mainly Georgia, South Carolina, and Maryland, wore more fashionable, modern-style clothing, in the Jeffersonian "Jacobin" mode. A former student reminisced, "Bold was the youth who defied custom, for tight trousers ... pantaloons, disheveled hair and laced shoes had an unholy significance; they were the trademarks of Sabbath-breakers, tipplers, and 'ruff-scuff,' in short, of the followers of the 'atheist and libertine,' Thomas Jefferson."[5]

The Reverend Timothy Dwight, president of Yale, denounced his cousin, Aaron Burr, as a Republican "Jacobin." Young John C. Calhoun, an ardent Democratic-Republican, attended Yale and Litchfield Law School. Although Calhoun was sickened by Dwight's conservative Federalist diatribes, Dwight, showing greater tolerance for challengers and dissent than many professors in our own times, respected Calhoun's brilliant arguments for his own populist opinions, and said his intelligence entitled him to be president of the United States one day.[6] However, Southern Republicans (whom Federalists usually called "democrats" after 1800) like Calhoun could not help but feel uneasy in a generally unfriendly atmosphere.

Judge Reeve vigorously expressed his negative feelings about Jefferson. In 1800, he predicted that if Jefferson were elected president, the streets would run red with blood within two years. In 1801, behind the scenes, he encouraged Federalist members of Congress to hold out for the election of his brother-in-law, Aaron Burr, as president instead of Jefferson. In 1804, he joined Senator Uriah Tracy in attempting to convince Connecticut leaders to join an independent "Eastern Confederacy" under Burr's nominal leadership. In 1805, when Republican publisher Selleck Osborne, editor of the *Litchfield Witness*, was jailed, Calhoun and one other law student, his friend John Felder, defying Reeve, joined a crowd of over a thousand Jeffersonians in marching past the window of Osborne's cell to applaud him.[7] According to the recollections of Calhoun, who spent more than a year at Reeve's school, as well as other law students, Reeve did not mention current politics in his law lectures, or attack Jefferson.[8]

Most of Connecticut's lawyers were Federalists and Congregationalists. For admission to the Connecticut bar, a candidate had to be favorably reviewed by the Federalist-controlled county courts. In order to get ahead, a young lawyer had to be friendly with the clergy and support the state's ruling Federalist oligarchy. Most Connecticut attorneys went to Yale College, then apprenticed in a law office or studied at Litchfield Law School, which was presided over by Judges Reeve and James Gould, both men devout Federalists.[9]

To a certain extent, Jefferson respected the legal profession, although he regarded most attorneys as corrupt moneygrubbers. Nonetheless, it was due to his efforts that his alma mater, the College of William and Mary, instituted the first law professorship. In 1779, as governor of Virginia, Jefferson was automatically a member of the Board of Visitors of the college. The "godless" Jefferson succeeded in getting rid of the two professorships of Divinity, and installing professorships of law and medicine in their place. George Wythe, Jefferson's close friend and law teacher, became its first law professor, a position he served in from 1779 to 1789, when he left for Richmond to resume his lucrative legal practice and become Chancellor of the state. St. George Tucker replaced him as professor of law at William and Mary.[10]

Using Collier's *Litchfield Monitor* as a mouthpiece, Reeve wrote about thirty anti–Democratic Republican articles accusing President Jefferson of various crimes. He targeted Jefferson for violating the Constitution by refitting the French frigate *Berceau*, seized by U.S. warships after peace was made with France, without specific appropriations from Congress, and then returning it to the French. Reeve was especially active from 1801 to 1803. During this period, his pseudonyms included "Phocion," "Asdrubal," and "Marcellus." Reeve called the "Democrats" immoral blasphemers who sought to abolish the clergy and the Constitution. Their secret objectives were to severely reduce the Army and Navy and blight Federalists' laudable hopes for an alliance with Britain.[11]

In 1806, the Hartford federal grand jury indicted Reeve for libelous statements in his much earlier November 25, 1801, article about the *Berceau*, in which he wildly charged that Jefferson had destroyed the people's liberties by perverting the Constitution and the Judiciary, deprived the people of trial by jury, illegally spent public money, and attempted to establish a despotic government. Reeve promised to continue to denounce Jefferson as a "democrat" and a "Jacobin." (His prosecution for this 1801 piece was actually barred by a statute of limitations.)[12]

Employing the pseudonym, "Hampden," Reeve used a name popular among both Republicans and Federalists. It recalled a prominent Puritan republican foe of Charles I who was killed in battle in 1643 during the English Civil War. The judge titled the pamphlet *Letter to the President of the United States*. It was published in October 1808, after all the prosecutions had been discontinued except for a Supreme Court test case to determine whether the federal government could prosecute cases of seditious libel in federal courts, *United States v. Hudson and Goodwin.* Barzillai Hudson and George Goodwin, publishers of the Federalist *Hartford Connecticut Courant* were indicted by a grand jury for reprinting an article from the *Utica Patriot,* a New York Federalist paper, denouncing Jefferson's secret request from Congress in February 1806 for $2 million to bribe Napoleon to support U.S. acquisition of West Florida from Spain. The author derided Jefferson for keeping the measure secret from the voters, whom he supposedly trusted because of his democratic proclivities.[13] That case, decided by the Marshall Court in 1812, acquitted Hudson and Goodwin. The Supreme Court determined that there was no federal common law of libel. This stand in favor of freedom of the press, although it coincidentally exonerated anti–Jefferson newspaper publishers, accorded with Jefferson's lifelong belief in freedom of thought and his insistence that the national government could not claim a common law right to prosecute individuals for libel or sedition.

· · · · ·

Far from being a political novice, elderly Thomas Seymour (1735–1829) was among the most prominent, well-educated and well-connected politicians in Connecticut. He married Mary Ledyard (1735–1807) of the wealthy mercantile Ledyard family, a family most renowned for her nephew, John Ledyard's scientific explorations to Alaska and Russia, which Jefferson endorsed as secretary of state in 1790. A Yale College graduate (1755), Seymour was a successful lawyer. He served as a royal attorney during the 1760s, and later became Connecticut's state attorney. A veteran office-holder, he served in the militia both before and during the Revolution, rising to the rank of lieutenant-colonel. He was Hartford's delegate to the general assembly from 1774 to 1793. When Hartford became an incorporated city in 1784, he was elected its first mayor, holding that position for a record twenty-eight years, until he resigned in May 1812. The "first mayor" (his nickname) also served as the chief judge of the court of common pleas at Hartford from 1798 to 1803, concomitant with the mayoralty. He was a member of the council of assistants, the upper house of Connecticut's legislature, from 1793 to 1803, and chief judge of the Hartford County Court from 1798 to 1803. A devout Congregationalist despite his Republican Party membership, Seymour was deacon of Hartford's Second or South Church from 1794 to 1809. The Marquis de Lafayette reportedly resided at Seymour's house during his nationwide tour in 1824. When Seymour died, he was the oldest Yale graduate on record.[14]

Despite Seymour's political prominence, apparently his family was financially insecure. The father of seven children, six of them sons, he sought government jobs for himself and his family as rewards for his activities on behalf of the Democratic-Republican Party in Connecticut. After Jefferson's great victory in the 1804 presidential election, Seymour, glossing over the fact that he had not carried Connecticut, wrote him a letter of political advice. He indirectly blamed Jefferson's failure to remove Federalists from office for the party's weakness. Since the election, Connecticut Federalists, in their "notorious" legislature had stepped up persecution of Republican printers. They demonstrated anew "the intollerant [sic] and alarming Spirit of the predominant party." He was disappointed at Jefferson's inertia, his failure to use his appointive powers to "abate opposition to the measures of Government." Seymour claimed that he suffered great "privations" from Federalist persecution; torment "of which, Sir, you may have been apprized." "No one has, more ceaselessly, felt its malignant effects." At the same time, on a more fraternal note, Seymour "congratulated" Jefferson on the party's recent victories elsewhere: "Permit me, Sir, most cordially to congratulate you, & our happy Country, upon the late success of our Friends in Massachusetts & Ne. Hampshire.—May its benign influence be soon shed on this Section of the Union, so as to dispel the cloud of Delusion, in which it hath been so long, involved." He called himself Jefferson's "affectionate & obedient Servant."[15]

Jefferson would certainly have agreed that Connecticut voters were "deluded" in continuing to elect Federalists, but he ostensibly did not feel very "affectionate" toward Seymour. There is no record of him answering his letter. However, he did appoint one of Seymour's sons, Henry, to a minor federal post, commissioner of bankruptcy, shortly before the law creating it expired.[16]

Undeterred by Jefferson's silence, in August 1807 Seymour again wrote asking for government patronage. Recommending Henry for commissioner of the Connecticut federal loan office, he informed Jefferson that his son was a capable merchant, accountant, and a man of incorruptible integrity. Moreover, Henry had been annually elected secretary of state for Connecticut by the "unanimous suffrages of the friends of government." Now more reserved, Seymour, who did not know Jefferson personally, closed the letter expressing his "very great esteem & consideration."[17]

As the first signature on a letter to the president bearing the names of seven leading Connecticut Democratic-Republicans, Seymour, who probably authored the hard-hitting epistle, informed him of the indictments of Reeve, Osgood, Backus, Collier, and Hudson and Goodwin. Apparently, Seymour originated the idea of the federal prosecutions. Assuming that distorted reports of events in Hartford had reached Washington, Seymour began, "Apprehending that communications have been made to you, tending to misrepresent the sentiments of the Republicans in this State, on the subject of the prosecutions depending before the Circuit Court in this district, for Libels against the President & administration of the General Government; we submit the following observations, expressive of the opinions of the Republicans in this town, and of the Friends of Republican Government in this State."[18]

Sounding much like his political opponents would have if they were conducting the prosecution and the defendants were Republicans, Seymour continued, "Bills were found against a Judge, two political Priests, & three Federal printers, who were corrupting the taste and morals of the People." Seymour emphasized that most observers supported the Republican court's actions: "Public opinion had decided on the correctness of the procedure; moderate Federalists approve it; the violent are silent; and Republicans, with a few solitary exceptions, applaud it." Reporting that the prosecutions had already caused Federalist printers to exercise greater restraint in their personal abuse of Jefferson, while they continued to denounce "the measures and principles of the Administration," Seymour happily reported that lately the "Intolerant Majority softened in its asperity." Meanwhile, the Republican minority, though "despairing of Justice to itself from the State Courts," optimistically "anticipate[d] from the Courts of the U States, exact Justice to its enemies." Connecticut Republicans found revenge sweet.[19]

Distinguishing between legitimate federal common law prosecutions for calumnies of Jefferson's personal character and what Republicans considered unconstitutional federal lawsuits against critiques of government policy, Seymour and his colleagues defended the state party's actions as in accordance with Jeffersonian free speech principles. Fearing that they had been "misrepresented," they explained that they intended to defend the president's "reputation as a man" rather than his "official conduct" as a government official against Federalist defamation.[20]

After Seymour wrote Jefferson about the indictments in December 1806, the president confessed that he did not know what he was talking about. He had been slow to reply to the letter, probably because he was involved in delicate negotiations to preserve peace with Britain, and in suppressing Burr's rumored revolt. Manifesting little interest in the indictments one way or the other, he said, "The mass of business which occurs during a session of the Legislature, renders me necessarily unpunctual in acknowledging the receipt of letters, and in answering those which will admit of delay." That was his "apology" for remissness in replying to the letter from Connecticut's Jeffersonian activists, whom he called "republican characters … of high respectability."[21]

Above all, Jefferson wanted Connecticut and Massachusetts to join the rest of the country in becoming part of the Jeffersonian "family," along with their "sister states." Following his election victory, he began constant use of this filial rhetoric. Thus, he said he understood the reasons for the Connecticut Republicans' initiative. He sympathized with the great odds they faced in confronting Federalist domination of the state. Since Federalist newspaper editors fought dirty, and their newspapers showed the same unscrupulousness wherever Federalists controlled the government, he agreed that Republicans were justified in retaliating. "I have seen with deep concern the afflicting oppression under which the republican citizens of Connecticut suffer from an unjust majority," he wrote. "The truths expressed in your letter have been long exposed to the nation through the channel of the public papers, and are the more readily believed because most of the States during the momentary ascendancy of kindred majorities in them have seen the same spirit of opposition prevail."[22] Jefferson was irked that Federalists mercilessly castigated him whenever they gained a "momentary" majority, no matter how tenuous or temporary. They should instead admit defeat and seek conciliation with his nationally dominant administration.

At the same time, Jefferson probably felt that, in good conscience as a Democratic-Republican and a staunch advocate of freedom of the press, he could not support federal prosecution of libelous newspapers. Therefore, he made clear that he had never given the go-ahead to any Connecticut officials in their desire for revenge. "With respect to the countervailing prosecutions now instituted in the Court of the United States in Connecticut, I had heard but little, and certainly, I believe, never expressed a sentiment on them," he insisted. Nonetheless, he understood that, in the dark recesses of the human heart, most people desired revenge on their enemies. He condoned such emotions: "That a spirit of indignation and retaliation should arise when an opportunity should present itself, was too much within the human constitution to excite either surprise or censure," he asserted, "and confined to an appeal to truth only, it cannot lessen the useful freedom of the press." If the federal prosecutor based his lawsuit solely on "an appeal to truth" (even though according to the views expressed in the Kentucky Resolutions the federal government had no business trying sedition cases), Jefferson now opined, "it cannot lessen the useful freedom of the press."[23] For Jefferson, one way of viewing the impending Connecticut prosecutions was as a salutary quest for "truth." His friends were simply defending his personal morality in court, which it would be improper and inconvenient for him to do in a state court while serving as president of the United States at a critical time.

However, he was somewhat embarrassed that *his* reputation and character were on the line. He loftily reiterated his determination, publicly expressed in his second inaugural address, to conduct the first large-scale "experiment" in freedom of the press in the modern world. Had the Federalist propagandists confined their abuse to his public policies, Jefferson was sure that he would emerge victorious in public opinion; he had nothing to fear from a detailed examination. "As to myself, conscious that there was not a *truth* on earth which I feared should be known, I have lent myself willingly as the subject of a great experiment, which was to prove that an administration, conducting itself with integrity and common understanding, cannot be battered down, even by the falsehoods of a licentious press," he said, alluding to Federalist pamphleteers, "and consequently still less by the press, as restrained within the legal and wholesome limits of truth." If only the newspapers confined themselves to printing the truth about him, everyone would be happy (and Republican), he sighed, and his conviction that freedom of the press was a harmonious support for a stable democratic government would be validated. As he put it, "This experiment was wanting for the world to demonstrate the falsehood of the pretext that freedom of the press is incompatible with orderly government," a dictum expounded by conservatives in Britain and the world over. He self-righteously asserted that in his quest to prove the viability of freedom of the press, he had "never ... even contradicted the thousands of calumnies so industriously propagated against myself."[24] (Nevertheless, his friends and supporters had often done so.)

He argued that as long as the state's federal (Republican) prosecutors' goal was the truth, "the universal freedom of the press" remained unsullied. He insisted that he personally had nothing to hide, either of his public or private life. Although he reiterated his belief that the freedom of the press was too important for him to worry about the abuse he suffered, after years of humiliation he was starting to reconsider his position. He began to feel that the numerous calumnies the Federalists had invented about his personal life—perhaps thinking of the charges of his atheism, that he had defrauded an old widow of her savings, and (maybe) that he had been involved in regular sexual relations with a slave girl named Sally—justified his followers' intervention on his behalf to thwart the continued propagation of such insults. Thus, with the bevy of Connecticut libelers in mind, he bluntly stated, "the fact being once established, that the press is impotent when it abandons itself to falsehood, I leave it to others to restore it [the integrity of the press] to its strength, by recalling it within the pale of truth."[25] Feeling empowered by his reelection victory, he assured Seymour that he had his *carte blanche* in punishing the liars who sullied his reputation.

Always expecting that his policies and principles would convert all but the most extreme New England Federalists into Democratic-Republican voters, Jefferson believed that most citizens were ripe for change. He hoped that the people would reject the "interested aristocracy of priests and lawyers" who brainwashed them into a "voluntary degradation of mind." Fearing that these angry words might reach his opponents, he cautioned Seymour to keep the letter "private." On an optimistic note, he advised Seymour that, once Connecticut's newspapers got into the habit of printing the truth (which, in his view, would happen when most of them became Republican), its "citizens [would] rally to the republican principles of our Constitution, which unite their sister-States into one family." It was all a question of literate people exercising their intelligence to think for themselves, rather than do what the "rich, the wise, and the able," as they were generally called, told them to do: "It would seem impossible that an intelligent people, with the faculty of reading and right of thinking, should continue much longer to slumber under the pupilage of an interested aristocracy of priests and lawyers, persuading them to distrust themselves, and to let them think for them."[26] Since the residents of Connecticut were among the best-educated in the country, Jefferson was probably wondering what was taking them so long.

Meanwhile, Federalists objected that, although Edwards nominally presided over the

April 1806 court sessions, state party manager Wolcott regularly attended the proceedings and was the force behind them. Moreover, he temporarily served as the government's counsel in the September 1807 court term. Apparently on orders from Granger, Jefferson and Madison, Wolcott recommended that the case against Backus be discontinued. Newspaper reports erroneously stated that witnesses against Jefferson's chastity had arrived from Virginia. Wolcott objected to rumors that this had caused the president to order the case closed, and the witnesses to return home. Backus's counsel said that he had subpoenaed these witnesses, but they had not arrived because Jefferson sent them information that "the prosecution would be put an end to, and consequently their attendance would be unavailing." The counsel demanded a "special" trial, and said he would once again subpoena the witnesses. Judge Edwards ruled that this would be an extraordinary procedure, inconvenient to him. He declared that Backus should either wait for the decision in the case of Hudson and Goodwin, on which hinged the question whether the federal courts had common law jurisdiction, or consent to an end to the prosecution. Although Backus's lawyer asserted that his client wanted to prove his innocence and uphold his "character" as a matter of "fact," not merely law, Edwards said that Backus might have a trial if he wished, but that the district attorney would not force him and his witnesses could not be subpoenaed for a "special court." When Edwards offered to subpoena the Virginia witnesses by charging them with contempt of court for non-attendance, Backus' counsel emphasized Jefferson's culpability, asserting that the witnesses "failed to attend not from want of respect to the process of the court, but in consequence of the interference of the Executive of the United States." All parties then agreed to end Backus' prosecution.[27]

In later recounting the proceedings in a vituperative pamphlet published in October 1808, "Hampden" (a pseudonym for Reeve, or perhaps David Daggett), the Federalists' main spokesperson in the press, claimed that Wolcott controlled District Attorney Huntington and generally dominated affairs. "Hampden" derided the district attorney's incompetence, but praised Edwards for his fairness. He especially applauded Edwards' immediate dismissal of the proceedings against Reeve, and his acknowledgment that they were superseded by the statute of limitations and that he would not allow his niece's husband to be humiliated. On the other hand, Edwards permitted the proceedings against the other five Federalists to continue, asserting that the "licentious press" of the Federalists, who practically recommended overthrowing the Constitution, mocked freedom of the press, which ideally ought to teach the people loyalty to their government. Emphasizing that the United States was the only legitimate government because it was the only one that relied on "the will and choice of the people," Edwards warned that the republic could not survive if "forward and wicked" calumniators went unpunished. Using the press for purposes of "party revenge" and bringing the government into "contempt," he said, deserved "exemplary punishment."[28] With the power of hindsight, "Hampden" later taunted Jefferson, "After it became known at Washington that *the truth would be received in evidence* for these prosecutions, Mr. Jefferson gave unequivocal assurances, that the several actions should never come to trial; and accordingly, so soon as *decorum* permitted, they, one after another, made an *easy* exit."[29]

Implying that the federal courts possessed the common law power of punishing seditious libel, Edwards asserted that the U.S. Supreme Court agreed with him (as most Federalists did). Federal district courts prosecuted leading Republican editors like Benjamin Franklin Bache under the common law in the months before the Sedition Act of 1798; in fact, Bache died of yellow fever on September 10, 1798, awaiting trial. Ironically, in 1801 William Duane, Bache's successor as publisher of the Philadelphia *General Advertiser: Aurora,* was sentenced to thirty days in jail for contempt of court by the Philadelphia district court, controlled by Federalists, even though he was a leading Democratic-Republican and Jefferson was recently elected president. Jefferson seemed uncertain himself what he thought about the federal judiciary's common law jurisdiction in libel cases (as opposed to congressional legislation, which was barred by the First Amendment). Influenced by conservative Republican chancellor Robert R. Livingston of New York, who advised him to avoid provoking Federalists at the outset of his administration, Jefferson did not dismiss the prosecution or pardon Duane.[30]

After the Republican grand jury indicted the Federalist writers, their friends feared that the prosecution would employ the common law and prohibit the use of truth as evidence. Although Edwards at first asserted he would exert his powers under common law as the Federalists did under the Sedition Act, he was trying to frighten the Federalists with a dose of their own medicine. He announced that he would accept truth as a defense in accordance with Connecticut law.[31]

During the Alien-Sedition Act crisis of 1798–1800, Republican ideologues like Tunis Wortman, George Hay, and George Blake wrote pamphlets insisting that the press must be absolutely free. All Republicans agreed that truth must be permitted as a defense in all libel cases, contrary to the dictums of English common law. Accordingly, Edwards asserted that he would allow truth as a defense in the case. Packed by the Jeffersonian marshal with Republicans (rather than chosen by lot by town clerks as was done in the state court), the grand jury indicted Tapping Reeve for charging that Jefferson had pursued unconstitutional measures as president, but Edwards refused to issue a warrant for his arrest. Thomas Collier, editor of the *Litchfield Monitor,* was indicted for reprinting an article from Alexander Hamilton's *New-York Evening Post* claiming that Jefferson's administration was "profligate" and publishing Reeve's article charging that Jefferson had violated the Constitution by returning a French frigate seized by the U.S. Navy. A young Congregational minister named Thaddeus Osgood was indicted for reportedly delivering a slanderous sermon against Jefferson, defaming him as "a base, traitorous infidel, debaucher and liar." On several different Thanksgiving days, Osgood and Azel Backus preached that Jefferson would bring down the wrath of Heaven on the country because he was "not a believer of Christianity." In "Hampden's" words, directly addressing the president, "In support of this fact, they quoted from your Notes on Virginia; they instanced your appointments to office, and your bosom friends, particularly the infamous Thomas Paine." Collier was bailed out of jail by Federalist leaders Elias Shipman and David Daggett. With fewer friends, Osgood reportedly languished in prison for two days.[32]

Between the April and September 1806 sessions, when hearings resumed, Republican newspapers stressed that their champion editor, Selleck Osborne, was a victim of party vengeance. Perhaps because Federalist travail could not bear comparison with the actual imprisonment of Osborne, their newspapers were relatively silent about alleged Republican injustices to Osgood and Collier, who were out on bail. Republicans were chagrined by their failure to attract Litchfield's farmers, who they assumed had been brainwashed by their clergy, judiciary, and other officials. Seeking to rally the people, they decided to hold a big celebration, which became known ignominiously as the Sixth-of-August Festival. A multitude of Republicans gathered at Litchfield to hear a short prayer and rousing address by the Reverend Jonathan Law, after which they visited the town jail, where Osborne was held for refusing to pay his fine for libel. The Jeffersonian crowd appeared to Federalists as a "most signal exhibition of the rage of democracy." Federalists charged that during the festival Republicans beat up an old Federalist preacher who crashed their party. The propagation of this rumor lost Republicans votes. Thomas Robbins, a leading Litchfield cleric, asserted that it proved that the Republicans were "Jacobin" revolutionaries.[33] Consequently, in the September 1806 state elections, Republicans lost seats and they elected no town representatives for Litchfield, Reeve's stronghold.

Deriding Democratic-Republicans' insistence that it was necessary for the state government to harmonize with the national administration, Federalist campaigners argued that such reasoning was like advocating a "consolidation" of the states within the national government. Touting states' rights, they claimed that the Republican position violated the U.S. Constitution's contract with the states. They pointed out that the Republican ranks themselves were disunited, especially in the case of the former Jeffersonian leader, Congressman John Randolph of Roanoke, who now did all in his power to embarrass Jefferson. They argued that the Republicans had never harmonized with Washington and Adams, men more virtuous than Jefferson. They labeled "state-manager" Alexander Wolcott a dictator who forced all Republicans to bend to his will.[34] According to one Federalist pamphleteer, Jefferson sent Wolcott, a latter-day "Robespierre," to Connecticut to "revolutionize the State," undermine the "federalists," and "penalize their exertions against the inroads of democracy."[35]

The state's Federalist leaders asserted that the people were happy and prosperous, and would resist Republican attempts to "revolutionize" the state government. "The people have often been told that oppressive inequalities existed in taxation, that there was intolerance in matters of religion, and that a new constitution would be beneficial," they observed; yet they rejected the movement for changing the ancient law. "They have heard this clamour, reflected on their prosperity, and refused to join the standard of visionaries."[36]

· · · · ·

From the beginning of 1807, Jefferson had more important things on his mind than the persisting opposition to him in Massachusetts and Connecticut. This was the time of Aaron Burr's arrest and trial for conspiracy and treason. Jefferson feared that a secessionist movement in the West might be underway.[37] As early as November 27, 1806, Jefferson proclaimed the existence of a conspiracy against the United States and Spanish neighboring territories. Burr was arrested in March 1807. Less aggressive than his successor Abraham Lincoln, who unilaterally suspended habeas corpus during the Civil War, Jefferson, through the medium of Senator William Branch Giles, asked Congress to suspend it in order to procure additional evidence against Burr and his co-conspirators. Ironically, fellow Virginians, his son-in-law John Wayles Eppes and his nemesis John Randolph, led the battle against him in the House of Representatives, leading to the overwhelming rejection of his proposal by his own party, by a vote of 113 to nineteen.[38]

Obsessed with having Burr imprisoned and perhaps even executed as a traitor, Jefferson thought of nothing else for months. In an address to Congress on January 22, 1807, he said that Burr's guilt was "beyond question," in effect denying Burr the ancient legal right of being considered innocent until proven guilty.[39] Seeking congressional permission to use the Army and Navy to suppress Burr's conspiracy (which in accordance with the Constitution, he labeled an "insurrection"), Jefferson sent a draft of a bill to that effect to his friend, Congressman John Dawson of Orange County, Virginia. Congress approved Dawson's proposal.[40]

When a Richmond federal jury found Burr "not guilty" in September 1807, Jefferson had little time to sulk, however, since war with Britain and France resulting from their maritime depredations had become increasingly likely.

In light of such emergencies, Jefferson summoned a special session of Congress to meet for October 26, 1807. He feared that war with the powerful British nation was unavoidable. As he wrote his son-in-law, Congressman Eppes, "We have no information from England which is decisive of what we are to expect. The little circumstances which come to us give preponderance rather to the scale of war; in the expectation of that no man can wish so much as I do to be mistaken."[41] In December 1807, Congress approved his proposal for an embargo on all U.S. exports as a deterrent to immediate war.[42] Recognizing that war with England or France, or both, was possible during this period, Jefferson had little time for involvement in either thwarting or promoting the Connecticut prosecutions.

When it appeared that the attorneys for Azel Backus intended to subpoena testimony from the president's ex-friend John Walker, Madison, and other Cabinet members supposedly familiar with Jefferson's sexual harassment of Elizabeth Walker in 1769, the ordinarily suave president became agitated. He did not relish his dirty laundry being aired again. It had caused him ample embarrassment only a few years earlier, when Callender exposed his affairs and Massachusetts legislators and newspapers derided his alleged sexual encounters with Mrs. Walker and Sally Hemings. Concluding that it would be better for him and the Republican Party if the Connecticut indictments were discontinued, he ordered Postmaster General Gideon Granger to contact Judge Edwards and tell him to end the prosecution. As the editor of the *Letter* to Jefferson charged, Backus's attorneys had subpoenaed Walker and he had allegedly agreed to come to Hartford to testify. Subpoenas had also supposedly been issued for Madison and other members of Jefferson's Cabinet with whom he had earlier discussed the Walker Affair. These reports were the primary reason that Jefferson notified Madison that "the indictment against Mr. Backus was to receive a *quietus*," as a Federalist writer put it.[43]

Indeed, writing Madison about the incident, Jefferson adopted a self-righteous, macho stance. Apparently, his masculine pride had priority over his dedication to the press's unrestricted freedom from scrutiny by the federal government. He insisted that it was only to save Mrs. Walker from embarrassment that he ordered Backus's prosecution to cease. For himself, he would have preferred the public to judge whether he was a rake or not. He was not much impressed by the integrity of Backus and his lawyers, who seemed ignorant of Southern principles of honor: "I had not supposed there was a being in human shape such a savage as to have summoned Mr. W. [Walker] in such a case," he declared. "On account of the feelings of that family, I shall spare nothing to have this article [of indictment] withdrawn. Were it not for them, I would rather the whole should be gone into that the world might judge for themselves and the scoundrel parson [Backus] receive his punishment."[44] Nevertheless, he had seemingly delegated Postmaster General Granger as his envoy to quash the sedition cases.

On his way to Boston, Connecticut native Granger stopped at Hartford to deliver Jefferson's message. He consulted with district attorney Huntington, who seemed agreeable to halting the prosecution. "The Attorney acknowledged the utility of an early dismission [*sic*], and suggests that it was most probable that he should follow my advice," he wrote the president. "Be assured, sir, the prosecutions will be dismissed." Although Granger was "convinced of the Integrity" of Huntington and his friends, he surmised that they did not completely understand that their activities violated Democratic-Republican concepts of the Constitution and freedom of speech. However, Granger downplayed the usefulness of his actions for preserving Jefferson's reputation.[45]

For his part, Jefferson seemed relieved that Edwards and Huntington had ostensibly discontinued the Connecticut prosecutions. Edwards employed the Republican rationale that federal courts lacked jurisdiction, even on the basis of common law, to prosecute libel cases. Although Jefferson had previously regarded the exclusion of federal courts from prosecuting libel suits as integral to the First Amendment, he now seemed less motivated by the principle of freedom of the press than to preserving himself and his former friends from embarrassment. He again tersely wrote his closest confidant, Madison, about the latest developments in the Backus case. Probably alluding to Granger, he said, "I have a letter from Connecticut. The prosecution there will be dismissed this term on the ground that the case is not cognisable by the courts of the U.S." Implying that Madison should inform Mr. and Mrs. Walker of the outcome, he instructed him, "Perhaps you can intimate this where it will give tranquility."[46]

Somehow, Jefferson's orders that the Connecticut district attorney end Backus's prosecution had not been completely followed. In January 1808, Granger, who had probably talked with Jefferson shortly before about the Backus case, the only one still pending, was in New York City, on his way to Hartford. From New York, he wrote the president, "If you should be of opinion that it would be best to put an end to the prosecutions in Connecticut while I am there, I will endeavour to effect it."[47]

The Backus case was not in the forefront of Jefferson's thoughts in January 1808. He had signed the Embargo Act a few weeks before and was pondering the possibility of war with England, France, and American Indians. He now made amply clear to Granger that he wanted the prosecution cancelled, and to be on good terms with Backus. Revealing his fear of further public humiliation, he immediately replied to Granger's letter. "I received last night your favor of the 19th," he wrote. "I certainly wish the prosecutions you allude to put an end to, for the reasons explained in my former letters on that subject, and these are strengthened by the verbal declarations you communicated to me from the defendant [Backus]."[48] In earlier conversations, Granger assured Jefferson that Backus told him he had not denounced his morals the way some people claimed he had, but had only criticized his political actions. Now taking these statements at face value, Jefferson seemed much more forgiving than he usually was of the calumnies against him. "I have never considered the political hatreds pointed at me, as meant against me personally," he asserted, "but rather as the representative of the [Democratic-Republican] party, the real object of hatred, for what could there be personal between that gentleman & myself." He claimed to feel only kind feelings for Backus: "I am sure I wish him no injury, and if he intended one to me, I know it must have been from false impressions made on him. Peace therefore be with him."[49]

Even in writing Granger, his closest confidant in the matter of the sedition trials, Jefferson expressed greater concern with the major crises he confronted than with saving face in the dispute with Federalists. Unburdening himself on questions of war and peace to an official involved exclusively with mail deliveries, Jefferson discussed the recently-passed Embargo Act and British and French seizures of U.S. ships. He believed that to properly end such seizures, the country would probably have to go to war. Therefore, he praised the Embargo, which had only been in effect a few days. "We must have gone to war to avenge the wrong," he declared. "It was certainly a better alternative to discontinue all intercourse with these nations till they shall return to some sense of moral right." He was aware that merchant seamen would suffer severe unemployment as a result of the ban on American shipping overseas, but they were threatened with potentially fatal capture and impressment into the British Navy when they went abroad. "I only lament the situation of our seamen, and wish it could relieved," he said, probably expecting the Embargo to cost his party votes in the maritime states, especially New England. "As to the sacrifices of the farmers & citizen-merchants," he optimistically observed, tacitly contrasting native-born merchants with those of Scottish and English lineage who had dominated Virginia's tobacco trade in his youth, "I am sure they will be chearfully [*sic*] met."[50] Controversial policies like the Embargo would undoubtedly injure the president's popularity, especially in Massachusetts, Vermont, New York, and Connecticut, more than public dismay at his pursuit of women as a young man and possible senescent sexual escapades with his slave girls when he vacationed at Monticello.

In foregoing revenge on Backus, Jefferson emphasized his chivalry and desire to spare the Walker Family's feelings. However, it is likely that, in addition to his dread of public disgrace, the burdens of office that he mentioned to Granger and Madison, including the possibility of a large-scale conflict with Native Americans in Missouri and Louisiana; the thwarting of Burr's plots and his trial for treason; and the likelihood of war with Britain after the recent *Chesapeake* outrage also played a role.[51]

In April 1808, the federal circuit court, over which Supreme Court Justice Brockholst Livingston now presided, resumed consideration of the old sedition case of Hudson and Goodwin and some new matters involving state interruption of the mail by Connecticut's lieutenant governor John Treadwell, a devout Congregationalist and extreme Federalist, whose officers arrested a stagecoach driver for carrying the mail on Sunday ("the Sabbath"), a violation of state but not federal law. Of the grand jurors in the latter case, "Hampden" contemptuously observed, "One of these gentlemen was largely concerned in the rebellion of Shays, in Massachusetts, in 1786. Several of them were the enemies of Governor Treadwell, and all of them, one or two excepted, were furious jacobins."[52]

The case involving Treadwell, a popular and highly respected politician who was elected governor a few years later, reveals Democratic-Republican attempts to conciliate their bitterest foes, especially at a time when Jefferson was unpopular in Connecticut because of the Embargo Act. In September 1808, the case of Constable Joseph Porter, who had arrested Isaac Kellogg, the stagecoach driver who was delivering mail on Sunday, went to trial. Porter's attorneys included David Daggett and some of the state's leading Federalists. They were confronted by the allegedly incompetent District Attorney Hezekiah Huntington, "assisted by Mr. [Alexander] Wolcott." Despite being a Democratic-Republican, Judge Livingston wasted little time in determining that the lieutenant governor and his associates were not guilty of stopping the mail (although they had done just that), and directed the jury to acquit them. It promptly did so.[53]

A larger question emerged from the Republican district attorney's prosecution of the Federalist pamphleteers, lukewarmly supported at the outset by Judge Edwards: Was there a federal common law of seditious libel, and could U.S. government officials, whether in the executive, legislative or judicial branches, prosecute individuals for libel and slander? In the Hartford, Connecticut, cases, all six defendants were indicted for libeling the president of the United States, although they were not prosecuted, except for the publishers of the Hartford *Connecticut Courant*, Hudson and Goodwin, and that was rather as a test case to decide the major issue rather than as a serious court case.

As representatives of their clients, the Federalist defense attorneys now intended to deny that U.S. courts had common law jurisdiction in criminal cases. They argued that, in accordance with the law, the *Connecticut Courant* case should be "continued" (postponed) until two federal judges were present. Edwards attempted to placate them. He said that he would not pursue the case, but would agree that the Supreme Court should decide the matter. The district attorney and the defense attorneys accepted this solution. Meanwhile, the Backus and Collier indictments were "quashed."[54]

In February 1812, in the case of *U.S. vs. Hudson and Goodwin*, the Supreme Court, with Hudson and Goodwin agreeing to a trial (since Edwards told them in advance they would not be convicted) and Jefferson's appointee, Justice William Johnson, writing the majority opinion, concluded that federal courts lacked common law jurisdiction in cases of libel against the U.S. government.[55] Earlier, "Hampden" had made clear that Connecticut's Federalist majority felt little gratitude to Jefferson or the Republicans (whom they called "democrats," a term of abuse) for discontinuing the prosecutions. The editor of "Hampden's" *Letter* praised Pierpont Edwards' display of independence from the president's apparent goal of invoking a federal common law of sedition. Edwards accepted Connecticut's libel law, which employed truth as a defense. In general, however, "Hampden" felt only contempt for the "Jacobin" "harpies," as he called the Republicans, who desired a "banquet of revenge" on their opponents.[56]

· · · · ·

Shortly after leaving the presidency, Jefferson faced a painful and embarrassing situation. Leaders of his own party in Congress, including his son-in-law John Wayles Eppes, raged against the efforts of Democratic-Republican officials in the Connecticut courts to devise a federal common law of sedition to protect Jefferson.

The volatile Eppes often rejected Jefferson's views. In 1806, defying Jefferson's support for unrestricted U.S. trade with Haiti's revolutionary black dictatorship, Eppes stridently advocated suspending commerce with the island. He obtained a one-year embargo in February 1806. When Jefferson's followers attempted to persuade Congress to suspend the writ of habeas corpus against two of Burr's co-conspirators during his treason trial in 1807, and succeeded in the Senate, Eppes engineered a crushing vote against him in the House of Representatives.[57]

Two years later, Eppes again joined the renegade Jeffersonian party whip, John Randolph of Roanoke, now the president's most bitter enemy, in expressing shock that the Connecticut libel cases had gotten so far without presidential intervention to halt them. Even the Federalists, such as Connecticut congressman Samuel W. Dana (who was later Hudson and Goodwin's attorney when the case came before the U.S. Supreme Court), were less critical of Jefferson. During an earlier session of Congress, in 1807, Dana had briefly mentioned the Connecticut indictments, proposing that Congress take up the question whether the federal government had a common law power to punish crimes. His statements aroused Randolph's curiosity. Unlike Randolph and most Republicans, who insisted that Congress could not prosecute newspapers, Dana considered the Federalist Sedition Act of 1798 constitutional. He hesitated to deny that the government was barred from instituting common law suits against seditious libel. Perhaps relieved that there had been no convictions, but that the district attorney had issued a *nolle prosequi* (withdrawal of the prosecution) in all cases except the test case of *Hudson and Goodwin*, Dana told Randolph that he did not think that Jefferson personally initiated the indictments. On the national level Federalist pamphleteers wrote comparatively little about the Connecticut incident.[58]

In a debate he instigated in May 1809, after Jefferson left office, Randolph hoped to embarrass Jefferson. He charged that Jefferson was behind the attempt to prosecute the Connecticut Federalists for seditious libel. Jefferson thereby flouted his electoral platform of 1800, which denounced the Sedition Act as an unconstitutional arrogation of congressional power, Randolph asserted. Randolph was undeterred even after Connecticut Federalist congressman Dana defended Jefferson and pointed out that there had been no federal court prosecutions for libel, since Edwards discontinued the case against Azel Backus.[59] Coming to Jefferson's aid once more, Granger, using the pseudonym "Veritas," defended Jefferson against charges of hypocrisy in the *National Intelligencer.*[60]

Once out of office, Jefferson apparently was little respected by his party. Randolph was not the only Republican who impugned Jefferson as an ultra-nationalist violator of states' rights and freedom of speech. Democratic-Republican Representative George M. Troup of Georgia implied that Jefferson, though already retired, might justifiably be impeached by Congress if he had instigated the indictments of Azel Backus and the other Federalist agitators.[61] Troup demanded that either Jefferson or the Connecticut district attorney face impeachment. He argued that, if Jefferson had instructed the district attorney to institute English common law-type prosecutions "against a citizen for the purpose of oppression, while the defendant was prevented from giving in evidence the truth of his words or writing," Congress should put him on trial. Troup continued, "In such a case, I have no hesitation in saying that I would consider the President giving such an order as not only highly censurable, but as meriting an impeachment, as guilty of high crime and misdemeanor." "But if a different result should convince me that so far from being directed by the President of the United States," the district attorney had proceeded with the indictments on his own, Troup added, "the criminality would not rest with the President of the United States, but with the District Attorney; but more especially if not only unauthorized but unsanctioned."[62] Thus, Troup was reluctantly prepared to give Jefferson the benefit of the doubt.

In contemplating Jefferson's impeachment even though he was no longer in office, the congressmen, rather shockingly, appear to have been recurring to legal processes in the former mother country. In England, impeachment trials of government officials were sometimes conducted after they left office, although this was not generally the case in the United States. For most of the nineteenth century, Britain's legal system employed both impeachment and bills of attainder. Capital punishment was seldom the outcome of an impeachment trial in Britain, although one seventeenth-century and six eighteenth-century indictments ended in the death sentence. (In cases of bills of attainder, legislative trials which the King and Parliament resorted to primarily to punish treason, the death sentence was far more common.) The danger to the government or to the public safety in the alleged offense, not the official position of the offender, precipitated the impeachment.[63]

In England, anyone could be indicted by impeachment, officeholders and private citizens alike. The impeachment was conducted in the House of Commons, the trial in the House of Lords. The House of Lords heard the Commons' case, then decided on the punishment, which usually involved a criminal penalty, including seizure of property, prison, fines, and removal from office. With bill of attainder, which constituted a trial for treason conducted by Parliament, a more serious crime, the Commons conducted the prosecution and rendered the decision, although the Lords had to consent to a bill of attainder being issued for a legislative trial. Unlike cases of impeachment in the United States, in which the executive took no part, in England the king's consent to a bill of attainder was necessary and his officers were responsible for enforcing the punishment. In bills of attainder and the less serious "bills of pains and penalties," in which only seizure of property and not capital punishment was involved, a majority of the House of Commons and the House of Lords, as well as the king, had to agree on the precise punishment the defendant would suffer. Under bills of attainder, the lands and goods of the convicted defendant were forfeited to the Crown, and he was often executed. Indeed, attainder often fell upon the estates of traitors killed in battle. The suspect did not have a guaranteed right to defend himself in court; this depended on the Commons' permission.[64]

Fortunately, Jefferson's opponents did not recommend bringing back bills of attainder, which were outlawed by the Constitution for both the state and national governments, to convict him.[65] However, Randolph presented a barrage of resolutions implicating Jefferson in the Connecticut common law indictments. Congress's attention concentrated on the proposal, "That a committee be appointed to inquire whether any and what prosecutions have been entertained by the courts of the United States for libels at common law, and to report such provisions as in their opinion may be necessary for securing the freedom of speech and of the press."[66] Seeking to narrow the investigation, Thomas Gholson, another Virginia Republican and a friend of Randolph, proposed to insert the adjective "criminal" before the word "prosecutions" in the resolution, precipitating a lengthy debate. Randolph observed that, at least in Virginia, federal marshals chose grand juries in federal cases: as a presidential appointee, a marshal could not be considered impartial. Randolph histrionically desired to extend the debate to include safeguards for the Bill of Rights. He presented a resolution stating, "That provision ought to be made by law to secure the right of an impartial jury, in all cases, civil and criminal, maintained in the courts of the United States."[67]

Perhaps in dealing with the former president they intended to apply Virginia's constitution of 1776, which stipulated regarding the state's executive, "The Governor, when he is out of office, and others, offending against the State, shall be impeachable by the House of Delegates." The governor would be prosecuted by the state attorney general, and tried by the Judges of the General Court. If found guilty, he would be permanently barred from officeholding. If he held any public office at the time, he would be removed "pro tempore, or subjected to such pains or penalties as the laws shall direct."[68]

Randolph continued to dominate the debate. He was the undisputed leader of the strictly orthodox, states' rights, anti–Northern "Old Republican" party of Virginia and points south. The Federalists could not help but be amused as he did the dirty work of disrupting the Jeffersonian Republican Party. Joining Randolph in indicting Republicans, Connecticut High Federalist Timothy Pitkin pointed out that district judge Edwards, a Jefferson appointee, was the "sole acting judge in the court" during the prosecution of the Connecticut Six (as I shall humorously call them). He noted that Edwards delivered an inflammatory rant against seditious enemies of the government in his charge to the first New Haven grand jury, inciting them to choose to make a "presentment" (indictment).[69] (Pitkin did not mention that a few weeks later, Edwards said that he would accept truth as a defense in these cases, and that he eventually dismissed them.)

One Connecticut Federalist, Congressman Benjamin Tallmadge, stigmatized the Jeffersonians as hypocrites. They should have taken action to thwart the libel prosecutions much sooner, so that the defendants would not have had to endure the anxiety and expense of a court case. He pointed out that in Congress as early as January 1807 Dana had mentioned that Federalists were under indictment at common law for sedition in Connecticut. Tallmadge touted himself as protector of freedom of the press, an unusual identity for a New England Federalist to assume. He "took occasion to quote the journals [of Congress], to show that several mentions on the subject of those prosecutions had been made in the House in January, 1807; and he observed, that after them, how any gentlemen in public life could to this day have remained ignorant of the fact, was to him astonishing." Sounding a falsely conciliatory note, he said, apparently with some sarcasm, that he was "highly pleased that this subject was at length taken up, and hoped that no delay would obstruct an inquiry or prevent the passage of a law for the protection of the citizen in future."[70]

As a result of all the agitation in the House, the Speaker, veteran Massachusetts Republican Joseph B. Varnum, appointed a committee consisting of Randolph, James Holland, Samuel W. Dana, Benjamin Howard, and Uri (not Uriah) Tracy to investigate the Connecticut libel cases. James Holland was a venerable North Carolina Republican farmer who had served in Congress for over a decade, Uri Tracy came from Chenango County, New York, and Benjamin Howard represented Kentucky. Except for Dana, all the committee members were Jeffersonians. Finding Randolph increasingly irritating, especially in his opposition to military preparations after 1810, the committee ignored his agitation. It never reported, burying the embarrassing incident in oblivion.[71]

Jefferson was hardly pleased by the failure of members of his own party to let sleeping dogs (and ex-presidents) lie. Writing to his friend Wilson Cary Nicholas, congressman from Jefferson's Albemarle County, in June 1809, Jefferson self-righteously insisted that he had not instigated the prosecution of the Connecticut Federalist libelers.[72] According to him, his ex-friend Randolph was up to no good, as usual. Randolph and his claque in Congress made speeches that strongly implied Jefferson's complicity in the indictments, so "as to leave on every mind the impression that they [the Connecticut common law prosecutions for libel] had been instituted either by my direction, or with my acquiescence, at least." He wanted to assure Nicholas that his allies had been slow to deny the charges against him because they did not know the facts. "I shall state it for their satisfaction," he asserted, "and leave it to be disposed of as they think best." Other than having seen in the newspapers "dark hints" and "obscure" reports of Republicans prosecuting their enemies in Connecticut, he was ignorant of what was happening, and "paid little attention to it." When much later, he discovered that the federal court had indicted a "clergyman ... for calumnies uttered from the pulpit against me" (probably alluding to Backus), he claimed to have immediately taken up the matter with Connecticut resident Gideon Granger, his postmaster general. "I immediately wrote to mr Granger, who I think, was in Connecticut at the time, stating that I had laid it down as a law to myself to take no notice of the thousand calumnies issued against me," he insisted, "but to trust my character to my own conduct & the good sense & candor of my fellow citizens; that I had found no reason to be dissatisfied with that course, & I was unwilling it should be broke through by others as to any matter concerning me." Consequently, he had instructed Granger to tell the district attorney to "dismiss the prosecution." Unfortunately, something went wrong, because he soon heard that subpoenas were being issued by the Federalist agitators' defense attorneys for Jefferson's old foes Henry Lee, Richmond marshal David Meade Randolph, and others who knew about the Walker Affair to testify at the impending trial.[73]

Making no effort to disguise his alarm from a friend who knew all about the Walker Affair, Jefferson continued, "I then conjectured for the first time the subject of the libel. I immediately wrote to mr Granger to require an immediate dismission of the prosecution." (A strange proceeding, since Granger was not a legal or judicial official.) Ostensibly, Jefferson initially assumed that the prosecution issued the subpoenas. He soon learned (how is not clear) that District Attorney, "mr Huntington," was not responsible, but that the defendant had sent out the subpoenas "without his knoledge [sic]." Like a good Republican, Huntington reportedly told Granger (or wrote Jefferson) that he intended all along to "dismiss all the prosecutions at the first meeting of the court & to accompany it with an avowal of his opinion that they could not be maintained because the federal court had no jurisdiction over libels." Professing ignorance that there were five other defendants in addition to Backus, Jefferson was glad when he discovered that all the prosecutions were dismissed at the same time. His conscience apparently clear, he further verified his innocence by telling Nicholas that Granger soon showed him a "letter written by the Clergyman," apparently Backus, in which the Federalist preacher assured everyone that he had "no personal ill will" toward Jefferson and that the reports that he had vilified him in a sermon were false. Jefferson claimed that Granger "either shewed me, or said there were affidavits of at least half a dozen respectable men" at the sermon who said Backus had not denounced him, while as many other "respectable men" swore the opposite. Seemingly not considering the incident very important, Jefferson confessed that his memory was blurry, but he advised Nicholas that Granger "can confirm every thing substantial" about his testimony. He was on rather shaky ground, since the affair had occurred less than two years earlier.[74]

Eager to reestablish his image as the unwavering defender of freedom of the press and newspapers' immunity from harassment by the national government under the First Amendment, Jefferson declared, "Certain it is that the prosecutions had been instituted & had made considerable progress without my knolege [sic], that they were disapproved by me as soon as known, and directed to be discontinued." Confusing the Federalists' Sedition Act, a positive law restricting freedom of the press, with his party's recourse to common law in Connecticut, Jefferson weakly continued, "The [district] attorney did it [stopped the prosecutions] on the same ground on which I had acted myself [as president] in the cases of Duane, Callender & others, to wit that the sedition law was unconstitutional and null, & that my obligation to execute what was law, involved that of not suffering rights secured by valid laws [the Bill of Rights], to be prostrated by what was no law."[75]

Unconvincingly, Jefferson blamed Edwards for the prosecutions. Revealing familiarity with the case's details despite gaps in his memory, he wrote, "I always understood that these prosecutions had been invited, if not instituted, by judge Edwards, & the Marshal, being republican, had summoned a grand jury partly, or wholly republican; but that mr Huntington declared from the beginning against the jurisdiction of the court & had determined to enter Nolle prosequis before he received my directions to do it."[76] These statements seem inaccurate or false, as Huntington was ostensibly more determined than Edwards to continue the indictments.

Thus, Jefferson sought to depict Connecticut Republicans, as well as himself, as devout followers of the extreme version of the Jeffersonian doctrine, complete freedom of the press from interference by the central government. Indicating that he was not dismayed by the stigma the incident might leave on his unblemished record as champion of freedom of the press, Jefferson turned to a personal gripe: Congress's neglect to provide him with freedom from postage for the letters he mailed (called the franking privilege), which all ex-presidents were entitled to receive.[77]

Seeking to be of assistance to his friend and in-law Jefferson, Nicholas went to work in Washington. He buttonholed Granger about the matter, and found that he had not thought Jefferson as innocent as he claimed to be. According to Nicholas, Granger observed that "it was believed by some of those who had some agency in directing them [the prosecutions], that altho' you did not direct the commencement of them, you had no objection to their being carried on." Eventually Nicholas convinced Granger to write an anonymous article in the newspapers exonerating Jefferson in the matter, thereby defanging Randolph and some of Jefferson's other Republican adversaries.[78]

· · · · ·

To Jefferson's renewed chagrin, after he had been retired for five years, Granger reminded him of this embarrassing incident of his presidency. Granger claimed that because he had followed Jefferson's secret instructions and directed the termination of the Connecticut lawsuits, many Republicans in the state viewed him (Granger) as a pro–Federalist pariah. Others called him a "Burrite" and said that he had been on close terms with Burr during his western conspiracy. Treating Jefferson disdainfully, Granger demanded that he compose a letter exonerating him from these accusations, thereby enabling him to resume his political career. He implied that otherwise he would publicly denounce Jefferson and charge that the ex-president had acted like a lowly political operator, disregarding the protection of free speech when he had the opportunity to punish his enemies in Connecticut. Jefferson indignantly replied that he had directed Granger to have the *nolle prosequis* instituted on the basis of principle: devotion to freedom of the press and his belief that the federal government could not institute criminal libel suits. Because they violated Republican principles and consisted only of charges against him, and he always made it a rule to ignore calumny against himself, he immediately advised Granger and Edwards to dismiss the indictments.[79] His private letter to Madison at the time indicated that this may not have been the case.

Although Jefferson reproached Granger for the threatening tone of his letter, he wrote him a note attesting to his Democratic-Republican respectability, which Granger never made public. After this, the two Republican Party leaders never contacted each other.[80] Seeming more concerned that Granger would accuse Dolly Madison of premarital debauchery than that he would revive interest in his youthful escapades, Jefferson wrote, "You may give pain perhaps where you wish it; but be assured it will react on yourself with double tho' delayed effect; and that it will be one of those incidents of your life on which you will never reflect with satisfaction." Coining a phrase, he concluded, "Remember that we often repent of what we have said, but never of that which we have not."[81]

Perhaps Jefferson's memory was failing. He admitted to Madison that Granger's "appeals to my very defective memory" about Granger's role in thwarting Burr's western conspiracy in 1806 "are very painful." Granger and Madison had become political enemies. Granger supported the radical Duane-Leib faction in Pennsylvania against the mainstream McKean group, and it was rumored that in 1812 he had favored DeWitt Clinton rather than Madison for president.

In Jefferson's case, however, the Postmaster General had been "ever friendly and faithful, and I on several occasions used his services to the advantage of the public." Jefferson believed that he had succeeded in convincing Granger not to publish documents insulting to Madison or himself, even concerning rumors of Dolly Madison's premarital promiscuity.[82]

• • • • •

As Seymour's December 1806 letter to Jefferson hinted, Edwards' and Huntington's common law prosecutions in Connecticut may have temporarily weakened the state's Federalists. During the spring of 1806, Republicans briefly controlled the lower house of the legislature.[83] In August 1806, a Federalist circular warned that in Connecticut, "The effects of the thorough organization of the State by the Democratic party, were proved last spring, by the addition of more than twelve hundred votes for their candidate for Governor."[84]

Unsurprisingly, the Republican position in Connecticut greatly deteriorated during the years of the Embargo and the War of 1812. Connecticut's voting regulations were designed to keep members of the Standing Order in power. The list of candidates for the upper house of the state legislature (council of assistants) traditionally placed current and former assistants at the top of the ballot, thereby encouraging voters to reelect them, perpetuating the Federalist oligarchy. In 1801, to tighten Federalist control, the state assembly adopted the "Stand-Up Law," by which nominations of assistants at the town meeting had to be done by the voters' standing up or a show of hands. This procedure increased the likelihood that most voters, intimidated by the Federalist patriarchy and the Congregationalist Establishment, would fear to show sufficient independence and integrity to nominate a member of the detested Republican Party for the Council. This procedure enabled the Federalists to retain control of the legislature.[85]

The Federalist governor and assembly refused to allow the Connecticut militia to serve outside the state during the War of 1812. British troops invaded Connecticut twice in 1814, and British ships bombarded the town of Stonington. They burned the ships at Pettipang Point in the town of Essex when the citizens resisted British incursions and prevented their landing. The heroic defenders thereby earned the praise of Jeffersonian editor Philip Freneau, who composed a poem about them. Despite this outburst of patriotism, in December 1814 Connecticut sent a delegation to the Hartford Convention. Protesting the acts of the Madison Administration, the Convention urged amendments to the Constitution to reduce the political power of immigrants and the Southern and Western states and limit Congressional control of commerce. It hinted that the New England states would consider leaving the Union if their demands were not met.[86]

After the Battle of New Orleans and the Treaty of Ghent ended the war on a relatively successful note for the United States and its Democratic-Republican leadership, the New England Federalists suffered a humiliation from which they never completely recovered. In 1817, Connecticut's Congregationalist religious establishment was weakened when the state's Episcopalians turned against it because the government failed to supply them with expected funding. Thereafter, Episcopalians joined Methodists and Baptists in overthrowing the Federalists. In the 1817 state elections, their coalition defeated the Federalists for control of both the governorship and the lower house of the General Assembly. In October 1817, the Republicans succeeded in repealing the Stand-Up Law. In 1818, seizing their opportunity, the Republicans successfully called for a constitutional convention to repeal the colonial charter of

1662, the state's frame of government for over 150 years. The constitution of 1818, ratified by the voters, disestablished the Congregational Church. It provided for the separation of church and state and the equality before the law of all Christian denominations, although Jews were not permitted public worship until 1843.[87]

Although an improvement over the ancient charter, the Constitution of 1818 was not outstandingly liberal. It increased the suffrage, gave the governor more power, created a more independent judiciary, and continued the traditional annual elections and legislative sessions. However, like Virginia's constitution and others, it unfairly apportioned the legislature, giving the eastern districts hegemony over the interior. It allowed each existing town two delegates to the House of Representatives (lower house of the legislature), while new towns established after the Constitution of 1818 went into effect would be permitted only one delegate each.[88]

In Connecticut, seeing the political handwriting on the wall, Federalist leaders converted to Democratic-Republicanism to revive their political careers. The state's voters witnessed the spectacle of Oliver Wolcott, Jr., one of the foremost Hamiltonian Federalists, running for governor in 1818 on the Democratic-Republican (often called Democratic) ticket. He was succeeded by Gideon Tomlinson, a conservative Jeffersonian. The Democrat-controlled General Assembly did not adopt these men's recommendations for a more activist state government. It rejected their proposals for more state aid to agriculture and industry, new taxes to build roads and canals, improved Connecticut River navigation, prison reform, and tax increases to support public education. Implementing a Jeffersonian tendency toward economic egalitarianism, the Democratic legislature imposed a more equitable tax structure, taxing the wealthy more heavily and including stocks and bonds as taxable assets.[89]

Even after the Hartford Convention's failure, New England Federalists remained hostile to the lower classes. They believed their Jeffersonian opponents fawningly courted them. Massachusetts and Connecticut Federalists ascribed their political defeats to Republican pandering to base self-interest and the lowest elements of human nature, while Federalists upheld classical republican "virtue." Diehard Federalists mocked Jeffersonians' use of ex-Federalists like Wolcott as their gubernatorial candidate and Republican attempts to recruit other Federalists. Priding themselves on their disinterested probity, they imputed demagogic ambitions to the Republicans.[90]

· · · · ·

Unfortunately, the Connecticut common law prosecutions fiasco may have had the long-term effect of embittering state residents against Democratic-Republicanism. On the surface, the legal incidents made it appear that Jefferson and his followers had contempt for Connecticut's leading public figures, such as Governor Treadwell and Judge Tapping Reeve, its most venerable newspapers, and its hallowed Congregationalist Church. In concluding his *Letter* to Jefferson, "Hampden," sensing the partisan advantage Federalists might reap from the trials, stressed that the president had permitted his minions, federal marshals, attorneys, and jurors to persecute "the most respectable citizens of Connecticut." He took especial note of the manner in which Marshal Phelps manhandled the Reverend Backus, treating him "as a felon," displaying him on "the public road to Hartford, as the object of the scorn and derision of an infamous rabble." Alluding to Alexander Wolcott's alleged Robespierre-like political role in the proceedings, "Hampden" depicted Backus as being indicted like a criminal "under the direction of a bloody minded State Manager." Likewise, the indictments of Treadwell and Reeve, "a highly respected Judge of our Superior Court," evinced Jefferson's "political intolerance."[91]

Plainly, in prosecuting Backus, "Hampden" emphasized, Jefferson's motivation was "a malignant spirit of revenge, the constant inmate of little and depraved hearts." Happily, Backus's "superior talents," "piety" and "eloquence ... frustrated the diabolical schemes of a few unprincipled Jacobins of his neighborhood," and he retained the support of the "friends of [George] Washington." Intent on reviving the memory of the first president, despite his being a Virginia slaveholder like Jefferson, "Hampden" claimed that Republicans targeted Lieutenant Governor Treadwell and Judge Reeve for "destruction," because they were "unshaken supporters of Washington, and strong pillars in our political fabric."[92]

Ignoring Jeffersonian efforts to court Connecticut Federalists by ending the prosecutions, "Hampden" mocked Jefferson's failure to gain a conviction in any of the eleven cases against magistrates, clergyman and printers, which were all abandoned or lost by the "public prosecutor." "Hampden" lacked sympathy for lawsuits he viewed as the result of both the district attorney's ignorance and "the malice of Connecticut Jacobinism." He concluded that Jefferson revealed his naivety in appointing as district attorney the most stupid, obstinate and "unskillful" lawyer and the most "unsuitable person for the office" possible. For Jefferson, the only qualification Huntington needed, "Hampden" asserted, was "his democracy." Ignoring Jefferson's more recent and aggressive Second Inaugural Address, he charged that Jefferson's actions in Connecticut belied the promises of his First Inaugural Address to cooperate with his opponents. He had failed to respect the minority's "equal rights." Instead of welcoming them with "harmony and affection," he had displayed the "political intolerance" that he vowed to abolish.[93] More precisely, Jefferson's Inaugural had guaranteed to protect freedom of the press, trial by juries impartially selected, and the right of habeas corpus. The manner in which the Connecticut prosecutions were conducted encroached on all of these, according to "Hampden," revealing that Jefferson's words were insincere posturing.[94]

Perhaps aware of Seymour's correspondence with Jefferson or of Dana's brief mention of the Connecticut cases in Congress, "Hampden" charged that Jefferson had not squelched the proceedings even though he knew about them as early as the winter of 1806–1807. In contrast to Jefferson's eagerness to reimburse Callender's fine under the Sedition Act, "Hampden" pointed out, the president had been remiss in shielding the Federalists "from the fangs of persecution." Allowing the indictments to continue instead of withdrawing them, Jefferson flouted the conciliatory overtures of his First Inaugural.[95]

"Hampden" adroitly claimed that Jefferson, abandoning his small-scale "reign of terror," personally ordered the libel cases discontinued because they would have revived public interest in his unsuccessful attempt, as a young man in his twenties, to seduce his friend John Walker's wife Elizabeth. Since John and Elizabeth were both Federalists, it was rumored that they were willing to endure the "shame" of recounting Jefferson's disgraceful conduct. "Hampden" observed that the defense attorneys had subpoenaed both "Colonel" Walker and Secretary of State James Madison (who did not know Jefferson when these incidents occurred) to testify. (Madison had acted as the mediator between Jefferson and Walker a few years earlier, after Callender revived talk about the Walker Affair in the *Richmond Recorder* and it was rumored that Walker would challenge President Jefferson to a duel.) "Hampden" bluntly charged that Jefferson failed to prosecute the case against the Reverend Backus because he did not want the Walker scandal revived in the public eye. Much of "Hampden's" concluding statement referred to Jefferson's First Inaugural. He mocked the Republicans as "democrats," demagogues who, with Jefferson's collusion, hypocritically violated his First Inaugural Address's promises of harmony and conciliation between the parties. Directly addressing Jefferson, "Hampden" denounced the various abortive prosecutions conducted by the federal district attorney from 1806 to 1808 as evidence of Jefferson's vindictiveness and waste of taxpayers' money: "Thus, you perceive, that eleven prosecutions have been instituted by your officers in Connecticut against our Magistrates, Clergymen and Printers, all of which, one excepted [that of Hudson and Goodwin], have been defeated, or voluntarily abandoned by the public prosecutor."[96]

Quoting at length from Jefferson's First Inaugural, "Hampden" pointed out that Jefferson's failure to immediately cancel the prosecutions showed the insincerity of his claim that "we are all republicans, we are all federalists." "If your own solemn declarations, made in the face of the nation, had the least influence on your practice, you would have exhibited the magnanimity of an elevated understanding, and ordered them [the prosecutions] to be withdrawn," Hampden charged, "instead of the weakness of a pigmy mind, in endeavoring to prevent the proofs from Virginia [that is, the witnesses to his indiscretions] being laid before the Court and Jury."[97] He re-emphasized that the whole process, which ended when the intimidated President belatedly ordered the prosecutions discontinued, wasted taxpayers' money to the tune of $10,000, "a sum greater than the whole amount of the salaries for a year of the Judges of our Superior Court."[98]

Pleased to ridicule Jefferson's administration, "Hampden" reiterated that Tapping Reeve had never been formally arrested in 1806, because the offense alleged in the indictment occurred over two years earlier and was not eligible for prosecution under U.S. law. Pointing to this and other technical and typographical errors made by District Attorney Huntington at the beginning of the prosecutions, "Hampden" assumed that Jefferson's attorney general was at fault: "This *trifling* circumstance was probably overlooked by the learned Attorney-General, and by Capt. Vanduerson, the foreman of the jury."[99]

In fact, there was no active attorney general in Jefferson's Cabinet in 1806, when Huntington initiated the prosecutions. Levi Lincoln had recently resigned. His replacement, John Breckinridge, former U.S. senator from Kentucky, fell ill at his plantation in June 1806, and was unable to return to Washington. He died on December 14, 1806, probably from tuberculosis. Thomas Seymour did not write Jefferson to inform him of what was happening at New Haven and Hartford until his letter of December 20, 1806, four days after Breckinridge died. It is evident that Breckinridge, the first Cabinet member from west of the Allegheny Mountains, never knew about the case. He was in Kentucky, dying. Although "Hampden" ridiculed Jefferson's attorney general's ignorance of the law, Breckinridge could hardly be held accountable.[100]

Not only did "Hampden" seek to humiliate Jefferson, he wanted to make the upsurge in favor of the common man that Jefferson's movement represented appear vulgar, ridiculous, and even criminal. He wrote of the witnesses that federal marshal Frederick Phelps recruited to testify against Backus, and those allegedly called on to testify to *their* good characters: "With all fidelity to the United States, he brought forward from the grog-shops and taverns, all that could avail on such a trial."[101] Like most Federalists, "Hampden" defended the legality of the Sedition Act, a "positive law" passed by Congress. On the other hand, he viewed the common law prosecutions begun in Connecticut as illegal because, after all, the Sedition Act which would have permitted them expired many years before. "Thus terminated the prosecutions for sedition at common law," he reminded the president in a mock-melodramatic tone. "You will constantly bear in mind that the sedition act (so called) had expired."[102]

In fighting back against Jefferson's alleged political persecutions, "Hampden" said, Connecticut's Federalists upheld the virtues of orderly middle-class republicanism against anarchical, rabble-driven Jeffersonian "democracy." With the help of such "democrats," the Jeffersonians, with their "always mischievous, but often inefficient" tactics sought, among other things, "to ruin printers, old and respectable ... who had fearlessly made a noble stand against the desolations of democracy." Along with other policies of his "administration," Jefferson's support for these "proceedings" revealed "an open and palpable design to insult the State of Connecticut." Connecticut had nobly participated in the Revolutionary War to "achieve the independence of this nation," and "always co-operated with the Union in all wise and just measures." It was undoubtedly a "State in which the *genuine* rights of man are amply secured, and where every man sits under his own vine and fig-tree." By defying Jefferson's legal officials, Connecticut's citizens had, with "immortal honor," "successfully resisted, a reign of terror; and persecutions, wicked and despotic."[103]

· · · · ·

For his part, while acknowledging the Federalists' continued power in New England and the rift between Connecticut and the rest of the country, which supported Democratic-Republicans, Jefferson emphasized New England's importance to republican political culture. He consistently stressed that a happy and Republican Massachusetts and Connecticut were vital to the success of the American experiment. He hoped their citizens would soon emerge from the pro-monarchical, pro–Federalist "delusions" imposed on them by their clergy and their ultra-Federalist politicians.

He felt no remorse for the Connecticut circuit court's actions in commencing common law indictments of his Federalist enemies, which, perhaps to his secret regret, he soon called off. In 1810, after he had settled into retirement, he wrote Granger, gently complaining about the mail service in the neighborhood of Monticello while praising his diligence and "valuable services" as postmaster general. Almost as an afterthought, alluding to Granger's "Veritas" articles a year earlier, he concluded, "I must add my acknolegements [*sic*] for your friendly interference in setting the public judgment to rights with respect to the Connecticut prosecutions, so falsely & maliciously charged on me. I refer to a statement of the facts in the *National Intelligencer* of many months past, which I was sensible came from your hand."[104] Jefferson expressed no alarm that members of his party, whether with or without his instructions, had begun prosecutions that if completed would have violated his nearly-sacred principle that the First Amendment prohibited the federal government from conducting common law sedition trials.

Although in theory Jefferson was a "states' rights" president, in reality, as Henry Adams and numerous others have pointed out, his actions told a different story. Had he been an authentic "states' righter," he would not have authorized the Louisiana Purchase, conducted secret negotiations for Florida, or proposed the ill-fated, albeit brief Embargo. As he explained after he retired from the presidency, there were times when necessity forced even the head of a democratic republic to wield undelegated powers. "A strict observance of the written laws is doubtless *one* of the highest duties of a good citizen, but it is not *the highest*," he said. "The laws of necessity, of self-preservation, of saving our country when in danger, are of higher obligation."[105]

In implementing this aggressive philosophy (in some ways a precursor of what Arthur M. Schlesinger, Jr., later called the "Imperial Presidency") with the least possible damage to the rights of his fellow citizens, Jefferson revealed that he was not merely an opportunistic politician, but a statesman. Rather than an instance where Jefferson wielded his power to crush peaceful if obnoxious opposition to his politics and personality, the fruitless Connecticut prosecutions comprise an *opéra bouffe* that, with amply ludicrous overtones, confirmed his lifetime devotion to unlimited freedom of the press.

10

Jefferson and James Sullivan, Shooting Star of Massachusetts' Political Firmament

After his 1804 reelection victory, which, employing military phraseology Jefferson termed a "winter campaign," he received numerous letters of congratulation. One lengthy and rambling letter from Congregationalist minister Thomas Allen of Pittsfield depicted his arrival on the American political scene as an intervention of Divine Providence. Allen was not only a radical Jeffersonian of Congregationalist denomination, a rare bird in those days. He was also a Revolutionary War hero, having distinguished himself at the Battle of Bennington in 1777. Allen depicted his and Jefferson's most extreme Federalist opponents as demonic Monarchists, in terms more bitter than even Jefferson himself used. Relieved that Jefferson had defeated "malevolent" Federalists, exemplars of the "human Depravity" of "expiring Royalty," Allen fulsomely continued, "Your name has been cast out and trodden under foot of Federalists. But you have been superior to their Calumnies and Machenations [sic], their reproaches have brightened your Character, and afforded room for the Exercise of the noblest Virtues that adorn human Nations [sic?]."[1]

Replying graciously to the Republican clergyman, Jefferson indicated that he had been severely injured by the most recent Federalist calumnies. These had occurred in the Massachusetts legislature. Turning the tables on Republican demands that the assembly fire the state printer, a Federalist publisher who recently libeled Jefferson by mentioning his sexual affairs, Federalists in the state assembly revived Callender's charges of Jefferson's sexual relationship with Sally Hemings.[2] At first taking a high-minded attitude, Jefferson, thanking Allen for his "friendly dispositions," asserted, "The last thirty years are probably more pregnant of instruction to mankind than any equal period which history furnishes." The U.S. had taught the world lessons "most pleasing to the friends of man. For those who live under it certainly no government can be more eligible." For himself, however, though he admitted he was largely responsible for the people's happiness, the insults he endured during his presidency imposed "a fiery ordeal." To endure it, he said, required "all the devotion of patriotism which inspired a Decius. His sacrifice was life. With us character must be offered on the altar of public good."[3]

While lamenting the disrespect shown him by Federalist militants, Jefferson emphasized that he did not consider these tormentors representative of the people of Massachusetts, who were good-natured and on the verge of turning Republicans. "A few malicious men, availing themselves of the licentiousness of the press, are able to test by the severest trials the firmness of a public man," he concluded. However, he believed that his noble "experiment" in unshackling the press had succeeded: "The justice which our citizens have shown themselves capable of exercising and their discernment between facts & falsehood will hold up an encouragement to future functionaries, which our late experiment warrants." In other words, Jefferson's electoral victory signified that, despite Federalist newspapers' rage, his "experiment" in freedom of the press was justified. Exposing his self-pity, he benignly observed, "After so much misrepresentation, to see my countrymen coming over daily to a sense of the injustice of a certain party towards me, is particularly gratifying & will sweeten the latest hours of retirement & life."[4] News that James Sullivan, Republican candidate for governor of Massachusetts, had racked up an impressive number of votes despite losing the election, increased Jefferson's exhilaration at his party's popularity and his expectation that all New England would soon become Republican.

A native of Maine, James Sullivan (1744–1808) was one of the most intellectually complex and politically significant Democratic-Republican leaders. He deserves more attention from historians than he has received. Brother of the Indian-hating General John Sullivan, who taught him the practice of law, James Sullivan, unlike most successful politicians during that deferential era, was essentially self-educated. He never attended college. He was a brilliant, erudite and successful lawyer in Maine, and later in Boston, where he moved in 1783. Not averse to engaging in risky businesses, he invested in the Yazoo lands in Georgia and in various manufacturing and canal companies. At the same time, he denounced big financiers who speculated in the public debt, perhaps envying their inordinate wealth. He implied as much in his book, *The Path to Riches* (1992), where he argued that political parties arose because of the resentment the less-rich felt for the rich. During the Revolution, Sullivan held numerous government posts, among them serving in the state assembly and as judge in Massachusetts' Supreme Court and admiralty court. He was also a member of the governors' council, which was chosen by the legislature. Sullivan ardently supported American independence, though because of lameness (and possibly epilepsy) he was unable to serve in the military. He was a delegate to the Massachusetts constitutional convention of 1780, and supported the U.S. Constitution. Disappointed that he was not elected to the state ratifying convention, he briefly joined up with the state's politically prominent Antifederalists, John Hancock and Samuel Adams. A major contributor to the state's cultural life, Sullivan was among the founders of the American Academy of Arts and Sciences in 1780 and the Massachusetts Historical Society in 1791.

Despite Sullivan's general conservatism, he opposed excessive concentrations of wealth and believed that big corporations and banks controlled by a small minority should be terminated by state governments for the public good. In Massachusetts he favored replacing private banks with a state bank. A measure popular with middling merchants, it finally became law in 1812, after his death. Sullivan was probably the most popular Democratic-Republican candidate in Massachusetts. He ran for governor as early as 1797, and in 1804 was narrowly defeated by the popular incumbent, Caleb Strong. He made a better showing than any Republican before him, winning his home district of Maine. He created a statewide party organization, and lost again in 1806 by an even smaller margin.[5]

Finally defeating Strong, Sullivan won the governorship in April 1807. His cultivation of a party organization had borne fruit. Out of 81,500 votes cast, the greatest number in Massachusetts history, he won by a total of 42,000 to 39,000 for the incumbent. In addition,

Massachusetts for the first time elected a Republican legislature. Of the New England states, Connecticut alone remained Federalist. This was at a time when Jefferson's party was at its zenith. The 10th Congress was controlled by Republicans, and even most of the New England members supported Jefferson. The lukewarm New Hampshire Federalist senator William Plumer, who despite his support for secession in 1804 would soon become a Jeffersonian, was succeeded by a Republican. John Quincy Adams abandoned even nominal Federalist loyalty. He favored resistance to British insults, and charged his Federalist opponents with disloyalty and secessionist sympathies. Meanwhile, the staunch Connecticut Federalist Uriah Tracy had died, and there were no Federalists of equal caliber in the state to replace him. Nonetheless, a few diehard Federalists from the 1790s remained in Congress. Though there were only five Federalist senators, among them were the extremist anti-populist, anti–Southern Timothy Pickering of Massachusetts and James Hillhouse of Connecticut, along with the less fanatical, albeit mediocre Chauncey Goodrich of Connecticut and James A. Bayard and Samuel White, senators from Delaware.[6]

Jefferson's relationship with Sullivan, a conservative Republican whose attitudes probably had more in common with the Federalists than with Jefferson, was somewhat rocky. Perhaps appositely, his son, William, became a leading Federalist politician, although he was less strongly devoted to the Union than his father, going so far as to support the Hartford Convention in 1814. As a self-made businessman and lawyer who served as Massachusetts' attorney general (an officeholder chosen by the governor and his council, not by popular vote) from 1790 to 1806 under both Federalist and Republican governors, James Sullivan generally took a middle-of-the road position. Although he opposed the Jay Treaty of 1794, he won the admiration of Federalists for trying to disperse a Boston riot against the Treaty in 1795. Historian Ronald Formisano considers him representative of the "Revolutionary Center," a politician capable of attracting both Federalists and Jeffersonians. Paul Goodman, another expert on Massachusetts politics during the Jeffersonian period agreed, writing of Sullivan's long tenure as attorney general: "Socially respectable, he was considered a restraining influence by Federalists, who did not discharge him when they assumed power." An adherent of the Congregationalist Church, although as an attorney he defended Baptist dissenters in Maine, he was not overzealous about expanding religious freedom in Massachusetts. In Formisano's words, he was an "eighteenth-century moderate" with a "studied ambiguity on the question of religious taxes." Sullivan hoped that both Federalists and Republicans would unite under conservative leadership, preferably his own. To that extent, he favored nonpartisanship. His entire political career centered on Massachusetts. Except for brief service in the Continental Congress in 1782–1783 and in 1796 in connection with settling a boundary dispute between Massachusetts (Maine) and Canada, he never held national office. Sadly, he died shortly after he reached the apogee of his political success and fame as governor of Massachusetts.[7]

Sullivan may have become doubtful of the president's support as early as 1805, when Jefferson did not offer him a government job when he asked for one. Despite being the perennial Republican candidate for governor of the state and its foremost party organizer, Sullivan heard rumors that Jefferson opposed his candidacy in 1804, even as Republican prospects in Massachusetts brightened and Sullivan made a better showing than any previous Republican gubernatorial candidate. He amassed twenty-four thousand votes against thirty thousand for his opponent, the popular Caleb Strong. Impressed by the "result of the contest in your state," Jefferson, recurring to his tendency toward anticlerical witticisms, advised him to accept "the federal unction of lying & slandering" in good grace. Violent Federalist abuse had become *de rigueur* for Republican candidates. "Who has not" been subjected to it? Jefferson observed. "Who will ever again come into eminent office unannointed [*sic*] with this chrism?"[8]

Sullivan was especially alarmed by rumors ostensibly spread by Republicans that Jefferson disliked him. Jefferson attempted to convince Sullivan that the rumors were false. Exhilarated by news that Sullivan's numbers had been impressive, Jefferson wrote him that he expected him eventually to win the governorship and Massachusetts to join the Republican fold. Anticipating that this bedrock of the republic would soon unite with the rest of the country as a Jeffersonian community, Jefferson predicted that Sullivan's strong showing made it a "certain prospect ... that another year restores Massachusetts to the general body of the nation." Sullivan was dismayed by Federalist attacks on his "moral character," among them charges that he was a dishonest lawyer. The Federalists and his personal enemies also claimed that he had written the constitution for Boston's Democratic-Republican Society in 1793 and was an early member, but then publicly withdrew from it in 1794 when it became unpopular. The Federalists also accused him of taking bribes as attorney general, defrauding his creditors, and attempting to cheat the land speculators Phelps and Gorham of money he owed them for land in upstate New York.[9]

The president consoled him.[10] He emphasized the amorality of Federalist propaganda, and advised Sullivan to accustom himself to it. Otherwise, Federalist pamphleteers would gloat over their success in driving a formidable Republican adversary from politics. As Sullivan was well aware, for Massachusetts Federalists "falsehood & calumny" had become the "ordinary engines of opposition." In many cases, they had succeeded in discouraging potential Republican candidates from risking abuse and humiliation in pursuit of public office. Implying that he did not consider public opinion infallible, Jefferson pointed out, "The circle of characters equal to the first stations is not too large, & will be lessened by the voluntary retreat of those whose sensibilities are stronger than their confidence in the justice of public opinion." Some of the most upright and "exalted" statesmen demurred at holding office, out of disgust with "the brutal beatings & hewings of these heroes of Billingsgate," he confided to Sullivan. However, rather than citing leading Republicans who abstained from politics in retreat from Federalist calumny, Jefferson recalled his "intimate knoledge" [*sic*] of the "greatest character of our country," the deceased ex-president, George Washington, whose abnormal sensitivity to newspaper vituperation (his rage at Republican criticism) he had personally witnessed. As far as Jefferson was concerned, Washington's reaction was that of a crybaby, since he was not subjected to nearly as much press vilification as Jefferson endured: "Had he been assailed with the degree of abandoned licentiousness now practised [*sic*]," Jefferson assured Sullivan, Washington would have resigned the presidency in anger. "The torture he felt under rare & slight attacks proved that under those of which the federal bands have shewn themselves capable he would have thrown up the helm in a burst of indignation." Implying that Sullivan, like Jefferson, could be a better, more virtuous and *masculine* man than even the great Washington, he said they should shrug off Federalist vituperation. "This effect of sensibility must not be yielded to," he warned; or the Republican cause in New England would be defeated. "If we suffer ourselves to be frightened from our post by mere lying, surely the enemy will use that weapon: for what one so cheap to those of whose system of politics morality makes no part?" After exaggeratedly depicting the Federalists as the epitome of evil, Jefferson drew analogies between the news-paper abuse endured by Democratic-Republican "patriots" and the persecution of the early Christians under the Roman Empire in the era of Jesus and the Apostles: "The patriot, like the Christian, must learn that to bear revilings & persecutions is a part of his duty: and in proportion as the trial is severe, firmness under it becomes more requisite & praiseworthy."[11] Thus, Jefferson, reiterating Revolutionary-era concepts, combined ideas of Christian and masculine republican virtue. Asserting that the Democratic-Republican leader must possess both, he assured Sullivan that he was a paragon who could meet the Federalist challenge in his state. If Sullivan did not waver under Federalist abuse, he would inevitably become governor, Jefferson was sure.

In pursuit of that objective, the president assured Sullivan that the rumors Federalists had planted, "insinuations of any want of confidence in you from the administration generally, or myself particularly," had no factual basis, and would, "like their other falsehoods, produce in the public mind a contrary inference." Despite assuring Sullivan that the Federalist rumors would backfire, he had to admit that he had no government appointments to offer him, but only because none were available. In any case, Sullivan had more important things to do, such as organizing the Republican Party in his state in preparation for the impending gubernatorial contest. Implying that he wanted Sullivan to stay exactly where he was, Jefferson observed that to appoint him to a job in Washington and remove him from the Massachusetts scene would be counterproductive, because he was destined "for the most distinguished mark of their affection & confidence," the governorship. "To the nation in general your election will be as gratifying as to that particular state," he was sure, "for never can we consider our union as solid while so important a member as Massachusetts is disaffected. That we may not fail to obtain this accession to our harmony & prosperity, nor you so honorable a testimony of the esteem & approbation of a respectable state, no one prays more sincerely than I do."[12] Extolling Sullivan as a figure of potentially national importance, Jefferson thus emphasized that Massachusetts was more than a great state. In the recent past, it had been a foremost symbol of the American Revolution and the rational republicanism the new nation embodied at its best.

Nonetheless, the optimistic president must have been shocked when Sullivan informed him that Federalist agitators in Massachusetts, ostensibly sinking even lower than usual, plotted civil war and an alliance with Great Britain. This was even more alarming than their claims that Jefferson opposed his candidacy. Probably to Jefferson's dismay, Sullivan reported that some Federalist agitators, deciding to become more refined, had abandoned charges that Jefferson was a rake who had children by his slaves. They now accused *him* of wanting to be king of the United States! This was a unique charge, and Sullivan was sure that the Federalists rather than Jefferson wanted monarchy. Although like Jefferson, he thought that the rank-and-file Federalists of the state respected the president and were on the verge of conversion to Republicanism, his doleful scenario must have depressed Jefferson. "There will never be an end to the malice and falsehoods of the wicked combination who assume the appellations of federalists [instead of royalists] in order to deceive the people," Sullivan wrote: "Those of them who hold the higher grade have become ashamed of low abuse in regard to the chief national magistrate. They are now representing him as being in favor of a monarchy; but the people are too wise to listen to them. They [the Federalist leaders] want a civil war, but they have no way to introduce it; their praetorian guards [the regular army formed during the undeclared war with France?] are disbanded and the [state] militia will not make war on their own freedom. The hope from England declines as the misfortunes of that nation are multiplied."[13] Thus, Sullivan adopted the role of Jefferson's confidant. He was obviously convinced that the president, at least for the time being, was his friend. Both Republicans appreciated the importance of Massachusetts and the desirability of all branches of its government coming over to the Jeffersonian ranks.

In the spring elections of 1806, Sullivan was again the Republican candidate for governor. He believed that he would have won the election had the Federalists not employed fraud, trickery, intimidation, and bribery to gain unfair advantage. They went to such extremes as putting Sullivan's name as governor at the head of a legislative ticket that was composed only of Federalists, deceiving unwary voters. At other times, they pretended to be Republican canvassers writing out election ballots, as the law required, and deliberately spelling Sullivan's name "Sullan" so that the votes would be disqualified. In Sullivan's opinion, the Massachusetts Federalists were the embodiment of evil; or at least that was what he told Jefferson, who had earlier said something similar. Sullivan often depicted them as monarchists who wanted to return to English dominion. They plotted to provoke war with France and Spain, align with Britain, and break up the republic. Sullivan detested the big banks, the clergy, and the lawyers, considering them Federalist stalwarts. "The Lawyers are numerous and the greater part of them openly avow their sentiments against the present government," he said. "The numerous corporations for bribery and other money purposes are decided against elective government." He predicted that the banks and big creditors would manipulate the financial system against their numerous debtors when peace arrived in Europe. They would call in their loans, resulting in a scarcity of specie and bank notes consequent to diminished overseas trade. Federalist bankers would blame the Republicans for the ensuing economic depression, demand a "more energetic government, and an objection to the national [Jefferson] administration." Federalist agitators would urge the people to revolt "until force becomes necessary to maintain the government," precipitating civil war.

Observing that the Federalists were encouraged by the expectation that Jefferson would "retire at the end of three years," Sullivan assured Jefferson that he hoped that he would serve a third term. He reported that the Federalists looked to Jefferson's bitter foe (and distant relative) John Randolph of Roanoke as their leader, but their plans were far more odious than even that volatile Virginian would support. "Randolph has become great among them," he observed. "And if a war with France or Spain can be provoked our form of constitution will be blasted, and perhaps the nation divided and subjugated by foreign powers."[14]

Sullivan's near-hysteria in his letters to Jefferson did not actually match his political practices. In general, he sought conciliation between moderate Federalists and Republicans. It is possible he thought that by adopting such a strident tone he would gain Jefferson's confidence. In June 1806, after he had been narrowly defeated by what he called Federalist "legerdemain," he wrote Jefferson that the Federalists considered him the strongest Republican gubernatorial candidate, and targeted their most vehement personal abuse at him to force him to abandon politics. However, he assured Jefferson that he considered the Democratic-Republican mission to preserve peace and maintain popular rule too vital for him to leave politics before the Jeffersonians had gained a greater foothold in Massachusetts. Appalled at the thorough Federalist dominance of the state government and courts, he warned that Jeffersonians lacked legal recourse to fight libels against them: "There is no pretence for a civil remedy for injuries done to the persons or characters of the republicans," he lamented. "All the benches are filled with men, to use your expression, in another case, of whose System morality makes no part."[15]

Sullivan was probably aware that his moderate outlook was typical of the majority of Massachusetts Jeffersonians. A master politician, and among the earliest professional politicians, he presented his views in a deliberately vague manner, so as to gain support from both Federalists and Republicans. For instance, his noncommittal views on religious freedom were designed to draw a large following. After his death, the Republican-controlled legislature passed a Religious Freedom Act (1811), which, despite its name, still imposed restrictions on Baptists and Methodists who did not exactly follow its certificate and registration rules. William G. McLoughlin, the leading authority on Massachusetts religion in the early republic observes, "The success of Sullivan's studied ambiguity on the question of religious taxes was demonstrated by a dispute after his death on precisely what his stand would have been on the Religious Freedom Act adopted in 1811." Some Republican advocates of religious freedom interpreted his words to mean that he would have supported complete religious disestablishment, while Federalists argued that he would have condoned continued moderate religious establishments like that of the 1811 Act.[16]

Unlike Jefferson and Madison's conduct in Virginia during the Revolution, the Massachusetts Republican Party was relatively apathetic on the question of equal rights for Dissenters. According to McLoughlin, Sullivan and Massachusetts Republican generally supported Article 3 of the Massachusetts Constitution of 1780, which granted a preferential position to the Congregationalist Church in the matter of receiving state taxes. They "believed that compulsory religious taxes were not equal to an Establishment so long as the law was equitably exercised to exempt bona fide dissenters from such taxes."[17]

Again unlike Jefferson, Sullivan, more akin in this respect to Massachusetts Federalists, felt contempt for immigrants and the lower classes. He argued that, if Jefferson spent more time advancing Massachusetts' interests and following the advice of conservatives, he could succeed in abolishing political parties. At the beginning of Jefferson's presidency, he advised him to make "every exertion ... to destroy the lines of party distinction." Not being a member of Jefferson's inner circle, he had the misconception that Jefferson wished to severely reduce the Navy. He pointed out that New Englanders favored a strong navy ("armed naval force"), since "the pride of the people, conversant on the ocean, is delighted with the idea." New Englanders also preferred some kind of standing army, he said. Sullivan thought that, by retaining a military force, Jefferson would remove some likely bases of "party division." However, it was not Jefferson but Old Republicans in Congress who opposed a substantial navy; Sullivan apparently did not know very much about Jefferson's programs.[18]

Furthermore, by inaccurately interpreting Jefferson's first annual message to Congress as proposing to remove all restrictions on immigration, when Jefferson only asserted that the Federalists' harsh Naturalization Act was unfair, Sullivan revealed xenophobia. In effect, like the Pennsylvania Jeffersonians Alexander James Dallas and Thomas McKean, in ideology he was a closet Federalist, a would-be elitist who because he came from a lower-class social background and was considered an "outsider" despite his wealth, joined the Republicans to get ahead in politics.[19] Agreeing with conservative New Englanders on the evils of immigration, he wrote to Dr. William Eustis, a leading Republican and U.S. senator from Massachusetts, "We are full of people, and want no accession. We know no way to open the door, without the admission of the very dregs of Europe." In an effort to gain support for his party, he tried to convince Massachusetts Federalists that Jefferson also opposed immigration.[20]

Many of Sullivan's attitudes were conservative. Despite being a self-made man, he had many of the viewpoints of an arrogant snob, a wealthy merchant and lawyer with contempt for the common man. His grandfather was a famous Roman Catholic Irish rebel, Major Philip O'Sullivan, and when his parents emigrated from Ireland they apparently maintained the Roman Catholic faith. However, Sullivan, perhaps for social advantage, converted to Congregationalism. In 1806, as attorney general of Massachusetts, he exploited anti–Catholic prejudice for political advantage, according to some observers. Personally prosecuting a Northampton murder case against Dominic Daley and James Halligan, two Irish immigrant laborers, Sullivan denied defense attorney Francis Blake's claim that Massachusetts' natives dislike for Irish Catholics made it impossible for them to get a fair trial. He argued that there was no religious or ethnic prejudice in Northampton County. After two hours of deliberation, despite the lack of compelling evidence, the jury convicted the two Irish Catholics of murder, and they were sentenced to hang.[21]

Despite his popularity with the voters, Sullivan personally believed that the people were too ignorant and passionate for self-government. He was reluctant to support disestablishment of the Congregationalist Church, despite eventually changing his religion to Unitarianism. Politically opportunistic, he recommended that Jefferson retain Federalists in office when they performed their jobs well; at the same time, in order to build a personal political base, when he became governor in 1807 he appointed Republicans to the state courts, displacing Federalists.[22]

When the Embargo Act commenced, Sullivan, who had finally won election as governor a few months earlier, gave Jefferson at least nominal support. In February 1808, he sent him resolutions of Massachusetts town meetings that approved the law. Strongly nationalistic and anti-monarchical, Sullivan found intolerable Senator Pickering's defense of British contempt for American neutral rights, lives, and property on the high seas. In March 1808, Pickering, in his capacity as senator, wrote the new governor a semi-official letter charging that Jefferson had proposed the Embargo in December 1807 at the behest of Napoleon, as a covert means of cutting off all trade with Britain in accord with French policy. In Pickering's view, this provocation was a preliminary to a U.S. declaration of war on England.[23]

An irate Sullivan refused to send Pickering's letter to the assembly, but "Essex Junto" member George Cabot, a member of the Governor's Council, obtained a copy and published it. In retaliation, Sullivan wrote a public letter attacking Pickering as a would-be secessionist. Senator John Quincy Adams denounced Pickering's letter for ignoring British atrocities and violations of American neutral rights, among them the *Chesapeake* Incident, impressment, and the Orders in Council prohibiting American trade with Europe except on British terms. In Adams' view, the U.S. had no choice but the Embargo or war. He warned that the Federalists preferred to kowtow to the British and were ready to abandon any "pretence to national sovereignty." Concurring with Adams, Sullivan charged Pickering planned to excite sedition and rebellion and tear the Union apart.[24]

Despite Pickering's venerable reputation with old Federalists, Sullivan narrowly won reelection against Strong. However, assisted by the unpopularity of the Embargo, the Federalists gained a majority in the state legislature. They voted to replace Adams with James Lloyd, and at the same time adopted resolutions condemning the Embargo. This virtual repudiation caused the sensitive Adams to resign his seat before his term ended.[25] In his ground-breaking *History*, Henry Adams denounces the Federalists, who humiliated his grandfather. He merges criticism of Jefferson with disgust for his bitter foes, writing, "Thus, the great State of Massachusetts fell back into Federalism. All, and more than all, that Jefferson's painful labors had gained, his embargo in a few weeks wasted." Still, the president had the satisfaction of knowing that the Federalists were no longer a national party, and might even be considered traitors: "The Federalists of 1801 were the national party of America; the Federalists of 1808 were a British faction in secret league with George Canning [British foreign secretary]."[26] Ironically, Sullivan's most assertive act during his brief governorship of Massachusetts (the governor served a one-year term) was to grant excessive numbers of permits to merchants for importing flour into the state during the Embargo Act, which they covertly sold abroad in violation of the law.[27]

Though Sullivan (who in late 1808 was bedridden and close to death) insisted that the flour was solely for the use of the state's residents, Jefferson was skeptical. Discovering that speculators sold the Massachusetts permits as far south as Washington and Alexandria, Virginia, he requested Lieutenant Governor Levi Lincoln, his former attorney general, to investigate. Lincoln, who spent most of his time on his farm in Worcester, undertook a brief investigation for Jefferson in Boston but did not want to take on the task of supplying permits full-time. "My impressions were that there had been a great abuse of the indulgencies granted to the citizens of Massachusetts," he wrote. After returning to Boston, he found that "much [flour] which has been imported has been fraudulently carried out of the state. The enemies to the embargo or at least some of them seem to countenance this violation of law."[28] To Jefferson's dismay, after Sullivan became governor of Massachusetts, he, along with Supreme Court Justices Brockholst Livingston and William Johnson and Boston federal district attorney George Blake (whom Leonard W. Levy considered the foremost Republican defender of liberty of the press during the Sedition Act crisis of 1798–1800) was among the Jeffersonian leaders who refused to enforce the Embargo Act in 1808–1809.[29]

It did not take long for Jefferson to become disillusioned with the Embargo and prefer war as an alternative. "Our situation is truly difficult," he wrote Lincoln. "We have been pressed by the belligerents to the very wall, and all further retreat is impracticable."[30] He was not sure whether England or France would ultimately be the enemy. He seemed more willing to confide in Lincoln than in Lincoln's official superior, Governor Sullivan, whom he did not entirely trust.

11

President Jefferson and New England
From Embargo to War

Despite his partiality toward New England's town meeting form of government, Jefferson had contempt for what he considered the amoral greed of its people, especially its merchants. He considered Massachusetts shippers especially obsessed with profiting by the carrying trade, no matter how much their fellow citizens suffered from British ship seizures, impressment of sailors into the Royal Navy, and ultimately—after numerous exacerbating incidents—war between the ex-Mother Country and the United States. During Jefferson's presidency, Eastern merchants reaped impressive profits in the perilous carrying trade. They transported tropical goods and manufactures between European mother countries like Spain, France, and England and their Caribbean colonies. The Jefferson Administration and the merchants themselves insisted (to no avail) that the United States, as a neutral country, should enjoy unimpeded free trade with belligerents in time of war. Nonetheless, historians estimate that even if only one in three cargoes reached their destination without being confiscated, American merchants would still handsomely profit.[1]

Ex-president John Adams apparently backed up this assessment. Writing in 1815, while giving himself most of the credit he asserted that Jefferson's (pre–Embargo) presidency was the best time Eastern merchants had ever experienced. "The halcyon days of New England prosperity were the first six years of Mr. Jefferson's administration," he observed: "Was this felicity owing to the wisdom, the virtue, or the energy of Mr. Jefferson? Or was it the natural, necessary, and unavoidable effect of the universal peace and tranquillity abroad and at home, and with universal nature, civilized and savage, entailed upon him by his predecessor, in spite of friends and enemies?"[2]

That Jefferson as president was undoubtedly aware of the profits that Eastern merchants reaped increased his frustration at their refusal to endure the self-sacrifice entailed by obeying the Embargo. Toward the end of his presidency, Jefferson was especially irate at the smuggling and violations of the Embargo Act committed by New Englanders.

At the beginning of 1809, Congress finally repealed the Embargo Act. Jefferson privately proposed that it simultaneously abolish the preferential drawbacks of import duties on sugar, coffee, tea, molasses, and other tropical produce the "trading States" re-exported to the Continent. At times, he considered the best solution was restricting American ships to the carriage of domestically produced and manufactured goods ("our own produce"), even though by this stance the United States might eventually permanently surrender its claims to freedom of the seas in wartime. Shortly before leaving the presidency, Jefferson denounced Massachusetts "federalist" merchants, who he claimed thwarted his selfless, nationalistic efforts to promote American manufacturing during the Embargo. These "ship-owners" and merchants, he charged, sought profits from transporting domestic raw materials to Europe for conversion into manufactured goods there. He argued that U.S. prosperity as a whole could be better advanced by exporting crude domestic manufactures to Europe in exchange for more sophisticated goods America could not produce itself.[3]

In January 1809, with nationalistic zeal, Jefferson raged against selfish eastern Federalists. He charged that their clamor against his nationalistic attempts to encourage domestic manufacturing had converted profit-obsessed Massachusetts merchants to the Federalist point of view: "This absurd hue and cry has contributed much to federalize New England, their doctrine goes to the sacrificing of agriculture and manufactures to commerce; to the calling all our people from the interior country to the sea-shore to turn merchants, and to convert this great agricultural country into a city of Amsterdam."[4]

Unlike his earlier exhortation in *Notes on Virginia* that all Americans become farmers, Jefferson now proclaimed himself the advocate of a balanced economy: "But I trust the good sense of our country will see that its greatest prosperity depends on a due balance between agriculture, manufactures, and commerce, and not in this protuberant navigation which has kept us in hot water from the commencement of our government, and is now engaging us in war. That this may be avoided, if it can be done without a surrender of rights, is my sincere prayer."[5] Thus, Jefferson acknowledged his responsibility as president to preserve America's neutral rights on the high seas. He doubted that, unless in defense of national honor, the profits of Massachusetts merchants abroad were worth a war.[6]

At the end of his presidency, Jefferson felt vindicated when Secretary of War William Eustis, a staunch Massachusetts Jeffersonian re-appointed by Madison, sent him a eulogistic address from members of Boston's Republican Party. Jefferson was pleased that the "sons of Massachusetts" were ready to unite behind a strong national government and protest Europe's degrading treatment, which seemed likely to make war the only alternative to national humiliation. "The moment for exerting these united powers, to repel the injuries of the belligerents of Europe, seems likely to be pressed upon us," he observed. In a moment of unusual candor, he assured Eustis that he never intended the Embargo to be permanent, but employed it so that ships belonging to U.S. citizens would be safely in U.S. ports when war was declared. He insisted that one of his major objectives was to protect New England's seamen and commerce. "After exhausting the cup of forbearance and conciliation to its dregs, we found it necessary on behalf of that commerce, to take time to call it home into a state of safety," he admitted, "to put the towns and harbors which carry it on into a condition of defence, and to make further preparation for enforcing the redress of its wrongs, and restoring it to its rightful freedom."[7]

Insisting that the Embargo did not discriminate against Massachusetts but affected all parts of the country equally, Jefferson hoped its Federalist citizens would soon join in support of the administration's efforts along with their Republican "brethren" in the "sister states." He was confident that the people of Massachusetts respected the "will of the majority," which dictated their obedience to the Embargo. "Associated with her sister States in a common government, the fundamental principle of which is, that the will of the majority is to prevail, sensible that, in the present difficulty, that will has been governed by no local interests or jealousies," he declared, "that to save permanent rights, temporary sacrifices were necessary, that these have fallen as impartially on all, as in a situation so peculiar they could be made to do, she [Massachusetts] will see in the existing measures a legitimate and honest increase of the will and wisdom of the whole."[8]

· · · · ·

Despite his reasonable and conciliatory rhetoric and his conviction that the Embargo was impartial, Jefferson did not entirely trust the people of Massachusetts. He was disappointed that they had not immediately embraced his election in 1801. From the beginning of his presidency, he paid a great deal of attention to political trends in the state. The most politically powerful Massachusetts leader was probably Governor Caleb Strong. Despite being an Anglophile Federalist, Strong, a native of Northampton, Massachusetts, who strongly endorsed town meeting democracy, low official salaries and annual elections of legislators, was a humble man of moderate wealth. He was popular with the voters. After he defeated Gerry in 1800, many Republicans were willing to accept him as the representative of both parties. In the gubernatorial election of 1803, eastern Republicans had no objection to him heading their ticket, but Berkshire and Essex County Republicans were less willing to abandon their partisan identity. They wanted Gerry to challenge him again, while other Massachusetts Republicans, such as Henry Dearborn, preferred Levi Lincoln as their candidate, and gathered some western support. On the other hand, a caucus of Boston Republicans in February 1803 reached the conclusion that Strong was unbeatable. They supported Strong for governor, but nominated Republicans to compete in state legislative contests. The general passivity of the Boston group resulted in Republicans losing assembly seats in Suffolk County, particularly Boston, while gaining a few elsewhere. In 1804, William Eustis, Boston's Democratic-Republican congressman, lost his bid for reelection. Historian Paul Goodman observes, "Failure undermined the influence of the eastern faction, which could no longer resist demands for new leadership to rally the faithful." As we have seen, the party eventually turned to James Sullivan of Maine for salvation.[9]

Writing from Stockbridge in April 1803, western Massachusetts congressman John Bacon informed Jefferson of the state party's disarray. Admitting that Republicans were poorly organized, he regretted the poor communication between Washington and Boston. By the time the capital's Jeffersonians became aware that Boston Democrats intended not to oppose Strong's reelection, "the system [was] so far advanced that it was judged most prudent to proceed as they had first proposed." Glad to report that his congressional district, which included Stockbridge and western Massachusetts, comprised "a decent majority in favor of *democratical republicans*," nonetheless Bacon expected Strong to win the governorship and the Federalists to gain a majority of the state legislature in recently concluded elections. While stressing Strong's popularity as a major factor in Federalist success, he believed that Republican political fortunes "are not less favorable than they have been for two years past." "I do not consider the number of votes given for Governor, or even for Counsellors or Senators, as an accurate criterion by which to judge of the real state of political sentiment with us," he explained. "Mr. Strong's *personal* popularity is such as has, apparently, considerable influence on the votes which are given for all public officers who are elected by the same men, and at the same time, with the Governor." Strong easily won reelection, and a Federalist majority of fifty joined him in the state house of representatives when that body convened in May 1803.[10]

Depressed that Bacon confirmed his fears that Massachusetts remained Federalist, Jefferson tried to minimize his disappointment that recent state elections had not produced a Republican majority. "Your favor of the 11th has been received…. I observe what you say on the aspect of your elections," he said. "Altho' federalism appears to have boasted prematurely of it's [sic] gains, yet it does not appear to have yielded as we might have expected to the evidence either of their reason or their senses." Jefferson suspected that the Federalists exaggerated their power in Massachusetts after two years of his rule, but he recognized that the people had not converted *en masse* to his party. He was hopeful for the future. He accurately predicted that, in light of New Englanders' love of frugality and devotion to liberty, they would inevitably overthrow their established church and soon join the rest of the nation in adopting the Jeffersonian creed. He considered Massachusetts citizens' political outlook incompatible with their personal philosophies. "Two facts are certainly as true as [they are] irreconcilable," he continued. "The people of Massachusetts love economy & freedom, civil & religious. The present [national] legislature & executive functionaries endeavor to practice economy & to strengthen civil & religious freedom. Yet they are disapproved by the people of Massachusetts." He suspected that part of the answer to this enigma was that the people's habitual subservience to their leaders, among them Connecticut Valley political veterans like the devout Calvinist and populist Strong, the current state governor, retarded their progress toward Republicanism. "It cannot be that these had rather give up principles than men," he wrote edgily. "However the riddle is to be solved, our duty is plain, to administer their interests faithfully & to overcome evil with good."[11] Thus, at least before the repercussions of Embargo and war marred his expectations, his general outlook on Republicans' future in Massachusetts was positive.

Jefferson considered it possible that in wartime, New Englanders would favor the British enemy. Had he been privy to the reports of John Howe, a native Bostonian who had moved to Nova Scotia after the Revolution and in September 1808 was employed by George Prevost, the governor of Nova Scotia as a spy, his fears would have been confirmed. Howe claimed that disgust with the Embargo was general throughout New England, especially in Massachusetts. He said that many New England Federalists favored the section's secession from the Union as an independent confederation. Howe believed that Jefferson and the "Democrats" were inveterate Anglophobes who really wanted war with England. He was confident that, in light of recent Federalist successes in elections for Congress and presidential electors in New Hampshire and Rhode Island, the Federalists would soon gain a majority in Congress. "The Embargo has completely federalised [sic] all the New-England States," he gleefully observed, "and may eventually lead to a division of the Southern and Northern States." Howe hoped that the Federalists would nominate Charles C. Pinckney of "North Carolina" (he was actually from South Carolina) for president and Rufus King for vice-president, should they acquire enough confidence to run a ticket after Jefferson's great victory in 1804. Aware of the disunity in the Democratic Party, he considered the possibility that George Clinton, though Jefferson's vice-president and ostensibly ready to continue in that office under Madison, the Democratic presidential candidate, was being courted by Federalists and was considering running for president under their banner; in that case he thought Monroe might become the Democratic candidate for vice-president. Sadly, a British spy's observations corroborated the likelihood of national rupture should war occur.[12]

Almost clairvoyantly, Jefferson wrote as if Howe's letters were right in front of him. He urged Eustis to ensure that his state's "citizens, faithful to themselves and their associates, will not, to avoid a transient pressure, yield to the seductions of enemies to their independence, foreign or domestic, and take a course equally subversive of their well being, as that of their brethren."[13] Even at this early date in the road to war between British and Americans, Jefferson wanted to make clear that it would be self-destructive for Massachusetts to betray the Union.

When President Madison, hoping to advance national unity, unexpectedly appointed the inexperienced Eustis to the important post of secretary of war, Jefferson's tone grew urgent. He wanted to impress upon the new Cabinet member his fear that Massachusetts Federalists might eventually use the excuse of war to secede from the Union. Congratulating Eustis on his appointment, Jefferson said, "Besides the general advantages we may promise ourselves from the employment of your talents and integrity in so important a station, we may hope peculiar effect from it towards restoring deeply wounded amity between your native state & her sisters."[14]

Nonetheless, Jefferson predicted that if extremist Federalists gained control of the entire Massachusetts government, the state might secede from the Union. "The danger of the leading Federalists then having direction of the state, to take advantage of the first war with England to separate the N.E. states from the union has distressingly impaired our future confidence in them," he opined. Perhaps Jefferson wanted Eustis to use his influence in Massachusetts and possibly the threat of U.S. military intervention to tame the Federalists leadership. That a violent option was not on Jefferson's mind was evident in his concluding remarks, in which he expressed anger at the Federalists who he suspected wanted to divide the Union, but failed to recommend force to keep them in. As was his wont, he stressed that the fate of democracy and republicanism in the world depended on the success of the U.S. republic's example. He wanted the Federalists to admit their culpability should they force the New England states out of the Union, thereby weakening it and making its decline and fall to foreign invaders or domestic subversion possible. Rather than touting military force, he emphasized the moral force a strong union represented: "In this, as in all other cases, we must do them [the Federalist secessionists] full justice, and make the fault their own, should the last hope of human liberty be destined to receive its final stab from them."[15]

That Jefferson had conducted a neutral foreign policy between England and France was evident even to one of his most bitter adversaries, Abigail Adams, wife of John Adams. She had become more favorable to the Jeffersonians, including the recently elected President Madison, after Madison appointed her son John Quincy Adams minister to Russia in March 1809. She wrote her daughter Abigail ("Nabby") that she considered both Jefferson and Madison impartial in their attitudes to Britain and France. "No one can accuse Mr. Madison for want of a frank and honourable spirit of accommodation with Great Britain," she insisted. "When she held out her hand with a spirit of conciliation, he received it with true magnanimity; and I rejoiced sincerely that our causes of animosity were to be removed. I own I am not satisfied with the subsequent conduct of the British Ministry; what powers the new ministry may be clothed with, time must disclose. I feel at present safe in the hands of Mr. Madison. I presume he will not permit himself to be cajoled into any relinquishment of our national rights, or infringement of our independence."[16]

Although Abigail had written Jefferson vindictively in 1804, charging him with deliberately removing her son John Quincy from a minor federal court office and bribing Callender to write defamatory pamphlets about her husband during the election campaign of 1800, she now told her daughter that Jefferson, like Madison, was a good man and a patriot; indeed, it was the New England Federalists who were the real enemies of the country, because they favored the interests of England against those of the United States. "Whatever predilection Mr. Jefferson had in favour of France, or has against Great Britain, I believe, in his public transactions, he strove to act with impartial justice towards both," she remarked. Apparently ready to take office herself, she continued, "I read all the dispatches with care and attention, expecting to find what had so often been declared, a blind partiality towards France, and hatred towards England; but justice requires me to say, that I could discover no such thing; and when party spirit yields to reason and sober sense, this will be the equitable decision." Although willing to admit Jefferson's impartiality in his conduct of foreign affairs—something that conservative Federalists then and conservative historians now would not concede—she was unwilling to fully exonerate him. "I wish I could notice all Mr. Jefferson's measures with the same candour," she darkly concluded. "But to his own Master, he must stand or fall."[17]

On the other hand, Abigail charged her husband John's Federalist fair weather friends with forcing him to act in a partisan fashion as president in doling out government jobs, so that in this respect her beloved, "dearest friend" was no better than Jefferson. "For it is very true, that the federal party were as hungry and rapacious after office, as ever their opponents have been, and of a spirit quite as selfish and intolerant," she vividly wrote Nabby. Recalling one of the nasty letters she wrote Jefferson during his presidency, in 1804 (but stating its contents far more euphemistically), she observed, "I once said, or rather wrote to Mr. Jefferson, 'if you are a freeman, and can act yourself, you can do more than either of your predecessors could' to remove hostility between the parties." "Such was the bitterness of the federal party, or rather the leaders of it, and [Pickering?] was one of them, that they would not hear a word of any nomination to office, of even the cool and moderate republicans," she reminisced concerning her husband's administration. Now she felt only contempt for the New England High Federalists. "There will never be any harmony between parties, until public offices can be shared; and this your father used to tell them," she asserted. In terms that even Jefferson might have found extreme, Abigail charged that the Federalists who controlled Massachusetts had usurped the powers of the national government within their state, intending to convert Massachusetts into a British colony.[18]

Pointing out that John Adams had recently written articles in a Democratic-Republican newspaper, the *Boston Patriot*, defending the nation's right to freedom of the seas and Jefferson's foreign policy, Abigail complained that in return he was "maligned and abused by the Anglo-American party," her term for his former Federalist allies.[19] Advocating a more aggressive policy toward the British and French than even Jeffersonian radicals espoused, she favored the repeal of the Embargo and Non-Intercourse Acts and the abandonment of all restrictions on U.S. commerce. She proposed that the national government dispatch frigates to convoy U.S. merchant ships and help them "defend themselves as neutrals," as well as back them up in refusing to pay tribute to the British government for licenses to carry on trade in Europe. On a more peaceful note, she hoped that the incoming Madison Administration would "calm the just fears and apprehensions of the people; [and] disarm party spirit if possible. That I fear is the hardest labour of all, whilst pride, envy, and ambition are the predominant passions of man."[20] Jefferson would undoubtedly have shared her sentiments.

• • • • •

The final crisis with England was precipitated by its unrestricted confiscations of American shipping in the West Indies after the *Essex* decision in 1805, and British sea captains' impressment of American sailors to serve aboard British warships in the struggle against Napoleon. Britain's desperate need for sailors for its formidable navy and its contempt for the United States, whose merchant ships hired runaway British seamen in American ports, culminated in an extreme insult to the U.S. flag in June 1807, when the British warship *Leopard* fired without warning on the American frigate USS *Chesapeake* in Chesapeake Bay. The American warship's commander, Commodore James Barron, initially refused the British captain's demands that he surrender several deserters from the Royal Navy. The British killed two sailors and seized four alleged British navy deserters (two of them American blacks) from the government vessel.[21]

The road to war with England was simultaneously the path to greatest alienation between the New England states and the Jefferson and Madison administrations. It led to passage of the Embargo Act, which Jefferson proposed in December 1807, during the last year of his presidency. Jefferson did not regard the Embargo as a long-term measure, or as an ideal solution to British attacks on American trade, impressment of U.S. citizens into the British Navy, and Britain's contempt for U.S. national honor. British contempt for American sovereignty, akin to its scorn for Denmark, Sweden, and other weak military powers, was amply revealed by the *Chesapeake* Affair, the British peacetime blockade of U.S. harbors including New York, and other maritime incidents that took American lives. The Embargo was designed to forestall war with Great Britain until the U.S. was better prepared militarily and merchant ships came home safely from abroad.[22]

Never enthusiastic about the legislation that historians consider the greatest failure of his presidency (which he actually proposed at Madison's insistence), Jefferson was ambivalent in predicting New Englanders' response. With family members and people who lacked political influence, he confided his lack of faith in the Embargo a year after it went into effect. The possibility that Congress would soon repeal it did not disappoint him. He wavered between confidence that New England citizens' patriotism would override their devotion to material gain, and fear that their selfishness—so contrary to the image of Massachusetts republican "virtue" he imbibed during the Revolutionary period—would lead them to secession and alliance with Britain in case of war.[23]

In November 1807, a few weeks before Congress passed the Embargo Act, Jefferson perceived that public opinion's outrage after the *Chesapeake* Affair had abated. "The war-fever is past, & the probability against it's return rather prevalent," he wrote his daughter. He observed the formation of a caucus of dissident congressional Republicans led by John Randolph of Roanoke and Joseph Clay of Pennsylvania. He viewed them as obstructionists without specific plans or preferences for dealing with Britain, but he was confident that, "in neither house, even with the assured aid of the Federalists, can they shake the good sense & honest intentions of the mass of real republicans." Jefferson apparently had no plan of his own at this time. Eager to leave office, he was "tired of … being the personal object for the hatred of every man who hates the present state of things."[24]

Historians have generally ascribed greater enthusiasm to Jefferson's enforcement of the Embargo than he actually felt. For example, Brian Steele claims that he considered the Embargo an important example of American exceptionalism: the republic's superiority to monarchies in searching for a better means of securing its rights than war. Steele invents examples of Jefferson's rigorous enforcement of the Embargo that never occurred. On Gallatin's advice, Steele says, Jefferson in April 1808 proclaimed the Lake Champlain region of Vermont and New York in a state of insurrection, which would allow him to enforce martial law there. Steele also asserts that Jefferson thought it might be necessary to proclaim martial law throughout Massachusetts, occupy Boston, and use the regular army to crush opposition. This does not sound like Jefferson. He generally believed in live-and-let live, as he said in his first inaugural address, upholding "a wise and frugal government, which shall restrain men from injuring one another, shall leave them otherwise free to regulate their own pursuits of industry and improvement, and shall not take from the mouth of labor the bread it has earned." A source Steele cites, Merrill D. Peterson's unannotated but commendable biography of Jefferson, says nearly the opposite of Steele: "Jefferson did not contemplate use of the army, though he possessed the authority under the act of Congress provoked by the Burr Conspiracy."[25]

Always reluctant to encroach on the economic freedom of his fellow citizens, Jefferson never employed the army or navy in a meaningful way to enforce the Embargo. On April 19, 1808, after learning of widespread smuggling by boat from Lake Champlain to Canada, he issued an order for potential "insurgents" to "disperse" to their homes. He instructed any "civil or military officials" in the "vicinage" to deliver would-be "insurgents" who engaged in violence to the nearest "civil authority." This haphazard proclamation made no mention of sending Army or militia regiments to the area and did not give orders to a specific military or civilian official. This is very different from proclaiming the Lake Champlain area to be in a state of insurrection.[26]

In keeping with current conservative tendencies among historians of the early republic, it appears that scholars have taken at face value the belated assertions of Vermont's Federalist congressmen during the Tenth Congress that Jefferson had earlier insulted their state by proclaiming its residents rebels. On November 10, 1808, Martin Chittenden, a Federalist congressman from Vermont, who as the state's governor in 1814 refused to permit the militia to leave its borders, presented a resolution to repeal the Embargo, which he complained, should have already been revoked. He felt especially responsible for getting rid of the Embargo because of "its interesting nature to his constituents, who, in addition to the common sufferings, had the extreme mortification of being represented as in a state of insurrection."[27] Chittenden himself did not call for the text of Jefferson's proclamation, which was old news. Two weeks later, apparently seeking to embarrass Jefferson, his Vermont Federalist colleague, James Elliot, proposed that Jefferson furnish the House of Representatives with a copy of his "proclamation issued in April last, in consequence of the opposition to the embargo laws near Lake Champlain."[28] Congress agreed to the proposal, and on November 30 it received the text from Jefferson.[29]

Likewise, Jefferson later sought to give an impression of firmness to Secretary of War Dearborn, who was alarmed by violations of the Embargo in Massachusetts. Writing in August 1808, he told Dearborn that he too had received "accounts … from others that the infractions of the embargo in Maine and Massachusetts are open." Mentioning some collectors of the customs, he assured Dearborn, "I have removed Pope, of New Bedford, for worse than negligence. The collector of Sullivan is on the totter." Making a few removals from office hardly constituted effective enforcement of the Embargo, but Jefferson apparently did nothing else besides angrily referring to his Federalist opponents as "parricides" seeking to destroy the

Union. Alluding to his executive order that no state be permitted to receive more than its usual imports of flour, thereby hindering attempts to smuggle the product to Canada or abroad, which Governor James Sullivan threatened to ignore, he asserted, "The tories of Boston openly threaten insurrection if their importation of flour is stopped. The next post will stop it. I fear your Governor is not up to the tone of these parricides, and I hope, on the first symptom of an open opposition of the law by force, you will fly to the scene and aid in suppressing any commotion."[30] The elderly Dearborn had no intention of "flying" anywhere. Jefferson probably did not expect him to; and Jefferson did nothing to enforce the law when Sullivan permitted Massachusetts merchants to import more flour than they were legally allowed. Writing to Gallatin about the possible need to use force in Boston and other Massachusetts towns, Jefferson seemed unwilling even to call out the militia. He wrote, "As to ordering out militia, you know the difficulty without another proclamation." He was probably referring to something like the April 1808 Lake Champlain proclamation.[31]

Notwithstanding his reputation among many historians as a fervent supporter of the Embargo, Jefferson never used regular troops on a large scale to enforce the law. When troops went against the resisters, they were defeated. In August 1808, after the Embargo aroused increased hostility to the Democratic-Republican Party, especially in New England and New York, he confided to the Embargo's foe, Secretary of the Treasury Gallatin that he had grown to dislike the law. He sought to blame Congress for the measure, even though he had originally proposed it. "This embargo law is certainly the most embarrassing we have ever had to execute," he admitted. Still, he agreed with Gallatin that if Congress did not propose to adopt some other alternative, it should save face by seeking stricter enforcement. "I did not expect a crop of as sudden & rank growth of fraud & open opposition by force could have grown up in the U.S.," he bluntly described violations of the Embargo. "I am satisfied with you that if [British] orders & [French] decrees are not repealed, and a continuance of the embargo is preferred to war (which sentiment is universal here), Congress must legalize all *means* which may be necessary to it's *end* [i.e., objective]." Thus, although he claimed that Congress considered the Embargo preferable to war (and implied that he was not an avid supporter of the Embargo), he wanted the legislature to bear responsibility for it. He emphasized that he opposed spending additional sums on military and naval implementation of the law: "I am clearly of opinion that this law ought to be enforced at any expence, *which may not exceed our appropriations*," he wrote.[32] Such policy statements showed little dedication to efficiently executing the Embargo.

During August 1808, despite New Englanders' systematic evasions of the Embargo, Jefferson remained apathetic about enforcement. He wrote Governor Sullivan that he trusted to the conduct of "my fellow citizens of Massachusetts, which has, I think, been emphatically marked by obedience to law, and a love of order." He expected them not to engage in food riots on the pretext that they were not being allowed to import enough flour, nor in smuggling of flour abroad.[33]

As a democratic leader, Jefferson probably perceived that he lacked a popular mandate for enforcing the Embargo. He was reluctant to enforce a law that could only cause him headaches and diminish his political capital. Although Leonard W. Levy and other historians insisted that he enforced the general Embargo rigorously, his implementation of the law (which among his Cabinet only James Madison favored) was weak. He made a few extreme private statements, such as fantasizing that judges would sentence lumber smugglers from

Vermont to death for treason, but that he would benevolently pardon most of them. (They were acquitted in the courts.) In attempting to enforce the Embargo, a federal customs employee and two U.S. Army soldiers were killed in Maine and Vermont, respectively. Particularly in Vermont, shootouts took place between large numbers of smugglers on rafts heading for Canada and small detachments of soldiers or militia and revenue officers, in which the government's enforcers, heavily outnumbered, usually had to retreat. In one case in St. Albans, Vermont, in the summer of 1808, thirty smugglers fought twelve soldiers for a stash of potash, and beat them back. At Rutland, Vermont, smugglers killed two soldiers. Eight suspects were reportedly arrested, and four escaped. One of the shooters, named Dean, was executed for murder.[34]

The paltry armed forces sent to implement the Embargo, and Jefferson's indifference to the whole matter, strongly suggest that, once he became aware of the widespread violations and unpopularity of the law, and the way it brought to the surface the underlying conflict between disinterested "republican virtue" and the capitalist pursuit of profit, inherent in a free, "liberal" state of the type he supported, he decided the law should be repealed. The Embargo lasted only a little over a year before Congress abandoned it, an extremely brief time when compared to most other legislation, or with U.S. wars, which often have lasted for many years. Jefferson did nothing to advocate the Embargo's existence after witnessing a groundswell of opposition to it in the Northern and Eastern states, although his administration retained most of its original Democratic-Republican supporters there.[35]

More surprising until one remembers Jefferson's desire for territorial expansion into Canada, Florida, and possibly Texas and Cuba, at this time he showed greater eagerness to pursue his obsession with seizing Florida from Spain than with enforcing the Embargo. He hoped to use the Embargo Act as an excuse to annex West Florida, which he considered legitimately part of the Louisiana Purchase. Jefferson was interested in taking advantage of Napoleon's reversals at the hands of nationalist rebels in Spain, which decreased his ability to dispatch an Army to the New World, to undertake a U.S. invasion of Spanish Florida. As he wrote the Secretary of the Navy, "I am glad to see that Spain is likely to give Bonaparte employment. *Tant mieux pour nous.*"[36]

Jefferson's letters to government officials in August 1808 emphasized his desire to employ Southern volunteers, recently recruited in case of war with Great Britain, for an invasion of Florida. Despite a barrage of letters from government officials complaining about violations of the Embargo, he was more disposed to conduct war against Spanish Florida in his most blatantly Machiavellian manner. After superficially discussing enforcement of the Embargo, merely recommending the removal of Mr. Jordan at the port of Sullivan, he wrote Gallatin, who was responsible for enforcing the Embargo, that he expected Charles Pinckney, U.S. minister to Spain, to report soon on his failed negotiation to obtain compensation for American merchants' claims. "If England should be disposed to continue peace with us, and Spain gives to Bonaparte the occupation she promises," he suggested, "will not the interval be favorable for our reprisals on the Floridas for the indemnifications withheld?"[37]

Indirectly indicating his sympathy for New England interests despite his rhetoric against Federalist "parricides," Jefferson was more determined to use American military and naval forces against Osage Indian "banditti" and especially against Spanish Florida, than against his "fellow citizens." Informing Dearborn that Pinckney would soon be conducting conferences in

London with Foreign Secretary George Canning, he deviously outlined his expansionist intentions:

> Should England make up with us, while Bonaparte continues at war with Spain, a moment may occur when we may without danger of commitment with either France or England seize to our own limits of Louisiana as of right, and the residue of the Floridas as reprisal for spoliations. It is our duty to have an eye to this in rendezvousing and stationing our new recruits and our armed vessels, so as to be ready, if Congress authorizes it, to strike in a moment. I wish you to consider this matter in the orders to the southern recruits, as I have also recommended to the Secretary of the Navy, as to the armed vessels in the South. Indeed, I would ask your opinion as to the positions we had better take with a view to this with our armed vessels as well as troops. The force in the neighborhood of Baton Rouge is enough for that. Mobile, Pensacola and St. Augustine, are those we should be preparing for. The enforcing the embargo would furnish a pretext for taking the nearest healthy position to St. Mary's, and on the waters of Tombigbee.[38]

Aware that Massachusetts' Democratic-Republican governor James Sullivan permitted smuggling in Boston and elsewhere, Jefferson, though exasperated, intended to do little about it. "I have some apprehension that the tories of Boston, etc., with so poor a head of a Governor, may attempt to give us trouble," he warned Secretary of the Navy Robert Smith. "I have requested General Dearborn [secretary of war, also from Massachusetts] to be on the alert, and fly to the spot where any open and forcible opposition shall be commenced, and to crush it in embryo." Although such vague instructions bore little resemblance to martial law, Jefferson professed confidence that the common people of Massachusetts were loyal to him and would obey the Embargo. "I am not afraid but that there is sound matter enough in Massachusetts to prevent an opposition of [*sic*] the laws by force," he wrote.[39]

Ironically, Jefferson entrusted Gallatin, who opposed the Embargo, with *carte blanche* in enforcing it. The president took no direct action himself. However, letters the secretary of the navy sent him from a Bostonian, warning that the city's Federalists were organizing riots against the Embargo, made him uneasy. The author claimed "that there is ground to apprehend insurgency in Massachusetts." Jefferson, who on hearing about Shays' Rebellion in the Massachusetts backcountry twenty-one years earlier preached, "the tree of liberty must be refreshed from time to time with the blood of patriots and tyrants," was less inclined to give that advice when in charge of the government. He was suspicious of the informant, not knowing "his politics," and thought he might be a trouble-maker. He knew that Governor Sullivan courted popularity, and speculated that he might flee if a full-scale "federalist insurrection" took place. However, he believed that Boston's citizens were loyal to the government they had chosen, and they respected its temporary nonviolent efforts to assert the nation's rights. "That the federalists may attempt insurrection is possible, and also that the Governor would sink before it," he wrote Gallatin. "But the republican part of the State, and that portion of the federalists who approve the embargo in their judgments, and at any rate would not court mob-law, would crush it in embryo." He informed Gallatin of his recent ("flying") letter to Dearborn. Unlike the Bowdoin government in Massachusetts at the time of Shays' Rebellion, Jefferson would never hire a private army to disperse "insurgents": "I have some time ago written to General Dearborn to be on the alert on such an occasion, and to take direction of the public authority on the spot. Such an incident will rally the whole body of republicans of every shade to a single point—that of supporting the public authority."[40]

Jefferson showed no alarm about the rumored "insurrection" in Boston or about smuggling in New York, advising Gallatin that he should retain enough gunboats in New York harbor "to preserve order" and send the rest to Boston. But he considered the "state of things" generally "tranquil." He trusted that Bostonians loved law and order more than they hated the Embargo. He also favored modifying the Embargo to allow ships of large tonnage to depart the country in ballast if they agreed to return with cargoes of salt, which was essential for New England's farm animals.[41]

It did not take long for Jefferson to decide to abandon the Embargo. When the irascible French minister, Louis Turreau, complained after the law had been in effect for six months that it placed England and France on the same ground, even though England seized far more U.S. ships than the French and, even worse, kidnapped ("impressed") thousands of American sailors into the British Navy, Jefferson agreed. He replied, "It is possible that Congress may repeal the embargo, the continuation of which would do us more harm than a state of war." He alluded to privateers, a traditional means by which New England seamen gained wealth in war, particularly from capturing the merchant ships of a commercial power like Britain, as they had done in the Revolution. "For us in the present situation all is loss," he told Turreau, "whereas, however powerful the English may be, war would put us in a way of doing them much harm, because our people are enterprising [by which he probably meant the privateersmen]."[42]

When the Republican-controlled Congress repealed the Embargo on March 1, 1809, two days before his presidency ended, Jefferson eagerly signed the measure. He confessed that he had considered it temporary all along. "The belligerent edicts," he explained to John Armstrong, U.S. minister to France, on his first day of retirement, "rendered our embargo necessary to call home our ships, our seamen and our property" in expectation of war with Britain, France, or both powers. Jefferson admitted his original hope was that the European powers' self-interest would lead them to repeal their decrees against American commerce when faced with the Embargo. However, Jefferson lamented, widespread smuggling and "evasion" reduced its impact. "After fifteen months' continuance, it is now discontinued because, losing fifty million dollars of exports annually by it, it costs more than war, which might be carried on for a third of that, besides what might be got by reprisal [privateering]. War therefore must follow if the edicts [against neutral commerce, the British Orders in Council and the French Berlin and Milan decrees] are not repealed before the meeting of Congress in May." He looked forward to a declaration of war upon some nation. He was hopeful that one positive result would be U.S. annexation of Florida.[43]

In early 1809, the Madison Administration unexpectedly resumed trade with Britain while maintaining non-intercourse with France. It accepted British envoy David Erskine's false assurances that the British government had repealed its prohibitions on U.S. trade with its enemies. At that point, ex-president Jefferson revealed himself less "Anglophobic" than most historians, with only superficial knowledge of his views, acknowledge. He proposed that the U.S. declare war on France and use that as an excuse to take over Florida and Cuba, colonies of Napoleon's nominal ally Spain. He believed that the inhabitants of those colonies would voluntarily offer themselves for annexation to the United States if war occurred between the United States and France, acquisitions welcomed, like British Canada, by both Madison and Jefferson. Conscious of Federalists' hostility to France, Jefferson sardonically expected them to offer no objections to war with France rather than England, the country they extolled.[44]

By the end of 1808, Jefferson was ready to abandon the Embargo, which had been law for less than a year, for limited or full-scale war. The Embargo had seemingly been ineffective, except in impoverishing Southern planters (including himself) and Northern wheat farmers who had nowhere to sell their produce, and enriching the New England, Vermont, and New York merchants who smuggled goods to Canada, Europe, and the West Indies, unfairly rewarding those who lacked "republican virtue." Although he believed that both England and France deserved punishment for violating U.S. neutral rights and flouting American national honor, he understood that the country was too weak to fight both great powers simultaneously.[45]

While expecting Congress to soon repeal the Embargo and replace it with non-intercourse with Britain and France, Jefferson heard rumors that a majority of Congress favored all-out war. At this point, he was uncertain if he wanted war. "This [war] party will perhaps lose ground by time, and especially as a suggestion has been made to make another effort by offering to both belligerents to elect between a repeal of these edicts and war, tightening the embargo in the meantime," he wrote his son-in-law, Thomas Mann Randolph. The idea, however, was "only in embryo."[46]

Within a few months, Jefferson had become disgusted by the Embargo and preferred war. However, his primary interest was to leave office and let Madison handle the crisis, to which the secretary of state had contributed by advocating the Embargo. To his eldest granddaughter Anne's husband, the violent drunkard Charles L. Bankhead, he wrote in November 1808, "We are all politics here." He believed that three-fourths of Congress rejected "submission & tribute" to England, but that one-fourth (the Anglophile "Essex Junto" Federalists) secretly preferred subservience to the British. Comparing the foremost alternatives, "embargo & war," Jefferson expected Congress to continue the Embargo until the "close of the session," when it would probably choose war. Of the "schismatic fourth" composed of dissident, "Quid" Republicans united by personal animus toward Jefferson resulting mainly from patronage disappointments, and New England Federalists, Jefferson predicted they would support "whatever proposition leads to war with France & submission to England." He noted that one of the factions (probably Giles') "has already proposed" war with France.[47]

It is likely that Jefferson cursed the final days of his presidency, especially after a lady friend contacted him. She was a young woman named Catherine Cruger, daughter of Alexander Hamilton's lovely sister-in-law, Angelica Schuyler Church. Now the wife of a New York merchant, Catherine wrote President Jefferson begging him to allow her husband to violate the Embargo by sending ships to his plantation in the West Indian colony of Santa Cruz to supply it with provisions and bring back sugar for him to sell at home and abroad.[48] Jefferson was not prepared to break his administration's laws even for an attractive woman. He promptly replied that his hands were tied. "Living as we do, in a country governed by fixed rules, nothing can be done for one which is not done for every other in an equal case," he said.[49] He was sure that she would agree with him that in a republic, the rules of fairness were unbreakable. She never wrote back.

Acutely aware that the Southern states, among them his own Virginia and the slaveholding entrepôt South Carolina, patriotically obeyed the Embargo while suffering more from its effects than New England did, Jefferson may have begun to feel bitter toward the cradle of town meeting democracy. He gratefully received news from Thomas Lehré, a Democratic-Republican Charleston politician and member of South Carolina's state assembly, that the state remained firmly in Jefferson's camp. In October 1808, Lehré sent the president local newspapers with reports that Charleston's Republicans had won the state legislature by a great majority over the Federalists. He assured Jefferson that South Carolina's citizens loyally obeyed the Embargo, and that Madison would get all of its electoral votes in the upcoming presidential race. "The true friends of America, were never more determined than at present, to support you and your Administration, in whatever measures you may think proper to adopt for the welfare and happiness of our Country," he concluded.[50]

As a lame-duck president on his way out of office, and suffering a loss of popularity because of the Embargo Act, which he had never fully supported, Jefferson was glad to receive this cheering news. He angrily contrasted Southern patriotism with "eastern" disloyalty, observing that even South Carolina's Federalists generally supported the Embargo law. Trying to maintain his reserve, his reply to Lehré exaggerated the degree of national unity behind the Embargo. "While the opposition to the late laws of embargo has in one quarter amounted almost to rebellion and treason, it is pleasing to know that all the rest of the nation has approved of the proceedings of the constituted authorities," he asserted. The old revolutionary now perceived himself as the symbol of law and order against criminal elements. "The steady union which you mention of our fellow citizens of S. Carolina, is entirely in their character," he commented, not foreseeing that within twenty years the state would be in the forefront of disobedience and nullification of laws. "They have never failed in fidelity to their country and the republican spirit of its constitution. Never before was that union more needed or more salutary than under our present crisis."[51]

Contending that war was the only viable solution to the current stalemate with the European powers, and noting that his recent annual message to Congress had recommended war, Jefferson emphasized the need for national unity. Charging that the Northeastern Federalists preferred to submit to British domination for the sake of commercial profit, he argued, "You will see that we have to choose between the alternatives of embargo and war; there is indeed one and only one other, that is submission and tribute. For all the federal [i.e., Federalist] propositions for trading to the places permitted by the edicts of the belligerents, result in fact in submission, although they do not choose to pronounce the naked word." Pejoratively referring to his Federalist political opponents as a "sect," he favorably compared South Carolina's Federalist minority with the majority Federalists in Massachusetts' legislature. "I do not believe, however, that our fellow citizens of that sect with you will concur with those to the east in this parricide purpose, any more than in the disorganizing conduct which has disgraced the latter. I conclude this from their conduct in your legislature in its vote on that question."[52] With his tendency to exaggerate at this time, Jefferson equated New England merchants willing to suffer British harassment of their trade in return for likely profits with "parricides," killers of the republican virtue for which their venerable fathers and region were renowned.[53]

Jefferson must have been aware of the election losses his Democratic Party had suffered in New England, largely because of the Embargo. Federalists regained control of the Massachusetts legislature in the spring 1808 elections, although Democrats claimed that many towns with Democratic majorities were too stingy to send delegates to Boston because they did not want to pay their salaries. In Connecticut, where they had always been a minority, Democrats lost seats in the state legislature too. But Governor John Langdon and a Democratic legislature maintained control in New Hampshire. In 1808, Democrats lost their dominant position in Rhode Island. Although Democrats held on to the state governorship through the popular Fenner family, Federalists gained a majority of the Rhode Island state legislature. In Vermont in 1808, Federalists took over the governorship and the upper house, but Democrats kept control of the lower house. Ironically, Republican newspapers that sought to arouse support for the Embargo in Federalist locales pointed out that former President John Adams, who was personally hostile to Jefferson at this time, supported it.[54]

Growing increasingly disillusioned with the Embargo, Jefferson thought it was now supported, ironically, only by Federalists. They dreaded war with England and preferred to continue the Embargo. Moreover, they often broke the law by smuggling; New England was the only section of the country where incomes increased during the trade stoppage.[55] Writing to his confidant Thomas Mann Randolph, he denounced not only the Federalists but Bonaparte, who he suspected had made peace with Russia and Sweden to enable him to "execute his murderous purposes on Spain & Portugal at his leisure." Maintaining his belief in Federalist duplicity, Jefferson wrote, "There is a sincere wish to take off the embargo before Congress rises, prevailing with every body but the Federalists, who (notwithstanding their clamours) it is perfectly known would deprecate it as their greatest calamity." Jefferson favored an effort to distinguish between the belligerents, resuming trade with whichever one was less obnoxious. He finally concluded that war (and the abandonment of the Embargo) was the only sensible option. "The difficulty is how to separate the belligerents so as to have trade with one while we have war with the other," he advised, "because a war with both continues the embargo in effect, with war added to it." He expressed a feeble hope that by the summer of 1809, either England or France would repeal its decrees against U.S. commerce; Congress would then "declare war" against the refractory nation.[56] (Macon's Bill Number Two, passed in May 1810, which precipitated the War of 1812, partially implemented Jefferson's ideas.)

Concurring with what he perceived were the intentions of the Democratic majority, Jefferson favored limited war. He expected Congress to meet in special session in May 1809 to repeal the Embargo and replace it with "letters of marque & reprisal," legalizing privateering against belligerents who continued to harass American shipping. "This will let Europe see that our purpose is war, while not expressing it authoritatively," he wrote Randolph. He believed that the unleashing of privateers, which had seriously harassed British trade during the American Revolution, would intimidate England and France. Representing a prelude to war, "at the same time it would quiet our own people by letting them see the term when the embargo is to cease."[57]

By January 1809, Jefferson thought that the purposes of the leading New England Federalists had grown more sinister. He warned that the extremists, expecting that the Republican congressional majority would soon replace the Embargo with war, had revived their plot for the New England states and possibly New York to secede from a Democratic-controlled Union and join the British Empire or form an independent country. Although congressional Democrats expected their proposal for limited war to appease public opinion and "keep every thing quiet," Jefferson was less optimistic. In the waning days of his presidency, he exaggerated the power that diehard Federalists had acquired in the state legislatures. He learned that "the monarchists of the North (who have been for some time fostering the hope of separation) have been able to make so successful use of the embargo as to have federalized the 5 Eastern States & to endanger N. York, and they mean now to organize their opposition by the regular powers of their State governments." Instead of praising the Embargo as preferable to war, Federalists were now manipulating public hostility to the law in order to encourage disunion. Jefferson claimed that the Massachusetts legislature was about to call a convention whose objective was secession of the "whole country east of the North [Hudson] River, & they are assured of the protection of Gr. Br." Perhaps through Secretary of War Dearborn, Republican Massachusetts legislators had informed Jefferson that they hoped that congressional repeal of the Embargo "will satisfy so great a portion of their people as to remove the danger of a convention." Expecting Congress to repeal the Embargo and authorize privateering in May or June, Jefferson's Republican informants still feared that self-centered New England merchants might denounce even this moderate defiance of their favorite trading partner, Britain.[58]

Jefferson had reached the conclusion that Massachusetts merchants' support for measures to preserve national honor could not be taken for granted. He was unwilling to appease them by abandoning letters of marque and non-intercourse with England and France. "We must save the Union; but we wish to sacrifice as little as possible of the honor of the nation," he asserted. Expecting war with England rather than France, he justifiably feared that Britain would offer inducements to convince the New England state legislatures to stay out of the conflict. "If war takes place with England," the philosopher-politician presciently observed, "we have no security that she will not offer neutrality & commerce to N. England, & that the latter will not accept it." His hopes rested on Britain's leaders, who he hoped would be "rational" enough to comprehend that they could not simultaneously fight Napoleon and the United States. He thought that, after assessing Madison's victory in the recent presidential election; reviewing documents his administration had recently published demonstrating his government's "fair conduct towards both countries," in an effort to allay British suspicions that he preferred France; "the failure, so far, of expected insurrections in Massachusetts," on which he suspected the British depended; and Napoleon's projected "ultimate" triumph in Spain despite persisting nationalist opposition, the British ministry would choose negotiation rather than war.[59] For Jefferson, continuation of the Embargo was out of the question.

Jefferson remained torn between his general belief in the patriotism and virtue of New Englanders and his awareness, arising from their widespread violations of the Embargo, that they considered the pursuit of profit among their "natural rights," above the law. He expected Congress to meet in special session in May 1809 to end the Embargo and issue "letters of marque & reprisal against the nations which shall have decrees against our rightful commerce." With the likelihood of war increasing, Jefferson feared that his political opponents would attempt to renew the Embargo, an option he opposed. Among these he included "the Federalists, the Apostates, & 2 or 3 honest Republicans from the South, who (these last I mean) wish to try the embargo till the fall." Reiterating his earlier view that the monarchical Federalist extremists were more loyal to England than to the United States, he feared that war with Britain might lead those in "the North" to secede. He wrote, "In the mean time the disquietude in the North is extreme, & we are uncertain what extent of conflagration a spark might occasion." As usual, he distinguished between the "republican" rank-and-file New England voters and the political and mercantile elite, whom he seldom identified by name. "A line now seems to be drawing between the really republican Federalists & the English party," he lamented, "who are devoted, soul & body, to England & monarchy." Unless England repealed its maritime decrees, he expected war with Britain to be declared in May.[60]

At this point, Jefferson was packing up and preparing to leave Washington for Monticello. Now merely an ex-president, he was no longer the respected head of his party, and few Congressmen requested his advice. He most candidly stated his views to family members, such as Thomas Mann Randolph, Jr. On January 31, 1809, he wrote him that he intended to sell land to help pay his debts. Claiming that getting rid of one's debts was the source of greatest "happiness," he hoped to sell unremunerative timber land. He wrote, "A property yielding so little profit had better be sold and converted into more profitable form, and none can be more profitable, that is, yield so much happiness, as the paiment [*sic*] of debts, which are an insufferable torment." Perhaps he was really thinking about the last year of his presidency when he referred to "insufferable torment." Congress was about to repudiate his Embargo policy, but he had already rejected it himself. He now preferred war. Indeed, he now implied that the Embargo had been Congress's idea. As he wrote Randolph in February, "I thought Congress had taken their ground firmly for continuing *their* embargo till June, and then war."[61]

Seeking to update Randolph on recent events, Jefferson's January letter informed him that Congress had passed a resolution to convene in special session for May 1809, when he expected it to consider more drastic measures. He reported that John Nicholas of Virginia had presented a bill for repealing the Embargo and replacing it with letters of marque and reprisal. Jefferson hoped that the Embargo would be feebly enforced until it was repealed, so as not to further alienate the "people of the Eastern States." He expressed anxiety for the preservation of the Union, suspecting that, despite their "ostensible" wrath at the Embargo, the "Essex Junto" really desired "separation & annexation to England" as "their real object" and would not be pacified by the law's repeal. Nonetheless, Jefferson ended with a hopeful assessment. He thought that most of "the people, or even the real Federalists of the prominent kind," desired to remain in the Union. He did not want to antagonize moderates by rigidly enforcing the Embargo in the few remaining weeks of its existence. As he put it, "If we can avoid deeds of force on the land (in the execution of the law) the difficulty may pass over." At the same time, he noted the possibility that the commerce-obsessed "Eastern states" might refuse to join a war against England if the former mother country tempted them with a preferential trade treaty: "I am not certain that if war be commenced against England, they will not accept neutrality & commerce if offered by England. Thus we are placed between the alternatives of abandoning our rights on the ocean, or risking a severance of the Union. My ultimate hope is in the good sense of the body of the people to the eastward who will think more dispassionately when the final question is proposed to them."[62]

A few weeks later, when Jefferson discovered that Congress would repeal the Embargo before his presidency ended, he seemed surprised. He thought that increased military preparations should take place first, and that war should naturally succeed the failed Embargo. He was under the impression that Congress would repeal the Embargo in June 1809, when he would be at home in Monticello, and follow it with war. However, in early February he was initialy stunned to learn that "a sudden and unaccountable revolution of opinion took place the last week, chiefly among the New England and New York members, and in a kind of panic they voted for the 4th of March for removing the embargo, and by such a majority as gave all reason to believe they would not agree either to war or non-intercourse."[63]

Ostensibly, Jefferson had not been kept informed of his party's intentions, so much had his power in the Republican hierarchy declined as a result of his status as a lame-duck president whose apparently bumbling Embargo had diminished the party's popularity. Unconsciously returning their contempt, he thought that popular opposition to the Embargo had intimidated them into an abrupt retreat. He apparently assumed Congress had not thought out an alternative to replace it, and would probably automatically return to the dangerous route of unrestricted trade with the world. For his part, Jefferson no longer feared that the New England states would rebel against continuance of the Embargo or any other policy the Democratic-Republicans devised. In the past few months, he had become convinced that the vast majority of New Englanders were loyal to the Union, and he now disdained the secessionist rumblings of the extreme Essex Junto Federalists. As he put it, writing Randolph in February, Republican rejection of the Embargo occurred "after we had become satisfied that the Essex Junto had found their expectation desperate, of inducing the people there to either separation or forcible opposition." Manifesting no regret that Congress intended to remove the Embargo, his latest information now led him to believe that it would pass a non-intercourse bill against England and France, a policy to which he did not object. "The majority of Congress, however, has now rallied to the removing the embargo on the 4th of March, non-intercourse with *France* and *Great Britain*, trade everywhere else, and continuing war preparations," he informed his son-in-law. "The further details are not yet settled, but I believe it is perfectly certain that the embargo will be taken off the 4th of March," he matter-of-factly concluded.[64]

The erratic tone and wording of this letter, which he began by stating that Congress was undecided about what it would do after repealing the Embargo, and ended by informing Randolph that Congress would implement non-intercourse, revealed that at this point Jefferson was ignorant of what was going on and played little role in the Democratic-Republican Party. He no longer associated himself with the Embargo, but seemed dismayed that Republicans had not shown more backbone in retaining it for a slightly longer period. Evidently, as the words of his letter revealed, Democratic-Republican congressional leaders had kept him "out of the loop" on policy-making in the final days of his administration. Even as president, Jefferson's clout with his party was ephemeral. This suggests that it was puerile for abolitionists to harass him during his retirement with demands that, in light of his alleged overwhelming popularity and influence, it was morally incumbent on him to initiate a campaign to abolish slavery.[65] (Even greater puerility characterizes many historians today, who incessantly charge Jefferson with proslavery racism because he did not make the abolition of slavery part of his party's platform or publicly demand that the state and national governments abolish slavery in his old age.[66])

For his part, with only a few days left in office, Jefferson seemed more satisfied with his presidency than he had been for a long time. Unlike his doubts the year before, he now believed that the citizens of New England would unwaveringly support the government in the event of war, and that only the implacable "Essex Junto" of Federalist extremists would attempt to thwart Republican measures. Along with dozens of other cities and towns, localities in Massachusetts, Connecticut, and other New England states had recently sent Jefferson numerous congratulatory addresses praising his presidency and his services to his country. For someone as sensitive to criticism and needy of public approval as Jefferson had always been, these messages must have been something of a tranquilizer.[67]

On the eve of his retirement, Jefferson perhaps pondered that, as fate would have it, he had been a stronger, more aggressive, "usurping" chief executive than his predecessors, despite his identification with states' rights and strict construction of the Constitution. Through such daring measures as the Louisiana Purchase and the Embargo, he acted on the public will as he conceived it, relying on the people's judgment for vindication or repudiation at election-time. In other words, in many respects he was what political scientist William Nisbet Chambers called a "plebiscitarian" politician, a term that Chambers applied to Jefferson's Federalist opponents. At the same time, he was fundamentally a "popular" leader, as Chambers called his Democratic-Republican Party. As president, he merged "popular" and "plebisci-tarian" identities. After the Embargo had been in force for little more than a year, he admitted his administration's error in proposing it and concurred with popular demands, especially noisy in New England, for ending it. Jefferson yielded to the popular will when it seemed to oppose him. He was not ashamed to acknowledge his mistakes, especially when New England's continued membership in the Union was at stake.[68]

12

The "Sage of Monticello" Views New England at War

Like John Taylor, Jefferson was inspired by New England's political institutions, especially its town meetings. He conceived of them as little democracies enforcing the will of the majority. He was mortified that the popular town meetings of Massachusetts, Connecticut, and Vermont voted against his administration and vigorously resisted its harsh policy of Embargo on Great Britain from 1807 to 1809. The New England states nullified the Embargo by overland smuggling through Canada, and blatantly violated its transatlantic non-shipment provisions.[1] The hardheaded opposition to Jefferson's policy in New England, even among members of his own Democratic-Republican Party, played a major role in the repeal of the measure in March 1809 and the earnest, though ultimately unsuccessful efforts by the Madison Administration to reach agreement with British minister David Erskine on British wartime trade regulations.

Nevertheless, Jefferson had hardly been out of office a year when he reached the conclusion that the New England town meeting was the *ideal* form of government, and should be emulated by his state and throughout the nation. Ironically, his admiration grew especially out of his perverse respect for their effective negation of his administration's most important measure, the Embargo. He merged his new desire to emulate the New England town meetings' direct democracy with his eternal quest for a system of public education in Virginia, which he had tried to enact since 1776. He believed both projects would further democracy and perfect popular government. As he explained to state court Judge John Tyler, a leading Tidewater Democratic-Republican, owner of Greenway plantation in Charles City County, and father of the later president: "I have indeed two great measures at heart, without which no republic can maintain itself in strength. 1. That of general education, to enable every man to judge for himself what will secure or endanger his freedom. 2. To divide every county into hundreds [the Southern name for wards], of such size that all the children of each will be within the reach of a central school in it."[2] He also intended the "hundreds" to be the "fundamental" seat of local government and town meetings. "Every hundred, besides a school, should have a justice of the peace, a constable and a captain of militia," he advised. "These officers, or some others within the hundred, should be a corporation to manage all its concerns, to take care of its roads, its poor, and its police by patrols, &c. (as the select men of the Eastern townships)."[3] Expressing this surge of admiration for New England institutions, Jefferson preferred to regard the section as an integral part of the Union ("the Eastern townships") rather than as external and alien to it ("New England").

Advancing the radical idea of selection of Virginia's jurors by the voters instead of the county sheriff, Jefferson believed that contests for these and all other state positions should take place in the towns, or "hundreds." He suggested that local militia units ("captaincies") temporarily perform the functions of wards, "with a power to the courts to alter them occasionally." "These little republics would be the main strength of the great one," he exultantly predicted, admitting that the political power and success of his Eastern political opponents had inspired this idea. Giving them perhaps more credit for the "spirit of '76" than they deserved, at the expense of his own state he asserted that they had initiated the Revolution of 1775 as well as the counterrevolution of 1808. "We owe to them the vigor given to our revolution in its commencement in the Eastern States," he said, "and by them the Eastern States were enabled to repeal the embargo in opposition to the Middle, Southern and Western States, and their large and lubberly division into counties which can never be assembled." And, he may have speculated, merging public education (with a democratic-republican slant, of course) with their town meetings might even convert stubbornly Federalist New Englanders to his way of thinking. Perhaps with the increasing likelihood of war with Great Britain in mind, Jefferson viewed these miniature town democracies as analogous to an invincible national military machine. As he envisioned it, "General orders are given out from a centre to the foreman of every hundred, as to the sergeants of an army, and the whole nation is thrown into energetic action, in the same direction in one instant and as one man, and becomes absolutely irresistible." Should such local military/political democratic institutions form in the Democratic-Republican South, Jefferson proclaimed that he would "consider it as the dawn of the salvation of the republic."[4]

On the eve of war in 1812 and a possible Massachusetts Federalist alliance with England, Jefferson, notwithstanding his melodramatic scenarios of civil strife, staunchly opposed a preemptive "first strike" (a term used by a later, more powerful generation of Americans engaged in foreign wars) against a sister state. Though alarmed by its large number of apparently pro–British leaders, he was confident that the mass of its citizens would be loyal to the Union. Jefferson had met Massachusetts congressman, signer of the Declaration of Independence, and independent Federalist Elbridge Gerry many years earlier in New York City in 1766, on his way home from Philadelphia, where he had traveled to be inoculated for smallpox. Gerry and he had become close friends, and Gerry was the first person to send him a copy of the U.S. Constitution in 1787 (by way of their mutual friend John Adams), when he was minister to France.[5]

Gerry, who was considering switching from the Federalists to the Democratic-Republicans, had abruptly initiated a correspondence with Jefferson on the eve of war. Jefferson warned Gerry that Massachusetts contained an "English faction" that wanted to run the United States government, whether by means of popular elections or not; and that it was prepared to leave the Union if its demands were not satisfied. "The [pro–British] newspapers say rebellion, and that they will not remain united with us unless we will permit them to govern the majority," he asserted. Although he believed that their "anti-republican spirit" should "be met at once," he advised the exercise of moderation by the other states of the Union rather than the employment of military force against their potentially disloyal neighbor. As he often did, he reiterated the views of Madison's *Federalist Number 10*. He exhorted Americans to rely on the territorial extent and cultural diversity of their nation, which differentiated it from the ancient, ill-fated Greek city-states, for protection against threats to democratic rule. "The extent of our country secures it, I hope, from the vindictive passions of the petty corporations of Greece," he said. Projecting a worst-case scenario, he predicted that if the radical Massachusetts Federalists led by Timothy Pickering and Christopher Gore succeeded in taking their state out of the Union, the British would reject their aspirations to become part of the Empire and enjoy its trading privileges. Distrusting these High Federalist leaders, Jefferson suspected them of urging their state to join Britain because only in this mode would they gain the increased power that the Massachusetts electorate would deny them even under "an independent government." Inevitably, he thought that an independent Massachusetts would beg the British in vain for union "and a dispensation with their navigation act" after losing their wonted role in U.S. commerce. On the other hand, Jefferson thought Massachusetts Republicans were numerous enough to defeat pro-monarchical elements in the unlikely event of civil war in that state, after which the "other seventeen States" would restrain them from wreaking vengeance on the monarchical minority.[6]

Returning from these imaginary flights he apparently enjoyed, Jefferson believed that even most of the "federalists of Massachusetts" were "honest and well-meaning." Thus, he sarcastically expected that Pickering and Gore would be able to recruit only "silk stocking gentry, but no yeomanry—an army of officers without soldiers," in their "perverse" probe for "separation and rebellion" from the United States. He firmly rejected a military confrontation between Massachusetts and the other states on the question of resisting Britain. Alluding to the internal struggle between Whigs and Loyalists during the American Revolution, Jefferson was optimistic that he and Gerry "shall sink to rest, without having been actors or spectators in another civil war." Viewing Massachusetts and Virginia as symbiotic, natural economic allies, "faithful companions in the war of Independence, peculiarly tallied in interests, by each wanting exactly what the other has to spare," Jefferson argued that their recent estrangement merely resulted from disagreement over the correct national response to British harassment of neutral trade, which really made Britain "the common enemy of both." Hoping for ultimate "re-union" between mercantile, Federalist Massachusetts and agricultural, Republican Virginia as in Revolutionary days, he was encouraged that a congressional Republican caucus had nominated Gerry for vice-president after his defeat for re-election as governor of Massachusetts. Though ready to subdue rebellion, Jefferson proposed to minimize the seriousness of radical Federalist newspapers' secessionist threats, with their likely expectation of British aid: "A government like ours should be slow in believing this, should put forth its whole might when necessary to suppress it, and promptly return to the paths of reconciliation."[7]

Writing about New England to a former Massachusetts Federalist like Gerry, Jefferson was apt to be more charming and forgiving than when he wrote non–New Englanders, like Philadelphian Thomas Leiper. To this rich Philadelphia tobacco manufacturer he complained that, by demanding special privileges for merchants and insisting that Jefferson abandon his projects to encourage domestic manufacturing and the exportation abroad of manufactures produced at home, Massachusetts Federalists hoped "to convert this great agricultural country into a city of Amsterdam." However, in 1809 Jefferson was not arguing that America remain an "agricultural country," as he did in *Notes on the State of Virginia* almost thirty years earlier. Ironically, he was now charging that the merchant-dominated Federalist Party of the Eastern states wanted to hinder their fellow citizens from producing and exporting cheap manufactures, which would make the United States economically independent. Insidiously, the New England Federalists had convinced the voters that they ought to confine themselves to supplying raw materials for their merchants to ship abroad, and for their ships to bring back foreign manufactures to sell at high prices at home. This comprised part of the Federalist attack on the Embargo. Irate that the Federalists had seemingly succeeded in obstructing his new campaign for domestic manufacturing, Jefferson angrily commented, "Yet this absurd hue and cry has contributed much to federalize New England, this doctrine goes to the sacrificing agriculture and manufactures to commerce; to the calling all our people from the interior country to the sea-shore to turn merchants, and to convert this great agricultural country to a city of Amsterdam."[8]

Southerners, especially Republicans, generally agreed that New England merchants and shippers received preferential treatment in the Union and benefited from carrying tobacco, cotton, rice, and other Southern agricultural products. Even during the disputed presidential election of 1800–1801, when New England congressmen persisted in voting for Aaron Burr to deprive Jefferson of victory, Virginia Republican James Monroe viewed their obstructionism as a sham threat to "disorganize" the Union. He thought they were bluffing. Arguing that New England Federalists really had no desire to secede, since they reaped great benefits from union by cheating the Southern farmers and planters who traded with them, he said. "The Eastern people have no thoughts of breaking the Union, & giving up the hold they have on the valuable productions of the South. They only mean to bully us, thereby preserve the ascendancy, and improve their profits." He expected them eventually to acquiesce in Jefferson's election.[9]

Unlike Monroe in 1801, Jefferson harbored no particular hostility toward New England on the eve of his first election. During the Embargo crisis of his presidency, he believed that his policy to encourage domestic manufacturing would help most New Englanders as well as the rest of the country, especially if he preserved peace by causing the collapse of the British economy, which depended on exporting manufactures. In general, Jefferson had long thought that Virginia and the rest of the country should emulate New England's political institutions. One could hardly disagree with John Ferling's conclusion (although he is discussing Jefferson's activities during the Revolutionary War period, when he seldom referred to "New England" *per se*): "Whether or not he realized it, what Jefferson sought was to make Virginia more like Massachusetts."[10]

The War of 1812 marked the end of Jefferson's illusion that the democratic form of New England's government would overcome the "monarchical" attitude of many of its leaders. Their refusal to assist the national government with men or money; permitting defiant smuggling in violation of non-intercourse laws; and indeed treasonous rumblings of secession and perhaps even alliance with the British, furnished ample reason for Jefferson to fear what Massachusetts and its sister states might do. By December 1813, Boston Federalist newspapers contended that the war was lost and urged President Madison to negotiate peace with Great Britain. Timothy Pickering and Josiah Quincy, Massachusetts Federalist leaders, demanded Virginia give up its domination of the presidency.[11] Meanwhile, Massachusetts, farmers and businessmen sent out an illegal flow of foodstuffs to Canada for which they were paid in hard cash and imported British manufactured goods. Although by late 1813 there was little specie to be found south of the Potomac, New England had a specie surplus resulting from the illegal cash and carry import and export business its citizens conducted with the enemy, although bankers and the state government refused to lend money to the Union. Rejecting Madison's requests to assist the Union with volunteers, the Massachusetts legislature instead paid for seventy thousand state militiamen, whether to fight the British or the United States was unclear. The governors of Massachusetts claimed that their refusal to assist the war effort was constitutional, and the state never sent even a single militiaman against the British during the entire war. When Congress passed an embargo in December 1813 to hinder the trade between New England and Great Britain, Massachusetts wrath increased, and town meetings petitioned for its repeal and an end to excessive Southern influence in the government. Even congressional repeal of the Embargo at Madison's urging in April 1814, both because it was poorly enforced and as a peace offering to Massachusetts, failed to pacify the New England extremists.[12]

After British troops burned Washington in August 1814, the Massachusetts government became even more aggressively disloyal. Town meetings petitioned for a regional convention to consider such options as a separate peace with the British. During the summer of 1814, British troops occupied most of Maine without resistance. Massachusetts Federalist governor Caleb Strong, who was annually elected to that office from 1812 to 1816, when he retired, must have considered his constituents willing to buy peace at almost any price. Only reluctantly, he called up the state militia to prepare for a possible British invasion of the mainland. Rather than fight the British, Federalists preferred peace and perhaps an alliance with them against the United States. Benjamin Russell, Boston Federalist publisher of the *Columbian Centinel*, after fraternizing with British naval officers aboard a frigate, informed his readers that the British would favorably regard Madison's resignation, which he advocated. In late 1814, John Low, Maine's representative in the state assembly, proposed that Massachusetts send a delegation to Washington to ask Madison to resign from office. In October 1814, the state legislature proposed a regional convention, 260 to 90, and sent twelve delegates to meet on December 15, 1814, at Hartford, Connecticut, with representatives from the other New England states (Rhode Island and Connecticut alone showed up; Vermont and New Hampshire did not officially attend). Learning of the burning of Washington, Massachusetts leaders assumed that the U.S. had lost the war, in which their state luckily had not participated.[13]

Massachusetts' refusal to participate in the war and its virtual treason in expectation of America's defeat provided the context in which the most egregious of Governor Strong's acts took place. Unlike Jefferson, who seemed to think access to the Newfoundland fisheries was vital to Massachusetts' economy, in order to deter a British invasion Strong was prepared to yield to the British the right to the fisheries as well as give up some territory in Maine disputed with Canada. In September 1814, after the British took over northern Maine, Strong sent an emissary to Sir John Coape Sherbrooke, the British commander at Halifax, whose troops had overrun Maine, to offer a separate peace, and possibly Massachusetts secession, if the British agreed to protect an independent Massachusetts from U.S. retaliation. The British government agreed to these terms. Lord Bathurst, Secretary of War, and Prime Minister Lord Liverpool, were enthusiastic about them, hoping to use them to prod concessions from President Madison, until the Treaty of Ghent and Jackson's victory at New Orleans vitiated the proposal. Rumors of New England secession were quite common toward the end of 1814. The Democratic mouthpiece, Samuel Harrison Smith's (Washington) *National Intelligencer*, constantly warned from October to December 1814 that the United States would impose discriminatory duties against New England's produce if it seceded, and would encourage its inhabitants to migrate to loyal parts of the Union.[14]

Like Jefferson, S. H. Smith correctly read the less than virtuous motives of Massachusetts

Federalists. Renouncing the old Puritan concept of the individual's subordination to the well-being of the community in economic affairs, embodied in such dicta as the "just price," leading Federalists bluntly declared that New England could not, or would not support the war because Madison flouted its self-interest by pursuing it. The Boston *Columbian Centinel*, the foremost Federalist newspaper, rhetorically asked, "Who tries to save the Union, MR. MADISON, who has destroyed all those New England Interests for which alone she entered into the *Union*, or the New England Patriots, who are about to assemble [at the Hartford Convention] to see if they cannot regain the rights they have lost?"[15]

In Onuf's interpretation, Jefferson, enraged by Massachusetts opposition to the war effort, desired thoroughgoing revenge against the errant New Englanders: he hoped the U.S. Army would invade the region and, after evacuating its Republican "moiety," "destroy" New England rather than tolerate its continued resistance to the national will and war effort. (Perhaps Onuf was mistakenly thinking about the Union's treatment of the South as a "conquered province" after the Civil War, a topic which he briefly covered in a book he wrote with his brother Nicholas.[16]) After summarizing several letters Jefferson wrote, mostly at the time of the Hartford Convention, and silently (and misleadingly) inserting phrases Jefferson used five years later, when his hopes for the union palled during the Missouri Crisis, Onuf notes:

> Jefferson's imaginative scenario enabled him to remove the good republicans of Massachusetts out of harm's way and so enact a ritual humiliation on the remaining "army of officers." ... The practical effect of this exercise was to draw a "geographical line" between the traitors who stayed and the good republicans who moved on to friendlier climes. Jefferson was eager to draw such a line at this time both because its extent was so limited (he persisted in the belief that the "Essex Federalists" would succeed only in Massachusetts and that the other New England states would remain loyal) and because it justified the projection of his own "deadly hatred" against his "fellow citizens."[17]

Asserting, based on his reading of these few letters, that Jefferson employed neurotic/psychotic defenses of projection and denial, Onuf powerfully concludes, "Jefferson made Federalists foreigners and gave them a country of their own (Massachusetts) so that he could imagine making war on them–and so persuade himself that he was not violating the republican gospel of peace and affectionate union."[18]

According to Onuf, Jefferson psychopathically tried to convince himself that he was justified in recommending the unpardonable extermination of his fellow citizens in a venerable section of the Union. (Luckily, he was out of power at the time, and he was suggesting this course to individuals who lacked political influence.) Onuf concludes that Jefferson justified making war on fellow citizens because it was essential to exterminate "monarchists" who would vitiate republican principles and undo all of Jefferson's work. In a worst-case scenario, they might even reunite with the ex-Mother Country. After examining and interpreting a few of Jefferson's letters written during the War of 1812, Onuf sweepingly concludes that Jefferson was obsessed with "destroying New England," thereby promoting the Republican South's uncontested sway in the Union. "Jefferson's ruminations about the fate of New England during the War of 1812 prefigured his response to the Missouri crisis," Onuf explains, contrasting Jefferson's cheerful bloodthirstiness during the war with his melancholy caution amidst the postwar dispute over slavery expansion:

> In both cases advocates of dangerously unrepublican principles held sway within a specific geographical region; having lost their national base of support, these unreconstructed "monarchists" exploited sectionalist

grievances in order to prepare the way for disunion and foreign alliances. Yet, despite these apparent parallels, Jefferson's response to the earlier crisis was profoundly different. In 1813 and 1814, he welcomed a war with the New England Federalists that he knew the loyal Republican states would easily win. The subsequent restoration of the union, purified of the last vestiges of monarchical corruption, would redeem the promise of the American Revolution.[19]

But do Jefferson's letters really say what Onuf imputes to them? He only cites three: to James Martin, Sept. 20, 1813, to William Short, November 28, 1814, and to John Melish, December 10, 1814. A careful examination of these letters, which will be undertaken below, reveals that, far from expressing a desire for the violent suppression of Massachusetts resistance or New England's extermination as a section, Jefferson's attitude is one of watchful waiting. He advocated a defensive posture, if resistance to military invasion by a hypothetical alliance between Britain and New England became necessary. Nowhere did he suggest a U.S. military expedition to "destroy" New England, as Onuf argues.[20]

In the months leading up to the War of 1812, Jefferson, like many other War Hawks, seemed frustrated by New England obstruction. Jefferson was confident that his fellow Virginians favored war with Great Britain and the seizure of its huge Canadian colony. A few weeks before President Madison asked Congress for war, Jefferson wrote him, "Your declaration of war is expected with perfect calmness, and if those in the North mean systematically to govern the majority it is as good a time for trying them as we can expect."[21] Historians hostile to Jefferson use this quotation to depict him as a saber-rattling warmonger eager for the U.S. Army to invade antiwar New England, much as commanding general Alexander Hamilton recommended "putting Virginia to the test of resistance" by invading it in 1799. However, this was not the case. Despite Jefferson's belligerent tone, the context of his letter indicates that he was merely suggesting that the impending debate on a declaration of war would reveal the unpopularity of New England's peace policy and the consequent lack of credibility of its claim to "govern the majority." Jefferson might also have been alluding to the upcoming presidential election.

In the presidential election of 1812, Madison's leading opponent was the "peace candidate," New York's governor DeWitt Clinton. Clinton was a former Democratic-Republican who sought to form an antiwar coalition of commerce-oriented Northern Federalists and export-oriented Northern Republican farmers against Madison and the "Virginia Dynasty," which Clinton's supporters claimed had governed too long on behalf of Southern agrarians and slaveholders.[22] Perhaps Jefferson had the election contest in mind, and his expectation that Clinton represented a minority and would be defeated, when he alluded to "those in the North" who hoped "to govern the majority." Although Madison won the election, it was by a smaller majority of electoral votes than he and Jefferson won their two previous elections.

Jefferson was ready to support war with Great Britain in 1812 despite the likelihood that it would further derange his fluctuating personal economic fortunes. The embargo during his presidency had caused him and other Southern planters great financial loss, probably greater than was endured by the North.[23] As he observed to President Madison about the ninety-day embargo that Congress imposed in April 1812, the price of "flour, depressed under the first panic of the embargo," had only gradually recovered and would again fall with the domestic glut produced by the erection of wartime blockades and embargoes.[24]

Except for the finest grades, tobacco had become nearly worthless; even corn was more profitable to cultivate because of its soil-restorative properties. Jefferson recommended wheat as a more profitable crop. Having just returned from Poplar Forest, he reported to Madison that, notwithstanding economic privation, Virginia was united in favor of war. "I am just returned from Bedford," he wrote. "I believe every county South of James river, from Buckingham to the Blue ridge (the limits of my information) furnished its quota of volunteers. Your declaration of war is expected with perfect calmness" in Virginia, he said.[25]

· · · · ·

When Congress declared war on June 18, 1812, by narrower margins than would characterize its vote on most future conflicts, Jefferson's zeal remained undiminished. Like most Republicans, he was exasperated by New England's continued opposition. Lending Madison advice and encouragement, he assured him of the war declaration's popularity in Virginia, "the only opinion being that it should have been issued the moment the season admitted the militia to enter Canada." With mordant waggery, he admitted some minor opposition to war in his state: "The federalists indeed are open mouthed against the declaration, but they are poor devils here, not worthy of notice. A bunch of tar to each state South of the Potomac, will keep all in order," he advised, "and that will be freely contributed without troubling government."[26] Remembering that revolutionary crowds had tarred and feathered loyalists during the American Revolution, a conflict he often compared to the present one, Jefferson drolly assured Madison that this time-tested remedy for would-be traitors and sunshine patriots would be inexpensive to a cash-strapped government.

If timid Virginia Tories deserved this nonlethal punishment, the more vigorous New England opposition required something stronger. At this point Jefferson, again humorously, anomalously recommended violence against New England. In phrases that the editors of the early printed editions of his writings deleted, perhaps for fear of damaging his reputation for benign statesmanship, Jefferson wrote Madison, "To the North they will give you more trouble. You may then have to apply the rougher drastics of Governor Wright [Robert Wright, Republican former governor of Maryland and a congressman during the War of 1812], hemp and confiscation."[27] Surprisingly, Onuf does not mention Jefferson's ostensibly murderous recommendation, probably the closest remarks he ever made to justify the professor's claim that he wished to "destroy" New England.

Jefferson was obviously jesting. In fact, he was only quoting Congressman Wright, further diluting the sincerity of his sentiments. In a speech in Congress several weeks before war was declared, Wright had advised that, if "the signs of treason and civil war discover themselves in any quarter of the American Empire … the evil would soon be radically cured, by hemp [for hanging traitors] and confiscation [of property]."[28] Certainly, both Wright and Jefferson were aware that the U.S. Constitution, which prohibited use of bills of attainder by either the state or national governments, made such action by Congress illegal.

Other Republicans, albeit with less extreme proposals than hanging, also desired to punish Federalist obstructionism. Implying that war would silence partisanship, the *Boston Yankee*, one of Massachusetts' few Jeffersonian newspapers, supported it as a means to "insure peace at home, if not with the world." Madison's brother-in-law, Virginia congressman John George Jackson, advised, "The war will separate the partisans of England from the honest federalists & *Tar & Feathers* will cure their penchant for our enemy."[29] Like 1860–1861, it was a period of unprecedented tension and divisiveness in the new nation's history. Rash statements were to be expected from nationalists (in this case Southern Republicans) who sought to preserve the republic's independence from what they considered obstructive, potentially secessionist Northern states.[30]

Although Jefferson wrote his letter to James Martin more than a year before the Hartford Convention, New England's militias and governors had already been refractory, refusing to serve under federal military authorities, pay their quotas of national taxes, or contribute to national loans and treasury notes. Obviously aware of Massachusetts' particular irascibility, Jefferson favored permitting the state to leave the Union peacefully if that was what its people wanted. However, he was confident that this would never occur. Half of Massachusetts citizens were "republicans," he estimated, and many of the remainder were aware that Massachusetts needed the Union more than the Union needed Massachusetts. He anticipated that the state would remain in the Republic, if only for fear of losing domestic markets for its manufactures in the South and Middle States and the privilege of carrying those regions' exports abroad, both of which he predicted the United States would withhold if Massachusetts chose seces-sion. Moreover, American ships and produce were excluded from most European ports because of various blockades by Britain and France. Jefferson expected New England would continue to suffer these restrictions even if it declared its independence. Jefferson even pre-dicted that Great Britain, eager to destroy an enfeebled potential competitor, would manip-ulate the situation to negotiate an anti–Massachusetts commercial treaty with a cooperative rump Union.[31]

Thus, Jefferson theoretically agreed with his old foe Alexander Hamilton's interminable predictions, in *Federalist Papers* 6, 7, and 8, that wars would take place between individual or partially-confederated leagues of states in the absence of a strong federal union, since, as Hamilton put it, neighboring states were "natural enemies."[32] In *Federalist* Number 6, Hamilton warned: "A man must be far gone in Utopian speculations who can seriously doubt that, if these States should either be wholly disunited, or only united in partial confederacies, the subdivisions into which they might be thrown would have frequent and violent contests with each other. To presume a want of motives for such contests as an argument against their exis-tence, would be to forget that men are ambitious, vindictive, and rapacious. To look for a continuation of harmony between a number of independent, unconnected sovereignties in the same neighbourhood, would be to disregard the uniform course of human events, and to set at defiance the accumulated experience of ages."[33] On the other hand, Jefferson did not think that things would reach such an extreme between the Union and Massachusetts. He predicted that Massachusetts would prudently reject secession, aware "that in case of war with the Union, which occurrences between coterminous nations frequently produce, it would be a contest of one against fifteen."[34]

In considering the possibility of war between Massachusetts and the Union, therefore, Jefferson was not being unduly aggressive. He was merely taking a page from Hamilton, a man who appeared to him in this, as in other instances during the War of 1812, in the unwonted role of mentor. Indeed, Jefferson was sympathetic toward the Eastern states' reluctance to pay war taxes. In arrears on his federal and state taxes throughout the War of 1812, he believed that the Democrats were misguided in levying high land taxes to pay for the conflict. Writing to William Short on November 28, 1814, while Congress considered a six-million-dollar tax on houses, lands, and slaves, he urged it to adopt, for the duration of the War of 1812, the old Hamiltonian principle of "funding" the debt—merely paying the interest on it—rather than employing a "sinking fund" which paid installments of both interest and principal. In light of the conflict's heavy expenses, the latter would be too burdensome during wartime. His correspondent, Short, a politically unpopular Virginian who admired Hamilton, was a Federalist in all but name despite his lifelong friendship with Jefferson. Short blamed Madison for the war, thought it had been a mistake and ruined the economy. Thus, Jefferson probably thought he would find a sympathetic reader when he bluntly wrote that he thought that Congress's fiscal policies were unwise (even though his son-in-law, John Wayles Eppes of Virginia, chaired the House Committee on Ways and Means). "I wish I could see them [Congress] get into a better train of finance," he said. "If anything could revolt our citizens against the war, it would be the extravagance with which they are about to be taxed. It is strange indeed, that at this day, and in a country where English proceedings are so familiar, the principles and advantages of funding should be neglected, and [tax] expedients resorted to."[35]

Nearly as mercilessly as a New England Federalist, Jefferson denounced the Democratic Congress's fiscal policies: "Their new bank, if not abortive at its birth, will not last through one campaign; and the taxes proposed cannot be paid." He believed the patriotic Southern states suffered most from the wartime embargoes and British blockades, while the Easterners smuggled goods across borders and overseas. "How can a people who cannot get fifty cents a bushel for their wheat, while they pay twelve dollars a bushel for their salt, pay five times the amount of taxes they ever paid before?" he protested, perhaps contemplating his own predicament. "Yet that will be the case in all the States south of the Potomac. Our resources are competent to the maintenance of the war if duly economized and skillfully employed in the way of anticipation. However, we must suffer, I suppose, from our ignorance in funding, as we did from that of fighting, until necessity teaches us both."[36]

Although critical of the Democrats, Jefferson was most bitter toward the "Eastern" states during the War of 1812, especially in its first two years. At this time, because of a tacit bargain with the British, the New England states remained unblockaded. In exchange, they traded with British troops and ships, violating the 1812 embargo act and lending little support to the United States Army. Such blatant disloyalty aroused Jefferson's alarm and contempt. Writing in December 1813 to David Bailie Warden, an Irish radical who was in England during the war, he vented his anger. Updating him on the struggle, he argued that Massachusetts-born General William Hull, although a Republican, deserved death by court-martial for his cowardly surrender of the fort at Detroit and refusal to obey presidential orders to invade Canada. But he felt even greater outrage at the "Eastern states" refusal to contribute their "resources" to the Canadian campaign, especially since they were closest to the battlefield. Consequently, the "Middle & Southern states, most remote from the scene of action," had to bear the burden, impeding the dispatch of a formidable force at the outset. Jefferson assured Warden that the British were lying for propaganda purposes in claiming great victories over the Americans, and were indeed suffering defeats. Unfortunately, American ships, under embargo and British blockade, lacked access to the ocean and could not tell Europeans the truth. He was especially angry that New England's Federalist governments bargained with the British, deceiving them with promises of eventual secession in order to gain exemption from the blockade. Although he distrusted Massachusetts' government, he retained his respect and confidence in the republican integrity of its citizens. "The game playing by a few base & cunning leaders in Massachusetts, however degrading to the state, is a compleat dupery of the English," he believed. "If the question of separation, with which they are tantalising the English were ever to be proposed to the people of that state not one tenth even of the federalists would countenance it. Yet by decieving [sic] the enemy on this head they keep themselves unblockaded and their trade little disturbed."[37] Thus, Jefferson showed no animosity toward the people of Massachusetts, and apparently continued to admire their democratic town meeting-style government. On the other hand, he was painfully aware that their legislatures and governors were more interested in the region's economic self-interest than its political freedom and autonomy; perhaps he feared they confused the two.

Calculating that Massachusetts' monarchical Federalists who "bear deadly hatred to their republican fellow-citizens" and would prefer British "despotism" to republican government numbered less than one-fourth of the state's voters, Jefferson doubted that they would be able to manipulate the republican majority to favor secession and civil war. Even should the "monarchical" minority somehow carry the rest of the state for secession, Jefferson professed little alarm. "I see, in their separation, no evil but the example" they would serve for other states in promoting the legality of leaving the Union, he observed in a letter to James Martin. In the event of the state's secession, Jefferson envisioned a mass exodus from an independent Massachusetts to the more fertile (and democratic) soils of the other states. He thought that rational discussion of the pros and cons of secession, even during wartime, would have salutary consequences. But if Massachusetts *did* finally secede, Jefferson warned, "Their refractory course ... will not be unpunished by the indignation of their co-States, their loss of influence with them, the censure of history, and the stain on the character of their State."[38]

Rather than eagerly advocating a preventive war against a secessionist "monarchical" Massachusetts, as Onuf suggests, Jefferson expected the state to remain in the Union. Nevertheless, he would not interfere if Massachusetts chose to peaceably depart, although he believed the rest of the states would be justified in imposing economic sanctions and other hostile diplomatic measures against it. Of course, should Massachusetts become Britain's ally and invade the United States, Jefferson expected Americans to defend their country.

The latter scenario was the topic of Jefferson's letter to Short on November 28, 1814, at the same time that the New England states were preparing for their momentous convention at Hartford, with its secessionist overtones. On October 18, 1814, the Massachusetts legislature (known as the General Court) called for a convention of the New England states to meet at Hartford, Connecticut, to consider "a radical reform in the national compact." It took the initiative by choosing a set of delegates. The General Court's resolutions and report were widely reprinted, in Hezekiah Niles' popular *Niles Weekly Register* (Baltimore) on November 12, and elsewhere. Jefferson had probably seen them by the time he wrote his letter of 28 November 1814 to his old friend Short.[39]

Jefferson transferred scenarios from post–Periclean ancient Greece, when leaders of conflicting factions in the city-states often called in stronger foreign powers to support them against their enemies, to the situation in his own country. After all, he knew his Montesquieu, who had written in *The Spirit of Laws*: "If a republic be small, it is destroyed by a foreign force; if it be large, it is ruined by an internal imperfection."[40]

In light of the dire military situation, with British troops stationed in Castine, Maine, and parts of Michigan and upstate New York, Jefferson considered the possibility that a seceded Massachusetts might attack the rest of the Union. Hardly awestruck by Massachusetts military power, he rejected a preemptive Union attack on the Anglophile bastion. "If they [Massachusetts] become neutral," he bluntly asserted, "we are sufficient for one enemy without them, and in fact we get no aid from them now." Thus, the United States would be no worse off militarily even if Massachusetts did leave the Union to assume a posture of "neutrality." Should the Massachusetts governor or legislature attempt to join the English army, Jefferson expected that the majority of the state's citizens' opposition to such a course would precipitate intrastate war. As he put it, "If their administration determines to join the enemy, their force will be annihilated by equality of division among themselves. Their federalists will then call in the English army, the republicans ours, and it will only be a transfer of the scene of war from Canada to Massachusetts." As he earlier told James Martin, he believed that Great Britain would make peace with the United States in exchange for its promise *not* to support Massachusetts' right to the fisheries and to give up demands for freedom of the seas (which were made primarily to protect New England shipping, according to Jefferson). He expected that Britain would then turn its forces against an independent Massachusetts.[41]

Still, Jefferson was confident that no internecine conflict would take place between the United States and Massachusetts. "It will not come to this," he assured his friend. "Their [Massachusetts] own people will put down these factionists as soon as they see the real object of their opposition [i.e., secession]; and of this Vermont, New Hampshire, and even Connecticut itself, furnish proofs." He was heartened by the refusal of the Vermont and New Hampshire legislatures to appoint delegates to the Hartford Convention.[42] Jefferson's prediction proved accurate.

13

Jefferson and John Melish

A Scottish Pro–American
and New England in the War of 1812

Like many Americans, Jefferson had long feared the consequences of "foreign influence" in disrupting the new republic's political stability and undermining its independence.[1] He was especially intent on convincing foreign observers that the republic was strong and that national unity would overcome individual or sectional preferences for England or France. This was especially true of English immigrants and travelers, natives of the former mother country who tended to disparage the United States' democratic institutions as anarchical. He was acquainted with John Melish, a prolific Scottish historian, geographer, and liberal reformist writer who traveled through and wrote about the United States during the War of 1812. Melish sent Jefferson a copy of his *Travels* through the United States (1813), seeking to drum up subscriptions for the book. Jefferson discovered new information about the extent of domestic manufacturing in the Western states since the commencement of his Embargo Act in that volume, confirming his belief in the growth of national unity and uniformity. "The candour with which you have viewed the manners & condition of our citizens, is so unlike the narrow prejudices of the French & English travellers preceding you, who, considering each the manner and habits of their own people as the only orthodox," he wrote, "have viewed every thing differing from that test as boorish and barbarous, that your work will be read here extensively, and operate great good."[2]

However, Jefferson was disappointed that, in discussing the disputes between the Federalist and Republican parties over the decades, Melish, after comparing Washington's Farewell Address and Jefferson's first inaugural address, concluded that little ideological difference between the parties existed; they were merely motivated by a quest for votes and the perquisites of public office. Jefferson concealed his anger at Melish's conclusion, which called into question the *raison d'être* of his political life: the struggle for democracy and self-government against the threat of aristocracy and monarchy that he took for granted much of the Federalist leadership embodied, particularly the Massachusetts "Essex Junto." "The primary motive" in the parties' struggle for power was not political patronage, he informed Melish, but "a real and radical difference of political principle." "I sincerely wish our differences were but personally who should govern, and that the principles of our constitution were those of both parties. Unfortunately it is otherwise." Insisting, as he often did, that the Democratic-Republicans properly interpreted the Constitution and were its true and only "friends," he continued, "The question of preference between monarchy and republicanism, which has so long divide mankind elsewhere, threatens a permanent division here."[3]

Jefferson evaded analysis of disputes within the Republican Party between states' rights and nationalist elements; pro- and antislavery segments; and Northern, Southern and Western factions.[4] Instead, he concentrated on the ideological conflict he perceived between monarchical and anti-monarchical factions of the Federalist ("federalist") party, especially in New England. As he usually did, he claimed that there were significant disagreements between the "*leaders* and the *people*" within the Federalist Party. He observed that the people favored representative government, but as generally conservative individuals, rejected the extremism of the French Revolution. Thus, they often favored the British in foreign affairs. As he summarized things for Melish: "Among that section of our citizens called federalists, there are three shades of opinion—distinguishing between the leaders and people who compose it, the leaders consider the English constitution as a model of perfection, some, with a correction of its vices, others with all its corruptions & abuses." He claimed that it was well known that Alexander Hamilton idolized the English constitution and considered the prime minister's ability to gain support by "corrupting" the House of Commons through bribery and political appointments among its greatest strengths. Jefferson pretended to be shocked by such ideas, although as president he was not above attempting to manipulate Federalist legislators by his intimate and ornate dinners, although he seldom if ever offered bribes or political patronage to gain their support. Jefferson assured Melish that he and many others had often heard Hamilton express the opinion "that a correction of what are called its vices would render the English an impracticable government."[5]

He explained to Melish that even Hamilton, despite his great services to the country, always intended for the U.S. to evolve into a monarchy. He and his followers hoped to establish a government like Britain's "here, and only accepted and held fast, at first, to the present constitution, as a steppingstone to the final establishment of their favorite model," England, the country that they favored in foreign policy and relied on to help them "effect this change." In this letter, Jefferson was unclear about exactly how England was to assist the Federalists in converting the U.S. to a monarchy, merely stating that it was "their prototype and great auxiliary." An influential minority of the Federalist leaders, mainly in Massachusetts, were prepared for their state to eventually secede from the Union, "considering the voluntary conversion of our government into a monarchy as too distant if not desperate." They contemplated the secession of the "Eastern fragment" of "our union," which was "in truth the hot bed of American monarchism, with a view to a commencement of their favorite government," monarchy. They relied on the rest of the states to eventually come around to their way of thinking. As Jefferson unflatteringly put it, they expected the other states "may gangrene by degrees" to support of monarchy, "and the whole be thus brought finally to the desired point."[6]

Although Jefferson regarded the so-called "Essex Junto" as instigators of secessionist plots in Massachusetts, he doubted that the state would permanently leave the Union. He emphasized Massachusetts' dependence on the other states for food, raw materials, and markets. Viewing Massachusetts as unable to exist on its own, he anticipated that, once its leaders comprehended that they were not attracting any other states to their confederation, they would humbly return to the republic they had left for their failed monarchical project. Ignoring the Maine forests, and the state's wheat-fields and fisheries, he exaggeratingly observed: "For

Massachusetts, the prime mover in this enterprise, is the last state in the union to mean a final separation, as being of all the most dependant [*sic*] on the others. Not raising bread for the sustenance of her own inhabitants, not having a stick of timber for the construction of vessels her principal occupation, nor an article to export in them, where would she be, excluded from the ports of the other states, and thrown into dependance [*sic*] on England, her direct & natural, but now insidious, rival?"[7] Jefferson was probably alluding to British diplomatic efforts, including neglecting to extend its blockade of the United States to New England, to court Massachusetts to join it in the war with the Union.[8]

Contending that advocates of Massachusetts secession comprised only a small minority within the state, Jefferson, perhaps with Timothy Pickering primarily in mind, revived the seldom-used epithet "Essex Junto" for these villains. Compared to these plotters, even Hamilton was politically virtuous, he informed Melish, because he eschewed secession and was willing to wait for the majority of the people to see the light and demand that the republic become a monarchy. As Jefferson explained, "At the head of this minority is what is called the Essex junto of Massachusetts. But the majority of these leaders, do not aim at separation. In this they adhere to the known principle of General Hamilton, never under any views to break the union." Thus, Hamilton, who unknown to Jefferson was actually the main author of Washington's farewell address, which Jefferson considered a model of Americanism, had become for the Virginian something of a nationalistic hero nine years after his death.[9]

Taking for granted that most Massachusetts citizens preferred England to France, and for that reason might hesitate to join the war effort, Jefferson insisted that they were in other respects loyal to the Union, at least in not favoring secession. Summing up Massachusetts political opinion, he wrote, "Anglomany, Monarchy, & Separation then are the principles of the Essex federalists, Anglomany & Monarchy, those of the Hamiltonians, and Anglomany alone that of the portion among the people who call themselves federalists." He stressed that the vast majority of Massachusetts "federalists" preferred republican government to a king, "are as good republicans as the brethren whom they oppose, & differ from them only in the devotion to England and hatred of France, which they have imbibed from their leaders." He blamed the Federalist rank-and-file for adopting their demagogic leaders' Francophobia, but was sure that they would never join the Essex Junto in plans to set up an independent country. "The moment that these leaders," who comprised a minority even of the Federalist political elite, "should avowedly propose a separation of the union, or the establishment of regal government, their popular adherents would quit them to a man, & join the republican standard, and the partisans of this change, even in Massachusetts, would thus find themselves an army of officers without a soldier."[10] Jefferson considered it desirable that the Massachusetts secessionist clique come clean about its intentions; for then the people of the state would reject it *en masse* and enthusiastically join the Republicans and the crusade against British domination that Jefferson perceived the War of 1812 to be.

Hoping to help Melish comprehend the vital differences between Federalists and Republicans, Jefferson continued his capsule history of the parties. He maintained that the Republicans, not the Federalists, were the party that wanted to preserve and enforce the Constitution (with a Bill of Rights added), while the Federalists, especially their leaders, hoped to eventually convert the country into a monarchy and abandon the original form of government. "The party called republican is steadily for the support of the present constitution," he reassured Melish (who may have heard Republicans being referred to as "antifederalist disorganizers" and "Jacobins" by their enemies). Indirectly acknowledging that many Republicans had originally been Antifederalists who opposed an unamended Constitution, he said that now they only objected to its failure to give the people enough direct power to democratically run the government: "They [the Republicans] obtained at it's commencement all the amendments to it they desired. These reconciled them to it perfectly, and if they have any ulterior view, it is only perhaps to popularise it further, by shortening the Senatorial term, and devising a process for the responsibility of judges more practicable than that of impeachment."[11] (Jefferson favored six-year terms for judges, and their dismissal by the president with concurrence of two-thirds of Congress.[12])

After making clear that the Jeffersonian Republicans were the Good Guys and the Federalists the Bad Guys, because the Republicans were confident in the people's virtue and good sense and wanted them to wield power rather than rich minorities, while the Federalists favored rule by a wealthy elite and plotted either to leave the Union or convert it eventually into a royal government, despicable objectives, Jefferson wanted the Briton Melish to know that he and his Republican colleagues were not hostile to Old Albion, despite rumors to the country. He wanted Melish to understand that there was nothing "personal" in the fact that the second war in thirty years between the two kindred peoples was in progress. As Jefferson put it, "They [the Republicans] esteem the people of England and France equally, & equally detest the governing powers of both."[13] By this, Jefferson meant that he detested both Napoleon and the British oligarchs, for mocking American independence and harassing American trade.

During his retirement, Jefferson grew increasingly fond of writing and talking about the period when he became a party leader, before taking over the country as third president. To Melish he described himself as a shy, private man who really did not want power for itself, but had to become party leader and president in order to save the republic from would-be monarchists. "After an intimacy of 40 years with the public councils & characters," he assured Melish that he had provided him with an accurate account of the sources of party division. "[This] is a true statement of the grounds on which they are at present divided, and that it is not merely an ambition for power," as Melish charged in his book. Becoming semiautobiographical, he emphasized that he was the people's choice for president, that he did not seek office or power but that the people and their leaders had sought him out to guide them. He was not the ambitious man that Melish implied. "An honest man can feel no pleasure in the exercise of power over his fellow citizens," he advised him. Probably alluding to his refusal to consider a third term, he added, "Considering as the only offices of power those conferred by the people directly, that is to say the Executive & Legislative functions of the General & State governments, the common refusal of these, & multiplied resignations, are proofs sufficient that power is not alluring to pure minds, and is not, with them, the primary principle of contest." Attempting to justify his political career, he asserted that he had acted on self-sacrificing principles, "and had it been a mere contest who should be permitted to administer the government according to it's genuine republican principles, there has never been a moment of my life in in which I should have relinquished for it the enjoiments [*sic*] of my family, my farm, my friends & books."[14]

Somewhat disingenuously, Jefferson praised George Washington as the greatest exemplar of republicanism. In fact, especially in the first president's last years, Jefferson was convinced that Washington had gone over to the anti-republican leaders of the Federalist Party, particularly his great protégé Hamilton. Assuring Melish that he agreed with the principles of Washington's Farewell Address, and that his first inaugural address contained similar ideas, he was apparently unaware that Hamilton wrote most of the Address, despite its generally republican tone. Jefferson claimed Washington for the Republican Party, as if to make clear that the Massachusetts "Essex Junto" was alien to the Father of his Country. "General Washington did not harbor one principle of federalism," Jefferson insisted. "He was neither an Angloman, a monarchist nor a Separatist [i.e., secessionist]."[15]

On second thought, Jefferson confessed the first president's skepticism of the people's ability to govern themselves: Washington opposed the Democratic Societies as threats to his view that rulers should do what they thought was best for their constituents whether the latter agreed with them or not. "He [Washington] sincerely wished the people to have as much self-government as they were competent to exercise themselves," Jefferson explained: "The only point in which he and I ever differed in opinion was that I had more confidence than he had in the natural integrity and discretion of the people; and in the safety and extent to which they might trust themselves with a controul over their government. He has [sic] asseverated to me a thousand times his determination that the existing government should have a fair trial, and that in support of it he would spend the last drop of his blood. He did this the more repeatedly, because he knew General Hamilton's political bias, and my apprehensions from it."[16]

In 1800, Jefferson, in conversing with Dr. Benjamin Rush, who revealed his contempt for Washington during the Revolutionary War by participating in the notorious Conway Cabal that sought to remove Washington as commander-in-chief of the Continental Armies, spoke unkindly of the first president. He shockingly expressed relief that Washington's death the year before had eliminated a potentially dangerous foe of republicanism; so his statement to Melish was euphemistic.[17] Probably aware that he was stretching the truth, Jefferson misleadingly implied that Washington felt increasingly alienated from Hamilton's anti-republican ideology toward the end of his life. Returning to his castigation of the pro-monarchical New England Federalist political minority, he powerfully concluded, "It is a mere calumny therefore in the Monarchists to associate General Washington with their principles, but that may have happened in this case which has been often seen in ordinary cases, that by often repeating an untruth men come to believe it themselves."[18]

In writing so forthrightly to Melish, who had visited him briefly in Washington during his presidency in 1806 but was otherwise a stranger, Jefferson was primarily concerned with making clear the distinction between Washington and the Massachusetts secessionist-monarchists, whom he referred to by the shorthand, "Essex Junto." By getting Washington on his side for posterity, beginning with contemporary writers like Melish, whose misconceptions he hoped to correct (probably expecting Melish to write a follow-up volume), Jefferson justified his political career and increased the likelihood that his party would survive into the future. Alluding to Massachusetts Federalists in general and the "Essex Junto" in particular, he concluded, "It is a mere artifice in this party to bolster themselves up on the revered name of that first of our worthies."[19]

Hardly as impressed with Washington's abilities as he claimed, Jefferson was being somewhat disingenuous. In 1814, in his famous letter to Walter Jones, a Virginia Republican who contemplated writing a biography of Washington, Jefferson composed one of the most insightful commentaries on Washington's character. Although less ardently attempting to transmute

Washington into a Republican for posterity, Jefferson recalled that when the first president died, he "felt on his death, with my countrymen that 'verily a great man hath fallen this day in Israel.'"[20]

In writing to Melish in 1813, apart from thanking him for the gift of his book, Jefferson wanted to convince him that Washington was closer in his political ideology to the Jeffersonian Republicans than he was to would-be Massachusetts secessionists like Pickering and Cabot. In the depths of war with Britain, which it seemed possible they would lose, and in which New England refused the government assistance, Americans needed to know that the great Washington would have opposed its secession. Though hoping that Melish (ironically a Briton) would spread the word, the ever-cautious Jefferson, unwilling to disturb his retirement by participating in political battles, requested him to keep his name out of it. "If I have dwelt longer on this subject than was necessary," he said, "it proves the estimation in which I hold your ultimate opinions, and my desire of placing the subject truly before them. In so doing I am certain I risk no use of the communication which may draw me into contention before the public. Tranquility is the summum bonum of a Septuagenaire." Effusively praising the "lively merits" of Melish's work despite his disagreement with its depiction of the Federalists and Republicans as two peas in a pod, Jefferson assured him that if he mailed him more copies he would send them to his friends in Europe to be translated in their respective languages, "as an antidote to the misrepresentations of former travellers." However, his primary concern was his own vindication, and the aspersion of his political enemies, the Massachusetts Anglophile and "monocratic" political extremists, such as Fisher Ames, Theodore Sedgwick, and Timothy Pickering, who had hounded him for two decades. He wanted it to be clear that *he* was the nationalist democrat and friend of the people, despite his ostensibly states' rights-oriented Kentucky Resolutions of 1798 against the Alien, Sedition, and Naturalization Acts; and *they* were the parochial-minded secessionists. As he mildly put it, "Whatever effect my profession of political faith may have on your general opinion, a part of my object will be obtained, if it satisfies you as to the principles of my own action."[21]

Ardently seeking Jefferson's patronage, Melish lost little time replying. Confiding that he was a thoroughgoing Democratic-Republican, he opined that Jefferson had misunderstood his seeming derision of both parties as political opportunists. What he *really* meant, he assured Jefferson, was that the Federalists, although monarchists and centralizers, touted Washington's Farewell Address as their political testament in a hypocritical attempt to gain votes. Mimicking Jefferson, he said, "I may add that while I hold the very worst opinion of the *British party*, and a number of *Monarchical Federalists* in this Country, Yet I consider the great body of people which composed the Federal party to be in truth Republicans at bottom."[22]

However, Jefferson thought that Melish did not adequately comprehend the urgent state of affairs the War of 1812 posed for the Union's survival. In another letter to Melish, in December 1814, Jefferson more angrily reiterated his suspicion of British intentions. Sounding less conciliatory to the mother country than in his letter to Melish two years earlier, he charged that the British, hoping to re-annex the United States, encouraged New England secessionism. Further, he charged that British negotiators adopted dilatory maneuvers at Ghent. They demanded an Indian buffer state in the Midwest as a *sine qua non* for peace in order to prolong the negotiations, because they expected to benefit from the outcome of the Hartford Convention and an ensuing alliance between Great Britain and Massachusetts. Jefferson thought that the United States should chasten the British by seizing Canada and eliminating British maritime superiority. Insisting that he and President Madison had always desired "an equal, a just and solid connection of friendship and intercourse" with Great Britain, he charged that the British preferred to disrupt the "federal system."[23]

Mixing physics and astronomical metaphors involving planets, stars, and solar systems, Jefferson hoped that Massachusetts would reject British overtures and remain peacefully within the republican "orbit." If Massachusetts ultimately seceded, he preferred to use economic coercion rather than military force to persuade it to return to the Union: "That [matter], of reducing, by impulse instead of attraction, a sister planet into its orbit, will be as new in our political as in the planetary system. The operation, however, will be painful rather than difficult." Nevertheless, Jefferson again predicted that the republican portion of Massachusetts (the state that he now called a "wandering star") would restrain the "monarchical" minority from seceding. Alluding to the dreaded possibility that the Union would be forced to fight a defensive war against an alliance between Massachusetts and Britain followed by an invasion of the Homeland, Jefferson speculated that dealing with this contingency might be preferable to American armies' invading distant, spacious Canada: "The sound part of our wandering star [Massachusetts] will probably, by its own internal energies, keep the unsound [the monarchical Federalists] within its course; or if a foreign power is called in, we shall have to meet it but so much the nearer, and with a more overwhelming force." Expecting that national unity and determination would thereby be accelerated, he predicted that an alliance between a seceded Massachusetts and Great Britain "will probably shorten the war." Deploring the British negotiators' meandering course at Ghent, Jefferson informed Melish that it was "probable that the *sine qua non* [Native American buffer state] was designedly put into an impossible form to give time for the development of their plots and concerts with the factionists of Boston, and that they are holding off to see the issue, not of the Congress of Vienna, but that of Hartford."[24] Despite numerous obstacles, Jefferson remained confident that the republic would prevail, and that the New England states would remain a vital part of it.

14

Jefferson Defends
New England's Interests
Despite the Hartford Convention

From the outset of the War of 1812 to its conclusion, Jefferson remained confident in New England citizens' loyalty to the Union despite their governments' rebelliousness and secessionist tendencies. Strongly expressing his nationalistic "affections" (Onuf's favorite word, but not used here by Jefferson) and sympathy for Massachusetts even at the nadir of American military fortunes, Jefferson hoped U.S. peace negotiators would uphold the state's claim to the fisheries. In a rarely cited but widely available letter to Adams from their much-quoted correspondence, Jefferson expressed alarm at rumors that Great Britain sought to deny Massachusetts rights to fish in Labrador and southern Newfoundland. He supported fighting for Massachusetts' right to retain the fisheries as a war aim, even though Massachusetts refused to assist the other states. Jefferson queried Adams, "What will Massachusets [sic] say to this? I mean her majority, which must be considered as speaking, thro' the organs it has appointed itself, as the Index of it's [sic] will. She chose to sacrifice the liberty of our seafaring citizens, in which we were all interested, and with them her obligations to the co-states, rather than war with England. Will she now sacrifice the fisheries to the same partialities?"[1]

Hoping the Union would exhibit its "affection" for Massachusetts by upholding its right to the fisheries, Jefferson expected Massachusetts to cooperate in defending its interests. In an imaginary conversation with the "refractory sister" state, Jefferson wrote: "I know what, as a citizen of the Union, I would say to her. 'Take this question ad referendum. It concerns you alone. If you would rather give up the fisheries than war with England, we give them up. If you had rather fight for them, we will defend your interests to the last drop of our blood, chusing [sic] rather to set a good example than follow a bad one.' And I hope she will determine to fight for them."[2] In this instance as in others, Jefferson recommended benevolent treatment of Massachusetts despite its refusal to cooperate during the war. Like Jefferson, Adams supported the war and deplored his state's conduct.[3]

Both men were relieved when the Hartford Convention disbanded on January 4, 1815, after proposing a long list of constitutional amendments.[4] Seeking to safeguard the carrying states from national embargoes or other prohibitions of foreign trade of the kind implemented by Jefferson and Madison, the Convention demanded that such laws require two-thirds vote of both houses of Congress, and that trade restrictions last no longer than sixty days. In another attempt to learn lessons from the recent past, the Hartford Convention recommended amendments it hoped would restrict the political power of the slave-holding South and the West and revive the waning influence of New England. Among these were constitutional amendments to prohibit future naturalized citizens from holding any national office, appointive or elective; abolish the "three-fifths clause," that counted a slave as three-fifths of a person in apportioning state seats in the House of Representatives; require a two-thirds vote of both houses of Congress to admit new states to the Union and declare war; limit the president to a single term, and prohibit the president from being consecutively elected from the same state, to prevent the recurrence of such disasters as the Virginian Jefferson and Madison administrations. More important at the time, the Convention decreed that its attendee states receive a portion of U.S. taxes to pay for their own defense, that they should not be responsible for sending militia or even "regular" U.S. Army troops stationed within them to any other parts of the country than New England, and that the U.S. government reimburse them for their military expenditures for their section's defense. In effect, the Hartford Convention required the national government to recognize New England as what political theorists called a "state within a state." It insisted that the other states recognize New England's self-interest by ratifying Constitutional amendments that most benefited it politically and economically. In the short term, the Convention decided to recommend a second convention take place if the war with Britain continued and the national government refused to allocate the New England states tax moneys for their self-defense and neglected their protection. This final resolution, which protested what the delegates framed as the perennial failure of the national government to defend the New England states during the war, warned that if the national government failed to distribute tax moneys to them for their defense, the legislatures would appoint delegates to another convention to meet in Boston in June 1815 "with such powers and instructions as the exigency of a crisis so momentous may require." Such language strongly hinted that their secession from the Union was possible.[5]

It is surprising that Jefferson did not express more alarm at such unacceptable proposals, which constituted an ultimatum to the national government, especially since the Convention kept its proceedings secret. Unfortunately, the Hartford Conventioneers blatantly refused to assist the Union in winning the only war in U.S. history where the invaders had secured a foothold within U.S. boundaries and burned its capital.

On the contrary, Jefferson advocated sympathetic treatment of Massachusetts despite its failure to cooperate during the national emergency. He threw what little political influence he possessed into the scale on the side of moderation toward an errant "sister state." In terms of policy-making, neither his proposals during the War of 1812 for a United States government monopoly on currency issuance, nor his recommendation in 1823 for cooperating with Great Britain against the Holy Alliance were adopted by the respective sitting presidents, his closest friends, Madison and Monroe. In matters of even minor political appointments, Jefferson's old friend President Monroe ignored his suggestions.[6] Whatever historians might assume, therefore, Jefferson's ideas played little role in New England's fate within the Union during the War of 1812.

In at least one respect Jefferson's wrath at the disunionism presaged by the Hartford Convention led to a persisting unflattering perception of New Englanders, especially in Massachusetts. As had been the case at least since *Notes on the State of Virginia*, Jefferson expressed prejudice against urban merchants and cities, claiming they were selfish, amoral and corrupt compared to the "virtuous" farmer. (But this was an old Southern complaint. As early as 1785, Richard Henry Lee denounced the "avaricious monopolizing spirit of commerce" in the North.)[7]

After the Hartford Convention, as before, Jefferson vented this antipathy in letters to several friends and acquaintances. He unburdened himself to ex-senator William Plumer, a former extreme New Hampshire Federalist who, partly from considerations of political expediency and desires for a patronage appointment, switched to Republicanism after the *Chesapeake* outrage in 1807. Plumer went so far as to support the Embargo Act. Revealing poor memory or a surprising degree of naïveté, Jefferson seemed unaware that as a New Hampshire U.S. senator, Plumer was among the most active Federalists in proposing New England's secession from the Union in 1803 and 1804 if Jefferson and his party won overwhelming majorities in upcoming elections.[8] Jefferson now accused the Hartford Convention delegates of being in British pay. Even more incredibly, he had long suspected that this was true of Robespierre and the most radical French Revolutionaries during the Reign of Terror (1793–1794), in part because his friend, James Monroe, U.S. minister to France at that time, influenced by the conservative Plain Party, had told him so.[9]

Seeking to encourage Plumer, a resident of rural New Hampshire, to complete his conversion to the Republicans, Jefferson told him that Massachusetts men cared only about "administering to their worldly gain," implying that Plumer was more unselfish. When Plumer enclosed him a copy of a pro-secessionist New England clergyman's sermon advocating disunion, Jefferson lamented that such writings violated his principle of the separation of church and state. Dismayed that New England parishioners would subsidize an unpatriotic minister, he said, "The paradox with me is how any friend to the union of our country can, in conscience, contribute a cent to the maintenance of any one who perverts the sanctity of his desk to the open inculcation of rebellion, civil war, dissolution of government, and the miseries of anarchy." Jefferson drew comparisons between Massachusetts traitors and the French Revolution's Maximilien Robespierre that were common at the time, even though they lacked factual basis. He claimed that Massachusetts anti-war leaders, like the Jacobin Mountain Party who directed the Reign of Terror, were "emissaries" employed by Britain as "incendiaries and anarchists in the disorganization of all government there." Ironically, Robespierre's enemy George Jacques Danton, who opposed the Reign of Terror, was in British pay, and was guillotined for it.[10]

Perhaps in order to convince Plumer of his political moderation, Jefferson discoursed on his opposition to the radical phase of the French Revolution that unfolded from 1792 to 1794. He continued to maintain that the Federalists who attended the Hartford Convention and had refused to support the Union throughout the war were no different from the French politicians who implemented the Reign of Terror. French radicals, Jefferson charged, while pretending to be zealous friends of "republican government and the rights of the people," were covert traitors, ranging from Danton and Marat to Robespierre and his Montagnard faction. Bribed by British Prime Minister William Pitt, Jefferson claimed, they took over the Jacobin clubs, "and overwhelming by their majorities the honest and enlightened patriots of the original institution, distorted its objectives, pursued its genuine founders under the name of Brissotins and Girondists unto death, intrigued themselves into the municipality of Paris [Paris Commune], [and] controlled by terrorism the proceedings of the legislature," already infiltrated by their "co-stipendiaries." They savagely persecuted and murdered thousands of their fellow-citizens. Exhibiting his moderate side, Jefferson even regretted that the Jacobin Mountain Party had "murdered their king," and ruled by means of a bloody dictatorship. Wreaking havoc and disorder, and discrediting the Revolution, they "accomplished their stipulated task of demolishing liberty and government with it."[11]

Plumer completed his switch to the Democratic-Republican Party shortly after Jefferson's letter. However, political expediency played a greater role in his conversion than Jefferson's skill at persuasion.[12] In any case, Plumer, who had always favored religious freedom and for most of his life was a deist, must have pleased Jefferson when, after reelection as governor of New Hampshire in 1816, a post he held since 1813, he persuaded the state legislature to grant acts of incorporation to any religious association that requested them. This was equivalent to enacting religious liberty.[13]

· · · · ·

The Hartford Convention delegates operated on a far smaller, comparatively more benign scale than France's revolutionary government during the Reign of Terror. Nevertheless, Jefferson seemed convinced that its members, like certain French counter-revolutionists, were hirelings of malevolent, mercantile, monarchical Britain, which, he thought, had never abandoned the idea of subjugating its rebellious North American colonies. Just as Britain had sought to quash French republicanism by employing subversive agents in 1793–1794, he dreaded it now intended to crush republicanism in the United States, assisted by New England antiwar and secessionist elements. "England now fears the rising force of this republican nation," Jefferson vigorously asserted, "and by the same means is endeavoring to effect the same course of miseries and destruction here; it is impossible when one sees like courses of events commence, not to ascribe them to like causes." Jefferson's ostensibly empirical approach, derived from Enlightenment rationalism, may have been imprecise. However, the suspicion that "foreign influence" and foreign conspiracy manipulated America's political leaders had a long history. Both Federalists and Democratic-Republicans accused each other of subservience to foreign governments.[14] Jefferson naturally applied this rhetoric to the Hartford Convention.

Jefferson explained the Hartford Convention by recourse to a conspiratorial *Weltanschauung*. He believed that leading antiwar Federalist politicians got rich through bribery and "corruption," funded by the British Government. Jefferson had regarded the ex-mother country's regime as amoral since George III's accession. "We know that the government of England, maintaining itself by corruption at home, uses the same means in other countries of which she has any jealousy, by subsidizing agitators and traitors among themselves to distract and paralyze them," he charged. "She sufficiently manifests that she has no disposition to spare ours." (And indeed, in recent times Britain had bribed American politicians like Silas Deane and William Blount.) In calling a convention of New England states to oppose the war and propose constitutional amendments during wartime, Jefferson insisted, the Massachusetts legislature showed "symptoms" of British anti-republican influence and bribery. Alluding to government intelligence ("information") about British spies operating in Boston, Jefferson warned, "we know as far as such practices can ever be dragged into light, that she [Britain] has practiced, and with success, on leading individuals of that State."[15]

As was his custom, Jefferson viewed opposition to the Democratic-Republican government and passivity in confronting monarchical invaders as a cardinal sin. It signified that New

England's governors were willing to blight the only experiment in man's self-government in modern times that had any prospect of success, and in furnishing an example for freedom to the world's oppressed and enslaved in the future. Jefferson denounced the Massachusetts Federalist government as a threat to democracy. He charged that it was guilty before "history" of "the crime of combining with the oppressors of the earth to extinguish the last spark of human hope, that here, at length, will be presented a model of government, securing to man his rights and the fruits of his labor, by an organization constantly subject to his own will." If New England's governments succeeded in the "crime" of impairing U.S. defenses and facilitating its defeat by England, the "perpetrators" would incur an infamous "immortality" comparable to that of "Robespierre and his associates, as the guardian genii of despotism, and demons of human liberty."[16]

Although Jefferson distrusted New England's state governments during the war, he denied that all the antiwar factions opposed republicanism. Rather, he suspected that many naïve citizens inadvertently cooperated with British spies. "I do not mean to say that all who are acting with these men are under the same motives," he assured Plumer. "I know some of them personally to be incapable of it." Intent on comparing New England's current "Federalist party perversions" with the Jacobin "demagogues and assassins of Paris" of twenty years earlier, Jefferson argued that propaganda "deluded" many supporters of the antiwar factions to "furnish unconscious assistance to the hired actors in these atrocious scenes," the Federalist politicos. But he believed that the "parricidal" schemes of New England's spies and British conspirators would fail. He concluded his letter to Plumer by professing confidence in the virtuous republicanism of the average Massachusetts man, who he believed was too "happy" within the Union to consider secession. "I have never entertained one moment's fear on the subject [Massachusetts secession]," he said. "The people of this country enjoy too much happiness to risk it for nothing; and I have never doubted that whenever the incendiaries of Massachusetts should venture openly to raise the standard of separation, its citizens would rise in mass and do justice themselves to their own parricides."[17]

Despite his suspicion and contempt for New England's avaricious merchants and power-seeking (and, he thought, greedy) established clergy and politicians, Jefferson regarded most New Englanders as decent, patriotic republicans. Indeed, Jefferson trusted (perhaps more than he should have) his correspondent, William Plumer, who had at least nominally turned from Federalism to Democratic-Republicanism, had been elected governor of New Hampshire and was writing a history of the American Revolution: "I am glad to learn that you persevere in your historical work," he enthused. "I am sure it will be executed on sound principles of Americanism, and I hope your opportunities will enable you to make the abortive crimes of the present, useful as a lesson for future times."[18] Apparently, Jefferson had nothing against *this* New Englander. He wanted to assure Plumer that he considered his fellow New Englanders sufficiently patriotic and virtuous to render "abortive" any future High Federalists' secessionist schemes.

Undeniably, Jefferson was angered by what he considered New England's treason against the United States during this period. Its citizens had violated his Embargo Act, then refused to help their sister states with troops or loans to the United States Government, though as a result of smuggling and placating the British they were financially in better shape than the others.[19] However, after the United States' relatively successfully concluded the War of 1812, albeit with little assistance from Massachusetts and its neighbors, Jefferson preferred to emphasize what New England had in common with the rest of the Union rather than their sources of conflict.

• • • • •

At the beginning of the War of 1812, Jeffersonian Governor Elbridge Gerry's seeming political strength led Jefferson to expect that Massachusetts would eagerly cooperate with the Madison Administration in prosecuting the conflict. Jefferson felt encouraged by the doughty Republican minority and the vigorous Republican opposition to the Federalists in the state. As recently as 1812, employing the famous Gerrymander (soon repealed by the Federalists), Massachusetts voters had reelected the neophyte Republican governor and several Jeffersonian Congressmen. Gerry was a paradoxical statesman, an "antiparty" politician who epitomized "classical republicanism" yet evolved into a bitter partisan before the War of 1812. Defeating Caleb Strong for the governorship by a narrow margin in 1810, Gerry proclaimed himself a moderate, who intended to represent both the Federalists and Jeffersonians. In his inaugural address as governor in 1810, he promised to retain Federalists in office. Anticipating Lincoln's more famous speech in using a Biblical phrase, he declared, "A house divided against itself cannot stand." He thereby alienated his Democratic-Republican allies, whom the Federalists excluded from state offices when they ran the government.[20]

Despite Gerry's overtures, Federalist politicians and newspapers continued to attack him bitterly during his reelection campaign in 1811, even threatening him with violence. This improper conduct aroused his wrath. He did not initiate the "gerrymander" that bore his name, a technique of redistributing election districts to benefit the party in power, previously employed by the Federalists; but he approved it when the Democratic-Republicans in the legislature pushed it through to increase the number of Republicans in the General Court. Unlike his message the year before, in his 1811 inaugural address Gerry denounced the Federalists as traitorous partisans, while still insisting that he stood above all parties. From 1811 to 1812 Massachusetts Republicans in the assembly exceeded even their Federalist predecessors in partisanship; the assembly Speaker distributed committee assignments exclusively to their leaders.[21]

Indignant at the persisting Federalist opposition, Gerry continued to view himself, according to historian Ronald Formisano, "as a no-party man, now forced to act by the irresponsibility of a fanatical party." He presided over the gerrymandering of congressional and state legislative election districts. More democratically-inclined than the conservative Gerry, the Republican legislature passed laws that made bank charters available to more people, instituted universal manhood suffrage for town elections, and incorporated a great number of new towns, which were expected to vote Democratic-Republican. Although radical Jeffersonians initiated these reforms, Gerry signed them into law.[22]

After his reelection as governor in 1812, Gerry instructed his attorney general to prosecute Boston Federalist newspapers for libel. However, the Federalists were still dominant in the city, and he could secure only ten indictments and three convictions from the juries. Despite Gerry's vociferous assaults on his opponents, he continued to deny that he was a partisan politician, although like many party leaders at this time, as Formisano notes, he "did not think in terms of a legitimate opposition."[23] After the unpopular declaration of war, Massachusetts Republicans were defeated, and the state abandoned the common cause. Jefferson had ample reason for disappointment at "our refractory sister," as he called Massachusetts in writing to John Adams.[24]

Toward the end of the war, even the usually temperate President Madison was alarmed. In November 1814, lacking sufficient tax money and troops, he denounced New England's recalcitrance, charging that the British "persevered" in the war because they expected that section's active support. Like Jefferson earlier, he compared the Federalists to the Salem witch-hunters of the 1690s, angrily observing, "The greater part of the people in that [eastern] quarter have been brought by their leaders, aided by their priests, under a delusion scarcely exceeded by that recorded in the period of witchcraft; and the leaders are becoming daily more desperate in the use they make of it." Convinced that Eastern politicians' and clergy's "object is power," Madison feared that the Hartford Convention would precipitate "revolts & separation" if Britain offered help to its leaders. He worried that the antiwar majority might physically attack the "respectable" number of pro–Union New Englanders who were "faithful to the nation." The Hartford Convention's peaceful adjournment, Jackson's victory at the Battle of New Orleans, and the Treaty of Ghent favorably resolved Madison's crisis.[25]

· · · · ·

For several years after the war ended, Jefferson pondered Massachusetts Federalist politicians' betrayal of the nation. Shortly before the conflict's resolution became public knowledge, Jefferson again voiced resentment of Massachusetts' militancy. He reiterated his varied suspicions in letters to his old friend, the Marquis de Lafayette, who resided in France throughout Napoleon's regime. As he had done in writing Plumer, Jefferson again speculated that the Hartford Convention, although called by the Massachusetts assembly, was the brainchild of British spies who bribed the state legislature. Writing to Lafayette in February 1815, he boasted that the defeat of the secessionists at Hartford had disappointed the British government, which would soon be "force[d]" to make peace with the United States. The war only continued because greedy British officials, hoping to "recruit their broken fortunes," profited from bribes they received from government war contractors. Jefferson was confident that the Hartford Convention's termination without Massachusetts' secession shattered British expectations of victory. "They [the British] have hoped more in their Hartford convention" as the means to gain victory than in the collapse of the U.S. government's finances, he reported to Lafayette. The British aimed to overthrow American republicanism as they had overthrown it in France, Jefferson asserted. "Their fears of republican France being now done away, they are directed to republican America," he said, "and they are playing the same game for disorganization here, which they played in your country." Reviving rumors about the French Revolution rife during the 1790s, Jefferson compared the conduct of Massachusetts' politicians with that of Robespierre during the Reign of Terror of 1793–1794. He believed that the British had bribed Robespierre and other French officials to disrupt national unity, conduct mass executions of their opponents, and suppress free speech. "The Marats, the Dantons and Robespierres of Massachusetts are in the same pay, and under the same orders, and making the same efforts to anarchise us, that their prototypes did there," he concluded.[26]

Nonetheless, Jefferson always believed that the majority of the people of New England, although they may have opposed the war, remained loyal to the Union. Reiterating the viewpoint of his earlier, famous dialogue with Adams on "natural aristocracy," Jefferson assured Lafayette that property-owning, democratically inclined New England farmers would never consent to reunite with the Mother Country and resume monarchical rule.[27] The British would inevitably find their efforts to foster secessionist sentiment floundering because "the yeomanry of the United States are not the *canaille* of Paris." (Apparently, by this, Jefferson meant that the city workers of Paris had initially supported Robespierre when he promised to advance their economic program of price and wage regulations.) Mockingly depicting the alleged flunkies of British conspirators and secret agents as "gambling merchants and silk-stocking clerks," he predicted that only they would join a British plot "to separate [New England] from the Union." He insisted that most New Englanders loved the republic. As he put it, "The cement of the Union is in the heart-blood of every American." In words reminiscent of his first inaugural address, he said, "I do not believe there is on earth a government established on so immovable a basis." He clearly included Massachusetts within this patriotic community, anticipating it would experience a nationalistic surge like that of the old Revolutionary Minutemen: "Let them [British sympathizers], in any State, even in Massachusetts itself, raise the standard of separation, and its citizens will rise in mass, and do justice themselves on their own incendiaries." Nor had the Madison Administration feared the Hartford Convention's outcome, Jefferson astutely observed, but merely greeted it with "silent contempt." The Convention failed even to provoke an attempt by Union troops to break up its proceedings, which might have aroused some sympathy for it elsewhere: "If they could have induced the [United States] government to some effort of suppression, or even to enter into discussion with them, it would have given them some importance, have brought them into some notice. But they have not been able to make themselves even a subject of conversation, either of public or private societies."[28]

Continuing to stress the alleged similarity between the Hartford Convention Federalists and France's political opportunists during the Reign of Terror, he admitted that not "all who met at Hartford were under the same motives of money, nor were those of France [during the Reign of Terror]." In any case, Jefferson observed, the Federalist leaders' obsession with party victory was hardly less execrable than their alleged affinity for bribery. He was exasperated by the ceaseless efforts of Federalist "Outs" to replace the Republican "Inns" [*sic*]; some the mere dupes of the agitators, or of their own party passions."[29] Perhaps Jefferson was now leaning toward labeling even Robespierre a mere political operator, rather than a fanatical ideologue or a traitor whose talents and influence were for sale to the highest bidder.

In the letter to Lafayette, Jefferson boasted of Jackson's January 1815 victory at New Orleans, exaggerating the extent of British "defeats at New Orleans by [Generals] Jackson, Coffee, and Carroll, with the loss of four thousand men out of nine thousand and six hundred, with their two Generals, Packingham [*sic*] and Gibbs killed, and a third, Keane, wounded, mortally, as is said." (Actually, twenty-five hundred British were killed, and only twenty-five of Jackson's soldiers, one of the greatest U.S. victories.) Jefferson was not aware that the Treaty of Ghent had been ratified until after he finished the letter. In a postscript, he informed Lafayette of the peace treaty, remarking, "I am glad of it, and especially that we closed our war with the eclat of the action at New Orleans. But I consider it as an armistice only, because no security is provided against the impressment of our seamen." He warned that until Britain abolished impressment of U.S. citizens into the Royal Navy, there would be continued likelihood of war, necessitating that the U.S. increase its fortifications, improve its militia, and expand "our domestic manufactures, which have taken such root as never again can be shaken."[30]

Confident that New England's citizens would resist secessionist movements, either by their legislatures or the Hartford Convention, Jefferson never considered proposing a

Bonapartist-type military action against the conferees. Historians like Onuf, who claim that the retired elder statesman, who actually exerted little political influence on his friends Madison and Monroe, made such a recommendation, are mistaken. Even with the hindsight of February 1815, several weeks after the Convention's adjournment, Jefferson expressed no regrets that the Army had missed an opportunity to disrupt the meeting and arrest the delegates. Such action would have violated the democratic ideals he stood for, ideals that the New England states whose town meeting model he revered had implemented through the Convention itself, despite its odious objectives.

In contrast with Jefferson, one major figure of the War of 1812, General of the Army Andrew Jackson, retrospectively favored hanging the Hartford Conventioneers. "I am free to declare, had I commanded the Military Department where the Hartford Convention met— if it had been the last act of my life I should have punished [the] three principle [sic] leaders of the party. I am certain an independent courtmartial would have condemned them" to death. As he explained to President-elect James Monroe in January 1817, he regarded the delegates as disloyal. "These kind of men altho called Federalists, are really monarchists, & traitors to the constituted Government," he concluded. "But, I am of opinion that there are men called Federalists that are honest, virtuous, and really attached to our government, and altho they differ in many respects and opinions with the republicans, still they will risque every thing in its defence."[31]

This is not to say that Jefferson passively regarded New England's attempt to intimidate the rest of the Union. Even in 1817, again writing to Lafayette, Jefferson bitterly lamented that Massachusetts had precipitated "civil schism" during the war. He rejoiced that the nation had proven its strength by repelling the British onslaught, "when, with four eastern States tied to us, as dead to living bodies, all doubt was removed as to the achievements of the war, had it continued." Despite New England's rejection of his party during the conflict, Jefferson argued that the "complete suppression of party" was the most salutary outcome—the "best effect"—of the war. From the outset of party contest in the early 1790s, he had insisted that most of the "federalists" were patriotic citizens who rejected the "mere Anglomen" in the party. Following the Hartford Convention fiasco and the humiliation of the would-be secessionists, Jefferson observed, contrite Federalists "are received with cordiality into the republican ranks" and helped elect Jeffersonian candidates. "Even Connecticut, as a State, and the last one expected to yield its steady habits (which were essentially bigoted in politics as well as religion), has chosen a republican governor, and republican legislature," he boasted. On the other hand, the continued Federalist resurgence in Massachusetts aroused his anxiety: "Massachusetts indeed still lags; because most deeply involved in the parricide crimes and treasons of the war. But her gangrene is contracting, the sound flesh advancing on it, and all there will be well."[32]

Notwithstanding his disappointments at the disunity uncovered by the war, Jefferson was willing to forgive—if not entirely forget—the indiscretions of the Federalist-controlled New England states. The message he conveyed in this letter to Lafayette, as in all of his correspondence during the War of 1812 period, was of the overriding importance of defeating the British invader and binding up the republic's wounds with the balm of Jeffersonian Republicanism.

Jefferson's letter to Lafayette of May 14, 1817, achieved an unintended kind of immortality. In *Democracy in America*, considered along with *The Federalist* the greatest book ever written about United States' institutions, Alexis de Tocqueville briefly quoted Jefferson's letter to demonstrate the validity of his own view that American national unity was extremely fragile. In elaborating the thesis of *Democracy in America*'s first volume that the state governments were virtually independent of the national government and could ignore it with impunity, Tocqueville misleadingly employed Jefferson's letter to Lafayette to prove the central government's weakness. Tocqueville was being duplicitous, since he must have been aware that Jefferson's epistle actually emphasized the Madison Administration's competence and success in defeating Great Britain. From Tocqueville's perspective, "The federal government, in spite of the efforts of its founders, is … one of such naturally feeble sort that it requires, more than any other, the free support of the governed in order to survive." Believing that the national government had repeatedly been too weak to confront resistance by state governments even when only "one of the states" was rebellious, he emphasized the Union's extreme tenuity. "Each time that determined resistance has been offered to the federal government [by a state], it has yielded," he argued. With South Carolina's recent "nullification" of federal tariffs in mind, he wrote, "Experience has proven that up till now, when a state has been obstinately determined on anything and demanded it resolutely, it has never failed to get it; and when it has flatly refused to act, it has been allowed to refuse."[33]

Writing in 1835, and basing his text on his experiences in the United States from 1831 to 1832, Tocqueville's negative assessment of the relations between the national government and the states was primarily inspired by South Carolina's revolt against the protectionist federal tariff laws of 1828 and 1832, climaxed by its "nullification" of the congressional Force Bill that demanded compliance with the law. To broaden his point, Tocqueville added a historical footnote referring to the War of 1812 and the Hartford Convention. Regarding Jefferson's statements as validating his own argument about state obstructionism, Tocqueville observed, "Seeing the conduct of the northern states in the War of 1812. Jefferson, in a letter of May 14, 1817 to General La Fayette, says: … 'with four eastern states tied to us, as dead to living bodies, all doubt was removed as to the achievements of the war, had it continued.'"[34]

After quoting Jefferson to show the national government's ineffectiveness in demanding help from the states, even during a war for national survival, Tocqueville concluded that the United States was powerless because it lacked a peacetime standing army to coerce disobedient states. Perhaps influenced by the example of European monarchies, Tocqueville asserted, "Without a permanent army, a government has nothing prepared in advance to take advantage of a favorable opportunity, overcome [local] resistance, and take over sovereign power by surprise." In addition, he opined, the republic's extensive physical terrain would "make it very hard to use" an Army to coerce a state.[35] Unlike Tocqueville's misuse of its contents, Jefferson's letter to Lafayette, as we have seen, actually praised the accomplishments of burgeoning U.S. nationhood and the likelihood of greater national unity.

Jefferson's conciliatory intent was the opposite of what modern historians have claimed. Instead of proposing the destruction of Massachusetts and recommending military incursions, Jefferson adhered to a peaceful, election-based strategy. He believed that eventually the state's voters would "see the light," although his phraseology was more starkly physical, laced with vivid metaphors of gangrenous flesh. Far from endorsing the propriety of executing New Englanders, he metaphorically accused *them* of a heinous type of murder: "the parricide crimes and treasons of the war." By opposing their *patrie*, trading with the British and refusing to assist the nation, their crime was equivalent to a son killing his father. Still, Jefferson opposed violent retribution against them.

15

New England and the South in the Mind of an Aging Jefferson

Despite New England's selfish conduct during the War of 1812, Jefferson was conciliatory in the conflict's aftermath. He liked New Englanders, among other reasons because they were generally more bookish and intellectual than those from other regions of the country.

For example, among the scholars he was most eager to hire to teach at his embryonic University of Virginia was Massachusetts native George Ticknor, whom he met through John Adams. He wrote Adams of his pleasure at the visit of two young New England scholars, Ticknor, a Federalist and a graduate of Dartmouth, and Francis C. Gray, a Republican graduate of Federalist-oriented yet deistic Harvard. Adams wrote letters of introduction to Monticello for these two friends. They spent three days at Jefferson's home in early February 1815, when Massachusetts' disloyalty during the recent war and its legislature's call for the Hartford Convention were fresh in Jefferson's mind. Alluding to these unpleasant events, Jefferson wrote Adams, "I thank you for making known to me Mr. Ticknor and Mr. Gray. They are fine young men indeed, and if Massachusetts can raise a few more such, it is probable she would be better counselled as to social rights and social duties." He was especially impressed by Ticknor's knowledge of books: "Mr. Ticknor is particularly the best bibliograph I have met with." Demonstrating his confidence in this New Englander, Jefferson commissioned Ticknor to buy rare editions of the classics for him when he went on a tour of Europe. Revealing that his bark was worse than his bite in the matter of inviting New Englanders to teach at his university (something he later implied that he would *never* do), Jefferson offered Ticknor the professorship of Spanish and French literature at his University of Virginia, but Ticknor's prior commitment to Harvard intervened.[1]

For the rest of Jefferson's life, Ticknor remained one of his favorite visitors. Jefferson so much admired his knowledge of the classics, expertise in foreign languages and in the art of collecting and evaluating rare books, that he persistently urged him to become a professor at his projected University of Virginia.[2] (Ironically, although one of the university's purported objectives was that its students develop increased loyalty to the South and the Democratic Party, Jefferson invariably preferred to hire professors from Federalist New England and "monocratic" Great Britain rather than Southern natives.) He effusively flattered Ticknor. "Would to god we could have two or three duplicates of yourself, the original being above our means and hopes," he wrote him after he rejected a professorship at the university.[3] He whined to John Adams, "I should have been much more pleased had he accepted the

Professorship in our University" instead of Harvard, where he became a professor of modern languages.[4]

Like many people who met Jefferson on their visits to Monticello, Ticknor found charming his veneer of plainness, humility, and ostensible respect for others' opinions. From the sloppiness and cheapness of Jefferson's clothing during his retirement, as reported by Ticknor and others, there are indications that, painfully aware of his debts, he was determined to economize on his wardrobe. His greatest debts consisted of those long ago incurred by his father-in-law in buying slaves, as well as the ones he ran up during his luxurious residence in Paris during the 1780s, when he spent extravagant sums on books, clothing and wine purchases. He continued to spend exorbitant sums on wine for entertainment purposes, particularly his semi-weekly dinners with Congressmen during his presidency, which he paid for out of his own pocket. After he retired from the presidency, the unceasing entertainment of strangers and fixed costs for the upkeep of hundreds of slaves, who because of declining prices for tobacco, flour, and wheat, became a fiscal burden for many of those who did not sell them down to the Lower South during his last years, further undermined his finances. This became the case especially after the 1819 depression, which lasted for several years. (In that year, he gave himself the "coup de grace," as he called it, by backing a huge bank loan to his friend, his grandson's father-in-law Wilson Cary Nicholas, which fell completely on his shoulders when the bankrupt Nicholas died in 1820.[5])

On his visit of February 1815, Ticknor had this to say about Jefferson's appearance: "There is a breathing of notional philosophy in Mr. Jefferson—in his dress, his house, his conversation. His setness [sic], for instance, in wearing very sharp toed shoes, corduroy small-clothes, and red plush waistcoat, which have been laughed at till he might perhaps wisely have dismissed [thrown them out] them."[6] It is hard to believe that this allegedly elegant aristocrat was dressed virtually like an eccentric old hobo.

Despite modern-day Monticello's breath-taking elegance as a leading tourist attraction, the reality in Jefferson's time was less impressive. The parlor seemed more like a museum or menagerie than a home, with its Indian hides, panther skins, moose heads, and other flora and fauna. In 1815, touring Europe, Ticknor was told by the Abbé Correa, a Portuguese statesman who had recently visited Virginia, that he considered Monticello unimpressive. Correa had once said this, very politely, in the presence of Jefferson's hot-tempered son-in-law, Thomas Mann Randolph, Jr., who felt so insulted by the remark that he nearly challenged him to a duel.[7]

Ticknor was hardly awestruck by Jefferson. He downplayed his greatness as an intellectual and political leader. With the arrogance of youth, he paid little attention to what Jefferson said. He wrote that Jefferson claimed that an obscure work by Pierre Charron, a skeptical sixteenth-century Catholic priest and disciple of Montaigne, titled De la Sagesse (Of Wisdom), was the finest treatise ever written on moral philosophy. Probably mistakenly, he claimed that Jefferson praised a "Review of Montesquieu" by Du Pont de Nemours as "the best political work that had been printed for fifty years." Jefferson must have said that Destutt de Tracy's Review of Montesquieu, which he greatly admired and translated into English, was his favorite old-age political treatise, as historians like Adrienne Koch and Joyce Appleby have noted.[8]

Ticknor's companion on the trip, Francis C. Gray, served as secretary to John Quincy Adams from 1809 to 1813 when he was U.S. minister to Russia. In his diary, Gray composed a detailed account of his impressions of Jefferson. Like Ticknor, he was surprised by the chintzy appearance of Jefferson's clothing and the dilapidated state of his furniture, indications that Jefferson was trying to economize and forego selling slaves despite his declining financial condition. "Mr. Jefferson soon made his appearance," Gray's irreverent record began: "He is quite tall, 6 feet one or two inches, face streaked & speckled with red [blotches], light grey eyes, white hair, dressed in shoes of very thin soft leather with pointed toes & heels ascending in a peak behind, with very short quarters grey worsted stockings, corderoy [sic] small clothes blue waistcoat & coat, of stiff, thick cloth made of the wool of his own merinos [sheep] & badly manufactured [probably by his own slaves], the buttons of his coat & small clothes of horn, & an under waistcoat flannel bound with red velvet—His figure bony, long with broad shoulders, a true Virginian."[9] Jefferson's legendary sloppiness and desire for personal comfort in his clothing (although it was sometimes made of expensive materials), famously attested to by the piqued British ambassador Anthony Merry in 1803, remains evident in these personal observations by Ticknor and Gray.

While Jefferson briefly departed the room to instruct their coachman to leave their baggage at Monticello and return to Charlottesville, Gray and Ticknor carefully inspected their surroundings in the "parlour." Gray seemed appalled at the virtual squalor in which Jefferson lived (similar to that of the original slaveholders of frontier Virginia described in Carl Bridenbaugh's *Myths and Realities*). "On looking round the room in which we sat the first thing which attracted our attention was the state of the chairs," Gray wrote. "They had leather bottoms stuffed with hair, but the bottoms were completely worn through & the hair sticking out in all direction; on the mantle piece which was large & of marble were many books of all kinds Livy Orosius, Edinburg review, 1 vol. of [Maria] Edgeworths moral tales &c. &c." Jefferson apparently preferred a cluttered environment with a diverse array of books scattered about to one of neat order. Gray continued, "There were many miserable prints & some fine pictures hung round the room."[10] It was not a very prosperous-looking milieu.

The puritanical Bostonians refused a glass of rum and sugar ("toddy") when a slave ("servant") offered it to them, after which no more hard liquor was served, in deference to the abstemious visitors. However, they drank beer and wine at dinner. Jefferson elaborated on his literary opinions, such as his admiration for the Saxon language and his distrust of Hume's history of England, for its "tory principles are to him insupportable," although he admired Hume's writing style and attention to detail. "The best mode of counteracting their effect is, he thinks, to publish an Edition of Hume expunging all those reflections & reasonings, whose influence is so injurious, this has been attempted by [John] Baxter, but he has injured the work by making other material abridgements."[11] Historians are well aware of these aspects of Jefferson's intellectual life; Gray probably accurately reported what he said.

Appositely enough, during his visit Gray witnessed Jefferson's dependence on the material culture of New England. Instead of walls, Monticello had many full-length windows in many areas on the first floor, which caused Jefferson no end of trouble. On their arrival, Gray and Ticknor observed "a servant occupied in substituting a wooden panel for a square of glass, which had been broken in one of the folding doors opening on the lawn. Mr. J. had procured the glass for his house in Bohemia [Czechoslovakia], where the price is so much the square foot whatever be the size of the glass purchased, & these panes were so large that unable to replace the square in this part of the country, he had been obliged to send to Boston to have some glass made of sufficient size to replace that broken, & this had not yet been received."[12] The palatial Monticello mansion seemed in surprisingly dilapidated condition with regard to both its furnishings and its external appearance. It is possible that Jefferson, were he to rise from the dead, might not recognize the present-day ornate tourist attraction visited by many thousands every year, whose revenues and accouterments provide income for dozens of workers, scholars, and pseudo-scholars.

More than the two New Englanders, the English radical, George Flower, who hoped to settle in the United States with his friend Morris Birkbeck, found Jefferson admirable when he visited Monticello in December 1816. Like Gray and Ticknor, he took note of Jefferson's simple attire. In one of the most detailed albeit overlooked descriptions of Jefferson (for this reason I will print it here), he said: "In person he is tall and thin and tho near 80 years old, as active as a Boy. A person of such sure acquirements & abilities I never met with, both in his dress and House there is the greatest plainness and simplicity. He wears a coarse Cloth Coat with large steel Buttons and in our old fashion a red plush Waistocat and a pair of dark brown corderoy [sic] Breeches with colored worsted Stockings. In his appearance like a respectable old English Gardener. Regular in his habits, methodical in his actions, temperate in living, affable and polite in his Manners, accessible to the most illiterate persons, and a companion for persons of polish'd Manners & the greatest literary Attainments."[13] Whether hailing from old or New England, Jefferson's visitors in his old age found a unique individual, who advocated constant change, scientific progress, and intellectual and political revolution in his philosophy while wearing worn-out (we might call it "retro") clothing from Revolutionary War days. Perhaps he wanted to be constantly reminded of the time he achieved two of his greatest goals: "author[ship] of the Declaration of American Independence and of the Statute of Virginia for Religious Freedom," as he wrote on his epitaph. His colleagues Madison and James Monroe followed his quaint example.

Whatever Ticknor and Gray might have thought of him, Jefferson had a soft spot in his heart for that bastion of conservatism and erudition, Harvard College, partly because its students and faculty led in expounding the Unitarian creed he advocated. This might explain why, when two merchants offered to send him garden seeds from Marseilles, not sure of their exact destination, Jefferson said he did not know anyone there, and directed them to ship the seeds to Harvard College. "I would request you to offer them to the acceptance of the botanical garden attached to the University of Cambridge [Harvard] and if charges, duties &c. are due on them, on your having the goodness to drop me a note of them," he replied, "I will immediately remit the amount."[14] Undoubtedly, he respected the institution that claimed the loyalties of his protégé Ticknor as a formidable center of learning.

Jefferson was always eager to help scholars researching U.S. History, especially when they were foreigners whose writings might affect the opinion of his country held overseas by intellectuals and politicians. He was also anxious that these writers not obtain inaccurate information by talking to the "wrong" people, i.e., his political opponents, the "monocratic" Federalists; or reading Federalist newspapers. In 1795, Christoph Daniel Ebeling (1741–1817), a German liberal professor and librarian at Hamburg's prestigious Gymnasium, who taught classes in the Greek language, U.S. history, and international finance, contacted Jefferson. He wrote him requesting assistance in writing a history of the United States, and sent him a list of the hundreds of sources he used in researching his study, and those American intellectuals, especially Jefferson's friend, the Reverend William Bentley of Salem, who sent him a great deal of information about the United States. Ebeling, who never visited the United

States, fervently admired the revolutionary republic. He said that the only legitimate governments were those whose citizens enjoyed unimpeded personal freedom. He believed in the right of revolution, and thought European peoples should imitate the United States' example by exercising it. His history of the United States, it remained unfinished at his death in 1817.[15] Ebeling eventually completed seven volumes of his *General History of America*, which was arranged by state and covered only ten of them, including Virginia. Ebeling relied on Jefferson's *Notes on the State of Virginia* for much of his account of Virginia's history, and for that reason considered dedicating his *History* to Jefferson; but finally did not. However, he did send him a complimentary Virginia volume, but it is doubtful that Jefferson read it because it was not translated from German.[16]

Jefferson was alarmed that Ebeling had written to and read books by such Federalist hard-liners as Congregationalist clergymen Jedidiah Morse of Yale College, who preached in New York Presbyterian and Charlestown and Newbury, Massachussetts Congregationalist churches; and newspaper editor Noah Webster, who later became famous for composing the first major American dictionary of the English language. In his "Notes on Professor Ebeling's Letter of July 30, 1795," commenting on the authorities on whom Ebeling relied for information about the United States, Jefferson showed contempt for these Northern Federalist writers, who denigrated the South. At the same time, he tried to be discerning in his evaluations. He considered his friend Ezra Stiles, President of Yale, "an excellent man, of very great learning, but remarkable for his credulity." He regarded Ebeling's other sources, Dr. Benjamin Smith Barton, Dr. David Ramsay, and famed Republican poet Joel Barlow, the last a native of Connecticut while the other two were born in Pennsylvania (although Ramsay had moved to South Carolina, where he ceased denouncing slavery), as more reliable. Next to their names, he wrote, "All these are men of respectable characters worthy of confidence as to any facts they may state, and rendered, by their good sense, good judges of them." Jefferson viewed Noah Webster, editor of the New York Federalist newspapers *American Minerva* and *New York Herald*, and the orthodox Calvinist preacher Morse, both Federalists of Connecticut extraction, as anti–Southern. However, he observed that they were "good authorities for whatever relates to the Eastern states, & perhaps as far South as the Delaware." With devastating sarcasm, he continued, "But south of that their information is worse than none at all except as far as they quote good authorities. They both I believe took a single journey through the Southern parts, merely to acquire the right of being considered as eye-witnesses."[17] Jefferson's statement was not entirely accurate. As a young man, Morse spent five months in 1787 as an evangelical minister to a congregation in frontier Midway, Georgia.[18]

Although Jefferson apparently only superficially investigated these two would-be authorities, he disliked their reactionary politics sufficiently to belittle their reputations. Continuing his critique for Ebeling's enlightenment, he even disparaged fellow Virginians. Admitting that some of them were vagrants, especially in the towns (he was not describing hard-working farmers), he suspected that Webster and Morse obtained their information from such types. As he explained, "To pass once along a public road thro' a country, & in one direction only, to put up at it's taverns, and get into conversation with the idle, drunken individuals who pass their time lounging in these taverns, is not the way to know a country, it's inhabitants, or manners. To generalize a whole nation from these specimens is not the sort of information which Professor Ebeling would wish to compose *his work* from."[19]

Observing the list of newspapers that Ebeling consulted in composing his study of the United States, Jefferson muted his shock that they were all Federalist; and all edited by natives of New England. They were John Fenno's *Gazette of the United States*, Alexander Hamilton's semi-official mouthpiece, published in Philadelphia; Webster's New York *Minerva*; and Benjamin Russell's twice-weekly Boston *Columbian Centinel*, New England's leading Federalist newspaper, reputedly with the largest circulation in the country. Initially not very explicit about the partisan orientation of these newspapers, Jefferson found it necessary to explain the party battle to his German correspondent. Alongside a list of these papers, he tartly observed, "To form a just judgment of a country from it's newspapers the character of these papers should be known, in order that proper allowances & corrections may be used. This will require a long explanation, without which, these particular papers would give a foreigner a very false view of American affairs." Jefferson then explained that, after the U.S. Constitution went into operation in 1789, two political parties developed. One of them embodied the vast majority of the people, especially the "Agricultural interest," who favored "Republican" government and outnumbered their opponents "500 to one." The latter, the "Anti-republicans" or "monocrats," consisted mainly of wealthy merchants, office-seekers, fiscal speculators, and bankers in the cities, who controlled a disproportionate share of the wealth and most of the newspapers. They favored converting the U.S. form of government to a British-style monarchy. Jefferson left no doubt that Ebeling had inadvertently chosen "Anti-republican" newspapers, among which he included, along with the *Centinel*, Webster's *Minerva, and* Fenno's *Gazette*, "the Hartford newspaper," by which he meant the *Connecticut Courant*, and the pro–Federalist Richmond *Virginia Gazette*, edited by Augustine Davis, which he called "Davies's Richmond paper." Thus, Jefferson's criticism was not directed solely at New England newspapers; he included the leading Federalist newspapers, many of which were located in New England.[20]

Jefferson supplied a more knowledgeable and detailed description of "Republican" newspapers. He apparently hoped that Ebeling would prefer to rely on them in his research. He was especially solicitous that Ebeling consult Quaker Samuel Pleasants, Jr.'s Virginia Democratic-Republican paper, the *Richmond and Manchester Advertiser*, whose name was changed to *Virginia Argus* in 1796. He was also aware that Thomas Larkin and Abijah and Thomas Adams edited a staunchly Republican paper in Boston, the *Independent Chronicle*, although he did not know such details as that it was semiweekly. Enumerating the Republican papers for Ebeling, he included "Adams's Boston paper, [Thomas] Greenleaf's of New York, [Peter] Freneau's of New Jersey, [Benjamin Franklin] Bache's of Philadelphia, Pleasant's [*sic*] of Virginia, &c." Demonstrating his knowledge of the Republican press, he continued, "Pleasant's paper comes out twice a week, Greenleaf's & Freneau's once a week, Bache's daily." Revealing less familiarity with Massachusetts papers, he admitted, "I do not know how often Adams's." He was especially eager that Ebeling read Pleasants' Virginia paper: "I shall according to your desire endeavor to get Pleasant's for you for 1794, & 95 and will have it forwarded through 96 from time to time to your correspondent at Baltimore."[21]

Rather than discrediting New England as the home of Federalism, in his correspondence with Ebeling Jefferson desired merely to inform him of the best sources of information on Democratic-Republican points of view. He mentioned Boston newspapers of both persuasions. He had nothing against New England *per se*. His object of aversion was the "monocratic" Federalist Party, as he called it. He feared this party wished to warp the U.S. Constitutional government into a monarchy and join the British to crush France's revolutionary attempts to "republicanize" Europe.

Twenty years later, Dr. William Bentley of Salem, Massachusetts, a foremost Unitarian scholar and Democrat, to whom Jefferson had offered the presidency of the University of Virginia, requested him to send Ebeling new source materials on Virginia to enable him to complete his project. After explaining that he had sold most of his books to the Library of Congress, Jefferson complained that he had neither time nor energy to investigate historical sources. Still, because of the numerous geographies and gazetteers hostile to the South authored by New Englanders, he hoped that Ebeling's books on U.S. history and geography would eventually be translated from German and published in the United States, so "that our selves and the world may at length have something like a dispassionate account of these States." Perversely blaming Morse and other malicious Federalist authors for the dearth of accurate writings about the state instead of Virginians' failure to take up the pen and write books favorable to Virginia, he lamented, "Poor human nature! when we are obliged to appeal for the truth of mere facts from an eyewitness [Morse?] to one whose faculties for discovering it are only an honest candor and caution in sifting the grain from the chaff."[22]

Writing to Bentley, Jefferson, perhaps unconsciously, ignored the horrors of Southern slavery. He predicted that white immigrants would choose to settle in Virginia rather than other states once they had accurate information. For him, the United States remained an idyllic land of liberty. He assumed that the "enslaved" peoples of Europe would unanimously desire to move there if offered the opportunity. He did not want New England's theological obscurantists to dampen newcomers' spirits. While regretting that Napoleon's egotism, dictatorship and wars had committed "parricide" on the French Revolution's liberal ideology of human rights and freedom of thought, he believed that the ideals of equality and democracy had survived there in muted form. Throughout the Atlantic world, "nations hitherto in slavery have descried through all this mist a glimmering of their own rights, have dared to open their eyes, and to see that their own power and their own will suffice for their emancipation."[23] Alluding to the disgraceful Hartford Convention, Jefferson feared that the "Hartford nation" ostensibly preferring the inferior, "mixed monarchy" brand of "republicanism" prevalent in Great Britain, the only other country with even a semblance of representative government and civil equality, retarded the freedom and progress of humanity at home and abroad.[24]

While regretting that many influential New Englanders had rejected his Democratic-Republican doctrines, Jefferson expected a mass migration of disgruntled, anti–Federalist Massachusetts citizens west, to states that were more liberal. When Benjamin Waterhouse wrote him that many educated Bostonians, disillusioned by the religious and political obscurantism in the city, were leaving the state, he wrote back, "The emigrations you mention from the Eastern states are what I have long counted on." Exaggeratedly assessing New England's political and religious quagmire, Jefferson said, "The religious & political tyranny of those in power with you, cannot fail to drive the oppressed to milder associations of men, where freedom of mind is allowed in fact as well as in pretence."[25]

Jefferson exaggerated the purport of Waterhouse's letter. He wishfully anticipated a flood of Northern would-be farmers from several "Eastern states," who would purchase land from Virginia's heavily indebted plantation owners and cultivate it with their labor. They would replace the slaves he hoped to have liberated and exiled by government fiat in the near future. The Republican Unitarian physician Waterhouse had merely said that many intellectual inhabitants of urban Boston had left the state, resenting the "Essex Junto's" religious Establishment which deprived them of freedom. "Their Hartford convention has been made the laughing stock of the publick," he wrote of the extreme Federalists. "Boston is already half ruined.

Emigration is fast draining off her best spirits. Those who can distinguish between business & bustle say, that she is rapidly on the decline."[26] Waterhouse did not suggest that a mass exodus of farmers from Massachusetts had occurred, but only of educated Bostonians.

Because Virginians lacked an adequate system of public education, Jefferson doubted their capacity for self-government would ever be equal to that of the people of Massachusetts. His fears remained unassuaged, although Virginians voted for his party consistently for over twenty years. In 1795, although his home state was already the established cradle of Democratic- Republicanism, he was unconvinced of the average Virginian's interest in public affairs. In his memorandum to Ebeling advising him to question his sources' credibility and warning that Morse of Connecticut and Webster of New York knew little about the South, and as Northern Federalists were biased against it, he more significantly admitted he distrusted the integrity of the average Southern men they interviewed. He asserted these "loungers" were unqualified to furnish accurate details. In noting Morse and Webster's ignorance of the South, Jefferson simultaneously disparaged the intelligence and poor work ethic of Southerners. As we have seen, he remarked, "to pass once along a public road thro' a country, and in one direction only, to put up at it's taverns, and get into conversation with the idle, drunken, individuals who pass their time lounging in these taverns, is not the way to know a country."[27]

Jefferson dreaded the possibility that such "drunken loungers," the uneducated vagrants and unskilled town laborers he distrusted, might somehow, once they became sober, gain control of the political process in Virginia. He was more receptive toward skilled artisans, as he explained in his "Population" chapter (known as "Query VIII") in *Notes on Virginia,* and in letters to John Lithgow in 1805 and Benjamin Austin in 1816.[28]

Jefferson indirectly expressed similar fears of illiterate and unproductive white male citizens in a letter to the Virginia geographer and political reformer Samuel Kercheval. He implied that seductive women too easily influenced men's political opinions, especially at election time. In general, Jefferson thought that women were as intelligent as men, but because of their physical weakness (what some people, like John Adams, called "delicacy"), it was not appropriate or safe for them, as child-bearers, to participate in the rough-and-tumble anxieties of politicking. This view was similar to Aristotle's application of the Greek term *akuron* to women.[29]

Unlike the ancient Greeks, Jefferson conceded that political justice required that, in apportioning seats in the Virginia legislature, slaveholders (himself included) must repudiate political advantages derived from the unethical practice of human bondage, such as the Constitution's "three-fifths clause." On the other hand, he applied classical republican principles to determine proper suffrage qualifications in Virginia. "Principle will, in this, as in most other cases, open the way for us to correct conclusion," he began. "Were our state a pure democracy, in which all its inhabitants should meet together to transact all their business, there would yet be excluded from their deliberations (1) infants, until arrived at years of discretion. (2) women, who, to prevent depravation of morals and ambiguity of issue, could not mix promiscuously in the meetings of men. (3) slaves, from whom the unfortunate state of things with us takes away the rights of will and of property."[30]

Extending his analysis from direct democracy, wherein every male citizen voted on every issue, to representative democracy, springing from Americans' "new science of politics," as Hamilton called it, Jefferson continued, "Those then who have no will could be permitted to exercise none in the popular assembly; and of course could delegate none to an agent in a representative assembly. The business in the first case [direct democracy], would be done by qualified citizens only; and in the second by the representatives of qualified citizens only."[31] In comparing direct democracy with representative republicanism, Jefferson's conceptions were influenced by such diverse institutions as the New England town meeting and the Native American tribal council.[32]

· · · · ·

During Jefferson's retirement, a major cause of controversy between the Founders was which one of them (and which state) had done most to promote the cause of Independence. Much to John Adams' chagrin, most people acknowledged Jefferson as the primary author of the Declaration of Independence, something Adams thought he should receive most credit for, because he believed his oratorical skills pushed the resolution for independence through Congress. He even claimed that Jefferson had copied the Declaration's wording from the Mecklenburg, North Carolina, declaration of independence, which, though later proved apocryphal, allegedly appeared at the end of 1775. In writing to Jefferson, Adams suppressed his competitive feelings over their respective roles in the Revolution. However, Jefferson made clear to Adams that he would not let newspaper reports that Adams had denigrated his achievement interfere with their octogenarian epistolary friendship.[33]

In contrast to Adams' ethnocentricity, Jefferson objectively assessed New England's contribution to the Revolution. When Samuel Adams Wells, Sam Adams' grandson, queried Jefferson about reports that Jefferson claimed that the prewar committees of correspondence originated in Virginia rather than Massachusetts, he protested his regard for Massachusetts' reputation. "So far as either facts and opinions have been truly quoted from me," he explained, "they have never been meant to intercept the just fame of Massachusetts, for the promptitude and perseverance of her early resistance." Further clarifying the point, he explained that Boston and its sister Massachusetts towns had organized the first intra-state committees of correspondence in 1772. The following year, Virginia's House of Burgesses, prompted by his closest friend, Dabney Carr, had initiated the first inter-colonial committees of correspondence to communicate with other colonies. He went on to attest his respect for John Adams's oratorical ability as "a speaker … whose deep conceptions, nervous style, and undaunted firmness, made him truly our bulwark in debate." Jefferson ended his letter by expressing confidence that Massachusetts would soon return to "sound principles" in politics.[34]

· · · · ·

Paradoxically, despite his awareness that New England remained the stronghold of conservative Federalism, restrictive suffrage, and an established church, Jefferson extravagantly praised the "perfectly" governed New England towns as his paradigm for extending local democracy in Virginia by creating wards. He asserted, "These wards, called townships in New England, are the vital principle of their governments, and have proved themselves the wisest invention ever devised by the wit of man for the perfect exercise of self-government, and for its preservation."[35]

A seeker for political stability despite his undeserved reputation for radicalism, Jefferson praised Federalist Connecticut for the consistent outcomes of its direct popular elections of local officials, which in other states were usually appointed. Proposing that Virginia adopt direct popular election of state judges, Jefferson advised it to follow Connecticut's example: "In one State of the Union, at least, it has long been tried, and with the most satisfactory success. The judges of Connecticut have been chosen by the people, every six months, for nearly two centuries, and I believe there has hardly ever been an instance of change, so powerful is the curb of incessant responsibility."[36] Thus, despite unusually frequent elections, which guaranteed the possibility of rotation in office to an extreme, Connecticut citizens were satisfied with their judges and continued to reelect the same men, who, aware that the people judged *them* every six months, apparently acted with probity.

Jefferson was convinced that New Englanders' political institutions contributed to their greater interest in politics, compared to Southerners. In New England towns, Jefferson said, direct involvement with the neighborhood's local government and services gave "to every citizen, personally, a part in the administration of the public affairs." He urged Virginia to adopt this "vital principle" of New England's government.[37] Other letters he wrote during his retirement from the presidency reiterated his opinion that the optimal republic was the direct democracy of the New England town, although he regretted that such a government was not feasible over a large land area.

Especially in old age, Jefferson, who had always insisted that at least three years of grade-school education were required in order to understand history and current events, had become convinced that only educated citizens were capable of voting and participating in politics.[38] He enthusiastically endorsed a provision in the Spanish *Cortes'* (legislature's) proposed constitution for revolutionary Spain that prohibited illiterate citizens from voting. "Enlighten the people generally," he wrote his friend Pierre Samuel Du Pont de Nemours in 1816, the same year as his illuminating letters to Kercheval, "and tyranny and oppressions of body and mind will vanish like evil spirits at the dawn of day." He continued: "Although I do not, with some enthusiasts, believe that the human condition will ever advance to such a state of perfection as that there shall no longer be pain or vice in the world, yet I believe it susceptible of much improvement; and most of all, in matters of government and religion; and that the diffusion of knowledge among the people is to be the instrument by which it is to be effected."[39]

This insistence on the importance of education was one basis of Jefferson's respect for New Englanders. It made it impossible for him to bear an enduring grudge against them.

16

Jefferson, *Federalist Number 10* and New England Dissent During the War of 1812

In his forgiving and gracious attitude toward New England, especially Massachusetts, during the War of 1812, Jefferson did not intend to display weakness or timidity. To pardon the region its transgressions was more than Christian benevolence on his part. His vision of American history entailed keeping the republic together and expanding its borders to include such diverse regions as Canada, Florida, Texas, and perhaps even Cuba. Intent on establishing freedom of thought and democratic institutions throughout the nation (at least for white men), Jefferson envisioned "an empire for liberty."[1]

From the American experiment's inception, Jefferson had been committed to expanding the borders of an "extended" federal republic whose emergence onto the world scene Madison famously envisioned in *Federalist Number 10*. Even more perhaps than his close friend, Jefferson was convinced of the "extended republic's" salutary effect in defusing, diffusing, and diluting mischievous factions. In 1795, temporarily retired from politics, he wrote from Monticello to an Anglophile Genevan political theorist who hoped the Swiss city-state would become a constitutional monarchy: "I suspect that the doctrine, that small States alone are fitted to be republics, will be exploded by experience, with some other brilliant fallacies accredited by Montesquieu & other political writers. Perhaps it will be found that to obtain a just republic (and it is to secure our just rights that we resort to government at all) it must be so extensive as that local egoisms may never reach it's greater part, that on every particular question, a majority may be found in it's councils free from particular interests, and giving therefore an uniform prevalence to the principles of justice. The smaller the societies, the more violent and more convulsive their schisms."[2]

The same year, writing to a Frenchman trying to collect debts that Jefferson owed the banker Ferdinand Grand dating from his years as U.S. minister to France, Jefferson reiterated these views. After claiming that he had paid this debt, Jefferson went on to assure his correspondent that France's large land area would enable it to succeed as a republic. Contrary to Montesquieu's dictum in *Spirit of the Laws*, Jefferson believed that large countries, by incorporating numerous diverse socioeconomic factions, were better suited for republics than small ones. By Jefferson's reasoning, not every state (in the U.S. federal union, for example) would be likely to harbor identical factional interests, influences, and seek the same objectives as its co-states. This would preserve minority rights at the same time that it enforced majority will. Employing a mixture of classical republican and modern liberal democratic theory, Jefferson asserted that large republics subdued "local passions" because within their confines, "the general views of the great body to which these local passions do not extend" predominated. The United States, which encompassed a relatively large land area, proved this, he contended.[3] (This was before multi-national corporations like BP, Exxon, Apple Computer, JP Morgan Chase, and Microsoft existed, which might have caused Jefferson to modify his optimistic conclusions.)

Jefferson's election to the presidency in 1801 confirmed his confidence that the republic's huge land mass and diverse social and economic interests would shield it from both monarchy and regional division. He reiterated, in a letter to a former Vermont Republican congressman, that his victory "furnishes a new proof of the falsehood of Montesquieu's doctrine, that a republic can be preserved only in a small territory. The reverse is the truth. Had our country been even a third only of what it is, we were gone. But while frenzy & delusion like an epidemic, gained certain parts, the residue remained sound & untouched, and held on till their brethren could recover from the temporary delusion; and that circumstance has given me great comfort."[4]

With the Democratic-Republican ascendancy and the triumph of the "Virginia Dynasty" from 1801 to 1824, as we have seen, New England Federalists sporadically threatened that their states would secede from the Union. Republicans reprimanded them for their disloyalty, especially during and after the War of 1812. Eastern Federalists had hatched secessionist schemes as early as 1794, when they bristled at Republican threats to defeat the Jay Treaty with Great Britain. As mentioned earlier, Pickering's efforts in 1804 to recruit Burr to secessionist schemes that would include New York, and secessionist talk inspired by Theodore Sedgwick and recorded by John Quincy Adams in 1808 during the Embargo Act are prominent examples.[5]

A prototypical sociologist who linked individual personality characteristics with occupational survival advantages, Jefferson increasingly perceived an affinity between the personalities of Massachusetts merchants and British shippers. In a letter in 1811 to the itinerant Scottish lecturer James Ogilvie, who instructed Jefferson's grandson Thomas Jefferson Randolph at his academy at Milton, a town near Monticello, Jefferson denounced what he perceived as the British people's growing obsession, mainly in the cities, with wealth ("gold"). "The English have been a wise, a virtuous and a truly estimable people," he asserted. "But commerce and a corrupt government have rotted them to the core." England's increasing corruption, precipitated by the agricultural majority's loss of power to the fiscal, mercantile, manufacturing and exporting interests, would end in "despotism," he pessimistically predicted. The British upper classes of the cities and their love for money would debase national morality and virtue and vitiate popular rule, even if the nation eventually adopted republican forms of government and abolished monarchy.[6]

When Ogilvie informed Jefferson that he intended to write a book about his travels throughout the United States that praised the open-mindedness, prosperity and happiness of its people under republican government, Jefferson was pleased, although predicting that the travelogue would anger aristocratic, anti–American circles abroad. He joined Ogilvie in applauding Americans' amiability in answering his questions about their views and lifestyle. This candid outlook attested their freedom of thought. "Much to their credit, however, unshackled by the prejudices which chain down the minds of the common mass of Europe, the experiment has proved that, where thought is free in its range, we need never fear to hazard what is good in itself," he observed. Jefferson reiterated his long-held view, an optimistic reworking of Madison's *Federalist Number 10*, that it was the Union's great territorial extent in comparison with European countries, and the widespread availability of cheap land, rather than any superior mindset, puritanical virtue, or mental development that made Americans more free, happy, and successful in self-government than their oppressed counterparts abroad. Americans' "prospects" were bright, he was certain, because "human nature has never looked forward, under circumstances so auspicious, either for the sum of happiness, or the *spread of surface* provided to receive it."[7]

Because Europeans, and especially English aristocrats who hated the masses' growing demands for freedom, were hostile to the United States, Jefferson feared that Ogilvie's narrative would not sell abroad. Britain's cities were "ripe for despotism," and he doubted that the farming areas could save them. Even a "reformation of government" could not redeem the British because of the powerful urban elements' obsession with profit, Jefferson argued. Although Americans were grateful for Ogilvie's praise of them, Europeans would greet his views with scorn.[8]

On the lecture circuit in the South, Ogilvie asked Jefferson for suitable topics for a speech. Jefferson could not resist a jibe at the Protestant clergy, most likely thinking of those of New England. He said that Ogilvie had been successful so far in selecting suitable topics by choosing whatever interested him. Adding an *ad hominem* comment, he said he thought that Ogilvie's lectures were far superior to preachers' Sunday sermons, "better adapted to the useful purposes of society, than the weekly disquisitions of their hired instructors. All the efforts of these people are directed to the maintenance of the artificial structure of their craft, viewing but as a subordinate concern the inculcation of morality," he charged. He was contemptuous of what he regarded as clergy's harping on religious dogma and their self-interested manipulation of their parishioners. "If we will but be Christians according to their schemes of Christianity, they will compound good naturedly with our immoralities," he sarcastically commented, implying that the only thing that clergymen cared about was profit, religious conformity, and power, not the moral behavior and good works of their constituents.[9]

At this time a more serious threat than the power-seeking Calvinist clergy alarmed Jefferson. Massachusetts congressmen were once again threatening their state's secession from the Union, pouting now over the anticipated admission of Louisiana as a state. This event would increase the number of slave states so that their senatorial representation would equal that of the Free States. Boston representative Josiah Quincy charged that the admission as a state of a portion of the Louisiana Purchase was unconstitutional because the vast territory had not been part of the United States when it declared its independence from Great Britain. He was especially angry that the sectional balance between North and South would be threatened if the Orleans Territory was admitted to the Union as the state of Louisiana. Speaking before the House of Representatives on January 14, 1811, Quincy declared, "If this bill passes, it is my deliberate opinion that it is virtually a dissolution of this Union; that it will free the States from their moral obligation, and, as it will be the right of all, so it will be the duty of some, definitely to prepare for a separation, amicably if they can, violently if they must."[10]

With reputable New Englanders like young Quincy, from one of the oldest families in Massachusetts, recklessly threatening secession merely if a new state derived from the Louisiana Purchase, Jefferson's signal accomplishment as president, were admitted, Jefferson's alarm is not surprising. That was perhaps why he suggested to Ogilvie as a topic for a lecture, the horrors of disunion, and how such Balkanization would inevitably lead to a recapitulation in this hemisphere of disunited Europe's wars. In tones recalling Alexander Hamilton's warning in *Federalist Number 6* that failure to ratify the U.S. Constitution would result in the thirteen states eventually going to war with each other over territorial and trade disputes, Jefferson, even more melodramatically, rhetorically asked: "What would you think of a discourse on the benefit of the union, and miseries which would follow a separation of the States, to be exemplified in the eternal and wasting wars of Europe, in the pillage and profligacy to which these lead, and the abject oppression and degradation to which they reduce its inhabitants?"[11]

Flattering Ogilvie's literary abilities, Jefferson considered it crucial to make all Americans aware that New England's secession would burst their present happiness and latent power. "Painted by your vivid pencil, what could make deeper impressions, and what impressions could come more home to our concerns, or kindle a livelier sense of our present blessings?"[12]

Jefferson's feelings for New England were not entirely conciliatory. He remained shocked by its pro–British conduct during the War of 1812. (He would have been further appalled had he known that Governor Caleb Strong had actually sent an emissary to the British at Halifax, Nova Scotia, in September 1814 to negotiate a separate peace.) Writing in March 1815 to an old Massachusetts colleague, his Secretary of War Henry Dearborn, a constantly loyal Democratic-Republican, he expressed his resentment at Massachusetts' aloofness from the Union. Employing metaphors, he said the state considered itself more important than the others. He charged that Massachusetts believed it could oppose the war, profess friendliness toward the enemy, and flout the rights of the rest of the nation, especially the Southern states. "Her Southern brethren are somewhat on a par with her in wisdom, in information, in patriotism, in bravery, and even in honesty, although not in psalm-singing," he wrote sarcastically if not irreverently, perhaps deliberately bestowing the masculine pronoun on his section of the Union and effeminizing Massachusetts. Thus, he implied that the people of Massachusetts were cowardly, possibly dishonest capitalists, as well as effeminate psalm-singers and religious fanatics. His final remarks were kinder, but still showed disappointment in what he considered the state's egotism and ethnocentricity: "With her ancient principles, she would really be great, if she did not think herself the whole."[13] In short, this letter reveals Jefferson's continued appreciation of Massachusetts' primary role in the American Revolution and his regret at its apparent backsliding. He maintained his friendship with Massachusetts man Dearborn, despite his disgust with Massachusetts following the war's relatively successful conclusion without the state's assistance.

In fact, Jefferson wrote his angriest letter about Massachusetts, again to Dearborn, in August 1811, almost a year before the War of 1812 began. His rancor was perhaps exacerbated because, as he told his friend, he was feeling the pains of an acute attack of rheumatoid arthritis. In any case, a fierce battle was raging between extremist Federalists of Timothy Pickering's ilk in Essex County and the Republican party led by Governor Elbridge Gerry, who had been a moderate or "Adams Federalist" for much of his political life, although invariably a "classical republican" political independent, according to his biographer George Athan Billias.

Jefferson was apprehensive that Massachusetts would make a separate peace with England if war ensued. Nonetheless, he remained confident that most Americans "are perfectly equal to the purposes of self-government, and that we have nothing to fear for its stability," despite the old age and death of many Revolutionary leaders and Founding Fathers. Even in

Massachusetts, he wrote Dearborn, the "tories" were in the minority in peacetime. However, he feared that should war occur, faint-hearted Republicans might join the Federalists on a peace platform that amounted to near-treason. Viewing many New Englanders as Anglophiles, excessively profit-oriented, and perhaps more cowardly than Virginians, he warned, "The spirit, indeed, which manifests itself among the tories of your quarter, although I believe there is a majority there sufficient to keep it down in peaceable times, leaves me not without some disquietude."[14]

Confused by the stance of Massachusetts merchants, Jefferson feared that their admiration for English culture and mores took priority even over their rational economic self-interest. They refused to admit that the British government, which ruthlessly advanced the interests of British merchants and financiers, aimed to secure a monopoly of world commerce at the expense of its American competitors, including New Englanders. Ironically, if the United States was forced to go to war, the primary reason would be to protect American commerce; yet New Englanders would seemingly oppose a war waged to defend their interests. "Should the determination of England, now formally expressed, to take possession of the ocean, and to suffer no commerce on it but through her ports, force a war upon us, I foresee a possibility of a separate treaty between her and your Essex men, on the principles of neutrality and commerce," he warned. By bargaining for a separate peace, Massachusetts merchants might try to gain crumbs from a British maritime monopoly. The Essex County High Federalists (whom Jefferson labeled the "Essex Junto" years before), led by Pickering, with "his nephew Williams, can easily negotiate" such a peace treaty for the state. This would probably gain them supporters among lukewarm Democratic-Republicans, whom Jefferson, employing a religious analogy, called "quietists." Fearing the strength of Pickering's faction, he warned, "Such a lure to the quietists in our ranks with you, might recruit theirs [antiwar Federalists] to a majority."[15]

As he would reiterate in the future, Jefferson thought that New Englanders' dedication to commercial profit would lead them to regret and eventually renege on any deals they made with the British in exchange for peace. Even if Massachusetts negotiated with the British to maintain neutrality for the duration of an Anglo-American war, he commented, "excluded as they would be from intercourse with the rest of the Union and of Europe, I scarcely see the gain they would propose to themselves, even for the moment." In Jefferson's prognosis, the other states could successfully fight a "defensive war" against Britain without Massachusetts' help. "The defection would certainly disconcert the other States," he admitted, "but it could not ultimately endanger their safety. They are adequate, in all points, to a defensive war."[16] (He was referring to a "defensive war" against the British, not against Pickering and his minions.)

Jefferson was unwilling to abandon Massachusetts Republicans' control of the state government to potential Anglophile Federalist traitors. He hoped that Republican leaders from other states would lend a helping hand in campaigning against Federalist secessionists in Massachusetts. Using military metaphors to depict the impending presidential contest of 1812, he wrote Dearborn, "I hope your [Democratic] majority, with the aid it is entitled to, will save us from this trial, to which I think it is possible we are advancing." The "trial" was for the sister states to suffer the possible neutrality or secession (which Jefferson called "defection") of Massachusetts, guided by Pickering, after the likely U.S. declaration of war on Great Britain. After hoping that the improbable simultaneous deaths of King George III and

Napoleon might bring peace in Europe and end British and French harassment of U.S. shipping, thus making war unnecessary, Jefferson returned to domestic affairs. He admonished his fellow Republicans to treat New England Federalists, despite their character as potential traitors, with respect for their civil rights, but not appease them with government appointments. On this score, he praised Gerry's conduct: "Tell my old friend, Governor Gerry that I give him glory for the rasping with which he rubbed down his herd of traitors. Let them have justice, and protection against personal violence, but no favor. Powers & preeminences conferred on them are daggers put into the hands of assassins, to be plunged into our bosoms in the moment the thrust can go home to the heart."[17] Occasionally, Jefferson projectively used strong metaphors, likening his opponents to "assassins," perhaps because he was not a very violent person himself. But they were only metaphors.[18]

Evidently (despite historian Brian Steele's strained interpretation of Jefferson's general outlook), Jefferson meant electioneering maneuvers, not military coercion, when he counseled Dearborn, "I hope your [Democratic-Republican] majority, with the aid it is entitled to, will save us from the trial, to which I think it is possible we are advancing."[19] Jefferson anticipated that Massachusetts Federalists, guided by Pickering, a perennial agitator for the state's secession since Jefferson was elected in 1801, might leave the Union if war took place.[20]

After devoting some of the rest of the letter to Dearborn to denouncing the uncivilized conduct of England and France toward other nations, Jefferson returned to Massachusetts politics. He praised Governor Gerry, his and Adams' old friend. Recently elected governor of Massachusetts, Gerry, formerly a moderate Federalist, became a zealous Jeffersonian Republican. He vigorously turned against the disunionists among the Federalists. He created the Gerrymander system of redistricting to deprive the Essex County Federalists of their fair share of representation in the legislature. Jefferson admired Gerry's triumph over "his band of traitors." Wracked by pain, he seemed to think he was fighting the Revolutionary War all over again. He recalled Federalist repression during the days of the undeclared war with France and the Alien-Sedition Acts, going so far as to charge that Pickering's Federalists, even now, would gladly "guillotine" their opponents. Predicting Gerry's victory over such reactionaries, he urged excluding them from office and concomitantly protecting them from violence, even though he believed they would inflict corporal punishment on others if they had the power.[21]

Such melodrama was not characteristic of Jefferson. Gerry and Dearborn scarcely needed reminders to avoid appointing Federalist secessionists to office. Perhaps thinking of such stinging events as the 1801 election stalemate, Massachusetts violations of the Embargo Act, and Chief Justice John Marshall's benign conduct at Aaron Burr's treason tiral, he warned that the extreme Federalists had no respect for compromise. "Moderation can never reclaim them," he asserted. "They deem it timidity, and despise without fearing the tameness from which it flows." Continuing to a frenzied crescendo, Jefferson, as would become habitual with him, compared the Essex Junto to Robespierre. Recalling his earlier resentment of the Alien and Sedition Acts, he warned that if the Junto gained control of the state, it might even institute a domestic Reign of Terror. "Backed by England," he frantically warned, with obvious exaggeration, "they never lose the hope that their day is to come, when the terrorism of their earlier power is to be merged in the more gratifying system of deportation and the guillotine."[22] Perhaps this was Jefferson's means of rhetorical vengeance on the Federalists. Especially during the 1790s, they had unfairly accused him and his party of fanatical partisanship for the French Revolution, especially the "Jacobin" Robespierre and the Reign of Terror's excessive use of the guillotine against the Revolution's foes.

The intense pains of rheumatoid arthritis also, perhaps, contributed to Jefferson's diatribe. He seldom complained about this affliction to his correspondents. After his explosion against the Federalists, he wrote wearily, "Being now *hors de combat* myself, I resign to others these cares. A long attack of rheumatism has greatly enfeebled me, and warns me that they will not very long be within my ken." Fearing the possibility of the republic's dissolution, he asked the modestly capable Jeffersonian Dearborn to carry on in his place, perhaps one day as president. "But you may have to meet the trial, & in the focus [*sic*] of it's fury," he warned excitedly, "God send you a safe deliverance, a happy issue out of all afflictions, personal and public, with long life, long health, and friends as sincerely attached as yours affectionately."[23]

Written on the eve of the second war with Great Britain, this was Jefferson's harshest philippic against Massachusetts. He compared the state's extremists with the radicals of the Reign of Terror and depicted them as demonic politicians. Nevertheless, he said they should receive the protection of the laws, but not be pacified with appointment to political office. In this letter, wracked by his physical pain, Jefferson seemed to abandon the thoughts of party reconciliation he had so abundantly expressed in his first weeks as president in 1801, immortalized in the Inaugural Address's, "We are all republicans, we are all federalists."

It may be more than coincidence that Jefferson's harshest words against New England were written when his physical health was at its nadir. Although he was only sixty-eight years old, he was increasingly aware that his mental faculties were decaying with age, and he feared senility. At this time, writing to his friend, the ubiquitous medical doctor, Benjamin Rush, early feminist, founder of psychiatry and a zealous advocate of bleeding yellow fever patients, he professed surprise that most people feared to admit to themselves "that their minds keep pace with their bodies in the progress of decay." For the first time, he confided that awareness that his mental acuity was in decline was among his reasons for leaving the presidency after two terms. "Had not a conviction of the danger to which an unlimited occupation of the Executive chair would expose the republican constitution of our government made it conscientiously a duty to retire when I did, the fear of becoming a dotard and of being insensible of it, would of itself have resisted all solicitation to remain," he said. He was in the middle of a severe attack of rheumatism, so painful, especially in his hip, that he could not walk. The disability was particularly distressing because he had always enjoyed walking and "taking exercise." Pondering the reciprocal deterioration of mind and body, he sometimes asked himself what his purpose had been in reading so many books. He said he engaged in exercise because its only objective was itself. He took for granted that Rush was in good health in body and mind because the physician's practice necessitated constant motion.[24] (In those days, doctors were expected to make house calls; in addition, Rush made charitable visits to poorhouses and the public hospital.)

Seemingly pondering suicide (as he did occasionally when he thought about sickness, old age and death), Jefferson continued, "The sedentary character of my public occupations sapped a constitution naturally sound and vigorous, and draws it to an earlier close, but it will still last quite as long as I wish it." Once again expounding his doctrine that the "earth belongs to the living, not the dead," he concluded, "There is a fullness of time when men should go, & not occupy too long the ground to which others have a right to advance." Attempting to shake off his depression, he ended the letter with poetic sentiments of epistolary friendship, expecting that he and Rush would not see each other again: "We must continue, while here, to exchange occasionally our mutual good wishes. I find friendship to be like wine, raw when new, ripened with age, the true old man's milk, & restorative cordial. God bless you & preserve you through a long & healthy old age."[25] In light of Federalist obstruction of war preparations, perhaps Jefferson thought that his death and the death of the republic would take place together.

For the time being, Jefferson did not anticipate civil war; and a U.S. declaration of war against Britain was almost a year away. Although Massachusetts Democratic-Republicans like Elbridge Gerry, as well as Jefferson, employed rhetoric of military combat when anticipating encounter with their extremist Federalist foes, they were referring to political campaigns, elections, and official appointments. This was true of Massachusetts governor Gerry's letter to Dearborn, through whom he sought to assure Jefferson that he did not intend to appoint pro-secession Federalists to office. Describing his patronage policy, Gerry said, "His [Jefferson's] sentiments in regard to the implacable tories of the State & of the Union, perfectly coincide with my own; as well in respect to the malady, as to the cure. My policy is directed to this point, a discrimination & as far as it can be effected, a separation, between the revolutional, & antirrevolutional federalists." In Gerry's opinion, the "revolutional" Federalists, i.e., those who had supported the American Revolution, might be cautiously trusted with appointments in some cases, while the "antirevolutional federalists" were potential secessionists and traitors who opposed the American Revolution. He continued, "The former, although some of them may pant for a monarchy, in order to be nobles, are generally disposed to preserve our Union & independence; the latter, with some disappointed expectants [who had not gotten government appointments], & visionary Burrites [supporters of Aaron Burr's secessionist plots in 1804–1807], are decidedly for a secession of the northern states, & the erection over them of an Hanoverian monarchy." Using violent terminology, Gerry assured his friends that he would refuse to appoint diehard Federalists of this stripe to office. "This at least is my decided opinion, & as the laconic scotch General said to his army ... 'if we do not kill them, they will kill us.'"[26]

Gerry felt that the belligerent antiwar tone of the New England extremists compelled him to reject them for political appointments. "The conduct of the 'Boston assemblage,' left me no alternative, but that of a decided opposition to them," he explained, "or an abandonment of the General Government, of our Union & Independence." Depicting himself as a duelist or medieval knight in combat, the elderly governor ended on a note of challenge: "I have entered the list with them, & will never retreat, or yield, before my last breath."[27]

During the War of 1812, Jefferson became increasingly exasperated with the New England states' refusal to contribute men, money, and supplies to the struggle for survival against Britain. In 1814, he wrote to Horatio Gates Spafford, a New York Democratic-Republican Quaker who supported the war while busily compiling gazetteers of the state. Jefferson was interested in finding out more about the natural resources of all the states. He believed that the United States' productive agriculture and extractive industries and its large land mass especially suited it for democracy and republican government. "I wish we had as full a statement as to all our states," he wrote Spafford, "we should know ourselves better our circumstances and resources, and the advantageous ground we stand on as a whole. We are certainly much indebted to you for this fund of valuable information."[28]

Earlier, Spafford reported to him that in Albany, New York's capital, where he lived, there was much opposition to the war. Spafford was shocked that Governor DeWitt Clinton had appointed antiwar politicians to office. Spafford regarded opponents of the war as Anglophile monarchists, a sentiment with which Jefferson could sympathize although he was slightly more tolerant of the opposition. Perhaps thinking of the infamous Dartmoor Prison in southwestern England, in which American sailors were held, Spafford advised that President Madison treat British prisoners of war with the same cruelty that the British treated Americans. After being mobbed in a local tavern for voicing these sentiments, Spafford pondered the severity of divisions over the war. "The Merchants, Lawyers, & priests, are almost all Monarchists & they & their tools are plunging into a preparation for a civil war," he warned. "I see it plainly, & know too well their designs; & I would to God that thou & all the Southern people knew it as well." He considered Southerners like Jefferson more patriotic than Northerners.[29]

Spafford was writing about New York, but Jefferson most closely associated antiwar activities and official opposition with Massachusetts and Connecticut. Their governments proclaimed that they did not intend to supply troops or conduct national direct tax collections to finance the war. Jefferson vigorously concurred with Spafford: "I join in your reprobation of our merchants, priests and lawyers for their adherence to England & monarchy in preference to their own country & it's [*sic*] constitution. But merchants have no country. The mere spot they stand on does not constitute so strong an attachment as that from which they draw their gains. In every country and in every age the priest has been hostile to liberty. He is always in alliance with the Despot abetting his abuses in return for protection to his own."[30]

At this point, as far as Jefferson was concerned, merchants, clergymen, and tyrannical kings were equally in league with one another, equally criminals conspiring against the lives and fortunes of citizens or subjects. The defeats that U.S. troops suffered during the war and the reluctance of many parts of the country to support the war effort embittered him. He considered many of the war's opponents, and many clergymen, motivated by greed and partisanship, especially in Europe with its established churches and in New England, where tottering church establishments remained. "It is easier to acquire wealth and power by this combination than by deserving them," he continued, decrying the alliance of "throne and altar," as it was called in Europe. As he often did, Jefferson protested that the established churches had besmirched Jesus' benign teachings in their efforts to crush and expropriate their rivals: "And to effect this they have perverted the purest religion [Jesus' ethical teachings] ever preached to man, into mystery & jargon unintelligible to all mankind & therefore the safer engine for their purposes."[31]

Jefferson's explanation of the lawyers' abrupt abandonment of republicanism for promonarchical views was more complex. He felt that Anglo-American lawyers were exemplary for their Whig ideology and devotion to "the free principles of their constitution." He ascribed their defection to the influence of British lawyers, who he believed had become pro–Tory and in favor of a stronger monarchy (or "executive branch" in the United States) because of the influential writings of William Blackstone, whose *Commentaries* they read instead of Sir Edward Coke's venerable republican *Institutes*. He especially decried the influence of David Hume's *History of England,* which he perhaps exaggeratingly considered one of the most eloquent, hypnotic treatises in defense of monarchy ever written. Absurdly, Jefferson claimed that Hume's works "have done more towards the suppression of the liberties of man, than all the million[s] of men in arms of Bonaparte." His greatest fear was that the American people would be converted to monarchy, not by British "assaults of force" during the war, but from their growing attraction to "English books, English prejudices, English manners, and the apes, the dupes, and designs among our professional crafts [e.g., attorneys and clergy]."[32]

At least in this letter, Jefferson did not single out New England as the primary offender advocating monarchy. According to Jefferson, the disposition to monarchy was widespread among U.S. merchants, clergy, and attorneys. Positing an antagonism between farmers and urbanites like lawyers and merchants, whom he associated with admiration for British books and culture, he stated his definite preference, as he had done earlier in *Notes on Virginia*, in favor of agrarians. He invariably viewed the future in the context of Madison's *Federalist Number 10*. He rested his confidence on the nation's survival as a republic in its federal form, comprising nineteen states and one national government, and its large land mass. Together, they restrained more than a few states at a time from abandoning republicanism or suppressing civil liberties. A surprisingly terse yet trenchant exposition of his optimistic reliance on the dictums of *Federalist 10*, with which his political thought is seldom associated, comes at the end of this revealing letter, with the mixture of paranoia and hope that characterized Jefferson in old age: "When I look around me for security against these seductions [of British culture], I find it in the wide spread of our Agricultural citizens, in their unsophisticated minds, their independance [*sic*] and their power if called on to crush the Humists [i.e., admirers of David Hume] of our cities, and to maintain the principles which severed us from England. *I see our safety in the extent of our confederacy, and in the probability that in the proportion of that the sound parts will always be sufficient to crush local poisons.* In this hope I rest."[33]

Although postmodern "Jefferson experts" would probably interpret this letter as Jefferson's call for a "war of extirpation" by "unsophisticated" hayseeds against the evil "Humists of the cities," Jefferson, as he frequently did, was merely writing figuratively of struggles that for him were intellectual and political. They were waged in books, newspapers, and at ballot-boxes (or *viva voce* in the South) rather than on the battlefields of a civil war, whose possibility he always viewed with anxiety. (He generally preferred peaceable secession to bloody internal conflict.) Similarly, some scholars might eagerly accuse Jefferson of "hypocrisy," pointing to his use of the (to our ears) pejorative term, "unsophisticated" to describe the farmers he supposedly admired and relied on to defend the country's freedom. However, in those days, the term "unsophisticated" meant "not artificial"; authentic; and had other virtuous, "republican" connotations. As early as 1664, it signified something that was "Not tampered with, uncorrupted, genuine." In 1790, Jefferson's contemporary, Edmund Burke, in his *Reflections on the Revolution in France* (1790), asserted, "We preserve the whole of our feelings still native and entire, unsophisticated by pedantry and infidelity."[34] Taking the dictums of Madison's *Federalist Number 10* at face value, Jefferson took comfort in the idea that continental expansion would preserve a farming society whose members had the right ideas about democracy, representative government, and "republican virtue."[35]

Even after the Hartford Convention's exasperating melodrama, Jefferson firmly believed that the republic's complementary geographic and economic sectors would generate a thriving society. He insisted that its diversity and extensive land area guaranteed its survival, and ultimately, world power. Once more disparaging the idea of Montesquieu's *Spirit of Laws* (1748) that republics and the virtuous citizenry that sustained them could exist only in small territories where everyone had identical interests and similar opinions, Jefferson, in a letter to

French treasurer Barbé-Marbois, said: "I have much confidence that we shall proceed successfully for ages to come, and that, contrary to the principle of Montesquieu, it will be seen that the larger the extent of country, the more firm its republican structure, if founded, not on conquest, but in principles of compact and equality. My hope of its duration is built much on the enlargement of the resources of life going hand in hand with the enlargement of territory, and the belief that men are disposed to live honestly, if the means of doing so are open to them."[36]

Jefferson regarded the War of 1812 not only as a war of military defense against the likelihood of British victory and the consequent surrender of some portion of sovereignty for the people and government of the United States. He also considered it a struggle to preserve American culture and democratic political life from the "corruptions" of would-be monarchists, foreign and domestic, whom he now eccentrically called "Humists." Indeed, confidence that the diverse interests within the new nation, whose bedrock majority remained the farmers in whom he confided for support of republicanism, would quash monarchical threats foregrounded his view of the political landscape in his last years. When he observed the New England states contributing to such enlightened cultural trends as Unitarianism and inclining more and more to the Democratic Party in their politics, he felt secure that a strong republic would survive into the indefinite future—until the issue of slavery in the territories tore serious fissures in national unity.

17

Jefferson and Adams
"Natural Aristocracy," Class Conflict and the Uses of New England

Despite being a slaveholder, Jefferson was surprisingly eager to portray himself as the friend of the people, especially the lower middle-class farmers and taxpayers. He said they paid too much in taxes, through excises and tariff duties on necessities. He preferred that imported luxuries bear most of the burden instead. As president, he proposed to abolish all excise taxes in his first annual message to Congress in December 1801, and the Republican-controlled Congress eagerly gratified his wishes. In April 1802, it abolished the unpopular whiskey excise tax, carriage tax (which actually hurt small Massachusetts farmers more than Southern slaveholders), and the whole litany of excises passed during the presidencies of Washington and Adams.[1] Later, with such tariffs on luxuries as the "Mediterranean duties," begun in 1804 to finance war against the Libyan pirate-state, pay tribute to their rulers and ransom captured American sailors, he continued to advance this goal.[2]

At the same time, Jefferson's thoughts on New England after he left office revealed his willingness to use taxation as a political weapon. Resenting Massachusetts merchants for violating his Embargo Act and voting against his party, he wanted to abolish the drawbacks (refunds on tariff duties) they got when they re-exported certain products.[3] Contrastingly, he idolized New England farmers as he did all cultivators of the earth, and wanted them to bear as little taxation as possible. Thus, as with many other areas of his policies, Jefferson exhibited ambivalence and self-contradiction.

· · · · ·

Jefferson had always considered most New Englanders as republicans devoted to majority self-rule. That was why he admired their town meetings and wished to have Virginia copy them in the shape of "wards" or "hundreds." He regarded local, democratic self-government as the most effective government, an inspiration to the people to take an interest in public affairs. Even at the beginning of the party conflict in the 1790s, although Jefferson lamented that the New England states tended to side with Hamilton and the Federalists, he doubted that their people, if accurately informed, would continue to approve of the Federalists. He suspected that a few self-interested leaders were misleading Massachusetts voters in particular. Indeed, he was confident that, once Philip Freneau's Jeffersonian newspaper, the *National Gazette*, begun in October 1791, gained wide circulation in Massachusetts the people would switch to the Republicans and vote against Federalist stalwart Fisher Ames' reelection to Congress. As he optimistically reported to his son-in-law in November 1792, "Freneau's paper is getting into Massachusets [*sic*] under the patronage of Hancock and Sam Adams, and Mr. [Fisher] Ames, the colossus of the monocrats and paper men, will either be left out or hard run. The people of that state are republican; but hitherto they have heard nothing but The hymns and lauds chaunted by Fenno," the last a reference to John Fenno, the Hamiltonian Federalist editor of the Philadelphia *Gazette of the United States*.[4]

In March 1793, although shocked by the overwhelming defeat of a set of resolutions he had secretly drafted proposing a congressional investigation of Hamilton for alleged misconduct as secretary of the treasury, introduced into the House of Representatives by his friend William Branch Giles, he remained optimistic. Indeed, he predicted that Massachusetts' voters would give the Republicans the margin of victory in the near future. Insisting that Massachusetts was as "republican" as any other state, he predicted that its voters would elect a Democratic-Republican to Congress. "The elections have been favorable to the republican candidates everywhere south of Connecticut; and even in Massachusetts there is a probability that one republican will be sent who possesses the confidence of that description of men in that state (and which forms the mass of the state) and who will fulfil [*sic*] the only object needed, that of carrying back to the faithful accounts of what is doing here [i.e., at the capital, Philadelphia]." He concluded, "This they have never had, and it is all they need."[5] He was right; for the first time Massachusetts elected a Republican, Henry Dearborn, to Congress.

Admiration for New England's town meeting democracy had long been integral to Jefferson's political schema. As early as *Notes on Virginia*, without specifically mentioning the New England town, he praised the concept of wards as the model for structuring his state's education and popular participation in government. Sometimes he called wards "hundreds," imitating the terminology of medieval England and colonial Maryland. But he had Connecticut and Massachusetts towns primarily in mind. Wards, microcosmic institutions in which each citizen voted in decision-making on the town level, enabled people to participate in the local sphere of government. They also helped train them for later roles in national politics.[6] On a sadder note, he was also painfully aware that cliques of powerful, often venerated Federalist political leaders unduly influenced the votes of the state's citizens. Foremost among such cohorts was the faction that Jefferson labeled the "Essex Junto."

Jefferson early employed the phrase "Essex Junto." He used the term to refer to right-wing Massachusetts Federalist politicians, not only in Essex County, which included Timothy Pickering's home town of Salem, but the whole state. For instance, in July 1801, Jefferson wrote, explaining to Massachusetts Democratic-Republican congressman Levi Lincoln, his appointee as attorney general, his desire to unite ("consolidate") the moderate New England Federalist masses and the Jeffersonians:

> The consolidation of our fellow-citizens in general is the great object we ought to keep in view, and that being once obtained, while we associate with us in affairs, to a certain degree, the federal sect of republicans, we must strip of all the means of influence the Essex junto, and their associate monocrats in every part of the Union. The former [i.e., the "federal sect of republicans"] differ from us only in the shades of power to be given to the executive, being, with us, attached to republican government. The latter wish to sap the republic by fraud, if they cannot destroy it by force, and to erect an English monarchy in its place; some of them (as Mr. [John] Adams) thinking its [i.e., the English constitution's] corrupt parts should be cleansed away, others (as Hamilton) thinking that would make it an impracticable machine.[7]

After Jefferson became president, his New England advisers joined him in searching for a strategy that would facilitate their section's transfer of allegiance to the Republican Party. Echoing the president's view that New Englanders were ripe for conversion to Republicanism, Gideon Granger of Connecticut, Jefferson's politically-connected postmaster general, was sure that Massachusetts and Connecticut farmers voted Federalist only because they lacked access to Republican newspapers. Likewise, Attorney General Lincoln argued that the deception, intimidation, and indoctrination employed by Federalist leaders had induced the people's Federalist convictions. "They [New Englanders] are republicans, in their sentiments, & habits," Lincoln wrote Jefferson after a little over a year in office, "they reason right on their principles, were these corrected, they would act right—the misfortune is, they have had imposed on them errors of fact."[8]

Earlier in Jefferson's presidency, Lincoln was more optimistic about the authenticity of Massachusetts and Connecticut Federalist leaders' expressed desire to conciliate Jefferson and their growing tendency to conform to Republican opinions. He even included Judge John Lowell and merchant Jonathan Jackson, both extremists and members of the "Essex Junto," among those amenable to conciliation. He heard that even they repudiated the abusive articles concerning Jefferson that "were continually issuing from the federal presses, that they were disliked, discountenanced, & [they] wished to prevent them." Lincoln concluded that extremist Federalist clergy, money-grubbing Federalist newspaper editors, and literary hacks, "desperate, and dying scribblers," who thrived on sensationalism produced the newspapers' anti–Jefferson scurrility. "The news paper clamor undoubtedly originates with the editors themselves and an inferior description of writers, aided by some busy clergy men," he said. "I am sure the leading & respectable federalists would think themselves slandered at the imputation of countenancing it."[9]

Perceiving Massachusetts as more than a sinkhole of his vitriolic critics, President Jefferson's positive thoughts centered on its town meeting form of government. Although Jefferson had visited Boston as early as 1784, and was presumably exposed to the town meeting phenomenon at that time, he first expressed enthusiasm about wards as president in 1802 and in greater detail in retirement, in a letter to John Tyler in 1810.[10] In his famous October 1813 letter to Adams elucidating his idea of "natural aristocracy," he implied that his 1779 state public education bill proposed to create wards with extensive powers to replace Virginia's counties and parishes. (In fact, the bill only proposed to give wards responsibility for erecting schools.) "My proposition had for a further object to impart to these wards those portions of self-government for which they are best qualified, by confiding to them the care of their poor, their roads, police, elections, the nomination of jurors, administration of justice in small cases, elementary exercises of militia, in short, to have made them little republics, with a Warden at the head of each, for all those concerns which, being under their eye, they would better manage than the larger republics of the county or state."[11]

Drawing analogies between his projected wards and New England town meetings, Jefferson explained to Adams their utility for conducting statewide referenda in terms flattering Adams' native soil. "A general call of ward-meetings by their Wardens on the same day thro' the state would at any time produce the genuine sense of the people on any required point," he noted, "and would enable the state to act in mass, as your people have so often done, and with much effect, by their town meetings."[12]

In Jefferson's view, his bill for public education, and presumably the ward governments to implement it, "would have raised the mass of the people to the high ground of moral respectability necessary to their own safety, and to orderly government; and would have compleated [*sic*] the great object of qualifying them to select the veritable aristoi [aristocrats], for the trusts of government, to the exclusion of the Pseudalists."[13] Public education administered by wards, combined with the laws he had drafted from 1776 to 1779 for religious freedom and abolishing primogeniture and entail, would prepare the average citizen for the responsibilities of government. They would simultaneously reduce the economic and political power of the state's colonial aristocracy.

In other words, Jefferson regarded universal public education as the way to encourage naturally intelligent and virtuous individuals from all socioeconomic strata ("veritable *aristoi*," or genuine aristocrats) to realize their potential and, hopefully, serve as elected officials. Those who gained power in the past by wealth and corruption, not true ability, comprised an inauthentic, phony aristocracy, which Jefferson dubbed "Pseudalists." Under Jefferson's system, they would lose their power. This letter to Adams, a direct response to Adams' thoughts on aristocracy, in many ways mimicked James Harrington's classic *Oceana* (1656). However, Jefferson's contemporary source of inspiration was the New England town. For the first time, he expounded his famous idea of the "natural aristocracy." Jefferson elaborated on this concept a few years later in his autobiography.[14] Thus, at the height of the War of 1812, Jefferson's analysis of New England's deferential yet democratic politics stimulated his creative political thought rather than fantasies of "destroying New England."

Jefferson addressed some of his most lucid commentary on Massachusetts town meeting democracy to that paragon of New England conservatism, his quondam friend John Adams. In the scintillating correspondence of their final years, Jefferson contributed significantly to American political thought. Discussing the "natural aristocracy of virtue and talents" in this famous letter to Adams of October 28, 1813, Jefferson shed praise on New England's institutions. First, he explained his objections to Adams's inclusion of those who possessed wealth, physical beauty, and noble lineage within the "natural aristocracy." Jefferson limited the "natural aristocracy" to those of exceptional intellectual and moral qualities ("virtue and talents"). He relegated the other categories to a "pseudo-aristoi," "an artificial aristocracy founded on wealth and birth, without either virtue or talents; for with these it would belong to the first class [the "natural aristocracy"]." Jefferson had misgivings about this aspect of Adams' political philosophy. He opposed Adams's concept that the "aristocracy," which for Adams comprised the wealthy, the beautiful, and the highborn as well as intellectuals and virtuous sages, should sit in a separate legislative house. In this "upper house," they would possess a veto power over laws passed by the assembly's "lower house," which represented the middle- and working-classes. In his *Defence of the Constitutions* and elsewhere, Adams insisted that a bicameral legislature would protect poorer, less articulate groups from the superior charm, power, wealth and intellect of the "aristocracy," thwarting its attempts to deceive and overwhelm them. Similarly, instituting a separate legislative chamber for the rich protected them from odious legislation to confiscate their property and distribute it among the poor (measures often called "agrarian laws").[15]

Adams apparently feared that the wealthy classes, albeit a minority, would dominate the naïve majority if they mingled in a unicameral legislature. However, Jefferson cogently pointed out that a separate branch of the legislature confined to the rich would automatically give the "artificial aristocracy" an unfair advantage, by enabling it to block beneficial legislation proposed by the "natural aristocracy," which ideally sought to promote the common good. Contrary to historian Joseph J. Ellis's interpretation, Jefferson thought the dispute between him and Adams rested on the best means to prevent the rich and powerful from dominating the government, not on the rightfulness of popular rule itself, on which Jefferson thought they both agreed.[16]

Though asserting that he had more confidence than Adams in the average person's ability to choose the best men ("natural aristocrats") as rulers, Jefferson suggested that this was the only major political difference between them. According to him, the voters would usually elect the "natural aristoi" to office. "It would have been inconsistent in creation to have formed man for the social state, and not to have provided virtue and wisdom enough to manage the concerns of the society," he asserted. Implying that direct democratic processes on the model of the town meeting would elect the best leaders, he rhetorically asked, "May we not even say that that form of government is the best which provides the most effectually for a pure selection of these natural aristoi into the offices of government?" By contrast, the "artificial aristocracy" was "a mischievous ingredient in government, and provision should be made to prevent it's [sic] ascendancy."[17] However, aside from direct popular elections, Jefferson did not suggest any legislation to ensure the "natural aristocracy's" rule, or impede the "artificial aristocracy's" ascendancy.

Fearful that a politics of deadlock might result were Adams's version of bicameralism implemented, Jefferson, himself a lifelong bicameralist, argued that "Senate cabals" would be likely in an upper house controlled by the rich. Perhaps he was also thinking of his near-defeat for the presidency in 1801 by Aaron Burr's "aristocratic" Federalist partisans, which had actually occurred in the popularly elected House of Representatives. Adams had recently reminded Jefferson of this event, which he would always find traumatic. "Had the voters for Burr, addressed the Nation, I am not sure that your Convention would have decided in your Favour," Adams observed. He was alluding to Republican proposals in 1801, which Jefferson favored, to immediately summon a convention to amend the Constitution to provide distinct ballots for president and vice-president, facilitating Jefferson's election. "But what Reflections does this suggest? What Pretensions had Aaron Burr to be President or Vice President?"[18] For Adams, Burr's substantial following in 1800 was evidence that the people were *not* particularly virtuous.

Pointing out that disaster had nearly occurred when the House of Representatives chose the president in 1801, the Braintree philosopher continued to insist that the "Pseudo-aristoi," in Jefferson's parlance, should have a separate, upper-class legislative chamber. According to Adams, such a legislative body would somehow restrict the upper classes' direct influence upon the more democratic chamber, while simultaneously empowering the rich, as Jefferson summarized his friend's views, to protect their "wealth against the Agrarian and plundering enterprises of the Majority of the people." Detecting the paradox implicit in Adams' theory (which even failed to explain how the rich would be kept from dominating both houses, since Adams never specified that only the middle classes and the poor would be eligible for election to the "lower house"), Jefferson pointed out that, "To give them [the wealthy pseudo-aristoi] power in order to prevent them from doing mischief, is arming them for it, and increasing instead of remedying the evil. For if the coordinate branches can arrest their action, so may they that of the coordinates. Mischief may be done negatively as well as positively." Disparaging Adams's recurring fear that popular assemblies might abolish private property, Jefferson noted that the relatively conservative state legislatures, "in action for 30. years past, have proved that no fears of an equalisation of property are to be apprehended from them."[19] Indeed, as a large land- and slave-holder, Jefferson would want his property protected.[20]

• • • • •

Earlier in his political life, Jefferson visited Massachusetts and Connecticut. He thought that these trips, assisted by reading the works of Adams and others, afforded him insight into New Englanders' psychology and enabled him to compare it with Virginians.' "It is probable that our difference of opinion may in some measure be produced by a difference of character in those among whom we live," he wrote Adams in his letter on "natural aristocracy" in 1813. "From what I have seen of Massachusetts and Connecticut, myself, and still more from what I have heard, and the character given of the former by yourself who know them so much better, there seems to be in those states a traditionary [*sic*] reverence for certain families, which has rendered the offices of the government nearly hereditary in those families." Alluding to the Adamses, Quincys, and Otises' replacement of the Hutchinsons and Olivers as Massachusetts' political aristocracy during the Revolution, Jefferson continued, "I presume that from an early period of your history, members of these families happening to possess virtue and talents, have honestly exercised them for the good of the people, and by their services have endeared their names to them."[21] He probably expected Adams to appreciate this oblique praise.

Fearing that Adams might find his linkage of Connecticut and Massachusetts offensive, Jefferson clumsily explained, "I mean it politically only, not morally." He proceeded to denounce the avarice of the citizens of the Nutmeg State, claiming, "they seem to have modelled their morality on the story of Jacob and Laban." Finally, he expressed his suspicion of Massachusetts politicians as well, commenting, "altho' this hereditary succession to office with you may in some degree be founded in real family merit, yet in a much higher degree it has proceeded from your strict alliance of church and state." He implied this union was based on sheer greed and ambition. In this connection, he praised Virginia's political system for reducing clerical influence. Indeed, the royal government had paid Virginia's Anglican Clergy at rates tied to the price of tobacco during the colonial regime; however, because of serious inflation during the colonial period and later, New England's Congregationalist clergy invariably had to cajole the members of their congregations for remuneration. Probably aware of these factors, Jefferson concluded that his colony's clergymen, "having been secured against rivalship by fixed salaries, did not give themselves the trouble of acquiring influence over the people."[22]

The clergy, never having sought political power during colonial times, Jefferson explained, lacked any motive to gain it under Virginia's new constitution of 1776, which explicitly prohibited their election to the state assembly.[23] Although Jefferson told Adams that his opinion of Connecticut was low because the clergy ostensibly dominated the government and the courts, in a letter to Samuel Kercheval a few years later he praised the state. He applauded Connecticut's method of popular election of judges, instead of their appointment by the legislature, the existing mode in Virginia and most other states.[24]

As Jefferson's tight-lipped smile and confident, twinkling eyes staring down at us from his portraits make clear, he was certain of one thing: he *was* a "natural aristocrat," even though he may never have said so. If he had, he would have lacked the humility and "virtue" required of a "natural aristocrat." It is difficult to tell from his portraits whether he is laughing with us or at us. But it seems obvious that he is pleased with and likes himself.[25] As a natural aristocrat, he highly valued freedom for himself and those citizens who recognized his greatness. Indeed, his educational program, with its goal of grooming an intellectual elite whether from the "rubbish" or the cream of society, was intrinsically aristocratic—just like his vision of New England's political culture.

Although he admired its town meetings, Jefferson found it difficult to avoid expressing his contempt for New England's established church. He believed the Church's religious sanctions had coerced and intimidated the voters. Even worse, the people obediently "cannonised" [sic] their ministers. By contrast, Virginia's colonial clergy "did not give themselves the trouble of acquiring influence over the people," although its secular aristocracy exercised awesome political power. During the Colonial Period, wealth accumulated in "particular families" under Virginia's old law of entail, endowing the rich with an aura of arrogant independence and inspiring brisk competition among them for seats on the "king's council" (governor's council). Jefferson charged that the wealthiest planters took the Crown's side in all disputes with the people. The voters punished their royalism by ostracizing them after Independence. He ascribed the Virginians' allegedly more democratic temperament, despite their less democratic political institutions, to the presence of such invidious, aristocratic Tories (a class that generally did not return after the Revolution, and which historians have pretty much ignored for Revolutionary Virginia). "Hence they were unpopular; and that unpopularity continues attached to their names," Jefferson explained, listing the names of a few prominent old families with Loyalist members. "A Randolph, a Carter, or a Burwell must have great personal superiority over a common competitor to be elected by the people, even at this day."[26]

To a degree, Adams corroborated Jefferson's suspicions of New Englanders' docility toward their social superiors. Confessing to their deferential demeanor, he noted that even the conservative, formerly Loyalist old families maintained the respect of the public. Despite their Tory or undemocratic reputations, whenever these venerable families decided to "fall in with the popular Sentiments, they are preferred, cetoris [sic] paribus to all others" in elections, he informed Jefferson.[27]

Spurred by Adams' account of the Massachusetts electorate's conservatism, Jefferson (perhaps considering himself the prime example) emphasized Virginians' tendency to embrace enlightened political thought and action. As further evidence of Virginians' revolt against their richest planters, Jefferson proudly listed laws passed between 1776 and 1785, "drawn by myself," abolishing primogeniture (descent of all landed property to the eldest son if the owner died intestate) and entail (prohibiting by one's last will and testament sale by descendants of any part of the landed estate or its slaves). This legislation destroying the "pseudo-aristocracy" had taken place in Virginia before it occurred in Massachusetts. In Massachusetts, Pennsylvania, and Connecticut dating from the colonial period, partible inheritance prevailed in cases of intestacy, but the eldest son got a double portion. Massachusetts courts based this procedure on precedents of Mosaic and English common law. Although various forms of entailed estates descending solely to the eldest son continued to exist into the twentieth century, Massachusetts and New Hampshire abolished the double portion in 1789, Pennsylvania in 1794, and Rhode Island in 1798.[28]

In retrospect, Jefferson regretted the defeat of his equally important bill creating wards for educational purposes, which he desired to expand for the purpose of administering local governmental concerns, and which he told Adams he had modeled after the New England towns. As he put it, his proposal would have "divide[d] every county into wards of 5 or 6 miles square, like your townships," established a system of free elementary education, and offered scholarships enabling the most intelligent indigent students to pursue an advanced education.[29]

Harold Hellenbrand, a close student of Jefferson's educational thought, perceives the ward republics as proof of Jefferson's unconscious patriarchal tendency. He finds that Jefferson's Revolutionary War era reform program "consisted of pedagogy and parental solicitude writ large." As was the case in New England, Jefferson thought the state in Virginia might assume a paternalist and democratic edge. Hellenbrand believes that his 1776–1779 legislative platform evinced this intention: "Because these reforms required the consent of the legislature and the enactment of the public in local wards, and because they advanced the cause of reason, he did not conceive of them in *Notes on the State of Virginia* or elsewhere as laws imposed from above on the people." Ironically, Jefferson's educational reforms had their roots in British common law and the "patrimonial customs that he otherwise sought to displace." Rather than seeking extreme radical change, Jefferson envisioned his projects as "encouraging deference to reasoned precedent and legal forms." As Hellenbrand explains, his bills for the more general diffusion of knowledge and for religious freedom alike embodied "his central drama of a father/teacher who influenced his wards by reason, not brute compulsion. Essentially, Jefferson interpreted the pastoral function of God and his ministers [and of himself as legislator/minister] in pedagogical and Lockean terms."[30] That Jefferson ardently embraced the town meeting despite its conservative tendencies reveals that he was not as radical as some historians, invariably resorting to his "Adam and Eve" letter to William Short in 1793 or his "tree of liberty" letter to William Stephens Smith after Shays' Rebellion in 1787, insist.[31]

For Jefferson, New England was more than just another part of the country. It was a *model* for the political structure of the rest of the states, especially at the local level. Humiliated that New Englanders had flouted his presidential administration's embargo acts by conducting widespread illegal trade with Canada and Great Britain, he hoped to utilize their political vehicle—the town meeting—to convert his following into something like the New England Federalist small-town juggernaut that overthrew his Embargo. Using the Federalists' own weapon against them, so to speak, he would prevent them from repeating their success in negating national policies.[32] Thus, he pictured the town meeting as embodying a form of *levée en masse* or *rage militaire* like that attributed to the French and American revolutionary armies. Although Jefferson castigated the Massachusetts town meeting as a "selfish minority" for opposing the national will as expressed by Congress's Embargo Act, his resentment was blunted by admiration for the town meetings' democratic unity, even if in an un–Democratic cause.[33]

• • • • •

In 1816, Jefferson often wrote about democratic participation and public education. He was impelled by rumors of an impending Virginia constitutional convention or perhaps because his plans for a state university were taking shape. He explained his matured views on the functions of local and national government in letters to Albemarle County state legislator Joseph C. Cabell. He reiterated that the national government ought to be entrusted with foreign, interstate and military affairs, and the state governments with civil liberties, police and administration. The local wards would be involved with the affairs appropriate to the citizens of a small town, "until it [governmental devolution] ends in the administration of every man's farm by himself, by placing under every one what his own eye may superintend, that all will be done for the best."[34]

Jefferson had an ulterior motive for instituting ward meetings, identical with Massachusetts town meetings, in his state. He believed that ward governments, by exerting pressure upon the state legislature for better educational facilities, would inevitably assist him in obtaining money for his brainchild, the University of Virginia. By improving young Virginians' education, Jefferson hoped to expand its political power within the Union, which he felt had declined in proportion to Massachusetts, a state that placed greater emphasis on educating its citizens. As Jefferson emphasized in 1820 in a letter to state senator Joseph C. Cabell, his ardent spokesperson for the university in the state legislature, Massachusetts' educational system had enabled it to acquire great influence over the rest of the Union, despite a land area only one-tenth of Virginia's. He hoped that such reasoning would convince the Virginia legislature to provide additional funding for his budding University.[35]

Jefferson often pointed to Massachusetts' example to demonstrate education's importance in strengthening state governments, especially in light of what he perceived as the struggle between North and South for national hegemony after the Missouri controversy. He hoped this sectional logic would increase support for his fledgling University of Virginia in the parsimonious state assembly. By 1820, during the crisis over Missouri's admission to the Union as a slave state, Jefferson professed to fear that Southern youth who attended Northern universities like Harvard (which he usually called "Cambridge") would imbibe hostility to Southern institutions. He even recommended that they attend the University of Kentucky instead, "because she has more of the flavor of the old cask [Virginia] than any other."[36]

Jefferson was more concerned with improving the quality of Virginia's educational system and making his fellow citizens better informed and more capable of running a democratic ward-government than with creating a states' rights bastion when he founded the University of Virginia. Jefferson was eager to secure most of his professors from such institutions as Oxford, Cambridge, and Edinburgh. He sent his young friend attorney Francis W. Gilmer to recruit them in 1824, on a quest that precipitated the frail young man's death. It is difficult to accept the claims of some historians that Jefferson was obsessed by an "Anglophobia" which drove his public and private attitudes. He was also enthusiastic about procuring scholars from Massachusetts, like the mathematician Nathaniel Bowditch and the Romance literature expert George Ticknor, even though his efforts failed. Jefferson was not at all deterred by Ticknor and Bowditch's Unitarianism, a creed repellent to the Presbyterian clergy Jefferson needed to pacify in order to gain funding and legislative approval for his university. He was not biased against New England scholars despite the region's Federalism. Notwithstanding his political opponents' charges that he favored France in all things rather than England, he generally preferred teachers from the former mother country. He only insisted that an American professor run the school of law and government, where he expected the superior virtues of representative democracy to be expounded.[37]

Jefferson's preference for New Englanders and scholars from Great Britain remained constant. Shortly before his death, he wrote the Marquis de Lafayette, "You know how much I have at heart the success of our university. Its opening now awaits only the arrival of three professors engaged in England who were to have sailed in October or November last, but of whose actual sailing we have not yet heard. Still we hourly expect them and in the moment of their arrival shall announce the opening of the university."[38] Jefferson's actions incited protests in Virginia newspapers, irritated by his seeming lack of Americanism in openly recruiting Britons and New Englanders to teach at his university.[39]

If Jefferson were thoroughly convinced that Northern colleges were a dangerous influence, he would not have been eager to hire graduates of Northern institutions like Ticknor to teach at his university. He was also probably aware that many leaders of the Republican Party had attended prestigious Northern colleges, equivalent to today's "Ivy League." James Madison, foremost among Jefferson's political allies, graduated from the College of New Jersey (Princeton University), while the lesser-known states' rights Virginia congressman John Dawson had attended Harvard College. Other leading Republican politicians, such as Nathaniel Macon of North Carolina, Wilson Cary Nicholas, John Randolph, and William Branch Giles of Virginia, all zealous advocates of states' rights and Virginia's interests, had attended Princeton (in addition, Randolph briefly attended Hamilton's *alma mater*, Columbia). Ironically, the greatest states' righter and most famous advocate of nullification, John C. Calhoun of South Carolina, was born in Connecticut and attended Yale College.[40] However, Jefferson, shrewdly warning that Southerners who attended Northern colleges came back opposed to the Southern way of life (and by implication the institution of slavery), had a peg on which to hang his requests for state funds for his college.

There is little doubt, however, that Jefferson's primary concern in urging Virginia to adopt an improved system of primary and secondary education that would reach every member of society, capped by his precious brainchild, the University of Virginia, was to increase his fellow citizens' political aptitude. He was sure that education, especially in the fields of history and politics, would make Virginians more competent to run the affairs of a democracy of the type he envisioned in his "ward-republics." He held a low opinion of the average Virginian, whom he regarded as a lazy "lounger" susceptible to bribes and grog (rum mixed with water). In January 1816, in a revealing letter to his state assemblyman, Albemarle County's Charles Yancey, urging him to support a new "college" for Virginia in the neighborhood of Monticello, he made clear that his objectives transcended the creation of a university that would attract Southerners who would otherwise go north. Despite his modest critique of New England's mindset, his goal was to preserve and advance republicanism and democracy in his state and in the nation as a whole. His famous letter to Yancey, illuminating his views, deserves quotation at length:

> I am a great friend to the improvements of roads, canals & schools.... The literary fund [an annual appropriation for educating the children of the poor] is a solid provision, unless lost in the impending [state] bankruptcy. If the legislature would add to that a perpetual tax of a cent a head on the population of the state, it would set agoing at once, and for ever maintain a system of primary or ward schools, and an university where might be taught in it's highest degree every branch of science useful in our time & country: and it would rescue us from the tax of toryism, fanaticism, & indifferentism to their own state which we now send our youth to bring from those of New England. If a nation expects to be ignorant & free, in a state of civilisation, it expects what never was & never will be. The functionaries of every government have propensities to command at will the liberty & property of their constituents. There is no safe deposit for these but with the people themselves; nor can they be safe with them without information. Where the press is free and every man able to read, all is safe.[41]

Jefferson's derogatory passing reference to the metaphorical "tax of toryism, fanaticism, & indifferentism to their own state" that Northern colleges imposed on their Virginian students was extrinsic to the letter's basic meaning. As he made clear, his primary goal was to improve his fellow citizens' literacy and education. He assumed that educated voters would more competently supervise and regulate their governmental representatives, whose evil inclinations to defraud them of their "liberty & property" would be deterred. At the same time, he hesitated to advertise his distrust of the virtue and honesty of politicians, who might not appreciate this assessment when they voted on funding his university. Thus, while he asked Yancey to reveal the letter's contents to Thomas Walker Maury, a personal friend, Albemarle County delegate to the House of Delegates, and advocate of the university, he advised him not to show it to his enemies in the legislature. Suspecting that he was not especially popular with Virginia politicians, he advised Yancey, "The frankness of this communication will, I am sure, suggest to you a discreet use of it. I wish to avoid all collisions of opinion with all mankind. Shew it to Mr. Maury with expressions of my great esteem. It pretends to convey no more than the opinions of one of your thousand constituents, and to claim no more attention than every other of that thousand."[42] Jefferson insisted that the children in every state in the Union, especially his own Virginia, whose legislature lagged in providing funds for public primary and secondary education, must be well-educated in order to protect their liberty and property. He looked to Massachusetts and the other New England states as models to guide them.

In a Christmas Day 1820 letter to Cabell, Jefferson deliberately exaggerated the extent to which Massachusetts' superior educational system had enabled it to acquire unwarranted power in the Union despite its small size. Lending his remarks a semi-official veneer, he observed that he "lately saw in a newspaper an estimate in square miles of each of the states." It disclosed that Virginia, encompassing 70,000 square miles, was the largest state in the Union, and Massachusetts, only a tenth as big, was the fourth smallest. Jefferson's remarks betrayed a quantum of jealousy: "She is the 21st only in the scale of size [there were only twenty-three states in the Union at this time, so Jefferson slightly erred], and but one-tenth that of Virginia yet it is unquestionable that she has more influence in our confederacy than any other state in it." He claimed that Massachusetts' power derived from its educational facilities: "Whence this ascendancy? From her attention to education unquestionably. There can be no stronger proof that knoledge [sic] is power, and that ignorance is weakness. Will our legislators always be dead to this truth?"[43]

Thus Jefferson, as in recommending a ward system of local government emulating Massachusetts town meetings, which he considered far more efficient and democratic than the South's counties, paraded Massachusetts as a paradigm whose educational institutions Virginia should emulate if not surpass. In this case, he hoped that emphasizing New England's success and power in the government might procure the Virginia legislature's financial support for his new university. The veneer of hostility barely masked the reality of Jefferson's admiration and hope for Virginia's imitation of a Northern sister state.

18

Jefferson's Late-Life Ambivalence Toward New England

During his presidency, Jefferson had favored New England mercantile interests. He implemented naval war with the Libyan (Tripolitian) pirates from 1801 to 1805 and the 1807 Embargo Act to protect New England shipping. He had also favored passage of legislation exempting New England ships from lighthouse fees; lower tariff and tonnage duties for U.S. ships, and other measures that would favor U.S. as opposed to foreign vessels. Later, perhaps because New Englanders were politically hostile, violated the Embargo Act, and had in large numbers pursued evangelical, revivalist religions (which he lumped together under the label "Presbyterian"), Jefferson at times seemed resentful of them. Perhaps for political reasons, he concealed this feeling during his presidency. However, he made it evident in old age, when he charged New England politicians with monopolizing power and economic benefits bestowed by the national government. His image was the reverse of Northerners' later obsession with the Southern "Slave Power."[1]

On October 19, 1822, writing to William Short, Jefferson deplored New England's alleged selfishness, mirroring the accusations of Northerners (and modern historians like Garry Wills), who accused the South of dominating the national government through the Constitution's "three-fifths clause." Tracking the government's expenditures during his retirement, he complained that most lighthouses were built in New England at the nation's expense. "I wish with you that Congress had the power of expending our *surplus* monies (if ever we are to have them) on public improvements, and have long wished for such an amendment to the constitution; with the condition expressed that the federal proportion of each state should be expended on improvements within the state," he averred. "Otherwise all, like our lighthouses &c. would go to New England."[2] But Jefferson invariably admitted that New England's superior educational facilities and astutely managed democratic town meeting form of government facilitated its earning whatever advantages it had acquired on the national political stage.

In accord with his yardstick, by which the greatest degree of direct individual participation equaled the best form of government, Jefferson could not help but praise the New England town meeting *prima facie*. It was the highest point that direct democracy could attain, he eloquently wrote in a letter to Cabell in 1816, urging him to promote a state university in the Virginia legislature: "Where every man is a sharer in the direction of his ward-republic [he wrote], or of some of the higher ones [county or state], and feels that he is a participator in the government of affairs, not merely at an election one day in the year, but every day; when there shall not be a man in the State who will not be a member of some one of its councils, great or small, he will let the heart be torn out of his body sooner than his power be wrested from him by a Caesar or a Bonaparte."[3]

Jefferson discovered that his classical republican desire that each citizen become a part-time politician had achieved greatest realization, not in ancient Athens, but in the town meeting governments of Massachusetts that opposed his presidency. He reminded Cabell of the recent past: "How powerfully did we feel the energy of this organization in the case of embargo? *I felt the foundations of the government shaken under my feet by the New England townships."* Thus, Jefferson admitted the enervating effect that New England's opposition during the days of the Embargo had upon him during the most frustrating period of his presidency. But, rather than utilizing their (possibly treasonable) opposition during his presidency as a pretext for crushing the New England towns, Jefferson retrospectively praised their conduct as epitomizing political authenticity. "There was not an individual in their States whose body was not thrown with all its momentum into action; and although the whole of the other States were known to be in favor of the measure [the Embargo Act], yet the organization of this little selfish minority enabled it to overrule the Union."[4]

Southern states' righters' hostility to Northern antislavery, anti-Southern and pro-commercial educators and politicians further impelled Jefferson's quest for a great university for his state. Alienated by such events as the Marshall Court's nationalizing decisions, congressional anti-slavery attempts to intimidate Missouri, and the proliferation of banks across the nation, which precipitated the Panic of 1819 that ruined him and his friends, Jefferson bitterly lashed out at Northern centralizers. He and John Taylor of Caroline, adopting the rhetoric of the Antifederalists and the Republicans of the 1790s, usually called them "consolidationists." As he wrote Taylor, seeking to recruit his support for the university, he did not intend for it to compete with the state's private academies and elementary schools, whose rectors felt threatened by its existence. He wanted his university to teach Southerners the proper way to think about politics and government and furnish an alternative to the dominance of Federalist, Northern (and antislavery) educational institutions. "We shall receive only those subjects [i.e., students] who desire the highest degree of instruction, for which they now go to Harvard, Princeton, N. York, & Philadelphia," he explained. In a blatantly sectional pitch, he argued, "These seminaries are no longer proper for Southern or Western students. The signs of the times admonish us to call them home." As he had earlier informed Cabell, he wanted Virginia to possess a knowledge resource independent of the "free" states. "If knolege [sic] is power, we should look to it's advancement at home, where no resource of power will be wanting" if his university received support. Alluding to Taylor, ten years his junior, Jefferson concluded reassuringly, "This may not be in my day; but probably will in yours."[5]

Despite their prudish Federalism and obstinate disobedience to government, Jefferson regarded the Boston town meeting's members as more admirable than his own fumbling supporters, organized in counties. Describing a hypothetical "county meeting" that might have been summoned during the prewar crisis with Great Britain, he derided his agrarian supporters in an unseemly manner. "What would the unwieldy counties of the middle, the south, and the west do? Call a county meeting, and the drunken loungers at and about the court houses would have collected, the distances being too great for the good people and the industrious generally to attend." He assumed that many of his supporters in the counties were despicable ne'er-de-wells: "The character of those who really met would have been the measure of the weight they would have had in the scale of public opinion."[6] It would not have been very impressive.

Jefferson concluded by purveying a new slogan, "divide the counties into wards." He considered the ward or town meeting form as a panacea for political evils, especially the danger of excessive centralization of power, "the degeneracy of our government, and the concentration of all its powers in the hands of the one, the few, the well-born or the many."[7] His admiration for the Massachusetts town meeting persisted till the end of his life.

In 1816, in numerous letters about republicanism and democracy in response to rumors of a new Virginia constitutional convention and the revolutionary upsurges in Latin America, Jefferson acclaimed the New England townships as his political ideal. Even to his old anti–Massachusetts friend John Taylor, to whom in 1798 he had first vouchsafed his belief that New England "town meetings" were a good thing despite their contentiousness, Jefferson bluntly praised their direct democracy. Jefferson's new, eccentric political lexicon applied the term "republic" to governments whose citizens took "direct action," like the town meetings, rather than representative institutions. "Such a government is evidently restrained to very narrow limits of space and population," he explained, echoing Montesquieu. "I doubt if it would be practicable beyond the extent of a New England township."[8]

Jefferson was also admittedly thinking of the New England states when he argued that the next best type of republic was one where the people acted through popularly elected conventions, or annually chose their representatives "for such short terms as should render secure the duty of expressing the will of their constituents." Endorsing the Madisonian idea of the extended federal republic, he said, "This I should consider as the nearest approach to a pure republic, which is practicable on a large scale of country or population. And we have examples of it in some of our State Constitutions, which, if not poisoned by priest-craft, would prove its excellence over all mixtures with other elements; and, with only equal doses of poison, would still be the best." He was undoubtedly alluding to Massachusetts and Connecticut, which despite their odious "priest-craft," popularly elected their governors and legislatures. By contrast, Virginia's governor was a figurehead, chosen by a malapportioned state legislature under a restrictive suffrage.[9]

Following the War of 1812's satisfying conclusion, Jefferson's resentment of Massachusetts merchants was at its height. The state government, under Federalist Governor Caleb Strong, had not only refused to contribute men or materials to the war effort; it had expedited the smuggling and illegal trade that New England shippers carried on with Britain and its colonies. At this point, Jefferson was ready to confide to fellow Southerner William H. Crawford of Georgia, who was abroad as U.S. minister to France, the depth of his disappointment in the Massachusetts citizenry. He damned the New England shippers as selfish mercantile schemers who put their own desire for unrestricted wartime trade ahead of the nation's peace and well-being. He repeatedly denounced the policy of granting shippers drawbacks on re-exports of tropical produce abroad, regarding such refunds as special favors to merchants similar to those that had ultimately embroiled the British government in endless wars to promote its merchants' interests overseas. There was no reason for the United States, which was "essentially agricultural," to emulate its bad example. Jefferson believed that the U.S. should have only a restricted commercial presence abroad: "The exercise, by our own citizens, of so

much commerce as may suffice to exchange our superfluities for our wants, may be advantageous for the whole," he reflected. "But it does not follow, that with a territory so boundless,
it is the interest of the whole to become a mere city of London, to carry on the business of
one-half the world at the expense of eternal war with the other half."[10] Jefferson's anger rose
as he contemplated Massachusetts' aggressive pursuit of commercial profit as a permanent
scourge on the peace of its sister states whenever Europe was engaged in a major war.

Seeking to discourage future wars to promote New England commerce, Jefferson went
so far as to suggest that the U.S. Government's "fundamental principles" should limit foreign
commerce. He proposed denying entry into the country to any immigrants or would-be citizens who intended to embark on risky trading ventures that might provoke war with other
governments, arguing that "we want no citizens, and still less ephemeral and pseudo-citizens,
on such terms. We may exclude them from our territory, as we do persons infected with disease." Ostensibly, Jefferson would ideally have liked to deport some citizens of New England
as carriers of the "disease" of mercantile avarice. He intended to prohibit Massachusetts merchants from provoking future wars for free trade in wartime. Their selfishness caused suffering
to the rest of the country: "We have most abundant resources of happiness within ourselves,
which we may enjoy in happiness and safety without permitting a few citizens, infected with
the mania of rambling and gambling, to bring danger on the great mass engaged in innocent
and safe pursuits at home."[11]

In retirement, while continuing to resent New England merchants' obstruction of his
Embargo policy's efforts to avert or postpone full-scale war with Great Britain until the U.S.
was better prepared militarily, Jefferson appreciated the "Eastern states'" desire for an equitable national tax system. He was aware that many sections of New England benefited from
his policy of promoting domestic manufactures. With a keen perception of national political
economy, he understood New Englanders' ostensibly eccentric tax preferences. Although the
Southern states were seemingly hard hit by national direct taxes (as historians like Robin
Einhorn and David Waldstreicher insist) because the "three-fifths clause" imposed land and
other direct taxes (including poll taxes on slaves) in proportion to a state's total free population
together with three-fifths of its number of slaves, the Eastern states in fact were more likely
to object to direct taxes, and congressmen from the Southern states preferred them. In this
way, Southern politicians appeased their poorer, non-slaveholding constituents, who wanted
the wealthy slaveholders taxed.[12]

In light of their often scrabbly acreage, New England farmers often had trouble paying
their state taxes, which were generally imposed on land and farm produce. This was especially
true during the Articles of Confederation period, when the conservative state government
forced farmers to pay their taxes in specie in order to reimburse the state's creditors and pay
the Congressional requisitions. The direct state land tax payable in silver was a major cause
of Shays' Rebellion.[13]

Jefferson had long been aware that New England farmers opposed the national direct
land tax. In 1798, when the direct tax on land and slaves was imposed for the first time, mainly
by Federalist votes, during the presidency of John Adams to finance the military preparations
for the undeclared war with France, Jefferson predicted the opposition of small farmers in
Massachusetts and other states. He wrote Madison that the "quotas," by which he meant the
levying of the tax on land and slaves in proportion to a state's population, were so unpopular
with New Englanders that its congressional representatives might defeat the land tax in

Congress.[14] Southern farmers, on the other hand, although they also often had to pay state land taxes, were gratified by the fact that the big slave-holders had to pay poll taxes on their slaves and higher taxes on their more valuable land, which distributed the burden more fairly.

In 1811, writing to his antislavery French physiocrat friend, Pierre Samuel Du Pont de Nemours, about U.S. tax policy, Jefferson carefully explained (without mentioning the taxes on slaves, a subject that probably embarrassed him) the diverse tax systems of New England and the South. He assured Du Pont that national revenues would not suffer from the increased manufacturing of crude domestic goods, which the Frenchman assumed would consequently reduce imports of those goods, adversely affect tariff revenues, and make recourse to unpopular excises and direct taxes essential. "I do not believe the change of our system of taxation will be forced on us so early as you expect, if war be avoided," Jefferson observed. "It is true we are going greatly into manufactures; but the mass of them are household manufactures of the coarse articles worn by the laborers & farmers of the family. These I verily believe we shall succeed in making to the whole extent of our necessities. But the attempts at fine goods will probably be abortive." He most likely was referring to Massachusetts and Rhode Island factories, which were most numerous. "They are undertaken by company-establishments, & chiefly in the towns; will have little success, & short continuance in a country where the charms of agriculture attract every being who can engage in it." Thus, Jefferson was not much impressed by the New England textile manufacturers. While acknowledging that revenue from imports of "coarse goods" would decline, Jefferson was confident that U.S. population and productivity would increase in all areas, not only that of manufacturing, and the nation's exports must remain stable or increase; "& the imports must be equivalent to them, & consequently the revenue on them be undiminished."[15] Interpreting the laws of the balance of trade, Jefferson assumed that the value of American exports and American imports must be equal. Although homes, plantations, and small American factories would produce coarse manufactured goods for domestic consumption, the luxury items would still come from Europe, and they would be bought by America's wealthy, who would thus pay most of the nation's taxes. Jefferson also believed that, if war could be avoided, the Madison Administration would be able to pay off the public debt within a few years, and then only one-third of the current national revenue would be required. He somewhat perversely regarded national fiscal solvency as essential to national strength, even more so than a strong army and navy.[16]

As Jefferson continued his discussion of national political economy, he expressed his democratic tax views and his knowledge of the diverse tax preferences of the states. Although he corrected some of Du Pont's errors, he made a few of his own in the process. "Your information that a commencement of [national] excise had been again made, is entirely unfounded," he reported. Showing an affinity with small Southern and western farmer/distillers' hostility to excises, he continued, "I hope the death blow to that most vexatious & unproductive of all taxes was given at the commencement of my administration, & believe its revival would give the death blow to any administration whatever."[17]

Jefferson then informed Du Pont of the tax structures of the diverse sections of the Union. As a taxpayer himself, he was undoubtedly aware that Virginians paid taxes on their land and slaves, though not on individual family members. In New England, there were usually poll taxes on family members as well as land taxes. Excise taxes were uncommon. Jefferson wrote, "In most of the middle and Southern states some land tax is now paid into the State treasury, and for this purpose the lands have been classed & valued, & the tax assessed according to that valuation. In these an Excise is most odious." Jefferson also expressed knowledge of New England tax preferences: "In the Eastern states land taxes are odious, excises less unpopular."[18]

Adopting the arguments of John Taylor of Caroline and other Republican political economists, who claimed that farmers and especially Southerners, who produced few manufactures, generally paid most of the import duties, Jefferson pointed out that under Democratic-Republican congresses during his presidency, taxes on imports were paid mainly on luxury goods bought by the rich. Of course, the tariff was a mode of revenue confined to Congress, and prohibited to the states. But, according to Jefferson, all parts of the Union preferred the tariff over direct (land or poll) taxes because it was more equitable and paid largely by those who could afford to buy expensive imported luxuries. As he told Du Pont, "We are all the more reconciled to the tax on importations, because it falls exclusively on the rich, and, with the equal partition of intestate's estates, constitute the best agrarian law."[19] (The "agrarian law" was a term that originated in England and France; it generally meant the forced distribution of the land of the rich among the poor, undertaken by mob violence or civil war.)

The tariff was hardly a "leveling," agrarian law; Jefferson revealed old-age political conservatism in socioeconomic matters by considering it as such. Although touting himself and his presidency as advancing economic democracy and the well-being of the average farmer, Jefferson tended to exaggerate the radicalism of his ideas. An aging statesman, he also seemed to be losing his memory. He apparently forgot that the salt tax had been repealed during his presidency, and at his recommendation.[20]

He had proposed the repeal of the salt tax in his sixth annual message to Congress on December 2, 1806, the same one in which he asked Congress to outlaw the slave trade. Secretary of the Treasury Gallatin was reluctant to abandon the salt tax. It constituted a reliable source of revenue at a time when war with Great Britain was possible and tariff income from England was threatened by congressional passage of a Non-Importation Act (the Gregg-Nicholson Act) in retaliation for British seizures of U.S. ships and impressment of U.S. seamen. However, Jefferson considered it advisable, for reasons of economic democracy and political expediency, to advocate the repeal.

Eight months earlier, in April 1806, one of Jefferson's most bitter foes, the eccentric and self-righteous chairman of the House Ways and Means Committee, his former ally John Randolph of Roanoke, sought to make political capital and embarrass Jefferson's Administration by proposing the repeal of the salt tax in his committee, an abortive effort that backfired against him. He intended to deprive Jefferson of revenues from both the "Mediterranean duties" (increased tariff duties imposed for the purpose of fighting the Tripolitan pirates) and the salt tax. He wanted to deprive Jefferson of funds to increase the number of ships and gunboats in the Navy for a possible war with England. (Although a Democratic-Republican, the unpredictable Randolph, like the Federalists, argued that the British were fighting civilization's battle against the dictatorial Bonaparte.) He also wanted to thwart Jefferson's efforts to obtain $2 million to bribe Napoleon to facilitate the purchase the Floridas from Spain's puppet monarchy for $5 million, suspecting these sums would end up in Napoleon's coffers. The salt tax, in effect since 1789 and almost annually increased, was a burdensome and unpopular tax that produced half a million dollars in revenue.[21] Because the salt tax was so unpopular with their constituents, few Republicans were eager to speak in favor of keeping it. Randolph, leader of the "Quid" opposition to Jefferson, brought in a bill repealing the salt tax and renewing the "Mediterranean Fund," which was scheduled to expire with the end of the Tripolitian War but whose renewal Jefferson had successfully requested in January 1806.

Hoping to split the Republicans and embarrass Jefferson, the minority Federalists in Congress supported Randolph. On April 17, 1806, the bill to repeal the salt tax passed the House of Representatives by the resounding vote of 84 to 11, and was sent to the Senate despite its embarrassment to the Jefferson Administration. Even this apparent victory was actually a partial defeat for Randolph, since the more lucrative "Mediterranean fund" tax was renewed. Indeed, when the bill reached the Senate, where Jefferson's support was stronger, even the repeal of the salt tax was struck out, allowing Jefferson abundant funds to pursue his schemes. On April 21, 1806, the Senate returned the bill to the House with its emendations, but Randolph convinced the House members of the conference committee to reject the Senate bill, and the process started over. Jefferson reasserted his leadership, and the tables turned on Randolph. On April 26, 1806, the last day of the congressional session, Randolph, insisting on the need to keep the Executive dependent on the legislature for revenue, demanded that the House repeal both the salt tax and the Mediterranean duties. Now that his anti-administration stance was clear, the Jeffersonian Republicans in the House defeated him, although the margin was close: 47 to 40. However, in the aftermath of Randolph's salt tax debacle, Jefferson was more powerful than before: he had gained both renewal of the "Mediterranean duties," even though the war with Tripoli had ended; and continuation of the heavy salt tax.[22]

Perhaps Jefferson had learned political lessons from this undocumented but evidently bitter fight within his own party over the salt tax, in which the "Quid" leader Randolph sought to reduce his power. He apparently concluded that political expediency and public happiness made it desirable for him to propose repeal of the salt tax. Thus, assuming a role convivial to him, Jefferson once more showed himself "The Friend of the People." In his annual message to Congress on December 2, 1806, he said: "The duties composing the Mediterranean fund will cease by law at the end of the present season. Considering, however, that they are levied chiefly on luxuries, and that we have an impost on salt, a necessary of life, the free use of which otherwise is so important, I recommend to your consideration the suppression of the duties on salt, and the continuation of the Mediterranean fund, instead thereof, for a short time, after which that also will become unnecessary for any purpose now within contemplation."

Jefferson suggested that in the future, surplus funds in the treasury should be used to build roads, canals, and other "objects of public improvement," and to support a model national university and specialized educational institutions. He urged Congress to immediately pass the necessary constitutional amendments and send them on to the states for ratification.[23] Congress repealed the salt tax in March 1807, two years before Jefferson retired from office.[24]

Jefferson was eager to proclaim himself the advocate of the poor against the rich; and compared with the Federalists, Republican administrations may have been justified in making this claim. Indeed, Jefferson forgot one of his administration's most important contributions to the well-being of poor farmers and fishermen, the latter mostly from New England, who preserved their catches with salt. Mistakenly believing that the salt tax, which burdened the poor farmers who fed salt to their animals and preserved their meat with it, was still in effect, he nonetheless exuberantly wrote Du Pont:

> In fact, the poor man in this country who uses nothing but what is made within his own farm or family, or within the U.S. pays not a farthing of tax to the general government, but on his salt; and should we go into that manufacture, as we ought to do, he will pay not one cent. Our revenues once liberated by the discharge of the public debt, & its surplus applied to canals, roads, schools, Etc and the farmer will see his government supported, his children educated, & the face of his country made a paradise by the contributions of the rich alone without his being called on to spare a cent from his earnings. The path we are now pursuing leads directly to this end which we cannot fail to attain unless our administration falls into unwise hands.[25]

Now viewing the war with Great Britain as unnecessary, in his June 1816 letter to Crawford Jefferson retrospectively blamed it on "Massachusetts, who had produced it, [and] took side with the enemy waging it." The war was fought to advance the commercial prospects of ungrateful New Englanders, and Jefferson, reviving a proposal he had made before the war, thought that congressional abolition of drawbacks might prevent a recurrence of a similar conflict with Great Britain. Still espousing a nationalist creed, he considered it unfair for the rest of the country to get involved in wars to defend Massachusetts merchants' unrestricted trade. He told Crawford that he preferred that the states that demanded to pursue war-provoking trade (i.e., New England) would secede from the Union rather than that the other states be forced to sacrifice themselves to advance "gambling speculations for a few, with eternal war for the many." Jefferson did not demand that these selfish states be kicked out; he merely professed a hope that they would leave voluntarily. Those states whose citizens insisted on pursuing their "licentious commerce" in the carrying trade, he asserted, were welcome to leave the Union: "If any State in the Union will declare that it prefers separation with the first alternative [unrestricted commerce and war], to a continuance in union without it, I have no hesitation in saying, 'let us separate.' I would rather the States should withdraw, which are for unlimited commerce and war, and confederate with those alone which are for peace and agriculture."[26]

Jefferson made these tepid remarks during his retirement, at a time when secession was an acceptable idea and the Union was not considered sacrosanct.[27] Without recommending means of enforcement or government action to make New Englanders leave the Union, and considering his politically quiescent status, his words were essentially rhetoric. They hardly merit the vilification he has received from Onuf and others. Moreover, these are his most bitter and aggressive comments concerning New England. Ironically, Onuf does not cite them, perhaps because they reveal Jefferson's consistent aversion to the use of force.

Again resorting to the example of Great Britain's drawback system, Jefferson wished to prevent his people from becoming, like the British, impoverished from wars in defense of mercantile avarice. Moreover, he had contempt for the carrying trade, which shipped Latin American and European goods rather than those produced in the U.S. Indeed, he depicted the Massachusetts carrying-trade merchants as an unproductive blight on the republic. They provoked wasteful wars: "Our commercial dashers, then, have already cost us so many thousand lives, so many millions of dollars, more than their persons and all their commerce were worth."[28] These were the harshest words Jefferson ever directed at New Englanders, and they were aimed solely at its shipping-merchant minority, rather than at the republican, farming majority of its people, whom he continued to celebrate.

Nonetheless, Jefferson continued to have bitter feelings toward Massachusetts merchants, who had been disloyal and shown an un-republican selfishness and callousness toward the public good during the years of embargo and war. In mutedly eloquent tones, he expressed his aversion to his old Braintree friend, John Adams. He began by praising the two-fisted, virile Kentuckians, who he claimed (probably incorrectly, considering the Second Great Awakening's popularity there) were more attuned to "rational Christianity" than people from the older states. "They are freer from prejudices than we are, and bolder in grasping at truth," he argued. "The time is not distant, though neither you nor I shall see it, when we shall be but a secondary people to them." He concluded on a bitter note, probably aimed more at Adams's Federalist, mercantile Massachusetts than at his agrarian Republican state of Virginia: "Our greediness for wealth, and fantastical expense, have degraded, and will degrade, the minds of our maritime citizens. These are the peculiar vices of commerce."[29]

Even John Adams occasionally questioned the virtue of his fellow New Englanders. In 1776, when he was more optimistic than he would be later, he wrote a Revolutionary colleague, "Our dear Americans perhaps have as much of it [virtue] as any Nation now existing, and New England perhaps has more than the rest of America." He was always willing to give Massachusetts the benefit of the doubt. "But I have seen all along my Life Such Selfishness and Littleness even in New England, that I sometimes tremble to think that, altho we are engaged in the best Cause that ever employed the Human Heart yet the Prospect of success is doubtful not for Want of Power or Wisdom but of Virtue."[30]

With his unwavering theoretical faith in the people's virtue and essential decency and his commitment to popular rule and direct democracy, Jefferson could not maintain his sour outlook on the New England personality in earnest for too long. He regarded "democracy" and "republicanism" as synonymous, a stance at variance with most of his contemporaries and at the opposite pole from John Adams' *Defence of the Constitutions of Government of the United States* (1786–1787). Probably with the New England town meeting foremost in his thoughts, Jefferson asserted, "The further the departure from direct and constant control by the citizens the less has the government of the ingredient of republicanism."[31]

However, the Massachusetts town meetings were not the only inspiration for Jefferson's infatuation with ward-republics. In a letter to the English democratic reformer John Cartwright two years before his death, he broadly hinted that the study of medieval history in his youth, which led him to idealize the quasi-mythical Saxon *Witan*, played a role. He informed Cartwright that he considered his ward idea analogous to "the hundreds of your Saxon [King] Alfred." This time, he failed to mention the New England townships.[32]

Further attesting his conversion to a philosophy of strong local government in his final years, Jefferson rejected federal judicial review of unconstitutional legislation or federal oversight of disputes involving state and national governments' concurrent powers. During the constitutional debates from 1787 to 1789, Jefferson had seemingly favored the Supreme Court's hegemony, in accordance with Article 6, section 2. By 1824, he preferred that the states request a constitutional convention (an option under the Constitution) if a dispute arose between the competing powers of the state and national governments.[33] He no longer perceived any merit in the Supreme Court or federal judicial review.

Therefore, Jefferson took his concept of "ward-republics" seriously. Seemingly at odds with Adams, he thought that the American people's virtuous national character preserved their insufficiently democratic, republican institutions, not the other way around.[34] At the same time, he argued that "the Man of these States" was not inherently more virtuous than the European *canaille*; rather, it was the abundance of available land and the prosperous expanding economy that enabled Americans to avert class warfare, bypass the need for an institutionalized aristocracy, and sustain representative democracy. As he explained to Adams, in the United States, unlike revolutionary France, "every one, by his property, or by his satisfactory situation, is interested in the support of law and order. And such men may safely and advantageously reserve to themselves a wholesome controul over their public affairs, and a degree of freedom, which in the hands of the Canaille of the cities of Europe, would be instantly perverted to the demolition and destruction of every thing public and private."[35]

Jefferson thereby again politely refuted Adams's position that inevitably a long-term, perhaps hereditary aristocracy must be ensconced in its own house of the legislature, even in a middle-class republic like the United States, where most people were relatively comfortable and did not pose a perpetual threat to the propertied classes. And, in Jefferson's opinion, the New England towns, where most families owned a little piece of land, although they had opposed his presidency and Embargo Act, epitomized democracy at work and would ultimately substantiate his conclusions.[36]

Although he admired New England's forms of local government, Jefferson could not avoid a jab at their persisting deference to the oldest families. He contrastingly praised Virginia, where, or at least so he told Adams, voters were more discerning and even rebellious. Replying to Adams' confession that most of the same men were repeatedly re-elected to office in Massachusetts, Jefferson maintained that in the South "family distinction" had less of a mystique. "You surprise me with the account you give of the strength of family distinction still existing in your state," he wrote, perhaps half-playfully. "With us it is so totally extinguished that not a spark is to be found but lurking in the hearts of some of our old tories. But all bigotries hang to one another; and this in the Eastern states hangs, as I suspect, to that of the priesthood." Taking a shot at his favorite enemy, the evangelical Congregational clergy, Jefferson hyperbolically defended the political institutions of his home state, where (he knew) the old eastern families actually retained much power. "Here youth, beauty, mind and manners are more valued than a pedigree," he unctuously boasted of Virginia.[37]

When discussing constitutional reform with other Virginians, however, Jefferson argued that the state government was insufficiently democratic. This had occurred partly because its founders were inordinately influenced by pessimistic, misanthropic European political philosophers, "whose fears of the people have been inspired by the populace of their own great cities," such as Paris and London, "and were unjustly entertained against the independent, the happy, and therefore orderly citizens of the United States."[38] To Jefferson's chagrin, the law-abiding character of the propertied majority of Americans gave conservatives in his state an excuse to argue that democratic political reforms would disturb its peaceful homeostasis. "We are always told that things are going on well; why change them?" Jefferson parroted them. "This is true; and I verily believe they would go on as well with us under an absolute monarch, while our present character remains, of order, industry, and love of peace, and restrained as he would be by the proper spirit of the people." Restating views he had expressed over thirty years earlier in *Notes on Virginia*, Jefferson insisted that democratic change might be attempted more easily at junctures when the people were moral, virtuous, and relatively satisfied. "But it is while it [the people's character] remains such, we should provide against the consequences of its deterioration," he said. "And let us rest in the hope that it [a democratic revision of Virginia's constitution] will yet be done, and spare ourselves the pain of evils which may never happen."[39]

During an 1816 controversy over proposals for revising Virginia's constitution, Jefferson fervently supported the call for a constitutional convention. He reminded Samuel Kercheval, an agitator for reform, that in *Notes on Virginia* he had advocated representation for counties in the legislature proportionate to their population, as well as modification of various "republican heresies" that marred the Constitution of 1776. In defining republicanism, he obviously had in mind the New England townships. As he put it, "let it be agreed that a government is republican in proportion as every member composing it has his equal voice in the direction of its concerns, (not indeed in person, which would be impracticable beyond the limits of a city, *or small township*,) but by representatives chosen by himself, and responsible to him at short periods." For him, as he stressed in a July 1816 letter to Kercheval, the optimal republic was the direct democracy of the New England town, although he regretted that it was not feasible over a large area.[40]

Jefferson wrote Kercheval again in September 1816 regarding the Virginia convention project, which, rejected by the legislature, would not take place until October 1829, three years after Jefferson's death. He reiterated his egalitarian democratic view, first expressed in *Notes on Virginia*, that representation in the state legislature should be apportioned solely according to white population. He wanted to deprive the plantation owners of the inordinate power they wielded by virtue of their large slave holdings. Jefferson denied the validity of Southern conservatives' admonition that, if Virginia adopted such revision, Northern abolitionist congressmen would demand elimination of the U.S. Constitution's "three-fifths" compromise. However, he explained, the United States Constitution was itself a "compromise," whose provision for a slave component in congressional representation ought to be rejected in a democratic revision of Virginia's county representation. Assuring Kercheval that New Englanders had scant legal basis to insist on terminating the "three-fifths" clause, Jefferson said, "There is no inconsistency in claiming representation for them [slaves] from the other States [in the United States Constitution] and refusing it within our own." He used the analogy of Connecticut, which imposed suffrage restrictions upon propertyless white males while counting them along with similarly disfranchised women and children in calculating that state's national congressional representation. Even though the New England states lacked universal male suffrage, restricting the town vote to "freemen," all of its people were counted in its "quantum of representation and taxation in the General Government."[41]

According to Jefferson, Virginia's slaves must likewise be considered part of the society: "So, slaves with us have no powers as citizens; yet, in representation in the General Government, they count in the proportion of three to five." Briefly analogizing the United States government to a "foreign" country, Jefferson argued that Congress had no power to alter Connecticut's (or Virginia's) suffrage regulations or arbitrarily reduce its congressional representation. "In truth, the condition of different descriptions of inhabitants in any country is a matter of municipal arrangement, of which no foreign country has a right to take notice," Jefferson concluded.[42] Therefore, Jefferson argued, it did not follow that the U.S. Constitution should be amended to abolish the three-fifths slave representation in Congress even if Jefferson's recommendation to exclude it from the state constitution were approved. It was like comparing apples and oranges.[43]

However, Jefferson's admiration for New Englanders' political character had its limits.

Although he had read Adams's *Defence of the Constitutions of Government of the United States* (1787–1788), and even purchased it for the budding collections of the University of Virginia in 1825, by that time he had apparently reached the conclusion that its ideas were pro-monarchical. At least, he wanted his disturbingly pro–Federalist friend William Short, whom he had been reproaching for his conservatism for years, to think so. "Can any one read Mr. Adams's defence of the American constitution without seeing that he was a Monarchist?" he queried him. "And J. Q. Adams the son was more explicit than the father in his answer to Paine's rights of man. So much for leaders. Their followers were divided."[44] In questioning John Quincy Adams's republicanism, Jefferson was alluding to the newspaper articles he wrote in the summer of 1791, at age twenty-four, under the pseudonym "Publicola" attacking Thomas Paine's revolutionary democratic manifesto, *The Rights of Man*. However, he may have attacked *Defence* for Short's benefit, to impress upon him the need to convert to Democratic-Republicanism. That Jefferson purchased Adams's work for the university indicates he sympathized with Adams's ideas of balanced government and the separation of powers, including a role for the executive in legislation. Moreover, Jefferson thought Adams' *Defence* significant enough to repurchase it after he sold the original copy that Adams had given him to the Library of Congress (along with 6,300 other books) in 1815. Adams' *Defence* formed part of Jefferson's library holdings at the time of his death.[45]

In connection with evaluating the republicanism of New Englanders, the commentary rendered by William Short, Jefferson's multi-millionaire railroad and stock investor protégé, is especially illuminating. A shrewd speculator in land, stocks, banks, and railroads, Short was a founder of Phi Beta Kappa and a political conservative who, despite his sympathy for Alexander Hamilton and the Federalists, was a lifelong friend of Jefferson, who called him his adoptive son. A paradoxical figure, Short deserves more attention than he has received. In December 1824, inspired by his reading of some recently published correspondence of Robert Goodloe Harper, a leading South Carolina and Maryland Federalist who was a vice-presidential candidate in 1816, he wrote Jefferson a letter defending the Federalists' republicanism; Jefferson responded with the letter quoted above.[46]

Having returned to Philadelphia a few years before after a long stay in Paris, Short was appalled by the charges of treason that Democratic-Republicans had leveled against the members of the Hartford Convention, more especially in light of the fact they were New Englanders. He insisted that New Englanders were the best republicans in the United States, no matter their political affiliation. He told Jefferson that it was ridiculous to accuse Adams or any New England politician of monarchical sympathies. He was disconcerted by the recent publication of the correspondence between Monroe and Jackson in 1816–1817, in which both Democratic leaders had agreed that the Hartford Convention participants were Anglophile monarchists (Jackson even said the leaders should be hanged). Short asserted that he had been on terms of friendship with many Federalists and that none were monarchists. He was sending Jefferson some recently published letters written by long-time Federalist Robert Goodloe Harper that in his opinion proved Federalists' republicanism: "You will find inclosed two of [Robert] Walsh's papers, containing each a letter from Gen. Harper. There are three others containing each a similar letter, which I do not send in the present packet lest the volume should be increased to too great a size."[47]

Short was impressed by the temperate tone of Harper's writing, and by the general republican credo of the Federalist Party. As he explained to Jefferson, "I do not insist on your reading these letters. Their length is rather appalling—but they are written with so much moderation, that I have read them with pleasure, but perhaps not more on that account, than on their corroborating the opinion I had already myself formed on my first return to this Country, more than twenty years ago." Launching an impassioned (for him) defense of the Federalists, the ordinarily dour Short continued, "It so happened that I formed at that time an intimate acquaintance with several of those who had been considered leaders of the federal party, & against whom I had seen as well in our papers as in the French which copied them, the same accusations which are now reported by Mr. Monroe. I was surprized [*sic*] not to be able to discover the least disposition in any of their leaders towards a monarchical system & most especially in this country. My mode of life & habits of intimacy with them were such that they could not have concealed from me such sentiments had they existed even in the innermost recesses of their heart."[48]

Even more accommodating toward New England than his friend Jefferson, Short believed that the moment was ripe for sectional concord between New England and the South. Perhaps unaware that the "Era of Good Feelings" of Monroe's first administration had dissipated, Short advised that Virginians recognize New Englanders as even more sincere republicans than themselves and make sectional peace with them: "And at this moment, now that these heats of party contention have passed off, which so much blind the soundest judgements, I have no doubt our Southern friends must be as much surprized, as I always was, that they should have had any serious idea of attributing a monarchical propensity to the Praise God Barebones inhabitants of the East. There is certainly & always has been more of the Anti-monarchical principle on the borders of the Connecticut river, than in the whole region South & West of the Susquehanna."[49]

Unlike Jefferson, Short regarded the New Englanders as if anything excessively republican. This may be seen by his reference to the semi-mythical Praise God Barebones, a radical Puritan of the English Civil War era. This was an epoch when such extreme measures as the confiscation of the property of the Anglican Church and the redistribution of the property of the rich among the poor were considered for the first and only time on the floor of the House of Commons. The parties of Levellers, Diggers, and Fifth Monarchists competed for control of the House of Commons; the House of Lords was abolished. It was the most radical period in English history.

Short's political sentiments are paradoxical. Despite his friendship for Jefferson, he embraced anti-democratic, pro–Federalist political views. He was a nationalistic conservative, who favored government centralization. Perhaps because of personal jealousy of Jefferson's close friendship with Monroe and especially Madison, he eventually broke off all personal contact with these two friends and even blamed Madison's Virginia Resolutions for the alleged triumph of states' rights in the United States during the 1820s and 1830s. At the same time, along with Jefferson's grandson-in-law Nicholas Trist, he outrageously denied that Jefferson, who coined the term "nullification" in his 1798 Kentucky Resolutions, had ever supported that extreme doctrine. Despite his pro–Federalist inclinations, Short, like many former Federalists, voted for the hard-nosed backwoods Democrat Andrew Jackson for the presidency in 1828, believing that the country needed a strong leader of his ilk who allegedly desired to appoint Federalists to office. Although Short objected to Jackson's veto of the recharter of the Bank of the United States in 1832, he admired his stance against South Carolina's nullification movement, which he considered the strongest opposition to states' rights manifested by any president thus far (perhaps he overlooked Jefferson's ill-fated Embargo Act, having been in Paris at the time). Ultimately, Short, like Alexander Hamilton and even John Adams at pessimistic periods in his career, confessed that he did not believe the United States would survive as a republic. In 1833, Short wrote, "From the first time of my first reading of the [U.S.] Constitution when we received it in Europe, I never did believe that it could be supported, & its having lasted beyond my expectation has been a very agreeable surprise to me. All the respect I had for Mr. J[efferson], who firmly believed that the Republic would be perpetual, was insufficient to satisfy me that the centrifugal would not be too strong for the centripetal force; & nobody I think can doubt it now." He eventually regretted his praise of Jackson, whom he considered too submissive to the special interests of the western farmers in vetoing the recharter of the Bank of the United States.[50]

In some ways, Jefferson's viewpoint diametrically opposed that of his conservative friend. Jefferson argued that, although the people of New England had more democratic *institutional structures* than Virginians, their *temperament* was more conservative and deferential than that of their sister state; this led them to politically incorrect Federalist choices. He thoroughly analyzed New Englanders' often anti–Republican voting trends in his famous 1813 letter to Adams, who must have been flattered when Jefferson cited chapter and verse from *Defence*, specifically page 111 of Volume I (in Jefferson's shorthand, "vol. I. pa. III"). Adams's "Defence of the American Constitutions" is listed in the catalog of Jefferson's library auctioned off in 1829, when his bankrupt family was forced to sell his assets. Examining page 111 of Volume I of the 1787 London edition, which Adams had sent Jefferson the same year it was published, one indeed finds, in Letter XXV, titled "Dr. Franklin" (the relevant portion of which extended from 109–111) Adams's remarks about New Englanders' veneration for old, distinguished families. Page 111 includes Adams' famous statement, "Will any man pretend that the name of Andros, and that of Winthrop, are heard with the same sensations in any village of New England? Is not gratitude the sentiment that attends the latter, and disgust the feeling excited by the former?" Apparently, Jefferson was impressed by Adams' observations on Massachusetts voters' docility, such as, "Go into any village in New England, and you will find that the office of justice of the peace, and even the place of representative, which has ever depended only on the freest election of the people, have generally descended from generation to generation, in three or four families at most."[51] Jefferson had these deferential characteristics of New Englanders in mind (which Virginians apparently shared) when he wrote to Short near the end of his life.[52]

Although the "leaders," Jefferson wrote Short, were "monarchists," the rank-and-file Federalists who "followed" "monocrats" like Adams, Hamilton, Robert G. Harper, and Harrison Gray Otis "were divided. Some went the same lengths, others, and I believe the greater part, only wished a stronger Executive." He reminisced that, after his return to New York from France in the spring of 1790, he found himself outnumbered by the capital's social and political leaders. They lauded the virtues of monarchy as the best form of government, "in so much that in maintaining those of republicanism, I had always the whole company on my hands." He mentioned Joseph Dennie ("Denny"), originally from Boston, editor of the prestigious review *The Port Folio* as a prominent monarchist. He was uncertain whether "the Essex junto of Boston were monarchists but I have always heard it said, and never doubted."[53] He had been saying the same thing for over twenty years.

· · · · ·

In his consistently favorable commentary on New England town meetings' system of participatory democracy, Jefferson embraced a concept of the General Will that, like

Jean-Jacques Rousseau's *Du contrat sociale* (1762), melded individual and social well-being. For participants in ward governments and local educational and transportation networks, as *The Social Contract* put it, there was "not one who does not think of *each* as meaning him."[54] Thus, even in old age, when he reputedly reverted to conservatism in many ways, Jefferson affirmed the individualistic and democratic path on which America was heading.

19

Jefferson Bares His Teeth Against Lyman Beecher and New England's "Priests"

Upon retiring from the presidency, the violently anticlerical Jefferson bared his teeth, denouncing both Massachusetts and Connecticut citizens' servility toward religious leaders like Connecticut Congregationalists-turned-Presbyterians Timothy Dwight and Lyman Beecher, who stigmatized him as an atheist during his presidential contests. Beecher, minister at the Federalist haven of Litchfield, sincerely regarded Jefferson and Madison as "political and moral atheists." With his stern Calvinist view of human nature, Beecher thought that men were basically evil. He believed that it was impossible for them to instinctively organize society for the common good, as Jefferson claimed. Only a government dominated by religion could secure rational liberty and public order, he warned. Beecher was especially alarmed when the evangelical "minor sects," as he called them, the Baptists and Methodists, joined the Jeffersonian "atheists" to accomplish the disestablishment of Connecticut's Congregationalist Church in 1818. He believed that the evangelical churches should be natural allies of the Presbyterians and Congregationalists. Beecher was relieved when the temporary alliance of the Baptists and the secular humanists, as we might call them today, broke down after Disestablishment. He was gratified to discover that the "minor sects" then abandoned the alliance with the deistic Jeffersonians and joined the Presbyterians to defeat the Republicans in the political arena. As historian David Sehat incisively puts it, "The realignment made perfect sense. Evangelicals had never wholly shared Madison and Jefferson's view of religious liberty as an inalienable individual right. They agreed with Christian republicans that religion needed a connection to state governance. Once the issue of state support was out of the way, their more natural alliance with Christian republicans such as Beecher would reemerge, not just in Connecticut but across the new nation."[1]

Jefferson's contempt for the Trinitarian clergy increased with age, especially when, under the leadership of Congregational-Presbyterian revivalists like Beecher and Dwight they espoused an aggressive policy of converting those of other faiths. Jefferson could hardly have endorsed Beecher's vitriolic opposition to the Unitarians' denial of original sin. It is hardly likely that Jefferson would have agreed with historian K. Alan Snyder, who praised Dwight, Morse, and their ilk. "Dwight and Morse were not manipulators grasping for political authority, nor part of a reaction against the American Revolution," Snyder concluded. By opposing the autonomy of the individual and the extension of political democracy, "Within

228

the dominant Congregationalist Federalist framework of the early national period, they were, quite simply, champions of liberty" as a Protestant Dissenter would understand it.[2] Jefferson would have laughed at such *non sequitur* reasoning, which would claim that obedience to law and order and established church dogmas took precedence over the individual's natural rights, right to self-government, and sense of justice.

Conversely, Jefferson found extremely entertaining the attacks of English Unitarians such as Samuel Cooper Thacher and Thomas Belsham on "Athanasian jargon," as he called the orthodox belief in the Trinity. In 1818, he thanked two publishers for sending him Thacher's sermon, *The Unity of God*, a Unitarian discourse. Convincing himself that Unitarianism was more popular in the United States than it actually was, he asserted, "I make you my acknolegement for the sermon on the Unity of God, and am glad to see our countrymen looking that question in the face. It must end in a return to primitive christianity, and the disbandment of the unintelligible Athanasian jargon of 3 being 1 and 1 being 3. This sermon is one of the strongest pieces against it. I observe you are about printing a work of Belsham's on the same subject, for which I wish to be a subscriber, and inclose you a 5 Dollar bill, there being none of fractional denominations. The surplus therefore may stand as I shall be calling for other things."[3]

On the other hand, in old age Jefferson recognized the danger in the tyranny of the majority as well as "selfish minorities." Along with his friends Madison and Monroe, he was at all times deeply concerned with protecting the rights of minorities against aggressive majorities. That concern impelled his struggle to overthrow the established church in Virginia during the 1770s, and motivated his stress on religious freedom. In this context, Massachusetts assumed special significance for him in his final years. He was thrilled when John Adams, whose views had grown closer to his own, was elected a delegate to the state's constitutional convention in 1820. Adams unsuccessfully proposed modification of the third article of the Massachusetts bill of rights, which established Protestant Christianity as a tax-supported religion and denied full religious freedom to non–Protestants. Adams favored religious freedom for all, although he still wished to maintain the tax-supported status of the Congregational Church. Jefferson kept himself informed of his friend's activities. "I was quite rejoiced, dear Sir, to see that you had health and spirits enough to take part in the late convention of your state for revising it's [*sic*] constitution, and to bear your share in it's debates and labors," he said.[4]

In 1813, however, when Adams warned him that the Unitarian clergy were as intolerant as the Congregationalists and the Roman Catholics, Jefferson, who adhered to many Unitarian tenets, was not alarmed. In many ways still an orthodox Puritan (Daniel Walker Howe calls him a "Liberal Congregationalist"), Adams feared that Unitarian ecclesiastical tyranny had reared its ugly head in Massachusetts. "I wish You could live a Year in Boston, hear their Divines, read their publications, especially the *Repository*," he wrote Jefferson, alluding to the Unitarians' short-lived magazine. "You would see how spiritual Tyranny and ecclesiastical Domination are beginning in our Country: at least struggling for birth."[5]

Unappreciative of Jefferson's political and religious moderation, Adams chided him, "Checks and Balances, Jefferson, however you and your Party may have ridiculed them, are our only Security."[6] (Neither Jefferson nor the Democratic-Republicans opposed checks and balances between the three branches of government; and in practice Jefferson had extended the executive power over Congress.) Eventually, Jefferson began to share Adams' alarm that the Unitarians, once they had sufficient strength, might suppress other denominations.

For the time being, age only increased Jefferson's wrath at New England Presbyterians and Congregationalists' attempts to proselytize foreign peoples, from Chinese to Native Americans. He feared these obstinate clergy would obstruct national scientific advancement. When Peter H. Wendover, a New York City congressman and minister of the Dutch Reformed Church in New York City's Greenwich Village, sent him a printed copy of his colleague Alexander McLeod's sermon defending the Democratic Party and the War of 1812, Jefferson appreciated the clergymen's political sympathies. However, this did not stop him from raging as in younger days against clergy employing their religious authority to undertake a pseudo-divine, semi-official interference in political questions. Warming to the topic—whether religious comprehension benefited when clergymen delivered politically oriented sermons—Jefferson pronounced a shrill negative. Since clergy were hired solely to discuss matters of religion, not medicine, politics, or other extraneous issues, they must stick to that topic in their sermons, rather than seek to influence their parishioners' political opinions under false, theologically based premises.[7]

In the course of expressing his views on this matter, Jefferson vented his hatred for the revivalists who had harried him during his political career. In his last years, their Presbyterian Virginia followers had pressured him to dismiss the theologically agnostic but brilliant Thomas Cooper as professor of chemistry and natural philosophy at his brainchild, the University of Virginia. As vigorously as ever, Jefferson insisted on prohibiting clergymen from employing the pulpit to promulgate their ideas, although they were entitled to speak and write freely outside their workplace, like everyone else. However, he prohibited publication of this philippic in opposition to the clergy expounding their political opinions in their sermons and violating separation of church and state. (He thought that their job was to teach religion.) "Tranquillity, at my age, is the balm of life," he wrote. "While I know I am safe in the honor and charity of a McLeod, I do not wish to be cast forth to the Marats, the Dantons, and the Robespierres of the priesthood; I mean the Parishes, the Ogdens, and the Gardiners of Massachusetts." He specifically named these Medford, Massachusetts Congregationalist preachers—John S. J. Gardiner, Eliphalet Pearson, Solomon Ogden, and Elijah Parish, as the greatest offenders.[8] Thus, as he had with the Essex Junto and the Hartford conventioneers, Jefferson ironically likened Massachusetts Puritanical religious extremists to their fanatical, deistic opposites, the radicals of France's anti–Christian Reign of Terror of 1793–1794. Perhaps aware of this letter's controversial tenor, Jefferson, who was particularly timid about getting involved in explosive disputes in his frail old age, never mailed it.

More surprisingly, when Horatio Gates Spafford, a New York Democratic-Republican magazine editor informed him of New England Congregationalists' plans to propagandize their religion in Virginia, Jefferson, though confessing alarm, avoided participating in a public controversy. "From contest of every kind I withdraw myself entirely," he wrote. "I have served my hour, and a long one it has been. Tranquility is the object of my remaining years, and I leave to more vigorous bodies & minds the service of which has rightfully, & in succession devolved on them." However, he sent his friend, Thomas Ritchie, editor of the *Richmond Enquirer*, Virginia's leading Democratic newspaper, a letter warning of a possible invasion of the state by Lyman Beecher's "Presbyterian" fanatics. He instructed him to print it anonymously in his paper. Jefferson called them "Presbyterians," probably because the Congregationalists and Presbyterians had united, much to his chagrin, under Connecticut Presbyterian minister Lyman Beecher's leadership in the Andover Seminary. After reading the copy that

Spafford had mailed him of Beecher's *Address*, in which he impressed newly minted Connecticut clergy with the need to go abroad and convert new ministers in the South and West to their creed, Jefferson denounced its aggressive proselytizing activities. He sent the pamphlet to Ritchie, warning, "I think the pamphlet of such a character as not to be unknown, or unnoticed by the people of the United States. It is the most bold and impudent stride New England has ever made in arrogating an ascendancy over the rest of the Union."[9]

At least to a fellow Virginian, Jefferson did not disguise his fear that New England revivalists intended to regain control of the nation. At the same time, he perceived religious salvation as coming from Boston's Unitarians, who ironically emerged from the same Harvard College, which, along with Yale, was the breeding ground of evangelicals.[10] In his twilight years, Jefferson deplored the progress of the Second Great Awakening, dreading it as an irrational, intolerant religious revival. He feared Connecticut clergymen such as Lyman Beecher and warned that Pennsylvanian "Presbyterianism" and Virginia "fanaticism" dominant in the churches would eventually outlaw free thought. He despised both established and evangelical churches, charging that they consisted of greedy, power-hungry "priests." He also feared the Second Great Awakening's spread to Virginia, under the guidance of such Presbyterian clergy as John Holt Rice.[11]

More modern in his thinking than some other revivalists, John Holt Rice, a member of the Board of Trustees of Jefferson's University, wanted to prove that Presbyterians were liberal and intellectual. He felt that they competed with the more rationalistic Episcopalians on this score. He edited the *Literary and Evangelical Magazine* from 1818 until his death. Though he attacked Episcopalians as refractory backsliders, he nonetheless claimed that Presbyterians supported diversity among Christian sects more than Episcopalians did. Insisting on his respect for freedom of religion and Christian brotherhood, Rice styled himself an intermediary between evangelical Baptists and Methodists and the more intellectual Episcopalians.[12]

Rice was offended when the better-educated Episcopalians derided the Presbyterians. Somewhat embarrassed at the irrational religious enthusiasm Presbyterians exhibited at revivals, Rice wanted to maintain his denomination's venerable reputation for being well educated. He favored "sound learning and true piety" for his parishioners, and asserted that they were better-educated, more intellectually sophisticated, and more personally reserved than other religious sects. Their theology was more esoteric than that of the Baptists, he noted with approval, and they distinguished themselves from the Methodists, who valued personal experience, piety, and emotion more than sound thought. As far as Rice was concerned, the Presbyterians maintained the ideal middle ground between reason and emotion they had held since the creation of the College of New Jersey and the days of John Witherspoon in the 1740s and 1750s.[13]

Jefferson did not exaggerate the threat that Lyman Beecher's and other revivalist orthodoxies posed to intellectual freedom. Almost overnight, Beecher became among the most popular theologians in the United States. In 1810, he began preaching in the Litchfield, Connecticut Congregational Church. His parishioners were worried about the growth of immorality and New Englanders' emigration to the West. A leading figure of the Second Great Awakening, Beecher stressed the "subordination" of children to their parents, their proper indoctrination in Christianity, and the cultivation of moral peer groups among them. His expostulations against vice using the language of hellfire and damnation, gained numerous converts to his revivalism.[14]

Beecher was more moderate than some other Calvinist Congregationalists. For instance, he argued that man was not depraved by nature, but sinned by choice. He argued that men were responsible for their own salvation. Beecher participated in National Bible Societies and Education Societies. The American Education Society was formed in 1815 and the American Bible Society in 1816.[15]

Beecher played a major role in founding the Andover Theological Seminary in 1808, which organized a three-year program of theological seminars independent of universities. The seminary was founded after Unitarians took over Harvard in 1805 and elected Henry Ware Hollis Professor of Divinity. In 1806, Unitarian Samuel Webber was elected Harvard's president. He replaced Acting President Eliphalet Pearson, an orthodox revivalist who served from 1804 to 1806. After his rejection for the presidency of Harvard, Pearson resigned from the faculty in protest and went on to found the Andover Seminary, seeking to defeat the Unitarians. The Reverend Jedidiah Morse of Charlestown, the Reverend Leonard Woods, pastor of the West Newbury congregation, and Samuel French of Andover assisted him. They intended to engraft a clergy-training institution onto Phillips Academy in Andover. Their project gained significant support when Samuel Abbot, a Boston merchant, left his fortune to Andover Seminary instead of to Harvard College.[16] A theological school similar to Andover was begun at West Newbury, Massachusetts, at the same time, under the guidance of R. V. Samuel Spring and Woods.[17]

Intent on reviving Congregational orthodoxy under the label of Presbyterianism, the revivalists founded an evangelical journal titled the *Panoplist*. Jedidiah Morse was editor, and Leonard Woods contributed many articles. Morse and Woods conceived the idea of uniting the Andover and West Newbury institutions. Newbury Congregationalists followed the teachings of Samuel Hopkins, who had studied with Jonathan Edwards himself. Hopkins was more orthodox in his beliefs than even the Andover clergy. The two factions agreed to combine the endowments of Andover and West Newbury and use the funds to construct the Andover Theological Seminary on the grounds of Phillips Academy in September 1808. The three hundred thousand-dollar endowment was twice as great as Harvard's total endowment.[18]

Arguing that their main concern was to undermine Unitarianism, Morse proposed to use the Andover Seminary for post-college education of ministers. Indeed, the Andover Seminary was the first truly post-graduate professional school in the United States. It would hire three professors. The Reverend Timothy Dwight, the president and "Pope" of Yale, was very enthusiastic about the new Seminary. Large numbers of students enrolled in the program from the outset, around a hundred annually. One of Jefferson's foremost denouncers, John Mitchell Mason, who had famously attacked him as an atheist in a New York City pamphlet during the election of 1800 titled "The Voice of Warning," participated in the Seminary's creation and inspired some of its educational ideas. He had begun a seminary as an associate reformed Presbyterian minister in New York City, but it was a four-year program with only one professor, Mason, and it combined secularized college courses with religious training. The Andover Seminary was more theologically-oriented.[19] The terms for admission as a student at Andover were piety, a college degree, a highly moral character, and membership in a "Christian Church." Nevertheless, the Seminary founders did not want to teach the classics or the Hebrew language, which they thought should more properly be learned by undergraduates. Woods took the appointment as Abbot Professor of Christian Theology, honoring the Boston merchant, which he held from 1808 to 1847. Pearson became Professor of Sacred Literature, but served a single year, preferring to remain as a fund-raiser and chairman of the board of trustees. He was succeeded by Moses Stuart, a self-made scholar, who taught himself Hebrew and German and demanded that his students learn these languages. Ebenezer Porter was professor of Sacred Rhetoric and Ecclesiastical History from 1812 to 1834. James Murdock was hired to relieve Porter of some of his course load; he taught Ecclesiastical History from 1819 to 1828, but was relieved of his duties, alienating the faculty because he included too much secular history in his lectures.[20] Jefferson undoubtedly found this formidable array of Christian scholars intimidating, both intellectually and politically. Despite their learning, he viewed them as threats to the advancement of learning, because their knowledge was rooted in tendering the old rather than cultivating the new.

The Second Great Awakening, spearheaded by these new Presbyterians, was on the move. The greatest clerical minds of the century were involved in the Andover Seminary and its offshoots. Their success in gaining converts among the people was impressive. Yale President Dwight was in the forefront of the movement. In 1812, he convinced New Jersey Presbyterians to adopt the Andover system of three years of post-graduate theological seminary study and to include three or four professors of theology on their faculty when they set up the Princeton Theological Seminary. Revivalists wanted to convert their ostensibly elitist organization into a mass movement. For this purpose, they founded the American Education Society (AES) in Boston in 1815, to provide substantial scholarships to indigent ministry students. Pearson, as president of Andover's Board of Trustees, along with two faculty members, Ebenezer Porter and Moses Stuart, drafted the society's constitution. Between 1815 and 1865, the AES assisted nearly five thousand candidates for the ministry, about one-fourth of all who attended the Andover Seminary during that period. The AES also provided money to kindred seminaries that adopted Andover's three-year post-graduate model.[21]

The virtual Bible of these revivalists was Lyman Beecher's *Address of the Charitable Society for the Education of Indigent Pious Young Men for the Ministry of the Gospel* (1814). The address described the aims of this offshoot of a New Haven organization, the Education Society of Connecticut, devoted to helping poor ministry students in Connecticut to complete their studies at Andover. This institution and its sister organization, the Female Education Society of New-Haven, were precursors of the American Education Society, formed a year later. The prestigious attorney Tapping Reeve of Litchfield, Connecticut, was the Charitable Society's president. Remembered primarily for his legal scholarship and for founding the first law school in the United States, in his own day Reeve was notorious for his violent pseudonymous diatribes in Connecticut newspapers against Jefferson and the Democratic-Republicans as threats to religion and public order. Beecher, the brains of the Society, headed the Charitable Society's Committee of Supplies, devoted to fund-raising and to composing the Society's public statements. Among the most distinguished members of the Society were the Reverends Timothy Dwight and Nathaniel W. Taylor, who served on its Committee on Appropriations.[22]

Beecher's address alarmed Jefferson when Horatio Gates Spafford sent it to him in 1816. He began to fear that the evangelicals were plotting a nationwide campaign to convert everyone in the United States, north and south, to revivalist Presbyterianism. For Jefferson, such a victory would spell the end of freedom of thought and scientific advance in the United States. It was intrinsically anti-republican as well.[23] In light of its importance in arousing Jefferson's dread, it is appropriate for us to analyze Beecher's *Address* at considerable length.

Beecher's first major point was that there were dangerously few competent Presbyterian clergy in the United States. Insisting that ministers should be well-educated, he warned, "Religion is the last thing that should be committed to the hands of ignorant and incompetent men, and the real deficiency of competent religious instructors is at least *five thousand,* and the population unsupplied is five millions."[24] Beecher explained that the Society's goal was to provide "a sufficient number of competent religious instructors" to supply the entire republic with an "evangelical Ministry." For any one of the eight million people of the United States to be deprived of an "evangelical light" would be "calamitous," Beecher instructed his readers. According to his calculations, "To provide competent religious instruction for the United States, would demand at least one pastor for every thousand souls; which, estimating the family at seven members, at a medium, will be one pastor for one hundred and fifty families."[25] According to Beecher, the devout ancient Jews, and the early colonial Connecticut Puritans, had an even higher ratio of Christian teachers to families. Beecher stated that, at present, there was only one educated minister for every 1500 people in the New England states, instead of the recommended one to one thousand; and his home state, Connecticut, was the only one in the U.S. that could boast a minister for every thousand people. Consequently, morality and virtue throughout the nation declined. According to Beecher, the average for European congregations was one minister to "every 1000 souls." The Russian Orthodox Church, which had a minister for every 450 people, performed far better. (It did not seem to matter to Beecher that Russia was ruled by an oppressive monarch, who denied his people the most basic rights.) He reluctantly admitted that the population of the United States was so scattered that it would be difficult in many areas for a minister to find it convenient to preach to as many as a thousand parishioners.[26]

Jefferson took note of, and was angered by, Beecher's presumption that only Yale Congregationalist ministers were sufficiently well educated to preach throughout the nation.[27] Indeed, Article 1 of the Constitution of the Charitable Society for the Education of Indigent Young Men, for the Ministry of the Gospel stipulated that Yale College was the only institution the "indigent young men" would be assigned to attend.[28] Beecher said, "To supply then a population of 8,000,000 with competent religious instructors, at the ratio of one for a thousand, demands the agency of 8000 ministers. But according to the best information which can be obtained, and which to a great extent is obtained from the authentic printed documents of ecclesiastical bodies, there are not, according to the largest computation, more than 3,000 educated ministers of the Gospel in our land; leaving a deficiency of 5,000 ministers, and a population of five millions destitute of proper religious instruction."[29]

In Beecher's opinion, many ministers were so unqualified as to be unworthy of being counted among the clergy. He claimed there were 1500 of these so-called clergymen, "who are nominally ministers of the Gospel," but "are generally illiterate men, often not possessed even of good English education, and in some instances unable to read or write."[30] Continuing pessimistically, he claimed that only 1200 "organized congregations" in the United States (the majority were undoubtedly in New England) could adequately support a pastor. "The remainder [of churches] is either in the hands of illiterate men, or like primeval Chaos, without form and void, and darkness resting upon it."[31] He castigated "illiterate" preachers, who knew nothing about theology, and preached only on the Sabbath, working at other jobs the rest of the week. Despite their ostensible piety and good intentions, such illiterate ministers inevitably failed to contribute to society and civilization generally in the same way that "an educated Ministry" would.[32] Beecher went so far as to warn that educated youth would "despise religion" and turn to atheism or Unitarianism out of contempt for these ignorant preachers. If "illiterate pastors" gained hegemony, "education, religion and literacy will be neglected, civilization will decline, and immoralities multiply."[33]

Since religious knowledge was the most important knowledge of all, Beecher asserted, he was disgusted that an intensive education was required for attorneys, physicians, merchants, and even farmers and mechanics; but not for religious instructors. With the exception of Connecticut, Beecher moaned, the Union was deplorably underserved by an educated and virtuous clergy.[34]

While insisting that all the states were lacking in educated ministers, Beecher particularly regretted that New York lacked well-informed and moral clergymen. "On the right hand and on the left [New York State's boundaries with Connecticut], Connecticut is bounded by a moral wilderness, and her sympathies are demanded by a famine of the word of life," he dramatically declared. The new states in the West, as well as Louisiana, were deplorably sunk in immorality. On the other hand, New Jersey seemed well-supplied with ministers by comparison with most of the states outside New England.[35]

In words that Jefferson may have considered a back-handed compliment, Beecher confessed that, although he lacked information about the religious proclivities of Pennsylvania and Delaware, he knew enough about Virginia to warn that it was in profound moral danger. He did not deny that, as "the centre of the Union," Virginia "must always exert a powerful influence on our national concerns." Therefore, he considered it especially important to inform his readers that exactly 914,000 of Virginia's residents (in a state that the U.S. Census of 1810 listed as having 970,000 people) were, as far as religious teaching went, "in the hands of unlettered men, or totally destitute of the means of grace." Even Maryland required additional ministers, and North and South Carolina's situations were as bad as Virginia's.[36] Beecher did not hide his despair: "Such, then, is the state of our nation, more deplorably destitute of religious instruction than any other Christian nation under heaven."[37]

Beecher reluctantly concluded that too few respectable theological colleges existed to supply the deficit of minsters in the United States. He spoke as if (pre–Unitarian) Harvard and Yale Colleges were the only acceptable institutions from which competent ministers could emerge. In the years before 1800, he informed his listeners, there was a greater ratio of ministers to people, at least in New England, than currently existed. Reiterating his calculation that of eight million Americans, five million lacked access to religious preachers, he advised that the solution to this crisis was to educate the pious poor for the ministry; this would both fill the glaring gap and save the virtuous poor from a life of crime.[38]

Beecher's statistics blatantly depicted the current crisis. According to Beecher's reasoning, since Yale College provided one-sixth of all national college graduates headed for the ministry, it was responsible for supplying one-sixth of the U.S. population with ministers. In order for it to do so, thereby fulfilling Beecher's desired quota of a minister for every thousand people, it would have to graduate eighty ministers annually, compared with its current rate of graduating only nine ministers per year. A greater number of colleges and institutions for training ministers was immediately needed. "The evangelizing of the nation" concerned everyone.[39]

Even more than "foreign missions" to convert non–Protestants overseas, Beecher advised, "domestic missions" must be set up, whose goal was "a Bible for every family, a school for every district, and a pastor for every 1000 souls." It was imperative, Beecher insisted, that the entire country be aware of the dangerous shortage of ministers through the dissemination of newspapers, tracts, and pamphlets. He bewailed the "perishing millions," who died spiritually for lack of correct Christian upbringing and education. Neglecting to mention daughters, Beecher urged parents to assume the responsibility for educating "pious sons," whom they should encourage to leave home and become preachers, even though it was natural for aging parents to want their sons to remain at home and nurse them "in the decline of life."[40]

In order to fulfill these objectives, Beecher hoped to incorporate members of the lower and middle classes into the Church fold. He proposed to recruit them for the clergy, along with upper-class Harvard and Yale graduates, whose number was inadequate to supply all the ministers that were needed. Sounding like a twenty-first century politician, he enthusiastically observed, "The great mass of talent, and piety, and zeal, and hardy enterprise, lies in the middle class of society, and downward to the cottage of the poor." Although the lower classes embraced religious revivals, Beecher noted, poverty prevented them from receiving a religious education.[41]

The goal of providing the worthy poor with money for a religious education inspired the formation of the Charitable Society for the Education of Indigent Pious Young Men for the Ministry. The Charitable Society's funding would "open this inexhaustible fountain" of poor, albeit pious youth to the opportunity to become candidates for the ministry. Beecher was confident that the churches would cooperate with the Charitable Society. Calculating that $100 per year was needed to support a divinity student, he urged every member of the revivalist churches to contribute a dollar to the Charitable Society. Indeed, he desired every church in Connecticut to pledge to contribute to the Charitable Society.[42]

Beecher did not hesitate to request women to contribute the money they accumulated from their various charitable efforts to aiding young men in undertaking a theological education. He urged the various Female Charitable Associations in Connecticut to contribute money as well as donate their labor to produce clothing and other materials for sale, contributing the money they raised to help young men in the worthy goal of becoming Protestant ministers. Women should also urge their friends to contribute to the Charitable Society. Even frivolous non-religious young men should see the wisdom of contributing their savings to the Charitable Society, instead of wasting their money on dissolute pursuits and alcohol.[43]

Targeting the interest of the wealthy in an orderly society, Beecher urged those who could most easily afford it to help the worthy poor become Presbyterian ministers. "Men of wealth! Help us; we intreat you help us to save your country from ruin, and the souls of your countrymen from death," he poignantly exclaimed. In accordance with the will of Jesus, the rich should remember that if they were not kind and just they would not reach the heavenly gates. "Freely ye have received; freely give," he concluded. Beecher implored the state legislature to contribute to the Society as well, with influence and funding. He urged alumni of Yale College to contribute.[44]

As Jefferson feared, Beecher made clear that the young ministers he hoped to educate would unite the republic under the banner of evangelical Christianity. "The intercourse of good men, in the blessed enterprise, of evangelizing our land, will do more than every thing beside to make the different parts of the land acquainted, to do away local jealousies, to consolidate the nation, and perpetuate its liberties," he said. In his opinion, his goal of a harmonious, community-oriented Christian republic accorded more with the meaning of the American Revolution and its "sacred cause of liberty" than Jefferson's ideal of intellectual, spiritual and political freedom and economic opportunity for all.[45] Bluntly acknowledging his awareness that the states had little "affection" for each other (obviously, he was referring to the "slave" and "free" states), he claimed that one of his objectives was to promote national unity. At the same time, like a good Connecticut localist who opposed assisting the national government in fighting against the British invaders during the War of 1812, especially with Democratic-Republicans in control, Beecher observed that "consolidation of the State Governments would make a despotism." As a states' righter and conservative Federalist, Beecher concluded that the best way to effect national unity was by means of religious organizations and the clergy.[46]

A theological imperialist, Beecher hoped to found the American "empire, upon a rock" of religious conformity, which would impose upon the nation a "more homogeneous character, and bind us together by firmer bonds." He relied on the New England clergy and their associated academies and schools to convert the whole nation to evangelical Christianity, through the process of creating "institutions of homogeneous influence." "The fulfillment of the Charitable Society's goal of a minister for every thousand persons" was the primary means by which theological and social uniformity would be attained. Although Benjamin Rush, at a moment of unwisely merging his revivalist Presbyterianism with his republicanism, rather mildly urged Americans to become "republican machines," Beecher more blatantly exhorted them to become Presbyterian machines, employing rhetoric guaranteed to alarm Jefferson. The implementation of his recommendations, Beecher assured his hearers, "would produce a sameness of views, and feelings, and interests, which would lay the foundation of our empire upon a rock. Religion is the central attraction which must supply the deficiency of political affinity and interest."[47] More succinctly, Beecher warned that, without a number of ministers more proportionate to the rapidly increasing U.S. population, the young republic would decline into "a state of absolute heathenism."[48]

Insisting on his republicanism, Beecher made clear that the republic's survival depended on increasing the number of evangelical clergy and sending them on their domestic mission of conversion. Otherwise, the future of American republicanism would be short. "If knowledge and virtue be the basis of republican institutions, our foundations will soon rest upon the sand," he warned, "unless a more effectual and all-pervading system of religious and moral instruction can be provided." It is likely that Jefferson's projected secular-oriented University of Virginia would not fulfill Beecher's specifications.[49]

One of Beecher's gravest fears was that, if an increasing number of young men did not choose the ministry as their profession, there would be a growing scarcity of ministers to satisfy the needs of the greatly expanding U.S. population. According to Beecher's off-the-mark calculations, by the end of seventy years (in 1884), the U.S. would contain seventy million people, "and there will be only *six thousand* competent religious teachers; that is, SIXTY-FOUR MILLIONS out of the SEVENTY, will be wholly destitute of proper religious instruction."[50] If these pathetic individuals received any Christian instruction at all, it would be minimal, hardly worth more than education in "idolatry" for the soul's beatification. As Beecher graphically explained, "There is a brutality and ignorance, and profligacy always prevalent where the Gospel does not enlighten and restrain, as decisively ruinous to the soul, as Idolatry itself."[51]

Beecher linked political and religious salvation; education and Christian morality. Equating knowledge of the Gospel and general literacy, he perceived little difference between them. He thought that those who did not read the Bible regularly should not be allowed to vote. "The right of suffrage in the hands of an ignorant and vicious population, such as will always exist in a land where the Gospel does not restrain and civilize, will be a sword in the hand of a maniac, to make desolate all around him, and finally to destroy himself," he warned. Beecher was convinced that education in revivalist Presbyterian Christianity was the only way to prevent individual ignorance and damnation and social anarchy. Adopting an anti-political stance, he advised, "It is no party in politics that can save this nation from political death, by political wisdom merely." The people no longer looked to God for guidance; this could only be changed by an influx of new Protestant ministers. "The disease is upon the vitals, and the remedy must be appropriate."[52]

Although he purportedly opposed political "consolidation," Beecher certainly approved the efforts of new, young revivalist ministers to cement a metaphorical "consolidation" of the states through love of Christianity, creating "a more homogeneous character" for the Union. Beecher was acutely aware of the prevalence of national disunity, amply demonstrated by widespread, active opposition to the War of 1812 among high state government officials. He proposed that the only way to create "affection" between the people of the different states was to establish Protestant Christianity through the proselytizing activities of his projected eight thousand ministers traveling on circuit throughout the United States preaching the Gospel.

In Beecher's world-view, national unity and "affection" among the people of the diverse states could only be restored by uniting them under the same religion: revivalist Christianity. Too much psychological conflict existed between the sections for Beecher's taste. "United as they [the states] are, chiefly for defence and commercial purposes," he said (although little unity for national defense existed among the New England states at this time), "there is not sufficient intercourse to beget affection, nor a sufficient solidity of the whole nation to counteract the danger of local repulsion in times of public commotion." Once his eight-thousand-man Presbyterian ministry went into action, it would generate the requisite national harmony and feeling of community. Infiltrating all the states, it would "establish schools, and academies, and colleges and habits, and institutions of homogeneous influence." Beecher relied on his ministerial cohort to change even the "habits" of its constituents. Through Protestant Christianity, undoubtedly in alliance with New England Federalism, Beecher hoped to see the nation unified and ultimately saved for God. Moral "friendship" would thereby be "diffused through the nation."[53]

Perhaps Beecher thought it might be necessary for his upstart elite of poor but honest ministers to use their muscle to "convert" recusants. He assumed that the sturdy, intelligent poor for whose education his fund was intended would be physically strong; a byproduct of the hardships they endured in their lives of honest, hard-working poverty. "They will be taken from a state of society where bodily vigour, resolution, and a capacity of enduring hardships, will be found in their best estate," he said, and finally emerge as "intelligent and pious young men."[54]

Beecher had second thoughts about sending these paragons of intelligence and virtue to Harvard, which by this time had become a Unitarian citadel. The Charitable Society's constitution specified that the only college to which they could apply for admission was Yale. These pious poor, funded by scholarships to Yale College, were equivalent in their way to Jefferson's "natural aristocracy." (Jefferson's abortive constitutional plan for Virginia, described in *Notes on the State of Virginia* during the 1780s, would have funded the most intelligent economically disadvantaged students with full scholarships for a secularized education at the College of William and Mary.) Beecher was confident that the clerical candidates would provide a shining example to their fellow students, whom Beecher expected to imitate their virtue and diligence. He thought they would lead many religious "revivals." Although Presbyterian revivals and seminaries had already sprung up in New England, Yale College's current lack of funds to educate prospective impoverished candidates for the ministry impeded the growth of religious enthusiasm. Even worse, Beecher warned, unless Yale immediately obtained additional money for "charitable education" of ministerial candidates, the entire nation faced "relapse into heathenism," and would "positively" be "crushed by the hand of despotism."[55] It was hard to understand the meaning of Beecher's bloated rhetoric, unless he considered the Madison Administration's request for assistance from Massachusetts militia in meeting the British invasion of that state as evidence of Democratic-Republican "despotism."

Beecher said that only the training of many new ministers, especially from the habitats of the poor, could preserve America's republican government. "The necessities of your country and the world, and the high authority of heaven, bind you to give, committing the event to GOD," he urged potential contributors. Those near death who desired to go to Heaven were advised to contribute to the charitable fund. Tragically, Beecher pointed out, each year 150,000 Americans died without access to a Protestant minister, and were perhaps unwittingly doomed to damnation. Beecher ended his address, somewhat like Johan Tetzel selling indulgences in 1500, confidently predicting that contributors to his Charitable Society would avert this fate.[56]

Unlike Beecher and his followers, and unlike most Americans, Jefferson, particularly near the end of his life, enthusiastically preferred deism. Spurred by disillusionment with New England's disloyal conduct during the war, he expressed contempt for New England Presbyterian revivalists like Beecher in his letters, beginning in 1815. In addition to their opposition to the patriotic war, Jefferson believed, the Massachusetts clergy were atavistic opponents of scientific progress and useful knowledge. He charged them with opposition to the new, safer practice of cowpox vaccination (instead of inoculation with weakened human virus) against smallpox, which Dr. Benjamin Waterhouse of Harvard College introduced into Massachusetts. As far as Jefferson was concerned, the evangelical clergy like profit-obsessed physicians, opposed all progress. In the course of a congratulatory letter to Dr. Waterhouse, he applauded him for "bearing up with firmness and perseverance against the persecutions of your enemies, religious, political and professional. These last I suppose have not yet forgiven you the introduction of [cowpox] vaccination and annihilation of the great variolous [i.e., the practice of inoculation with weakened human smallpox virus] field of profit to them: and none of them pardon the proof you have established that the condition of man may be meliorated, if not *infinitely*, as enthusiasm alone pretends, yet *indefinitely*, as bigots alone can doubt." He despised these "bigots," but praised their fellow New Englander Dr. Waterhouse, whose progressive views of medical knowledge he shared. "In lieu of these enmities you have the blessings of all the friends of human happiness, for this great peril [smallpox] from which they are rescued."[57]

In demonizing the evangelical clergy in writing Waterhouse, Jefferson was preaching to the choir. Waterhouse supplied Jefferson with one of the most detailed summaries he received of the connection between political and religious divisions in Massachusetts. Writing that the state's Calvinists had divided into orthodox Calvinists and Unitarians, he sarcastically informed him, "our restless Levites are now at open & bitter war among themselves, on account of the old & tedious subject of the *unity, trinity* & *atonement.*" Jefferson may have been shocked to learn that the most extreme Federalists, members of the "Essex Junto," most vehemently advocated his preferred religion, Unitarianism. "The Essex-Junto are the revivers & patrons of the imputed heresy of Unitarianism," Waterhouse wrote him.[58]

That Massachusetts' political religion was complex was evident from Waterhouse's brief description. He observed that Caleb Strong and William Phillips, the governor and lieutenant governor of Massachusetts, were members of the politically conservative Essex Junto, but unlike their Unitarian colleagues, they were "two of the most rigid Calvinists in New England." Labeling himself a "mischievous," "wicked Unitarian Republican" waiting to see the outcome of the clash between Federalist Unitarians and orthodox Calvinists, and how it might weaken the party's political power, he noted the paradox that Harvard College was the "fortress" of both Federalism and Unitarianism.[59]

By contrast with these clerical "bigots," Jefferson praised the nationalistic Massachusetts Democrats, John Holmes of Maine and James Trecothick Austin of Lexington. He admired their recent patriotic Fourth of July orations. Instead of harking back to the Revolutionary War, Jefferson said, they creatively "made the present state of things the subject of annual animadversion and instruction." He even had a favorable word about his old, once-reactionary foe, the expatriate Briton, William Cobbett. Now a radical in hot water with the authorities at Whitehall, Cobbett publicly hoped for America's success in the war against Britain. Thus, Jefferson now extolled "Cobbet's [sic] address," probably *An Address to the Clergy of Massachusetts* (1814) in favor of religious freedom for Roman Catholics, a position that Cobbett had only recently adopted. Jefferson said that Cobbett's work "would of itself have mortified and humbled the Cossac [sic] priests; but brother Jonathan has pointed his arrow to the hearts of the worst of them."[60]

Renewing his disdainful attack on the leading Massachusetts clergy and other New England antiwar protesters, he coined for them the nickname, "Hartford nation" and implied that they were not only unpatriotic but immoral. (An intense religious conflict prevailed between orthodox Calvinists and Unitarians, although both sects were mainly Federalist in their political sentiments.) "These reverend leaders of the Hartford nation it seems then are now falling together about religion, of which they have not one real principle in their hearts," he angrily observed. "Like bawds, religion becomes to them a refuge from the despair of their loathsome vices. They seek in it only an oblivion of the disgrace with which they have loaded themselves, in their political ravings, and of their mortification at the ridiculous issue of their Hartford convention." As anti-republican and anti–American, in Jefferson's eyes the New England clergy could not redeem themselves. His acrimony increased as the memory of the war grew more distant. After deriding their "disgrace," he again emphasized, as he had months earlier, the mercy and broad-mindedness that the republican United States government presided over by his comrade Madison had exercised, forgiving their Christmas Eve aberrations. Such benevolence distinguished the United States under Democratic-Republican guidance from every other existing government, he was sure. As he put it: "No event, more than this [the abortive Hartford Convention and the national government's noninterference with it], has shewn the placid character of our constitution. Under any other their treasons would have been punished by the halter. We let them live as laughing stocks for the world, and punish them by the torment of eternal contempt."[61] Thus, like the American Indians, whose attitude in this respect Jefferson admired, the United States government punished traitorous conduct by ridicule and ostracism rather than bloodshed.[62]

At the same time, Jefferson believed that the potentially disloyal minority of New Englanders (the "Hartford nation" of extremist Federalists) required continued surveillance. His anxiety over a recurrence of Anglophile secessionism after the Hartford Convention led him to recommend U.S. abstention from international affairs. His often meddlesome pacifist friend, Dr. George Logan, naively believing that the brutal despot Tsar Alexander I was truly a force for peace in the world, and convinced that several autocratic monarchs planned to attack the United States, proposed that the U.S. negotiate commercial and military alliances with the "republican" Emperor as well as with Great Britain. On the other hand, Jefferson, in a letter that Logan had published in *Poulson's American Daily Advertiser* without his permission, viewed Alexander I as the detestable conqueror of Poland and other fledgling states despite his ostensible affability toward the U.S. He advised Logan to pay more attention to domestic affairs. He feared that the New England states contemplated rejoining Britain now that the former Mother Country was the world's most powerful nation. Explaining his concept of the balance of power to Logan, he said, "We were safe ourselves from Bonaparte because he had not the British fleets at his command. We were safe from the British fleets, because they had Bonaparte at their back; but the British fleets and the conquerors of Bonaparte being now combined, and the Hartford nation drawn off to them, we have uncommon reason to look to our own affairs."[63]

In the aftermath of the War of 1812, Jefferson continued to resent New Englanders' frequent disparagement of Southern mores and morals. This was especially the case with Connecticut native Jedidiah Morse. The revivalist Presbyterian and extreme Federalist partisan insulted Virginians in his geography books. He invariably praised New England. Jefferson had long resented what he called "the libel of [Dr.] Morse on this State."[64] Jefferson must have been particularly enraged because Morse insisted that there was a greater difference between the incomes of rich and poor there than in any of the Northern states, and that the average Virginian was more ignorant. Ironically, he plagiarized his negative remarks on Virginians from the private journal of his friend and correspondent Ebenezer Hazard, second postmaster general of the United States, written during the late 1770s. Morse himself briefly visited Williamsburg in 1786.[65]

First published in 1789, Morse's *American Geography* went through numerous editions. Morse denounced Virginia for persecuting Quakers during the colonial period, but ignored the fact that Quakers were executed for their beliefs in New England during the 1650s. In the 1794 edition of his book, Morse erroneously asserted that the majority of Virginians were Presbyterians, although it was well-known that the Episcopalians outnumbered them. In discussing the American Revolution and the making of the Constitution, Morse grudgingly admitted that Virginia "has produced some of the most distinguished and influential men that have been active in effecting the late great and important revolutions in America. Her political and military character will rank among the first in the page of history: but it is to be observed, that this character has been obtained for the Virginians by a few eminent men, who have taken the lead in all their public transactions, and who, in short, govern Virginia." Contending that most Virginians were apathetic toward politics (an observation that Jefferson might have reluctantly seconded), Morse continued, "The great body of the people do not concern themselves with politics; so that their government, though nominally republican, is, in fact, oligarchical or aristocratical."[66]

Acclaiming those Virginians with wealth, most of it from plantations, who participated in public affairs, Morse nonetheless regretted that their leisure rested on the "pernicious" institution of slavery. (However, Morse only lamented that slavery harmed Virginians' morals.) Wealthy Virginians, Morse wrote, copying from Hazard without mentioning him, "are in general sensible, polite, and hospitable, and of an independent spirit." Like most elitist Federalists, Morse had less regard for the lower classes. He wrote, "The poor are ignorant and abject, and all are of an inquisitive turn. A considerable proportion of the people are much addicted to gaming, drinking, swearing, horse-racing, cock-fighting, and most kinds of dissipation." Continuing to copy Hazard's analysis from his trip in 1777–1778, Morse observed, "There is a much greater disparity between the rich and poor, in Virginia, than in any of the northern States."[67] Jefferson intensely disliked when outsiders mocked his state, especially when they were evangelical Presbyterian Federalists.

Shifting his emphasis from the ministry's political to its religious aberrations, Jefferson insisted that its irrational adoption of neo-Catholic, Platonist idealism to prove Jesus' divinity distorted the Bible's original teachings about Jesus, which was that he was a mortal moralist and benign preacher. "The subject of their present clawings and caterwaulings is not without it's interest to rational men," he haughtily remarked. "The priests have so disfigured the simple religion of Jesus that no one who reads the sophistications they have engrafted on it, from the jargon of Plato, of Aristotle & other mystics, would conceive these could have been fathered on the sublime preacher of the sermon on the mount." They called themselves Christians instead of Platonists to deceive their parishioners: "Knowing the importance of names they have assumed that of Christians," he charged, "while they are mere Platonists, or any thing rather than disciples of Jesus."[68]

More optimistically, Jefferson thought that Virginia had up to this point resisted the irrational, evangelical scourge.[69] He considered it vital to warn his fellow Virginians of Beecher's plan to send Presbyterian clergy from Yale for the purpose of evangelizing them and eventually the whole nation. Jefferson sent Thomas Ritchie, editor of the distinguished newspaper, the *Richmond Enquirer* a brief diatribe, one paragraph long, against the New England evangelists for him to publish anonymously in his paper. Jefferson received several pamphlets, written by leading revivalists Beecher and Pearson, from Horatio Gates Spafford, a New York Unitarian. Although Spafford unsuccessfully solicited Jefferson to publicly denounce the New England evangelicals, Jefferson, outraged by what he conceived as New Englanders' plot to achieve national religious uniformity, anonymously exposed their project in the *Richmond Enquirer*. Beecher and his cohort are "to send among us their Gardiners, their Osgoods, their Parishes & Pearsons, as apostles to teach us their orthodoxy," he warned. "This is the outline of the plan as published by Messrs. Beecher, Pearson & Co."[70]

Jefferson considered the evangelical New England clergy a mainstay of reactionary Federalism. In retrospect, composing the introduction to his brief memoir of the 1790s, the *Anas*, in 1818, he imputed to these Federalist clergy much of the paranoia and political persecutions of what he called the Federalist "reign of terror" during the Quasi-War with France from 1798 to 1800. He considered Adams, although president at the time, as merely the unwitting pawn of the High Federalist politicians and clergy, most of whom came from New England. As he reminisced, describing the plots of Federalist extremists to permanently subdue their Republican enemies with the Alien and Sedition Acts and other measures in 1798, "In the fervor of the fury and follies of those who made him[Adams], their stalking horse [pawn], no man who did not witness it, can form an idea of their unbridled madness, and the terrorism with which they surrounded themselves." He specifically mentioned the Puritan preachers: "The horrors of the French revolution, then raging, aided them mainly, and using that as a raw head and bloody bones they were enabled by their stratagems of X.Y.Z. in which this historian was a leading mountebank [villain], their tales of tub-plots, Ocean massacres, bloody buoys, and pulpit lyings, and slanderings and maniacal ravings of their Gardiners, their Osgoods, and Parishes, to spread alarm into all but the firmest breasts."[71]

In 1815, writing to Dr. Benjamin Waterhouse, who with Jefferson's help, disseminated Edward Jenner's smallpox vaccine throughout the United States and among the Indian tribes, saving thousands of lives, Jefferson derided prominent Massachusetts Congregationalist and Presbyterian preachers. Listing several Connecticut and Massachusetts orthodox clergy, he drolly claimed that because of his reputation among them for atheism and immorality, they abhorred his home, Monticello, which Waterhouse hoped to visit, as "the Sodom and Gomorrah of parsons [Thaddeus] Osgood, [Elijah] Parish and [John] Gardiner." For Jefferson, even this cloud had a silver lining. He claimed that the efforts of the fanatical evangelicals would backfire. Spearheaded by Democratic Republicans, the people's reaction against these theologians' "meretricious trappings" would result in more conversions to Unitarianism and "restore to us the figure [of Jesus Christ] in its original simplicity and beauty" as the "sublime preacher of the sermon on the mount." With a light-heartedness that was becoming increasingly rare for him, he wrote, "The effects of this squabble [between Jeffersonian Unitarians and Federalist Congregationalist-Presbyterians] therefore, whether religious or political, cannot fail to be good in some way."[72]

Apparently overlooking the fact that a greater number of Federalists than Republicans were Unitarians, among them his irreconcilable enemy Timothy Pickering, Jefferson mistakenly equated political and religious "faith." He pretended that Democratic-Republicanism and Unitarianism were virtually synonymous. Thus, Jefferson unrealistically expected that Unitarianism would eventually become the "national" religion. One of his most famous statements of this prediction was in a letter to Waterhouse in 1822, in which he asserted, "I trust that there is not a *young man* now living in the U.S. who will not die an Unitarian."[73]

At the same time, Jefferson demanded that all sects respect competing denominations' equal rights. He may have heard about Dedham's Unitarian Church's high-handed efforts to take over the establishment prerogatives and state funding of the town's Congregationalist Church, actions upheld by the Massachusetts Supreme Court in the *Baker v. Fales* decision in 1821. He wrote Waterhouse that he feared that Unitarians might eventually become as despotic as their current religious foes, the Congregationalists and Presbyterians. Anticipating the Unitarians' ultimate victory over those benighted sects, he advised Waterhouse, a Unitarian, to prevent members of his faith from oppressing Trinitarians, or breaking up into disparate contentious factions once they held power. "Much I fear that when this great truth [belief in 'one God' rather than the Trinity] shall be re-established, it's Votaries will fall into the fatal error of fabricating formulas of creed, and Confessions of faith, the engines which so soon destroyed the religion of Jesus, and made of Christendom a mere Aceldama," he warned, and "that they will give up morals for mysteries, and Jesus for Plato."[74]

Chagrined at his beloved Unitarians' power-plays and possible tyrannical propensities, Jefferson went so far as to declare his preference for the Quakers, despite his frequent criticism of what he considered their Anglophile, pro–Federalist politics. (He apparently preferred to forget that most New England Unitarians were Federalists.) "How much wiser are the Quakers," he continued, "who, agreeing in the fundamental doctrine of the gospel, schismatize about no mysteries, and keeping within the pale of Common sense, suffer no speculative differences of opinion, any more than of feature, to impair the love of their brethren." And he advised: "Be this the wisdom of the Unitarians, this the holy mantle which shall cover within it's charitable circumference all who believe in one God, and who love their neighbor."[75] Jefferson's motto, in religion as in life, was "Live and let live."

20

Jefferson's Old-Age Affinity for New England's Unitarian Theology

Jefferson viewed the Unitarians based at Harvard College as performing a heroic role in what he hoped would be the upcoming conversion of the people of the United States to deism. He much preferred to see Unitarian preachers invade Virginia instead of the Presbyterian ministers that Lyman Beecher dispatched there. Convinced that Virginians were amenable to Unitarian theology preached by Harvard-educated ministers, he regretted that few had visited. "That doctrine has not yet been preached to us," he informed Waterhouse. "But the breeze begins to be felt which precedes the storm; and fanaticism is all in a bustle, shutting it's doors and windows to keep it out." Eagerly anticipating that Unitarian preachers would expel "the foggy mists of Platonism" characteristic of Protestant Christianity, he was anxious to hear their "evangelical" message, hoping that they would convince his fellow Virginians to abandon the actual evangelical dogmas that many had recently embraced. "I am in hopes that some of the disciples of your institution [Harvard] will become missionaries to us, of these doctrines truly evangelical, and open our eyes to what has been so long hidden from them," he wrote, sounding almost mystical himself. "A bold and eloquent preacher would be no where listened to with more freedom than in this state, nor with more firmness of mind," although it might take some of the revivalists a while to "unlearn the lesson that reason is an unlawful guide in religion." Some of the orthodox "might startle on being first awaked from the dreams of the night, but they would rub their eyes at once and look the spectres boldly in the face." Although it was possible that the "hierophants" of the established churches would exclude a Unitarian teacher from sharing their pulpits, Jefferson predicted that (like Jesus in the Sermon on the Mount?), he "would be attended in the fields by whole acres of hearers and thinkers." He wittily concluded, "Missionaries from Cambridge would soon be greeted with more welcome, than from the tritheistical [*sic*] school of Andover [Beecher's Calvinist seminary]. Such are my wishes, such would be my welcomes, warm and cordial." He was glad to report that Jared Sparks, Harvard-educated writer, editor, historian, and Unitarian minister of Baltimore, had written an "inestimable book on the subject" of religion. Sparks was the newly elected Chaplain to the House of Representatives.[1]

In religious matters, Jefferson was eager for union with his Massachusetts friends, especially if it would imbue Virginians with Unitarian ideology. Apparently, he did not care whether they were Federalists or Democratic-Republicans. George Thacher and Timothy

Pickering, two diehard Federalists, were Unitarians with whom he corresponded in his last years on religious topics.[2]

Jefferson favored harmony within the nation and between the sections in matters of politics as well as religion. Apart from his vituperation against the Connecticut Charitable Society and Beecher's organization in 1816, he seldom singled out New Englanders for condemnation as being uniquely fanatical in their religion.[3] He viewed revivalism, or "fanaticism" as he pejoratively called it, as a nationwide phenomenon. In 1822, he wrote several letters to Thomas Cooper, a radical deistic professor of chemistry and natural philosophy, whom he had wanted to hire at the University of Virginia, but whose appointment the religiously orthodox state legislature opposed. He described his anxiety at the Second Great Awakening's increasing popularity. He ascribed the crisis to the power of "Presbyterianism," by which he probably meant the unification of Calvinist Protestant denominations spurred by the famous Andover meeting in 1809. As he often did, he denounced the benightedness of Calvinism, which now occupied the foreground of his fears. His rancor at New England's disloyalty during the War of 1812 was dimmed by the gift of forgetfulness.[4]

As we have seen, Jefferson's enthusiasm for the growth of Unitarianism in Boston was nearly unbounded. He made this clear in a letter in November 1822 to Cooper, the English émigré and radical Republican freethinker, intellectual and scientist who began his career an abolitionist and ended it as president of South Carolina College, where he became a devout supporter of slavery and the South. Because of his affinity for Unitarianism, he effusively praised Boston, the denomination's power center. He explained his feelings to the brilliant English scientist and polymath Cooper, an anticlerical agnostic and colleague of Joseph Priestley. Cooper resided in Philadelphia. Surveying the national religious scene, Jefferson found Boston's Unitarianism a welcome exception to the growing extremism in other parts of the republic. "The atmosphere of our country is unquestionably charged with a threatening cloud of fanaticism," he melodramatically observed, "lighter in some parts, denser in others, but too heavy in all." Shocked by Cooper's report, confirmed by Waterhouse, that Pennsylvania had become the stamping ground for evangelicals, he lamented: "I had no idea, however, that in Pennsylvania, the cradle of toleration and freedom of religion, it could have arisen to the height you describe. This must be owing to the growth of Presbyterianism. The blasphemy and absurdity of the five points of Calvin, and the impossibility of defending them render their advocates impatient of reasoning, irritable & prone to denunciation."[5]

By contrast, he glowingly praised the Bostonians, who had chosen the deistic theology of Unitarianism over the revivalist orthodoxy of Presbyterianism. "In Boston however and it's [sic] neighborhood, Unitarianism has advanced to so great [sic] strength as now to humble this haughtiest of all religious sects; insomuch that they condescend to interchange with them and the other sects the civilities of preaching freely & frequently in each other's meeting houses." Revealing his attention to religious trends and the significance he attached to them for the future of the nation's intellectual freedom, he continued, "In Rhode Island on the other hand, no sectarian preacher will permit an Unitarian to pollute his desk." Turning to his home state, Jefferson told Cooper that he had managed to implement an equality of religious rights among the chapels near his university in Charlottesville, but that in the state capital of Richmond revivalism was gaining popularity, especially among the women. With an appreciation for sexual humor, he commented: "In our Richmond there is much fanaticism, but chiefly among the women—they have their night meetings, and praying-parties, where attended by their priests, and sometimes a hen-pecked husband, they pour forth the effusions of their love to Jesus in terms as amatory and carnal as their modesty would permit them to use to a mere earthly lover."[6] Jefferson revealed surprising impartiality between sections of the Union in his critique of religious trends. He impugned his home state and the impressionability of its women while bestowing high praise on Boston Unitarians, although they were often Federalist in politics.

During Jefferson's last years, a new object of fear, emanating from New England Federalist preacher Jedidiah Morse, arose. Morse invited Jefferson to join an organization he had created, the Society for the Civilization and Improvement of the Indian Tribes, to consist of most governmental officials including the vice-president, former presidents, and the members of Congress, and of which all the clergy in the United States would be members. Under the guise of this mammoth "voluntary society" to "civilize" the American Indians, Jefferson feared that Morse planned to eventually overthrow the United States government. He was not flattered when Morse offered him membership as a former chief executive. Though politely rejecting Morse's offer, he bluntly reminded him that such a gigantic organization would potentially constitute an *imperium in imperio* that could compete for power with the legitimate national government elected by the people. He unhesitatingly pointed out to Morse "that the clergy will constitute nineteen twentieths of this association, and, by the law of the majority," would monopolize the organization. Jefferson considered Morse's group a potentially revolutionary organization, perversely similar to the conventions and committees of public safety that the thirteen colonies had utilized to resist Great Britain early in the American Revolution. But while extralegal modes of government were necessary then, there was no need for such an extra-governmental institution now, when the people were happy under their elected leaders. He also compared the potential dangers of the society with the Jacobin societies of France during the French Revolution, whose members, despite their good intentions, ended up taking over the National Convention and instituting the totalitarian Reign of Terror.[7]

Doubtful that such a large organization would confine its mission to advising the government on relations with Native Americans, Jefferson suspected that Morse and his colleagues intended to attempt to secure New England's "Presbyterian" hegemony in government and society through such institutions. He kept these thoughts hidden from Morse (who probably surmised what Jefferson felt), but voiced his warnings to Madison and Monroe, who also feared Morse's motives. As Jefferson wrote Madison, stating his fear of Morse's plan, "I acknolege the expediency, for revolutionary purposes, of general associations, coextensive with the nation. But where, as in our case, no abuses call for revolution, voluntary associations so extensive as to grapple with & controul the government, should such be or become their purpose, are dangerous machines, and should be frowned down in every regulated government."[8]

When President Monroe asked Jefferson for permission to make the letter to Morse public, Jefferson was cautious. He said he did not want Morse to think he was throwing down the "gauntlet" to him in the press, because, as an old retired statesman, he "should certainly prove a recreant knight, and never meet him in that field." However, amply aware of the Society's potential dangers, Jefferson told Monroe, "Do in this whatever you please. I abandon the letter to any good it may answer."[9] Once more Jefferson had reason to fear the power of New England reaction. However, he did not frame the threat as a sectional one, but rather as an effort by the clergy to gain national power and influence.

Jefferson had hoped that the Massachusetts constitutional convention of 1820–1821, under Adams' guidance (the Convention chose him its president out of politeness, but he refused the offer), would repeal the Congregational church establishment. Alluding to the unlimited freedom of thought he perhaps erroneously ascribed to pagan philosophers, he employed the neologism, "liberalism," in writing to Adams. "The amendments of which we have as yet heard prove the advance of liberalism," he said, "and encourage a hope that the human mind will some day get back the freedom it enjoyed 2000 years ago." Stressing the threat he believed revivalism posed to freedom of thought, he continued, "This country, which has given to the world the example of physical liberty, owes to it that of moral emancipation also. For, as yet, it is but nominal with us. The inquisition of public opinion overwhelms in practice the freedom asserted by the laws in theory."[10] Jefferson's tone was angry. He had expected that the town meeting democracies of New England, where Unitarianism flowered and the people seemed more ready than ever before for freedom, would have made more progress in adopting rational religion. Instead, the Convention did little in this regard, although it managed to pass a liberalized suffrage, extending the vote to all taxpaying adult males.[11]

Contrary to the views of scholars such as Richard K. Matthews, who emphasizes Jefferson's radicalism, or, like Joseph J. Ellis and Conor Cruise O'Brien, portray him as a totalitarian democrat determined to enforce the will of the majority, Jefferson demanded security for the rights of the minority. He was disappointed that the state constitutional convention in Massachusetts in 1820 failed to abolish the Congregational Church's special privileges. (Even Adams, who in the past fervidly defended the Establishment, now demanded greater religious freedom, including the end of blasphemy's status as a felony. He did not go so far as to recommend abolishing the Congregational Church's special privileges.) Jefferson, who apparently had kept up with the Boston convention's activities, criticized its failure to promote religious liberty. Although he recognized Massachusetts' vital contribution to the success of the American Revolution–what he now called "physical liberty"—he regretted that its leaders were not yet prepared to endorse "moral liberty"—religious freedom. And he lamented that the mass of the voters seemed to submit to the will of their social superiors on this issue. As he put it, "the inquisition of public opinion overwhelms in practice the freedom asserted by the laws in theory."[12]

Jefferson's ambivalent, love-hate relationship with New England was especially evident after he retired from political life. In the immortal correspondence of their twilight years, appositely enough, he occasionally wrote to John Adams regarding his friend's native region. He praised the disestablishment of Connecticut's "popedom" after its Congregational Church was overthrown in 1817–1818, fifteen years before that happened in Massachusetts. He also confided to Adams his conviction that the town meeting, "ward" form of government would suit Great Britain, once its long-anticipated republican revolution, which Jefferson had fruitlessly predicted for over twenty years, occurred.[13] His long-distance friendship with Adams was stronger, and dealt with more critical issues, than his in-person contacts with him when they served together in Philadelphia, Adams as president and Jefferson as vice-president. At that time, they were competitors for power and the nation's highest office. In their last years, they unburdened themselves on the most vital matters, including the all-important question of slavery. That issue erupted with all its force in 1820, over Missouri's entry into the Union.

21

Jefferson, the Missouri Compromise Crisis and the University of Virginia

During the period of the Embargo Act and the War of 1812, Jefferson uncomfortably witnessed New Englanders' demand that the national government put their interests, especially merchants' involvement in the carrying trade, ahead of national honor and the long-term public good. The New England states' resistance to embargoes and trade restriction laws before the War of 1812 and to the U.S. government's request for military and economic assistance during the conflict, climaxed by the Hartford Convention, hardly reassured him of its citizens' national feeling. Although Jefferson was painfully aware that New England had successfully defied the rest of the nation, he chose to forgive its near-treason in the interest of future harmony and national unity. A few years after the war ended, he was even more shocked by "a momentous question, [which], like a fire bell in the night, awakened and filled me with terror."[1] This was the congressional and national debate over slavery, whose synecdoche was the conflict over admitting Missouri to the Union as a slave state in 1820.

Although the New England states were not in the forefront of this crisis, in some of their leaders' participation in opposing slavery in the Louisiana Purchase he detected the resurgence of New England's rejection of his concept of the national interest. In general, he, like other aging Democratic leaders, including Madison and Monroe, interpreted the congressional controversy over admitting Missouri to the Union as a reckless attempt by the Federalist Party to resurrect itself by emphasizing the divisive moral question of outlawing slavery in those territories the Jefferson Administration acquired in 1803. One "slave" state derived from the purchase had already been admitted, Louisiana itself. Federalists in Congress had not seriously opposed the entry of Alabama (split-off from Georgia in 1798) into the Union as a "slave" state in 1818. However, the incoming state of Missouri was a "Border State" to which relatively few slaveholders had moved. Perhaps for this reason a freshman Republican congressman from New York, James Tallmadge, fortuitously proposed in 1819 that Congress refuse Missouri entry as a state unless it agreed to gradually abolish slavery, by not allowing any new slaves into the state and emancipating the slaves already there when they reached the age of twenty-five.[2]

For Jefferson and many others, especially in the South, the idea that Congress could legislate on slavery in a territory like Missouri, whose population was sufficient to apply for admission as a state, and had written a state constitution (unlike the raw territories of the

Old Northwest, in which Congress had prohibited slavery in 1787) brought up an explosive issue. It also encroached on the vital principle of states' rights in every state in the Union. Desiring to impress the relevance of this point of view for New England on Massachusetts congressman John Holmes, Jefferson demonstrated his familiarity with the local politics of the region. He used the example of the institution of freemanship prevalent in Massachusetts, Connecticut, and Rhode Island towns since colonial times. As Jefferson euphemistically put it in his famous letter to Holmes, after the issue of Missouri's admission was settled by allowing its entry into the Union as a slave state while Maine came in as a "free" state, and the rest of the Louisiana Purchase north of Missouri was barred to slavery:

> Of one thing I am certain, that as the passage of slaves from one State to another, would not make a slave of a single human being who would not be so without it, so their diffusion over a greater surface would make them individually happier, and proportionally facilitate the accomplishment of their emancipation, by dividing the burthen on a greater number of coadjutors. An abstinence too, from this act of power [congressional power to prohibit slavery in nascent states], would remove the jealousy excited by the undertaking of Congress to regulate the condition of the different descriptions of men composing a State. This certainly is the exclusive right of every State, which nothing in the constitution has taken from them and given to the General Government. Could Congress, for example, say, that the non-freemen of Connecticut shall be freemen, or that they shall not emigrate into any other State?[3]

Possibly aware of Holmes' enlightened racial attitudes—as a delegate to Maine's constitutional convention in 1819, he advocated free black suffrage in the new state—Jefferson clarified his lifelong opposition to slavery. Jefferson objected to Congress' risking the existence of the American republic by raising the sensitive issue (for Southerners) of the immorality of slavery and prohibiting slavery in a new state without taking action to permanently abolish the odious institution. In that sense, he metaphorically considered the Missouri Compromise "a reprieve only, not a final sentence." As he passionately explained to Holmes, despite the existence of the line 36°30' temporarily demarcating free and slave states, the Union's survival would face similar challenges whenever a new state applied for admission if the slavery issue was raised. "A geographical line," he warned, "coinciding with a marked principle, moral and political, once conceived and held up to the angry passions of men, will never be obliterated; and every new irritation will mark it deeper and deeper." After thus clairvoyantly predicting the Dred Scott decision and the Civil War, Jefferson went on to insist that he favored the abolition of slavery, followed by the freed slaves' exile from the United States. Reiterating views he had first publicized during the 1780s in Notes on the State of Virginia, he declared, "I can say, with conscious truth, that there is not a man on earth who would sacrifice more than I would to relieve us from this heavy reproach [slavery], in any practicable way. The cession of that kind of property, for so it [the slave] is misnamed, is a bagatelle which would not cost me a second thought, if, in that way, a general emancipation and expatriation could be effected; and with due sacrifices, I think it might be."[4]

Stressing his disappointment that Congress had not attempted to find a more lasting solution to the blight of slavery, Jefferson famously wrote, "But as it is, we have the wolf by the ear, and we can neither hold him, nor safely let him go. Justice is in one scale, and self-preservation in the other." He claimed to be convinced by Holmes' argument that "diffusion" of the Upper South's surplus slaves to the west would not ultimately increase the number of slaves in the country. He suggested that, at least theoretically, westward migration would improve their living conditions, by allowing masters who could not afford to take care of them to sell them to others. In addition, he objected to Congress' expanding its powers to include the condition of individuals within a state, even if they were only slaves. Congress might eventually employ such reasoning to encroach on the Bill of Rights, as the Sedition Act of 1798 had done. He considered the lower house of Congress irresponsible for outlawing slavery in new states like Missouri, where it was a legal and established institution when it was a European colony and at the time France sold the territory. Indeed, the Louisiana Purchase treaty had guaranteed slaveholders their property, albeit slaves were not numerous in Missouri.

Jefferson preferred that Congress pursue the mature path of abolishing slavery *in toto*, rather than adopt half-baked measures whose defects would become evident in the future. For this reason, he considered the present generation of politicians inept, with the exception of Holmes and a few others who put the Union ahead of sectionally divisive measures like prohibiting slavery in the territories. "The generation of 1776" had meaninglessly sacrificed itself "to acquire self-government and happiness to their country," Jefferson lamented, when by such measures as outlawing slavery in slaveholding territories, it "is to be thrown away by the unwise and unworthy passions of their sons," who were more interested in partisan advantage than in permanently abolishing slavery. Jefferson supported the Missouri Compromise as "hush[ing] for the moment" the explosive issue of slavery. However, he feared that under the guise of antislavery principles, partisan rivals would break up the republic without ending slavery in the "slave states." The latter, he argued, would be more likely to abolish slavery within a North-South Union than in an independent Southern Confederacy outside it. Alluding to antislavery theorists and politicians who provoked disunion without devising constructive abolition proposals, Jefferson insisted: "If they would but dispassionately weigh the blessings they will throw away, against an abstract principle [abolition of slavery] more likely to be effected by union than by scission, they would pause before they would perpetrate this act of suicide on themselves, and of treason against the hopes of the world."[5]

Jefferson emphasized that the "abstract principle" of abolition would not achieve realization through interminable, violent debates over slavery in the territories comprised in the Louisiana Purchase. On the contrary, he believed, such debates would probably so exacerbate relations between North and South that secession and probable civil war would ensue. Jefferson regarded Congress's initial conduct as precipitating the "suicide" of the United States as a single nation, dashing the hopes of oppressed peoples throughout the Atlantic World that revolution against their monarchical oppressors would lead them to happy independence and self-government. He welcomed Holmes as his nationalist ally in seeking to perpetuate the republic's wholeness: "To yourself, as the faithful advocate of the Union, I tender the offering of my high esteem and respect."[6]

At the outset of the Missouri controversy in February 1819, when Tallmadge introduced his amendment to the Missouri statehood Enabling Bill to prohibit slavery there after newborn slaves reached the age of twenty-five, he acted alone.[7] Ostensibly, New York and New England Federalists decided to latch onto the issue of slavery, revived by a Jeffersonian congressman, as their only hope of regaining political power. Antislavery New York and Pennsylvania Republicans joined them. Imbued with cynicism about the Federalists since the 1790s, and even more so since their disloyalty during the Embargo and War of 1812, Jefferson automatically viewed the Missouri controversy when it appeared in 1820 as constituting a similar Federalist challenge to national unity motivated by political opportunism. In the case of the Republican

Tallmadge, there was some ground for Jefferson's mistrust, although he never mentioned him by name. Tallmadge became an ally of the renegade Republican, New York governor Dewitt Clinton, and his brother married a member of the Clinton family. Perhaps thinking he had more of a future in state politics, Tallmadge served only one term in Congress, from June 6, 1817, until March 3, 1819. He declined renomination. Clintonians nominated him for the New York state senate in 1819. During the campaign, Tallmadge's supporters depicted him as a hero who dared defy the "Southern aristocrats," although the office of state senator had little bearing on national issues. Although Tallmadge campaigned for black votes and courted the antislavery Quakers and the New York Manumission Society, he lost the election. The Tammany Democrats, also known as the "Bucktails" and later the "Albany Regency," led by Martin Van Buren, successfully opposed him.[8]

Tallmadge did not prove to be much of an antislavery idealist. After his defeat, he abandoned the Clintonians, since Clinton had not offered him a good patronage job, and joined the Tammany Democrats. Elected to the state assembly in 1824, he appeased Van Buren by voting to remove Clinton as a director of the Erie Canal Commission, a petty act that led the state's voters to reelect Clinton governor. Ironically, Clintonians led by Thurlow Weed, a former admirer of Tallmadge, thwarted Tallmadge's nomination as governor, but agreed that he could stand for lieutenant governor as Clinton's running mate.[9]

In early 1820, Tallmadge's Amendments to the Missouri enabling bill seemed popular in New York. The state legislature voted 117 to 4 in favor of instructing its congressmen to oppose Missouri's admission into the Union as a "slave state." Clinton gained the votes of many free blacks by opposing slavery in Missouri. In 1820, he was reelected governor, defeating Vice-President Tompkins.[10] Like Clinton, who is remembered more for the Erie Canal than for being a Great Emancipator, Tallmadge was not single-mindedly devoted to the cause of emancipation. In 1821, as a delegate to New York State's constitutional convention, Tallmadge was silent when the Van Burenites removed the $250 freehold requirement ("100 pound freehold") for white voters for governor and state senators while retaining it for blacks. The state convention enacted virtually universal white male suffrage, granting the vote to white males who resided in the state for a year, irrespective of wealth or tax payments (if they were exempt from taxes by law). However, Tallmadge did make an antislavery speech at the Convention. He proposed the liberalization of the gradual emancipation laws passed in 1799 and 1817. He thought that the law should be changed to free all slaves immediately, except for minors and those born after July 4, 1799, who would still have to wait until July 4, 1827. His proposal was defeated.[11]

New York Federalists took the lead, engaging in antislavery polemics under the leadership of Rufus King and DeWitt Clinton to recoup their political losses. New England Federalists and Massachusetts Republicans also opposed Missouri's admission to the Union as a slave state. This controversy ended with the Missouri Compromise, shepherded through Congress by Jefferson's protégé President James Monroe. Nominal Democratic-Republican congressmen like Arthur Livermore of New Hampshire supported the Tallmadge Amendment. In 1800, as a New Hampshire presidential elector, Livermore voted for Adams. However, he was elected as a nominal Republican to the Fifteenth and Sixteenth Congresses (March 4, 1817–March 3, 1821) He lost his bid for re-election in 1822, but returned to Congress as an Adams-Clay Republican in the Eighteenth Congress.

Jefferson could not blame Massachusetts or Connecticut for the imbroglio. Tallmadge a Jeffersonian Republican congressman from New York and early protégé of former New York Governor and current Vice President Daniel Tompkins, introduced the two amendments to the Missouri enabling bill. They barred Missouri from statehood unless its territorial legislature agreed to prohibit the entry of slaves in the future and provide for the emancipation of all slaves born there when they reached the age of twenty-five. Thus, Tallmadge's Amendments, which only concerned Missouri, were actually less antislavery than the Missouri Compromise that replaced it, which prohibited slavery throughout the Louisiana Territory except for the states of Missouri and Arkansas. Although the textbooks emphasize that under the Missouri Compromise, Maine entered the Union as a "free" state, while Missouri entered it with slavery, this was actually less important than the other portions of the Compromise. Moreover, Maine entered the Union immediately after the "compromise," on March 15, 1820, while Missouri only obtained permission to apply for admission once its constitutional convention completed a constitution for the state. Missouri did not enter the Union until August 10, 1821, following a second battle over Missouri's prohibiting the entry of free blacks in which Congress nearly reneged on the first bargain allowing Missouri into the Union. In both cases, Jeffersonian Republicans, Kentucky Representative Henry Clay, along with Illinois senator Jesse B. Thomas (who devised the 36°30' compromise), played decisive roles in defusing a crisis that might have led to civil war.[12] After briefly serving as lieutenant governor, Tallmadge participated in various public causes. He was one of the founders of present-day New York University, serving on its presidential council from 1834 to 1846. He became a Whig ideologue and traveled to Europe promoting the protective tariff, modernization, and economic development as far east as Russia.

· · · · ·

It was appropriate that Jefferson make his first extended comments on the Missouri crisis to his oldest confidant, a New Englander, John Adams. At diverse times, Adams had been his firm friend and bitter opponent. Despite having recently regarded Massachusetts as the prime fomenter of disunion, Jefferson could now spread the blame for the republic's instability among representatives of other Northern states, inspired by Tallmadge, a New York Democratic-Republican congressman. Adams was the first correspondent to bring up the topic of Missouri with Jefferson, although at first the New Englander did not seem to think the issue of slavery divisive or important. When he wrote Jefferson in November 1819, he merely jumbled it together with a bunch of other national issues. "Congress are about to assemble and the Clouds look Black and thick, Assembling from all points, threatening thunder and Lightning," he wrote with feigned melodrama. "The Spanish Treaty [to purchase Florida], the Missouri Slavery, the encouragement of Manufactures Act, the plague of Banks, perhaps even the Monument for Washington," but especially "the bustle of Caucuses" to decide nominees for president and vice-president, would "produce an effervescence."[13]

Perhaps because as a Southerner he knew the explosiveness of the issue of slavery for his section, Jefferson took the Missouri crisis more seriously than Adams did. He considered the outcome of Missouri's admission to the Union decisive for the United States' continuation as a republic. At least temporarily, he accepted slavery as a concomitant of republicanism. He regarded the "Missouri question," the issue of whether Congress had the right to exclude slavery from states cut from the Louisiana Purchase, as the most significant the country had yet faced. In his opinion, Missouri, which was applying for admission to the Union and whose territorial legislature had written a state constitution, was no longer a fledgling territory, unlike the Northern and Southern territories bordering the Ohio River that he recommended closing to slavery in 1784. He expected Missouri to reject admission to the Union if it had to give up slavery; it would instead choose to become a separate country. He expressed his fears to Adams, responding more quickly than usual after receiving his letter. After acknowledging the country's many problems, including an economic depression partly caused by the Bank of the United States' unpredictable behavior and frauds committed by some of its officers; and President Monroe's frustration in his negotiations to purchase Florida from Spain, he concluded: "The banks, bankrupt law, manufactures, Spanish treaty, are nothing. These are occurrences which, like waves in a storm, will pass under the ship. But the Missouri question is a breaker on which we lose the Missouri country by revolt, and what more, God only knows."[14]

Thus, Jefferson thought that Missouri would leave the Union ("revolt") and become an independent country if Congress refused to admit it as a slave state. Bitter arguments between the North and South over Missouri's status and the general issue of slavery would inevitably follow, possibly ending in the breakup of the Union. "From the battle of Bunker's hill to the treaty of Paris, we never had so ominous a question," he warned.[15]

Despite his venerability, Adams lacked political influence even in Massachusetts. Jefferson may nonetheless have hoped to rouse him to action to restrain King and other Federalist leaders, such as Massachusetts Congressman Joshua Cushman, who wanted to bar slavery from the Louisiana Purchase. Reflecting on his old age and nearness to death, as he often did at this time, Jefferson morosely assured Adams, "It [the Missouri crisis] even damps the joy with which I hear of your high health, and welcomes to me the consequences of my want of it. I thank God that I shall not live to witness its issue."[16]

Feeling a need to express his anxiety over the Missouri crisis to the chief executive, his old friend James Monroe, Jefferson wrote him in March 1820. At the same time, he requested Monroe to find a government job for a New England Republican, Christopher Ellery of Rhode Island. Ellery (1768–1840) joined the Republican Party in opposition to the Federalists in a state where they long held power. He was a U.S. senator from 1801 to 1805. After Ellery's defeat for re-election to the Senate, Jefferson appointed him Commissioner of Loans (the job of paying public creditors under the funding act of 1790) for Providence in 1806. Ellery achieved notoriety when South Carolina Federalist leader John Rutledge, Jr., as he described in his pamphlet *A Defence Against Calumny; or Haman, in the Shape of Christopher Ellery* (1803) called him a scoundrel, allegedly slapped him around and challenged him to a duel, from which, Rutledge wrote, he had reportedly abstained like a coward. Jefferson was aware that Rutledge, who had been Jefferson's protégé as a youth, had become one of the most fanatical Federalists. Jefferson therefore considered Ellery worthy of government patronage. However, Jefferson was cautious about asking Monroe for favors; and his later request, in 1824 that Monroe appoint his friend Bernard Peyton postmaster at Richmond was indeed ignored, leading Jefferson to feel that his friendship with Monroe was over. Nevertheless, in asking Monroe's assistance for Ellery, Jefferson declared, "I am often placed under the dilemma of either alienating my old friends, or of giving you the trouble of reading a letter, and I have had too many proofs of your friendship not to know you will take that trouble to save me from so painful an alternative."[17]

Since Ellery was not a close friend, Jefferson professed relative indifference to the outcome. Acknowledging that Monroe, like all presidents, faced numerous "difficulties," political and personal, in choosing appointees, he continued, "after giving my testimony, I pay no attention to the result, leaving that to yourself who alone have a view of the whole ground." Still, his support for Ellery was evident. He wrote, "Christopher Ellery ... was one of the most active of our friends in R.I. in the times of our trials whether our government should be republican in practice as well as profession. He came into the Senate when I came in to the administration and assisted in giving us a majority in that body, nor was there a more zealous or active one in it. He is a good republican, a good man and of good understanding."[18] Monroe gratified Jefferson's wishes by appointing Ellery collector of customs at Newport, a job he held until 1834.

If Jefferson was reading the newspapers where he might have found the text of King's speeches in the Senate on slavery in Missouri, he would have been shocked to discover that King justified the exclusion of slavery on the basis of states' rights, rather than national power. King argued that slavery made it more difficult for the country to defend itself against foreign aggression and domestic revolts. (Perhaps he remembered that antislavery delegates to the great Constitutional Convention in 1787, which he attended, stressed that the slave states imposed an unnecessary burden on the rest of the Union by making a national standing army necessary to repress the inevitable slave uprisings.) King did not seem chagrined by the injustice of slavery. With regard to Missouri, he argued that the perpetuation of slavery in the new states and future territorial acquisitions would require the national government to claim additional powers to regulate the institution. The unrestrained exercise of such powers might precipitate federal encroachments on the rights of all states, and "may prove fatal to the public liberties." King's legalistic stance is not surprising. He had not opposed slavery in 1790 as a senator in the First Congress, when the Quakers presented antislavery petitions, nor at the Philadelphia Convention itself.[19]

Adams probably intended to cheer up his distraught friend. Less nationalistic than Jefferson, he had never been as interested in territorial expansion, or even in increasing the country's military and naval strength, as Jefferson had been, even during the 1780s. In old age, Adams resigned himself to the Union's mortality: its disintegration, whether as a result of the slavery issue, the ambitions of domestic demagogues, or some other reason. In writing to Jefferson at this time, Adams cared little whether Missouri entered the Union as a free or slave state. He preferred to discourse (perhaps allegorically) on the decline and fall of the Roman Empire. While the Northern-dominated House of Representatives and the Southern-controlled Senate fought over Missouri's fate, Adams was comparatively unperturbed. He accepted the possibility of the Union's breakup over the issue. "The Missouri question, I hope, will follow the other waves under the ship, and do no harm," he wrote, taking up Jefferson's earlier nautical metaphor. "I know it is high treason to express a doubt of the perpetual duration of our vast American Empire and our free Institution[s]," he said, assuring Jefferson he desired an "everlasting" republic. "But I am sometimes Cassandra enough to dream that another Hamilton, another Burr might rend this mighty Fabric in twain, or, perhaps, into a leash, and a few more choice Spirits of the same stamp might produce as many Nations in North America as there are in Europe."[20] Adams expected that unscrupulous power-brokers ready to sell out to European governments, or Napoleonic military adventurers would one day overthrow the American republic.

It was difficult for Jefferson to stomach such an idea. He did not reply to Adams' blithe acceptance of disunion. Perhaps sensing that he had gone too far after Jefferson ceased writing to him for several months, Adams mustered up more nationalist zeal in a letter in February 1820, which was mainly concerned with his "prejudice against ... Metaphysics" and his disagreements with Jefferson on the likelihood of human progress, a topic on which Jefferson was generally optimistic. "I wish the Missouri question may not sett too narrow limits to the Power and Respectability of the United States," he wrote. "Yet I hope some good natural way or other will be found out to untie this very intricate knot."[21] He seemed ready to accept Missouri with slavery for the sake of the Union; or perhaps for the sake of Jefferson's epistolary friendship.

When Jefferson first learned in detail that New York Republicans had joined Northern Federalists in demanding the prohibition of slavery in the Louisiana Purchase, he viewed it as the harbinger of civil war over an institution that a large and influential Southern minority regarded as vital to their interests. In February 1820, he wrote his congressional representative, Hugh Nelson, who had told him what was happening, "I thank you for your information on the progress & prospects of the Missouri question. It is the most portentous one which ever yet threatened our Union. In the gloomiest moment of the revolutionary war I never had any apprehensions equal to what I feel from this source."[22]

He was relieved by the peaceful congressional settlement that permitted slavery in Missouri but prohibited it throughout most of the rest of the Louisiana Purchase, a slap in the face to Southern slavery. But Jefferson opposed slavery and wanted it abolished in any case, so this was not a source of discontent for him. However, he doubted that the Compromise would endure; and predicted that similar controversies would arise whenever a slaveholding group petitioned for admission to enter the Union along with their bondspersons. The result would be the breakup of the Union into Northern and Southern confederacies. As he wrote Nelson in March, immediately after he heard that a compromise had passed Congress, "I thank you, dear Sir, for the information in your favor of the 4th inst. of the settlement, *for the present*, of the Missouri question. I am so compleatly [sic] withdrawn from all attention to public matters that nothing less could arouse me than the definition of a geographical line, which on an abstract principle is to become the line of separation of these states, and to render desperate the hope that man can ever enjoy the two blessings of peace & self government. The question sleeps for the moment, but is not dead."[23]

Despite his dire prediction that the Union would fall apart over the issue of human bondage, Jefferson maintained a sense of humor that suggested that he was more optimistic about the republic's survival than these words suggest. He believed that the Union was rooted in the economic self-interest of its member states, which would transcend the dispute over slavery. Thus, he could at least temporarily view with amusement the bitter controversies in Congress over the tariff, internal improvements, and banks, now that the most critical source of division, slavery, had been peacefully resolved. Aware that North and South, Massachusetts, and Virginia, were united in pursuing self-interest, Jefferson was prepared for the transition of his countrymen's *mentalité* from "classical republicanism" to "liberalism," as modern historians call it. Despite his anxiety over Missouri, he concluded his February 1820 letter to Nelson on a strangely upbeat note: "I observe you are loaded with petitions from the Manufacturing, commercial & agricultural interests, each praying you to sacrifice the others to them. This proves the egotism of the whole, and happily balances their cannibal appetite[s] to eat one another. The most perfect confidence in the wisdom of Congress leaves me without a fear of the result." Ending with the bizarre theme, "Our cannibals, ourselves," Jefferson optimistically hoped that the self-interested diversity of Americans might be a source of the republic's redemption.[24]

Jefferson did not hide from John Holmes the truth that the peace of his last years was shattered by the congressional battle over slavery in Missouri. Holmes represented the Massachusetts frontier district that would become the "free" state of Maine in 1820, shortly before Missouri entered the Union as a slave state, as part of a bargain between sections. Jefferson praised Massachusetts' congressmen—Maine's Democratic representative Mark Langdon Hill and former Federalists Holmes of Maine and Jonathan Mason of Boston—who supported the Missouri Compromises (1819–1821) permitting slavery in the new state. He charged that New York Federalists, led by Senator Rufus King and Governor De Witt Clinton, fomented sectional hostility by demanding slavery's prohibition in the Louisiana Purchase. When the crisis ended with Maine's admission as a "free" state to balance Missouri's entry with slavery, Jefferson congratulated Hill on "the sleep of the Missouri question," and applauded the election of pro–Missouri Democrat William King (Rufus's half-brother) as Maine's first governor. Jefferson insisted that the "laws of nature" limited slavery's expansion. Concluding that "both parties" opposed slavery as a "hideous evil," he predicted that "duty and interest" would eventually lead to "a practicable process of cure." He continued to distrust New York "Federalists." He feared they would foment "eternal discord" in their quest for political gain by "seducing" antislavery Democrats. In October 1820, expressing his nationalism, he predicted that any break-up of the Union would be temporary. The voters, if not Congress, would demand a "convention" to restore the Union, reconciling the sections "like quarrelling lovers to renewed embraces, and increased affections." He appreciated the role played by the three Massachusetts congressmen, whose vote to admit Missouri as a slave state had provided the margin of victory for preserving the Union.[25]

· · · · ·

Torn by ambivalence over the issue of slavery, Jefferson knew that in maintaining this immoral and benighted labor system the South stigmatized republican government. Yet he was also painfully aware that he and many other Southerners depended on slave labor and feared the social and economic consequences of immediate emancipation. He was especially alarmed by numerous threats of secession during the Missouri debates, hurled by New England antislavery politicians and Virginia proslavery legislators alike. Both groups were dissatisfied with the Missouri Compromise's outcome in terms of future restriction of slavery. Jefferson never manifested opposition to prohibiting slavery in the Louisiana Purchase for those parts of the region that had only entered the territorial stage, just as in Congress he had proposed to outlaw slavery south of the Ohio River in the defeated Ordinance of 1784, which would have made Kentucky and Tennessee "free" states. However, he opposed prohibiting it in Missouri because the state constitution had already validated it, and hundreds of slaveholders had moved there.[26] Despite his initial opposition to prohibiting slavery in the Louisiana Purchase (in which President Monroe and Madison agreed with him, although Monroe abandoned his personal biases and threw his support behind the compromise), Jefferson accepted the agreement because he considered it necessary to preserve the Union.[27]

Later, he explained his views to Richard Rush, U.S. minister to Great Britain, son of his old friend Benjamin Rush. Informing him of current events at home, he reminded him, "The boisterous sea of liberty is never without a wave." He clearly perceived that Northerners and Southerners held bitterly opposed perspectives on slavery expansion, even though both sections theoretically abhorred it as "a hideous evil." Because of their intimate involvement with slavery, Southerners "more sorely felt and sincerely deplored" the institution, Jefferson argued, but they were more aware of "the difficulty of the cure." Jefferson convolutedly warned that the New England Federalists were defeating their own antislavery purposes, because, by blocking the expansion of slavery into new areas of the west and south, they "prohibit[ed] willing States from sharing the evil." According to Jefferson, if slavery remained bottled up, thereby increasing the number of slaves in the states where it already existed, their inhabitants would become more and more desperately dependent on it, and would inevitably oppose "its final eradication."[28] However, Jefferson was confident that a permanent settlement would be reached and the Union would be preserved. Otherwise, both the current generation of Americans and posterity would irreparably suffer. Viewing both the Southern Republican and Northern Federalist parties as too hotheaded, he hoped they would become more cooperative and less preoccupied with "visionary fears"; it was more important that each sincerely opposed slavery and that "the duty and interest of both is to concur also in divining a practicable process of cure." Elaborating a worst-case scenario, Jefferson argued that even if irresponsible leaders precipitated a "separation" of the Union, the "schism" would last only a few years. Bitter experience would convince North and South of their symbiotic interdependence, and they would reunite "like quarrelling lovers to renewed embraces, and increased affections." As Jefferson had asserted since the early 1790s, the Union functioned best as an indissoluble extended republic. Returning to his prognostications, he said, "The experiment of separation would soon prove to both that they had mutually miscalculated their best interests."[29]

As was often the case when he compared the weak-kneed Unionism and republicanism of New England's politicians with its citizenry's more devout nationalism, he professed greater confidence in the good sense and patriotism of the common people than of their leaders. Even if Congress "in a passion" voted to dissolve the Union, he reiterated, their "soberer" constituents "would call a convention and cement again the severance attempted by the insanity of their functionaries." Feeling no misgivings about the unconstitutional or "revolutionary" nature of this remedy, Jefferson, who had long ago envisaged a special convention as a last resort to install him in the presidency in 1801, favored direct action by the people to "refresh" (as he notoriously wrote in 1787) their democratic "tree of liberty" in emergencies. In any case, he considered partisans of secession "insane," whether from Massachusetts or Virginia.[30]

For Jefferson, preservation of the Union, inevitable harmony between New England and the South, and the indispensability of the successful republic to world liberation were "moral facts." Although "consoled" by believing that the Union would never permanently split, Jefferson said, "my greatest grief would be for the fatal effect of such an event on the hopes and happiness of the world." To Jefferson, harmony between the sections was the "sacred duty" of American republicanism: "We exist, and are quoted, as standing proofs that a government, so modelled as to rest continually on the will of the whole society, is a practicable government. Were we to break to pieces, it would damp the hopes and the efforts of the good, and give triumph to those of the bad through the whole enslaved world. As members, therefore, of the universal society of mankind, and standing in high and responsible relation with them, it is our sacred duty to suppress passion among ourselves, and not to blast the confidence we have inspired of proof that a government of reason is better than one of force."[31]

But the Missouri question was not over for Jefferson. His dread of disunion revived when antislavery elements in Congress threatened to refuse Missouri admission to the Union unless it expunged from its constitution a prohibition of the entry of free blacks into the state, even though several states already in the Union, among them Virginia, Ohio, and South Carolina, had similar laws.[32] He feared that Missouri, if denied entry into the Union, would become an independent republic. If Congress decided to "force" it into the Union, Missouri might attract sympathetic Southern and western states and undertake a new Midwestern confederacy. As he usually did, Jefferson saw the big picture. He despaired for the future of republican government throughout the world. He wrote his old colleague Gallatin, who observed the results of the restoration of monarchy in France: "Should this scission take place, one of it's [*sic*] most deplorable consequences would be it's discouragement of the efforts of the European nations in the regeneration of their oppressive and Cannibal governments."[33]

Despite his fears that the Eastern states would provoke disunion by their uncompromising attitude on slavery, Jefferson still desired to conciliate New England. He was aware that its people's commitment to democratic-republicanism was shaky, and that they might secede from the Union if they thought their interests were inadequately supported. He considered it essential to preserve the loyalty of the Democratic-Republican stalwarts who had stood with the Party from the beginning of the 1790s, such as his Massachusetts colleagues, Henry Dearborn and Levi Lincoln. After serving in Jefferson's Cabinet, Dearborn and Lincoln continued to represent the Republican Party in their states. With the Missouri crisis still in his thoughts, Jefferson in a letter in August 1821 let Dearborn know that he was always happy to hear from him. Since the Missouri crisis had ended without any state leaving the Union and with Missouri getting its way on retaining slavery and barring the entry of free blacks, Jefferson's anxieties were somewhat eased. He still resented New England Federalists' threats of secession during the Hartford Convention and the Missouri Controversy, especially because they had gained numerous Democratic-Republican antislavery recruits by hypocritically (in his opinion) emphasizing the "moral" question of slavery during the Missouri debates. Jefferson doubted the Federalists were sincere in stressing their antislavery objectives, believing they opportunistically sought to regain political power. At the same time, he acknowledged that their budding alliance with Northern Democratic-Republicans might ultimately take control of the government. In an unusual reversal of attitude, perhaps because he thought that once the Federalists took political power they would no longer stress the extremely divisive issue of slavery, he told Dearborn that he was resigned to such an outcome. "It is indeed of little consequence who governs us, if they sincerely and zealously cherish the principles of union and republicanism," he asserted.[34] If Republicans and Federalists shared power, the Republicans would moderate Federalist tendencies to tarnish "principles of union and republicanism."

Despite the renewal of questions on the Louisiana Purchase's constitutionality precipitated by the debate over Missouri's statehood, Jefferson did not regret that as president he had doubled the nation's territory. Echoing Madison's *Federalist Number 10*, he continued to believe that an "extended republic" that covered a great deal of space and embraced diverse social, ethnic, religious, and economic interests would endure longer than a small republic where only a handful of different interests contested for power. "I still believe that the Western extension of our confederacy will insure its duration, by overruling local factions, which might shake a smaller association," he asserted. "But whatever may be the merit or demerit of that acquisition [the Louisiana Purchase], I divide it with my colleagues, to whose counsels I was indebted for a course of administration, which, notwithstanding this late coalition of clay and brass, will, I hope, continue to receive the approbation of our country."[35]

Jefferson felt no shame at his grandiose act of purchasing Louisiana, especially when writing to Dearborn, who was secretary of war in his Cabinet at the time and who to an extent shared the credit or blame (as Jefferson satirically put it) for one of the greatest accomplishments of an American presidency. (Perhaps imitating John Randolph, who more famously called proslavery Northern congressional representatives "doughfaces," Jefferson now labeled antislavery Northern Democratic-Republicans "clay," molded by the demagogic "brass" of the Northern Federalists).

In the debate over Missouri's admission to the Union, however, Jefferson thought that Northern Federalists were abusing Congressional (national) power for sectional (Northern) purposes, depriving Southerners of their rights as slaveholders within the individual states. After witnessing how close the debate over slavery had come to rupturing the Union, Jefferson became more favorable to a permanent two-party system to dampen serious conflicts. He preferred that it consist of old-style Federalist advocates of "monarchy" and "aristocracy" against "democratic" and egalitarian (at least for white males) Democratic-Republicans, believing it threatened national harmony less than the slavery issue.[36]

During the 1790s, Jefferson hoped that eventually all citizens, including those of New England, would adopt the Republican credo. At that point, he considered the party system a temporary organization. The Republican Party was a temporary vehicle to stamp out the remnants of "monarchism" represented by the Federalists. After the Missouri crisis, he viewed permanent national parties of "aristocrats" versus "democrats" as positive forces that would mute sectional hatreds and prevent them from fracturing the nation, as they threatened to do over slavery. He preferred the disputes over "monarchy" versus "republicanism," which as late as his memoirs of the political warfare of the 1790s, written in 1818 and posthumously titled the *Anas*, he considered threats to the republic's survival. However, he considered these disputes less dangerous than the sectional animosities over slavery exposed in the Missouri crisis.[37]

Jefferson revealed his evolving points of view to his old friend William Short. In a letter in April 1820, mainly concerning religion, he claimed that because of the Missouri crisis he was far more anxious about sectional disputes over slavery than he had been regarding the Federalist/Republican conflict over the powers of the national government during the 1790s. Although claiming to have lost interest in politics, he confessed that the slavery question revived his fears for the Union's survival. "Although I had laid down as a law to myself, never to write, talk or even think of politics," he wrote exaggeratedly, "to know nothing of public affairs, and therefore had ceased to read newspapers, yet the Missouri question aroused and filled me with alarm." He now minimized the previous dichotomy between Federalists and Republicans, which when it confronted him in the form of Hamiltonian policies had actually caused him extreme dread. "The old schism of federal and republican threatened nothing because it existed in every State," he reminisced, "and united them together by the fraternism of party."[38] Thus, Jefferson asserted, before the slavery issue made party divisions sectional rather than national the presence of Federalists and Republicans in every state, no matter whether they composed the majority or the minority, left sectional conciliations in place. The two conflicting parties had more or less balanced each other out.

More ominously, he viewed the current struggle over slavery as squarely framed as an inherently irreconcilable contest between North and South. As he convolutedly put it, "The coincidence of a marked principle, moral and political, with a geographical line, once conceived, I feared would never more be obliterated from the mind; that it would be recurring on every occasion and renewing irritations, until it would kindle such mutual and mortal hatred, as to render separation preferable to eternal discord." The bitterness of the conflict over slavery, he implied, would lead either to a peaceful dissolution of the Union or interminable civil wars ("eternal discord") between separate Northern and Southern nation-states. Averring his conviction that an indissoluble Union (at least of the original thirteen states) was meant to last, he lamented, "I have been among the most sanguine in believing that our Union would be of long duration. I now doubt it much, and see the event at no great distance, and the direct consequence of this question." He perceived a future separation of the Union between North and South, in which the Midwestern states, because of their reliance on the Mississippi River for the shipment of their goods, would join the Southern "slave" states rather than the "free" states. The division would not rest "by the line which has been so confidently counted on [the 36°30' of the Missouri Compromise]; the laws of nature control this; but by the Potomac, Ohio, and Missouri, or more probably the Mississippi upwards to our [Virginia's] Northern boundary."[39]

Bitter over what he foresaw as the eventual implosion of a united federal republic, he preferred to die before it occurred. "My only comfort and confidence is, that I shall not live to see this; and I envy not the present generation the glory of throwing away the fruits of their fathers' sacrifices of life and fortune, and of rendering desperate the experiment which was to decide ultimately whether man is capable of self-government," he opined. He charged that future generations would be guilty of betraying the experiment in self-government if they failed to abolish slavery peacefully. As he put it, "This treason against human hope, will signalize their epoch in future history, as the counterpart of the medal of their predecessors."[40] Jefferson was temporarily pacified after the Missouri crisis was resolved, although he expected that a similar struggle would erupt the next time a "slave" state requested admission to the Union.

Surprisingly, several scholars ascribe proslavery and fiercely pro–Southern views to Jefferson during the Missouri Crisis, distorting his generally nationalist attitude on the issue. Even during the 1950s, before the currently dominant anti–Jefferson historiography gained sway, Southern-based historians like Glover Moore and Charles H. Moffat demonized Jefferson as a states' righter, virtually a forerunner of the "fire-eaters" of the 1850s. In his standard work, *The Missouri Controversy*, Moore depicted Jefferson as a pro–Southern fanatic who created the University of Virginia because he feared that Southern students who went to Northern colleges would learn to hate slavery and the South. Moore overlooked the obvious: that Jefferson had been agitating for the university for nearly a decade before the Missouri crisis. (On the other hand, Jefferson probably understood that he might be able to gain funding for the university more easily if he appealed to state legislators' fear of Northern attacks on slavery.) According to Moore, who relies somewhat on an earlier article by Moffat in *West*

Virginia History, in 1822 Jefferson boasted that he had received letters from people in nearly every state south of the Potomac stating that they looked forward to the opening of the university as an alternative to sending their sons to Northern institutions.[41] In Moore's summation, Jefferson, Madison, John Randolph, and Monroe all reacted as Southern states' righters to the Missouri crisis, and there is little reason to think they would have adopted a more high-minded outlook on the eve of Civil War in 1860 had they been alive.[42]

Ostensibly, Jefferson had developed a great hatred for Harvard College, just at the time that he was directing French merchants to send their wine there and was trying to recruit Ticknor to his Virginia faculty. In 1821, months after the Missouri controversy had been settled, he complained to Joseph C. Cabell, a Virginia state senator and the strongest legislative supporter of the University, that even with a $60,000 grant from the legislature, the college would only be able to pay six professors, while Harvard would lord it over them "with her twenty professors." He emphasized the threat to proslavery sentiment if Virginia students who went to Northern institutions became abolitionists. As he put it, "How many of our youths she [Harvard] now has, learning the lessons of Anti-Missourianism, I know not; but a gentleman lately from Princeton, told me he saw there a list of the students at that place, and that more than half were Virginians. These will return home, no doubt, deeply impressed with the sacred principles of our holy [Northern congressional] alliance of [slavery] Restrictionists."[43] It seems likely that Jefferson was impelled more by a desire for increased funding for his University than by dread of Harvard and Princeton's alleged abolitionism, for which they had no reputation at this time. Moreover, the "restrictionists" were now quiet, since they had gotten most of what they wanted by the Missouri Compromise's prohibition of slavery in the territories north of 36°30'.

A year later, Jefferson again found himself defending requests for more money from the legislature for his university and denying predictions that it would be a financial and educational fiasco. Contradicting reports that only a hundred students had shown an interest in admission, Jefferson claimed more applicants than that had appeared from Virginia alone, which "will immediately furnish far beyond that number." Seeking increased state support, Jefferson emphasized the university for Southerners as a desirable alternative to Northern institutions, though he failed to defend slavery. He claimed that parents from many Southern states were eager to send their children there. "The letters I have received from almost every State south of the Potomac, Ohio, and Missouri, prove that all of these are looking anxiously to the opening of our University as an epoch which is to relieve them from sending to the Northern universities." Although stressing the sectional nature of his university, he did so mainly to get more state aid and to convince the legislature that it would support itself largely from tuition, from Virginia and neighboring Southern states as well as the North, so that it would easily become a self-financing, profitable enterprise. He emphasized the quality-education he intended to promote there. He argued that it would be superior to Northern colleges, which he now considered only as "preparatory" schools. "And when we consider that the colleges of those States, considered as preparatory only for ours, have one, two, or three hundred students each, we cannot doubt that ours will receive the double and treble of their numbers," he said with unusual optimism. Estimating that he would instantly recruit 218 students, he informed Cabell of an enthusiastic letter from Maryland. Obviously, he wanted to convince the legislature that his university would be a good investment and a self-sustaining enterprise. He did not imply that it would be devoted to upholding slavery.[44]

In January 1826, shortly before he died, Jefferson composed an essay, "Thoughts on Lotteries." He sent it to his friends in the legislature to help them convince the assembly to pass a bill permitting him to stave off bankruptcy by auctioning off his plantations *via* a nationwide lottery.[45] Even in a document devoted to demonstrating his services to the state, he stressed that the university would uphold principles of nationalism, republicanism, and freedom of thought, rather than dedication to such peculiar Southern institutions as slavery. In the essay, while grandiosely listing his contributions to Virginia, he made clear that he considered the university a national institution that would raise his state's reputation with the rest of the country and imbue its graduates with virtue and loyalty to the whole nation.[46]

In "Thoughts on Lotteries," Jefferson argued that the university he had created would make Virginia a center of enlightenment and nationalism in which citizens of other states would enroll. By means of its advanced educational practices and its widespread and influential alumni, it would eventually play a significant role in cementing national unity and friendship between Virginia and its "sister states." At the outset of his discussion of the university, he referred to Virginia as "our country." As the essay progressed, he made clear that he believed the whole nation would unite for liberal ends through the university's influence. "The effects of this institution on the future fame, fortune, and prosperity of our country, can as yet be seen but at a distance," he admitted, initially referring to his home state. Shifting emphasis, he then elaborated on his lifelong goal, to create an educational institution that would imbue its graduates with genius, brilliance, and devotion to republican virtue and that would make Virginia a national leader in the democratic republic. He predicted that state and national leaders would graduate from his institution. "An hundred well-educated youths, which it will turn out annually, and ere long," he assured his readers, "will fill all its offices with men of superior qualifications, and raise it [Virginia] from its humble state to an eminence among its associates which it has never yet known; no, not in its brightest days."[47]

Perhaps Jefferson exaggerated Virginia's decline as a source of national leadership; after all, Monroe had just retired from the presidency. On the other hand, he was prescient in anticipating that Monroe would be the last two-term president from Virginia for almost a century. Moreover, few of the most prominent figures in Congress other than the irksome John Randolph were Virginians. In any case, Jefferson asserted, his college would renew Virginia's political and intellectual distinction. "That institution," he continued, favorably comparing the university's free-thought with the benightedness of other colleges (perhaps in New England), "is now qualified to raise its [Virginia's] youth to an order of science unequalled in any other State." He believed that "this superiority will be the greater from the free range of mind encouraged there, and the restraint imposed at other seminaries by the shackles of a domineering hierarchy, and a bigoted adhesion to ancient habits."[48] Assembly members and others currently involved in Virginia politics "will enjoy the ineffable happiness of seeing themselves succeeded by sons of a grade of science beyond their own ken." The university's alumni would inevitably emerge as optimal national leaders.

Thus, Jefferson considered his university a nationalist vehicle. Attracting students from all over the country, it would cement national unity. "Our sister States will also be repairing to the same fountains of instruction, will bring hither their genius to be kindled at our fire, and will carry back the fraternal affections which, nourished by the same *alma mater*, will knit us to them by the indissoluble bonds of early personal friendships," he dramatically observed. His conclusion merged the rhetoric of state loyalty and national patriotism. "The good Old Dominion, the blessed mother of us all, will then raise her head with pride among the nations, will present to them that splendor of genius which she has ever possessed, but has too long suffered to rest uncultivated and unknown," he said, "and will become a centre of ralliance to the States whose youth she has instructed, and, as it were, adopted."[49]

Since Jefferson's objective was to obtain financial assistance from the state government, he naturally emphasized the benefits the university would procure for Virginia's reputation. Nonetheless, the purport of Jefferson's remarks was to solidify Virginia's greatness within the nation, not apart from it, and to unite it with the Northern states whose students would be its alumni. He made clear that he considered the university a tool of republican rebirth for the state and the nation. As he put it, "I claim some share in the merits of this great work of regeneration. My whole labors, now for many years, have been devoted to it, and I stand pledged to follow it up through the remnant of life remaining to me."[50]

Even in writing to the extreme states' righter, William B. Giles, Jefferson depicted his university as an institution of national and international significance, not merely local in its range. He boasted that he had obtained five professors from England, the recent enemy and cultural parent. "Our University has been most fortunate in the five professors procured from England," he wrote. "A finer selection could not have been made." Underlining his cosmopolitan motives, he was sure that the university's graduates would become political leaders. "A great proportion of them are sincerely devoted to study, and I fear not to say that within twelve or fifteen years from this time, a majority of the rulers of our State will have been educated here." They would be indoctrinated with loyalty to ideas of democracy, popular government, and republican virtue, which Jefferson considered "the correct principles of our day." As Jefferson put it, "They shall carry hence the correct principles of our day, and you may count assuredly that they will exhibit their country [Virginia?] in a degree of sound respectability it has never known, either in our days or those of our forefathers." For Jefferson, these "correct principles," as he listed them in his July 1816 letter to Kercheval, included direct democracy to the greatest extent possible, with universal manhood suffrage, direct election of executive and judicial officials, equal apportionment of the state legislature, "ward divisions" on the New England model, and "periodical amendments of the constitution." On the national level, for Jefferson they implicitly encompassed opposition to recent Supreme Court decisions' encroachments on the powers of the states as well as the powers of Congress, for instance in the *Marbury v. Madison* decision in 1803. In Jefferson's opinion, especially in his later years when the Marshall Court developed aggressive tendencies, the Supreme Court, an appointive body, should not be able to ride roughshod over popularly elected branches of government such as the state legislatures and Congress. (Ironically, had Jefferson's antipathy to "judicial review," a constitutional feature he had actually recommended during the 1787 ratification debates, become national policy, the Taney Court's *Dred Scott Decision* [1857], invalidating the Missouri Compromise and legalizing slavery in the territories, thus precipitating the Civil War, might never have occurred.) These "correct principles" also included, for Jefferson though not for Giles, opposition to slavery.[51]

In another letter to Short, in 1825, Jefferson seemed to calmly accept political parties. He explained to Short, who had spent most of his adult life in Europe, his view of Federalist politics and strategy. Attempting to recoup their losses following their disgrace in the War of 1812, pro-monarchical Federalists boldly denied ever advocating monarchy or secession, "yet the spirit is not done away," Jefferson insisted. "The same party takes now what they deem the next best ground, the consolidation of the government, the giving to the federal member of the government ... a controul over all the functions of the states, and the concentration of all power ultimately at Washington." At this time, a little more than a year before his death, Jefferson predicted that, after all the Federalist leaders had died and their papers were open to the public, everyone would see that they covertly espoused monarchism. But Jefferson expected that both he and Short would be dead before these papers were made available.

Jefferson believed political parties were a constituent part of human nature, because it was natural for people's ideas to differ: "Where not suppressed by the rod of despotism, men, according to their [physical] constitutions, and the circumstances in which they are placed, differ honestly in opinion. Some are Whigs, liberals, democrats, call them what you please. Others are Tories, Serviles, aristocrats etc. The latter fear the people, and wish to transfer all power to the higher classes of society; the former consider the people as the safest depository of power in the last resort."[52]

According to Jefferson, this latent class conflict, with each party ascribing different levels of intelligence and ability to the average man, and trusting his political acumen to divergent degrees, was the point of contention between the Federalists and Jeffersonian Republicans. It constituted "the common division of Whig and Tory." In terms of public policy, he argued, the difference manifested itself in a dispute between supporters of strong, centralized government ("consolidationists") and advocates of states' rights and weak government. This was the most honest, valid, and safe political bifurcation, "the most salutary of all divisions, and [it] ought therefore to be fostered, instead of being amalgamated. For take away this and some more dangerous principle of division will take it's [*sic*] place."[53]

Jefferson was probably thinking of recent sectional controversies, particularly the burgeoning alliance between Northern Federalists and Republicans. Adopting an anti-Southern stance, they united against the expansion of slavery in Missouri and in support of higher tariffs. These sectional conflicts threatened to disrupt the Union by creating bilateral divisions between North and South. Jefferson feared these more than he did disputes on issues over which Federalists and Republicans, dispersed through all the states of the Union, might differ among themselves. The latter had the effect, predicted in Madison's *Federalist Number 10* and elsewhere, of mollifying antagonistic sectional and economic interests.

Surprisingly, in the 1825 letter to Short the elderly Jefferson forgave the Federalists for their antidemocratic ideology. Although he derided recent attempts by veteran Federalist leaders like Harrison Gray Otis and Robert G. Harper to "white wash" (Jefferson's phrase) their party's historic image by claiming that Hamilton and other former party leaders had rejected monarchy, he was no longer disturbed by their supposed preference for it. "Their followers," he said, "were divided. Some went the same lengths; others, and I believe the greater part, only wished a stronger Executive." As he had often insisted in the past, he regarded the Federalist rank-and-file as more moderate in their views than their leaders.[54]

As he did in his *Anas* and letters to other friends during this period, he reminisced to Short about the widespread support for monarchy he found on arriving in New York City to assume the duties of secretary of state in 1790. During dinner conversations, he "was astonished to find the general prevalence of monarchical sentiments, insomuch that in maintaining those of republicanism, I had always the whole company on my hands." He forgave Short, who objected that Federalists were as republican as anyone else, rationalizing that Short's long absence as a U.S. minister abroad had left him out of touch with events in his country. More dramatically, Jefferson assured him that, despite Federalists' current protestations that they never favored monarchy, his Republican Party saved America's representative democracy from their aristocratic clutches: "Had it not been for the firm and determined stand then made by a counter-party [to the Federalist monarchists], no man can say what our government would have been at this day."[55]

Jefferson conceded that the Federalists now recognized that it was "desperate" for them to expect the American people to accept monarchy after so many years of republicanism. Still, he suspected that, even though it was no longer their "direct aim," they considered a broad construction of the Constitution *via* the Marshall Court's judicial decisions the "next best ground" for achieving a stronger, "consolidated" national government. (Jefferson defined "the consolidation of the government" as "giving to the federal member of the government, by unlimited constructions of the Constitution, a control over all the functions of the States, and the concentration of all power ultimately at Washington.")[56]

As his life reached a close, Jefferson, at least when writing to states' rights advocates like Thomas Ritchie, Spencer Roane, and John Taylor, concurred with their belief that the Federalists sought, through Supreme Court decisions and extending the power of Congress and the president, to eviscerate states' rights. The Federalists intended the national government to dominate the states, causing the dissipation of the democratic impulses and closeness to the local voter with which he and other Republicans identified the states. Apparently, he chose to forget that one of his oldest friends, James Monroe, was president at this time of increasing national power in the government. Indeed, as president Jefferson himself had exercised greater executive power than any of his predecessors, by means of such high-handed measures as the Louisiana Purchase, an undeclared war with Arab pirates, and the Embargo Act, all of which were arguably unconstitutional.[57] Nevertheless, Jefferson insisted that, once the private letters and other documents of the Republican and Federalist leaders were published long after they died, future generations would finally ascertain that Harper and his colleagues were "monarchists."

Although Jefferson had found the Federalists' ostensible monarchical sympathies exceedingly disconcerting during the 1790s, when he fought Hamilton and his cronies, now that his party had been in power for twenty-five years, it no longer worried him. Gratified that "time will, in the end, produce the truth," he stoically observed that differences of opinion, in politics as in every other sphere of life, were inevitable aspects of human nature "in every country, where not suppressed by the rod of despotism." And he hoped that the United States' governing authorities would never dare to suppress freedom of speech and expression. Surmounting his earlier apprehension, he applauded the antagonism between centralizers and states' righters. "This is the division of sentiment now existing in the United States," he observed. "It is the common division of Whig and Tory, or according to our denominations of republican and federal; and is the most salutary of all divisions."[58]

Ironically, in his dying months Jefferson almost wistfully desired to encourage the old-style differences of opinion between Hamilton and himself, rather than replace them with the prevailing hostility between pro- and anti-slavery forces. (Indeed, antislavery was an aspect of political and social reform in which the would-be aristocrat Hamilton never showed any interest.) As Jefferson tersely (and euphemistically) put it, "Take away this [dichotomy of opinion between Whigs and Tories] and some more dangerous principle of division will take its place."[59] What he was presciently referring to was the division between "free" and "slave" states, pro- and antislavery parties that would smolder and eventually sunder the Union. He now considered this basis of political and ideological conflict, which had arisen in all its blatant power during the Missouri crisis as never before, a deeper source of political and ideological conflict than the proverbial division between "monarchy" and "republicanism" that he had stressed for most of his political life. Earlier than most politicians, the superannuated Jefferson was aware that this was the most crucial division in the country.

Jefferson wanted to convince himself that the North-South conflict over slavery would soon disappear. He assured Short that the old division between Hamiltonian Federalists and Jeffersonian Republicans now superseded the Missouri debates' struggle between abolitionists and anti-abolitionists. As he put it: "There really is no amalgamation [between Federalists and Republicans]. The parties exist now as heretofore. The one, [Federalists] indeed has thrown off its old name, and has not yet assumed a new one, although obviously consolidationists. And among those in the offices of every denomination I believe it to be a bare minority."[60]

As in the days of the Alien and Sedition Acts, he considered protecting dissenting political opinions as vital as preserving religious freedom in maintaining individual and national self-respect and uniqueness. "I am no believer in the amalgamation of parties," he proclaimed, "nor do I consider it as either desirable or useful for the public; but only that, like religious differences, a difference in politics should never be permitted to enter into social intercourse, or to disturb its friendships, its charities, or justice." He praised political parties' role in protecting the people against oppressive government: "In that form, they are censors of the conduct of each other, and useful watchmen for the public."[61]

Aware that competitive, popularly oriented political parties existed only in the United States, Jefferson hoped that, as organs of public opinion, these parties could divert political struggles away from the explosive though urgent issue of slavery into less divisive paths. (Great Britain's rudimentary party system confined the suffrage to fewer than ten percent of the population; and politicians were primarily aristocrats who used bribery to attain their objectives.) Jefferson wanted to use political parties to preserve a unique republic whose leaders would eventually find a peaceful solution to eliminate what he called the "hideous blot" of human bondage. He said about slavery, "We feel & deplore it morally & politically, and we look without entire despair to some redeeming means not yet specifically foreseen" for abolishing it. He believed that political action could achieve emancipation. "I am happy in believing that the conviction of the necessity of removing this evil gains ground with time," he wrote Short. He noted two events that he thought would facilitate abolition. "Their emigration [of slaves] to the Westward lightens the difficulty by dividing it [among numerous small slaveholders] and renders it more practicable on the whole: and the neighborhood of a government of their own colour [Haiti] promises a more accessible asylum than that from whence they came."[62]

As Jefferson's letter to Short implied, Holmes' arguments convinced him that slavery's "diffusion" to points west like Missouri would help the parties to end slavery; with "diffusion," human bondage's presence would be diluted, less concentrated in a few states like South Carolina and Virginia, whose planters would otherwise fight to the death for its preservation because they owned so many slaves. Thus, Jefferson discovered additional reasons to support the Missouri Compromise. Holmes inspired Jefferson with the idea that the "diffusion" of slavery into Missouri would help terminate the peculiar institution, a view that Jefferson had never advocated until Holmes mailed him his "Letter to the People of Maine," dated April 10, 1820, which expounded the concept. He mailed this circular letter to Jefferson, in handbill form, from Washington, D.C., on April 12, 1820, scribbling a brief note at the end that he hoped Jefferson would read it if he had the time.[63]

Jefferson had additional reason to be grateful for the support and initiatives on Missouri of New England Democratic-Republicans like Holmes, Hill, and Mason. They viewed the situation more objectively than Southern proslavery fanatics and Northern abolitionists. He fixed his hopes on such pragmatic, democratic-minded politicians for a peaceful end to slavery that would maintain the Union intact. He also looked to the black government of Haiti as a sanctuary for the emancipated ex-slaves; a country where they could live under rulers of their own color, secluded from white domination.

22

Jefferson, the Missouri Compromise and the Haitian Paradox

Virginians and New Englanders

In old age, Jefferson, seeking to assuage his fears of national catastrophe, tried to convince himself that the struggle between pro- and antislavery factions was no longer paramount. The contest between those in favor of states' rights and those who urged greater national governmental powers and "consolidation" had resumed the priority it held since the battles between him and Hamilton over the Bank of the United States during the 1790s. However, Jefferson was certainly conscious that underlying this divergence was the deadly struggle between proslavery forces in the South and antislavery elements in the North. More and more, Southern slaveholders were employing "states' rights" as a shibboleth to protect their Peculiar Institution from future interference by Congress or the president, orchestrated by Northern antislavery politicians to bludgeon the South into eventually giving up slavery. This was the way that Southerners viewed the various resolutions against slavery in Missouri and Arkansas in the House of Representatives.

· · · · ·

In his last years, Jefferson stumbled upon a way to end the possibility of future conflict between North and South over slavery. He proposed that Congress abolish slavery by law, and then send the freed slaves on an all-expenses-paid, one-way trip to that cauldron of racial revolution and "liberty, equality, and fraternity" for blacks: the world's only black-controlled nation-state, Haiti (or "Hayti," as it was usually spelled at the time).

An advocate of self-government for all, Jefferson privately supported the Haitian Revolution almost from its beginning in 1791. However, he made no protest as secretary of state when Secretary of the Treasury Alexander Hamilton and President George Washington initially decided in 1792 to support the white French royalists on the island, who claimed that they represented the United States' ally, Louis XVI's tottering monarchy. As soon as Jefferson became president in 1801, he eliminated all obstacles to trade with Haiti imposed by John Adams' Administration during the Federalists' "Quasi-War" with France. Colluding with the British, Adams and his secretary of state, Timothy Pickering, agreed to limit trade with Saint Domingue (Haiti) to only two ports, Cap Français and Port-au-Prince. Although U.S. warships' naval bombardment of Jacmel proved decisive for Toussaint Louverture's triumph over the pro–French mulatto leader, General André Rigaud, in southern Haiti in 1800, Adams

269

afterward sought to weaken Louverture's military power. In December 1800, he refused to assist Louverture in taking over Santo Domingo (the present-day Dominican Republic) which was still in Spanish hands, although transferred to France by treaty in 1795.[1]

During Jefferson's presidency, American merchants sold weapons and other contraband items to the Haitian government, provoking numerous protests from Napoleon and his foreign minister, the notorious Talleyrand. In 1801, Jefferson went so far as to urge Virginia's Governor, James Monroe, to send the rebellious slaves convicted of conspiracy and sentenced to death after the abortive "Gabriel's Rebellion" to Haiti instead of hanging them. He even hinted that he would ask Congress for funds to transport the blacks. Careless historians, on the basis of slight evidence, have charged that Jefferson opposed the Haitian Revolution. They emphasize Congressional passage of a "suspension of trade" with Haiti in 1806 and 1807, in which the legislature reacted to pressure from Napoleon. The French emperor futilely desired to regain France's once-rich sugar colony (although, preoccupied as he was in Europe after 1803, he never did anything about it) and hinted he might support U.S. annexation of West Florida if the government cut off trade with the island. Jefferson and his secretary of the treasury Gallatin did not even bother to enforce the restriction, and trade continued virtually uninterrupted.[2]

For Jefferson, once freed from the responsibilities of office in 1809, the future of Haiti seemed even more beckoning to his purposes. He perceived the infant country's fate as a gauge by which history would judge African American intellectual equality with whites and their aptitude for self-government. He desired to defend himself against public distortions of his widely-publicized "suspicion" that blacks were mentally and physically inferior to whites, expressed in his famous book, *Notes on the State of Virginia*, during the 1780s, of which the French antislavery bishop Henri Grégoire had recently angrily reminded him. In 1809, Jefferson explained to the old Connecticut radical Joel Barlow, whom Grégoire had recently harassed about something else: "It was impossible for doubt to have been more tenderly or hesitatingly expressed than that was in the Notes of Virginia, and nothing was or is farther from my intentions than to enlist myself as the champion of a fixed opinion, where I have only expressed a doubt. *St. Domingo will, in time, throw light on the question.*"[3]

Although, considering the Haitians' record of submission to black dictatorships and "empires," Jefferson might justifiably harbor "doubts" about black aptitude for self-government, rather than point-blank denying that blacks could accomplish self-rule in Haiti or elsewhere he steadily hoped for African Americans' success. From 1801 onward, he proposed that the U.S. government indirectly assist the courageous black struggle in Haiti with an infusion of relatively skilled former slaves (and rebels), and then force slaveholders to emancipate their newborn slaves and deport them to Haiti when they became teenagers. He went so far as to specify that the U.S. Treasury pay the living expenses of the freed persons, educate them at government expense, and pay their transportation costs to Haiti. Since his project was obviously unconstitutional, Jefferson advised that the states pass an amendment to the U.S. Constitution if necessary to further his objective. The United States would thereby support the black experiment in self-government and simultaneously abolish the "hideous evil" of slavery, which mocked its claims as a bastion of liberty and equality. None of his contemporaries, including the reputed abolitionist John Quincy Adams, who during his presidency opposed U.S. recognition of Haiti, even though for the first time the country was united in peace and stability under General Jean-Pierre Boyer, voiced greater support for abolition.[4]

Jefferson was impelled by a desire, relatively widespread among politicians in the North and the South during the 1820s, to simultaneously rid the United States of slavery and African Americans, transporting them to their own "country" where they need not worry about white persecution and whites need not worry about living with them. Such colonization projects were recommended even by the abolitionist foe of the Missouri Compromise, Senator Rufus King.[5]

On the other hand, Jefferson's motives were in some ways "Pan-American" and modern. As he pointed out, both in *Notes on Virginia* and his letter to Jared Sparks in 1824, he was willing that the United States help the black exiles in their new home with food, supplies and technical assistance. During his presidency, Jefferson permitted U.S. merchants to conduct unrestricted trade in arms and supplies with the first Caribbean revolutionary regime, Saint-Domingue despite the vehement opposition of the world's greatest power, Napoleonic France. And during his retirement, as he quietly proposed that Virginia and the U.S. government support emancipated Southern blacks in their projected haven (or exile, depending on how one looked at it), Haiti, Jefferson envisioned a prototypical "Alliance for Progress," as it would be called later, although he claimed no role for the U.S. as an omnipotent Superpower. Indeed, as Steven Hahn has observed, by supporting the idea that former slaves must have their own country Jefferson anticipated the Black Nationalism advocated by such African American avatars as David Walker in the nineteenth century and Black Muslims, Marcus Garvey, and Malcolm X in the twentieth.[6]

Jefferson invariably associated the success of American union and republicanism with the worldwide victory of liberty. During this critical period, he also linked it with the abolition of the "hideous evil" of slavery. Indeed, he perceived "one good effect" from the threats and counter-threats of secession during the Missouri restriction debate: that it would further illuminate the festering problem of slavery. "It has brought the necessity of some plan of general emancipation & deportation more home to the minds of our people than it has ever been before," he believed. He considered it increasingly urgent to liberate the slaves, now that Northern majorities in the House of Representatives indicated they would eventually force it upon the Southern states, perhaps by an "immediate" law by which all slaves, children and adults, would be freed, probably without provisions for deporting them or providing for their livelihood if they remained in the South. For Jefferson, such a result would be the worst of all possible worlds. Spurred by the Missouri debacle, his kinfolk were already at work promulgating plans to emancipate and deport Virginia's slaves. In December 1820, Jefferson's son-in-law, Governor Thomas Mann Randolph, Jr., of Virginia had introduced a proposal for uncompensated gradual emancipation into the Virginia legislature.[7]

At the same time, Jefferson privately advanced his own plan, similar to the one he had urged in the 1780s in *Notes on Virginia*. He advised that Virginian slaveholders surrender their newborn slaves to the state's "guardianship," holding them as its wards under their mothers' care until they could be "sent at a proper age to S. Domingo [Haiti]." In *Notes* Jefferson had vaguely suggested sending emancipated slaves into the Virginia wilderness to set up their own country under the state's "protection." Now, rather ironically, he favored deporting the emancipated blacks to Haiti. A black dictatorship, Haiti's rulers had killed most of the whites on the island shortly after the country's creation in 1804. Its black "emperors," Dessalines and Henry Christophe, had reduced their black citizens to sharecroppers working for the government. Nevertheless, it was black-ruled, despite being a dictatorship. Jefferson may have

reasoned that, although Haiti's inhabitants had been transported there from Africa involuntarily to be slaves, like those of the American South, at least in Haiti they had achieved liberty
and a semblance of self-rule, although not democracy. Jefferson never said it in so many
words, but he may have justified his callous policy of emancipating and then deporting Southern slaves by reasoning that, unlike most whites, they had arrived involuntarily and therefore
it was ethical that they should be forced to leave, whether they liked it or not.

Although some white slaveholders abhorred Haiti's government as an incendiary symbol
of slave revolt, Jefferson regarded it as a convenient refuge. He had learned from reading the
popular *Niles Weekly Register* or some other paper that Haiti's new ruler, Jean-Pierre Boyer,
had proposed to grant land to black émigrés.[8] "There they are willing to receive them, & the
shortness of the passage brings the deportation within the possible means of taxation aided
by charitable contributions," Jefferson wrote to Albert Gallatin, U.S. minister to France. The
ex-president had already decided how the costs of transportation would be paid. He unrealistically believed that contributions from the governments of Europe, combined with national
taxes that he assumed ostensibly antislavery New Englanders would gladly help pay, and proceeds from the sales of public lands would be available for this worthwhile task. "In this I
think Europe, which has forced this evil on us, and the Eastern states who have been it's chief
instruments of importation, would be bound to give largely," he reasoned, with unrealistic
expectations of human goodness. In any case, Jefferson thought, "the proceeds of the land
office, if appropriated, would be quite sufficient."[9]

Thus, Jefferson expected New Englanders to subsidize African American freedom and
the preservation of the Union. Once more, as in Revolutionary times, the value of the connection with New England manifested itself to him. His optimism that Easterners would be
willing to contribute tax moneys or other funds to compensate Virginia slaveholders or pay
for the subsistence and deportation of the manumitted slaves grew following the vigorous
demonstration of antislavery sentiment in New England during the Missouri crisis of 1819–
1821.[10]

As recently as 1817, Jefferson had dismissed the possibility that Easterners would agree
to help finance a projected national plan of gradual slave emancipation and settlement "on
the coast of Africa," probably in Liberia or Sierra Leone, including "the patronage of our
nation until the emigrants shall be able to protect themselves." He doubted that New England
and the Middle states would generously agree to contribute tax dollars to finance an African
colony of manumitted slaves, or to compensate slaveholders for the loss of their human
property. "The bare proposition of purchase [of slaves] by the United States generally,
would excite infinite indignation in all the States north of Maryland," he predicted. He anticipated that the slave states themselves would end up bearing the burden of compensating
owners. As he wrote to a pro-colonization Lynchburg, Virginia, physician, "The sacrifice
must fall on the States alone which hold them; and the difficult question will be how to
lessen this so as to reconcile our fellow citizens to it." Nor was Jefferson convinced that
Southerners were eager to manumit their slaves or to compensate slaveholders. Although he
was "ready and desirous to make any sacrifice" for the emancipation of his state's slaves, so
long as they were "establish[ed] … elsewhere in freedom and safety," and kept apart from
the white population, he was alarmed that "the rising generation, of which I once had
sanguine hopes," was either apathetic or opposed to antislavery measures. He considered the
American Colonization Society's project to set up a West African colony to which free blacks

disillusioned with America's racist society might emigrate as a step forward, encouraging legislative action to emancipate and deport all slaves to a black nation-state. As he put it, "Perhaps the proposition now on the carpet at Washington to provide an establishment on the coast of Africa for voluntary emigrations of people of color, may be the corner stone of this future edifice."[11]

Thus, prior to the great conflict over Missouri in 1819–1821, Jefferson was doubtful that New Englanders and Northerners in general possessed sufficient republican virtue to participate in funding the abolition of Southern slavery. He remained distrustful, as he had been since the 1790s, of leading Federalists' devotion to the Union. His skepticism, intensified by the War of 1812, was strengthened by the Missouri crisis. This was a "fire-bell in the night, [which] awakened and filled me with terror," as he said in a letter to Maine congressman John Holmes, a Federalist-turned-Republican who supported statehood with slavery for Missouri in exchange for Maine's entry into the Union as a "free state."[12]

Along with Madison, Monroe, and most Virginians, Jefferson theoretically favored the spread of slavery into Missouri, because the state's inhabitants wrote a constitution that said they wanted it. Some Southerners, including Jefferson and Madison, contended that the "diffusion" of slavery into diverse regions of the country whose white inhabitants desired it accorded with the Constitution's provision that each state was entitled to the same rights and privileges as the original thirteen. Jefferson did not coin the term "popular sovereignty." However, he probably would have viewed legalizing slavery in Missouri, whose state constitution permitted it, as adhering to that doctrine. Nonetheless, Jefferson accepted the Missouri Compromise when Monroe signed the bill into law on March 6, 1820, even though it barred slavery in the territories north of the line 36°30'. His main interest was in preserving the Union, as he explained to Holmes in his letter of April 1820, congratulating him on the admission of Maine as a free state and the passage of the Missouri Compromise. On the other hand, Jefferson presciently believed there would be future controversies over the existence of slavery in the territories. What he especially feared was that Congress might arbitrarily decide to abolish slavery in the states where it already existed, including the original thirteen. He believed that such action would lead to the separation of the Union and even civil war. Referring to the possibility that Congress might arrogate the power to abolish slavery in the South, thereby violating the Southern states' confidence that the Constitution protected human bondage, Jefferson advised Holmes, who shared his views, that the Southern states might abolish slavery voluntarily in the future. Therefore, the Northern states should not risk the Union's survival by using their congressional majorities to force emancipation upon them. As we saw in the preceding chapter, stressing Congress's fatal foolishness if it proclaimed immediate emancipation for Southern slaves, he coldly labeled abolition an "abstract principle." Exaggerating the likelihood that Congress would arbitrarily decree emancipation (especially since pro–Southern votes still controlled the Senate), he warned that coercing the Southern states to abolish slavery would precipitate disunion and civil war, ending America's republican experiment and blighting the hopes of oppressed peoples everywhere that popular self-government was practicable. "If they [Congress] would but dispassionately weigh the blessings they will throw away, against an abstract principle more likely to be effected by union than by scission," he asserted, "they would pause before they would perpetuate this act of suicide on themselves, and of treason against the hopes of the world."[13]

Nevertheless, disgusted by slavery, Jefferson favored creatively using the Missouri

Compromise as a springboard for emancipation. He hoped New Englanders like Holmes and Jared Sparks, an active colonizationist and editor of the influential Boston periodical, *The North American Review*, would help him achieve an objective vital to preserving the republic. On the eve of death, he had little personal economic motive to defend the "Peculiar Institution." (He was aware that he had only a short time to live, and that after his death his estate and his slaves would probably be confiscated to pay his debts, leaving his daughter Martha tragically impoverished.) The most he could hope was that gradual emancipation of the slaves would eliminate a civil war over slavery, which he considered the greatest future threat to the Union's survival. He supported Missouri's admission as a slave state, since its white inhabitants had expected slavery to be permitted when they applied for entry into the Union. At the same time, he favored the prohibition of slavery in the rest of the Louisiana Purchase, and praised the handful of New England Republican congressional representatives that voted in favor of compromise. He disagreed with the majority of congressmen from his own state, who voted against the Compromise and muttered threats of secession, resentful of the stigma the Compromise placed on slavery.[14]

For Jefferson, emancipation and emigration of the freed blacks from the United States were two sides of the same coin. First expressed in Query XIV of *Notes*, Jefferson's anxiety on this topic persisted. Obsessed by dread that, if all slaves were emancipated as young adults without being immediately exiled abroad, they would attempt to annihilate their former white masters in revenge for past servitude, in a horrid bloodbath, he perhaps would even have preferred slavery's continuance to such a prospect. He expressed himself bluntly to his distant Massachusetts friend, John Adams, who sympathized with his point of view and agreed that the preservation of the union must not be risked to emancipate the slaves. Jefferson stigmatized the anti–Missouri faction as "the Holy Alliance in and out of Congress." He thus likened the Federalist-led group to European autocrats such as Russia's Tsar or the Emperor of Austria, considering them unconcerned about sacrificing the world's only democratic republic in exchange for the abolition of slavery. Insisting that congressional Federalists intended to manipulate the Missouri issue and eventually abolish slavery in all the states, empowering their commercial and manufacturing interests at the risk of dividing the Union into "Athenian" and "Lacedemonian," or ancient Spartan republics, he dramatically argued: "The real question, as seen in the States afflicted with this unfortunate population [slaves], is, are our slaves to be presented with freedom and a dagger? For if Congress has the power to regulate the conditions of the inhabitants of the States, within the States, it will be but another exercise of the power, to declare that all shall be free. Are we then to see again Athenian and Lacedemonian confederacies?"[15]

Exercising his imagination in predicting that war would follow the separation of the two sectional republics, Jefferson admitted his countrymen's violent, power-seeking propensities, exhibited not only in the institution of slavery but in pioneer expansion into Louisiana and the Floridas. Alluding to the Spartans and Athenians in their wars in fifth-century B.C. Greece, Jefferson speculated there might be "another Peloponnesian war to settle the ascendancy between" North and South. Or perhaps only the black slaves would rise up and kill the whites in the seceded South, as had recently happened in Haiti (although Jefferson overlooked its poignant example)? As he rhetorically inquired, "Or is this to be the tocsin of merely a servile war? That remains to be seen; but not, I hope, by you or me. Surely, they [North and South] will parley awhile, and give us time to get out of the way. What a Bedlamite is man!"[16] He hoped that he and Adams would be dead before the Union's sectional ordeal over the curse of slavery exploded in maniacal violence.

Despite his ostensible predilection in this controversy for the South, slavery and states' rights, Jefferson was essentially a nationalist.[17] Invariably opposing disunion, he conceived the federal union as an association of "sisters," as he called Massachusetts. Jefferson well understood that the voluntary fraternity of states he envisioned could be attained only if they treated each other with mutual respect, reciprocity, and even self-sacrifice. In the early republic, neither he nor any other statesman, including Adams, who viewed Southern secession with equanimity during the Missouri crisis, proposed coercing New England or other disgruntled states to remain within the Union. The Constitution had not outlawed secession, and fifty years later, only a bloody civil war would make it illegal.[18]

On the "Missouri question," as he called it, Jefferson was of two minds. He thought that Northern Federalists, not only those from Massachusetts and Connecticut but perhaps even more so congressional leaders from New York and Pennsylvania, intended to use national (that is, congressional) powers against states' rights (in this case, primarily the rights of Southern slaveholders). By this means, they would secure their selfish sectional (Northern) purposes of greater power in the national government. More portentously, he feared that Federalist and quasi-Federalist schemes for political power and their leader Rufus King's election to the presidency would blow up in their faces and lead to the secession of Southern states, including Virginia, from the Union. In the long run, therefore, as Stuart Leibiger notes, Jefferson's anxiety over the Missouri crisis, rooted in the explosive issue of slavery, reconciled him to a two-party system based on what he considered the less onerous issue of "consolidationists" versus "states' righters" or, in their eponymous form, "Federalists" versus "Democratic-Republicans."[19]

The issue of monarchy versus republicanism no longer seemed real to him, since he regarded it as having evolved into a conflict between those who wished to increase the power of the national government over the states and those who sought to maintain the *status quo*. That was preferable to a potential fight to the death between North and South over slavery, even though both issues involved states' rights. At heart Jefferson was a nationalist, especially when the national government wished to advance objectives he favored, such as territorial expansion (including the acquisition of territories as diverse as Canada, Texas, and Cuba) and the peaceful, gradual abolition of slavery.[20]

Writing in September 1820 to South Carolina congressman Charles Pinckney, a proslavery foe of the Missouri Compromise, Jefferson explained his (probably unwelcome) view that all parts of the nation must participate in devising and financing a plan of gradual abolition. He persisted in charging that "the leaders of federalism" throughout the North, not only in New England, plotted to regain national power by manipulating the explosive "local" issue of slavery expansion against the Democratic-Republicans, who were equally repelled by the institution. "They are wasting Jeremiads on the miseries of slavery, as if we were advocates for it," he protested. "Sincerity in their declamations should direct their efforts to the true point of difficulty, and unite their councils with ours in devising some reasonable and practicable plan of getting rid of it [slavery]."[21]

At this time, Jefferson usually complained to his correspondents that he was too old and sickly to keep up with public affairs and anticipated that he would not live long enough to be affected by them. Complaining to Pinckney of his "prostrate health," he wrote pathetically,

"I now am unable to write but with pain, and unwilling to think without necessity. In this state I leave the world and its affairs to the young and energetic, and resign myself to their care, of whom I have endeavored to take care when young." Jefferson had less influence with his peers than one might expect: the general fate of ex-presidents, with few exceptions. He seemed not even to want to exert influence. When Pinckney asked Jefferson his opinion of a speech he had recently made in Congress about the Missouri question, in which he also opposed a protective tariff, Jefferson weakly observed, "I read but one newspaper and that of my own State, and more for its advertisements than its news. I have not read a speech in Congress for some years. I have heard, indeed, of the questions of the tariff and Missouri, and formed *prima facie* opinions on them, but without investigation."[22]

It hardly seems likely that Jefferson was unaware that the New England states, particularly Massachusetts, virtually unanimously opposed the admission of Missouri to the Union as a slave state. They were recalcitrant even when compromise seemed necessary to preserve the Union. Likewise, most Virginians in Congress stubbornly insisted that the Thomas proviso prohibiting slavery in all territory north of the line 36° 30' with the exception of Missouri was unconstitutional.[23] Nonetheless, Jefferson avoided singling out Massachusetts or its New England confreres for condemnation, probably because he perceived acrimony's adverse effects on national unity at this critical period.

In Jefferson's schema, Northern Federalist politicians were split between those who favored preserving the Union and those who advocated their states' secession. Some would-be secessionists were motivated by hatred of slavery. More often, they expected to wield greater political power in a New England Confederacy. Indeed, Jefferson regarded the anti-slavery furor over Missouri as "a mere party trick," by which leading Federalists switched their party's *raison d'être* from "the principles of monarchism, a principle of personal not of local division," to the more dangerous "local principle," opposition to slavery. Their position took advantage "of the virtuous [antislavery] feelings of the people to effect a division of parties by a geographical line," the boundary between "slave" and "free" states. "They expect that this will ensure them, on local principles, the majority they could never obtain on principles of federalism," he charged. However, their "local principles" of antislavery rested on a spurious virtue, since Northerners owned no slaves while Southerners did.[24]

If secessionists gained power in New England and New York, Jefferson argued, no other states would join them, and they would soon return to the Union. Bitter at the prospect of Northern secession, whose likelihood he exaggerated at this time, Jefferson predicted, "If they push it to that, they will find the line of separation very different from their 36° of latitude, and as manufacturing and navigating States, they will have quarrelled with their bread and butter." Once they recognized that such a limited Northern confederacy was not politically or economically viable, Jefferson was confident that these demagogic "leaders of federalism" would, "after a little trial ... return to the embraces of their natural and best friends."[25]

· · · · ·

In the final analysis, Jefferson's confidence that the Union would survive rested on New England's farmers and townsmen, average people who considered national union the source of their happiness. He attempted to assuage his fear that posterity would relinquish the "state of happiness," liberty, and union he and his colleagues had endeavored to obtain for them and eventually extend to the world's inhabitants. Praising the naïve antislavery Northern rank and file, he denied that they desired disunion: "I must hope, nevertheless, that the mass of our honest and well-meaning brethren of the other States, will discover the use which designing leaders are making of their best feelings, and will see the precipice to which they are led, before they take the fatal leap."[26]

Isaac Briggs, who had worked for Jefferson during his presidency as surveyor of the Mississippi Territory, visited Monticello in late 1820, shortly after the most intense Missouri debates. Briggs spent a few days with Jefferson, his daughter and grand-daughters. Jefferson did not fear to speak frankly in front of him and the female members of his family. He told Briggs that he feared the Missouri crisis would disrupt "the safety and happiness of his country." He anticipated a rupture of the Union and the "horrors of Civil War." More graphically than he did with others, Jefferson warned, "Bloodshed, rapine and cruelty will soon roam at large." Expressing fears for the lives of the slaves if the South seceded in response to Northern harassment, Jefferson expected "a war of extermination against the African[s] in our land." Jefferson opined that Northern abolitionists' demand to prohibit slavery in the territories increased slaveholders' fears that Congress might seek to abolish slavery in the South itself. He thought that, if Northern agitation ceased, Southerners would eventually agree to free their slaves and even grant them "equal rights." He objected to Congress's denying slavery to Missouri, in which bondage had been ensconced under the Spanish and French before the U.S. obtained it through the Louisiana Purchase. (Moreover, under Article Three of the Louisiana Purchase treaty the United States had pledged not to disturb the territory's inhabitants in the possession of their property.) Jefferson feared that if Congress made another attempt to abolish slavery in Missouri at its next session, "All the horrors of civil war, embittered by local jealousies and mutual recriminations, will ensue. Out of such a state of things will naturally grow a war of extermination toward the Africans in our land." Instead of assisting the slaves in making progress toward "equal rights," Jefferson predicted, Northern abolitionists' demands for the slaves' immediate emancipation "would involve them [the slaves] as well as us in certain destruction." Briggs assured his wife and children that he conveyed "the substance" of Jefferson's words.[27]

23

Reconciling New England and the South to the Revolutionary Heritage, Old and New

George Ticknor, Daniel Webster and Andrew Jackson's Reputation

If Jefferson seemed prejudiced against one state's history and politicians, it was New York, home of Alexander Hamilton and John Jay. When his former ward and "adoptive son," William Short, hinted that he intended to move to New York City, Jefferson defined it for the ages as "a Cloacina of all the depravities of human nature." He seemed to have particularly hard feelings toward Jay, perhaps because he had been willing to sell out Southern interests in the abortive Jay-Gardoqui Treaty of 1786 with Spain and the renowned Jay Treaty with Great Britain in 1794. Jefferson wanted to disseminate the knowledge that Jay held pro-loyalist opinions at the outset of the American Revolution and had opposed a declaration of independence in 1776.[1]

Nevertheless, Jefferson occasionally agreed with Jay. He assured one student of the Revolution, who had just read Carlo Giuseppe Guglielmo Botta's somewhat inaccurate *History*, of the truth of Jay's comment that most colonists—Virginians, New Yorkers, and New Englanders alike—opposed seceding from the British Empire before the Battles of Lexington and Concord. As he put it:

> I have just received your favor of Jan. 30 and confirm, by my belief, Mr. Jay's criticism on the passages quoted from Botta. I can answer for it's truth from this state Southwardly, and Northwardly, I believe, to New York, for which state Mr. Jay is himself a competent witness. What, eastward of that, might be the dispositions towards England before the commencement of hostilities I know not. Before that I never had heard a whisper of disposition to separate from Great Britain. And after that, it's possibility was contemplated with affliction by all. Writing is so slow and painful to me [Jefferson suffered from rheumatism and two broken wrists] that I cannot go into details, but must refer you to Girardin's history of Virginia page 134 and Appendix No. 12, where you will find some evidence of what the sentiment was at the moment, and given at the moment.[2]

Indeed, Jefferson himself had not been eager to revolt against the Mother Country. In 1775, writing to a relative from a prominent Virginia family who had chosen the path of loyalism and emigrated to England, he asserted, "I would rather be in dependence on Great Britain, properly limited, than on any other nation on earth, or than on no nation." Even Samuel Adams, considered the hottest firebrand of the Revolution, was reluctant to end the connection with the British Empire.[3]

The Revolutionary heritage was much on Jefferson's mind in the years before his death. Botta's history of the Revolution was linked with this heritage and with the emerging tensions between North and South, tensions personified to a degree by Adams and Jefferson. Always ready to assert his primacy as a Revolutionary leader, Adams felt that some chroniclers of the War for Independence, including his old friend Mercy Otis Warren and Botta, had belittled his role, and that Southerners like Jefferson and Richard Henry Lee arrogated credit that he deserved. In the realm of revolutionary diplomacy, Adams charged, Benjamin Franklin received historians' praise that *he* merited.[4]

George A. Otis, a Bostonian relative of James Otis, married to a Virginian and living in Virginia, translated Botta's *History*. He sent Jefferson a copy of his work. He reported that John Adams, while praising Jefferson's "labors," had charged that Botta's account unduly favored the South (probably meaning that Botta gave Jefferson more credit for the Declaration of Independence than Adams got). "I have not been sensible of the Southern partiality imputed by Mr. Adams to the author," Jefferson observed. "The Southern States as well as Northern did zealously whatever the situation or circumstances of each, or of their sister States, required or permitted, and a relation of what they did is only justice." Perhaps expecting that Otis would report his observations to Adams, Jefferson included remarks that would be congenial to his aged correspondent. He agreed with Adams's criticism of the "factitious speeches" that Botta put into the mouths of Richard Henry Lee and other Revolutionary figures in order to convey their positions on the issue of independence during the Second Continental Congress, "speeches which he and I know were never made." Emphasizing the New Englander's oratorical talents, Jefferson wrote reassuringly, "Many acted abler parts than R. H. Lee, as particularly Mr. Adams himself did." Although Lee was a "good pioneer" in the independence movement, known for his "eloquence," he was "not an efficient reasoner." Lee's superficial discourse, characterized by "frothy, flimsy, verbose, musical voice and chaste language," lacked the requisite depth to convince the doubters "in such an assembly of men as that Congress." "This, Mr. Adams can tell you as well as myself," Jefferson pointed out, implying that Adams's oratory, passionate as well as rational, convinced waverers to support independence.[5]

In his declining years, Jefferson often sought to alleviate and conciliate sectional antagonisms (in earlier times personified by his old colleague John Adams) rather than exacerbate them in some destructive quest for a Southern Cavalier's revenge against the Puritans of the North.[6] When Massachusetts resumed electing Democratic-Republican congressmen in the 1820s and its intellectual leaders adopted Unitarianism, he believed that the state's "regeneration" was at hand. He relied for wine supplies on Joshua Dodge, a Boston merchant of Republican sympathies. In July 1823, Dodge informed him, after traveling through the United States, of "the general ascendancy of republicanism." Jefferson was especially pleased to learn of "the republican regeneration of Massachusetts," which "gives me great joy."[7]

As he often did, Jefferson reminisced about the unity between Virginia and Massachusetts in resisting Great Britain and in pushing through a declaration of independence at the Second Continental Congress, in which he and Adams played key roles. "The union of New

England and Virginia alone carried us through the revolution," he pointed out. Without being more specific, he continued, "Five steady votes were given by them on every question, and we picked up scatterers [sic] from the other less decided States which always secured a majority."[8] "Since that we are become aliens and almost hostile; and why?" he sadly acknowledged. "I know not." Feeling compelled to acknowledge Massachusetts' refusal to participate in fighting Great Britain in the War of 1812, already known as the "Second War for Independence," Jefferson continued to maintain his view that only a minority of people in Massachusetts had opposed the war or harbored disunionist sentiments. He turned to his favorite topic, the vital need to preserve republicanism in the United States, the only republic on earth. (As usual, he neglected to mention the existence of black slavery in the Southern states, perhaps because, as in ancient Greece and Rome, slaves were not considered part of the political nation.) He considered his home state of Virginia the staunchest advocate of republicanism and consequently "Americanism," but hoped that New England's regression had only been temporary. Taking solace from Dodge's news that Massachusetts' citizenry now fully embraced the republican creed, he wrote: "Virginia has never swerved a hair's breadth from the line of republicanism and Americanism. Massachusetts has strayed a little into the paths of federalism and Anglicism; but a good portion of her citizens have always remained loyal to true principles; they have brought their wandering brethren back again to their fold, and we joyfully receive them with the fraternal embrace."[9]

Ending on a sober note, Jefferson, perhaps with Monroe's near-unanimous reelection in 1820 in mind, hoped that the recent harmony Massachusetts displayed in supporting Republicanism would extend to many other issues in the future. "We shall now, I hope, feel towards each other the sentiments which united us in the revolution and become again truly brethren of the same principle."[10]

Despite linking them as fathers of the modern Democratic Party, most historians claim that Thomas Jefferson and Andrew Jackson disliked each other. In *The Market Revolution*, the distinguished historian Charles Sellers quotes Jefferson's alleged (possibly spurious) statement to Daniel Webster when Webster and their mutual friend George Ticknor visited Monticello in December 1824. He accepts Webster's report that Jefferson told him that Andrew Jackson was "a dangerous man."[11]

Late nineteenth century historians, questioned the accuracy of Webster's memo. One of the most prolific early biographers of famous Americans, James Parton, implied that Webster's "Notes of Mr. Jefferson's Conversation at Monticello, 1824," were unreliable, possibly a canard. Later, Arthur Schlesinger, Jr., in his classic, *The Age of Jackson*, observed that the source for Jefferson's alleged objection when President Monroe proposed Jackson for U.S. minister to Russia was an entry in John Quincy Adams' *Diary* for March 9, 1820, which was only hearsay (a statement that Jefferson made to Monroe, and which, years later, Monroe repeated to Adams).[12]

Jefferson's first major biographer, Henry S. Randall, doubted the accuracy of the Webster version of Jefferson's attack on Jackson. Supposedly, because Jackson hated General James Wilkinson, he blamed Jefferson for allowing Wilkinson to go scot-free during Burr's trial. Randall doubted that Jefferson had denounced Jackson the way that Webster's notes said he did: "It would be most extraordinary," Randall wrote, "that, to a known and decided political opponent, like Mr. Webster, he should express himself with a severity towards a Republican, that those most absolutely in his confidence never heard him employ."[13]

Jefferson's entire conversation with Webster, apart from his abrupt impromptu denunciation of Jackson, consisted of reminiscences about the American Revolution, the Declaration of Independence, and his meetings with French naturalist George Buffon and the *salonniéres* of Paris during his residence as minister from 1785 to 1789. It is possible that Webster or his companions on the visit to Monticello in December 1824 made those few sentences up to mislead posterity, or perhaps considered it a joke. Jefferson claimed to be impressed with Webster's reputation, although he was probably repelled by the extreme nationalist and pro-business positions he took in appearing before the Supreme Court as a plaintiff's attorney in *McCulloch v. Maryland* (1819), *Dartmouth College v. Woodward* (1819), and other famous cases. After Webster and Ticknor departed Monticello, Jefferson wrote to President James Monroe, who had earlier sent Jefferson a letter of introduction for Webster and Ticknor, "Your letter by Mr. Ticknor & Mr. Webster has been duly received. With the former I had had acquaintance and correspondence of long standing; and I am much gratified by the acquaintance made with the latter. He is likely to become of great weight in our government."[14] This by itself does not say anything about Jefferson's opinion of Jackson, and displays standard courtesy for Webster.[15]

The question whether Jefferson disliked Jackson and vice versa is more important to American history and historiography than the personal relations of two major figures in the Early Republic. The Democratic Party's longstanding claim to direct descent from Jefferson's Democratic-Republican Party of the 1790s and to inheriting Jackson's legacy, is an integral part of the American political system. Throughout its history, the Democratic Party has purportedly followed Jefferson's example in its desire to restrain arbitrary governmental power, protect civil liberties and civil rights and advance democracy, and in claiming to inherit the charisma of The Founders from Jefferson, James Madison, James Monroe, and Albert Gallatin. It would embarrass the Democratic Party to confront historians' charges (or assumptions) that the refined, quintessentially civilian, aristocratic elitist Jefferson was contemptuous of the rough-hewn, ultra-democratic populist, vulgar General Jackson, famed for his violence and hot temper (although in later life, he was universally described as epitomizing the chivalrous gentleman, especially by the ladies).

Historians have made little effort to discover what kind of personal acquaintance existed between Jefferson and Jackson, or whether, apart from his alleged notorious statement to Webster that Jackson was a "dangerous man," he made other comments about Old Hickory. Even Sean Wilentz, one of the nation's leading historians and an expert on the early republic, in his voluminous book, *The Rise of American Democracy*, whose underlying theme is the continuity between the ideas of Jefferson and Jackson, surprisingly fails to mention their personal relations. He merely says that Jackson considered Jefferson his "hero," and called himself a "principled Jeffersonian." Wilentz demotes to a footnote Webster's anecdote about his visit to Monticello in December 1824, on which other historians place such great weight. "On a visit to Monticello," Wilentz writes, "Daniel Webster and George Ticknor found Thomas Jefferson deeply ill-disposed to the popular general [Jackson] whom, they claimed, he considered a man of 'terrible' passions, a warrior with little respect for law and constitutions." Wilentz offers the following commentary: "The notes were written in [George] Ticknor's hand, and their veracity is dubious."[16]

Despite little evidence, scholarly assertions of Jefferson's dislike for Jackson pop up in unlikely places. Sellers' predecessors and followers in declaiming on an antipathy between

Jefferson and Jackson include numerous outstanding scholars. Gordon S. Wood in *Revolutionary Characters*; Daniel Walker Howe in *Political Culture of the American Whigs*; Andrew Burstein in *Jefferson's Secrets* (2005); and David S. Brown in an article, "Jeffersonian Ideology and the Second Party System," in *The Historian* (1999), assert that Jefferson had a low opinion of Jackson. Jefferson ostensibly regarded Old Hickory as an intellectual philistine, a vulgar and violent authoritarian, and potentially a political despot. James P. Ronda, a specialist on the Lewis and Clark expedition and the culture of Native Americans, also noted Jefferson's alleged detestation of Jackson. But, like other scholars, his only evidence was Daniel Webster's already mentioned, posthumously published December 1824 memo of his visit to Monticello with George Ticknor and Anna Eliot, Ticknor's wife. In a brief article on an unrelated topic, Ronda roundly asserts that Jefferson ultimately regretted advancing Westward expansion through the Louisiana Purchase. Jefferson concluded that the outcome was the rise to power of uncivilized demagogues like Andrew Jackson, Ronda believes; a "dangerous man," "unfit for the presidency," as Jefferson supposedly told Webster.[17]

Even Celia Morris Eckhardt, in a biography of Frances Wright the English abolitionist, a book only remotely concerned with Jefferson and Jackson, assumes that Jefferson feared and opposed Jackson. Discussing the presidential election of 1824, a contest between Jackson and John Quincy Adams, she writes, "people like Jefferson thought Jackson dangerous, and many wanted him defeated."[18] Contrariwise, another book that has virtually nothing to do with Jefferson, Amy S. Greenberg's recent narrative of the Mexican-American War and its effect on various participants, among them Nicholas Trist, Jefferson's grandson-in-law and private secretary in his old age, claims that Jackson was devoted to the "Sage of Monticello." Discussing Trist, who, although only a State Department clerk, negotiated the treaty that ended the Mexican War in 1848, without any evidence, she excitedly writes, "After Jefferson, Andrew Jackson took him [Trist] under his wing. Jackson thrilled to Trist's stories of life with the first Democratic leader, and treasured him as a conduit to the president he venerated above all others."[19] (She is perhaps being metaphorical, since Jefferson had been dead for several years.)

One of the first prominent historians to claim that acrimony existed between Jefferson and Jackson, Daniel Walker Howe, argued that Jefferson's Democratic-Republicans found the Jacksonian Democrats "too egalitarian for their liking." He writes, "The old Democratic-Republicans, those who formed the nucleus of the original Jeffersonian movement in the 1790s, felt little kinship with the second generation of Democrats, who based their claims to political power on democracy, or worse, mere popularity." Presenting no evidence to support his assertions, Howe continues, "The archetypal representative of this brand of Republican [Clay-Adams National Republican Whiggery *qua* 'classical republicanism'] was James Madison. It is well known (or at least it should be) that Jefferson disapproved of Jackson's candidacy in 1824; it is even more significant that Madison and Gallatin, who were still alive in 1832, when the issues of the Jacksonian era had been clearly drawn, supported Clay for president that year."[20] These assertions lack factual basis.

Although Howe presents no specific evidence or sources for any of these assertions, it is likely that, like most historians, he had in mind Daniel Webster's memorandum of his conversation with Jefferson in December 1824, in which Jefferson allegedly called Jackson "a dangerous man." With regard to Madison, neither Irving Brant's nor Ralph Ketcham's excellent biographies mentions anything about Madison preferring John Quincy Adams to Clay in

1832, or disliking Jackson. Gallatin, who supported states' righter William H. Crawford in 1824 and was even willing to serve as his vice-president, was politically inactive by 1832. A prominent New York City banker, he disliked Jackson's fiscal policies and supported the recharter of the Second Bank of the United States. Nonetheless, he accused B.U.S. President Nicholas Biddle of irresponsibility and mismanagement after Jackson vetoed the Bank's recharter in 1832. Contrary to Howe's assertion, Gallatin and Clay were enemies. An extreme protectionist in 1832, Clay resented Gallatin's advocacy of a moderate tariff and eventual free trade. In 1832, on the Senate floor, Clay denounced Gallatin's proposals, telling him, "Go home to your native Europe, and there inculcate upon her sovereigns your Utopian doctrines of free trade." Gallatin never supported Clay for the presidency.[21]

More recently, Jefferson expert Robert M. S. McDonald, citing only Massachusetts Federalist congressman Daniel Webster's "Notes of Mr. Jefferson's Conversation 1824 at Monticello," asserts, "Democrats appropriated Jefferson despite the fact that the party of Jackson was hardly the party of Jefferson." Without presenting any information about Madison other than citing Howe's book, which has no facts to back up its assertions, McDonald continues, "Jefferson—and James Madison also—disliked the hero of the Battle of New Orleans."[22]

Like Howe and McDonald, historian David S. Brown insists that not only Jefferson but his colleagues Madison and Monroe opposed Jackson's presidential candidacy. But the evidence he presents points in the opposite direction. For example, as proof of Monroe's hostility, he cites, without quoting, a letter that Monroe wrote to Thomas Ringgold in May 1826. In this letter Monroe said he strove for impartiality between the candidates in the election of 1824, but admitted that William H. Crawford's states' rights partisans considered him (Monroe) too nationalistic. Of Jackson, Monroe asserted, "To General Jackson I gave many proofs of like confidence & respect during the war, and after it, through the whole term of my service. Nor did I express any preference to any one in favor of either of the candidates, wishing to deal with all impartially." Brown also claims that Monroe wrote a letter to John C. Calhoun in 1829 lamenting that as president, Jackson had thrown many of his friends out of office; but the letter he cites dates from 1827, when John Quincy Adams was president. In that letter, Monroe did not mention anything about Jackson or a spoils system, but (seeking a big pension from the government as reimbursement for his service abroad) protested that he had always been Jackson's friend, and decried Congressional rumors that he had earlier denounced Jackson. Monroe suspected that his political enemies were trying to turn Jackson and his supporters in Congress against him by false statements that he had criticized Jackson during the Battle of New Orleans and at the time of his Florida invasion in 1818. This would make it more difficult for him to get a substantial reimbursement from Congress. Although he professed impartiality in the ongoing presidential struggle between Jackson and Adams, in the letter to Calhoun he insisted that he had always supported Jackson's actions, both in order to advance "the public good" and because of "the interest I took in his fame, [and] the friendship which I had for him…. That any of the friends of Genl. Jackson should have been, or now be desirous of injuring me is cause of real astonishment to me. I not only never injured him, but certainly never injured any of them." Thus, the letter to Calhoun also proves the opposite of what Brown implies. In the letter, Monroe asserted his admiration and support for Jackson, rather than his hostility. (The quotation from Monroe that Brown inserts in his article does not exist.) With regard to Madison, Brown merely cites Howe's book as "proof" that Madison opposed Jackson's candidacy and favored Clay; but, as we have seen, Howe has no evidence on the point.[23] Thus, historians generally assume Jackson's unpopularity with Jefferson and his colleagues without presenting any proof other than Webster's memoir as evidence.

In the early twentieth century, Augustus C. Buell, a popular writer who often made up his "facts" and "sources," claimed that Jackson made an anti–Jefferson speech at Richmond in the summer of 1807 when he was allegedly subpoenaed to testify before a grand jury about Aaron Burr's treason. In this speech, which Buell printed verbatim with quotation marks as if it were completely authentic, Jackson, who briefly sympathized with Burr, mainly because he detested the roguish General James Wilkinson, denounced Jefferson. He called Jefferson a "persecutor" of Burr and a murderer of innocent American seamen for failing to respond to the June 1807 British attack on the U.S. warship *Chesapeake* with a declaration of war. It is difficult to believe that Jackson would use such harsh terms against Jefferson, whom he considered the patron saint of the Republican Party. Buell does not provide any citation to locate Jackson's intemperate speech. He murkily asserts that Thomas Ritchie, a Jeffersonian Republican and editor of the *Richmond Enquirer*, a respected Democratic newspaper, dug it up and printed it in 1824, during the presidential contest between William H. Crawford, Ritchie's candidate, and Jackson. Buell does not make clear whether Ritchie printed the speech in his newspaper or as a pamphlet or broadside (handbill).[24]

Most professional historians deny that Jackson ever made the speech. In light of Buell's reputation for making up false stories in his biographies of famous people, and lying about his personal life and military service in the Civil War, most responsible historians regard him as a fiction writer rather than a narrator of true events. Milton Hamilton, author of an article exposing his falsehoods, believed that his books dangerously propagated erroneous information about the nation's past.[25] Harold D. Moser, editor of the Andrew Jackson Papers, mentions Buell's quotation of Jackson's anti–Jefferson "speech." He writes that Buell was "noted for his inaccuracies and fabrications of letters and documents, reprinted in his *History of Andrew Jackson* (New York, 1904), 1: 204–206, the only text found of a speech that Jackson allegedly delivered" in Richmond during Burr's trial in June 1807. Contemporary reports mentioned Jackson's vituperation against Wilkinson, whom, like many, he considered as at least equally guilty of treason with Burr. On June 25, Jackson left Richmond to return to Nashville.[26] Since the *Chesapeake* incident occurred on June 22, only three days before he left, it is unlikely that he was aware of it or had pondered its meaning sufficiently to ascribe blame to Jefferson in any case.[27]

What all these commentaries on Jefferson's dislike for Jackson have in common is their failure to present convincing evidence that Jefferson actually said he disliked Jackson. Their only proof is a memoir of dubious reliability, allegedly dictated by Daniel Webster, written shortly after December 1824, during a period when Webster was Jackson's enemy, but surprisingly not published during the campaign or during their lifetimes. That Webster kept Jefferson's attack on Jackson secret during the elections of 1824 and 1828 despite his hostility to Jackson indicates that the statements were not true, and that they were inserted in the memorandum of his visit either by Webster, Ticknor, Ticknor's wife, or someone else.

Nor did Webster, a Federalist, have much liking for Jefferson. He opposed Jefferson's election as president in 1800.[28] Along with Timothy Pickering and other diehard New England Federalist foes of Jefferson, Webster led the opposition in the House of Representatives to the purchase of Jefferson's library by Congress in 1815, which was essential to enable him to stave off bankruptcy and destitution for a few years. It is difficult to believe that Jefferson, a man who did not easily forgive vindictiveness, had forgotten about Webster's spiteful conduct, although in December 1824, he was very old and in poor health.[29] On the other hand, in old age Jefferson may have become resigned to what his old foe Hamilton called the "ingratitude of republics." Amid his financial troubles, Jefferson did not even receive sympathy from the legislature of his own state, which only grudgingly passed a law allowing him to sell his Albemarle County properties by a lottery (merely permitting him and his family to live at Monticello during his lifetime), which ended up as a fiasco. (After his death, though Virginia did nothing, the legislatures of Louisiana and South Carolina each donated ten thousand dollars in bank stock for the support of his daughter Martha and her family. Jefferson was hardly idolized in his own state.[30])

Briefly quoting Webster's memo on his conversation with Jefferson, and mistakenly assuming that it was a *letter from Jefferson*, Jackson scholar Matthew Warshauer likewise writes, "In 1824, Jefferson wrote that Jackson had very little respect for laws or constitutions and 'is a dangerous man.'"[31] This is practically the only adverse commentary on Jackson by Jefferson that appears in secondary sources. However, historians of the "Age of Jefferson and Jackson," as it is often called, eagerly utilize it.

In late December 1824, Webster, then a Federalist senator from Massachusetts, undertook a pilgrimage to Monticello with his friend, Jefferson's scholarly confidant, young Harvard classics professor George Ticknor. Supposedly, during Webster's conversation with the elderly Jefferson, the Virginian uttered devastatingly negative comments about Andrew Jackson, who, before the "corrupt bargain" between Adams and Clay, was apparently the president-elect. According to Daniel's son Fletcher Webster's later published account of their December 1824 conversations, Jefferson told him that General Jackson was "one of the most unfit men I know of for such a place [as the presidency]. He has had very little respect for laws or constitutions—& is in fact merely an able military chief…. He is a dangerous man."[32]

In Jefferson's and Jackson's time, contemporaneous with the election of 1824–1825, the only one of Jackson's competitors to publicly stigmatize "The Hero" as a "military chieftain" was the Great Compromiser, Henry Clay. He did so in a public letter to a Virginia supporter of John Quincy Adams in January 1825, attempting to justify his order to his supporters in the House of Representatives to switch their support to Adams. He thus countermanded the Kentucky legislature's instructions to the state's congressmen to vote for Jackson. Clay charged that Jackson was a notorious "military chieftain," who would make himself a military dictator if elected president. Expounding the popular theory of the cyclical decay of governments from republics into despotisms, he said: "As a friend to the liberty, and to the permanence of our institutions, I cannot consent, in the early stage of their existence, by contributing to the election of a military chieftain, to give the strongest guaranty that this republic will march in the fatal road which has conducted every other republic to ruin."[33]

For his part, Jackson identified the phrase, "military chieftain," solely with Clay's diatribe. He wrote one of his New York campaign managers, in a letter that was likewise published in the newspapers, that Clay, who had never fought in war, revealed his disrespect for military heroism by belittling Jackson and the soldiers who stood with him at Horseshoe Bend, New Orleans, and other conflicts. "I am well aware that this term 'Military Chieftain' has for sometime past been a cant phrase with Mr. Clay and certain of his retainers," he declared, "but the vote with which by the people I have been honored, is enough to satisfy me, that the prejudice by them sought to be produced availed but little." Implying that Clay was unpatriotic, Jackson continued, "Mr. Clay has never yet risked himself for his country, sacrificed his repose, or made an effort to repel an invading foe." He sarcastically observed that Clay would consider any brave, successful warrior dangerous, even George Washington should he return from the dead.[34]

In attacking Clay, Jackson was joined by such newspapers as the *Washington Gazette*, which denounced Clay for calling Jackson a "mere 'military chieftain.'" It argued that Clay, not Jackson, threatened U.S. republicanism because he had flouted the voters' will and made a "corrupt bargain" with Adams. "Henry Clay himself has inflicted the deepest wound on the fundamental principle of our government," the *Gazette* charged. "*He* has insulted and struck down the majesty of the people.... A thousand 'military chieftains' could not have done so much harm to our constitutional principles."[35]

When Webster arrived in Washington in December 1824 to resume his duties as congressman from Massachusetts, his wife and children remained in Boston. His friend George Ticknor met him in the national capital. Soon after finding lodgings, he and the Ticknors made a trek to Virginia to visit former presidents Madison and Jefferson, a trip that lasted from December 9–21. Jefferson had often invited Ticknor, whom he had met once before in 1815, to visit him again because of his great knowledge of European literature and expertise in the book trade. Because of a severe rainstorm, they remained guests at Monticello for five days, rather longer than Webster, whose son had become gravely ill, wished. On the evening following their departure, Webster dictated to Mrs. Ticknor the lengthy account of his interview with Jefferson, who had talked mainly about his experiences during the American Revolution and as U.S. minister to France during the 1780s. Before arriving at Jefferson's home, Webster learned of the illness of his son Charles, then almost three years old, but not until after his return to Washington did he find out the boy had died on December 19.[36] When they arrived in Charlottesville en route to Monticello, Webster received a letter from his wife Grace informing him that their little boy Charles was very ill.[37]

According to Charles M. Wiltse, editor of Webster's papers, the only existing copy of Webster's reminiscences "is in Mrs. George Ticknor's hand." The memorandum was first published in Fletcher Webster's edition of *The Private Correspondence of Daniel Webster*.[38] The microfilm edition of the Papers of Daniel Webster, reel four, contains three pages of notes in Webster's "autograph" hand (frames 4495–4497), "from which he probably dictated his memorandum to Mrs. Ticknor." The notes do not list every topic on which Jefferson ostensibly spoke; and Jackson's name is not listed there.[39]

One Democratic-Republican statesman who lauded Webster was President James Monroe, who as president was a stalwart nationalist, and therefore might be expected to applaud Webster's post–War of 1812 nationalist views. Early in December 1824, Monroe learned, probably from Ticknor, who was visiting Washington, that he and Webster intended to visit Monticello. Monroe wrote Jefferson, "Hearing that Mr. Webster & Mr. Ticknor will call on you, and indeed that their visit is principally intended for yourself & Mr. Madison, I take much interest in recommending them to your kind attention. They are known to the public as citizens of great respectability & talents, and the latter, is well known to you personally in those lights, so that little is left to me to add, than to bear my testimony in their favor, to the same effect." He alluded to Jefferson's recent serious illness, probably with rheumatism or diarrhea (which perhaps clouded his judgment at this time, especially regarding his "favor" for Webster's "principles"). "I hope that you have entirely recovered from the indisposition, with which you still suffered, when I was with you," Monroe ended the letter.[40]

Jefferson's consistent desire to maintain harmony and avoid personal antagonism during his last years (extending even to writing a few friendly letters to Timothy Pickering, perhaps his most bitter opponent) is the only explanation for his kindness to Webster on his visit to Monticello and his denunciation of Jackson, if the report of the latter is authentic. Jefferson's friendship and respect for young Ticknor were sufficient reason for him to write the following effusive letter to his protégé, Webster's close friend, when Ticknor requested Jefferson's permission to bring Webster with him to visit Monticello: "Whether Mr. Webster comes with you, or alone as suits himself, he will be a welcome guest. His character, his talents and principles, entitle him to the favor and respect of all his fellow-citizens, and have long ago possessed him of mine."[41]

Jefferson certainly did not "favor" Webster's "principles," unless he had covertly become a "consolidating" nationalist. In 1819, Webster had been plaintiff's counsel in the Supreme Court cases of *McCulloch v. Maryland* and *Dartmouth College v. Woodward*, in both instances successfully asserting the centralizing powers of the national government and the business corporation, opinions anathema to the aging Jefferson. In Webster's letters to friends describing his consecutive visits to Madison and Jefferson in December 1824, he emphasized Jefferson's silence on political matters. He made no mention of Jefferson's alleged attack on Jackson, which would have been politically useful to the candidacy of John Quincy Adams if it was a fact. A few days after arriving home, Webster wrote to New Hampshire Federalist senator Jeremiah Mason, "We were two days at Mr. MADISON'S. He was very agreeable, & treated us with much hospitality. He keeps alive a stronger interest in passing events than his more advanced [in age] friend [Jefferson]. At Mr. Jefferson's, we remained five days. This was something longer than our intention, but there came rains, which prevented our departure." About the "Sage of Monticello", Webster remarked, "He talked less of present things than might be expected. He talked mainly about the American Revolution, his experiences in France, & his views of literature, as well as the University of Virginia."[42]

Webster was interested in Jefferson's plans for the University of Virginia. He eagerly inspected the grounds with Jefferson and Ticknor. Historian Robert V. Remini mentions the excursion, although he misreads Webster's recommendations to Jefferson about allowing the students to carry guns at the university in order to properly conduct their military training exercises. Remini claims that Jefferson planned to distribute real, loaded firearms to the students, but that Webster advised him that guns made of wood were safer. As one might expect from a liberal of Jefferson's stature, the opposite is the fact; Jefferson advocated gun control. Ticknor recalled that Webster's prediction that the students would reject the idea of using wooden rifles and demand iron weapons proved accurate: "Mr. Webster took much pleasure in witnessing the beginning of the enterprise [University of Virginia]. He did not, however, fail to discover some of the defects of the system; he especially suggested to Mr. Jefferson that a project he had introduced into his laws for the university, to train the scholars in military exercises with guns made wholly of wood, because he did not think it safe to trust them with the usual fire-arms, would fail from the ridicule of the young men. It proved so."[43]

To his congressional colleague, William Plumer, Jr., of New Hampshire, an Adams supporter, Webster wrote a brief letter on December 18, 1824, just as he was departing from

Monticello. He primarily discussed the rainy weather that hindered his prompt departure, but also mentioned his impression of Jefferson, which had become favorable. "If I am inquired for, have the goodness and say I may be expected either on Tuesday or Wednesday morning," he wrote. He continued: "We should have left here yesterday [Friday] morning for Washington, but for the rain, which fell in torrents all day. This morning the streams are very full, & we doubt the expediency of setting out. I have found my visit here very pleasant. It has not only gratified a natural desire to see a distinguished & extraordinary man, but allowed an opportunity for much interesting & instructive conversation." He added the postscript, "The rain fell here yesterday & last night 5 inches."[44] If Jefferson had denounced Jackson in conversing with Webster, Webster would have mentioned it. Perhaps Jefferson only discussed his views of Jackson with his confidant Ticknor.

Ticknor was visiting Washington, D.C., in the late fall of 1824, enabling him to visit Monticello. Jefferson was interested in conferring with the New Englanders because they were involved in the educational progress of their state, and he thought they might give him useful advice on running the University of Virginia. Ticknor and Edward Everett were engaged in raising academic standards at Harvard College, where Webster had been an overseer since 1822. Because of Jefferson's venerability if no other reason, Webster was eager to meet him. Perhaps Jefferson wanted Ticknor's help in obtaining books for the University of Virginia, or merely to get his opinion of the buildings and grounds of the pride and joy of his last years. Perhaps from the weariness of old age, he seemed willing to let bygones be bygones as far as Webster's opposition to the Democrats in Congress was concerned. Writing to Ticknor, he invited Webster to come along, although he never wrote a letter to Webster himself. Since Monroe had informed Madison that Webster and Ticknor were visiting Jefferson, they decided that, out of politeness, they ought to drop by Montpelier on their way.[45] (To judge from Webster's violent opposition to Madison during his presidency, this was probably one visit "Little Jemmy" could do without.)

A sentence in Webster's previously-quoted letter to Mason indirectly indicated that Mrs. Ticknor's notes may have falsely, deliberately ascribed his words to Jefferson. (She allegedly composed the account of the conversation between Jefferson, Ticknor, and Webster from the information provided by the latter two visitors.) George Ticknor Curtis, a distant relative and friend of George Ticknor, in an appendix to his later biography of Ticknor, claimed that Mrs. Ticknor recorded their conversation the day after they ended their visit to Monticello. In fact, Mrs. Ticknor recopied the notes in 1869; and that was the only extant copy. After stating his belief that John Quincy Adams would win the presidential election in the House of Representatives, Webster wrote Mason, "It seems to me that there is, at this moment, rather a re-action against General Jackson—a *feeling*, somewhat adverse to giving the Presidency to [a] *mere* military character."[46] The phrase "mere military character" was nearly identical to the terms used by Mrs. Ticknor in recording Jefferson's hostile opinion of Jackson.

In another letter describing his visit to Jefferson, Webster again made no mention of Jefferson's opinion of Jackson. To Joseph Hopkinson, a leading Philadelphia Federalist lawyer and polemical *littérateur*, Webster described Jefferson as an entertaining conversationalist, but surprisingly inarticulate about current politics. "Mr. Jefferson is full of conversation," he wrote, "as it relates, pretty much, to by-gone times, it is replete with information & useful anecdote." Jefferson spoke mainly about the past, perhaps because he wanted to keep out of trouble and out of the newspapers: "Mr. Jefferson's conversation is little on present things;

partly perhaps from the prudence of forbearing to engage in questions which now divide the community, but mostly from a greater love for other topics." Reiterating what he told Jeremiah Mason, he said, "Early Revolutionary events, political occurrences, in both Hemispheres" during the period that he was in France in the 1780s, "& general literature & the University of Virginia would seem to be his favorite subjects."[47] In accord with the Stoic *mentalité* of the times, Webster only briefly mentioned that while he was journeying home from Monticello, his three-year old son died.[48]

Although most of the factual information about Jefferson's life in Webster's "memoir" is accurate, much was public knowledge by the 1850s, when Webster's reminiscences were first published. Since the words ascribed to Jefferson expressed such extreme distaste for Jackson, it seems difficult to believe that Webster would forego mentioning them in discussing his visit to Monticello with anti–Jacksonians like Plumer, Joseph Hopkinson, and Mason. Perhaps the younger George Ticknor, not Webster, imputed these words to Jefferson as a bad joke on posterity and the historical record. They were not made public until many years after Jefferson's and Webster's deaths. Webster was certainly not friendly toward Jackson during the 1820s, although he briefly became less hostile after Jackson defied the South Carolina nullifiers in December 1832. Apparently Webster was not pledged to secrecy regarding Jefferson's words. Moreover, the date of the notes' composition is not December 1824: at the top of the page is listed "1825," which makes it unlikely that the date can be exactly known. Without corroboration, it is possible that the account was written much later. Thus, it is impossible to be certain of the date or the accuracy of the record.

George Ticknor Curtis (1812–1894) was the step-grandson of Ticknor's father.[49] He compiled the *Life of Daniel Webster*, which contains information about the origin of Webster's notes on his conversation with Jefferson. He explained that George Ticknor's widow, Anna Ticknor, copied out for him the "Appendix," the title of the printed version of her record of Webster's statements when she, her husband, and Webster waited for the rain to subside at a Charlottesville inn. In a statement dated May 1, 1869, Anna Ticknor said that she recopied the material from her original manuscript before handing it over to Curtis: "These are notes about a visit of three or four days to Mr. Jefferson, in December 1824. They were written down, on the very evening on which we left Monticello, at a little tavern kept by a Mrs. Clarke, where we stopped for the night, early in the afternoon, because it was the only tolerable inn within our reach." She claimed that Webster, not her husband, was responsible for most of the dictation: "As far as what relates exclusively to Mr. Jefferson, his appearance and conversation, the work is Mr. Webster's. The rest is a sort of joint-stock contribution."[50] George Hilliard, who edited Ticknor's published letters, fell ill early in the progress of the work, and Anna Ticknor edited the portion that concerned Ticknor's life during the 1820s and 1830s. Hilliard's preface explained, "When the work was resumed, it was undertaken by Mrs. Ticknor and her eldest daughter, who, thenceforward, devoted themselves conscientiously to the task." Thus, Mrs. Ticknor was actively engaged in facilitating her husband's reception by posterity.[51]

If Jefferson spoke disparagingly of Jackson's presidential candidacy to anyone, it was most likely to George Ticknor and his wife. He relied on Ticknor for advice relating to faculty and book purchases for the University of Virginia, and perhaps thought it advisable to humor Ticknor's anti–Jackson prejudices. According to Webster's letters, Jefferson, who Webster suspected maintained silence on the election because he did not want any publicity, said little about current affairs; instead he reminisced about his role in the American Revolution and the early days of the French Revolution. The reminiscences of George Ticknor printed in George Ticknor Curtis's *Life of Daniel Webster* said nothing about Jefferson criticizing Jackson.[52] Paradoxically, George Ticknor Curtis wrote that George Ticknor furnished him Webster and Ticknor's memoir of their visit to Montpelier and Monticello, in which no anti–Jackson commentary by Jefferson appeared.[53]

Webster and Henry Clay, his senatorial colleague, Whig party leader and competitor, were not averse to encouraging lies and slander against Jackson, especially during the election of 1828. At that time, they subsidized newspapers that charged that his wife Rachel was an adulteress and that his mother was a common prostitute, so desperate were they to reelect John Quincy Adams against seemingly hopeless odds.[54] Perhaps if Jefferson disparaged Jackson, he did so in order to ingratiate himself with his guests Webster and Ticknor, Adams Federalists. Madison must have remembered that Webster was one of the bitterest opponents of the War of 1812, when he served in Congress from New Hampshire and mercilessly harassed him during his presidency. Yet even he was extremely friendly to the two New Englanders when they visited him at Montpelier on their way to Jefferson's home.[55] He freely drank choice wines with Ticknor and Webster, and uninhibitedly discussed politics with them.[56]

According to Ticknor's printed memorandum, Madison was friendly to Webster. At Montpelier, Ticknor wrote, "We were very hospitably received. Mr. Madison and Mr. Webster were old acquaintances, and evidently well pleased to see each other again. Mr. Madison talked well, and laid himself out to be agreeable to Mr. Webster."[57] Nonetheless, Ticknor admitted that they steered clear of disputation relating to politics. "Though every thing [*sic*] of a party nature was avoided between persons whose opinions were so opposite, yet both were too much interested in the country and its history not to talk about its affairs." Strange to relate, Ticknor recorded that Webster considered Madison a more intelligent president than Jefferson was, and second only to Washington in greatness. "After we returned to Washington," Ticknor wrote, "Mr. Webster told me that he had been very much impressed by Mr. Madison's conversation, and that it had fully confirmed him in an opinion he had for some time entertained, that Mr. Madison was 'the wisest of our Presidents, except Washington.'"[58]

Like Jefferson's alleged denunciation of Jackson, Webster's reported praise of Madison is difficult to believe. Webster despised Madison during the War of 1812, and was one of the most vigorous obstructionists of the war effort in Congress. He opposed raising taxes for the war, urged the New England states not to contribute their militia to the conflict, and advocated state nullification of national laws when it seemed that Congress might pass a draft. He supported the Hartford Convention, although he was reluctant to favor New England's secession from the Union. As for Madison, he called him "a faint-heated, lily-livered runaway" after he fled Washington, D.C., in October 1814 during the British invasion.[59] (Webster was in Portsmouth, New Hampshire, at the time.) Jefferson and Madison's graciousness and hospitality toward Webster despite his deep hostility toward them in the past is hard for a twenty-first century mind to comprehend.

Writing to his young friend William H. Prescott, who later became a renowned historian of Spain and Spanish America, especially the conquests of Mexico and Peru, and a Spanish literature expert, Ticknor described at length his visit to the two Virginia sages. He mentioned nothing about Jefferson's alleged alarm at Jackson's election. Ticknor's letter revealed that Madison was a better farm manager and perhaps possessed more slaves than Jefferson at this time. Ticknor said that Madison owned 180 slaves, but that he humbly viewed his plantation at Montpelier as a "farm." "Mr. Madison's farm—as he calls it—consists of about three thousand acres, with an [sic] 180 slaves, and is among the best managed in Virginia," Ticknor reported. He observed that most other Virginia plantations had a "very squalid appearance." Ticknor noted that Philip Barbour, a nearby planter and politician and U.S. senator, did not know how to use his great monetary wealth to make his mansion a "refined" habitation, despite its "luxurious" accouterments and brick construction. Ticknor was disappointed that Jefferson lived less opulently than he expected. "Early on Tuesday we arrived at Monticello," he wrote. "Everything here is on a larger scale than at Montpelier; the house, the grounds, and the arrangements. There is, too, nothing that marks the residence of an Ex-King." The young Massachusetts intellectual was more impressed with Jefferson's University, which he said contained "more beautiful buildings than anything architectural in New England, and more appropriate to an university than can be found perhaps, in the world." Ticknor mentioned nothing about Jefferson's opinion of Jackson. However, he reported that Jefferson was happy and healthy. Although Jefferson told him he would be ready to die when he could no longer read or ride a horse, Ticknor expected him to live "another nine or ten years." He said that Jefferson was primarily interested in launching the University of Virginia; he had little interest in politics. As Ticknor viewed him: "Mr. Jefferson is entirely absorbed in it [University of Virginia], and its success would make a *beau finale* indeed to his life. He is now eighty-two years old, very little altered from what he was ten years ago, very active, lively, and happy, riding from ten to fifteen miles every day, and talking without the least restraint, very pleasantly, upon all subjects."

Surprisingly, politics was not one of them. "In politics, his interest seems nearly gone," Ticknor observed. "He takes no newspaper but the *Richmond Enquirer*, and reads that reluctantly; but on all matters of literature, philosophy, and general interest, he is prompt, and even eager. He reads much Greek and Saxon. I saw his Greek Lexicon, printed in 1817; it was much worn with use, and contained many curious notes."[60]

Often quoted by scholars, Webster's memorandum was supposedly recorded sometime at the end of 1824 or the beginning of 1825 by Mrs. Ticknor, *née* Anne Eliot. Along with her Harvard professor husband George Ticknor, she accompanied Webster on his pilgrimage, from December 9 to December 21, 1824, to visit Jefferson and James Madison on their Virginia estates. Apparently, Webster did not feel sufficiently moved to preserve a record of his visit to Madison for posterity. However, his "notes" of his visit to Jefferson, especially Jefferson's unusually hostile comments about Webster's political opponent Andrew Jackson, have garnered much attention from historians. Ticknor was not only Jefferson's friend but was friendly with John Adams, who had first introduced him to Jefferson. Thus, in addition to ingratiating himself with Ticknor, the "Sage of Monticello" may have castigated Jackson in order to please his old friend John, father of Jackson's competitor, John Quincy Adams. John would be likely to ask Ticknor what Jefferson had said about the election.

The direct source of Jefferson's negative commentary is neither Webster nor Jefferson, but Mrs. Ticknor, to whom her husband and Webster allegedly dictated their reminiscences shortly after the visit ended. She was aware that Jefferson constantly invited her husband to Monticello, and she was interested in meeting the third president despite her family's antipathy to his policies. On September 28, 1824, exhilarated by the Marquis de Lafayette's visit to Boston in the course of his famous nationwide tour (Ticknor had met him in Europe years earlier), Ticknor suddenly manifested interest in once again seeing the great patriot Jefferson. He felt an urge to travel with his wife Anna, who, although reluctant to go to Charleston, South Carolina, "seems willing to go to Washington, Richmond, and Monticello, where Mr. Jefferson has again and again written to invite us to make a visit."[61]

As we have already seen, the Ticknors and Webster had to stay at an inn for a few days after visiting Jefferson because of heavy rainfall, and decided to record their experiences in a journal that they dictated to Mrs. Ticknor. "We had therefore a long winter evening before us," she explained, writing in the first person plural, "and we got rid of it by making these notes, which are here copied with care, and without a change of any sort, from the identical manuscript in which they were originally recorded, chiefly by Mrs. Ticknor, under the dictation of Mr. Webster and Mr. Ticknor. As far as what relates exclusively to Mr. Jefferson, his appearance and conversation, the work is Mr. Webster's. The rest was a sort of joint-stock contribution." As she explained, "In the course of the evening [late December 1824] when the preceding was written, from Mr. Webster's dictation [i.e., a description of Jefferson's physical appearance, conversation, and general demeanor], the gentlemen by uniting their recollections, preserved the following anecdotes of several great men, from Mr. Jefferson's recollection."[62] Apparently, the original set of notes were composed by Mrs. Ticknor, recording Webster's and her husband's words about Jefferson's statements, in the inn where the trio passed the night before heading back to Washington.[63]

Indeed, Mrs. Ticknor ostensibly considered Webster's (and/or Mr. Ticknor's) remarks about Jackson so interesting that, alone of her records of Webster's commentaries about his visit to Jefferson, she twice copied down Jefferson's anathemas about Jackson: the first time in advance of the rest of the "Notes," segregating them from the body of the text in their own place of honor. This suggests there may have been something contrived about this entry regarding Jackson. As they appeared on page twenty-four of Webster's "Notes," as recorded by Mrs. Ticknor, Jefferson said: "I feel much alarmed at the prospect of seeing General Jackson, President. He is one of the most unfit men I know of for such a place. He has had very little respect for laws or Constitutions—& is in fact merely an able military chief. His passions are terrible—When I was President of the Senate, he was a Senator, & he could never speak from the rashness of his feelings. I have seen him attempt it repeatedly, & as often choak with rage. His passions are no doubt cooler now—he has been much tried since I knew him—but he is a *dangerous man*."[64]

Jefferson's alleged comments are so extremely hostile to Jackson, more intemperate and bitter than anything Jefferson ever said about anyone, even Alexander Hamilton (about whom the most violent remarks he made were "[He is a] man whose history, from the moment at which history can stoop to notice him, is a tissue of machinations against the liberty of the country which has not only received and given him bread, but heaped it's honors on his head") that it is hard to believe he uttered them.[65] It is even possible that Mrs. Ticknor made them up herself, mimicking Webster's opinion of Jackson, and ascribed it to Jefferson to confuse contemporaries and posterity.

Ironically, even those who became Jackson's greatest enemies praised his rationality, *politesse*, and moderation. At the end of 1823, John Quincy Adams, conversing with one of Jackson's political foes, voiced the opinion that Jackson would make the best president of the

United States; he "preferred him decidedly to any of the other candidates."[66] After meeting Jackson for the first time in January 1824, Daniel Webster's wife was impressed and delighted by his politeness and civility.[67] Since Mrs. Ticknor's notes are the only source of Jefferson's defamatory quotation, which was published long after Webster and Jefferson were both dead, it is surprising that Webster, often Jackson's political foe, never used them to embarrass Jackson during his lifetime. Indeed, the possibility exists that George Ticknor's wife, Anna Eliot Ticknor, daughter of wealthy Boston Federalist merchant Samuel Eliot, who was a devout conservative and enemy of Jackson, may have invented these remarks out of whole cloth. They are not to be found anywhere else.[68]

Most of the material Webster allegedly recorded was factually accurate. For example, Jefferson reminisced with him and Ticknor about a panther skin he bought in Philadelphia on his way to Paris in 1784 to prove to French scientists like Georges Buffon and Abbé Raynal that, contrary to their assertions, American mammals were at least as big, actually bigger, than European.[69] Webster himself was not irreconcilably hostile to Jackson. He only turned against him at the final moment in the presidential election of 1824, lending decisive support to John Quincy Adams in the House of Representatives in the infamous "corrupt bargain" election. He had earlier viewed Jackson in a favorable light. In February 1824, he wrote his brother Ezekiel about Jackson in flattering terms. "Mr. Adams's chance seems to increase," he wrote, in light of the unpopularity of congressional caucus nominations for the presidency, which had settled on William H. Crawford, "and he and General Jackson are likely to be the real competitors at last. General Jackson's manners are more presidential than those of any of the candidates. He is grave, mild, and reserved. My wife is for him decidedly."[70] Thus, Webster was not initially an anti–Jackson partisan.

On the other hand, Webster vigorously opposed Jefferson, Madison and the War of 1812 when he served as a New Hampshire Federalist congressman from 1813 to 1816, although he eschewed participation in the quasi-secessionist Hartford Convention in December 1814. In 1816, Webster returned to Boston, where in 1804 he had been Christopher Gore's law clerk. He resumed the practice of law, convinced that Federalist opposition to the War of 1812 had doomed the party's prospects. Boston Federalist merchant Thomas Handasyd Perkins, whose investments in the opium trade between Turkey and China he shared in and facilitated, was one of his few friends.[71] Sydney Nathans, a careful student of Webster's early political career, writes, "Webster joined the alliance opposed to Andrew Jackson belatedly and reluctantly, and his belief persisted that conflict was best resolved by consensus among leaders rather than by competition between parties." At first, he refused to submit to party discipline.[72]

It is conceivable that the Ticknors or Webster invented Jefferson's remarks, or greatly exaggerated them to support their campaign against Jackson at some future date after Jefferson's death, since these damaging comments about Old Hickory were not published during Jefferson's lifetime. This may be because, until well into his first term, Jackson was considered an unknown quantity by Webster and his proto-Whig friends. Indeed, they had no distinctly established policies of their own, except for hoping that the next president would be a New Englander after twenty-four years of Virginian captivity. Early in his political life, according to his biographer Sydney Nathans, Webster prided himself on being above the political fray, a nonpartisan statesman who sought only the public good.[73]

Writers closer in time to the events that transpired tended, more than modern historians, to doubt the authenticity of the statements ascribed to Jefferson. They acknowledged that Webster and his friends visited Monticello in December 1824, and the accuracy of his physical description of the aging polymath. Judging from the remarks of the transcriber, Mrs. Ticknor, Jefferson's alleged comments about Jackson were likely in part her creation (what she called a "joint-stock contribution"), not a verbatim record. James Parton, an early biographer of both Jackson and Jefferson, considered Webster's "Notes" unreliable. He asserted, "All of Mr. Webster's Monticello notes have been called in question, and some of them are known to be incorrect." In a 1911 biography, a prominent Jackson scholar, John Spencer Bassett, questioned the veracity of Jefferson's "alleged" remarks (his term) to Webster about Jackson at their meeting in December 1824. Referring to an affable letter from Jefferson to Jackson dated December 18, 1823, only a year before the Webster-Ticknor junket, he observed, "Webster's report has been widely quoted; but it is hardly to be reconciled with the following expression," which he quoted from Jefferson's letter. Arthur M. Schlesinger's famous narrative, *The Age of Jackson* also suggests that Webster's "Notes" were not an accurate depiction of what Jefferson said about Jackson.[74]

Although early Jackson biographers hinted that Webster's memorandum was inaccurate or spurious and genteelly alluded to its "incorrectness," they failed to pursue the point. For example, according to the Webster/Ticknor notes, Jefferson praised Patrick Henry and belittled Henry's nephew and biographer, William Wirt, a renowned lawyer and writer who served as attorney general under Presidents James Monroe and John Quincy Adams. Reminiscing about the Revolutionary War period, Jefferson allegedly told Webster: "After all, it must be allowed that he [Patrick Henry] was our leader, in the measures of the Revolution, in Virginia. In that respect, more is due to HIM than to any other person. If we had not had *him*, we should probably have got on *pretty* well, as you [in New England] did, by a number of men of nearly equal talents, but he left us all far behind."[75]

About William Wirt, with whom Jefferson was personally friendly (although one could not tell that from the following remarks recorded by Mrs. Ticknor), Jefferson acerbically said, "His [Henry's] biographer, sent the sheets of his work to me, as they were printed, & at the end asked for my opinion. I told him it would be a question hereafter, whether his work should be placed on the shelf of *history,* or of *panegyric.*" He sarcastically continued, "It is a poor book, written in bad taste, & gives so imperfect an idea of Patrick Henry, that it seems intended to show off the *writer,* more than the subject of the work."[76]

Students of the period are aware that, contrary to Jefferson's statements in his "conversation" with Webster, Jefferson in his old age was critical of Patrick Henry.[77] He blamed Henry for a smear campaign against him in the House of Delegates in 1782 that insinuated that he was a coward who fled from the British army as governor of Virginia. Moreover, despite what he "said" to Webster, Jefferson did not view William Wirt as a fool. Jefferson considered Wirt a learned intellectual, and recommended him for law professor at the University of Virginia, despite his being Henry's nephew.[78]

Such questionable statements by "Jefferson" in his conversation with Webster indicate that he may not have said everything Webster or his amanuensis ascribed to him. More basically, a few paragraphs before his diatribe against Jackson, Jefferson told Webster, in the course of his narrative of the Revolution, "Richard Henry Lee, moved the Declaration of Independence, in pursuance of the Resolutions of the Assembly of Virginia, & only because he was the oldest member of the Virginia delegation."[79] This simple datum is the most revealing evidence that Webster's memoir is not entirely trustworthy.

Especially in his declining years, Jefferson tracked the deaths of the signers of the Declaration of Independence. A year before, he had reminded John Adams that only four were left. Undoubtedly, Jefferson was aware that in 1776, Richard Henry Lee (1732–1794) was *not* the oldest member of the Virginian delegation; his close friend and beloved law school teacher, George Wythe (1726–1806), whose tragic murder by his grandnephew in 1806 was etched in Jefferson's memory, was eldest.[80] Wythe attended Congress on June 7, 1776, when Lee moved that the colonies should become "free and independent states." Along with John Adams, he ably defended Lee's motion. Wythe, together with Lee, left for Virginia on June 13, while Jefferson, left behind to serve on the committee that wrote the Declaration of Independence, asked Wythe to present the Virginia constitutional convention with a draft of a state constitution he had written in his spare time.[81]

As recently as 1820, Jefferson had reason to think about his beloved friend and mentor Wythe. He responded to a query from historian John Sanderson asking him if he could supply any details about Wythe and other signers of the Declaration of Independence for a book he was writing. Intent on avoiding public controversy in his last years, Jefferson was not eager to commit himself, perhaps fearing he might offend someone and antagonize their family members or political supporters. He begged off from supplying information about John Hancock, saying that as Congress's second youngest member, he did not have much contact with the renowned first signer of the Declaration and president of the Second Continental Congress. However, he did not hesitate to write a few sentences in praise of Wythe, the person for whom, along with Dabney Carr, James Madison and John Page, he perhaps felt greatest affection. In the letter to Sanderson, dated August 31, 1820, Jefferson mentioned Wythe's age, indicating that he thought that Wythe was born in 1724, making him two years *older* than he actually was. He wrote, "I became acquainted with Mr. Wythe when he was about 38 years of age. He directed my studies in the law, led me into business, and continued until death my most affectionate friend. A close intimacy with him during the period of forty odd years, the most important of his life, enables me to state it's leading facts." Although he ended the letter without giving more information on Wythe, perhaps intending to do so at a future date, he asserted, "In the year of his birth, I may err a little, stating that from the recollection of a particular incident, the date of which, within a year or two, I do not distinctly remember."[82]

In addition, around this period, in July 1821, Jefferson was engaged in composing his *Autobiography*, which, despite its brevity, lack of new information, and impersonal nature, contains a few words about Wythe that show his significance for Jefferson. He said he greatly admired Wythe, and recalls that he discussed Wythe's virtues in a letter to "John Saunderson [*sic*]," which he misdates as August 31, 1821. A few pages earlier in the manuscript, he mentioned his letter to Sanderson in a footnote, giving its correct date: "For a sketch of the life and character of Mr. Wythe see my letter of Aug. 31, 1820 to Mr. John Saunderson."[83] Thus, during the 1820's, Jefferson had Wythe on his mind.

Jefferson was in his late seventies and early eighties during this period. His memory was probably not as good as it once was. Nevertheless, he erred in thinking that Wythe was *older* than he really was. He wrote Sanderson that Wythe became his law teacher at the age of thirty-eight, which would have put his birth date at 1724. Dumas Malone, the foremost

Jefferson scholar, wrote that Jefferson began to study law under Wythe in 1762, when Jefferson was nineteen years old.[84]

That such information was hardly arcane seems obvious. Although Webster, who was born after the American Revolution, probably did not ponder the deaths of signers of the Declaration of Independence, those personally connected with the momentous event like Jefferson and John Quincy Adams, whose father, the "Colossus of Independence," invariably took credit for its passage, certainly did. In his diary in 1820 John Quincy Adams wrote, that of the Declaration's fifty-six signers, "only four are at this day numbered among the living: John Adams, of Mass., my father, Thomas Jefferson of Virginia, William Floyd, of New York, and Charles Carroll of Carrollton, Maryland."[85]

Judging from these errors, and there are probably others, it is likely that, aside from its initial description of Jefferson's physical appearance, which Mrs. Ticknor said Webster "dictated" to her, some of Webster's "Notes of Mr. Jefferson's Conversation" were either false or a lark composed by Mrs. Ticknor. She was hostile to Jackson, and could have composed spurious "notes" with or without the active collaboration of her husband and Webster. Several outstanding historians have accepted this text as their sole basis for positing hostility between Jefferson and Jackson. They use it as their point of departure for arguing that Jefferson's aristocratic version of deferential, ersatz democracy was a far cry from Jackson's rough-hewn, vulgar, sweaty, individualistic frontier egalitarian democracy. These same scholars often then pounce on either or both of the two statesmen, their parties, and their ideologies.

Despite Jefferson's alleged acrimonious words to Webster, he did not oppose generals for office *per se*. For example, Jefferson ardently supported General George Washington at the outset of his presidency and through his first term. He did not turn to opposition until Washington's condemnation of the Whiskey Rebellion and his support for Jay's Treaty in 1794–1795 made it evident that his policies had become strictly Federalist.[86] It is likely that Jefferson felt comfortable with Jackson's candidacy. He greatly admired his military prowess, especially the incredible victory at the Battle of New Orleans.[87] In addition, Jackson shared Jefferson's anti-aristocratic prejudices (although they were both slaveholders, Jackson was a self-made plantation owner, rising up from poverty), opposition to big business monopolies like the Bank of the United States, and a desire for free trade in foreign economic policy.

On the other hand, it is possible that Jefferson's eagerness in his last days to reconcile New England and the South, his friendship for George Ticknor, and his tendency to avert disputes by agreeing with what others said, may have prompted words hostile to Jackson. However, this is unlikely, since Jefferson's policy was to avoid openly stating his personal preference for presidential candidates because he wanted to avoid public controversy. (Privately, he favored William H. Crawford, who was incapacitated by a stroke in October 1824.) Thus, he had no reason to defame Jackson as Ticknor's notes assert he did. Indeed, Jefferson's alleged comments were not made public during and after the 1824 election, suggesting that Ticknor and Webster might have feared he would deny that he said them. The most likely explanation for Jefferson's brusque words is that one or all of his visitors made them up. What rings true is Jefferson's eagerness to reconcile North and South, East and West in order to preserve the Union and extend its pattern of democracy, liberty and freedom of thought across the Atlantic world.

24

Jefferson's Political Map
and Terminal National Union
Include New England

As death neared, Jefferson's lifelong desire to uphold the ideal of national unity revived. He was fully aware that tense North-South relations resulted primarily from differences over slavery expansion; the Supreme Court's broad constitutional construction; the national bank; protective tariffs; and internal improvements. Although in letters to a few Southern extremists like one he wrote in December 1825 to William Branch Giles, he theoretically endorsed a call for Virginia's secession from a Northern-dominated Union, he invariably concluded with requests for patience. He told Giles that he hoped Virginia would remain in the Union until it was faced with "submission to a government without limitation of powers." In a tone echoing that of his letter to John Taylor in June 1798, he chided Giles, "If every infraction of a compact of so many parties is to be resisted at once, as a dissolution of it, none can ever be formed which would last one year." He boldly advised the irascible states' righter Giles to support a constitutional amendment, recently proposed in Congress, granting that body power over internal improvements. This amendment was similar to recommendations that Jefferson, Madison, and Monroe had made in several annual messages to Congress.[1]

Perhaps because he was near death, Jefferson's nationalism suddenly intensified to the extent of supporting federal *intrastate* internal improvements, with the consent of the state involved, as well as those between states. As he wrote Giles, he favored giving Congress, "by a regular amendment of the constitution [*sic*], a right to make roads and canals of intercommunication between the States, providing sufficiently against corrupt practices in Congress, (log-rolling,&c.,) by declaring that the federal proportion of each State of the moneys so employed, shall be in works within the State, or elsewhere with its consent, and with a due *salvo* of jurisdiction. This is the course which I think safest and best as yet."[2] Jefferson suddenly upheld an extreme nationalist view on internal improvements, which would permit the national government to erect roads and canals within individual states. (President Jackson opposed this type of internal improvement when he vetoed the Maysville, Kentucky Road bill in 1830.)

Jefferson wrote in a similar vein to William Fitzhugh Gordon, a conservative western Piedmont member of the House of Delegates, which had power to propose amendments to the U.S. Constitution. He argued that, despite its unpopularity with Virginia states' righters, such an extremely nationalistic amendment would "save and at the same time improve our constitution, for I think that with sufficient guards it will be a wholesome amendment."[3] Probably to appease states' righters like Gordon and his allies, he added a "Solemn Declaration and Protest of the Commonwealth of Virginia" which insisted, in opposition to the controversial proposals in John Quincy Adams' inaugural address, that the federal government could not construct internal improvements within a single state or erect a national university without constitutional amendments. However, on Madison's advice he concluded that the controversy was none of his business, and did not send Gordon the manifesto.[4]

In the last years of his life, perhaps because he was no longer involved in politics, Jefferson's proposals were more boldly nationalistic and politically radical than ever before, belying his protests against "consolidation." In an effort to promote Union, he proved willing to abandon Southern and Virginian prerogatives, including the sacred institution of black slavery, and adopt measures advocated by liberal activists in other parts of the country. In February 1824, writing to states' rights Virginia congressman Robert Selden Garnett, he started out by thanking Garnett for a copy of John Taylor's latest polemic against the "consolidation" of government in the Supreme Court, *New Views of the Constitution* (1824). "I shall read them with the satisfaction and edification which I have ever derived from whatever he has written," he politely promised. As was his custom, he said that the present-day "federalists" actually desired a "consolidationist" program. Though he warned that "the friends of consolidation" were becoming increasingly powerful, he evidently supported their objectives, as long as they were accomplished by what he considered the legitimate mode of amending the constitution rather than broad, arbitrary "construction."[5]

Intent on upholding the public will, Jefferson conceded that internal improvements were popular with most people in the states, as long as the money was spent for the benefit of the state and within the state. Pretending more sincere agreement with Garnett and Giles than he actually felt, Jefferson continued, "The friends of consolidation would rather take these powers by construction than accept them by direct investiture from the States" by means of constitutional amendments. Indicating that he was a strong supporter of national roads and canals (after all, it was under Jefferson's administration that the construction of the "National Road" began), he argued, "As to internal improvements particularly, there is probably not a State in the Union which would not grant this power on the condition proposed, or which would grant it without that [i.e., to spend the money within the state]." Expounding a relatively broad construction of the Constitution, Jefferson observed that the Constitution intended for the national government control over interstate and foreign affairs, while the individual states had charge of their constituents' domestic needs. According to Jefferson, the only "instance of control vested in the federal, over the State authorities, in a matter purely domestic" was in issuing "metallic tenders" as currency. (The Constitution prohibited the states from coining money or "emit[ting] bills of credit.") He did not depict the national government as alien to the states when he wrote Garnett, "The federal is, in truth, our foreign government, which department alone is taken from the sovereignty of the separate States."[6] He was merely explaining his view that the national government alone was in charge of "foreign" affairs—relations with other ("foreign") nations, although scholars in the past have misguidedly quoted this phrase to demonstrate Jefferson's "hostility" to the national government.

Jefferson vigorously supported democratic, nationalistic constitutional amendments: for limiting the president's term of office; direct popular election of the president, which necessitated abolishing the Constitution's proslavery "three-fifths clause"; and giving Congress control over internal improvements "on condition that each State's federal proportion of the moneys so expended, shall be employed within the State." Endorsing constitutional amendments enforcing direct election of the president by the people, limitation of the president to two terms in office, and internal improvements, Jefferson praised the amendment process. It was the road to peaceful progressive change, and the means by which the United States would avert European-style violent revolution, followed by anarchy. At the same time, Jefferson was not especially confident that, even were the value of amendments recognized, the Union would inevitably stick together and be "immortal." As he sagely put it, "The real friends of the Constitution in its federal form, if they wish it to be immortal, should be attentive, by amendments, to make it keep pace with the advance of the age in science and experience."[7]

Foreshadowing what in the 1950s was called "American exceptionalism," Jefferson argued that the amendment process was the route of peaceful reform that distinguished the U.S. from fledgling European republics that eventually returned to monarchy. Instead of adopting amendments, he pointed out, "the European governments have resisted reformation, until the people, seeing no other resource, undertake it themselves by force; their only weapon, and work it out through blood, desolation, and long-continued anarchy." Jefferson predicted that individual states would choose to secede from the Union unless the Constitution were amended in a more populist direction. They would prefer to leave rather than participate in what they might consider internal disorder. Although he did not say so, he may have had Southerners' desire to protect slavery in mind when he observed regarding disunion, "Here [in the United States] it will be by large fragments [i.e., groups of states] breaking off, and refusing re-union but on conditions of amendment, or perhaps permanently."[8] He understood the possibility of secession, which both the North and South threatened at different times, most recently during the Missouri crisis. He regretted that likelihood, but he did not think the Constitution prohibited it.

Slavery was a fulcrum of the Southern economy. It was a popular institution in such states as South Carolina, Mississippi, and Louisiana, where nearly half of the white families owned slaves, as Kenneth Stampp and others have pointed out. In several states most people had friends or relatives who were slaveholders. The proportion of whites who were slaveholders had increased in Virginia from the 1780s to the 1820s, as had the more widespread distribution of land, in part because of Jefferson's strenuous efforts to abolish primogeniture and entail in 1776–1778. According to Jackson Turner Main's analysis of Virginia tax lists for 1787 and 1788, a majority of adult white males were not landowners. Between one-half and three-fourths of adult white males were landless. Most white men were tenants or farm laborers on the lands of yeomen or wealthy planters. On the other hand, even thirty percent of the landless owned slaves, while half of them owned a cow. Although Main paints a picture of widespread economic desperation in Virginia farm areas during the 1780s, those who owned land owned a lot of it, especially compared to such parts of the country as rural Massachusetts, a state that was much smaller than Virginia in any case. The average Virginia farm was 230 acres. Three-fourths of Virginia landowners had slaves to help them cultivate their land, although most Virginia landowners possessed fewer than ten slaves.[9]

In examining the wealthiest one hundred Virginia planters of 1787 and 1788, Main finds that wealth was less concentrated in their hands than one might expect. They owned six percent of the land and six-and-a half percent of the slaves. The northern tidewater and the

Northern Neck, farmlands that bordered the James, Rappahanock and Potomac Rivers, had the best land and the wealthiest planters. The Piedmont and the southern tidewater below the James River had fewer wealthy men. Jefferson, whose plantations were in the Piedmont, was nevertheless the twenty-eighth richest man on the tax list. He inherited a great deal of land and slaves from his father-in-law John Wayles. (His close friend James Madison, who was only in his thirties, did not even make the top hundred at this time.) Jefferson owned a total of about ten thousand acres of land. The average land-holding of the wealthiest one hundred men was three thousand acres, although two on the tax list had over twenty thousand acres. The average number of slaves owned by the wealthiest one hundred was eighty. During the 1780s, at the height of his slave-holdings, Jefferson owned two hundred.[10]

Ironically, Jefferson had no thought of recommending a constitutional amendment protecting slavery, as Abraham Lincoln did after his election to the presidency in 1861. He emphasized the more pedestrian amendments under consideration in his time, some of which were favored by Northern Federalists, like restricting the president to two terms and other less dramatic reforms.

Adopting a position that seems naïve in hindsight, Jefferson believed that the Union would stay together if amendments passed for direct election of the president, a two-term limit to a president's tenure in office, and for promoting congressional supervision of internal improvements. With a sense of drama, he said, "If I can see these three great amendments passed, I shall consider it as a renewed extension of the term of our lease" as a united republic, "[and] shall live in more confidence, and die in more hope." At the close of his letter to Garnett he applauded the states' righter Taylor, perhaps hoping to gain both men's approval for his nationalist agenda. "And I do trust that the republican mass, which Colonel Taylor justly says is the real federal one, is still strong enough to carry these truly federo-republican amendments," he pleaded. "With my prayers for the issue, accept my friendly and respectful salutations."[11]

In view of the potential threat that democratic reforms in the presidential election process might pose to Virginia and the slave South's hold on the presidency, it took political courage for the generally reticent Jefferson to support such measures in letters to his conservative friends. A complex constitutional amendment for the president's direct election by the voters, introduced by Republican congressman Edward Livingston of New York on January 24, 1824, three weeks before Jefferson's letter to Garnett, did not formally repeal the "three-fifths" clause that was so objectionable to Northerners. The amendment would not outright reduce the number of slave-state electoral votes, but would effectively diminish the power of slaveholders. For presidential elections, each state legislature would create a number of districts "equal to the whole number of Senators and Representatives to which such State may be entitled in the Congress of the United States." By stipulating that the electoral districts must be equal in area and in number of eligible voters, the amendment eliminated numbers of slaves in apportioning electoral votes to districts. Equal electoral districts would reduce the weight of large slaveholders: "Each district shall be composed, as nearly as may be, of contiguous territory, and shall contain a number of persons entitled to vote, as nearly equal as circumstances will permit."[12]

In theory, Jefferson still believed that, except with regard to its monopoly over coinage and interstate and foreign commerce, the federal government's powers were primarily connected with U.S. relations with other countries. However, his nationalistic devotion to the

Union and his attachment to the states were linked *via* the constitutional amendment process, whereby state legislatures or state conventions ratified changes to the Constitution. In Jefferson's view, the only way to preserve the Constitution "immortal" was by constant amendment, "to make it keep pace with the advance of the age in science and experience."[13]

Although Jefferson may have been alluding to present discontents within Virginia and other Southern states, it is possible he also had the Hartford Convention in mind. Ironically, Jefferson supported several of the revisions proposed by that conclave, such as abolishing special privileges for slaveholders (in his case, in the apportioning of county representation in the state legislature); overriding the national "three-fifths clause," and limiting a president's tenure. (While he favored rendering the president ineligible after two terms, the Hartford Convention wished to restrict the president to a single term.)[14]

Among the other, even more controversial constitutional amendments Jefferson advocated at this time was one for the gradual abolition of Southern slavery. Although he made no recommendation for compensating slaveholders other than vaguely suggesting that the state pay the masters to provide food and shelter for newborn slaves and teach them a trade during their childhood, he said that the national government should subsidize the costs of "transporting" emancipated adult slaves to Haiti. Jefferson appositely disclosed the details of his plan not to a Southerner but a New Englander. Only a week before writing Garnett, Jefferson had sent this proposal for the gradual abolition of slavery to the Unitarian preacher and Harvard professor of classical languages Jared Sparks of Massachusetts, a Harvard College graduate and later president of the College. Like Jefferson a polymath, Sparks edited the *North American* Review, an influential periodical among New England intellectuals. After witnessing the brutality of slavery on his travels through North and South Carolina and Georgia, Sparks had become an antislavery colonizationist leader. There was a mutual trust between the aristocratic Jefferson and this young, brilliant New Englander who rose from poverty and virtually created the historical profession as an academic discipline.[15]

In his last years, Jefferson welcomed modernizing nationalist reforms. He seemed resigned to slavery's demise, but expected it to occur after his death. He was enthusiastic about proposed amendments for the direct popular election of a president limited to two terms (which he had always favored) and extensive federal internal improvements. As he explained to the localist Garnett, he believed that the Republican Party was "still strong enough to carry these truly federo-republican amendments," which, if passed, "I shall consider ... as a renewed extension of the term of our lease." He evoked the classical republican concept that all republics were doomed to eventually decline into anarchy, monarchy, and despotism, but hoped that reformist constitutional amendments, emulating the liberal spirit of the times, would give the republic a new lease on life.[16]

Such letters to states' rights politicians, which some historians have misconstrued as evidence that Jefferson turned increasingly reactionary with age and many others have ignored, seem rather to constitute his swan song to American nationalism. Jefferson balanced his contact with Virginia states' righters with communications with conservative New England nationalists like Sparks and Edward Everett, another Unitarian preacher and Harvard professor, renowned for his oratory and, during the Civil War, devotion to the Union despite his initial pro–Southern sympathies. During the 1820s, as congressman from Massachusetts, Everett combined several contradictory points of view. He supported Henry Clay's nationalistic American System, protective tariffs, and John Quincy Adams' program of activist federal government. At the same time, he theoretically upheld the rights of the states and supported Southern slavery. He ran for vice-president on the Constitutional Union Party ticket in the crucial election of 1860, and made a famous two-hour speech at Gettysburg battlefield in November 1863 before Lincoln's immortal two-minute address. He was a Massachusetts congressman when he wrote Jefferson in 1826 about a constitutional amendment that became popular with Southern delegates after John Quincy Adams defeated Andrew Jackson for the presidency in the House of Representatives in 1825, in an alleged "corrupt bargain" with Henry Clay that gained the latter's supporters. The constitutional amendment, proposed by South Carolina delegate George McDuffie in February 1826, would abolish the Electoral College and henceforth determine the president's election by means of popular vote in equal election districts throughout the country, eliminating any role for the House of Representatives or the Senate in cases where no majority was received by presidential or vice-presidential candidates.[17]

Everett initiated contact with Jefferson in 1822. Everett was probably aware of Jefferson's Unitarian sympathies. He sent him a book written by his brother, Alexander Hill Everett, U.S. *chargé d'affaires* at Amsterdam, about the political situation in Europe, titled *Europe; or a general survey of the present situation of the principal powers* (1822). Jefferson praised the volume, claiming that it gave him more accurate information than newspapers.[18]

Unlike the antislavery Jefferson, who supported Haiti's independence from France, Everett, despite his Massachusetts roots, was vigorously proslavery. On March 9, 1826, speaking in Congress in opposition to McDuffie's amendment, he simultaneously defended black bondage. "Domestic slavery is not, in my judgment, to be set down as an immoral and irreligious relation," he said. "I would cede the whole continent to any one who would take it— to England, to France, to Spain—I would see it sunk in the bottom of the ocean, before I would see any part of this fair America converted into a continental Hayti." Expounding a qualified version of the "Positive Good" argument justifying slavery, Everett asserted, "I know the condition of the working classes in other countries; I am intimately acquainted with it in some other countries, and I have no hesitation in saying, that I believe the slaves in this country are better clothed and fed, and less hardly worked, than the peasantry of some of the most prosperous States of the Continent of Europe."[19]

Jefferson was probably shocked by Everett's blatant proslavery sentiments. Yet, Jefferson maintained a tone of polite respect for Everett's opinion that Congress should not force abolition on the slave states. In his last years, Jefferson tended, as in his letter to Sparks, to believe that a coercive constitutional amendment might ultimately be necessary to effect abolition. After initiating correspondence with Jefferson, Everett sent him a copy of his proslavery speech, which included an analysis of McDuffie's amendment. Jefferson claimed to be impressed with it. "I have read it with pleasure and edification, and concurred with much of its contents," he replied. While concurring with Everett's defense of states' rights in the matter of slavery, he sternly rejected Everett's proslavery dicta. "On the question of the lawfulness of slavery that it is the right of one man to appropriate to himself the faculties of another without his consent, I certainly retain my early opinion," he said. "On that, however, of third persons to interfere between the parties, and the effect of conventional modifications of that pretension, we are probably nearer together." He affirmed his agreement with Everett's conservative Unionism: "I think with you also that the constitution of the U.S. is a compact of independent nations, subject to the rules acknowledged in similar cases, as well that of amendment provided within itself, as, in case of abuse, the justly dreaded but unavoidable *ultima ratio gentium* [by this, Jefferson must have meant secession or war]."[20]

Thus, Jefferson, albeit reluctantly, acknowledged the right of states to secede from the Union. He also remained interested in U.S. Inter-American policy. Apparently, he appreciated having Everett, chairman of the House committee on foreign affairs, as a conduit for current events. This was made evident when he wrote, "The Report on the Panama question mentioned also in your letter has as I suppose got separated by the way. It will probably come by another mail."[21]

Jefferson's communication with nationalistic New Englanders like Sparks and Everett made clear his solicitude for the opinion of New England's intellectual elite. He favored legislation that would help New England interests. His consistent support for a constitutional amendment on internal improvements was an implementation of loose constitutional construction of little use to the South. His advocacy of gradual abolition of slavery, the immediate termination of extra representation for Southern slave-holdings in the Electoral College, and his support for presidential term limits, reasserted his transcendent commitment to nationhood and acknowledged New England's vital role in the extended republic. Unfortunately, most studies of Jefferson's old age and retirement gloss over his political views at this time or depict him as an extreme state's righter and would-be secessionist. However, in many respects the dying Jefferson espoused more thoroughly democratic and Unionist ideas than at any time in his career. His political thought during retirement deserves to be more fully examined and taken more seriously, and not merely in terms of his correspondence with Adams.[22]

Douglass Adair, Drew McCoy, Julian Boyd and other historians have noted that Jefferson, by such means as the Louisiana Purchase (1803) and his refusal to submit to the aggression of either Napoleonic France, North African pirate states or the British Navy, more than anyone else guaranteed survival and world power for the federal union in his "empire for liberty."[23] For better or worse, Jefferson had always considered New England a vital and permanent part of that Union. He regarded its town meeting democracy, despite its threatened corruption by "priests" and conservative, would-be aristocratic leaders during the 1790s and the War of 1812, as a model for emulation by its sister states.

One of Jefferson's most consistent, indeed obsessive thoughts was that the future freedom of Europe's (and eventually the world's) peoples depended on their viewing the United States as a model of representative, democratic government worth following. As he said in his first inaugural address, he regarded the perseverance of the United States as a "successful experiment" in "republican government" as "the world's best hope" for ultimate liberation from despotism. After he left the presidency, he became even more convinced that the American example's endurance was crucial to future generations' choice of republican government. This conviction grew as a result of Jefferson's fear that the South American colonies, despite their revolution against Spanish monarchy, would fail at setting up republican governments because of their heritage of religious fanaticism and illiteracy. "The last hope of human liberty in this world rests on us," he wrote. "We ought, for so dear a stake, to sacrifice every attachment and every enmity."[24] In the context of worldwide struggle for democratic government, Jefferson preferred to minimize New Englanders' temporary anti-republican deviations, such as their recalcitrance during the Embargo years and the War of 1812.

Seldom naïve when it came to political issues, Jefferson in old age remained aware of the sectional sources of national strife. He anticipated that one of the candidates in the presidential election of 1824 would be William H. Crawford of Georgia, Monroe's Secretary of the Treasury, who had an undeserved reputation for advocating "Old Republican" states' rights principles. In fact, like Jefferson, he upheld an activist national government in practice despite his theoretical adherence to limited government. He had favored the recharter of the Bank of the United States in 1811, and supported such nationalist projects as extensive internal improvements, a protective tariff, and government-sponsored African colonization projects. Although Andrew Jackson was actually the most popular presidential candidate in 1824, Crawford's main competitor was thought to be John Quincy Adams, Monroe's competent Secretary of State, an avowed nationalist and former independent Federalist, whom Jefferson, though he never said so, may have considered too ambitious and too closely identified with New England. Like Crawford, he theoretically upheld the states' rights principles on which his Republican Party was founded during the 1790s, although in practice he treated them cavalierly during his presidency. Thus, Jefferson tended to prefer Crawford as a native-born Virginian and fellow Southerner.[25]

In November 1823, he wrote the Marquis de Lafayette about the impending election. Unaware that the royal troops of Lafayette's country, France, had recently overthrown a liberal monarchy in Spain and reinstalled its absolute monarch, Jefferson expressed optimism that Spain's "success will be the turning of the tide of liberty, no more to be arrested by human efforts." He stressed the importance of a "free press," to criticize government measures and express "the force of public opinion," for maintaining "honest and unoppressive government." "Who is to be the next President, is the topic here of every conversation," he informed Lafayette, who, living under a monarchy, did not enjoy that luxury.[26]

Jefferson perceived that the presidential election would be a contest between sections as well as governmental philosophies. "The question will ultimately be reduced to the northernmost and southernmost candidate," he predicted. "The former [Adams] will get every federal vote in the Union, and many republicans; the latter [Crawford], all of those denominated *of the old school*; for you are not to believe that these two old parties are amalgamated, that the lion and the lamb are lying down together." Forsaking the quixotic desire of his first term as president to unite the parties behind him as *the* Republican president of all the people, Jefferson accepted the idea that a system of at least two political parties voicing different ambitions and political objectives was inevitable in the United States.[27] Recalling the Hartford Convention, the most considerable attempt of any section to warn the rest of the Union that it might secede if its demands were not met, he gloated over its failure and the glorious outcome of the War of 1812 (at least compared with the possibility of British invasion and occupation).

In Jefferson's view, the Federalists' role as a national party was over because they flouted the republic's burgeoning nationalism. Especially during a war for survival, this was neither good morality nor good politics. "The Hartford Convention, the victory of Orleans, the peace of Ghent, prostrated the name of federalism," he reminded Lafayette, to whom he had said the same things eight years earlier. "Its votaries abandoned it through shame and mortification; and now call themselves republicans. But the name alone is changed, the principles are the same."[28] Jefferson admitted the necessity for a two-party system, because he was sure that if people were free to think and speak, they would differ in opinion. As he said long ago in an unpublished draft of his first Inaugural Address, "Where there are men there will be parties; and wherever there are free men, they will make themselves heard."[29]

Jefferson probably never expected that his election to the presidency would obliterate all political differences. His struggle for the office, even after he gained a majority of the popular vote, was a far from halcyon event. He experienced vituperation between his followers and those of Adams, and finally Federalist efforts to install Aaron Burr in the presidency during the roll call in the House of Representatives; capped off by Burr's watchful waiting, seeking the main chance.[30] Among his most indelible "first principles," which he applied to the sphere of religious liberty in *Notes on Virginia*'s Query XVII and in his Virginia Statute for Religious Freedom, was that no decent government could deny people the right to form their own ideas and opinions, in politics or religion.[31]

Jefferson often said that people would always differ in their political opinions. Without specifically mentioning New England, he explained to Lafayette: "The parties of Whig and Tory, are those of nature. They exist in all countries, whether called by these names, or by those of Aristocrats and Democrats, Coté Droite and Coté Gauche, Ultras and Radicals, Serviles and Liberals. The sickly, weakly, timid man, fears the people, and is a Tory by nature. The healthy, strong and bold, cherishes them, and is formed a Whig by nature."[32]

Jefferson had been making this point for years. As early as 1802, he thought that the name "Federalist" had been permanently discredited for use by a political party: "Freemen thinking differently and speaking and acting as they think will form into classes of sentiment, but it must be under another name, that of federalism is become so scouted that no party can rise under it." He considered Republicans and Federalists, or "whig and tory," two different types of personalities, with the Republicans bearing all the most admirable, courageous attributes. He argued, "As the division between whig and tory is founded in the nature of men, the weekly and nerveless, the sick and the corrupt, seeing safety and accessibility in a strong executive; the healthy, firm and virtuous, feeling confidence in their physical and moral resources, and willing to part with only so much power as is necessary for their good government, and therefore to retain the rest in the hands of the many, the division will substantially be into whig and tory, as in England, formerly."[33] Since he was of the opinion that New England voters had become inordinately accustomed to reelect their traditional leaders, which led to past rejections of his more progressive Republican Party, it is likely that in his final years, he had the realm of "Hartford nation," which had returned to the Federalists in the 1820s, primarily in mind.

The near-debacle of the conflict over Missouri's admission to the Union still irritated him. He considered it an example of the way Federalists, mainly from New York and Pennsylvania, were trying to deceive antislavery Jeffersonian Republicans in those states. They employed rhetoric about eventually abolishing slavery nationwide, through forcing all future states to enter the Union as "free" states. He considered this merely a ploy by which Federalists and some former Federalists expropriating the name of Republicans sought to regain political power. "On the eclipse of federalism with us, although not its extinction, its leaders got up the Missouri question, under the false front of lessening the measure of slavery, but with the real view of producing a geographical division of parties, which might insure them the next President," he charged. Jefferson resented such quondam Federalists, who made fools out of naïve Northern Republicans. "The people of the North went blindfold into the snare, followed their leaders for awhile with a zeal truly moral and laudable, until they became sensible that they were injuring instead of aiding the real interests of the slaves," he charged. He was probably alluding to his assumption that, if big planters were unable to sell their slaves to Southerners going to Missouri and other "new" slave states, they would have them permanently on their hands, and become increasingly insistent on protecting slavery. This was the basis for his support of "diffusion," the moot concept that, if slaveholders were permitted to bring their slaves into Missouri and other new states, the "old" slave states would be drained of many of their slaves and consequently their leaders would be less resistant to accepting legislation for gradual abolition within their states.[34]

Jefferson thought that the possibility of "diffusing" slavery by allowing new "slave" states into the Union would have salutary results. Their presence would enable the "old" slave states, like Virginia, which had more slaves than they needed, to sell their surplus bondspersons to them, thereby ultimately reducing the proportion of slaves in the population of the "old" slave states. This would make their economies less dependent on slavery, and render slaveholders more amenable to legislation that would abolish slavery after a specific year. As historians sympathetic to Jefferson's point of view point out, this was the strategy that Northern antislavery leaders in states such as New York, New Jersey, and Pennsylvania, with comparatively few slaves, employed. Indeed, there were still a few slaves in New Jersey as late as 1860.[35]

Neglecting to explain the logic behind his seemingly vacuous claim that "diffusing" slavery would promote abolition, Jefferson remained bitter that the Northern Republicans' "moral zeal" had been manipulated by the Federalists and ersatz Republicans and almost broke up the Union. He gloated that the Northern Republicans finally woke up to the fact that "they had been used merely as tools for electioneering purposes; and that trick of hypocrisy then fell as quickly as it had been got up." Relieved at the failure of the Federalist attempt to regain power through manipulating the volatile issue of slavery, Jefferson much preferred the revival of the conflict between states' righters and government centralizers ("consolidationists"), which he thought had less potential to destroy the Union. It revived the old, relatively harmless (at least, compared to slavery) "distinction, which, like that of Republican and federal, or Whig and Tory, being equally intermixed through every State, threatens none of those geographical schisms which go immediately to a separation."[36]

The United States having endured for fifty years as a republic, Jefferson no longer feared that the Federalists, after losing great leaders like Hamilton, would revive the idea that the republic should become a monarchy or rejoin the British Empire.[37] In 1824, he reminisced about the political battles of the 1790s in a letter to the new leader of the emerging Democratic Party, the "Old Fox of Kinderhook," Senator Martin Van Buren of New York. He discussed Hamilton objectively, reserving most of his anger for Timothy Pickering and Chief Justice John Marshall. Recalling his debates with the secretary of the treasury in the Cabinet and their struggle for Washington's support, he wrote of his great rival: "Hamilton frankly avowed that he considered the British Constitution, with all the corruptions of its administration, as the most perfect model of government which had ever been devised by the wit of man; professing however, at the same time, that the spirit of this country was so fundamentally republican, that it would be visionary to think of introducing monarchy here, and that, therefore, it was the duty of its administrators to conduct it on the principles their constituents had elected."[38]

Indeed, Jefferson recalled that after Washington's election to a second term, he and Hamilton agreed that there had been too much pomp and ceremony during his first four years in office, especially at his first inauguration; and that he should curtail it during his second term, beginning with the inaugural ceremonies. When Washington requested the members of his Cabinet to meet and discuss this issue and relay their proposals to him, Jefferson reminisced, "We met at my office. Hamilton and myself agreed at once that there was too much ceremony for the character of our government, and particularly, that the parade of the installation at New York [the first inauguration] ought not to be copied." However, Attorney General Edmund Randolph and Secretary of War Henry Knox "differed from us, the latter vehemently; they thought it not advisable to change any of the established forms." Since the vote was tied, and Hamilton and Jefferson had not prepared a detailed alternative option, Washington continued his levees and ceremonies into his second term.[39]

At the end of his life, Jefferson thus viewed Hamilton as a political moderate. Perhaps this was because Jefferson now directed his wrath at the abolitionists or pseudo-abolitionists who sought to bar the entry of slavery into the new states, an issue on which Hamilton was apathetic. Indeed, from Jefferson's end-of-life perspective, the brilliant and irascible New Yorker, who insulted him in the press until Burr killed him, had to his credit that, apart from his nominal membership in the New York Society for the Manumission of Slaves, an indecisive group that primarily sought to protect emancipated slaves from being kidnapped and resold into bondage, he never publicly attacked slavery. Perhaps hoping to encourage Van Buren to persevere in resurrecting a new Democratic Party under Crawford's nominal leadership, Jefferson continued, "I had meant to have added some views on the amalgamation of parties ... an amalgamation of name, but not of principle. Tories are Tories still, by whatever name they may be called."[40]

He felt happy that the sectional firestorm of slavery had been at least temporarily extinguished. Like mid-twentieth-century political scientists, he thought that the two-party system muted political controversies and provided a basis for compromise and coalition-building between antagonistic elements. However, he was less confident that when explosive issues like class conflicts between rich and poor or slaveholding and non-slaveholding groups and sections of the country became prominent, political parties would be able to defuse crises. For the time being, the "intermixture" within each state of political actors who favored a weak and those who favored a strong central government eased Jefferson's anxiety about an "immediate separation" of the states: "The line of division now, is the preservation of State rights, as reserved in the Constitution, or by strained constructions of that instrument, to merge all into a consolidated government." Writing to Lafayette, he anachronistically labeled advocates of a stronger president and national government "Tories," whereas the "Whigs" supported the rights of the legislative, "representative" branch of the national government (Congress) over those of the Executive. "Whigs" also advocated "the rights reserved by the States, as the bulwark against consolidation, which must immediately generate monarchy." While still unrealistically phrasing the partisan conflict as one that could potentially engender "monarchy," it is likely that Jefferson was not being literal, but, aware that his friend Lafayette, who lived under a monarchy, could empathize with such terminology, he used it to enlighten him. Returning to the topic of the presidential election, his conclusion was relatively upbeat: "Although this division [between consolidationists and states' righters] excites, as yet, no warmth, yet it exists, is well understood, and will be a principle of voting at the ensuing election, with the reflecting men of both parties."[41]

In his twilight years, Jefferson continued to insist that he and his party represented the will of the majority, while the Federalists and their successors represented the desires of the rich and the would-be-rich to exalt themselves by oppressing the people. (Perhaps Jefferson made the mental reservation that slaves were not members of the working poor citizenry, but part-property and part-people, or "human property."[42]) Jefferson did not hesitate to explain to the young Virginia politician Henry Lee, Jr., that he regarded differences of opinion between advocates of the rich and friends of the average person as the legitimate source of political parties, inevitable and ineradicable in every free government. "Men by their constitutions are naturally divided into two parties," he wrote. "1. Those who fear and distrust the people, and wish to draw all powers from them into the hands of the higher classes. 2ndly. Those who identify themselves with the people, have confidence in them, cherish & consider them as the most honest & safe, altho' not the most wise depository of the public interests. The last appellation of aristocrats and democrats is the true one expressing the essence of all."[43]

Jefferson sought to encourage young Lee, who, although the son of the devout Federalist General Henry Lee, was a Jacksonian Democrat, in his purported project of starting up a newspaper devoted to principles of freedom of the press. Lee said he was inspired to pursue this course after reading Madison's Report to the Virginia legislature in 1800 in defense of the Kentucky and Virginia Resolutions, which declared the Alien and Sedition Acts of 1798 unconstitutional and unenforceable within the state. As in 1798, Jefferson merged the concepts of democracy, political equality and freedom of speech with states' rights. Ignoring the deceased Henry Lee, Sr.'s orthodox Federalist credentials, vigorous support of the Alien and Sedition Acts, and hatred for him, Jefferson continued: "The paper which shall be governed by the spirit of Mr. Madison's celebrated report, of which you express in your prospectus so just and high an approbation, cannot be false to the rights of all classes. The grandfathers of the present generation of your family [Jefferson probably meant Richard Henry Lee and Francis Lightfoot Lee, signers of the Declaration of Independence] I knew well. They were friends and fellow laborers with me in the same cause and principle."[44] He said that he was no longer interested in reading newspapers, that he read only one (he probably meant Thomas Ritchie's *Richmond Enquirer*), but that he sometimes encouraged publishers of fledgling newspapers by subscribing for their first year, in order to promote the concept of freedom of the press. "I do the same now with pleasure for yours," the increasingly absent-minded Jefferson said, "and unwilling to have outstanding accounts, which I am liable to forget, I now enclose the price of the tri-weekly paper."[45]

As this letter and others written during this period make clear, Jefferson considered the support of states' rights against nationalist "consolidation" compatible with nationalist projects like internal improvements and the national government's abolition of slavery. He viewed such large-scale government activities as a means of upholding the rights of the lower- and middle-class majority against the encroaching "higher classes." Although disappointed that New England had not converted to the Democratic Party on the state level, he did not view New England as a particular haven of the "higher classes." At the same time, he respected the achievements of such institutions as Harvard College in the fields of science and education. His view of New Englanders remained essentially one of admiration.

Conclusion

New England Wins Jefferson's Heart

Jefferson was eager to hire New England scholars as professors at the University of Virginia, notwithstanding his reputation among New Englanders (and historians since) for hostility to the section. Although scholars often call Jefferson an "Anglophobe," he not only regarded the former mother country as the cradle of U.S. government, traditions, and culture; he also sought to hire Britons to teach at his university. He treated with respect English scholar Thomas Cooper, whom he hired to teach at his University, when Cooper recommended an Irishman named "Slack" or "Stack" as a "classical tutor" for the college.[1]

Writing to William Clark, the junior member of the famous Lewis and Clark Expedition, in 1825, not long before his death, he boasted of appointing English and Scots professors to the institution's faculty. He cared only about the quality of the faculty, not their national origins. "Some of our sister institutions in this country would have wished us with their refuse professors to have placed ourselves at the tail instead of the head of the line," he insisted. "We have however no cause to repent of the course we have pursued. The 5 Professors whom we obtained from abroad prove to be as happy a selection as we could have wished…. The 3 professors of our own country are too well known to need particular characterization." Exaggerating the students' docility and the popularity of his college, he wrote, "We have something upwards of 100 students of from 16 to 26 years of age and for order and good conduct, they have been nowhere surpassed."[2]

Actually, the students had been quite cantankerous and disrespectful, even violent toward the professors in the few months that the university had been in operation. Perhaps revealing that he was an anarchist at heart, Jefferson did not seem to mind their disgraceful antics. However, like Washington at Newburgh in 1783, he could put on a display of grief and dejection, as if choked up with emotion, when personally addressing those students who had attacked faculty members. The one hundred students attending the university in 1825 were a motley group, most of them spoiled children of the local gentry. The faculty members were not enforcing the rules of discipline, and students were often absent from class, including Jefferson's grandchildren Benjamin and James Randolph.[3]

Jefferson was unaware that his illusions about the tranquility, stoicism and dedication of the students at the University of Virginia were largely unfounded.[4] Nicholas Trist, Jefferson's grandson-in-law, informed him of the prevalence of disorders at the university and the failure of the faculty to enforce discipline.[5] Jefferson's evangelical foe and fellow member of the

Board of Visitors of the university, John Hartwell Cocke, said that the students were running roughshod and undisciplined over the campus. The exasperated professors, more interested in their research than instructing disruptive students, failed to take attendance and did not give the students examinations. By October 1825, Jefferson had become aware of the critical state of affairs. Despite extremely poor health, he took a carriage to the meeting of the Board of Visitors at Charlottesville. Robley Duglison, Jefferson's personal physician, who attended him on his deathbed, reported that the students were threatening the professors with violence and conducting alcohol-fused parties in the dorms, contrary to school regulations. On September 30 and October 1, 1825, students threw rocks and bottles at the professors who reported their wild party of the previous night. Masked students beat up professors. Jefferson was more tolerant of the students than his colleagues were. He thought that they were just having fun! In his old age, the anarchist disrespectful of authority finally emerged in full force. Sixty-five students signed a petition stating that the professors who accused them of an alcoholic debauch were lying, which precipitated the resignation of two professors originally from Cambridge University, George Long and Thomas Key. Finally becoming alarmed, Jefferson briefly, personally addressed the students, but apparently he was so choked up with emotion that he could not speak. The guilty masked students soon confessed their identities and culpability. This took place during the period from October 3 to October 7, 1825.[6]

Three of the fourteen masked students were expelled by the Visitors, of whom Jefferson was the head. Sadly, one of them, the leader of the troublemakers, was Jefferson's great-great-nephew, William Miles Cary. (At least, this indicates that Jefferson did not show favoritism toward his relatives.) Professors Long and Key, who ostensibly had better pedagogical experiences in London, objected to dealing with unruly students. But the Board of Visitors refused to accept their resignations. Meanwhile, other professors from the British Isles were happy being at the University of Virginia.[7]

Putting an optimistic spin on untoward events, Jefferson said he thought that the incidents had strengthened the school. At this time Jefferson was in pain and not far from death; his daughter administered 100 drops of laudanum (opium) to him daily, so it is likely he did not know what he was saying much of the time. He wrote William Short that age, infirmity, loss of memory and increasing deafness incapacitated him. Still, he persevered in persuading his young friend, Francis Walker Gilmer, who was dying of tuberculosis, to accept the professorship of law at the university. Sadly, Gilmer died before he could assume his duties.[8] Student vandalism against professors' homes continued.[9]

Writing to his Massachusetts in-laws, Jefferson minimized student violence. He wrote his grandson-in-law, Joseph Coolidge, Jr., who lived in Boston with his wife, Jefferson's granddaughter Ellen, that the students were paragons of virtue. "Our University is going on well," he said, exactly a month before he died. "The students have sensibly improved since the last year in habits of order and industry." He noted that the administrators had strengthened the rules and called the police to the campus when necessary.[10]

Jefferson tried to administer the university's affairs as Rector as best he could despite his declining health. The Board of Visitors sought to appoint U.S. Attorney General William Wirt, a native of Virginia and Patrick Henry's nephew, as professor of law after Gilmer's death. When the more tradition-minded Visitors, including James Madison, proposed that the university, like other universities, hire a president, Jefferson thought that this was an unnecessary expense. He also argued that the law creating the university had not authorized the Board of Visitors to hire a president. He believed that the faculty could jointly perform a president's duties. Perhaps Jefferson thought that the students should be controlled as little as possible by overpaid bureaucrats, in order for their creative juices to flow. However, defying Jefferson, Cocke offered the presidency to Wirt. When Wirt rejected the offer, they were back at square one. Jefferson continued to oppose creation of the presidency, pointing out that the school was strapped for funds and the legislature was increasingly reluctant to grant more. Jefferson's point of view won out: the University of Virginia had no president until 1904, when Edwin Alderman, after whom the university library is named, became its first chief executive.[11]

· · · · ·

Jefferson lacked the ingrained hostility to New England imputed to him by his Federalist opponents and recent historians. On the contrary, he exhibited pride and enthusiasm when his beloved granddaughter, Ellen Wayles Randolph, daughter of Martha Jefferson Randolph Chinn and Thomas Mann Randolph, Jr., married a rich Boston China merchant, Joseph C. Coolidge, Jr., in May 1825, about a year before Jefferson's death. Coolidge had graduated from Harvard College, an institution that Jefferson admired although he sometimes criticized it for anti-Southernism. Coolidge was a wealthy, cultivated Bostonian, a friend of Jefferson's Federalist protégé George Ticknor and nephew of the renowned architect and Boston Republican leader Charles Bulfinch. Ironically, Ellen and Joseph C. Coolidge's son, Thomas Jefferson Coolidge (1831–1921), became a multimillionaire New England businessman, gaining wealth from such diverse urban enterprises as textile manufacturing, banking, and railroad directorships. He married Hetty Sullivan Appleton, daughter of William Appleton, one of the founders of the Massachusetts textile industry, and ran the factory at Boott Hills near Lowell. Thomas Jefferson Coolidge went on to become director of numerous Massachusetts banks, as well as the Chicago, Burlington and Quincy Railroad and others.[12] Had Jefferson lived longer, one wonders how he would have reacted to his namesake personifying those things—manufacturing, banks, and that urban monster, the railroad—he had sometimes reviled.

Ellen W. Randolph married Joseph Coolidge, Jr., on May 27, 1825, in the parlor at Monticello. For their honeymoon, they traveled for five weeks across the Northern United States, from Monticello to Boston. She explained to her grandfather in a letter in August 1825, "Mr. Coolidge wished to give me an idea of the beauty and prosperity of the New England States," by setting out on an overland tour instead of taking a sea cruise from New York to Boston. They detoured across the Connecticut River Valley towns to the west. Emerging with a very enthusiastic opinion of New England, she wrote, "The journey has been long and somewhat fatiguing, but it has made me acquainted with probably the most flourishing portion of New England, and I do not regret having taken it." Her vehement attack on Southern slavery after experiencing the free air of Massachusetts perhaps disheartened her grandfather. She discerned in the western Massachusetts towns of Hampshire and Berkshire counties a "prosperity and improvement, such as I fear our Southern States cannot hope for, whilst the canker of slavery eats into their hearts, and diseases the whole body by this ulcer at the core." She regretted that, because of the blight of slavery, Virginia (in her opinion) was less agriculturally productive than New England despite its superior "soil and climate." Jefferson's granddaughter astutely observed, "I should judge from appearances that they [New England farmers] are at least a century in advance of us in all the arts and embellishments of life; and they are pressing forward in their course with a zeal and activity which I think must ensure success." Purveying a graphic, at times lyrical description of what she saw, Ellen praised New England's topography, farming, villages, roads, and inns, "the richness and beauty of the fields and meadows.... From the top of Mount Holyoke which commands perhaps one of the most extensive views in these States, the whole country as you look down upon it, resembles one vast garden divided into it's [sic] parterns [sic]."[13]

Ellen's unflattering comparison of New England with the South probably depressed Jefferson. He must have found particularly unwelcome her innuendo that Southerners lacked Northerners' virtuous moral fiber, as when she praised "the villages ... air of neatness and comfort that is delightful," and noted that the schoolchildren were unvaryingly polite, formal and deferential to strangers. Unlike Virginia, even the small country towns boasted colleges. Indeed, "the appearance of the people generally is much in their favor; the men seem sober, orderly, and industrious: I have seen but one drunken man since I entered New England, and he was a south carolinian [sic]!"[14] Although Ellen criticized the harsh working conditions of the local textile factories and decried the great disparity between the wealth of the cotton manufacturers as compared with the farmers and mill operatives, her general impression of New England was extremely enthusiastic. She minutely described the people and animals, as when she wrote: "There are two little spectacles I liked much to look out upon from the windows of the carriage; the one was, the frequent waggons [sic] laden high above their tops with hay (the country through which I have passed being principally a grass-growing one)."[15]

After receiving this letter, Jefferson's reply, largely overlooking Ellen's negative comments on Virginia, slavery, and the South, recalled his feelings about New England during his famous "botanizing" excursion northward in the summer of 1791 with James Madison. Ellen and Joseph's recent return from a similar trip gave Jefferson an excuse to reflect upon happier, younger days as well as the political lessons in freedom and prosperity that America had taught the world. "I am glad you took the delightful tour which you describe in your letter," he began. "It is almost exactly that which Mr. Madison and myself pursued in May and June, 1791." He enjoyed going back in time, narrating events as if they had occurred two weeks instead of thirty-four years earlier: "Setting out from Philadelphia, our course was to New York, up the Hudson to Albany, Troy, Saratoga, Fort Edward, Fort George, Lake George, Ticonderoga, Crown Point, penetrated into Lake Champlain, returned the same way to Saratoga, thence crossed the mountains to Bennington, Northampton, along Connecticut River to its mouth, crossed the Sound into Long Island, and along its northern margin to Brooklyn, re-crossed to New York, and returned. But from Saratoga till we got back to Northampton was then mostly desert. Now it is what thirty-four years of free and good government have made it."

His reminiscences evoked praise of the virtues of free labor, which had converted upstate New York from a "desert" (i.e., uncultivated and uninhabited territory) to fertile farm country. The growth and prosperity of upstate New York, fast-tracked by construction of the Erie Canal, "shows how soon the labor of men would make a paradise of the whole earth, were it not for misgovernment, and a diversion of all his energies from their proper object—the happiness of man,—to the selfish interests of kings, nobles, and priests." In this intimate letter to his granddaughter, seldom quoted by historians of his political ideas, Jefferson eloquently summarized the pith of his political philosophy. Perhaps the fact that she was now in the "free" state of Massachusetts, amid his idealized Boston town meetings, unconsciously increased his exultation in this letter. He referred to her husband, Joseph Coolidge, an avid abolitionist, as "the most excellent and amiable character to which we have committed your future well-being." He was pleased "by the kindness with which you have been received by the worthy family into which you are now engrafted." Aware that slavery's "fatal stain" might have rendered Virginia less pleasant for Ellen than Boston, he reluctantly admitted that she might prefer New England: "I have no doubt you will find also the state of society there more congenial with your mind than the rustic scenes you have left although these do not want their points of endearment.... One fatal stain deforms what nature had bestowed on us of her fairest gifts."[16] In old age, Jefferson's thoughts were actively engaged in formulating a plan that would permit Virginia and other Southern states to "get rid" of the stain of human slavery with least financial discomfort to the planters.

During his final years, elaborating upon thoughts in his letters to Gallatin, Pinckney and others at the time of the Missouri crisis, Jefferson formulated a revolutionary proposal: that the national government provide financial assistance to the Southern states in emancipating newborn slave children. He admitted this necessitated a "liberal construction" of the Constitution, perhaps even a constitutional amendment. He described this idea at length to the Massachusetts educator, abolitionist and editor Jared Sparks. Once more, Jefferson argued that Massachusetts and the other New England states, implementing the antislavery declarations of their leaders, should consent to utilize public land sales (including portions of his Louisiana Purchase) to amortize the massive expense of the unprecedented project of slave liberation and deportation to Haiti. "The object [emancipation], although more important to the slave States, is highly so to the others also, if they were serious in their arguments on the Missouri question," Jefferson chided Sparks. Jefferson expected that the slave owners, from patriotic motives, would gratuitously surrender neonates (he called them *post-nati* slaves). If they refused, he suggested that the young slaves should be seized by force in the guise of a special tax. He wrote, "The slave States, too, if more interested, would also contribute more by their gratuitous liberation, thus taking on themselves alone the first and heaviest item of expense."[17]

On the other hand, the pernicious influence of a states'-rights fire-eater like Giles, who constantly harassed Jefferson during his retirement years, perhaps caused him to question whether New Englanders were as loyal to the Union and republicanism as Virginians were. Seeking to mitigate Giles' demand that Virginia nullify congressional laws that injured its interests, such as protective tariffs and large-scale internal improvements, Jefferson composed a draft resolution by which the state legislature "acquiesced" in these objectionable laws while denouncing them as unconstitutional. Although he ultimately followed Madison's recommendation that he not mail Giles this provocative paper, Jefferson's contemplated protest reveals the underside of his nationalism. Condemning the Marshall Court's "consolidationist" decisions and congressional laws of moot constitutionality that extended interstate roads and canals, he nonetheless concluded that national unity and Congress's endorsement superseded legalistic doubts. He determined that the concept of the Constitution as a compact among the states could at least temporarily coexist with these aggressively nationalist trends.[18]

Jefferson's set of resolutions for consideration by the Virginia assembly "acquiesced" in these measures out of "affection" for its sister states: "We will breast with them, rather than separate from them, every misfortune, save that only of living under a government of unlimited powers," he asserted. Employing the idealistic, universalist approach that characterized many of his letters during his last years, his draft declaration and protest asserted, "We owe every other sacrifice to ourselves, to our federal brethren, and to the world at large, to pursue with temper and perseverance the great experiment which shall prove that man[kind] is capable of living in society, governing itself by laws self-imposed, and securing to its members the enjoyment of life, liberty, property, and peace."[19]

In addition, Jefferson's draft resolution proposed a constitutional amendment empowering Congress to construct internal improvements. He argued that this procedure accorded with the "common intendment of the time," and with the intent of the Founding Fathers "who framed it." By the terms of his resolution, pending a constitutional amendment, the Virginia assembly reserved the right to make a final decision on the constitutionality of congressional internal improvements, and "in point of fact," protested that their current unconstitutionality rendered them "null and void." For the time being, however, it instructed all persons to obey Congress's internal improvements laws, "in like manner as if said Acts were passed by the legislature of this commonwealth."[20] Thus, although Jefferson ostensibly sympathized with Giles's extremist views in principle, he gave the substance of his support to the current nationalist program, believing that preserving the Union was most important.

Perhaps Jefferson composed such an ambiguous document to get Giles off his back. He was close to death, and told Madison that he had not read any newspapers except for Ritchie's *Richmond Enquirer*, or paid attention to politics for many years. He said he did not feel much excitement even over the question of national internal improvements. "I have long ceased to think on subjects of this kind," he wrote, "and pay little attention to public proceedings." Anyway, he sent Madison a copy of a draft of his "Solemn Declaration and Protest" of the Virginia legislature against the acts of the national government for his comments.[21]

Surprisingly, Jefferson's "Solemn Declaration and Protest" was first and foremost a testimony of his and Virginia's devotion to the Union. His declaration, in the name of the Virginia general assembly, asserted that Virginia would remain united with its sister states under all circumstances, except those involving "submission to a government of unlimited powers." Virginia would remain part of the Union, at least temporarily, even if Congress passed unconstitutional measures, including erecting roads within a single state. "We will be patient and suffer much, under the confidence that time, ere it be too late, will prove to them also the bitter consequences in which this usurpation will involve us all."[22]

Jefferson was dedicated to the survival of the United States' "great experiment" to prove that men were capable of self-government, believing it was too important to break up the Union over a few disagreeable laws. "In the mean while we will breast with them, rather than separate from them, every misfortune save that only of living under a government of unlimited powers," his manifesto vowed.[23]

Jefferson emphasized that Virginians had no thoughts of leaving the Union. He asserted that the Virginia legislature, content to await the passage of constitutional amendments, desired "further to shew [sic] that even when the government of it's choice shall shew a tendency to degeneracy, we are not at once to despair but that the will & the watchfulness of it's sounder parts will reform it's aberrations, recall it to original and legitimate principles and restrain it within the rightful limits of self-government."[24]

He claimed that Virginia would be willing to pass a constitutional amendment for federal construction of roads and canals, provided the process was safeguarded "against abuses, compromises, and corrupt practices." For the time being Virginia would obey Congressional laws for constructing internal improvements. "To preserve peace in the meanwhile, we proceed to make it the duty of our citizens, until the legislature shall otherwise & ultimately decide, to acquiesce under those acts of the federal branch of our government which we have declared to be usurpations, and against which, in point of right, we do protest, as null and void, and never to be quoted as precedents of right."[25]

Ironically, Jefferson composed his declaration at the same time that President John Quincy Adams, in his first annual message to Congress in December 1825, proclaimed his hopes for a full-scale program of internal improvements as well as a national university and a national observatory. In the penultimate paragraph of the message, he said, "While foreign nations less blessed with that freedom which is power than ourselves are advancing with gigantic strides in the career of public improvement, were we to slumber in indolence or fold up our arms and proclaim to the world that we are palsied by the will of our constituents, would it not be to cast away the bounties of Providence and doom ourselves to perpetual inferiority?" In this same paragraph, he cited Jefferson's own University of Virginia and New York State's recently-completed Erie Canal as two great "undertakings" that showed what progressive state governments could do to help their constituents, and which, he said, put the current national government's inertia to shame.[26]

Despite his professed fears that Adams would complete the "consolidation" of the government, Jefferson, perhaps partly because he was flattered by his praise of the university in a major national address, was obviously generally willing to go along with him. His "solemn declaration and protest" concluded by asserting that the state legislature gave full approval to all acts of the government involving roads and canals. It promised "that all citizens of this commonwealth, and persons and authorities within the same, shall pay full obedience at all times to the Acts which may be past [*sic*] by the Congress of the U.S." on internal improvements.[27]

Jefferson's letters often possessed a chameleon-like character. Especially in old age, he often appeased and accommodated his correspondents' biases more than he would have had he expressed his thoughts with complete honesty.[28] That was the case with the letter he wrote Giles accompanying his draft resolution. Expressing fear that the federal government was usurping the rights of the states and intended eventually to exercise "unlimited power," Jefferson chastised the Supreme Court, President John Quincy Adams, and Congress. He charged that by means of the protective tariff, Congress was inordinately burdening farmers, who already suffered from declining prices for their goods in the world economy, and benefiting the wealthiest economic classes, merchants and manufacturers. On the other hand, Jefferson stood his ground even in the face of the irate would-be secessionist Giles, voicing his preference for a constitutional amendment legalizing internal improvements rather than rejecting that policy. Reiterating the Lockean republican ideology of his youth, he insisted that the separation of the Union "must be the last resource, not to be thought of until much longer and greater sufferings." In words reminiscent of those he had used to John Taylor in 1798, Jefferson instructed Giles: "If every infraction of a compact of so many parties is to be resisted at once, as a dissolution of it, none can ever be formed which would last one year." "We must have patience and longer endurance then with our brethren," he advised, "and separate from our companions only when the sole alternatives left, are the dissolution of our Union with them, or submission to a government without limitation of powers."[29] Even though the South was in an uproar over such measures as government threats to slavery; the protective tariff; internal improvements; and the national bank, Jefferson remained levelheaded. He gave primacy to Union and bestowed qualified support to nationalist policies, several of which he initiated, and which his friends Madison and Monroe amplified during their presidencies.

Unfortunately, perhaps from a desire to placate his volatile friend Giles, Jefferson criticized New Englanders in this letter in a more trivial manner than was his wont. Seeking to defeat John Quincy Adams's reelection prospects, Giles reminded Jefferson that, when Giles and Adams were senators in 1808, Adams divulged to members of Congress secessionist plots he suspected New England leaders were contemplating (similar to Pickering's efforts to recruit Burr in 1804) to escape the Embargo Act and create their own Anglophile confederation. Indeed, Giles said he advised Adams, who had feared that President Jefferson was conspiring with Napoleon against Britain, to inform Jefferson of his suspicions and generally clear the air with the president. Adams met with Jefferson on March 15, 1808, and Jefferson eliminated his suspicions that he was in league with France. (Jefferson did not remember the meeting when Giles mentioned it to him in 1825.) Giles' revival of old albeit vague memories of New England Federalist disloyalty rekindled Jefferson's anger at the town meetings' opposition to the Embargo, the most controversial law of his presidency. Giles' disclosure also revived Jefferson's memories of the Hartford Convention. Appalled by Giles' revelation of the 1808 incident which he had apparently forgotten, Jefferson observed, "They are historical facts which belong to the present, as well as future times." Giles was inclined to publicize the 1808 incident, an earlier, comparatively unknown instance of New England disunionism. He sought a statement from Jefferson that Adams had also divulged the plots of the "Essex Junto" to him during his presidency in 1808, although the aged Jefferson did not in fact recall the incident. And he seemingly had convinced Jefferson that the event had actually taken place. "I doubt whether a single fact, known to the world, will carry as clear conviction to it, of the correctness of our knowledge of the treasonable views of the federal party of that day, as that disclosed by this, the most nefarious and daring attempt to dissever the Union, of which the Hartford convention was a subsequent chapter," Jefferson angrily asserted. (As Adams' political enemy, Giles hoped, by publishing Jefferson's letter, to further embitter the old "Essex Junto" Massachusetts secessionists against the president in the upcoming election.)[30]

Evidently relieved that the slavery issue had temporarily ceased to inflame party conflict, Jefferson returned to his traditional attack on the Federalists as closet monarchists disdainful of republicanism. He suspected that the movement for "consolidation" of the national government's powers, like their previous secessionism, was a symptom of New England Federalists' contempt for republican government. However, Jefferson now feared that the monarchical branch of the "federal party" was increasing in popular support. This contrasted with his past insistence, especially during the War of 1812, that most New Englanders opposed, and would violently resist their leaders if they moved for secession or alliance with Great Britain. He feared that the program of "consolidation" had gained the centralizing Federalists "a vast accession of strength from their younger recruits, who, having nothing … of the feelings or principles of '76, now look to a single and splendid government of an aristocracy, founded on banking institutions, and moneyed incorporations under the guise and cloak of their favored branches of manufactures, commerce and navigation, riding and ruling over the plundered ploughman and beggared yeomanry. This will be to them a next best blessing to the monarchy of their first aim, and perhaps the surest stepping-stone to it."[31]

One area in which Jefferson envied New England's hegemony was higher education. As we have seen, among his reasons for zealously advocating the creation of the University of Virginia was to allow Southern students an alternative to Northern, anti-Southern institutions like Princeton, Harvard, and Yale, which to his mind imbibed "aristocratic," centralizing principles. In this endeavor to further public education, Giles, so unlike him in his hot temper and dogmatic states' rights ideology, was strangely to an extent Jefferson's bedfellow. In the same letter of December 26, 1825, in which Jefferson vaguely endorsed Giles's desire to thwart national internal improvements and high tariffs, and rally behind states' rights, Jefferson praised his efforts to erect a classical academy in Virginia that taught Greek and Latin. (In fact, Jefferson was not a fervent advocate for public instruction in these "dead" languages; although he read and spoke them proficiently, he considered French and Spanish more practical and useful for the aspiring politician or diplomat.) Confiding to Giles his disappointment that the students who had enrolled in his University's "classical school" were "shameful Latinists," he blamed this on the manner in which Latin was taught at Yale. "We must get rid of this Connecticut Latin, of this barbarous confusion of long and short syllables, which renders doubtful whether we are listening to a reader of Cherokee, Shawnee, Iroquois, or what," he complained to Giles. Still, he found that most of the students at Charlottesville were "fine youths," although "they committed some irregularities at first, until they learned the lawful length of their tether." He was confident that they would lead Virginia in a politically competent manner in the future: "A great proportion of them are severely devoted to study, and I fear not to say that within twelve or fifteen years from this time, a majority of the rulers of our State will have been educated here."[32]

Contrary to his reputation as an Anglophobe, Jefferson boasted of the brilliant scholars he had recruited from England to teach at the University of Virginia. "Our University has been most fortunate in the five professors procured from England," he informed Giles. "A finer selection could not have been made…. I verily believe that as high a degree of education can now be obtained here, as in the country they left."[33] Assisted by professors from old England and New England, Jefferson hoped his University would eventually surpass in excellence not only Harvard, but perhaps Oxford and Cambridge.

In his last letter to Giles, on the eve of death, bitterness toward New England finally erupted into Jefferson's consciousness. He granted priority in the Union to the South, and especially Virginia: its youth, its culture, and its burgeoning system of higher education, in which his role was preeminent. But his voice was now a mere whimper. He never proposed to subject the rest of the Union to the South—including New England, whose democratic town meeting institutions he always revered. For Jefferson, national union and freedom held the foremost place until he died. But, like a father with his children, he hoped that Virginia—and especially the graduates of his struggling offspring, the University of Virginia––would be *primus inter pares.* This helps explain his sporadic obsession with seeing Virginia emulate and eventually surpass the political and pedagogical achievements of its New England sisters.[34]

Only three months before his death, Jefferson sent his grandson, Thomas Jefferson Randolph, off to Quincy to visit a fellow old "Argonaut," John Adams. "Like other young people, he wishes to be able, in the winter nights of old age, to recount to those around him what he has heard and learnt of the Heroic age preceding his birth, and which of the Argonauts particularly he was in time to have seen," he wrote flatteringly to his old comrade. "Gratify his ambition then by recieving [*sic*] his best bow, and my solicitude for your health by enabling him to bring me a favorable account of it. Mine is indifferent, but not so my friendship and respect for you."[35]

From Quincy, after meeting young Randolph and young Bostonian merchant Joseph Coolidge, Jr., newlywed husband of Jefferson's granddaughter Ellen Wayles Randolph, Adams wrote back affectionately, "We New Englanders are but Pygmies by the side of Mr. Randolph. I was very much gratified with Mr. Randolph, and his conversation. Your letter [of March 25, just quoted] is one of the most beautiful and delightful I have ever received."[36] Adams was *one* New Englander who did not hate Jefferson.

In his efforts to "out-New England New England" by promoting progressive democratic political reforms within Virginia, Jefferson aimed to further legitimize and validate his fame and his Democratic-Republican program with the imprimaturs of direct democracy and popular rule. In a different context but with a similar purport, as a young man Jefferson had criticized John Locke's limited program of religious toleration, which although radical for its time denied religious freedom to atheists and Roman Catholics as threats to government. In 1776, Jefferson observed, "It was a great thing to go so far (as he [Locke] himself says of the parliament who framed the act of toleration) but where he stopped short, we may go on."[37]

Likewise, Jefferson wanted Virginia to "go on" by matching or surpassing its Northern "sisters" in implementing direct popular participation in governance. At least from the 1790s onward, amid partisan controversy between "democratic" Republicans and "aristocratic" Federalists, Jefferson needed to satisfy himself that the populist inclinations of Republican Virginians and his reputation as their democratic guide were at least as "self-evident" as those of their more "aristocratic," established-churched Eastern Federalist opponents.

For most of his life, but especially during his retirement years, Jefferson admired the New England town meeting's direct democracy as the ideal form of government. At the same time, he was dismayed by the arrogance and avarice of these same town meetings in Massachusetts, Connecticut, and Vermont in pursuing profit during the years of the Embargo and the War of 1812. Their citizens had not only violated the Embargo Act, but seemed to turn against the rest of the Union. To his even deeper disappointment, in the postwar years the success of such zealous religious revivalists as Lyman Beecher, Timothy and Theodore Dwight, Jedidiah Morse, and other "Presbyterians" in Connecticut and Massachusetts aroused his fears for religious freedom in the young republic. Their popularity cast a pall on his hope for the eventual triumph of "rational" deism embodied in Unitarianism, a religion that had likewise sprouted in New England.

Jefferson may well have wondered if his American Dream had metastasized into a nightmare. He was shocked by the ascendancy among New Englanders of selfish "ambition and avarice" and rampant individualism over traditional republican solicitude for the public good, although, ironically, their political practices most nearly approximated his communitarian democratic goals. At the end of his life as at the beginning of his political career, Jefferson was anything but indifferent to what was happening in the "sister states" of New England. Although present-day historians mercilessly chide the third president for inconsistency, his sentiments toward New England were unwavering. For it—in accordance with a nationalist vision responsible for writing the Declaration of Independence, purchasing Louisiana, defeating Middle Eastern pirate states, and establishing the United States as a democratic republic with a national tradition of religious freedom and secularized higher education—he always felt a preponderance of love over hate.[38]

Chapter Notes

Introduction

1. See Merrill D. Peterson, *The Jefferson Image in the American Mind* (New York: Oxford University Press, 1960), esp. chapter 4. Although most readers are probably aware of the difference between Abraham Lincoln's Republican Party and Jefferson's Republican Party, I will take the opportunity here to note that they were distinct entities. Indeed, Jefferson's Republican Party is usually considered the godfather of the present-day Democratic Party. This book will generally refer to Jefferson's party as the Republican or Democratic-Republican Party, and a few times as the Democratic Party, a name by which its political enemies referred to it as early as the 1796 elections, usually pejoratively. The party's adherents began consistently to adopt the name "Democrat" after Jefferson's election to a second term. Surprisingly, some professional historians seem confused about the names of the early parties. See, e.g., Robert J. Alderson, Jr., review of Arthur Scherr, *Thomas Jefferson's Haitian Policy: Myths and Realities* [Lanham, Md.: Lexington Books, 2011], *Journal of American History* 101, no. 4 (March 2015): 1250. For a study that emphasizes the use that Virginian right-wing racists and segregationists made of Jefferson's reputation during the 1950s, long after Jefferson's death, see Robert G. Parkinson, "First From the Right: Massive Resistance and the Image of Thomas Jefferson in the 1950s," *Virginia Magazine of History and Biography* 112 (2004): 2–35. Francis Cogliano, *Thomas Jefferson: Reputation and Legacy* (Edinburgh: University of Edinburgh Press, 2006), discusses historians' evaluation of Jefferson in the years since Peterson's work.

2. Ronald L. Hatzenbuehler, "Growing Weary in Well-Doing: Thomas Jefferson's Life Among the Virginia Gentry," *Virginia Magazine of History and Biography* 101 (Jan. 1993): 5–36; Robert E. Shalhope, "Thomas Jefferson's Republicanism and Antebellum Southern Thought," *Journal of Southern History* 42 (Nov. 1976): 529–56; James Roger Sharp, "Unraveling the Mystery of Jefferson's Letter of April 27, 1795," *Journal of the Early Republic* 6 (Winter 1986): 411–18; Sharp, *American Politics in the Early Republic: The New Nation in Crisis* (New Haven: Yale University Press, 1993); Stuart Leibiger, "Thomas Jefferson and the Missouri Crisis: An Alternative Interpretation," *Journal of the Early Republic* 17 (Spring 1997): 121–30; Peter S. Onuf, "Thomas Jefferson, Missouri, and the 'Empire of Liberty,'" in James P. Ronda, ed., *Thomas Jefferson and the Changing West: From Conquest to Conservation* (Albuquerque: University of New Mexico Press, 1997), 111–53; Onuf, *Jefferson's Empire: The Language of American Nationhood* (Charlottesville: University Press of Virginia, 2000), esp. chapter 3–5; K. R. Con-

stantine Gutzman, "The Virginia and Kentucky Resolutions Reconsidered: An Appeal to the 'Real Laws' of Our Country," *Journal of Southern History* 66 (Aug. 2000): 473–96; Andy Trees, "Private Correspondence for the Public Good: Thomas Jefferson to Elbridge Gerry, 26 January 1799," *Virginia Magazine of History and Biography* 198 (2000): 217–254; Joseph A. Fry, *Dixie Looks Abroad: The South and U.S. Foreign Relations, 1789–1973* (Baton Rouge; Louisiana State University Press, 2002), 12.

3. For example, see the laudatory reviews of *Jefferson's Empire* by James Roger Sharp in the *American Historical Review*, 106 (Dec. 2001): 1793–94, and James T. Kloppenberg in the *William and Mary Quarterly* 58, no. 1 (January 2001): 291–94.

4. Onuf, "Thomas Jefferson, Missouri, and the 'Empire,'" in Ronda, *Jefferson and the West*, 123, reprinted in *Jefferson's Empire*, 122 (quotation). "Hartford nation" was one of Jefferson' terms for New England following the War of 1812, alluding to the Hartford Convention in which Massachusetts and Connecticut defended their neutrality in the war and proposed various amendments to the Constitution designed to reconcile them to the Union.

5. Peter S. Onuf, *Jefferson's Empire: The Language of American Nationhood* (Charlottesville: University Press of Virginia, 2000), 75.

6. Onuf, *Jefferson's* Empire, 64, 65, 66–68.

7. Onuf, *Jefferson's Empire*, 68–70.

8. *Ibid.*, 70.

9. *Ibid.*, pp. 72, 77–78.

10. *Ibid.*, 121. Onuf's only basis for this conclusion is his misreading of a letter of 5 Sept. 1816, from Jefferson to Samuel Kercheval. Like Jefferson, Kercheval advocated reform of Virginia's undemocratic constitution. Jefferson used the "foreign country" analogy to depict the *national Congress* (not Connecticut). He accurately observed that the U.S. Government lacked constitutional power to dictate either Connecticut's or Virginia's suffrage regulations. Contrary to Onuf, in this letter Jefferson proposed to reduce slaveholders' power in Virginia's state government by amending its state constitution to prohibit counting the number of slaves in apportioning counties' representation in the legislature. He advised Kercheval to ignore tidewater conservatives' warnings that Northerners in Congress would demand that this principle be applied to repeal the national Constitution's "three-fifths clause," which included slaves in calculating state representation in Congress. He merely compared Connecticut's suffrage restrictions on women and propertyless males, who were counted in allocating its congressional representation despite lacking the right to vote, with the U.S. Constitution's clause counting

three-fifths of the slaves in computing Southern states' congressional representation. Paul L. Ford, ed., *Works of Thomas Jefferson* (12 vols., New York: Putnam, 1904–5), 12: 15–17; Thomas Jefferson Papers, Library of Congress. It is difficult to concur with Onuf's view (*Jefferson's Empire*, 121) that Jefferson's bland observation constituted an "imaginative leap into the abyss" of secession and civil war.

11. *Ibid.*, 123.

12. Onuf, *Jefferson's Empire*, 215n., citing Robert E. Shalhope, "Thomas Jefferson's Republicanism and Antebellum Southern Thought," *Journal of Southern History*, 62 (1976), 539–42. The same letter that Onuf cites to prove Jefferson's wish to "destroy" New England–the one to James Martin, Sept. 20, 1813, is cited by Shalhope to show that Jefferson hoped that the New Englanders would "depart in peace" if they refused to support the Union.

13. Onuf, *Jefferson's Empire*, 124. For the text of the letter on which Onuf based his extreme claims, see Jefferson to James Martin, 20 Sept. 1813, in Lipscomb and Bergh, eds., *Writings of Thomas Jefferson* (Washington, D.C.: Thomas Jefferson Memorial Foundation, 1903), 13: 382–83, and The Papers of Thomas Jefferson at the Library of Congress (online in "American Memory" series).

14. Onuf, *Jefferson's Empire*, 122.

15. *Ibid.*, p. 117.

16. Ibid., 115–116 (quotation).

17. *Ibid.*, p.116.

18. Brian Steele, "Jefferson, Coercion, and the Limits of Harmonious Union," *Journal of Southern History* 74, no. 4 (Nov. 2008): 823–854. Elizabeth R. Varon, *Disunion! The Coming of the American Civil War, 1789–1859* (Chapel Hill: University of North Carolina Press, 2009), 48–49.

19. The best brief summary of Jefferson's advocacy of the slaves' emancipation by government decree and their deportation to Haiti is Arthur Scherr, "Light at the End of the Road: Thomas Jefferson's Endorsement of Free Haiti in his Final Years," *Journal of Haitian Studies* 15 (Spring/Fall 2009): 203–216.

20. Francis D. Cogliano, *Emperor of Liberty: Thomas Jefferson's Foreign Policy* (New Haven: Yale University Press, 2014), 181. For some examples of urban Federalist newspapers' praise of the farmer's way of life by comparison with that of city inhabitants, see the *New York Herald*, Nov. 26 and Dec. 31, 1796, a New York City paper edited by the famous lexicographer, Noah Webster. On Federalist reliance on farm areas for votes, see, for example, Manning J. Dauer, *The Adams Federalists* (Baltimore: Johns Hopkins University Press, 1953), chapter 2.

21. Jefferson to Van Hogendorp, Oct. 13, 1785, in Julian P. Boyd et al., eds., *The Papers of Thomas Jefferson* (40 vols., in progress, Princeton: Princeton University Press, 1950–), 8: 633.

22. Cogliano, *Emperor of Liberty*, 182. Jefferson never recommended exterminating anyone, except in a few angry letters during the American Revolution and the War of 1812, when he suggested that those Indian tribes that waged merciless war against U.S. settlements in alliance with Britain deserved to be annihilated. See, for example, Jefferson to George Rogers Clark, Jan. 1, 1780, Boyd, ed., *Jefferson Papers*, 3: 258–59 and note. He always admired the American Indians' nearly anarchical form of government. He considered them potentially the intellectual equals of whites, and he always hoped they would be peacefully incorporated and assimilated into American society, in contrast with his opinion of black slaves, for whom he proposed gradual emancipation and emigration to Haiti. See Jefferson to James Madison, Jan. 30, 1787, in Adrienne Koch and William Peden, eds., *Life and Selected Writings of Thomas Jefferson*

(New York, 1944), 413, and Jefferson to Francis W. Gilmer, June 7, 1816, in Ford, ed., *Works of Jefferson*, XI, 535.

Chapter 1

1. For a poignant example of Jefferson's allusion to Virginia as a "country," see Query VI of *Notes on the State of Virginia*, in which, in the course of discussing the history of the colony's American Indian tribes, he admits, "An inhuman practice once prevailed in this country of making slaves of the Indians." *Notes*, in Merrill D. Peterson, ed., *Thomas Jefferson: Writings* (New York: Library of America, 1984), 186–87.

2. Thomas Jefferson to Edmund Pendleton, Dec. 16, 1783, May 25, 1784, quoted in Edward Dumbauld, *Thomas Jefferson: American Tourist* (Norman: University of Oklahoma Press, 1946), 57–58.

3. Jefferson to Chastellux, Sept. 2, 1785, in Peterson, ed., *Jefferson: Writings*, 826–827. (Spelling in the original). See also Joyce Appleby, *Inheriting the Revolution: The First Generation of Americans* (Cambridge, Mass.: Harvard University Press, 2000), 157–158.

4. Jefferson to Elizabeth Blair Thompson, Jan. 19, 1787, Boyd, ed., *Jefferson Papers*, 11: 587.

5. See Joanne Pope Melish, *Disowning Slavery: Gradual Abolition and 'Race' in New England, 1780–1860* (Ithaca: Cornell University Press, 1998).

6. See, e.g., Fred C. Luebke, "The Origins of Thomas Jefferson's Anti-Clericalism," *Church History*, 32, no. 3 (Sept. 1963): 344–56. For a recent discussion of religious practices in early Virginia, see Paul Rasor and Richard E. Bond, eds., *From Jamestown to Jefferson: The Evolution of Religious Freedom in Virginia* (Charlottesville, 2011).

7. See also David Waldstreicher, *Slavery's Constitution: From Revolution to Ratification* (New York, 2009), 64–65.

8. Jefferson warned his grandson Thomas Jefferson Randolph against horse-racing and dueling during his presidency. See Jefferson to Randolph, Nov. 24, 1808, Jefferson Papers, Library of Congress.

9. On Richard Price's racial prejudice, similar to Jefferson's, notwithstanding his abolitionism, see Anthony Page, "'A Species of Slavery': Richard Price's Rational Dissent and Antislavery," *Slavery and Abolition* 32 (March 2011): 53–73.

10. Richard Price to Jefferson, July 2, 1785, in Boyd, ed., *Jefferson Papers*, 8: 258–259.

11. Jefferson to Richard Price, Aug. 7, 1785, ibid., 8: 356.

12. Jefferson to Archibald Stuart, Dec. 23, 1791, in Peterson, ed., *Jefferson: Writings*, 984.

13. Pennsylvania abolished slavery in 1780, New Hampshire had never legalized slavery, Rhode Island abolished slavery in 1784, and Connecticut abolished slavery by law in 1784 and 1787. New York did not pass a law to abolish slavery until 1799, finalized in 1817; and New Jersey did not abolish bondage until 1804. Leon F. Litwack, *North of Slavery: The Negro in the Free States, 1790–1860* (Chicago: University of Chicago Press, 1961), 3.

14. Jefferson to Richard Price, Aug. 7, 1785, *Jefferson Papers*, 8: 356–57.

15. For helpful brief discussions of Adams' views, see John R. Howe, "John Adams's Views of Slavery," *Journal of Negro History* 49 (1964): 201–206; Bernard Rosenthal, "Puritan Conscience and New England Slavery," *New England Quarterly* 46 (1973): 62–81, at 80; and Richard S. Newman, *Transformation of American Abolitionism* (Chapel Hill: University of North Carolina Press, 2002), 33, 36, 37, 42. In his discussion of New England Jeffersonians' attitudes toward slavery, consisting of brief examinations of Abraham

Bishop, John Leland, and Levi Lincoln, Padraig G. Riley affects dismay that these individuals failed to emulate their Federalist political opponents by attacking Jefferson as a slaveholder and demanding repeal of the Constitution's "three-fifths clause." Riley argues that political expediency led them to abandon their earlier antislavery principles; however, they had *always* been Republicans, even when they denounced slavery. Padraig G. Riley, "Northern Republicans and Southern Slavery: Democracy in the Age of Jefferson, 1800–1819," Ph.D. dissertation, University of California, Berkeley, 2007), chapter one, "The Emancipation of New England." Moreover, Riley fails to recognize that the Federalists took no action against slavery when they ran the national government. Only Jefferson recommended antislavery measures, in proposing the abolition of the slave trade in 1806. Riley's puerility characterizes many historians' discussion of Jefferson and the early republic nowadays; it is certainly not confined to youthful authors of doctoral dissertations.

16. Jefferson to Richard Price, Aug. 7, 1785, *Jefferson Papers*, 8: 357.

17. Jefferson's Autobiography, online version, at htpp//libertyonline.hypermall.com; and in Peterson, ed., *Jefferson: Writings*, 5. Since Jefferson wrote his autobiography for personal reference and the information of his family, there was no reason for him to mention the manumission proposal if it were not true; besides which, he proposed the abolition of slavery a few years later in *Notes on the State of Virginia* and in his proposed constitution for Virginia in 1783, both of which were published under his name in 1787. In "Thomas Jefferson and Slavery," an article containing numerous factual errors concerning Jefferson's attitude towards slavery, historian Cassandra Pybus wrote that Jefferson never suggested manumission while in public life. She apparently wrote the article without reading Jefferson's *Notes on the State of Virginia*, or familiarizing herself with the Ordinance of 1784, his congressional resolution, which abolished slavery in the territories of the United States. She asserts, "As Paul Finkelman (1996) has observed, Jefferson was never sufficiently troubled by the injustice of slavery to risk proposing, or even supporting, efforts to provide for the emancipation of slaves, even as a voluntary, private matter." Cassandra Pybus, "Jefferson and Slavery," in Francis D. Cogliano, ed., *Wiley-Blackwell Companion to Thomas Jefferson* (Malden, Mass.: Wiley-Blackwell, 2012), 271–283, 273 (quotation). (In his *Autobiography*, though Jefferson recalled that he advocated laws for the private manumission of slaves as a Virginia legislator in his twenties, this was a far less controversial measure than government-enforced abolition, which he also proposed.) Pybus' carelessness in studying Jefferson is also evident in her laudatory review essay on a book that even those hostile to Jefferson admit is unreliable, Henry Weincek's *Master of the Mountain: Thomas Jefferson and his Slaves* (New York, 2012), in the journal, *Slavery and Abolition* 35, no. 2 (April 2014): 366–371. Here, her statistical statements about Jefferson's sales of slaves are undocumented and her footnotes are inaccurate.

18. *Autobiography*, in Peterson, ed., *Jefferson: Writings*, 33–34; "A Memorandum of Services to My Country," ibid., 702.

19. Jefferson to Richard Price, Aug. 7, 1785, *Jefferson Papers*, 8: 357.

20. *Diary of John Quincy Adams* (Cambridge, Mass., 1982), 1: 262 (May 4, 1785).

21. Good summaries of Jefferson's plantation management policies are contained in Malone, *Jefferson and the Ordeal of Liberty*, chapter 13, esp. 200–202, and Jack

McLaughlin, *Jefferson and Monticello: Biography of a Builder* (New York: Holt, 1988). Illuminating insights on this topic are in John B. Boles and Randal L. Hall, eds., *Seeing Jefferson Anew* (Charlottesville, 2010), 106, 165–67, and Lucia Stanton, "Perfecting Slavery: Rational Plantation Management at Monticello," in John Milton Cooper and Thomas J. Knock, ed., *Jefferson, Lincoln, and Wilson* (Charlottesville, 2010), 61–86.

22. Jefferson to Jared Sparks, Feb. 4, 1824, in Ford, ed., *Works of Jefferson*, 12: Jefferson to David Barrow, May 1, 1815, Jefferson Papers, Library of Congress.

23. See Maurice Jackson, *Let This Voice Be Heard: Anthony Benezet, Father of Atlantic Abolitionism* (Philadelphia, 2009).

24. Jefferson to Edward Carrington, May 27, 1788, in Julian P. Boyd et al., eds., *The Papers of Thomas Jefferson* (40 vols., in progress, Princeton: Princeton University Press, 1950–), 13: 208.

25. Jefferson to John Brown Cutting, July 8, 1788, *ibid.*, 13: 315.

26. Jefferson's Answers to Démeunier's First Queries, Jan. 24, 1786, in Boyd, *Jefferson Papers*, 10: 16. Jackson Turner Main, *The Antifederalists: Critics of the Constitution, 1781–1788* (Chapel Hill: University of North Carolina Press, 1961), 52–53 (quotation), 88–89; Main, *The Sovereign States, 1775–1783* (New York: Franklin Watts, 1973), 364–69, 453–54; Merrill Jensen, *The New Nation: A History of the United States During the Confederation, 1781–1789* (New York: Knopf, 1950), 323–25, 408–9; Herbert James Henderson, *Party Politics in the Continental Congress* (New York,: McGraw-Hill, 1971).

27. Jefferson to Edward Carrington, May 27, 1788, Boyd, ed., *Jefferson Papers*, 13: 209.

28. Jefferson's Answers to Démeunier's First Queries, Jan. 24, 1786, in Boyd, *Jefferson Papers*, 10: 16.

29. Charles A. Miller, *Jefferson and Nature: An Interpretation* (Baltimore: Johns Hopkins Press, 1988), 61.

30. Jefferson's Answers to Démeunier's First Queries, Jan. 24, 1786, in Boyd, *Jefferson Papers*, 10: 16. For Jefferson's nationalism and support for congressional regulation of interstate and foreign commerce, see Jefferson to Monroe, June 17, 1785, in Merrill D. Peterson, ed., *Thomas Jefferson: Writings* (New York: Library of America, 1984), 802–809. For his early statements that "cultivators of the earth are the most valuable citizens," see Jefferson to John Jay, Aug. 23, 1785 (quotation), Jefferson to G. K. van Hogendorp, Oct. 13, 1785, Jefferson to Madison, Dec. 20, 1787, and *Notes on Virginia*, Query 19, *ibid.*, 818–19, 836, 918, 290–91. On Rhode Island's farmers' opposition to the congressional impost, see Main, *Antifederalists*, 88–89.

31. Jefferson to Edward Carrington, May 27, 1788, Boyd, ed., *Jefferson Papers*, 13: 209.

32. For studies that stress an underlying sectional conflict at the Constitutional Convention and its aftermath, see Staughton Lynd, *Class Conflict, Slavery, and the U.S. Constitution: Ten Essays* (Indianapolis: Bobbs-Merrill, 1967), and Paul Finkelman, "The Founding Fathers and Slavery: A Covenant With Death," in Richard R. Beeman et al., eds., *Beyond Confederation* (Chapel Hill: University of North Carolina Press, 1986). Studies of Rhode Island during this period include Irving Polishook, *Rhode Island and the Union, 1774–1795* (Evanston: Northwestern University Press, 1969) and Peter J. Coleman, *The Transformation of Rhode Island, 1790–1860* (Providence: Brown University Press, 1963). Unfortunately, they include little about the party conflict between Democratic-Republicans and Federalists, and have no coverage of the presidential election of 1796.

33. Jefferson to William Stephens Smith, Nov. 13, 1787,

in Peterson, ed., *Jefferson: Writings*, 911. In an essay that reverses Jefferson's actual response the rebellion, Ronald Hatzenbuehler claims that he was shocked by the revolt and thought it showed that New Englanders were so accustomed to mindlessly obeying their clergy and big landholders that they could not rationally protest unjust laws, but reflexively exploded in violent upheaval: "Shays' Rebellion could occur only, Jefferson reasoned, in a state like Massachusetts where clergy and aristocratic families stifled freedom." Ronald L. Hatzenbuehler, "'Refreshing the Tree of Liberty with the Blood of Patriots and Tyrants': Thomas Jefferson and the Origins of the U.S. Constitution," in John M. Murrin and David E. Narrett, eds., *Essays on Liberty and Federalism: The Shaping of the U.S. Constitution* (College Station: Texas A & M University, 1988), 88–104, quote at 102. Hatzenbuehler imputes Jefferson's low opinion of Massachusetts citizens' political capacity to his disgust at Shays' Rebellion, but in fact he greatly admired the structure of their town meetings and hoped that Virginia would adopt a similar "ward" system.

34. For accounts of Jefferson's trip with Madison through New England in the spring of 1791, see Dumbauld, *American Tourist*, 7, 8, 19, 172–73; Alfred F. Young, *The Democratic-Republicans of New York: The Origins, 1763–1797* (Chapel Hill: University of North Carolina Press, 1967), 194–201; Adrienne Koch, *Jefferson and Madison: The Great Collaboration* (New York: Knopf, 1950), 114–16; Dumas Malone, *Jefferson and the Rights of Man* (Boston: Little, Brown, 1951), 359–63. See also Stanley Elkins and Eric McKitrick, *The Age of Federalism* (New York: Oxford University Press, 1993), 240–42.

35. Nathaniel Hazard to Hamilton, November 25, 1791, in Harold C. Syrett, ed., *The Papers of Alexander Hamilton* (27 vols.; New York: Columbia University Press, 1961–87), 9: 534. Pierpont Edwards's anomalous political career should be noted here. Despite his relationship to Aaron Burr, this New Haven lawyer, Connecticut legislator and member of the Continental Congress from 1787–88 favored the Constitution. He did not become a Jeffersonian Republican until 1800, after which he gained a reputation for extremism. Appointed district court judge of Connecticut by Jefferson, he prosecuted Federalist clergy and editors for libel until 1812, when Chief Justice John Marshall declared his activities unconstitutional. He was a driving force of the Connecticut constitutional convention of 1818, which disestablished the Congregational Church. *Dictionary of American Biography*, 6: 43–44.

36. Nathaniel Hazard to Alexander Hamilton, November 25, 1791, in Syrett, ed., *Hamilton Papers*, 9: 529–37.

37. *New York Herald*, Oct. 29, 1796.

38. *Acts and Laws of the Commonwealth of Massachusetts* (Boston: Young and Minns, 1796), 225–228. On the Boston electoral vote, see [Portsmouth] *New Hampshire Gazette*, Nov. 12, 1796, p. 3. For the Massachusetts legislature's actions, see Mary-Jo Kline, ed., *Political Correspondence and Public Papers of Aaron Burr* (2 vols., Princeton, 1983), 1: 276. Jeffrey L. Pasley, *The First Presidential Contest: 1796 and the Founding of American Democracy* (Lawrence: University Press of Kansas, 2013), 383, states that Massachusetts conducted popular elections for presidential electors in 1796, erroneously implying that the electors were all chosen at-large directly by the voters.

39. Lynn W. Turner, *The Ninth State: New Hampshire's Formative Years* (Chapel Hill: University of North Carolina Press, 1983), 151.

40. See Michael J. Dubin, *United States Congressional Elections, 1788–1997: The Official Results of the 1st through 105th Congresses* (Jefferson, N.C.: McFarland & Co., 1998), xv, 12, *passim*.

41. [Concord] *Courier of New Hampshire*, Oct. 4, 1796.

42. [Concord] *Courier of New Hampshire*, Nov. 29, 1796, p. 3.

43. Turner, *Ninth State*, 181, 183–84.

44. Turner, *Ninth State*, 14, 404 n.6.

45. *Greenleaf's New-York Journal and Patriotic Register*, Nov. 29, 1796, p. 3.

46. [Concord] *Republican Gazetteer*, Nov. 29, 1796, p. 3.

47. [Keene, N.H.] *Rising Sun*, Nov. 8, 1796, p. 3. Sprague, a staunch Federalist, served in the state legislature in 1797, and upheld President Adams' foreign policies there. In 1798, elected to Congress, he endorsed the Alien-Sedition Acts and proposed that U.S. ships be authorized to capture unarmed French merchant vessels, a measure so extreme that even some Federalists did not support it. See Turner, *The Ninth State*, 153, 425n.6.

48. *Greenleaf's New-York Journal & Patriotic Register*, Dec. 13, 1796, p. 3. The electors' names were also printed in the *Philadelphia Gazette*, Dec. 8, 1796, p. 3.

49. *New York Daily Advertiser*, Nov. i5, 1796, p. 2; and Thomas Greenleaf's Republican New York *Argus*, Nov. 18, 1796, p. 2. For Massachusetts as the foremost "localist" state during the 1780s, whose congressional delegates were more interested in the state's interests than a stronger national government, see H. James Henderson's path-breaking study, *Party Politics in the Continental Congress* (New York: McGraw-Hill, 1974).

50. Michael J. Dubin, *United States Presidential Elections, 1788–1860: The Official Records by County and State* (Jefferson, N.C.: McFarland & Co., 2002), xii.

51. Jefferson to Madison, Jan. 1, 1797, in Barbara Oberg, ed., *Papers of Thomas Jefferson*, 29: 247; Dubin, *United States Presidential Elections, 1788–1860*, xii.

52. Jefferson to Edward Rutledge, Dec. 27, 1796, in Barbara Oberg, ed., *Papers of Thomas Jefferson*, 29: 231–33, available online at National Archives "Founders Online" database.

53. Jefferson to Madison, Jan. 1, 1797, in Barbara Oberg, ed., *Papers of Thomas Jefferson*, 29: 247. See also Jean M. Yarbrough, *American Virtues* (Lawrence: University Press of Kansas, 1998), 228 n.138. For a study which emphasizes the prevalence of an incipient "totalitarian democracy" in colonial and Revolutionary Massachusetts, in which the town meetings enforced conformity to social mores in the absence of a viable police force, see Michael Zuckerman, *Peaceable Kingdoms* (New York, 1970).

54. Jefferson to Madison, Jan. 1, 1797, in Barbara Oberg, ed., *Papers of Thomas Jefferson*, 29: 247.

55. Jefferson to Volney, Jan. 8, 1797, Oberg, ed., *Jefferson Papers*, 29: 258. (I have changed some of the original punctuation for purposes of readability).

56. Jefferson to Madison, Jan. 1, 1797, in Boyd et al., eds., *Papers of Jefferson*, 29: 247. See also Jean Yarbrough, *American Virtues* (Lawrence: University Press of Kansas, 1998), 228 n.138. On British and American politicians' ambivalence toward political parties during the eighteenth century, see Isaac Kramnick, *Bolingbroke and his Circle: The Politics of Nostalgia in the Age of Walpole* (Cambridge, Mass.: Harvard University Press, 1968); Caroline Robbins, "'Discordant Parties': A Study of the Acceptance of Party Among Englishmen," *Political Science* Quarterly 73 (Dec. 1958): 505–529; Pat Rogers, "Swift and Bolingbroke on Faction," *Journal of British Studies* 9 (May 1970): 71–101; James H. Hutson, "The Origins of 'The Paranoid Style in American Politics': Public Jealousy from the Age of Walpole to the Age of Jackson," in David D. Hall et al., eds., *Saints and Revolutionaries: Essays on Early American History* (New York: Norton, 1984), 332–372; Richard Hofstadter, *The Idea of a*

Party System: The Rise of Legitimate Opposition in the United States, 1780–1840 (Berkeley: University of California Press, 1969); Lance Banning, The Jeffersonian Persuasion: Evolution of a Party Ideology (Ithaca, N.Y.: Cornell University Press, 1978); Ralph Ketcham, Presidents Above Party: The First American Presidency, 1789–1829 (Chapel Hill: University of North Carolina Press, 1984); and Arthur Scherr, "Inventing the Patriot President: Bache's Aurora and John Adams," Pennsylvania Magazine of History and Biography 119 (Oct. 1995): 369–399.

57. Dubin, United States Presidential Elections, 1788–1860, xii. Despite its general reliability, Kurtz, Presidency of John Adams, 409, was incorrect in this case. He mistakenly wrote that New Hampshire's legislature cast its electoral vote and that Rhode Island's town meetings chose that state's four electors, when the opposite was the fact. I have investigated these two states myself because no adequate account of the electoral processes and procedures during the presidential election of 1796 exists. Despite its length, Pasley's recent study, First Presidential Contest, does not carefully discuss the modes by which electors were chosen. It is more a general political history of the 1790s than a detailed account of the election campaign of 1796.

58. Jefferson to Madison, 1 Jan. 1797, in Boyd et al., eds., Papers of Jefferson, 29: 247. For Massachusetts Revolutionary–era town meetings as prototypical totalitarian democracies, enforcing "consensual communism" in the absence of a viable police force, see Michael Zuckerman, Peaceable Kingdoms: New England Towns in the Eighteenth Century (New York: Alfred A. Knopf, 1970). On the "classical republican" philosophical legacy descending from Plato and Aristotle through the Renaissance to the Enlightenment, which advocated the transcendence of selfish interests in pursuance of a consensual "common good," see, e.g., Zera S. Fink, The Classical Republicans (Evanston, Ill.: Northwestern University Press, 1945), and J. G. A. Pocock, The Machiavellian Moment: Florentine Political Thought and the Atlantic Republican Tradition (Princeton: Princeton University Press, 1975).

59. Jefferson to Aaron Burr, 17 June 1797, Boyd et al., eds., Jefferson Papers, 29: 439.

Chapter 2

1. Portions of this chapter have appeared in Arthur Scherr, "'The Most Agreeable Country': New Light on Democratic-Republican Opinion of Massachusetts in the 1790s," Historical Journal of Massachusetts 35, no. 2 (Summer 2007): 148–166.

2. Benjamin Franklin Bache to Margaret Bache, July 15, 1795, Bache Family Papers, Castle Collection, American Philosophical Society, reel 3 (microfilm). On Bache's "scoop," see Everette E. Dennis, "Stolen Peace Treaties and the Press: Two Case Studies," Journalism History, 2 (1975): 6–14. For accounts of Bache's Northern junket campaign against Jay's Treaty, see James Tagg, Benjamin Franklin Bache and the Philadelphia Aurora (Philadelphia, 1991), pp. 246–48, and Jeffery A. Smith, Franklin and Bache: Envisioning the Enlightened Republic (New York, 1991), pp.138–39. The relative socioeconomic equality on New England farms during this period is a theme of Robert E. Brown, Middle-Class Democracy and the Revolution in Massachusetts (East Lansing, Mich., 1955); Gloria L. Main, "Inequality in Early America: The Evidence from Probate Records in Massachusetts and Maryland," Journal of Interdisciplinary History 7 (1977): 559–581; and Jackson Turner Main, Society and the Economy in Colonial Connecticut (Princeton, 1985).

3. Tagg. Bache and the Aurora, p. 28; Smith, Franklin and Bache, p. 61.

4. Bache to Margaret Bache, July 15, 1795, Bache Papers, Castle Collection; Tagg, Bache and the Aurora, p. 248.

5. Bache to Margaret Bache, July 15, 1795, Bache Papers, Castle Collection.

6. For Vaughan's ordeal in England and France during the 1790s, see Craig Compton Murray, "Benjamin Vaughan (1751–1835): The Life of an Anglo-American Intellectual" (Ph.D. diss., Columbia University, 1989), 311–379; Dictionary of National Biography, s.v., "Vaughan, Benjamin"; Robert R. Palmer, Age of the Democratic Revolution (2 vols.; Princeton, 1959–64), 2: 121–22; and J. M. Thompson, Robespierre (2 vols.; New York, 1936), 2: 225.

7. Benjamin Vaughan to James Monroe, Sept. 2, 1797, James Monroe Papers, New York Public Library (Emphasis in original). It seems Vaughan is describing New Englanders' tendency to adopt "deferential" behavior toward their political and social leaders. See J. R. Pole's classic study, "Historians and the Problem of Early American Democracy," American Historical Review, 67 (1962); 626–646, and Edmund Cook, The Fathers of the Towns: Leadership and Community Structure in Eighteenth-Century New England (Baltimore, 1976). For studies of the clergy during the 1790s that corroborate Vaughan's opinion, see Gary B. Nash, "The American Clergy and the French Revolution," William and Mary Quarterly, 22 (July 1965): 392–412; Nathan O. Hatch, The Sacred Cause of Liberty: Republican Thought and the Millennium in Revolutionary New England (New Haven, 1977); and Henry F. May, The Enlightenment in America (New York, 1976).

8. Benjamin Vaughan to James Monroe, Sept. 2, 1797, James Monroe Papers, New York Public Library. Monroe and Vaughan had become acquainted during Monroe's ministry to Paris from 1794–1796. Murray, "Benjamin Vaughan," 377–79.

9. Roland M. Baumann, "John Swanwick: Spokesman for 'Merchant-Republicanism' in Philadelphia, 1790–1798," Pennsylvania Magazine of History and Biography, 97 (April 1973): 178–80; Arthur Scherr, "John Adams, Providential Rhetoric and Party Warfare: A Note on Massachusetts Politics in the Late 1790s," Mid-America: An Historical Review, 73 (Jan. 1991): 13–15; William Bruce Wheeler, "Urban Politics in Nature's Republic: The Seaport Cities in the Federalist Era, 1789–1801" (Ph.D. dissertation, University of Virginia, 1967), 89.

10. Benjamin Vaughan to James Monroe, Sept. 2, 1797, James Monroe Papers, New York Public Library (italics in original). Evincing his desire for compromise between the conflicting parties, Vaughan confided to Monroe that he possessed evidence aspersing Federalist John Jay's handling of the peace negotiations in 1782–83, but would not publish it out of friendship for Jay. Without much evidence, Michael Durey, Transatlantic Radicals and the Early American Republic (Lawrence, 1997), 224, claims that Vaughan gave "muted allegiance to Federalism."

11. For a biography of Vaughan, see Craig C. Murray, Benjamin Vaughan (1751–1835): The Life of an Anglo-American Intellectual (New York, 1982). In addition to those already mentioned, recent works which rehabilitate the New England Congregationalist clergy, depicting them as more liberal than their historical reputations would warrant are: Ruth Bloch, Visionary Republic: Millennial Themes in American Thought, 1756–1800 (Cambridge, 1985), pp. 168–207; David B. Davis, "American Equality and Foreign Revolutions," Journal of American History, 76 (Dec. 1989): 742–43; Kim Alan Snyder, "Foundations of Liberty: The Christian Republicanism of Timothy Dwight and Jedidiah

Morse," *New England Quarterly* 56, no. 3 (Sept. 1983): 382–397; and Robert J. Imholt, "Timothy Dwight, Federalist Pope of Connecticut," *New England Quarterly*, 73 (Sept. 2000): 386–411.

12. "Pelham," Hartford Connecticut *Courant*, Nov. 21, 1796.

13. Jefferson to Elbridge Gerry, May 13, 1797, in Peterson, ed., *Jefferson: Writings*, 1043.

14. Jefferson to St. George Tucker, Aug. 28, 1797, in Barbara J. Oberg, ed., *Papers of Thomas Jefferson*, 29: 519 (quotation). Jefferson to James Madison, Feb. 12, 1799, in James Morton Smith, ed., *Republic of Letters: The Correspondence between Thomas Jefferson and James Madison, 1776–1826* (3 vols.; New York, 1995), 2: 1095. Wolcott, Sr., argued that secession was desirable because the hypocritical Southerner Jefferson "will never have the northern confidence." He believed that the Union would be of "short duration" because of the ineradicable hostility between North and South. Oliver Wolcott, Sr., to Oliver Wolcott, Jr., Oct. 3, 1796; same to same, July 4, 1796, in George Gibbs, *Memoirs of the Administrations of Washington and Adams* (2 vols.; New York: Van Norden, 1846), I, 385–86 (first quotation), 372 (second quotation).

15. "PELHAM," in [Hartford] *Connecticut Courant*, Nov. 21, 1796. This first "Pelham" essay, dated Nov. 21, 1796, and specifically addressed to citizens north of the Potomac, was reprinted in the Democratic-Republican Philadelphia *Aurora: General Advertiser* on Dec. 19, 1796. The second installment of "Pelham" apparently did not appear there.

16. Ibid.

17. Ibid.

18. Ibid.

19. Ibid.

20. "PELHAM," *Connecticut Courant*, Dec. 12, 1796.

21. Ibid.

22. "Pelham," *Conn. Courant*, Dec. 12, 1796.

23. Jefferson to Elbridge Gerry, May 13, 1797, in Oberg, ed., *Jefferson Papers*, 29: 363.

24. Ibid.

25. "Greene," "To the Friends of Union," in Philadelphia *General Advertiser: Aurora*, Dec. 19, 1796 ("for the New-World"). "Pelham" was printed in the Philadelphia *General Advertiser: Aurora*, Dec. 19, 1796 ("From the Connecticut Courant") as well. For more on Democratic-Republican newspapers' response to "Pelham," see Donald H. Stewart, *The Opposition Press of the Federalist Period* (Albany: State University of New York Press, 1969), 348–350.

26. Jefferson to Elbridge Gerry, May 13, 1797, in Oberg, ed., *Jefferson Papers*, 29: 363–364.

27. Jefferson to Aaron Burr, June 17, 1797, in Mary-Jo Kline, ed., *Political Correspondence and Public Papers of Aaron Burr* (2 vols., Princeton, 1983), 1: 300.

28. Burr to Elbridge Gerry, Nov. 30, 1796, in Kline ed., *Political Correspondence and Public Papers of Aaron Burr*, 1: 278–79. See also ibid., 266–70; Jeffrey L. Pasley, *The First Presidential Contest: 1796 and the Founding of American Democracy* (Lawrence: University Press of Kansas, 2013), 385. On Thomas Pinckey's popularity with Republicans, see Arthur Scherr, "The Significance of Thomas Pinckney's Candidacy in the Election of 1796," *South Carolina Historical Magazine* 76, no. 2 (April 1975): 51–59.

29. On the New York City assembly elections of 1797, see Alfred F. Young, *The Democratic-Republicans of New York: The Origins, 1763–1797* (Chapel Hill: University of North Carolina Press, 1967), 493–495.

30. Jefferson to Aaron Burr, June 17, 1797, in Mary-Jo Kline, ed., *Political Correspondence and Public Papers of Aaron Burr* (2 vols., Princeton, 1983), 1: 300. Like Jefferson, Burr

was interested in Massachusetts political culture. After his election to the New York assembly in June 1797, he asked William Eustis, a Massachusetts Republican, to send him copies of the state's laws, both the current ones and those from before the Revolution. He was probably seeking ideas for legislative proposals. Burr to Eustis, Oct. 20, 1797, *ibid.*, 315.

31. Portions of Joshua Brookes' memoir were published in the *New-York Historical Society Quarterly* in 1947, as R. W. G. Vail, ed., "A Dinner at Mt. Vernon: From the Unpublished Journal of Joshua Brookes (1773–1859)," *New-York Historical Society Quarterly* 31, no. 4 (April 1947): 72–85, 82 (quotation). See also Kevin P. Hayes, ed., *Jefferson in His Own Time* (Iowa City: University of Iowa Press, 2012), p. xxviii; and Mary V. Thompson, *In the Hands of a Good Providence: Religion in the Life of George Washington* (Charlottesville, 2008), 1–2, 7–8.

32. For Jefferson's political "platform" (as we might call it today) in advance of the presidential election of 1800, see Jefferson to Elbridge Gerry, January 26, 1799, Peterson, ed., *Writings*, 1056–1057.

Chapter 3

1. Jefferson to James Madison, March 29, 1798, in Ford, ed., *Works of Jefferson*, 8: 392. For Jefferson's hope that a French invasion of Britain and its consequent "republicanization" would dampen Federalist eagerness for war with France, see Jefferson to Edmund Randolph, June 27, 1797, *ibid.*, 8: 320; Jefferson to Thomas Mann Randolph, Jr., Jan. 11, 1798, Jefferson Papers, Library of Congress; Jefferson to Peregrine Fitzhugh, Feb. 23, 1798, in Ford, ed., *Works of Jefferson*, 8: 377–78; Jefferson to Madison, June 7, 1798, *ibid.*, 436. As late as 1816, Jefferson was optimistic that Britain's poor would overthrow the monarchy out of despair at their poor living conditions, expropriate the wealthy on the model of France's Reign of Terror, and ultimately set up a democratic republic like that of the United States. Jefferson to John Adams, Nov. 25, 1816, in Cappon, ed., *Adams-Jefferson Letters*, 497–499.

2. Jefferson to Edmund Pendleton, April 2, 1798, *ibid.*, 395–96.

3. Jefferson to Peregrine Fitzhugh, Feb. 23, 1798, in Barbara B. Oberg, ed., *Papers of Thomas Jefferson*, 30: 130.

4. Jefferson to Peregrine Fitzhugh, Feb. 23, 1798, in Barbara B. Oberg, ed., *Papers of Thomas Jefferson*, 30: 130. For an interesting general discussion of the use of planetary models to explicate political systems during the eighteenth century, see Richard Striner, "Political Newtonianism: The Cosmic Model of Politics in Europe and America," *William and Mary Quarterly*, 3d ser., 52 (Oct.1995): 583–604.

5. See Jefferson's "Notes on the Formation of the Federal Government," 5 Jan. 1798, in Barbara B. Oberg et al., eds., *Papers of Thomas Jefferson*, 30: 13–14.

6. James Madison to Edmund Randolph, 25 Feb. 1787, in *Papers of James Madison*, ed. Hutchinson, Rachal, et al., 9: 299, quoted in Richard K. Matthews, *If Men Were Angels: James Madison and the Heartless Empire of Reason* (Lawrence, Kans., 1995), 14n. See also Lance Banning, *The Sacred Fire of Liberty: James Madison and The Founding of the Federal Republic* (Ithaca, N. Y.: Cornell University Press, 1995), 124.

7. Jefferson to James Madison, March 21, 1798, in Barbara Oberg et al., eds., *Papers of Thomas Jefferson*, 30: 190. See also Jefferson's "Notes on the Formation of the Federal Government," 5 Jan. 1798, ibid., 13–14.

8. Jefferson's "Notes on the Formation of the Federal Government," 5 Jan. 1798, *Jefferson Papers*, 30: 13–14. These notes are also in Franklin B. Sawvel, ed., *Anas of Thomas Jef-*

ferson (1903; reprinted, New York, 1970), 187–89. On the prevalence of pro-monarchical views among many political activists of the period, see Louise B. Dunbar, *A Study of 'Monarchical Tendencies' in the United States from 1776–1801* (Urbana, Ill., 1922). Most historians agree that several Massachusetts' legislators' early apathy toward the calling of a Constitutional Convention before Shays' Rebellion rested on localist or "parochial" opposition to a strong central government rather than to partiality for monarchy. See H. James Henderson, *Party Politics in the Continental Congress* (New York, 1974), 5–6, 268, 413. Indeed, contrary to Jefferson's suspicions in 1798, during the mid–1780s Massachusetts merchants turned Anglophobic. They resented the bitter competition they encountered from British merchants and factors who had returned to New England after the war. For reasons of political propaganda and sincere belief, Massachusetts Federalist merchants, lawyers, and politicians went so far as to charge that the Shays rebels wanted to return to the British monarchy and were supported by the British government. Stephen E. Patterson, "The Federalist Reaction to Shays' Rebellion," in Robert A. Gross, ed., *In Debt to Shays: The Bicentennial of an Agrarian Insurrection* (Charlottesville, 1993), 113–118.

9. Merrill D. Peterson, *Thomas Jefferson and the New Nation: A Biography* (New York, 1970), 605–606; Brent Tarter and Wythe Holt, "The Apparent Political Selection of Federal Grand Juries in Virginia, 1789–1809," *American Journal of Legal History* 49, no. 3 (July 2007): 257–283.

10. Jefferson to John Taylor, 26 Nov. 1798, in Barbara Oberg et al., eds., *Papers of Thomas Jefferson*, 30: 589–590.

11. Oberg, ed., *Jefferson Papers*, 30: 575, editorial note.

12. Petition to General Assembly of Virginia, Nov. 2–3, 1798, ibid., 571–574. A few months later, Taylor notified Jefferson that the legislature had postponed consideration of his Albemarle County petition for the direct election of jurors because the ongoing debate over those "unconstitutional laws," the Alien and Sedition Acts, and the problem of funding the arming of the militia had priority. He said the assembly was in a parsimonious mood, and did not want to spend money on implementing the district elections that popular election of jurors entailed. John Taylor to Jefferson, Feb. 15, 1799, Jefferson Papers, Library of Congress (online at American Memory). For Jefferson's support of annual, popular election of judges, see Jefferson to Samuel Kercheval, July 12, 1816. For his advocacy of local, popular election of jurors by "ward," see ibid., and Jefferson to John Cartwright, June 5, 1824, Jefferson Papers, Library of Congress.

13. James Madison, "Influence of Domestic Slavery on Government," in "Notes for the *National Gazette* Essays (ca. 19 December 1791–3 March 1792)," in Stagg et al, eds., *Papers of James Madison*, 14: 163–164.

14. For the persistence of Federalist Party strength in Massachusetts into the 1830s, especially on the state level, the standard work is Richard P. McCormick, *The Second American Party System* (Chapel Hill, 1967). For Federalist power in the wealthiest parts of the South during the 1790s, see Manning J. Dauer, *Adams Federalists* (Baltimore, 1953). See also Shaw Livermore, Jr., *The Twilight of Federalism* (Princeton, 1962). For the application of the concept of "secure" and "insecure" elites to the politics of the 1790s in much the same way that Madison used it in his notes, see Richard Buel, Jr., *Securing the Revolution: Ideology in American Politics, 1789–1815* (Ithaca: Cornell University Press, 1972).

15. John Taylor to Henry Tazewell, 13 June 1797, Tazewell Family Papers, Virginia State Library, quoted in Robert E. Shalhope, *John Taylor of Caroline: Pastoral Republican* (Columbia: University of South Carolina Press, 1980), 96.

16. John Taylor to Thomas Jefferson, n.d., received 13 May 1798, Thomas Jefferson Papers, Library of Congress.

17. Jefferson to John Taylor, 4 June 1798, in *Thomas Jefferson: Writings*, ed. Merrill D. Peterson (New York: Library of America, 1984), pp. 1049–50.

18. Jefferson to Taylor, 4 June 1798, in *Jefferson: Writings*, p. 1050. For Jefferson's favorable outlook on nature, see Daniel J. Boorstin, *The Lost World of Thomas Jefferson* (New York: Henry Holt, 1948), and Charles A. Miller, *Jefferson and Nature: An Interpretation* (Baltimore: Johns Hopkins University Press, 1988). On the pressures of growing population on the old New England town (with particular emphasis on Dedham, a small Suffolk county town near Boston), see Kenneth Lockridge, "Land, Population, and the Evolution of New England Society," *Past and Present* (April 1968): 62–80; see also Bettye Hobbs Pruitt, "Self-Sufficiency and the Agricultural Economy of Eighteenth-Century Massachusetts," *William and Mary Quarterly* 32, no. 3 (July 1984): 333–364.

19. John Taylor to Jefferson, 25 June 1798, Jefferson Papers, Library of Congress, reprinted with minor errors in William E. Dodd, ed., "Letters of John Taylor, of Caroline County, Virginia," *John P. Branch Historical Papers of Randolph-Macon College*, 2 (June 1908): 253–353, quote at 271. One historian, after a careless reading of Taylor's letter, has argued that Taylor was praising the undemocratic constitution of Virginia and hoping for the state's secession. But Taylor was actually praising the constitution of his nemesis, Connecticut. K. R. Constantine Gutzman, "The Virginia and Kentucky Resolutions Reconsidered: An Appeal to the 'Real Laws' of Our Country," *Journal of Southern History* 66 (Aug. 2000): 473–96, esp. 481–82.

20. Taylor to Jefferson, 25 June 1798, Jefferson Papers, Library of Congress, and Oberg, ed., *Jefferson Papers*, 30: 430–435, 434 (quotation).*See also* Shalhope, *John Taylor*, p. 98–99. Of course, Taylor's proposal was constitutional, since the fifth article of the U.S. Constitution permits two-thirds of the state legislatures to implement the call for a constitutional convention.

21. Jefferson to Madison, Feb. 5, 1799, in Barbara B. Oberg, ed., *The Papers of Thomas Jefferson* (Princeton, 2004), 31: 10.

22. Jefferson to Edmund Pendleton, April 22, 1799, ibid., 31: 97–98 and notes.

23. Jefferson to Edmund Pendleton, April 22, 1799, ibid., 31: 97–98.

24. After quoting this letter, historian Brian Schoen misleadingly comments, "Jefferson was fully conscious of the threat presented by the carrying trade, but party goals and his Anglophobia compounded to support the rights of the carrying trade." Brian Schoen, *The Fragile Fabric of Union: Cotton, Federal Politics, and the Global Origins of the Civil War* (Baltimore: Johns Hopkins University Press, 2009), 291–92, note 22. Obviously, Jefferson did not fulfill "party goals" by maintaining silence on the carrying trade during the election of 1800, which was not a matter of dispute between the parties in the election. He received no electoral votes from New England in any event. And it was not "Anglophobic" to feel responsible for protecting the carrying trade, which was profitable mainly to the pro–English, New England Federalist merchants who conducted it.

25. John Adams to Jefferson, 24 March 1801, in Cappon, ed., *Adams-Jefferson Letters*, 1: 264. This letter must have been especially painful for Adams to write. Not only had he been distressed by his defeat by Jefferson for the presidency, he had not recovered from the death of his son Charles, who had passed away, largely from alcoholism, on 30 November 1800. See also Edith B. Gelles, "The Adamses Retire," *Early*

American Studies 4 (Spring 2006): 1–15. In this letter, Adams bitterly informed Jefferson of Charles's death, probably expecting a commiserating reply in return. However, Jefferson failed to reply, as was his wont when deaths took place, which for him was an unpleasant topic he preferred to avoid discussing, for both his own benefit and that of others.

26. Moses Robinson to Jefferson, March 3, 1801, Jefferson Papers, Library of Congress (American Memory online). Spelling and punctuation are in the original.

27. *Ibid.*

28. Moses Robinson to Jefferson, March 3, 1801, Jefferson Papers, Library of Congress.

29. Jefferson to Moses Robinson, March 23, 1801, in Peterson, ed., *Jefferson: Writings*, 1087–1088. For biographical data on Moses Robinson, see J. Kevin Graffagnino, s.v., "Robinson, Moses," in *American National Biography* 18: 671–672.

30. Jefferson to Robinson, March 23, 1801, in Peterson, ed., *Jefferson: Writings*, 1087–1088.

31. Jefferson to Robinson, March 23, 1801, in Peterson, ed., *Jefferson: Writings*, 1087–1088.

32. Jefferson to Robinson, March 23, 1801, in Peterson, ed., *Jefferson: Writings*, 1088.

33. See Charles O. Lerche, Jr., "Jefferson and the Election of 1800: A Case Study in the Political Smear," *William and Mary Quarterly* 3rd ser., 5 (Oct. 1948): 467–491.

34. For Jefferson's patronage practices, see Carl E. Prince, "The Passing of the Aristocracy: Jefferson's Removal of the Federalists, 1801–1805," *Journal of American History* 57, no. 3 (Dec. 1970): 563–575; Carl E. Prince, *The Federalists and the Origins of the U.S. Civil Service* (New York: New York University Press, 1977); Sidney H. Aronson, *Status and Kinship in the Higher Civil Service* (Cambridge, Mass., 1964).

Chapter 4

1. Jefferson to the New Haven Merchants, July 12, 1801, in Oberg, ed., *Jefferson Papers*, 34: 554–557.

2. Levi Lincoln to Jefferson, July 28, 1801, ibid., 657–668, 658 (quotation). Spelling and punctuation in the original.

3. Levi Lincoln to Jefferson, Aug. 14, 1801, in Oberg, ed., *Jefferson Papers*, 35: 88.

4. Jefferson to Levi Lincoln, Aug. 26, 1801, in Oberg, ed., *Jefferson Papers*, 35: 146. I have modernized punctuation in some cases.

5. Jefferson to Pierre Samuel Du Pont de Nemours, January 18, 1802, ibid., 36: 390. For Jefferson's first annual message to Congress, Dec. 8, 1801, see ibid., 58–67.

6. Jefferson to Pierre Samuel Du Pont de Nemours, January 18, 1802, ibid., 36: 390.

7. Jefferson to Du Pont, January 18, 1802, ibid., 390–391.

8. Jefferson to Levi Lincoln, Aug. 26, 1801, in Oberg, ed., *Jefferson Papers*, 35: 146.

9. Ibid., 146–147.

10. Levi Lincoln to Jefferson, July 24, 1802, Oberg, ed., *Jefferson Papers*, 38: 125. (The online version of the Jefferson Papers at the Library of Congress at "Amrican Memory" dates this letter July 25, 1802.) Pasley, *'Tyranny of Printers,'* 206–15; William A. Robinson, *Jeffersonian Democracy in New England* (New Haven: Yale University Press, 1916), 36–51.

11. Jefferson to Joel Barlow, May 3, 1802, Jefferson Papers, Library of Congress, and Paul L. Ford, ed., *Works of Thomas Jefferson* (12 vols.; New York, 1904–5), 9: 370–72.

12. Jefferson to Joel Barlow, May 3, 1802, Jefferson

Papers, Library of Congress, and Paul L. Ford, ed., *Works of Thomas Jefferson* (12 vols.; New York, 1904–5), 9: 370–72.

Chapter 5

1. Jefferson to Elbridge Gerry, March 29, 1801, in Paul L. Ford, ed., *Works of Jefferson*, 9: 242–243. On Caleb Strong's "moderate" Hamiltonianism and popularity as a politician in what Ronald P. Formisano calls the "Revolutionary Center," see Ronald P. Formisano, *The Transformation of Political Culture: Massachusetts Parties, 1790s-1840s* (New York, 1983), 61–63.

2. John Quincy Adams to William Vans Murray, April 7, 1801, in Ford, ed., *Writings of John Quincy Adams*, 2: 535–526.

3. Ibid. I owe this reference to David Waldstreicher.

4. The best studies of Federalist frustration remain Fischer, *Revolution of American Conservaitsm*, and Livermore, *Twilight of Federalism.* James Roger Sharp, *American Politics in the Early Republic*, and Hofstadter, *Idea of a Party System* are also useful.

5. See, e.g., William A. Robinson, *Jeffersonian Democracy in New England* (New Haven, 1916); Paul Goodman, *The Democratic-Republicans of Massachusetts: Politics in a Young Republic* (Cambridge, Mass., 1964), and Formisano, *Transformation of Political Culture.*

6. See Jefferson to Dr. Benjamin Rush, Dec. 20, 1801, in Lipscomb and Bergh, eds., *Writings of Thomas Jefferson*, 10: 303–304, for an example of Jefferson's gratification at public acclaim for his annual message. For the text of his annual message, Dec. 8, 1801, see Peterson, ed., *Jefferson: Writings*, 501–509.

7. Danbury Baptist Association to Jefferson [after Oct. 7, 1801], in Barbara B. Oberg, ed., *Papers of Thomas Jefferson*, 35: 407–408. For Baptists' adoption of aspects of Quaker dress and mores, see Jane E. Calvert, *Quaker Constitutionalism and the Political Thought of John Dickinson* (New York, 2009), 227n.

8. Ibid. Jefferson to Benjamin Rush, Sept. 23, 1800, in Peterson, ed., *Jefferson: Writings*, 1081–1082.

9. Danbury Baptist Association to Jefferson [after Oct. 7, 1801], in Barbara B. Oberg, ed., *Papers of Thomas Jefferson*, 35: 407–408. Italics in original. In his Summary Journal of Letters, Jefferson listed the letter as being received on Dec. 30, 1801. Ibid., 409n. For Jefferson's letter to Rush, Sept. 23, 1800, which is printed in numerous collections, see Peterson, ed., *Jefferson: Writings*, 1082. Jefferson often used language nearly identical to that of the Danbury Baptists in deploring the union of church and state as an instrument of corruption and clerical self-interest. For example, see Jefferson to William Baldwin, January 19, 1810 (draft), in Looney, ed., *Papers of Thomas Jefferson: Retirement Series*, 2: 157–159.

10. Danbury Baptist Association to Jefferson [after Oct. 7, 1801], in Oberg, ed., *Papers of Thomas Jefferson*, 35: 408.

11. Ibid., 408.

12. Ibid. For Jefferson's doubts about human immortality and Jesus' divinity, see Arthur Scherr, "Thomas Jefferson versus the Historians: Christianity, Atheistic Morality, and the Afterlife," *Church History* 83, no. 1 (March 2014): 60–109. Apart from their mutual support of religious freedom, state noninterference in religious matters, and the voluntary nature of faith, the rational deist Jefferson and the emotional revivalist Baptists had little in common. See Andrew Koppelman, *Defending American Religious Neutrality* (Cambridge, Mass.: Harvard University Press, 2013), 61; and J. Judd Owen, "The Struggle Between 'Religion and Nonre-

ligion': Jefferson, Backus, and the Dissonance of America's Founding Principles," *American Political Science Review* 101, no. 3 (August 2007): 493–503. Koppelman, 61, observes, "Jefferson became an ally of Baptist proponents of disestablishment, notably Leland, but this alliance depended on a delicate silence about their dramatically different views of religious truth and therefore of what counted as corruption."

13. Jefferson to Messrs. Nehemiah Dodge and Others, a Committee of the Danbury Baptist Association, January 1, 1802, in Peterson, ed., *Jefferson: Writings*, 510.

14. See Oberg, ed., *Jefferson Papers*, 36: 253, for Leland's conveying the Danbury Baptists' address to Washington, D.C.

15. Jefferson's Draft Reply to the Danbury Baptist Association [on or before Dec. 31, 1801], in Oberg, ed., *Jefferson Papers*, 36: 255, note 2.

16. Jefferson to Levi Lincoln, January 1, 1802, in Oberg, ed., *Jefferson Papers*, 36: 256–257. Contrary to Johann Neem's thesis, there is no reason to think that by this phrase, Jefferson intended to publicly endorse Unitarianism, or "civil religion," or covertly spread his religious views among the people. Johann N. Neem, "Beyond the Wall: Reinterpreting Jefferson's Danbury Address," *Journal of the Early Republic* 27 (Spring 2007): 139–154,

17. Robert E. Lewis, "Ashbel Green, 1762–1848: Preacher, Educator, Editor," *Journal of the Presbyterian Historical Society* 36, no. 3 (1957): 141–156; Fred J. Hood, *Reformed America: The Middle and Southern States, 1783–1837* (Tuscaloosa: University of Alabama Press, 1980).

18. Jefferson's Draft Reply to the Danbury Baptist Association (on or before Dec. 31, 1801), in Oberg, ed., *Jefferson Papers*, 36: 255.

19. Ibid., 36: 255–256 note 5.

20. Levi Lincoln to Jefferson, January 1, 1802, ibid., 36: 257. On the Thanksgiving Day proclamations, see ibid., 36: 255 note to Jefferson's Draft Reply to the Danbury Baptist Association.

21. Jefferson to Levi Lincoln, January 1, 1802, in Oberg, ed., *Jefferson Papers*, 36: 257 (italics in original); and in slightly different form in Lipscomb and Bergh, eds., *Writings of Jefferson*, 10: 305.

22. Philip N. Mulder, *A Controversial Spirit: Evangelical Awakenings in the South* (New York: Oxford University Press, 2002), 106.

23. Jefferson to Levi Lincoln, January 1, 1802, in Oberg, ed., *Jefferson Papers*, 36: 257 (italics in original); and in slightly different form in Lipscomb and Bergh, eds., *Writings of Jefferson*, 10: 305.

24. Jefferson to Gideon Granger, Aug. 15, 1802, in Oberg, ed., *Jefferson Papers*, 38: 224–225. I have modernized Jefferson's capitalization. According to a pamphlet by anti–Burr Republican editor James Cheetham of New York, Eustis, at Burr's direction, had voted against Jefferson's proposal to repeal the Federalist Judiciary Act of 1801. Bishop had supposedly attempted to influence the Pennsylvania legislature in 1800 to cast its electoral vote equally for Jefferson and Burr, so that Burr would win the presidency. Cheetham made these charges in *A View of the Political Conduct of Aaron Burr, Esq. Vice-President of the United States* (New York, 1802). Ibid., 225 note.

25. Gideon Granger to Jefferson, Dec. 31, 1801, in Oberg, ed., *Jefferson Papers*, 36: 256.

26. Jefferson to Messrs. Nehemiah Dodge and Others, a Committee of the Danbury Baptist Association, January 1, 1802, in Peterson, ed., *Jefferson: Writings*, 510.

27. For an example of Dreisbach's errors in this matter, see Daniel Dreisbach, *Thomas Jefferson and the 'Wall of Separation' Between Church and State* (New York, 2002), 57–60.

28. Johann N. Neem, "Beyond the Wall: Reinterpreting Jefferson's Danbury Address," *Journal of the Early Republic* 27 (Spring 2007): 139–154, 142–143 (quotation).

29. Jefferson to William Greene Munford, June 18, 1799, in Peterson, ed., *Writings*, 1064–1066, 1065 (quotation).

30. *Notes on the State of Virginia*, Query XVIII, in Peterson, ed., *Writings*, 285.

31. Jefferson's *Autobiography*, Peterson, ed., *Writings*, 34–35.

32. David Barrow to Jefferson, March 20, 1815, and Jefferson to David Barrow, May 1, 1815, in Looney, ed., *Jefferson Papers: Retirement Series*, Vol. 8, Thomas Jefferson Papers, Library of Congress. For Barrow's antislavery activities in Virginia and Kentucky, see David B. Davis, *The Problem of Slavery in the Age of Revolution, 1770–1823* (Ithaca, 1975), 201, 202, 203, 552–555, and James David Essig, "'A Very Wintry Season': Virginia Baptists and Slavery, 1785–1797," *Virginia Magazine of History and Biography* 88 (1980): 170–185, and Essig, *The Bonds of Wickedness: American Evangelicals Against Slavery, 1770–1808* (Philadelphia, 1982).

33. Constance B. Schulz, "'Of Bigotry in Politics and Religion': Jefferson's Religion, the Federalist Press, and the *Syllabus*," *Virginia Magazine of History and Biography* 91, no. 1 (January 1983): 73–91, 84 (quotation).

34. William Linn, *Serious Considerations on the Election of a President, Addressed to the Citizens of the United States* (New York, 1800); John M. Mason, *The Voice of Warning to Christians, on the Ensuing Election of a President of the United States* (New York, 1800). For information on Linn and Mason, see Philip J. Anderson, "William Linn, 1752–1808: American Revolutionary and Anti-Jeffersonian," *Journal of Presbyterian History* 55, no. 4 (Nov. 1977): 381–394.

35. Jefferson to Benjamin Rush, Sept. 23, 1800, in Oberg, ed., *Jefferson Papers*, 32: 167.

36. Boston *Independent Chronicle*, January 21, 1799 ("COMMUNICATION"). The term "Reverend Cockader" was probably an allusion to the contrasting cockades, or military ribbons, worn by Republicans, who usually wore white, and Federalists, who generally wore black. The cockades supposedly signified devotion to the American or French revolutions, and the parties continued to argue over what the colors meant. Both parties invariably claimed that they wore cockades that appeared on the hats of U.S. troops during the American Revolution.

37. Benjamin Rush to Jefferson, Aug. 22, 1800, Oberg, ed., *Jefferson Papers*, 32:111.

38. See Jefferson to Charles Clay, January 29, 1815, in Looney, ed., *Jefferson Papers*, 8: 212; Jefferson to Ezra Stiles Ely, June 25, 1819, and Jefferson to Benjamin Waterhouse, July 19, 1822, in Bergh, ed., *Writings of Jefferson*, 15: 203, 391; Jefferson to James Smith, Dec. 8, 1822, in Dickinson W. Adams, ed., *Jefferson's Extracts from the Gospels* (Princeton: Princeton University Press, 1983), 408–409; Jefferson to George Thacher, January 26, 1824, in Ford, ed., *Writings*, 10: 289; and John Ragosta, *Religious Freedom* (Charlottesville: University of Virginia Press, 2013), 13.

39. Jefferson to Rush, Sept. 23, 1800, Oberg, ed., *Jefferson Papers*, 32: 167. I have modernized the letter's punctuation.

40. Ibid. See also Peterson, ed., *Jefferson: Writings*, 1081–1082.

41. Jefferson to Rush, Sept. 23, 1800, in Peterson, ed., *Jefferson: Writings*, 1082.

42. The "Syllabus" was enclosed in Jefferson to Rush, April 21, 1803, ibid., 1123–1126. Even in this survey and summary, Jefferson denied Jesus' divinity, viewing him only as an important "Jewish reformer" who "corrected the Deism of the Jews, confirming them in their belief of one only God, and giving them juster notions of his attributes

and government." Jefferson's admiration for Jesus, whom he compared to Socrates, was limited. He asserted that, because Jesus died at such a young age, "the doctrines which he really delivered were defective as a whole, and fragments only of what he did deliver have come to us mutilated, misstated, & often unintelligible." Ibid., 1125.

43. Benjamin Rush to Jefferson, May 5, 1803, Jefferson Papers, Library of Congress, quoted in Schulz, "'Of Bigotry in Politics and Religion,'" 90.

44. Jefferson to Benjamin Rush, June 13, 1805, in Founders Online database, National Archives.

Chapter 6

1. Providence [R.I.] *Impartial Observer*, Aug. 8, 1801.

2. Lyman H. Butterfield, "Elder John Leland, Jeffersonian Itinerant," *American Antiquarian Society, Proceedings* 62, no. 2 (Oct. 1952): 155–242, 220. See also Daniel Calhoon, "Leland, John," in *American National Biography*, which contains a few erroneous statements. For information on Jefferson's coat of arms, see the online *Thomas Jefferson Encyclopedia*, s.v., "Rebellion to tyrants is obedience to God."

3. *Hampshire Gazette*, Aug. 18, 1801; Baltimore *Federal Gazette*, Friday, January 1, 1802.

4. *Washington Federalist*, January 2, 1802, p. 3.

5. Oberg, ed., *Jefferson Papers*, 36: 254.

6. Benjamin Robinson to D. Robinson, January 1, 1802, quoted in C. A. Browne, "Leland and the Mammoth Cheshire Cheese," *Agricultural History* 18 (1944): 145–153, at 151.

7. Oberg, ed., *Jefferson Papers*, 36: 246–253.

8. The two versions of the Cheshire Committee's Address, the original, dated [30 Dec. 1801] and the one that appeared in Duane's *Aurora* on January 15, 1802, dated [1 Jan. 1802], are printed in Oberg, ed., *Jefferson Papers*, 36: 249–251.

9. Jefferson to Daniel Brown et al., January 1, 1802, Jefferson Papers, Library of Congress. See also Jeffrey A. Pasley, "The Cheese and the Words: Popular Political Culture and Participatory Democracy in the Early American Republic," in Jeffrey L. Pasley, Andrew W. Robertson, and David Waldstreicher, eds., *Beyond the Founders: New Approaches to the Political History of the Early American Republic* (Chapel Hill: University of North Carolina Press, 2004), 31–56, at 34. On the president as "mute tribune," see M. J. Heale, *The Presidential Quest: Candidates and Images in American Political Culture, 1787–1852* (London: Longman, 1982), chapter one.

10. Philadelphia *Port Folio*, January 23, 1802, pp. 23–24. Italics in original. Pedantically displaying his erudition, Dennie was quoting from Shakespeare' play *Henry VI, Part 3*, Act 3, Scene 2, line 148, in which the villainous Richard III says, "I'll make my heaven in a lady's lap." Dennie was applying it to the demagogue and widower Burr's alleged sexual exploits. What the deformed hunchback Richard III actually said, sarcastically denying that he intended to overthrow King Henry VI, was, "I'll make my heaven in a lady's lap, And deck my body in gay ornaments, And 'witch sweet ladies with my words and looks." By "*little Senate*," Dennie was of course referring to Vice President Burr's role as president of the U.S. Senate. Nancy Isenberg, *Fallen Founder: The Life of Aaron Burr* (New York: Viking, 2007), eccentrically views Burr as a virtually flawless, unjustly calumniated Founding Father.

11. Jefferson to the Committee of Cheshire, Massachusetts, January 1, 1802, in Oberg, ed., *Jefferson Papers*, 36: 252. Spelling in original.

12. Ibid.

13. Ibid. Spelling in original.

14. From the Committee of Cheshire, Massachusetts [30 Dec. 1801], ibid., 249.

15. Philadelphia *Port Folio*, January 23, 1802, p. 23. Emphasis in original. The Federalist magazine, (Walpole, N.H.) *Farmer's Weekly Museum*, January 26, 1802, p. 3, also published the *Aurora*'s version of the Cheshire Committee's address, under the derisive heading, "LAUGH WHERE WE MUST. The Mammoth Cheese."

16. Jefferson to the Committee of Cheshire, Massachusetts, January 1, 1802, in Oberg, ed., *Jefferson Papers*, 36: 252. Spelling in original. For the Cheshire Committee's remark, see ibid., 249. Italics in original.

17. Manasseh Cutler to Dr. Joseph Torrey, January 4, 1802, in William P. Cutler and Julia P. Cutler, *Life, Journals, and Correspondence of Reverend Manasseh Cutler* (2 vols.; Cincinnati: R. Clarke, 1888), 2: 66–67, quoted in Butterfield, "Elder John Leland, Jeffersonian Itinerant," 226–227. On Cutler's maneuvers as director of the Ohio Company Associates, see Louis W. Potts, "Manasseh Cutler, Lobbyist," *Ohio History* 96 (Summer/Autumn 1987): 101–123.

18. Manasseh Cutler to Dr. Joseph Torrey, January 4, 1802, in Cutler, *Journals*, 2: 66. My italics.

19. For example, see James H. Hutson, "Thomas Jefferson's Letter to the Danbury Baptists: A Controversy Rejoined," *William and Mary Quarterly* 56, no. 4 (Oct. 1999): 785–786; Hutson, *Religion and the Founding of the American Republic* (Washington, D.C.: Library of Congress, 1998), 84–97.

20. Cutler to Torrey, January 4, 1802, in Butterfield, "John Leland," 226–227.

21. On the goddess of reason and the Cult of Reason during the Reign of Terror, see Robert R. Palmer, *Twelve Who Ruled: The Reign of Terror in the French Revolution* (Princeton: Princeton University Press, 1941), chapter 5.

22. James H. Hutson, *Church and State in America: The First Two Centuries* (Cambridge: Cambridge University Press, 2008), 185–186. For more fully annotated presentations of Hutson's thesis, see his *Religion and the Founding of the American Republic* (1998; Hanover, N.H.: University Press of New England, 2002), and *Forgotten Features of the Founding* (Lanham, Md.: Rowman Littlefield, 2003). Hutson's most well-documented version of his (briefly notorious) thesis on Jefferson's religious devoutness, "Thomas Jefferson's Letter to the Danbury Baptists: A Controversy Rejoined," *William and Mary Quarterly* 56, no. 4 (Oct. 1999): 775–790, citing the High Federalist monthly publication, Joseph Dennie's Philadelphia *Port Folio*, January 23, 1802, as his source, adds the further imaginative detail that Jefferson sang Psalm 100 in the presence of Congress during Leland's attendance there. That sentimental tidbit appears nowhere in the *Port Folio* for January 23, 1802, which only covers Leland's presentation of the Cheshire cheese to Jefferson. However, Hutson claims that the *Port Folio* reported, "Mr. Jefferson has been seen at church, and has assisted in singing the hundredth psalm." Ibid., 785. Hutson seems confused on this score.

23. On the nearly unanimous vote for Republicans in Cheshire from 1800–1815, see Pasley, "Cheese and the Words," 46–48. During the War of 1812 years, more adult males voted than were legal voters in the town, Pasley points out. The habit of illegal voting went back to the colonial period. See John Cary, "Statistical Method and the Brown Thesis on Colonial Democracy," *William and Mary Quarterly*, 3d ser., 20, no. 2 (April 1963): 251–264.

24. Jefferson to Thomas Mann Randolph, Jr., Jan. 1, 1802, Jefferson Papers, Library of Congress (online at American Memory). See also Jeffrey A. Pasley, "The Cheese and

the Words: Popular Political Culture and Participatory Democracy in the Early American Republic," in Jeffrey L. Pasley, Andrew W. Robertson, and David Waldstreicher, eds., *Beyond the Founders: New Approaches to the Political History of the Early American Republic* (Chapel Hill: University of North Carolina Press, 2004), 31–56. Despite his excellent investigation of increased voter participation in Cheshire, Massachusetts during Jefferson's presidency, Pasley does not sufficiently appreciate the importance Jefferson attached to the cheese incident as evidence of the increasing devotion to the Republican Party in New England. Pasley also does not comprehend the extent to which Jefferson considered New England's conversion to Republicanism essential to the triumph of democracy and the defeat of monarchism in the nation.

25. Jefferson to John Wayles Eppes, January 1, 1802, Thomas Jefferson Papers, University of Virginia, reel five (microfilm). Eppes had been elected to the Virginia assembly the previous year.

26. Ibid. For Jefferson's familiarity with and admiration for the old modes of English governance, see Jefferson to Major John Cartwright, June 5, 1824, in Peterson, ed., *Jefferson: Writings*, 1490–1496; and H. Trevor Colbourn, "Thomas Jefferson's Use of the Past," *William and Mary Quarterly*, 3d ser., 15 (1958): 56–70.

27. Jefferson set down the "mammoth cheese" in the East Room of the President's House, where it remained for at least two years. James A. Bear and Lucia C. Stanton, eds., *Jefferson's Memorandum Books* (2 vols., Princeton: Princeton University Press, 1997), 2: 1062n. He paid Leland two hundred dollars for the cheese to show his appreciation, and because it was his policy to refuse gifts while in office. Ibid., 1062, under date of January 4, 1802. See also Butterfield, "John Leland," 226–227.

28. Jefferson to Constantin François Volney, April 20, 1802, in Barbara B. Oberg, ed., *Papers of Thomas Jefferson* 37: 295–97. On Volney's response to the Alien and Sedition Acts, see Gilbert Chinard, *Volney et l'Amérique* (Baltimore: Johns Hopkins Press, 1923); James Morton Smith, *Freedom's Fetters* (Ithaca: Cornell University Press, 1956), 51, 160–61; and Dumas Malone, *Jefferson and the Ordeal of Liberty* (Boston: Little Brown, 1962).

29. Jefferson to Constantin François Volney, April 20, 1802, in Barbara B. Oberg, ed., *Papers of Thomas Jefferson* 37: 295–97, 295 (quotation). I have modernized some of Jefferson's spelling and punctuation.

30. Ibid., 295.

31. Jefferson to Volney, April 20, 1802, ibid., 296.

32. Ibid.

33. Jefferson to Volney, April 20, 1802, ibid., 296.

34. Ibid., 297. I have modernized some of Jefferson's punctuation.

35. Jefferson to Benjamin Rush, January 3, 1808, Jefferson Papers, Founders Online database, National Archives.

Chapter 7

1. See Mary P. Adams, "Jefferson's Reaction to the Treaty of San Ildefonso," *Journal of Southern History* 21, no. 2 (May 1955): 173–188.

2. Manasseh Cutler, Journal, Dec. 13, 1802, in Cutler, *Journals*, 2: 113. My italics.

3. Claude G. Bowers, *Jefferson and Hamilton: The Struggle for Democracy in America* (Boston: Houghton Mifflin, 1925).

4. For Jefferson's witty use of the term, "incurable," quoted earlier, see Jefferson to Levi Lincoln, Aug. 26, 1801, in Oberg, ed., *Jefferson Papers*, 35: 146. I found the political

affiliations of the congressmen, with brief descriptions of their service, in the online version of the *Biographical Directory of the American Congress*. For Jefferson's dinners, see, Merry Ellen Scofield's general discussion, "The Fatigues of his Table: The Politics of Presidential Dining during the Jefferson Administration," *Journal of the Early Republic* 26, no. 3 (Fall 2006): 449–469.

5. Malone, *Jefferson the President: First Term*, 173–174, 192–200.

6. Cutler to Joseph Torrey, January 3, 1803, in Cutler, *Journals*, 2: 119.

7. Ibid., 120.

8. Margaret Bayard Smith, "Reminiscences [1837]," in Smith, *The First Forty Years of Washington Society* (New York: Scribner, 1906), 13–14.

9. Cutler to Joseph Torrey, January 3, 1803, in Cutler, *Journals*, 2: 120.

10. Samuel Taggart to his brother, Oct. 28, 1803, in George H. Haynes, ed., "Letters of Samuel Taggart, Representative in Congress, 1803–1817." *Proceedings of the American Antiquarian Society* 33 (April 1923): 113–226, 119 (quotation).

11. Taggart to his brother, Feb. 12, 1804, ibid., 33: 131.

12. Taggart to his brother, Feb. 12, 1804, ibid., 33: 131.

13. Taggart to ——, Feb. 8, 1807, ibid., 210.

14. Cutler to Joseph Torrey, January 3, 1803, in Cutler, *Journals*, 2: 120.

15. Elbridge Gerry to Jefferson, Oct. 27, 1803, Jefferson Papers, Library of Congress.

16. Elbridge Gerry to Jefferson, Oct. 27, 1803, Jefferson Papers, Library of Congress.

17. Jefferson to Elbridge Gerry, January 26, 1799, in Peterson, ed., *Writings*, 1055–1062.

18. Jefferson to Elbridge Gerry, March 3, 1804, in Lipscomb and Bergh, eds., *Writings of Jefferson*, 11: 15–16.

19. Ibid., 16.

20. Jefferson to Gideon Granger, April 16, 1804, Jefferson Papers, Library of Congress, excerpted in Lipscomb and Bergh, eds., *Writings of Jefferson*, 11: 24–26, at 24.

21. Ibid., 24.

22. Jefferson to Gideon Granger, April 16, 1804, in Lipscomb and Bergh, eds., *Writings of Jefferson*, 11: 24.

23. Ibid., 25.

24. Ibid., 25. On the topic of republicanism's decline as being analogous to the human lifecycle from infancy to youth, maturity, and old age, commencing as vigorous self-government and ending in despotic monarchy, see John R. Howe, Jr., "Republican Thought and the Political Violence of the 1790s," *American Quarterly* 19 (Summer 1967): 147–65; and Stow Persons, "The Cyclical Theory of History in Eighteenth Century America," *ibid.*, 6 (Summer 1954): 147–63.

25. Jefferson to Gideon Granger, April 16, 1804, in Lipscomb and Bergh, eds., *Writings of Jefferson*, 11: 25. On disorganizing elements in the Republican Party, such as the "Quid" party in Pennsylvania, composed of the Duane-Leib faction that desired more democratic state government; and other groups, like the "Invisibles" headed by Samuel Smith in Maryland, who desired increased patronage and political power, see Noble E. Cunningham, Jr., *The Jeffersonian Republicans in Power: Party Operations, 1801–1809* (Chapel Hill: University of North Carolina Press, 1963), and John S. Pancake, "The 'Invisibles': A Chapter in the Opposition to President Madison," *Journal of Southern History* 21, no. 1 (Feb. 1955): 17–37.

26. Jefferson to Gideon Granger, April 16, 1804, in Lipscomb and Bergh, eds., *Writings of Jefferson*, 11: 25.

27. Jefferson to Gideon Granger, April 16, 1804, in Lipscomb and Bergh, eds., *Writings of Jefferson*, 11: 25–26.

28. See, e.g., Dumas Malone, *Jefferson and the Ordeal of Liberty* (Boston: Little, Brown, 1962), chapters 25 and 26.

29. Jefferson to Gideon Granger, April 16, 1804, Jefferson Papers, Library of Congress.

30. Lynn Warren Turner, *The Ninth State: New Hampshire's Formative Years* (Chapel Hill: University of North Carolina Press, 1983), 214–216, 215 (quotation); Robinson, *Jeffersonian Democracy in New England*, 77.

31. Turner, *Ninth State*, 216.

32. Ibid., 217.

33. Granger to Jefferson, Sept. 2, 1804, Jefferson Papers, Library of Congress.

34. Granger to Jefferson, Sept. 2, 1804, Jefferson Papers, Library of Congress.

35. Turner, *Ninth State*, 217–218, quoting New Hampshire *House of Representatives Journal*, Nov. 1804; John Bach McMaster, *History of the People of the United States, From the Revolution to the Civil War* (New York: D. Appleton, 1910–1926), 3: 45

36. McMaster, *History of the United States*, 3: 45–47.

37. This information as available in standard sources, such as *Dictionary of American Biography* and *American National Biography*.

38. Lynn W. Turner, "The Impeachment of John Pickering," *American Historical Review* 54, no. 3 (April 1949): 485–507. For Federalist discriminatory practices, see Prince, *Federalists and the Origins of U.S. Civil Service*

39. In 1800, there were approximately 801 flour mills and 1,148 sawmills in New Hampshire, and 8,699 people engaged in manufacturing. There were 52,384 farmers. The only large town was Portsmouth. Elizabeth F. Morison and Elting E. Morison, *New Hampshire: A Bicentennial History* (New York: Norton, 1976), 92–93.

40. On New Hampshire's politics and economy, see the summary in Morison, *New Hampshire*. For the concept of "secure" and "insecure" elites, see Buel, *Securing the Revolution*, 79–90, and David Hackett Fischer, *The Revolution of American Conservatism: The Federalist Party in the Era of Jeffersonian Democracy* (New York: Harper and Row, 1965), Appendix. For diverse eccentric reasons, among them their affinity for dueling, an activity that New England legislators shied away from, Buel assumed that Southern Jeffersonian politicians were a more "secure elite" than New England's leaders. The latter, applying Calvinist pessimism to secular affairs, emphasized human depravity and opposed the "common man's" political participation. Buel contends that by endorsing popular rule, Southern Republicans demonstrated that they considered their political and social position secure. Buel also argues that the Democratic-Republicans, with their tendency to endorse democracy and representative government, epitomized the true meaning of the American Revolution. He overlooks the existence of anti-populist ideology among such Democratic-Republican slaveholding aristocrats as John Randolph of Roanoke and Thomas Mann Randolph, Jr. See Harry Ammon, "The Jeffersonian Republicans of Virginia: An Interpretation," *Virginia Magazine of History and Biography* 71, no. 2 (1963): 153–167, at 166–67. Buel also seems unaware that, as Jefferson occasionally pointed out, there was probably less turnover in the state legislatures and congressional representation in Connecticut and Massachusetts than in Virginia. This topic requires further study.

41. Lynn W. Turner, *William Plumer of New Hampshire* (Chapel Hill: University of North Carolina Press, 1962), 6–10, 146–148.

42. William Plumer to Jeremiah Smith, Dec. 18, 1803, William Plumer Papers, New Hampshire State Library, Con-

cord. By "dry-dock president," Plumer presumably alluded to Jefferson's recommendation to Congress to retain the warships built during Adams' presidency by storing them in dry docks until they were needed. However, Congress refused to build the dry docks and sold off most of the ships. The "salt mountain philosopher" refers to Jefferson's mention, in reporting to Congress on the Louisiana Purchase, that explorers had discovered a mountain made entirely of salt in the territory. See David Dzurec, "Of Salt Mountains, Prairie Dogs, and Horned Frogs: The Louisiana Purchase and the Evolution of Federalist Satire," *Journal of the Early Republic* 35, no. 1 (Spring 2015): 79–108.

43. William Plumer's Journal Entries, Dec. 20, 1803, printed as "Thomas Jefferson and Co. A Repository. A Collection of Facts, Anecdotes & Observations" (1803) in *Historical New Hampshire* 23, no. 2 (Summer 1968): 28–31. These incidents have been discussed in numerous works. See, for example, Catherine Allgor, *Parlor Politics: In Which the Ladies of Washington Help Build a City and a Government* (Charlottesville: University of Virginia Press, 2000), 35–47, and Robert R. Davis, Jr., "Pell-Mell: Jeffersonian Etiquette and Protocol," *Historian* 43, no. 4 (Fall 1981): 509–529. Allgor's account contains several factual errors, such as mockingly asserting that Jefferson issued a document called "Cannons of Etiquette" when the source she cites, Paul L. Ford's edition of *The Works of Jefferson*, 10: 47–48 (she mistakenly calls it by the name of his earlier collection, *Writings of Thomas Jefferson*) named it "Rules of Etiquette." In fact, Jefferson actually called his memorandum "Canons of Etiquette." Jefferson Papers, Library of Congress. More surprisingly, Allgor, having little knowledge of Jefferson, claims that he felt hostility to Elizabeth Merry, Anthony Merry's wife, because she "was an elite European woman—cultivated, charming, astute, and public—and thus everything Jefferson hated." *Parlor Politics*, 45. It is well known that Jefferson served for five years as U.S. minister to Paris during the 1780s, where, like Benjamin Franklin, he hobnobbed with the most intellectual women of the Continent, the famous *salonnières*, maintaining a lifelong correspondence with many of them. He may even have had a sexual affair with the young, beautiful and "cultivated" Maria Cosway. He never held the ignorant, misogynist viewpoint that Allgor imputes to him.

44. "Thomas Jefferson & Co.," 31.

45. William Plumer to Jeremiah Smith, Dec. 9, 1802, William Plumer Papers, Library of Congress.

46. Turner, *William Plumer*, 94–95; Lynn W. Turner, "Thomas Jefferson Through the Eyes of a New Hampshire Politician," *Mississippi Valley Historical Review* 30, no. 2 (Sept. 1943): 205–214, at 207.

47. Plumer, *Memorandum*, 453–455.

48. Sigmund Freud, *The Future of An Illusion* (New York: Norton, 1975).

49. Plumer, *Memorandum*, 543 (Dec. 27, 1806).

50. Turner, "Thomas Jefferson Through the Eyes of a New Hampshire Politician," 212–213.

51. Jefferson to William Plumer, July 21, 1816, Lipscomb and Bergh, ed., *Jefferson's Writings*, 15: 46; and Jefferson Papers, Library of Congress.

52. See Turner, *William Plumer*, 295–301.

Chapter 8

1. Jefferson's Second Inaugural Address, March 4, 1805, in Peterson, ed., *Writings*, 520–22.

2. Ibid., 521.

3. Jefferson's Second Inaugural Address, quoted in Mal-

one, *Jefferson the President: Second Term*, 8–9. On the increasing importance of the notion of public opinion among the Founders, especially James Madison, see Colleen A. Sheehan, *James Madison and the Spirit of Republican Self-Government* (Cambridge, 2009). As in many other things, David Hume probably inspired the Founders' emphasis on public opinion. In "Of the First Principles of Government," a text that likely influenced Jefferson, he famously wrote, "As FORCE is always on the side of the governed, the governors have nothing to support them but opinion. It is therefore on opinion only that government is founded; and this maxim extends to the most despotic and most military governments, as well as to the most free and most popular." Garry Wills, *Cincinnatus: George Washington and the Enlightenment* (Garden City, 1984), 99–100. Compare this with Jefferson's views in his famous letter to Edward Carrington, Jan. 16, 1787: "The basis of our governments being the opinion of the people, the very first object should be to keep that right; and were it left to me to decide whether we should have a government without newspapers or newspapers without a government, I should not hesitate a moment to prefer the latter." Peterson, ed., *Jefferson: Writings*, 880. Although the term, "public opinion," came into currency in the late eighteenth century, historians have only recently become fond of it, mainly because they often cite political theorist Jürgen Habermas's theory of the "public sphere."

4. See Fischer, *Revolution of American Conservatism*, 130–131; Stewart, *Opposition Press*, 30–31, 662 note165.

5. Thomas's figures are cited in Robinson, *Jeffersonian Democracy*, 69

6. Levy's chapter on Jefferson and seditious libel was so carelessly done that it is sometimes hard to take what he says seriously. Even concerning such a basic fact as the identity of Coray, a Greek political theorist who was interested in devising a constitution for Greece, which was struggling for independence against Turkey, Levy carelessly wrote that he was a French statesman involved in 1823 in writing a constitution for France.

7. Boyd, ed., *Jefferson Papers*, 1: 344.

8. Boyd, ed., *Jefferson Papers*, 1: 347, note 10. For Jefferson's drafting the state constitution, see Dumas Malone, *Jefferson the Virginian*, 235–36.

9. Ibid., 1: 344–45, 353, 363.

10. Ibid., 363 ("Rights Private and Public"). In order to depict Jefferson as a foe of freedom of the press, Levy's *Jefferson and Civil Liberties* omits these quotations. He quotes a private letter Jefferson wrote in 1823, which expressed identical sentiments to the ones in these constitutional drafts, but claims that this was the first time that Jefferson advocated unrestricted freedom of the press.

11. Levy, *Jefferson and Civil Liberties*, 47.

12. Albemarle County Instructions Concerning the Virginia Constitution, printed in Boyd, ed., *Jefferson Papers*, 6: 284–291, 288 (quotation); Levy, *Jefferson and Civil Liberties*, 46–47.

13. Jefferson's Draft of a Constitution for Virginia (1783), in Boyd, *Jefferson Papers*, 6: 304.

14. Jefferson to A. Coray, Oct. 31, 1823, in Lipscomb and Bergh, *Writings of Jefferson*, 15: 489, quoted in Levy, *Jefferson and Civil Liberties*, 69.

15. Levy, *Jefferson and Civil Liberties*, 53.

16. Ibid., 54. Ironically, in Richmond in 1803, after enduring newspaper insults and public harassment by Callender, Hay unsuccessfully prosecuted him for libel by forcing the Henrico County Court to legally bar him for one year from attacking the personal character of individuals, subject to fine and imprisonment. Hay reiterated his earlier opinion in 1799, which Levy extolled, that his interpretation

of freedom of the press would tolerate attacks on him as a public official, but not as a private man. (Among other things, Callender had accused Hay of cheating at cards.) Rebutting Hay's more moderate position, articles in the Richmond *Virginia Gazette* in January 1803 argued that the personal actions and character of public officials and candidates for office were fair game for newspaper examination and even abuse, since they enabled voters to better evaluate their credentials; newspapers should not be prosecuted for exposing public officials' private faults. Contrary to Levy's assumptions, these articles, not Hay's 1799 *Essay on the Liberty of the Press*, were the first defense of absolute freedom of the press in the United States. See Steven H. Hochman, "On the Liberty of the Press in Virginia: From Essay to Bludgeon, 1798–1803," *Virginia Magazine of History and Biography* 84, no. 4 (1976): 431–445.

17. Jefferson's Second Inaugural Address, March 4, 1805, in Peterson, ed., *Writings*, 521–22 (quotation).

18. Jefferson's draft of his second inaugural address, in Jefferson Papers, Library of Congress. Peterson, *Writings*, 522, has an erroneous transcription, "provided by the State against false," which might mislead readers into believing that Jefferson inconsistently recommended that the national "State" (in singular, capitalized orthography) exercise authority over the press.

19. Jefferson to Samuel Harrison Smith, May 21, 1803, Oberg, ed., *Jefferson Papers*, 40: 414–15. I have slightly modernized spelling and punctuation. For Granger's report to Jefferson, see Gideon Granger to Jefferson, with Jefferson's Note, May 13, 1803, ibid., 40: 366. The *National Intelligencer* printed Jefferson's information in its issue of May 23, 1803.

20. Jefferson to Levi Lincoln, June 1, 1803, with "Fair Play" article enclosure, Oberg, ed., *Jefferson Papers*, 40: 463–69.

21. Ibid., 467.

22. "Fair Play," ibid., 466–467 (quotation). Spelling and punctuation in original, except for minor changes.

23. Ibid., 466.

24. Jefferson to Lincoln, June 1, 1803, ibid., 464. For "Fair Play's" publication, see ibid., 467–68n. "Fair Play" has been discussed by few historians. Levy briefly mentions it in *Jefferson and Civil Liberties*, 59, as does Malone, in *Jefferson the President: First Term*, 85n. It is discussed at length in Noble E. Cunningham, Jr.'s excellent work, *Jeffersonian Republicans in Power: Party Operations, 1801–1809* (Chapel Hill, 1963), 255–57.

25. Jefferson to Comte de Volney, Feb. 8, 1805, Jefferson Papers, Library of Congress; reprinted in Lipscomb and Bergh, ed., *Writings of Jefferson*, 11: 68–69. By "constitutions" here, Jefferson meant healthy features within individual human physiques, not written charters of government.

26. Jefferson to Comte de Volney, Feb. 8, 1805, Jefferson Papers, Library of Congress. Jefferson probably borrowed the term, "genus irritabile vatum," from the famous ancient Roman poet Horace, at the beginning of the Roman Empire. It is Latin for "irritable race of poets." This was perhaps Jefferson's way of mocking orthodox Calvinism's religious dogmas as depicting fantasy rather than genuine faith.

27. Jefferson to Comte de Volney, Feb. 8, 1805, Jefferson Papers, Library of Congress. For Jefferson's report to Ebeling, see "Notes on the Letter of Christoph Daniel Ebeling" [after 15 Oct. 1795], in Julian P. Boyd, John Catanzariti, et al, *Papers of Thomas Jefferson*, 28: 506.

28. Malone, *Jefferson the President: Second Term* [Volume 5 of *Jefferson and his Time*], 11 (quotation).

29. Jefferson to the Rev. Thomas Allen, March 12, 1805, Jefferson Papers, Library of Congress, transcript available at Founders Online.

30. *Notes on the State of Virginia*, in Peterson, *Writings*, 251.

31. Jefferson to Edmund Randolph, Aug. 18, 1799, ibid., 1066.

32. Jefferson to Edmund Randolph, Aug. 18, 1799, ibid., 1068–69.

33. Ibid.

34. Jefferson to Gideon Granger, August 13, 1800, Peterson, *Writings*, 1078–79.

35. Jefferson to Gideon Granger, August 13, 1800, Peterson, *Writings*, 1079.

36. Ibid. See also Jefferson to Elbridge Gerry, January 26, 1799, in Peterson, ed., *Writings*, 1055–1062.

37. Jefferson to Levi Lincoln, March 24, 1802, in Oberg, ed., *Jefferson Papers*, 37: 119. I have modernized the original spelling and punctuation for purposes of clarity.

38. Jefferson to Levi Lincoln, March 24, 1802, in Oberg, ed., *Jefferson Papers*, 37: 119–20. Capitalization has been modernized. Italics in original.

39. Jefferson to Abigail Adams, Sept. 11, 1804 in Cappon, ed., *Adams-Jefferson Letters*, 279.

40. See James Morton Smith, "The Sedition Law, Free Speech, and the American Political Process," *Political Science Quarterly* 9, no. 4 (Oct. 1952): 497–511.

41. Jefferson to the Rev. Thomas Allen, March 12, 1805, and Jefferson to James Sullivan, May 21, 1805, quoted in Malone, *Jefferson the President: Second Term*, 12.

42. Jefferson's Draft of the Kentucky Resolutions, Oct. 1798, Peterson, ed., *Writings*, 450.

43. Gerard W. Gawalt, "'Strict Truth': The Narrative of William Armistead Burwell," *Virginia Magazine of History and Biography* 101, no. 1 (June 1993): 103–32, at 118–19; *New England Palladium*, Jan. 18, 1805; Dumas Malone, *Jefferson and his Time* (Boston, 1948–1981), 1: 153–55, 447–51; 4: 216–23; 5: 14–15, 386, 391.

44. Jefferson to Marc Auguste Pictet, Feb. 5, 1803, in Barbara B. Oberg, ed., *Papers of Thomas Jefferson*, 39: 457. Punctuation has been modernized for clarity.

45. Jefferson to Marc Auguste Pictet, Feb. 5, 1803, in Barbara B. Oberg, ed., *Papers of Thomas Jefferson*, 39: 457. For Jefferson's reminiscences about composing Query XIX of *Notes* while observing the starving city workers of Europe, see Jefferson to John Lithgow, Jan. 4, 1805, Jefferson Papers, Library of Congress.

46. Jefferson to Dr. Thomas Cooper, Feb. 10, 1814, and Jefferson to John Cartwright, June 5, 1824, in Peterson, ed., *Jefferson: Writings*, 1321–29, 1494–95.

47. Jefferson to Madison, July 31, 1788, Boyd, ed., *Jefferson Papers*, 13: 442–43, and Rutland, ed., *Madison Papers*, 11: 210–14; also available online. In *Jefferson and Civil Liberties*, 48–49, Levy deliberately distorts the contents of this letter. Claiming that it reveals Jefferson's political conservatism, Levy argued that Jefferson was trying to deter *Madison* from proposing radical concepts of freedom of the press in a bill of rights. Indeed, such distortions pervade Levy's entire, mercifully brief book.

48. Perhaps Jefferson foresaw the insanity, with its roots in the Middle Ages and the Inquisition, that later generations of Americans would witness during European governments' pogroms against the Jews, David Koresh's Waco Branch Dividians, Charles Manson's murderous cult, and Jim Jones' Guyana colony, although probably not the ultimate State-enforced barbarism of the Shoah, Hitler's near-annihilation of Europe's Jews, and Islamic terrorists' modern, worldwide war against Jews, Israel, and Christian "crusaders."

49. Malone, *Jefferson*, 5: 372.

50. Joseph Willcox to Jefferson, Oct. 20, 1801, and Pierpont Edwards and Ephraim Kirby to Jefferson, Oct. 22, 1801, in Oberg, ed., *Jefferson Papers*, 35: 475–76, 484–86; Malone, *Jefferson*, 5: 373.

51. *Connecticut Courant*, Nov. 27, 1805, quoted in Robinson, *Jeffersonian Democracy*, 64.

52. Malone, *Jefferson*, 5: 372–74; *Senate Executive Proceedings* (1805), 2: 10, 11.

53. Steven H. Hochman, "On the Liberty of the Press in Virginia: From Essay to Bludgeon, 1798–1803," *Virginia Magazine of History and Biography* 84, no. 4 (1976): 431–445, 431 (quotation).

54. [Hartford] *Connecticut Courant*, April 23, 1806. For the most recent scholarly examination of this episode, see Philip I. Blumberg, *Repressive Jurisprudence in the Early American Republic: The First Amendment and the Legacy of English Law* (Cambridge: Cambridge University Press, 2010), 156–166.

55. Malone, *Jefferson the President: Second Term*, 391. In 1811, after Levi Lincoln, who was going blind, declined the nomination, President James Madison nominated Alexander Wolcott to the Supreme Court, but the Senate, controlled by his opponents, defeated him. Madison was eventually forced to appoint the lukewarm Republican Joseph Story, who later became one of Marshall's strongest allies.

Chapter 9

1. Jefferson to Thomas Seymour, Feb. 11, 1807, Jefferson Papers, Library of Congress. For a detailed account of the Republican vendetta in Connecticut that takes a strong anti–Jefferson stance, see the article by Derek L. Mogck, an attorney in a law firm founded by descendants of George Goodwin, a publisher of the *Hartford Courant* and one of the defendants in the case, "Connecticut Federalists in President Jefferson's (Republican) Court: *United States v. Hudson and Goodwin*," *Connecticut History* 41, no. 2 (Sept. 2002): 144–72. Mogck argues that Jefferson probably initiated prosecution of the case, even though no evidence for this assumption exists. For Benjamin Franklin, see "An Account of the Supremest Court of Judicature in Pennsylvania, Viz. the Court of the Press," Philadelphia *Federal Gazette*, Sept. 12, 1789. Ironically, Levy, comparing Jefferson unfavorably with Franklin, wrote, "his eagerness to make America safe for democracy made him forgetful of Franklin's wise aphorism that they who seek safety at the expense of liberty deserve neither liberty nor safety." Levy, *Jefferson and Civil Liberties*, 169.

2. "Backus, Azel," in James G. Wilson, ed., *Appleton's Cyclopedia of American Biography* (New York: Appleton, 1895), 1: 129.

3. See the entries on "Reeve, Tapping," in *Dictionary of American Biography* and *American National Biography*, 18: 289–90, the latter by Kevin R. Cheney.

4. Marian C. McKenna, *Tapping Reeve and the Litchfield Law School* (New York, 1986); Hampden, *Letter to the President of the United States, Touching the Prosecutions Under his Patronage, Before the Circuit Court of the District of Connecticut* (New Haven: Oliver Steele, 1808; Shaw and Shoemaker #15422).

5. S. G. Goodrich, *Recollections of a Lifetime* (2 vols.; New York 1886), 1: 117, quoted in Marian C. McKenna, *Tapping Reeve and the Litchfield Law School* (New York: Oceana Publications, 1986), 73. Litchfield Law School attracted nearly as many students from Georgia, Maryland, and South Carolina as it did from the Northern states, but few came from Virginia, perhaps because of the presence of law professors at William and Mary and later the University of Virginia. Ibid., 145.

6. McKenna, *Tapping Reeve*, 125–126, 129.

7. Ibid., 130.

8. Ibid.

9. Ibid., 158.

10. Ibid., 143.

11. "Phocion," *Litchfield Monitor*, Nov. 25, 1801, March 24, 1802; McKenna, *Tapping Reeve*, 157.

12. Hampden, *Letter to the President of the United States*, 8; McKenna, *Tapping Reeve*, 157.

13. Hampden, *Letter to the President of the United States, Touching the Prosecutions Under his Patronage, Before the Circuit Court of the District of Connecticut* (New Haven: Oliver Steele, 1808; Shaw and Shoemaker #15422), 12.

14. Donald L. Jacobus, *History of the Seymour Family, Descendants of Richard Seymour* (New Haven, 1939), 153–161; Franklin B. Dexter, *Biographical Sketches of the Graduates of Yale College* (6 vols.; New York: Holt, 1885–1912), 2: 378–379.

15. Thomas Seymour to Jefferson, Nov. 20, 1804, Record Group 59, National Archives, available online at Founders Online database.

16. Thomas Seymour to Jefferson, August 6, 1807, RG 59, National Archives, available online at Founders Online database.

17. Thomas Seymour to Jefferson, August 6, 1807, RG 59, National Archives, available online at Founders Online database.

18. Thomas Seymour, Jonathan Bull, Sylvester Wells, Nathaniel Patten, Daniel Olcott, Thomas Tisdall, and Henry Seymour to Jefferson, Dec. 20, 1806, Jefferson Papers, Library of Congress, available online at Founders Online. The letter has been printed in Donald L. Jacobus, *History of the Seymour Family, Descendants of Richard Seymour* (New Haven, 1939), 156–158, 156 (quotation).

19. Thomas Seymour, Jonathan Bull, Sylvester Wells, Nathaniel Patten, Daniel Olcott, Thomas Tisdall, and Henry Seymour to Jefferson, Dec. 20, 1806, Jefferson Papers, Library of Congress, available online at Founders Online.

20. Ibid., also available in print in Jacobus, *History of the Seymour Family*, 156.

21. Jefferson to Thomas Seymour, Feb. 11, 1807, in Lipscomb and Bergh, ed., *Writings of Jefferson*, 11: 154.

22. Jefferson to Thomas Seymour, Feb. 11, 1807, in Lipscomb and Bergh, ed., *Writings of Jefferson*, 11: 154.

23. Ibid., 155.

24. Ibid.

25. Jefferson to Thomas Seymour, Feb. 11, 1807, in Lipscomb and Bergh, ed., *Writings of Jefferson*, 11: 155.

26. Jefferson to Seymour, Feb. 11, 1807, ibid., 156.

27. Hampden, *Letter to the President*, 17–20.

28. A Republican paper, the *Litchfield Witness*, April 30, 1806 ("The Charge") reprinted Edwards' instructions ("charge") to the grand jury.

29. Hampden, *Letter to the President of the United States, Touching the Prosecutions Under his Patronage, Before the Circuit Court of the District of Connecticut* (New Haven: Oliver Steele, 1808; Shaw and Shoemaker #15422), "Editor's Preface," p. iii.

30. On Bache's fate, see James Morton Smith, *Freedom's Fetters: The Alien-Sedition Acts and American Civil Liberties* (Ithaca, 1956), 200–204; on the harassment of Duane, see Kim T. Phillips, "William Duane, Revolutionary Editor" (Ph.D. dissertation, University of California, Berkeley, 1968), 128–32.

31. Hampden, *Letter to the President of the United States*, 9; Malone, *Jefferson*, 5: 375.

32. Hampden, *Letter to the President of the United States*, 26; Malone, *Jefferson*, 5: 376.

33. This paragraph is based on the account in Richard J. Purcell, *Connecticut in Transition, 1775–1818* (Washington, D.C.: American Historical Association, 19198), 275–76.

34. Hartford *Connecticut Courant*, Sept. 10, 1806.

35. Hampden, *Letter to the President of the United States*, 6.

36. Hartford *Connecticut Courant*, reprinted in *Boston Repertory*, Sept. 5, 1806.

37. See the account in Malone, *Jefferson the President: Second Term*.

38. Jon Meacham, *Thomas Jefferson and the Art of Power* (New York, 2014), 420–421; Adams, *History of the United States*, 836–837.

39. Meacham, *Jefferson*, 421.

40. Jefferson to John Dawson, Dec. 19, 1806, Jefferson Papers, Library of Congress. Meacham, *Jefferson*, 421; Malone, *Jefferson*, 5: 252–254.

41. Jefferson to John Wayles Eppes, Oct. 8, 1807, Jefferson Papers, Library of Congress.

42. The text of the Embargo Act, Dec. 22, 1807, is in *Statutes at Large*, 2: 451–453.

43. "Editor's Preface," p. iv.

44. Jefferson to Madison, Aug. 25, 1807, in Smith, ed., *Republic of Letters*, 3: 1491–92. Spelling modernized

45. Granger to Jefferson, Sept. 8, 1807, Jefferson Papers, Library of Congress. Unfortunately, much of the letter is illegible.

46. Jefferson to Madison, Sept. 18, 1807, Smith, ed., *Republic of Letters*, 3: 1497–98. The letter mentioned is probably Granger to Jefferson, Sept. 8, 1807, Jefferson Papers, Library of Congress.

47. Gideon Granger to Jefferson, January 19, 1808, Jefferson Papers, Library of Congress.

48. Jefferson to Gideon Granger, January 22, 1808, Jefferson Papers, Library of Congress. [The other letters of Jefferson to Granger have not been found.]

49. Jefferson to Gideon Granger, January 22, 1808, Jefferson Papers, Library of Congress.

50. Jefferson to Gideon Granger, January 22, 1808, Jefferson Papers, Library of Congress.

51. Jefferson to Madison, Sept. 18, 1807, Smith, ed., *Republic of Letters*, 3: 1497–98.

52. Hampden, *Letter to the President*, 20.

53. Ibid., 24.

54. Ibid., 14.

55. Malone, *Jefferson the President: Second Term: Volume 5 of Jefferson and his Time*, 388.

56. "Editor's Preface," p. iii.

57. A recent study of this incident claims that Jefferson inspired Senator William Branch Giles' request for a suspension of habeas corpus but presents no evidence that he had anything to do with it. Louis Fisher, "Jefferson and the Burr Conspiracy: Executive Power Against the Law," *Presidential Studies Quarterly* 45, no. 1 (March 2015): 157–174. More likely, the suspension of habeas corpus was traitorous General James Wilkinson's idea, since he wanted to distract attention from himself onto Burr and his co-conspirators Samuel Swartwout and Justus Erich Boulman. Jefferson warned Wilkinson that his conduct toward the Burr conspirators was unduly arbitrary. Jefferson to General James Wilkinson, Feb. 3, 1807, in Ford, ed., *Works*, 10: 336 note 1; also printed in Lipscomb and Bergh, eds., *Writings of Jefferson*, 11: 149; Kline, ed., *Papers of Aaron Burr*, 2: 991.

58. Malone, *Jefferson the President: Second Term*, 388–89. For Eppes' politically independent stance, see Arthur Scherr, *Thomas Jefferson's Haitian Policy: Myths and Realities* (Lanham, Md.: Lexington Books, 2011), 389–90, 506–7.

59. *Annals of Congress: House of Representatives*, May 25, 1809: 75–89.

60. "Veritas," in *National Intelligencer*, July 21, 1809.

61. *Annals of Congress*, 11th Congress, 1st sess., May 25, 1809, 75–89, at 84; Looney, ed., *Jefferson Papers: Retirement Series*, 1: 278.

62. George M. Troup, speech, *Annals of Congress*, 11th Congress, 1st sess., May 25, 1809, 88 (quotation).

63. Peter Charles Hoffer and N. E. H. Hull, *Impeachment in America, 1635–1805* (New Haven: Yale University Press, 1984), 3.

64. Ibid., 277n.

65. Brett Palfreyman's recent article, "The Loyalists and the Federal Constitution," *Journal of the Early Republic* 35, no. 3 (Fall 2015): 451–473, confuses bills of attainder with bills of pains and penalties. Therefore, it mistakenly argues that the state legislatures often employed bills of attainder during the Revolution. There were a few cases in which legislatures did authorize bills of attainder, such as in 1778, when Jefferson, at the request of Governor Patrick Henry, drafted a bill of attainder passed by Virginia's assembly, authorizing shooting on sight a loyalist bandit named Josiah Phillips. Unfortunately, the article does not discuss bills of attainder. That would have been an interesting study.

66. *Annals of Congress*, 11th Congress, 1st sess., May 25, 1809, 89.

67. Ibid., 81.

68. Virginia's constitution of 1776, available online at www.hinet.org (National Humanities Institute.)

69. *Annals of Congress*, 11th Congress, 1st sess., May 25, 1809, 88.

70. *Annals of Congress*, 11th Congress, 1st sess., May 25, 1809, 89. Tallmadge was correct. On January 2, 1807, when Congress was debating various means of thwarting treasonable conspiracies, particularly Burr's frustrated aspirations, Dana brought up the sedition prosecutions as evidence that Jefferson's federal government was exceeding its legal authority: "Mr. Dana observed that prosecutions, he understood, were depending in the courts of the United States, not arising under any existing statutes or treaty, but prosecutions sustained at common law." Thus indicating that he considered the 1798 Sedition Act legal, he continued, "In four cases warrants had been issued at the order of the court, the parties arrested and held to trial. Two of these prosecutions were against printers, for publications, which had appeared in their papers; two against clerical gentlemen, for words uttered by them. The charges extended to various questions respecting political conduct, morality, and religion. It was a subject of vast importance, whether this extensive range would be allowed to a public accuser, holding his place at the will of the Executive of the United States." *Annals of Congress*, House of Representatives, January 2, 1807, p. 247.

71. Ibid., 89. I have derived the party affiliations from the capsule biographies in *Biographical Directory of Congress*.

72. Jefferson to Wilson Cary Nicholas, June 13, 1809, Ford, ed., *Works of Jefferson*, available online by its date.

73. Jefferson to Nicholas, June 13, 1809, in Looney, *Jefferson Papers: Retirement Series*, 1: 276–277.

74. Ibid., 277. Spelling and punctuation in the original.

75. Jefferson to Nicholas, June 13, 1809, ibid., 277–78.

76. Jefferson to Nicholas, June 13, 1809, also in Looney, *Jefferson Papers: Retirement Series*, 1: 276–278; Jefferson Papers, Library of Congress, and available online at "Founders Online" National Archives database.

77. Jefferson to Nicholas, June 13, 1809, ibid., 278.

78. Wilson Cary Nicholas to Jefferson, July 18, 1809, in Looney, ed., *Jefferson Papers*, 1: 349–50; also available at "Founders Online" National Archives database.

79. Jefferson to Granger, March 9, 1814, in *Jefferson Papers: Retirement Series*, 7: 236–37; Malone, *Jefferson*, 5: 391.

80. Gideon Granger to Jefferson, Feb. 22, 1814, and Jefferson to Granger, March 9, 1814, both in Looney, ed., *Jefferson Papers: Retirement Series*, 7: 206–7, 236–37. The scant surviving Burr correspondence published in Mary-Jo Kline, ed., *Political Correspondence and Public Papers of Aaron Burr* reveals little contact between Burr and Granger. See also Irving Brant, *James Madison: Commander in Chief, 1812–1836* (Indianapolis, 1961), 242–245. Brant exaggerates Jefferson's innocence in this incident. He finds that Madison dismissed Gideon Granger as Postmaster General because he was insubordinate in desiring to appoint party activist Michael Leib as postmaster of Philadelphia, while Madison instructed him to appoint less controversial figures like Richard Bache or Return J. Meigs. (It is also possible that Madison fired him because he discovered that Granger supported DeWitt Clinton for president against Madison in 1812, and remained on good terms with his Clintonian opponents.)

81. Jefferson to Granger, March 9, 1814, in Looney, ed., *Jefferson Papers: Retirement Series*, 7: 237–238.

82. Jefferson to Madison, March 10, 1814, *Jefferson Papers: Retirement Series*, 7: 239–40.

83. Bruce P. Stark, "Universal Suffrage, the 'Stand-Up Law,' and the Wallingford Election Controversy, 1801–1818," *Connecticut History Review* 53, no. 1 (Spring 2014): 16–44, 40.

84. [Circular], enclosed in Timothy Dwight to Simeon Baldwin, Aug. 21, 1806, Baldwin Family Papers, Yale University, quoted in Noble E. Cunningham, Jr., *The Jeffersonian Republicans in Power: Party Operations, 1801–1809* (Chapel Hill: University of North Carolina Press, 1963), 131.

85. David M. Roth, *Connecticut: A Bicentennial History* (New York: Norton, 1979), 108–109.

86. David Morris Roth and Freeman Meyer, *From Revolution to Constitution: Connecticut, 1763–1818* (Chester, Conn.: Pequot Press, 1975), 110.

87. Stark, "Universal Suffrage, the 'Stand-Up Law,' and the Wallingford Election Controversy," 41; Roth, *Connecticut*, 112–113.

88. Ibid., 113.

89. Ibid.

90. Livermore, *Twilight of Federalism*, 40–45.

91. Hampden, *Letter to the President*, 27.

92. Hampden, *Letter to the President*, 27.

93. Ibid., 25.

94. Ibid., 26.

95. Ibid.

96. Ibid., 24.

97. Ibid., 26–27.

98. Ibid., 28.

99. Ibid., 23.

100. There are several discussions of John Breckinridge and his family: Lowell H. Harrison, *John Breckinridge: Jeffersonian Republican* (Louisville, Ky.: Filson Club, 1968); James C. Klotter, *The Breckinridges of Kentucky* (Lexington, Ky., 1986); and William C. Davis, *John C. Breckinridge: Statesman, Soldier, Symbol* (Lexington, Ky., 2010).

101. Hampden, *Letter to the President of the United States*, 24.

102. Ibid., 24.

103. Ibid., 28.

104. Jefferson to Gideon Granger, January 24, 1810, in Looney, *Jefferson Papers: Retirement Series*, 2: 179.

105. Jefferson to John B. Colvin, Sept. 20, 1810, in Looney, ed., *Jefferson Papers: Retirement Series*, 3: 99. Of

course, Jefferson was not referring to the Connecticut prosecutions in this letter, but to something he considered far more important: Burr's Conspiracy, which took place about the same time.

Chapter 10

1. Jefferson to Thomas Allen, March 12, 1805, and Thomas Allen to Jefferson, March 4, 1805, Jefferson Papers, Library of Congress. Transcripts of both letters are available at Founders Online database.

2. "Legislature of Massachusetts, House of Representatives, Tuesday, Jan. 31, 1805," and "The Monarchy of Federalism," the satirical title of the attack on Jefferson's morals, originally printed in the *New England Palladium*, were both reprinted in *Boston Repertory*, Feb. 8, 1805. The Reverend Thomas Allen's son, Thomas Allen, Jr., an assembly delegate from Pittsfield, introduced the resolution to fire the state printer. He was Jefferson's most ardent defender. See also Joseph E. A. Smith, comp., *History of Pittsfield (Berkshire County), Massachusetts* (Boston: Lea and Shepard, 1869–1876), 2: 72–73.

3. Jefferson to Thomas Allen, March 12, 1805, Jefferson Papers, Library of Congress. Jefferson's allusion to Decius was probably a reference to Decius Brutus, one of the assassins of Julius Caesar. Decius deliberately misinterpreted Caesar's wife Calpurnia's dream so that Caesar would show up on the Senate on the Ideas of March, where he was assassinated by Decius, Marcus Brutus and many others. Decius Brutus was himself murdered by Caesar's partisans shortly afterward.

4. Jefferson to Thomas Allen, March 12, 1805, Jefferson Papers, Library of Congress.

5. Much of the biographical information in this and the next few paragraphs comes from the biographical sketches of James Sullivan by James Truslow Adams in *Dictionary of American Biography*, 18: 190–91, and James M. Banner, Jr., in *American National Biography*, 21: 110–12.

6. Adams, *History of the United States*, 1027.

7. Formisano, *Transformation of Political Culture*, 70; Goodman, *Democratic-Republicans*, 100.

8. Jefferson to James Sullivan, May 21, 1805, Jefferson Papers, Library of Congress. "Chrism" is anointing oil (also called myrrh) used in important religious rituals such as baptism and confirmation in most Christian churches.

9. Jefferson to James Sullivan, May 21, 1805, Jefferson Papers, Library of Congress; Amory, *James Sullivan*, 2: 142–145.

10. Jefferson to Judge James Sullivan, May 21, 1805, in Lipscomb and Bergh, ed., *Writings of Jefferson*, 11: 72. On the Federalist campaign against Sullivan, see Robinson, *Jeffersonian Democracy in New England*, 50; and Amory, *James Sullivan*, 2: 142–152.

11. Jefferson to James Sullivan, May 21, 1805, Jefferson Papers, Library of Congress. Mark A. Kann, *A Republic of Men: The American Founders, Gendered Language, and Patriarchal Politics* (New York: New York University Press, 1998) and Pauline Schloesser, *The Fair Sex: White Women and Racial Patriarchy in the Early American Republic* (New York: NYU Press, 2000), are standard studies of the concept of masculinity as an integral component of "republican virtue" in the eighteenth century and how (upper-class) white women were affected by it.

12. Jefferson to James Sullivan, May 21, 1805, Jefferson Papers, Library of Congress. Lipscomb and Bergh, eds., *Writings*, 11: 72–74, prints a portion of this letter.

13. James Sullivan to Jefferson, June 20, 1805, Jefferson Papers, Library of Congress. Extrapolating from the text of

Jefferson's letter to Sullivan, May 21, 1805, it appears that Sullivan had asked for a government job and complained about Federalist calumny and rumors that Jefferson was unenthusiastic about his candidacy in a letter of April 14, 1805, that has not been found.

14. James Sullivan to Jefferson, April 21, 1806, Jefferson Papers, Library of Congress.

15. James Sullivan to Jefferson, June 20, 1806, Jefferson Papers, Library of Congress.

16. William G. McLoughlin, *New England Dissent, 1630–1833* (Cambridge, Mass.: Harvard University Press, 1971), 2: 1079. In general, see Formisano, *Transformation*, 153–159, 169–70; and Goodman, *Democratic-Republicans of Massachusetts*, 95–96, 165–66.

17. McLoughlin, *New England Dissent*, 2: 1079.

18. James Sullivan to William Eustis, January 13, 1802, quoted in Thomas C. Amory, *Life and Times of James Sullivan* (2 vols.; Boston, 1859), 2: 95. Jefferson's support for a strong navy is described in Gene Allen Smith, *For the Purposes of Defense: The Politics of the Jeffersonian Gunboat Program* (Newark: University of Delaware Press, 1996).

19. See for instance, Paul Goodman, *The Democratic-Republicans of Massachusetts* (Cambridge, Mass., 1964); G.S. Rowe, *Thomas McKean: The Shaping of an American Republicanism* (Boulder, Col., 1978); Ray Walters, Jr., *Alexander James Dallas* (Philadelphia, 1943); and Roland M. Baumann, "Philadelphia Manufacturers and the Excise Taxes of 1794: The Forging of a Jeffersonian Coalition," *Pennsylvania Magazine of History and Biography* 106, no. 1 (January 1982): 3–40.

20. James Sullivan to William Eustis, January 13, 1802, quoted in Amory, *Life and Times of James Sullivan*, 2: 95. See also Formisano, *Transformation of Political Culture*, 70.

21. Peter F. Stearns, "In 1806, James Sullivan Vaulted into the Governor's Office by Prosecuting to the Gallows Two Innocent 'Sons of the Ould Sod,'" *Boston Irish Reporter*, December 2005, p. 14, available online. However, historian Richard D. Brown denies that there was bias against the Irish Catholics in this case. His article, "'Tried, Convicted and Condemned, in Almost Every Bar-room and Barber's Shop': Anti-Irish Prejudice in the Trial of Dominic Daley and James Halligan, Northampton, Massachusetts, 1806," *New England Quarterly* 84, no. 2 (June 2011): 205–233, argues that in some trials in Massachusetts, immigrants received better treatment than native-born Massachusetts citizens, and that Sullivan's conduct of the case was exemplary.

22. Formisano, *Transformation of Political Culture*, 71–72.

23. Pickering to Governor Sullivan, March 1808, quoted in Adams, *History*, 1091–92. Apparently siding with Jefferson against Pickering, his family's inveterate foe, Adams ambivalently calls Pickering's "unscrupulous appeal to Jefferson's own official language" a singular "touch of genius." Ibid., 1091.

24. John Quincy Adams to Harrison Gray Otis, 1808, quoted in Adams, *History*, 1093.

25. Ibid., 1094.

26. Adams, *History*, 1094.

27. Formisano, *Transformation of Political Culture*, 71–72; Malone, *Jefferson the President: Second Term*, 566, 592–93.

28. Jefferson to Levi Lincoln, August 22 and Nov. 13, 1808, in Lipscomb and Bergh, ed., *Writings of Jefferson*, 12: 145–47, 194–95; Lincoln to Jefferson, Sept. 10, 1808, Jefferson Papers, Library of Congress (quotation); Adams, *History*, 1101–1103.

29. On Sullivan and Johnson's refusal to enforce the Embargo Act, see Malone, *Jefferson the President: Second*

Term: Volume 5 of Jefferson and His Times, 592–603; and
Levy, *Jefferson and Civil Liberties,* 55, 134 (Blake), 126–30
(Johnson), 126. 131–33 (Livingston), and 104–107 (Sullivan).
   30. Jefferson to Levi Lincoln, Nov. 13, 1808, in Lipscomb
and Bergh, ed., *Jefferson's Writings,* 12: 195.

Chapter 11

   1. Thomas A. Bailey, *A Diplomatic History of the American People* (6th edn.; New York: Appleton Century Crofts, 1964), 125–126.
   2. John Adams to James Lloyd, April 5, 1815, in Adams, ed., *Works,* 10: 155.
   3. Jefferson to Benjamin Stoddert, Feb. 18, 1809, Ford, ed., *Works of Jefferson,* 11: 98–99.
   4. Jefferson to Thomas Leiper, Jan. 21, 1809, in Paul L. Ford, ed., *Works of Thomas Jefferson* (12 vols.; New York, 1904–5), 11: 90–91.
   5. Ibid.
   6. Congress was ambivalent toward the Embargo from the start. It was one of the most short-lived pieces of legislation in U.S. history. After passing it in December 1807, Congress weakened it in April 1808 by authorizing the President to suspend it if he thought that was justified. In January 1809, Congress voted to make the Embargo more effective; and on March 1, 1809, it repealed the Embargo Act, replacing it with non-intercourse against Britain and France alone. *Statutes at Large,* 3: 490, 506, 528.
   7. Jefferson to William Eustis, January 14, 1809, Jefferson Papers, Library of Congress.
   8. Jefferson to William Eustis, January 14, 1809, Jefferson Papers, Library of Congress.
   9. Goodman, *Democratic-Republicans of Massachusetts,* 129–130.
   10. Bacon to Jefferson, April 11, 1803, in Oberg, ed., *Jefferson Papers,* 40: 163–164. Italics in original.
   11. Jefferson to John Bacon, April 30, 1803, in Ford, ed., *Works of Jefferson,* 9: 463–64.
   12. David W. Parker, ed., "Secret Reports of John Howe, 1808," *American Historical Review* 17, no. 2 (January 1912): 332–333.
   13. Jefferson to William Eustis, January 14, 1809, Jefferson Papers, Library of Congress.
   14. Jefferson to William Eustis, Oct. 6, 1809, Jefferson Papers, Library of Congress. Jefferson was probably not enthusiastic about Eustis's appointment. Madison appointed him mainly because he wished to conciliate New England Republicans by maintaining a sectional "balance" in the Cabinet after Eustis's fellow Massachusetts resident, Henry Dearborn, resigned as secretary of war at the end of Jefferson's second administration. Eustis remained secretary of war for three years until his ineptitude became evident during the War of 1812, and he resigned the post. Malone, *Sage of Monticello,* 111–113; Rutland, *Presidency of James Madison,* 32, 36, 107–108, 110, 120; Leonard D. White, *The Jeffersonians: A Study in Administrative History, 1801–1829* (New York: Macmillan, 1951), 217–218, 253.
   15. Jefferson to William Eustis, Oct. 6, 1809, Jefferson Papers, Library of Congress.
   16. Abigail Adams to "Nabby" Adams, June 19, 1809, in C. A. DeWindt, *Journal and Correspondence of Miss Adams* (2 vols.; New York, 1841), 2: 203–204.
   17. Ibid.
   18. Abigail Adams to "Nabby" Adams, April 10, 1809, in DeWindt, *Journal and Correspondence,* 2: 190–91. What Abigail actually wrote to Jefferson was that he had a greater public consensus behind him than either Washington or

Adams possessed, and could therefore pursue measures accommodating to the Federalists. "You can do more than either of your predecessors could, and are awfully responsible to God and your Country for the measures of your Administration." Abigail Adams to Jefferson, July 1, 1804, in Cappon, ed., *Adams-Jefferson Letters,* 273; and "Founders Online" database.
   19. Abigail Adams to "Nabby" Adams, May 13, 1809, in DeWindt, *Journal and Correspondence,* 2: 192–93.
   20. Abigail Adams to "Nabby" Adams, April 10, 1809, ibid., 192. Surprisingly, none of the biographies of Abigail Adams gives attention to her complete change of opinion on Jefferson and the party conflict during the period before the War of 1812 (following John Quincy Adams' appointment to the Russian post by Madison), and her sudden evolution into an ardent patriot and proto-War Hawk. For brief mention of her support for Madison's re-election in 1812, see Woody Holton's outstanding biography, *Abigail Adams* (New York, 2007), 380.
   21. On the context of the *Chesapeake* Affair and the long-term grievance of impressment, see Joshua Wolf, "'To Be Enslaved or Thus Deprived': British Impressment, American Discontent, and the Making of the *Chesapeake-Leopard* Affair, 1803–1807," *War & Society* 29, no. 1 (May 2010): 1–19.
   22. Jefferson to Benjamin Rush, January 3, 1808, Jefferson Papers, Founders Online database, National Archives.
   23. For Jefferson's antipathy to merchants at this time, see Jefferson to Thomas Leiper, 21 January 1809, in Ford, ed., *Works,* 11: 91.
   24. Jefferson to Martha Jefferson Randolph, Nov. 23, 1807, in "The Jefferson Papers," *Collections of the Massachusetts Historical Society,* Vol. 61 (1900): 119.
   25. Steele, *Thomas Jefferson and American Nationhood,* 281–82; Peterson, *Thomas Jefferson,* 891.
   26. The proclamation of April 19, 1808. "Proclamation by the President of the United States of America," is in Jefferson Papers, Library of Congress. It is printed in James D. Richardson, *Collection of the Messages and Papers of the Presidents,* 1: 450–451.
   27. Martin Chittenden's speech, Nov. 10, 1808, *Annals of Congress,* 10th Congress, 2d Session, Vol. 19, col. 474.
   28. James Elliot's resolution on The President's Proclamation, Nov. 25, 1808, ibid., col. 529.
   29. Ibid., Nov. 30, 1808, cols. 580–581.
   30. Jefferson to Secretary of War Dearborn, August 9, 1808, in Lipscomb and Bergh, ed., *Writings of Jefferson,* 12: 119. See also Henry Adams, *History of the United States,* 1101–1104.
   31. Jefferson to Gallatin, August 11, 1808, Lipscomb and Bergh, ed., *Writings of Jefferson,* 12: 122.
   32. Jefferson to Gallatin, August 11, 1808, Jefferson Papers, Library of Congress. Jefferson's italics. Jefferson to Gallatin, August 11, 1808, is also printed in Lipscomb and Bergh, eds., *Writings of Jefferson,* 12: 122–23. Brian Steele, "Thomas Jefferson, Coercion, and the Limits of Harmonious Union," *Journal of Southern History* 74 (Nov. 2008): 823–854, 830, misreads the letter as manifesting Jefferson's determination to acquire absolute power to enforce the Embargo. Steele exaggerates Jefferson's commitment to the Embargo, as did Levy, *Jefferson,* 105–141, who wrote, "As civil disobedience spread, Jefferson's resolution stiffened; he yielded increasingly to the temptation to employ any means, however draconic, to enforce compliance" (105). Mannix argues that Jefferson did nearly nothing to enforce the Embargo, despite his empty protests when smugglers murdered U.S. officials in Maine and Vermont. From the outset, Gallatin had opposed the Embargo Act. He said that

even war with Great Britain was preferable to a "permanent embargo." Gallatin to Jefferson, Dec. 18, 1807, Jefferson Papers, Library of Congress, available in transcript in "Founders Online" National Archives database.

33. Jefferson to Governor James Sullivan, August 12, 1808, ibid., 12: 127–30, 129 (quotation).

34. On Dean's execution, see [Richmond] *Virginia Argus,* Dec. 13, 1808, quoted in Walter Wilson Jennings, *The American Embargo, 1807–1809* (Iowa City: University of Iowa Studies in the Social Scences, 1921), 116, and the information in ibid., 115–116; Leonard W. Levy, *Jefferson and Civil Liberties: The Darker Side* (Cambridge, Mass., 1963), 116–131; 131 (for murdered soldiers); Joshua M. Smith, "Murder on Isle au Haut: Violence and Jefferson's Embargo in Coastal Maine, 1807–1809," *Maine History* 39 (March 2000): 17–39. For Jefferson's lack of enthusiasm for the worldwide Embargo, see Richard Mannix, "Gallatin, Jefferson, and the Embargo of 1808," *Diplomatic History* 3, no. 2 (April 1979): 151–172. Studies that suggest that Jefferson did little to enforce the Embargo despite his rhetorical support of additional enforcement legislation in 1808 include: Douglas Lamar Jones, "'The Caprice of Juries': The Enforcement of the Jeffersonian Embargo in Massachusetts," *American Journal of Legal History* 24, no. 4 (Oct. 1980): 307–330; William Jeffrey Bolster, "The Impact of Jefferson's Embargo on Coastal Commerce," *Log of Mystic Seaport* 37 (January 1986): 111–123. For the growth of bank deposits in Maine and western Massachusetts as a result of smuggling to Canada and the West Indies during the Embargo, see J. Van Fenstermaker and John E. Filer, "The U.S. Embargo Act of 1807: Its Impact on New England Money, Banking, and Economic Activity," *Economic Inquiry,* 28, no. 1 (1990): 163–84. On the comparatively minor hardships the Embargo caused in the United States, including New England and specifically the Port of Boston, by comparison with Great Britain, see Jeffrey A. Frankel, "The 1807–1809 Embargo Against Great Britain," *Journal of Economic History* 42, no. 2 (1982): 291–308; and Robin D. S. Higham, "The Port of Boston and the Embargo, 1807–1809," *American Neptune* 16, no. 3 (1956): 189–210. Burton Spivak, *Jefferson's English Crisis* (Charlottesville, 1979), interprets the Embargo as Jefferson's "classical republican" attempt to restore agrarian values by granting primacy to the direct exportation of American products and phasing out the carrying trade.

35. Jennings, *American Embargo,* 163–165, argues that Jefferson, despite favoring the Embargo, consented to its repeal out of fear that otherwise the secession of New England and civil war would ensue. But his sources consist of letters and other documents written many years after the War of 1812. Nevertheless, there is no doubt that Jefferson was influenced by the extent of smuggling going on in the North in his decision to end the Embargo, although he continued to insist that the majority of New Englanders obeyed the law and were devoted to the Union.

36. Jefferson to Secretary of the Navy, August 9, 1808, Lipscomb and Bergh, ed., *Writings of Jefferson,* 12: 121. The English translation of the French is: "So much the better for us."

37. Jefferson to Secretary of the Treasury Gallatin, August 9, 1808, ibid., 12: 120–21.

38. Jefferson to Dearborn, August 12, 1808, ibid., 12: 125–26.

39. Jefferson to Secretary of the Navy, August 9, 1808, Lipscomb and Bergh, ed., *Writings of Jefferson,* 12: 121. Since this is the only evidence that Steele cites, the only explanation for him interpreting this statement as a presidential order for martial law was that Steele wanted to mimic Onuf's

thesis about Jefferson's obsession with enforcing Virginia's domination of the Union by "destroying" New England.

40. Jefferson to Gallatin, August 19, 1808, Lipscomb and Bergh, ed., *Writings of Jefferson,* 12: 137–38.

41. Jefferson to Gallatin, August 19, 1808, Lipscomb and Bergh, ed., *Writings of Jefferson,* 12: 137–38. Sixty years before Levy's *Jefferson and Civil Liberties,* Henry Adams, the doyen of historians, depicted Jefferson as more enthusiastic about enforcing the Embargo than he actually was. Quoting this same letter to Gallatin, Adams labeled it an effort to provoke the Federalists, so that he could crush them: "Rebellion and disunion stared Jefferson in the face, but only caused him to challenge an outbreak and to invite violence." Henry Adams, *History of the United States during the Administrations of Thomas Jefferson* (1901; reprinted, New York, 1986), 1104. Although Adams did not emphasize his unconvincing observations on this point, he may have been one of Onuf's unacknowledged sources for the thesis in *Jefferson's Empire* that Jefferson intended to "destroy" New England.

42. Turreau to Champagny, June 28, 1808, in Archives des Affaires Étrangères, États-Unis, quoted in Adams, *History of the United S64tes,* 1140. On the success of privateering during the American Revolution, see William Bell Clark, *Ben Franklin's Privateers* (Baton Rouge: Louisiana State University Press, 1956), and Benjamin W. Labaree, *Patriots and Partisans: The Merchants of Newburyport, 1764–1815* (Cambridge, Mass.: Harvard University Press, 1962).

43. Jefferson to John Armstrong, March 5 [*sic*], 1809, in Lipscomb and Bergh, eds., *Writings,* 12: 261–62. Quoting this letter, a bemused Henry Adams admitted, "Jefferson submitted in silence, and even with an air of approval, to the abrupt abandonment of his favorite measure." Adams, *History of the United States,* 1244. For congressional repeal of the Embargo Act, to commence March 15, 1809, see *Statutes at Large of the United States,* 2: 531 (March 1, 1809).

44. Jefferson to Wilson Cary Nicholas, May 25, 1809, in Looney, ed., *Jefferson Papers: Retirement Series,* 1: 224.

45. See Lawrence S. Kaplan, "France and Madison's Decision for War, 1812," *Mississippi Valley Historical Review* 50, no. 4 (March 1964): 659–660.

46. Jefferson to Thomas Mann Randolph, Nov. 22, 1808, in "Jefferson Papers," *Collections of the Massachusetts Historical Society,* Vol. 61 (1900): 125.

47. Jefferson to Charles L. Bankhead, Nov. 26, 1808, "Jefferson Papers," Vol. 61: 126.

48. Catherine Cruger to Jefferson, Dec. 2, 1808, ibid., 127–128.

49. Jefferson to Catherine Cruger, Dec. 15, 1808, Jefferson Papers, Library of Congress.

50. Thomas Lehré to Jefferson, Oct. 14, 1808, Jefferson Papers, Library of Congress. On South Carolina politics at this time, see Margaret K. Latimer, "South Carolina: A Protagonist of the War of 1812," *American Historical Review* 61, no. 4 (June 1956): 914–929.

51. Jefferson to Thomas Lehré, Nov. 8, 1808, Jefferson Papers, Library of Congress.

52. Jefferson to Thomas Lehré, Nov. 8, 1808, Jefferson Papers, Library of Congress. See also Lipscomb and Bergh, eds., *Writings of Jefferson,* 12: 190–191, where Lehré's name is misspelled "Letue."

53. Catherine L. Albanese, *Sons of the Fathers: The Civil Religion of the American Revolution* (Philadelphia: Temple University Press, 1976).

54. William A. Robinson, *Jeffersonian Democracy in New England* (New Haven, 1916), 81–82, 155. For Republican newspapers emphasizing that Adams favored Jefferson's Embargo Act, see Boston *Independent Chronicle,* June 16,

1808, p. 2. According to my research in newspapers of the period, around 1808 the Democratic-Republicans began to regularly call themselves "Democrats." For example, the Philadelphia *Aurora* editorialized, "We can now say, by advices from all parts of Pennsylvania, that the *political ticket* of this state, will be MADISON for President, SNYDER for governor—and that all party distinctions are likely to be reduced under this ticket, to the old denominations of DEMOCRATS and FEDERALISTS—alias, WHIGS and *Tories*." Philadelphia *Aurora*, quoted in Boston *Independent Chronicle*, June 16, 1808, p. 2.

55. See Douglas Lamar Jones, "'The Caprice of Juries': The Enforcement of the Jeffersonian Embargo in Massachusetts," *American Journal of Legal History* 24, no. 4 (Oct. 1980): 307–330; William Jeffrey Bolster, "The Impact of Jefferson's Embargo on Coastal Commerce," *Log of Mystic Seaport* 37 (January 1986): 111–123. For the growth of bank deposits in Maine and Massachusetts as a result of smuggling to Canada and the West Indies during the Embargo, see J. Van Fenstermaker and John E. Filer, "The U.S. Embargo Act of 1807: Its Impact on New England Money, Banking, and Economic Activity," *Economic Inquiry*, 28, no. 1 (1990): 163–84. On the comparatively minor hardships the Non-Importation Act (originally passed in 1806) and Embargo caused in the United States, including New England and specifically the Port of Boston, by comparison with Great Britain, see Jeffrey A. Frankel, "The 1807–1809 Embargo Against Great Britain," *Journal of Economic History* 42, no. 2 (1982): 291–308; and Robin D. S. Higham, "The Port of Boston and the Embargo, 1807–1809," *American Neptune* 16, no. 3 (1956): 189–210.

56. Jefferson to Thomas Mann Randolph, Dec. 13, 1808, "Jefferson Papers," Vol. 61: 130.

57. Jefferson to Thomas Mann Randolph, Jan. 2, 1809, ibid., 130–131.

58. Ibid.

59. Jefferson to Thomas Mann Randolph, Jan. 2, 1809, ibid., 131, and "Founders Online."

60. Jefferson to Charles L. Bankhead, Jan. 19, 1809, ibid., 133.

61. Jefferson to Thomas Mann Randolph, Jan. 31, 1809, ibid., 134–135 (first and second quotations); Jefferson to Thomas Mann Randolph, Feb. 7, 1809, Lipscomb and Bergh, ed., *Writings of Jefferson*, 12: 248 (third quotation). My italics.

62. Jefferson to Thomas Mann Randolph, Jan. 31, 1809, "Jefferson Papers," Vol. 61: 134–135. On the Massachusetts situation, see Harlow W. Sheidley, *Sectional Nationalism: Massachusetts Conservative Leaders and the Transformation of America, 1815–1836* (Boston: Northeastern University Press, 1998), 76–77.

63. Jefferson to Thomas Mann Randolph, Feb. 7, 1809, Lipscomb and Bergh, ed., *Writings of Jefferson*, 12: 248.

64. Jefferson to Thomas Mann Randolph, Feb. 7, 1809, Lipscomb and Bergh, ed., *Writings of Jefferson*, 12: 248.

65. A well-known example is the young Virginia slaveholder Edward Coles, who freed his slaves and took them to Illinois. He became governor of the state and played a major role in preventing slavery from being legalized there. In 1814, Coles wrote Jefferson several letters urging him to write a manifesto publicly demanding the "general emancipation" of Virginia's slaves. He assured Jefferson that, as "the first of our aged worthies," his words would have an even greater impact after he died. Edward Coles to Jefferson, July 31 and Sept. 26, 1814, in Looney, ed., *Jefferson Papers: Retirement Series*, 7: 503–504, 704.

66. Ari Helo, *Thomas Jefferson's Ethics and the Politics of Human Progress: The Morality of a Slaveholder* (Cambridge:

Cambridge University Press, 2014), 44, reasonably points out that Jefferson had little success in converting Virginians or other Americans to his progressive views, not only on abolition but on universal manhood suffrage, complete freedom of religion, and equitable apportionment of legislative districts. He was less politically powerful than those historians who criticize him for passivity in publicly denouncing slavery assume.

67. A convenient sample of the replies to the patriotic addresses that New Englanders and other Americans, most of them Democratic-Republican partisans, sent Jefferson in 1808 and 1809, may be found in Saul K. Padover, ed., *The Complete Jefferson* (New York: John Day, 1943), 527–563, and Looney, ed., *Jefferson Papers: Retirement Series*, volume one, esp. 85, 88, for New Englanders' eulogistic addresses.

68. William Nisbet Chambers, "Party Development and Party Action: The American Origins," *History and Theory*, 3 (Feb. 1963): 91–120. On Jefferson as a strong president who took what John Locke called "prerogative" action when he considered the "self-preservation" (Jefferson's term) of the Union at stake, see Jeremy David Bailey, "Executive Prerogative and the 'Good Officer' in Thomas Jefferson's Letter to John B. Colvin," *Presidential Studies Quarterly* 34 (Dec. 2004): 732–754.

Chapter 12

1. See Burton Spivak, *Jefferson's English Crisis* (Charlottesville, 1979).

2. Jefferson to John Tyler, May 26, 1810, in Peterson, *Writings*, 1226.

3. *Ibid.*

4. *Ibid.* During the crisis over the Alien and Sedition Acts in October 1798, Jefferson had anonymously drafted Albemarle County's petition to the Virginia assembly requesting popular district elections of state (and ultimately federal) jurors instead of their appointment by the sheriff. He favored this mainly because Albemarle County federal jurors, had shown themselves to have pro–Federalist sympathies, notably by censuring Republican congressman Samuel J. Cabell. Dumas Malone, *Jefferson and the Ordeal of Liberty* (Boston, 1962), 398–99.

5. On Jefferson and Gerry, see Dumas Malone, *Jefferson the Virginian* (Boston, 1948), 100; and Malone, *Jefferson and the Rights of Man* (Boston, 1951), 164–65n.

6. Jefferson to Elbridge Gerry, June 11, 1812, in Paul L. Ford, ed., *Works*, 11: 256. Although Jefferson had probably not yet received the information, President Madison had requested Congress to declare war against Great Britain on June 1, 1812. The House of Representatives approved the declaration of war on June 4, the Senate passed it on June 17, and Madison signed the war declaration the next day. Reginald Horsman, *The War of 1812* (New York, 1969), 24.

7. Jefferson to Elbridge Gerry, June 11, 1812, in Paul L. Ford, ed., *Works*, 11: 256–57. After a superficial discussion of this letter, Andy Trees, "Private Correspondence for the Public Good: Thomas Jefferson to Elbridge Gerry, 26 January 1799," *Virginia Magazine of History and Biography* 198 (2000), 253–254, concludes that Jefferson was willing to break up the Union to escape from "monarchical" Federalists and anybody else who opposed his ideas. This seems to be exactly the opposite of Jefferson's purport in this letter to Gerry and much of his other correspondence during the War of 1812. For accounts of Pickering's secessionist goals and the general tendency toward disunion among conservative New England clergy (contrary to the claims of some scholars who should know better, these were not a paranoid

fantasy of Jefferson's), see Kevin M. Gammon, "Escaping 'Mr. Jefferson's Plan of Destruction': New England Federalists and the Idea of a Northern Confederacy, 1803–1804," *Journal of the Early Republic* 21 (2001): 413–443, and Jonathan D. Sassi, "The First Party Competition and Southern New England's Public Christianity," *Journal of the Early Republic* 21 (2001): 261–299.

8. Jefferson to Thomas Leiper, January 21, 1809, in Ford, ed., *Works*, 11: 91.

9. Monroe to Jefferson, January 6. 1801, in Stanislaus M. Hamilton, ed., *The Writings of James Monroe*, 7 vols. (New York, 1898–1903), 3: 254–55.

10. John Ferling, *Setting the World Ablaze: Washington, Adams, Jefferson, and the American Revolution* (New York, 2000), 165.

11. The best study of New England Federalist opposition to the war effort is Richard Buel, Jr., *America on the Brink: How the Political Struggle over the War of 1812 Almost Destroyed the Republic* (New York: Palgrave Macmillan, 2005).

12. Robert A. Rutland, *The Presidency of James Madison* (Lawrence, Kans., 1990), 141–143, 147.

13. Ibid., 175–176.

14. J.C.A. Stagg, *Mr. Madison's War* (Princeton, 1983), 472–473; Rutland, *Presidency of Madison*, 183–184; J.S. Martell, "A Sidelight on Federalist Strategy During the War of 1812," *American Historical Review* 43 (1938): 553–566; *American National Biography*, s.v., "Strong, Caleb."

15. *Columbian Centinel*, reprinted in *Boston Gazette*, Nov. 24, 1814, quoted in Allison L. LaCroix, "'A Singular and Awkward War': The Transatlantic Context of the Hartford Convention," *American Nineteenth-Century History* 6 (March 2005): 3–32, 18.

16. Nicholas G. and Peter S. Onuf, *Nations, Markets, and War: Modern History and the American Civil War* (Charlottesville, 2007).

17. Onuf, *Jefferson's Empire*, 124

18. Onuf, *Jefferson's Empire*, 124–25.

19. *Ibid.*, 123.

20. *Ibid.*, 123. The letters Onuf uses are Jefferson to James Martin, Sept. 20, 1813, Jefferson to William Short, Nov. 28, 1814, and Jefferson to John Melish, Dec. 10, 1814, all in Albert Ellery Bergh, ed., *The Writings of Thomas Jefferson* (20 vols., Washington, D.C., 1907), 13: 382–84, 14: 217–18, 220–21.

21. Jefferson to Madison, May 25, 1812, in James Morton Smith, ed., *The Republic of Letters: The Complete Correspondence Between Thomas Jefferson and James Madison*, 3 vols. (New York, 1996), 3: 1695. This letter is further discussed below.

22. On DeWitt Clinton's campaign to unite Northerners from both parties behind his commercial-oriented "practical republicanism" during the presidential election of 1812, see Craig R. Hanyan, "DeWitt Clinton and Partisanship: The Development of Clintonianism from 1812 to 1820," *New-York Historical Society Quarterly* 56, no. 2 (1972): 108–131; Steven Edwin Siry, "The Sectional Politics of 'Practical Republicanism': DeWitt Clinton's Presidential Bid, 1810–1812," *Journal of the Early Republic* 5, no. 4 (Winter 1985): 441–462.

23. For the Embargo's more severe effects on the South, which depended on exports to Britain of cotton, wheat, tobacco, and other staples, than on New England, see Garry Wills, *A 'Negro President': Jefferson and the Slave Power* (Boston: Houghton Mifflin, 2003), 156–157; Henry Adams, *History of the United States of America During the Administrations of Thomas Jefferson and James Madison*, 9 vols. (1891–1896; reprinted, New York: Antiquarian Press, 1962),

4: 281–283; Louis Martin Sears, *Jefferson and the Embargo* (Durham, N.C., 1927), 126, 228–252; Sears, "The South and the Embargo," *South Atlantic Quarterly* 20 (July 1921): 254–275; and Burton W. Spivak, *Jefferson's English Crisis* (Charlottesville: University Press of Virginia, 1979), 171–172, 203.

24. Jefferson to Madison, May 25, 1812, Jefferson Papers, Library of Congress. Jefferson was referring to "an Embargo on all Ships and Vessels in the ports and harbors of the United States," passed April 4, 1812. The ninety-day embargo applied only to domestically-owned U.S. vessels. *Statutes at Large of the United States* (Boston: Little and Brown, 1845), 2: 700. The best study of U.S. trade policies during the War of 1812 is Donald R. Hickey, "American Trade Restrictions during the War of 1812," *Journal of American History* 68, no. 3 (Dec. 1981): 517–538.

25. Jefferson to Madison, May 25, 1812, Jefferson Papers, Library of Congress. Jefferson used the same phrase, "govern the majority," in his letter to Gerry about the elections in 1812. Jefferson to Elbridge Gerry, June 11, 1812, in Paul L. Ford, ed., *Works*, 11: 256. Therefore, it seems obvious that for Jefferson the phrase signified political warfare, rather than armed warfare.

26. Jefferson to Madison, 29 June 1812, in Smith, ed., *Republic of Letters*, 3: 1698–99.

27. Ibid., 1699. Donald R. Hickey, in *The War of 1812: A Forgotten Conflict* (Urbana and Chicago, 1989), 345 n. 27, mistakenly claims that the early editors of Jefferson's writings omitted the entire letter. In fact, even more misleadingly, they only omitted the portion where Jefferson advocates violent reprisals against antiwar elements.

28. Robert Wright speech to Congress, 6 May 1812, in *Annals of Congress*, 12th Cong., 1st sess., 1413. Even Hickey, a historian unsympathetic to Jefferson, comments, "Doubtless Jefferson was speaking half in jest." Hickey, *War of 1812*, 56.

29. Boston *Yankee*, 15 May 1812, and John G. Jackson to Madison, 26 June 1812, Madison Papers, Library of Congress, both quoted in Hickey, *War of 1812*, 55–56.

30. For extended interpretations of the War of 1812 epoch as critical period for the republic, see Roger H. Brown, *The Republic in Peril: 1812* (New York, 1964) and Steven Watts, *The Republic Reborn: War and the Making of Liberal America, 1790–1820* (Baltimore, 1987).

31. Jefferson to James Martin, 20 Sept. 1813, in Bergh, ed., *Writings of Jefferson*, 13: 383.

32. See *Federalists* 6, 7, and 8, authored by Hamilton; see also Felix Gilbert's analysis, in *To the Farewell Address: Ideas of Early American Foreign Policy* (Princeton, 1961), 112–14.

33. [Alexander Hamilton], *Federalist No. VI*, in W. R. Brock, ed., *the Federalist; or, the New Constitution* (London, 1961), p. 20.

34. Jefferson to James Martin, 20 Sept. 1813, in Bergh, ed., *Writings of Jefferson*, 13: 383.

35. Jefferson to Short, 28 Nov. 1814, in Bergh, ed., *Writings of Jefferson*, 14: 217; and Peterson, *Writings*, 1357–58. Unfortunately, the best study of Short, George Green Shackelford, *Jefferson's Adoptive Son: The Life of William Short, 1759–1848* (Lexington: University Press of Kentucky, 1993), overlooks Short's Federalist sympathies.

36. Jefferson to Short, 28 Nov. 1814, in Bergh, ed., *Writings of Jefferson*, 14: 217; and Peterson, *Writings*, 1357–58.

37. Jefferson to David Bailie Warden, 29 December 1813, in Sigmund Diamond, ed., "Some Jefferson Letters," *Mississippi Valley Historical Review* 28 (Sept. 1941): 232. Spelling in the original. (Also in Jefferson Papers, Library of Congress).

38. Jefferson to Martin, Sept. 20, 1813, in Bergh, ed., *Writings of Jefferson*, 13: 383–84.

39. J. C. A. Stagg, *Mr. Madison's War: Politics, Warfare, and Diplomacy in the Early American Republic, 1783–1830* (Princeton, 1983), 471–72; *Niles Weekly Register*, 12 Nov. 1814.

40. *Spirit of Laws*, Book IX, chap. 1, in Thomas Nugent, trans., *The Spirit of the Laws* (1748; New York, 1949), 126. For Jefferson's view of Montesquieu, see David W. Carrithers, "Montesquieu, Jefferson, and the Fundamentals of Eighteenth Century Republican Theory," *French-American Review* 62 (1982): 160–68, and Joyce Appleby, "What Is Still American in the Political Philosophy of Thomas Jefferson?" *William and Mary Quarterly*, 3d ser., 39 (April 1982): 287–309. For general studies of the influence of the ancient Greco-Roman confederations on the early republic's political ideas, see, e.g., Meyer Reinhold, "Classical Influences and Eighteenth-Century American Political Thought," in Reinhold, *Classica Americana* (Detroit: Wayne State University Press, 1984), 94–115; Carl J. Richard, *The Founders and the Classics* (Cambridge, Mass., 1994), pp. 85–122; Edward M. Burns, "The Philosophy of History of the Founding Fathers," *The Historian* 16 (Spring 1954): 142–168; Richard M. Gummere, "The Classical Ancestry of the United States Constitution," *American Quarterly* 14 (Spring 1962): 3–18. However, it is likely that "the Founding Fathers' knowledge of Greek leagues was superficial and refracted at best, their applications of lessons therefrom generally partisan and opportunistic." Reinhold, *Classica Americana*, 103–104.

41. Jefferson to William Short, Nov. 28, 1814, in Bergh, ed., *Writings of Jefferson*, 14: 218.

42. Jefferson to Short, Nov. 28, 1814, in Bergh, ed., *Writings of Jefferson*, 14: 218; Robert A. Rutland, *The Presidency of James Madison* (Lawrence, 1990), 176.

Chapter 13

1. See, e.g., Lawrence S. Kaplan, "Toward Isolationism: The Rise and Fall of the Franco-American Alliance, 1775–1801," in Kaplan, *Entangling Alliances With None: American Foreign Policy in the Age of Jefferson* (Kent, Ohio, 1987), 79–95; Shlomo Slonim, "The Founders' Fears of Foreign Influence," *Mid-America: An Historical Review* 81 (Summer 1999): 125–146, and Arthur Scherr, "James Monroe on the Presidency and 'Foreign Influence': From the Virginia Ratifying Convention (1788) to Jefferson's Election (1801)," *Mid-America: An Historical Review* 84 (2002): 145–206.

2. Jefferson to John Melish, January 13, 1813, in J. Jefferson Looney, ed., *Papers of Thomas Jefferson: Retirement Series*, Vol. 5 (Princeton, 2008): 562–566, 563 (quotation).

3. Ibid., 563. For Jefferson's assertions that the Republicans were the true "friends" of the Constitution, who interpreted it as the Founders meant it to be interpreted, while the Federalists were its "enemies" because they had always really desired monarchy, and only pretended to support the Constitution to gain power, see, for example, Jefferson to Elbridge Gerry, Jan. 26, 1799, and Jefferson to William Johnson, June 12, 1823, in Peterson, ed., *Writings*, 1056–1057, 1469–1477.

4. See Kristofer Ray, "The Republicans are the Nation? Thomas Jefferson, William Duane, and the Evolution of a Republican Coalition, 1809–1815," *American Nineteenth Century History* 14, no. 3 (2013): 283–304.

5. Jefferson to John Melish, January 13, 1813, in J. Jefferson Looney, ed., *Papers of Jefferson*, 5: 563–564. As most Jefferson scholars know, in the introduction to his memoir

of his political role in the 1790s, the *Anas*, written in 1818, and in letters to Benjamin Rush in 1811 and to William Short in 1825, Jefferson described a dinner at his house in April 1791, at which Hamilton, in the presence of Jefferson and Adams, said that the British Government was "the most perfect government which ever existed," and that its "corruption" was what enabled it to work so well. *Anas* (Feb. 4, 1818), and Jefferson to Benjamin Rush, January 16, 1811, in Peterson, ed., *Writings*, 671, 1235–1236.

6. Jefferson to John Melish, January 13, 1813, in J. Jefferson Looney, ed., *Papers of Thomas Jefferson: Retirement Series*, Vol. 5: 564. Jefferson's underlining.

7. Ibid.

8. Ibid., 564. Jefferson's underlining. On British efforts to persuade Massachusetts to join in the war against the United States, see Bradford Perkins, *Castlereagh and Adams: England and the United States, 1812–1823* (Berkeley: University of California Press, 1964); Paul A. Varg, *New England and Foreign Relations, 1789–1850* (Hanover, N.H.: University Press of New England, 1980). For the revisionist argument that the delegates to the Hartford Convention in 1814 looked forward to Massachusetts' secession from the Union as an independent member of the "Atlantic community" with close ties to Britain, see Alison L. LaCroix, "'A Singular and Awkward War': The Transatlantic Context of the Hartford Convention," *American Nineteenth-Century History* 6 (March 2005): 3–32.

9. For Jefferson's inclusion of Washington's Farewell Address in the required readings at his college, see University of Virginia, "Regulations, Political Science," March 4, 1825, in Saul K. Padover, ed., *Complete Jefferson* (New York, 1943), 1112. On the embarrassment of mainstream Federalist leaders when they learned, years after Hamilton's death, that he was the main author of Washington's Farewell Address, and their fear that if this news got out it would harm their party's reputation and political chances, see Jeffrey J. Malanson, "'If I Had it in His Hand Writing I Would Burn It': Federalists and the Authorship Controversy over George Washington's Farewell Address, 1808–1809," *Journal of the Early Republic* 34, no. 2 (Summer 2014): 219–242.

10. Jefferson to John Melish, Jan. 13, 1813, in Looney, ed., *Papers of Thomas Jefferson: Retirement Series*, Vol. 5: 564. Underlining by Jefferson.

11. Ibid. Capitalization has been modernized. Spelling as in the original.

12. See Jeremy D. Bailey, "Constitutionalism, Conflict, and Consent: Jefferson on the Impeachment Power," *Review of Politics* 70, no. 4 (Fall 2008): 572–594.

13. Jefferson to John Melish, Jan. 13, 1813, in Looney, ed., *Papers of Thomas Jefferson: Retirement Series*, Vol. 5: 564–565.

14. Ibid., 565. Spelling in original. Punctuation modernized.

15. Ibid. For Washington's support of repressive Federalist measures during the undeclared war with France from 1798–1800, see, for example, Marshall Smelser, "George Washington and the Alien and Sedition Acts," *American Historical Review* 59, no. 2 (Feb. 1954): 322–334.

16. Jefferson to John Melish, Jan. 13, 1813, in Looney, ed., *Papers of Thomas Jefferson: Retirement Series*, Vol. 5: 564–565.

17. Benjamin Rush to Jefferson, March 12, 1801, Jefferson Papers, Library of Congress. See Jefferson Papers, Library of Congress, online at "American Memory." The letter is printed in Lyman H. Butterfield, ed., *Letters of Benjamin Rush* (2 vols.; Princeton, 1951–), 2: 832; and Julian P. Boyd et al., ed., *Papers of Thomas Jefferson* (40 vols., in progress; Princeton, 1950–), 33: 262. Jefferson mentioned

a desire for Patrick Henry's death as early as 1784, angry that Henry obstructed democratic reform of Virginia's constitution and opposed complete religious freedom. Jefferson to Madison, Dec. 8, 1784, in Boyd, ed., *Jefferson Papers*, 7: 557–560.

18. Jefferson to John Melish, Jan. 13, 1813, in Looney, ed., *Papers of Thomas Jefferson: Retirement Series*, Vol. 5: 565.

19. Ibid.

20. Jefferson to Walter Jones, January 2, 1814, in Ford, ed., *Works of Jefferson*, 11: 379.

21. Jefferson to John Melish, Jan. 13, 1813, in Looney, ed., *Papers of Thomas Jefferson: Retirement Series*, Vol. 5: 565–566.

22. John Melish to Jefferson, Feb. 11, 1813, Looney, ed., *Jefferson Papers*, 5: 625–630, 626 (quotation).

23. Jefferson to John Melish, Dec. 10, 1814, in Bergh, ed., *Writings of Jefferson*, 14: 220

24. Jefferson to John Melish, Dec. 10, 1814, in Bergh, ed., *Writings of Jefferson*, 14: 220–21.

Chapter 14

1. Jefferson to John Adams, July 5, 1814, in Cappon, ed., *Adams-Jefferson Letters*, 2: 432.

2. Jefferson to John Adams, July 5, 1814, in Cappon, ed., *Adams-Jefferson Letters*, 2: 432.

3. On Adams's support for the War of 1812, see Joseph J. Ellis, *Passionate Sage: The Character and Legacy of John Adams* (New York: Alfred A. Knopf, 1993), 107–12, and David McCullough, *John Adams* (New York: Simon and Schuster, 2001), 606, 616–617.

4. For the convention's conclusion, see [Washington] *Daily National Intelligencer*, Jan. 11, 1815, cited in C. Edward Skeen, *Citizen Soldiers of the War of 1812* (Lexington: University Press of Kentucky, 1999), 208n.

5. The Hartford Convention's resolutions may be found online at www.usconstitution.net, at Yale Law Center's Avalon website, and many other places. See Henry Steele Commager, ed., *Documents of American History* (New York: Meredith Company, 1973), 209–211, 211 (quotation). Surprisingly, John Charles Anderson Stagg's excellent study of the War of 1812, *Mr. Madison's War: Politics, Diplomacy, and Warfare in the Early American Republic, 1783–1830* (Princeton: Princeton University Press, 1983), erroneously asserts regarding the Hartford Convention's Report: "The convention also adjourned itself indefinitely—which could be taken to mean that the delegates might reassemble later to reconsider their course" (482). Stagg's interpretation, perhaps influenced by his mentor James M. Banner, Jr., depicted the Hartford Convention as a moderate movement with little thought of secession. Banner's work emphasizes the Conventioneers' motivations as republican ideology and a conviction of New England's "special character and role" in the Union and in history. Banner, "A Shadow of Secession? The Hartford Convention," *History Today* 38, no. 9 (Sept. 1988): 24–30, and Banner, *To the Hartford Convention: The Federalists and the Origins of Party Politics in Massachusetts, 1789–1815* (New York: Knopf, 1970).

6. For Jefferson's insignificant impact on Madison's and Monroe's policies in the instances mentioned above, see J. C. A. Stagg, *Mr. Madison's War*, 438–39; George Dangerfield, *The Era of Good Feelings* (New York: Harcourt, Brace and World, 1952), 293–301; Harry Ammon, *James Monroe: The Quest for National Identity* (New York: McGraw-Hill, 1971), 476–488. For Jefferson's failure to influence President Monroe's appointments to office, see, e.g., Dumas Mal-

one, *The Sage of Monticello* (Boston: Little, Brown, 1981; vol. 6 of *Jefferson and His Time*), 430, 449–451; Monroe to Jefferson, Feb. 7, 1820, in Stanislaus M. Hamilton, ed., *Writings of James Monroe* (7 vols.; New York: Putnam, 1898–1903), 6: 114–115; Jefferson to Monroe, Jan. 18, 1824, Ford, ed., *Works of Jefferson* 12: 373–374; Jefferson to Monroe, July 10, 1824, Jefferson Papers, Library of Congress; Jefferson to Monroe, 25 Aug. 1824, Jefferson Papers, Library of Congress; and Monroe to Jefferson, 26 Aug. 1824, Hamilton, ed., *Writings of Monroe* 7: 34–35. Donald F. Swanson, "'Bank-Notes Would Be But as Oak Leaves': Thomas Jefferson on Paper Money," *Virginia Magazine of History and Biography* 101 (Jan. 1993): 37–52, stresses Jefferson's fiscal competency.

7. Richard Henry Lee to Jefferson, May 16, 1785, in James C. Ballagh, ed., *The Letters of Richard Henry Lee* (2 vols.; New York, 1911–1914), 2: 358–59. See also Albert Tillson, "Friendship and Commerce: The Conflict and Coexistence of Values on Virginia's Northern Neck in the Revolutionary Era," *Virginia Magazine of History and Biography* 111(2003): 221–262.

8. Plumer resigned from the U.S. Senate at the end of 1806, intending to become a writer of history, but he discovered that he needed money. He soon ended up begging Jefferson and Democratic New Hampshire governor John Langdon for government employment, assuring them that he was no longer a High Federalist but had become a political independent. In May 1807, Jefferson ignored him when he claimed to have become a Republican and requested an appointment as collector of the customs at Portsmouth, New Hampshire. By July 1807, in the aftermath of the *Chesapeake* Affair, Plumer was publicly denouncing the British, alienating his old Federalist friends, and he was soon supporting Jefferson's Embargo Act of December 1807. As a reward, Langdon made him postmaster of Epping, the small town where he lived, and hinted that the Democratic Party had him in mind for more important offices. Lynn W. Turner, *William Plumer of New Hampshire, 1759–1850* (Chapel Hill: University of North Carolina Press, 1962), 173–184.

9. Jefferson to William Plumer, January 31, 1815, in Lipscomb and Bergh, ed., *Writings of Jefferson*, 14: 235–36. For Plumer's agitation in 1803–1804 for the secession of Federalist New England, see Lynn W. Turner, *William Plumer of New Hampshire* (Chapel Hill: University of North Carolina Press, 1964), 133–139, and Kevin M. Gannon, "Escaping 'Mr. Jefferson's Plan of Destruction': New England Federalists and the Idea of a Northern Confederacy, 1803–1804," *Journal of the Early Republic* 21, no. 3 (Autumn 2001): 413–443, at 435–436. On Monroe's ministry, see Arthur Scherr, "The Limits of Republican Ideology: James Monroe in Thermidorian Paris, 1794–1796," *Mid-America: An Historical Review* 79 (Winter 1997).

10. Jefferson to William Plumer, 31 January 1815, in Lipscomb and Bergh, ed., *Writings of Jefferson*, 14: 235–36. Throughout the Revolution, until Danton was guillotined in 1794, he pursued various revolutionary and counterrevolutionary conspiracies, giving and receiving bribes, acting as a double-agent, both pro- and anti-royalist, and speculating in the British East India Company. See Norman Hampson, *Danton* (1978; Oxford: Basil Blackwell, 1988), 92–97, 157–160, passim.

11. Jefferson to Plumer, 31 January 1815, Lipscomb and Bergh, ed., *Writings of Jefferson*, 14: 236.

12. See Lynn W. Turner, *William Plumer of New Hampshire* (Chapel Hill: University of North Carolina Press, 1962).

13. Elizabeth F. Morison and Elting E. Morison, *New*

Hampshire: A Bicentennial History (New York, 1976), 102. Among the provisions of New Hampshire's old constitution were stipulations that the law protected all Christians (Jews and Muslims were not included), and that only those who signed a Protestant test oath were eligible for office. In general, most taxpayers were required to support the Congregationalist Church as the legally chosen church of the town majority. Turner, *William Plumer*, 11.

14. Jefferson to Plumer, 31 January 1815, Lipscomb and Bergh, ed., *Writings of Jefferson*, 14: 236. On eighteenth-century thinkers' employment of empiricism and conspiracy theory to explain revolutionary political currents, see Gordon S. Wood, "Conspiracy and the Paranoid Style: Causality and Deceit in the Eighteenth Century," *William and Mary Quarterly* (July 1982): 401–441. See Robert H. Wiebe, *The Opening of American Society: From the Adoption of the Constitution to the Eve of Disunion* (New York, 1984), 71–80, 123–25, for incisive observations on the persistence of a "neocolonial" mentality in the United States until the relatively successful conclusion of the War of 1812.

15. Jefferson to William Plumer, 31 January 1815, in Lipscomb and Bergh, ed., *Writings*, 14: 237.

16. Jefferson to William Plumer, 31 January 1815, in Lipscomb and Bergh, ed., *Writings*, 14: 237. For Captain Stephen Decatur's suspicions in 1813 that New London, Connecticut traitors were using "blue light" lanterns to inform British warships of the position of his ship, the *United States*, in its attempts to escape the British blockade, see Buel, *America on the Brink*, 185.

17. Ibid.

18. Ibid., 238.

19. See Donald R. Hickey's discussion, "New England's Defense Problem and the Genesis of the Hartford Convention," *New England Quarterly* 50 (Dec. 1977): 587–604, and *The War of 1812: A Forgotten Conflict* (Urbana, 1989). Although Hickey attempts to defend Connecticut and Massachusetts' disloyalty, his wealth of detail undermines his argument.

20. Formisano, *Transformation of Political Culture: Massachusetts Parties*, 74, 112.

21. Formisano, *Transformation of Political Culture: Massachusetts Parties*, 74, 112; Thomas Lawrence Davis, "Aristocrats & Jacobins in Country Towns: Party Formation in Berkshire Country, Massachusetts (1775–1816)," Ph.D. dissertation, Boston University, 1975, 90–98.

22. Formisano, *Transformation of Political Culture: Massachusetts Parties*, 74 (quotation). Although Formisano's book is excellent, as is George Athan Billias's biography of Gerry, *Elbridge Gerry: Founding Father and Republican Statesman* (New York: McGraw-Hill, 1976), on which Formisano relies to a great extent, Jefferson is essentially absent from both of these volumes.

23. Formisano, *Transformation of Political Culture: Massachusetts Parties*, 75 (quotation). The best summary of the political leaders' role as antiparty party builders during this period is Hofstadter, *Idea of a Party System*.

24. Jefferson to John Adams, July 5, 1814, in Cappon, ed., *Adams-Jefferson Letters*, 2: 432.

25. Madison to Wilson Cary Nicholas, 26 Nov. 1814, in Gaillard Hunt, ed., *Writings of James Madison* (9 vols., New York, 1900–1910), 8: 319. See also Ralph Ketcham, "James Madison and the Nature of Man," *Journal of the History of Ideas* 19 (Jan. 1958): 65.

26. Jefferson to Lafayette, Feb. 14, 1815, in Peterson, ed., *Writings*, 1364.

27. Jefferson to Lafayette, Feb. 14, 1815, in Peterson, ed., *Writings*, 1364. Jefferson's famous letter to Adams on "natural aristocracy," discussed at length below, is Jefferson to

John Adams, Oct. 28, 1813, in Peterson, ed., *Thomas Jefferson: Writings*, 1308.

28. Jefferson to Lafayette, Feb. 14, 1815, *ibid.*, 1364–65.

29. *Ibid.*

30. Ibid., 1366. Because of poor communications, General Andrew Jackson did not receive news of peace until March 13, 1815, when he lifted martial law at New Orleans. Fighting continued between U.S. and British ships until July 1815. American prisoners were massacred at Dartmoor Prison in England on April 6. Donald R. Hickey, ed., *The War of 1812: Writings from America's Second War of Independence* (New York: Literary Classics of the United States, 2013), 682, 733. Hickey prints Jefferson's letter to Lafayette of Feb. 14, 1815, ibid., 682–688. Jefferson to Marquis de Lafayette, Feb. 14, 1815, ibid., 688 (quotation).On January 2, 1815, the British merchant ship HMS *Favorite* left London with a copy of the peace treaty, the Treaty of Ghent, for Senate ratification. Because of bad weather, *Favorite* first docked in New York on February 11. The Senate received the peace treaty on February 14, unanimously ratified the treaty two days later, and it was signed by Madison the same day. Hickey, ed., *War of 1812*, 733.

31. Andrew Jackson to James Monroe, Jan. 6, 1817, in Harold D. Moser et al., eds., *The Papers of Andrew Jackson* (Knoxville: University of Tennessee Press, 1980–), 4: 81. Original spelling and punctuation have been retained. Although David Brown, "Jeffersonian Ideology and the Second Party System," *The Historian: A Journal of History* 62 (Fall 1999): 18, interprets the letter as indicating that Jackson despised all Federalists as monarchists, on the whole its language was rather conciliatory. Indeed, Jackson had earlier recommended that President-elect Monroe appoint Colonel William Drayton, a prominent South Carolina Federalist, as secretary of war. Jackson to Monroe, Oct. 23, 1816 and Nov. 12, 1816, in Moser et al., eds., *Jackson Papers*, 4: 70, 74–75. During the presidential election of 1824, Jackson's opponents published those letters to back up their charge that he was pro–Federalist.

32. Jefferson to Lafayette, May 14, 1817, in Peterson, ed., *Writings*, 1407–8.

33. Alexis de Tocqueville, *Democracy in America*, ed. J. P. Mayer and Max Lerner, translated by George Lawrence (1835; 2 vols. in one, New York: Harper & Row, 1966), 1: 337–338.

34. Ibid., 338, note 53. Tocqueville cites as the source of his quotation a French edition of Jefferson's letters, *Correspondence of Jefferson*, published by M. Conseil.

35. *Democracy in America*, 1: 338, note 54.

Chapter 15

1. Jefferson to John Adams, June 10, 1815, in Lester J. Cappon, ed., *Adams-Jefferson Letters*, 2 vols. (Chapel Hill, 1959), 2: 443. For additional information on Jefferson's relationship with Ticknor, see Orie W. Long, *Thomas Jefferson and George Ticknor* (Williamstown, Mass., 1933), 11–34. By 1820, during the crisis over Missouri's admission to the Union as a slave state, Jefferson claimed to fear that Southern youth who attended universities in the Northern states would learn to be hostile to Southern institutions. He recommended that, until the University of Virginia opened, they attend the University of Kentucky instead, "because she has more of the flavor of the old cask [Virginia] than any other." It is probable that he recurred to sectional fears because the Virginia legislature was being stingy in giving him money to start up his university, and he wanted to frighten it into greater generosity. Jefferson to Joseph C.

Cabell, Jan. 22, 1820, in *Works of Thomas Jefferson*, ed. Paul L. Ford, 12 vols. (New York: Putnam, 1904–5), 12:155.

2. For more on Ticknor's February 1815 visit to Monticello, see his letters, especially George Ticknor to E. Ticknor, Feb. 7, 1815, in George S. Hilliard and Anne Elliot Ticknor, ed., *Life, Letters, and Journals of George Ticknor* (2 vols.; Boston: James R. Osgood, 1876), 1: 36–37.

3. Jefferson to George Ticknor, Nov. 25, 1817, in Ford, *Works*, 12: 76–79, 79 (quotation).

4. Jefferson to John Adams, July 9, 1819, *Adams-Jefferson Letters* 544.

5. Malone, *Sage of Monticello*, 301–315.

6. Ticknor, *Life, Letters, and Journals*, 1: 37 (Ticknor to E. Ticknor, Feb. 7, 1815).

7. See Ticknor, *Life, Letters, and Journals*, 1:16.

8. Ibid. See Adrienne Koch, *Philosophy of Thomas Jefferson* (New York, 1943), and Joyce Appleby, "What Is Still American in the Political Philosophy of Thomas Jefferson?" *William and Mary Quarterly*, 3d ser., 39 (April 1982): 287–309. Pierre Charron (1541–1603), was a French Jesuit priest who, becoming the friend and disciple of Montaigne, ended up a skeptic who believed that religion and morality were separate issues. In *Sagesse*, he advocated no particular religious doctrine, and a secular moral outlook.

9. "Francis C. Gray's Account of a Visit to Monticello" [Gray Diary, 4–7 Feb. 1815], in Looney, ed., *Jefferson Papers: Retirement Series*, 8: 232–236, 234 (quotation). The parenthetical comments are mine.

10. Ibid., 234. Original spelling in most cases retained; I have added some punctuation for purposes of clarity.

11. Ibid., 235 (quotation). For Jefferson's ambivalence toward Hume, see Leonard W. Levy's famous diatribe in *Jefferson and Civil Liberties: The Darker Side* (Cambridge, Mass., 1963). See also Douglas L. Wilson, "Jefferson vs. Hume," *William and Mary Quarterly* 46, no. 1 (January 1989): 49–70, and Craig Walton, "Hume and Jefferson on the Uses of History," in Donald W. Livingston, ed., *Hume: A Re-evaluation* (New York, 1976), 389–403.

12. Francis C. Gray's Account of a Visit to Monticello" [Gray Diary, 4–7 Feb. 1815], in Looney, ed., *Jefferson Papers: Retirement Series*, 8: 234–235 (quotation). Jefferson had briefly visited Bohemia in 1788 when he was U.S. minister to France.

13. George Flower to Richard Flower, Dec. 20, 1816, Flower Letters Copybook, Illinois Historical Society, printed in Mary Ann Salter, "George Flower Comes to the Illinois Country: A New Look at Motivations," *Journal of the Illinois Historical Society*, 69, no. 3 (August 1976): 213–223. I have made a few spelling and punctuation corrections.

14. Jefferson to Messrs. Binney and Ludlow, Feb. 5, 1820, Jefferson Papers, Library of Congress.

15. Christoph Daniel Ebeling to Jefferson, July 30, 1795, in Boyd et al., *Jefferson Papers*, 28: 423–428; Gordon M. Stewart, "Christoph Daniel Ebeling: America's Friend in Eighteenth Century Germany," *Monatshefte* 68, no. 2 (Summer 1976): 151–161.

16. See notes to Christoph Daniel Ebeling to Jefferson, July 30, 1795, in Boyd et al., *Jefferson Papers*, 28: 423–428

17. "Notes on Professor Ebeling's Letter of July 30, 1795," in Peterson, ed., *Jefferson: Writings*, 697.

18. For information on Morse's ministry in Georgia, see *Dictionary of American Biography*, 13: 245.

19. "Notes on Professor Ebeling's Letter of July 30, 1795," in Peterson, ed., *Jefferson: Writings*, 697. Italics are Jefferson's.

20. "Notes on Professor Ebeling's Letter of July 30, 1795," in Peterson, ed., *Jefferson: Writings*, 700–701. For histories of the party press at this time, see Stewart, *Opposition*

Press; David Hackett Fischer, *The Revolution of American Conservatism: The Federalist Party in the Era of Jeffersonian Democracy, 1801–1816* (New York: Harper and Row, 1965); Jeffrey L. Pasley, *The 'Tyranny of Printers"* (Charlottesville: University Press of Virginia, 2001); and Manning J. Dauer, *The Adams Federalists* (Baltimore: Johns Hopkins University Press, 1953). The essential reference source for identifying newspapers remains Clarence S. Brigham, *History and Bibliography of American Newspapers, 1690–1820* (2 vols.; Worcester, 1947).

21. "Notes on Professor Ebeling's Letter of July 30, 1795," in Peterson, ed., *Jefferson: Writings*, 700–701. Thomas Greenleaf edited two New York newspapers, the *New-York Journal and Patriotic Register*, a weekly, and the *New-York Argus*, a daily.

22. Jefferson to William Bentley, Dec. 28, 1815, in Lipscomb and Bergh, *Writings*, 14: 363.

23. Jefferson to William Bentley, Dec. 28, 1815, ibid., 14: 364.

24. Jefferson to William Bentley, Dec. 28, 1815, ibid., 14: 364. See, e.g., Jefferson's "Notes on Professor Ebeling's Letter of July 30, 1795," in Peterson, ed., *Jefferson: Writings*, 697–698, for one example of Jefferson's numerous comparisons of British and American liberty and constitutionalism. While emphasizing the superiority of Britain's "balanced government" and constitutional, "mixed monarchy" to the absolute monarchies of Europe, Jefferson invariably insisted that the U.S. form of representative government was vastly superior to Britain's "corrupt" balanced monarchy, with its ersatz checks and balances between legislative, executive, and judicial branches.

25. Jefferson to Benjamin Waterhouse, Oct. 13, 1815, in Ford, ed., *Writings of Jefferson*, 9: 533, and Looney, ed., *Jefferson Papers: Retirement Series*, 9: 78. Jefferson was replying to Waterhouse to Jefferson, Sept. 1, 1815, ibid., 9: 4–6.

26. Benjamin Waterhouse to Jefferson, Sept. 1, 1815, Jefferson Papers, Library of Congress; printed in Looney, ed., *Jefferson Papers: Retirement Series*, 9: 4–6.

27. Jefferson's "Notes on the Letter of Christoph Daniel Ebeling" [after 15 Oct. 1795], in Julian P. Boyd, John Catanzariti, et al, *Papers of Thomas Jefferson*, 28: 506. Jefferson continued to maintain a low opinion of Virginians who "lounged" around towns where county courts were held, believing that they were unproductive individuals. See Jefferson to Joseph C. Cabell, Feb. 2, 1816, Peterson, ed., *Writings*, 1381. (Perhaps these "individuals" were similar to those homeless who sit around Greyhound Bus stations nowadays.)

28. Jefferson to Joseph C. Cabell, Feb. 2, 1816, in Peterson, ed., *Jefferson: Writings*, 1381 ("drunken loungers"). For Jefferson's endorsement of small-scale manufacturing and the immigration of skilled European artisans to the U.S., see Jefferson to John Lithgow, January 4, 1805, quoted in Ford, ed., *Works*, 4: 86–88. Ford's lengthy discussion of *Notes on Virginia*, in Volume 3, pp. 313–45, describes how Jefferson said he would have revised *Notes* if he ever wrote a second edition; Jefferson to Benjamin Austin, January 9, 1816, in Peterson, ed., *Jefferson: Writings*, 1370–1372. *Notes on Virginia*, Query VIII, "Population," ibid., 212, recommended that Virginia offer special incentives to encourage the emigration of skilled workers who could teach Americans about new machinery ("Spare no expence in obtaining them"). Jefferson's ambivalence about foreign immigration is briefly discussed in Daniel J. Boorstin, *The Lost World of Thomas Jefferson* (New York, 1948), 291–92n.

29. Jefferson to Samuel Kercheval, Sept, 5, 1816, Jefferson Papers, Library of Congress. On Aristotle, see William W. Fortenbaugh, *Aristotle on Emotions* (New York: Barnes & Noble, 1975).

30. Jefferson to Samuel Kercheval, Sept, 5, 1816, Jefferson Papers, Library of Congress, Sept. 5, 1816.

31. Jefferson to Samuel Kercheval, Sept, 5, 1816, Jefferson Papers, Library of Congress, Sept. 5, 1816.

32. For Jefferson's admiration for American Indians' system of near-anarchical government, see, for example, Jefferson to Edward Carrington, January 16, 1787, Jefferson to Madison, January 30, 1787, and Jefferson to John Adams, June 11, 1812, all in Peterson, ed., *Jefferson: Writings*, 880, 882, 1261–1264.

33. Jefferson to Adams, Oct. 12, 1823, in Peterson, *Writings*, 1479–1481; Robert E. McGlone, "Deciphering Memory: John Adams and the Authorship of the Declaration of Independence," *Journal of American History*, 85 (Sept. 1998): 431–433.

34. Jefferson to Samuel Adams Wells, May 12, 1819, in Peterson, *Writings*, 1420–22. There is an account of this episode in Pauline Maier, *American Scripture: Making the Declaration of Independence* (New York: Knopf, 1997), 182. See also Jefferson to John Adams, May 15, 1819, in *Adams-Jefferson Letters*, 540. For Jefferson's praise of Adams's revolutionary services, see also Jefferson to John Adams, March 25, 1826, in Cappon, *Adams-Jefferson Letters*, 613–14. For further commentary on regional attitudes toward Great Britain before Independence, see Jefferson to George Otis, Feb. 15, 1821, in Paul L. Ford, ed., *Writings of Thomas Jefferson* (New York: Putnam, 1892–1899), 10: 187–88, and below.

35. Jefferson to Samuel Kercheval, July 12, 1816, in Peterson, ed., *Jefferson: Writings*, 1399.

36. Jefferson to Samuel Kercheval, July 12, 1816, in Peterson, ed., *Jefferson: Writings*, 1398.

37. Jefferson to Samuel Kercheval, July 12, 1816, in Peterson, ed., *Jefferson: Writings*, 1400 (first quote), 1399 (second quote).

38. See Jefferson's well-known proposal for three years of free public education for all free persons, male and female, in "A Bill for the More General Diffusion of Knowledge" (1778), in Boyd, ed., *Jefferson Papers*, II, 526–8.

39. Jefferson to Pierre Samuel Du Pont de Nemours, April 24, 1816, Jefferson Papers, Library of Congress.

Chapter 16

1. Jefferson to Madison, April 27, 1809, in Lipscomb and Bergh, ed., *Writings of Jefferson*, 12: 277.

2. Jefferson to François D'Ivernois, Feb. 6, 1795, in Julian P. Boyd, John Catanzariti, et al, *Papers of Thomas Jefferson*, 28: 263. Original spelling retained.

3. Jefferson to Jean-Antoine Gautier, Sept. 7, 1795, in Boyd, ed., *Papers*, 28: 453–54.

4. Jefferson to Nathaniel Niles, March 22, 1801, in Ford, ed., *Writings of Thomas Jefferson*, 8: 24.

5. See Gaillard Hunt, ed., *Disunion Sentiment in Congress in 1794* (Washington: W. H. Lowdermilk, 1905).

6. Jefferson to James Ogilvie, Aug. 4, 1811, in Bergh, ed., *Writings of Jefferson*, 13: 68–69, and Looney, *Jefferson Papers: Retirement Series*, 4: 72–74.

7. Jefferson to Ogilvie, Aug. 4, 1811, in Looney, *Jefferson Papers*, 4: 73. My italics.

8. Ibid., 4: 73.

9. Ibid.

10. Josiah Quincy, speech in House, Jan. 14, 1811, in *Annals of Congress*, Vol. 22, 11th Congress, third session, p. 525. See also Richard Buel, Jr., *America on the Brink: How the Political Struggle over the War of 1812 Almost Destroyed the Republic* (New York: Palgrave Macmillan, 2005), 11–14.

11. Jefferson to Ogilvie, Aug. 4, 1811, in Looney, *Jefferson Papers*, 4: 73–74, and Bergh, ed., *Writings of Jefferson*, 13: 70–71.

12. Jefferson to Ogilvie, Aug. 4, 1811, in Looney, *Jefferson Papers*, 4: 73–74, and Bergh, ed., *Writings of Jefferson*, 13: 70–71.

13. Jefferson to Henry Dearborn, March 1, 1815, in Lipscomb and Bergh, eds., *Writings of Jefferson*, 14: 289. See also Jefferson to Dearborn, Aug. 14, 1811, ibid., 13: 73, discussed below. For a different interpretation of these letters, see Brian Steele, "Thomas Jefferson, Coercion, and the Limits of Harmonious Union," *Journal of Southern History* 74 (Nov. 2008): 823–854, at 831, 835. For Massachusetts' peace feelers to the British before the end of the war, see J.S. Martell, "A Sidelight on Federalist Strategy during the War of 1812," *American Historical Review* 43 (1938): 553–566.

14. Jefferson to General Henry Dearborn, Aug. 14, 1811, in Albert E. Bergh, ed., *Writings of Thomas Jefferson*, 20 vols. (Washington, D.C.: Thomas Jefferson Memorial Association, 1907), 13: 73–74. In general, see George Athan Billias, *Elbridge Gerry: Founding Father and Republican Statesman* (New York: McGraw-Hill, 1976).

15. Jefferson to General Henry Dearborn, Aug. 14, 1811, in Albert E. Bergh, ed., *Writings of Thomas Jefferson*, 13:73.

16. Jefferson to General Henry Dearborn, Aug. 14, 1811, in Albert E. Bergh, ed., *Writings of Thomas Jefferson*, 13:73.

17. Jefferson to Dearborn, Aug. 14, 1811, in Looney, ed., *Jefferson Papers*, 4: 83. I have modified some of the punctuation to make it more readable.

18. For example, see Jefferson to William Short, Nov. 24, 1791, in Boyd, ed., *Jefferson Papers*, 22: 330–331; and Arthur Scherr, *Thomas Jefferson's Haitian Policy: Myths and Realities* (Lanham, Md.: Lexington Books, 2011), 30.

19. Jefferson to Dearborn, Aug. 14, 1811, ibid., 83 (quotation). For Steele's view (mimicking Onuf's thesis) that Jefferson favored some kind of armed invasion of Massachusetts, see "Jefferson, Coercion, and the Limits of Harmonious Union, " *Journal of Southern History* 74, no. 4 (Nov. 2008): 823–854, esp. 847–48.

20. See Sheidley, *Sectional Nationalism*; Kevin M. Gammon, "Escaping 'Mr. Jefferson's Plan of Destruction': New England Federalists and the Idea of a Northern Confederacy, 1803–1804," *Journal of the Early Republic* 21 (2001): 413–443.

21. Jefferson to General Henry Dearborn, Aug. 14, 1811, in Bergh, ed., *Writings*, 13: 73.

22. Jefferson to General Henry Dearborn, Aug. 14, 1811, in Bergh, ed., *Writings*, 13: 73. Jefferson said similar things about Federalist intentions during the Quasi-War with France in 1798, when the Federalist Congress passed such laws repressing internal dissent as the Sedition Act, the Alien Acts, and the Naturalization Act. He wrote, "At present the war hawks talk of septembrizing, Deportation, and the examples for quelling sedition set by the French Executive. All the firmness of the human mind is now in a state of requisition." Jefferson to James Madison, April 26, 1798, Jefferson Papers, Library of Congress. With reference to the French Revolution, "Septembrizing" probably alluded to the *coup* of Fructidor (the French Revolutionary calendar's word for the month of September) 1797, when Napoleon's Army voided the election of anti–Directory members of the legislature, driving them from the chambers. Or, it may have referred to the September Massacres in 1792, when radical French crowds dragged royalists and refractory Roman Catholic clergy from the Paris jails and summarily executed them. Ironically, in these cases, radical Jacobins rather than conservative royalists committed the violence.

23. Ibid.

24. Jefferson to Benjamin Rush, August 17, 1811, in Looney, ed., *Jefferson Papers: Retirement Series*, 4: 87–88.

25. Ibid. Rush died on April 9, 1813, thirteen years before Jefferson.

26. Elbridge Gerry to Henry Dearborn, Sept. 2, 1811, Dearborn Papers, Maine Historical Society, quoted in Looney, ed., *Papers of Thomas Jefferson: Retirement Series* (Princeton, 2007), 4: 84n. Jefferson to Dearborn, Aug. 14, 1811, is also printed in Looney, ed., *Jefferson Papers*, 4: 82–84. (Dearborn forwarded to Gerry the letter that Jefferson wrote him.)

27. Ibid.

28. Jefferson to Horatio G. Spafford, March 17, 1814, in Looney, ed., *Jefferson Papers*, 7: 248. For Spafford's life, see Julian P. Boyd, "Horatio Gates Spafford," in *Proceedings of the American Antiquarian Society* 51, no. 2 (Oct. 1941): 279–350.

29. Horatio G. Spafford to Jefferson, Dec. 17, 1813, in Looney, *Jefferson Papers*, 7: 57–58. On British atrocities in Dartmoor Prison, see Robin F.A. Fabel, "Self-Help in Dartmoor: Black and White Prisoners in the War of 1812," *Journal of the Early Republic*, 9, no. 2 (Summer 1989): 165–190.

30. Jefferson to Horatio G. Spafford, March 17, 1814, in Looney, ed., *Jefferson Papers*, 7: 248.

31. Jefferson to Horatio G. Spafford, March 17, 1814, in Looney, ed., *Jefferson Papers*, 7: 248.

32. Jefferson to Horatio G. Spafford, March 17, 1814, in Looney, ed., *Jefferson Papers*, 7: 249. For an illuminating history of Virginia's legal profession, see Anthony G. Roeber, *Faithful Magistrates and Republican Lawyers: Creators of Virginia Legal Culture, 1680–1810* (Chapel Hill: University of North Carolina Press, 1981).

33. Ibid., 249. My italics.

34. I obtained these references from the *Oxford English Dictionary* (online edition), s.v., "unsophisticated."

35. This interpretation of Jefferson's thought is far from original. Drew McCoy, *The Elusive Republic: Political Economy in Jeffersonian America* (Chapel Hill: University of North Carolina Press, 1980) is currently the standard work on this topic.

36. Jefferson to François de Marbois, June 14, 1817, in Peterson, ed., *Writings*, 1410.

Chapter 17

1. For payment of the excises, including the carriage tax, by each state, see *American State Papers: Class Three, Finance, Volume One* (Washington, D.C.: Gales and Seaton, 1832–1861).

2. On the "Mediterranean Fund," see Davis R. Dewey, *Financial History if the United States* (11th edn.; New York: Longmans, 1931), 121–122.

3. Jefferson to Benjamin Stoddert, Feb. 18, 1809, Ford, ed., *Works of Jefferson*, 11: 98–99.

4. Jefferson to Thomas Mann Randolph, Jr., Nov. 16, 1792, in Boyd et al, eds., *Papers of Jefferson*, 24: 623.

5. Jefferson to Randolph, March 3, 1793, *ibid.*, 25: 314. See Eugene R. Sheridan, "Thomas Jefferson and the Giles Resolutions," *William and Mary Quarterly*, 49 (Oct. 1992): 589–608, for a detailed examination of Jefferson's role in framing the resolutions.

6. Garrett Ward Sheldon, *The Political Philosophy of Thomas Jefferson* (Baltimore: Johns Hopkins University Press, 1991), 70, 82, 84, 67–72, 143–144; Adrienne Koch, *The Philosophy of Thomas Jefferson* (New York: Quadrangle Books, 1962), 162.

7. Jefferson to Levi Lincoln, July 11, 1801, in Lipscomb and Bergh, eds., *Writings of Jefferson*, 10: 264. The term "Essex Junto" is most often associated with Jefferson because it is attributed to him in Henry Adams' *History*, but it is possible that he picked up the term from President John Adams, under whom he served as vice-president from 1797–1801. According to Timothy Pickering, Adams employed the term in a derogatory fashion in talking with him in January 1797 after his narrow victory over Jefferson for the presidency. Adams complained about the "Essex Junto" as "some influential men in Massachusetts, who instead of zealously promoting were at best but *lukewarm* in regard to his election." Timothy Pickering Memoranda, in Timothy Pickering Papers, Massachusetts Historical Society, vol. 51, page 324 (Available on microfilm, with reel numbers corresponding to volume numbers). However, it is likely that John Hancock originated the term in referring to his political opponents in the 1788 gubernatorial election in Massachusetts. The best discussion of this alleged late eighteenth-century conspiratorial faction, David H. Fischer, "The Myth of the Essex Junto," *William and Mary Quarterly*, 3d ser., 21 (April 1964): 191–235, convincingly argues that the Essex Junto as an organized, unified body of extremist, anti-democratic disunionists in Massachusetts did not exist.

8. Levi Lincoln to Jefferson, July 24, 1802, Oberg, ed., *Jefferson Papers*, 38: 125. (The online version of the Jefferson Papers at the Library of Congress at "American Memory" dates this letter July 25, 1802.) See also Jeffrey L. Pasley, *'The Tyranny of Printers': Newspaper Politics in the Early American Republic* (Charlottesville: University Press of Virginia, 2001), 204.

9. Levi Lincoln to Jefferson, July 28, 1801, Oberg, ed., *Jefferson Papers*, 34: 659–61.

10. Jefferson to John Tyler, May 26, 1810, in Peterson, *Writings*, 1226. Jean M. Yarbrough emphasizes the originality of Jefferson's ward theories in her article, "Republicanism Reconsidered: Thoughts on the Foundation and Preservation of the American Republic," *Review of Politics* 41 (Jan. 1979): 61–95, and elsewhere.

11. Jefferson to John Adams, Oct. 28, 1813, in Merrill D. Peterson, ed., *Thomas Jefferson: Writings* (New York, 1984), 1308; Jefferson to John Tyler, May 26, 1810, *ibid.*, 1226–27. Cf. "A Bill for the More General Diffusion of Knowledge," *ibid.*, 365–73. Garrett Ward Sheldon, *Political Philosophy of Jefferson*, 68n.-69n., mistakenly takes Jefferson's statements in his letter to Adams at face value. He assumes that Jefferson's *Notes on Virginia*'s discussion of the local administration of charity and outdoor relief was a hypothetical proposal, to be eventually implemented by the creation of wards, but Jefferson was actually writing about how Virginia's parishes (counties) took care of their poor *at that time*.

12. Jefferson to Adams, Oct. 28, 1813, in Peterson, ed., *Jefferson: Writings*, 1308.

13. *Ibid.* The text of this letter, along with the rest of the significant correspondence between Adams and Jefferson, may conveniently be found in Lester J. Cappon, ed., *Adams-Jefferson Letters* (2 vols., Chapel Hill: University of North Carolina Press, 1959), 2: 390 (continuous pagination).

14. For Jefferson's comments in the *Autobiography*, written in 1821, which were virtually identical to those in his letter to Adams eight years earlier, see Peterson, ed., *Writings*, 32.

15. The most recent full-scale study of John Adams' political thought is C. Bradley Thompson's admiring *John Adams and the Spirit of Liberty* (Lawrence: University Press of Kansas, 1998).

16. Jefferson to John Adams, Oct. 28, 1813, in Peterson, ed., *Thomas Jefferson: Writings*, 1305. Joseph J. Ellis, *Passionate Sage: The Character and Legacy of John Adams* (New York: Knopf, 1993), 131–136.

17. Jefferson to John Adams, Oct. 28, 1813, in Peterson, ed., *Thomas Jefferson: Writings*, 1305–1306.

18. John Adams to Jefferson, June 14, 1813, in Cappon, ed., *Adams-Jefferson Letters*, 2: 330. Adams had learned about Republican plans to call a constitutional convention when Jefferson's letter to Joseph Priestley of March 21, 1801 (which also criticized Adams's conduct as president) was published in England in 1813. Jefferson to Priestley, March 21, 1801, in Peterson, *Writings*, 1085–86; Jefferson to Adams, June 15, 1813, Cappon, ed., *Adams-Jefferson Letters*, 333. On the electoral crisis of 1800–1801, see Dumas Malone, *Jefferson and the Ordeal of Liberty* (Boston: Little, Brown, 1962), 494–506, and Malone, *Jefferson the President: First Term, 1801–1805* (Boston: Little, Brown, 1970), 5–16.

19. Jefferson to John Adams, Oct. 28, 1813, in Peterson, ed., *Thomas Jefferson: Writings*, 1306. Numerous examples occur in Adams's *Defence* of his fear that the propertyless would take advantage of every opportunity to despoil the property of the rich. His chapter, "Marchamont Nedham," *Works*, VI, warns that if the poor possessed the vote they would use it to seize the property of the wealthy.

20. Adams considered private property sacrosanct: "The moment the idea is admitted into society that property is not as sacred as the laws of God, and that there is not a force of law and public justice to protect it, anarchy and tyranny commence." "Marchamont Nedham," *Defence*, in *Works*, VI, quoted in George A. Peak, ed., *The Political Writings of John Adams: Representative Selections* (Indianapolis, 1954), 148. With his enormous wealth in land, crops, and slaves, Jefferson would have little reason to disagree with this philosophy.

21. Jefferson to John Adams, Oct. 28, 1813, in Peterson, ed., *Thomas Jefferson: Writings*, 1307.

22. Jefferson to Adams, Oct. 28, 1813, *ibid.*, 1307. For the unstable financial situation of the Massachusetts clergy because of paper money inflation there during the eighteenth century and their reliance on their congregants' voluntary contributions despite government support, see Stephen Botein, "Income and Ideology: Harvard-Trained Clergymen in the Eighteenth Century," *Eighteenth-Century Studies* 13, no. 4 (Summer, 1980): 396–413.

23. Virginia Constitution of 1776, in Francis Newton Thorpe, ed., *Federal and State Constitutions* (7 vols., Washington: Government Printing Office, 1909), 7: 3817–18. Virginia was merely following a policy of clerical disbarment that had been in effect in England with respect to the House of Commons since 1642, and was thereafter instituted in thirteen other state legislatures, including six where the Anglican Church had been established before the Revolution. The motive of clerical exclusion from political office was to uphold the primacy of the secular state, rather than destroy existing religious hierarchies. See William M. Hogue, "The Civil Disability of Ministers of Religion in State Constitutions," *Journal of Church and State* 36 (Spring 1994): 329–55, and Daniel L. Dreisbach, "The Constitution's Forgotten Religion Clause: Reflections on the Article VI Religious Test Ban," *ibid.*, 38 (Spring 1996): 261–295.

24. See Jefferson to Kercheval, July 12, 1816, Peterson, *Writings*, 1398–99.

25. . Elizabeth W. Marvick, "Jefferson's Personality and his Politics," *Psychohistory Review*, 25 (1997), 127–163; Carl A. Binger, *Thomas Jefferson: A Well-Tempered Mind* (New York: Norton, 1970).

26. Jefferson to Adams, Oct. 28, 1813, in Peterson, ed., *Writings*, 1307.

27. John Adams to Jefferson, Nov. 15, 1813, in Lester J. Cappon, ed., *Adams-Jefferson Letters* (Chapel Hill: University of North Carolina Press, 1988), 402.

28. Jefferson to Adams, Oct. 28, 1813, in Peterson, ed.,

Writings, 1307. For Jefferson's role in abolishing entail and primogeniture, see Holly Brewer, "Entailing Aristocracy in Colonial Virginia: 'Ancient Feudal Restraints' and Revolutionary Reform," *William and Mary Quarterly*, 54 (1997), 307–346. George Lee Haskins, "The Beginnings of Partible Inheritance in the American Colonies," *Yale Law Journal* 51, no. 8 (June 1942): 1280–1315, esp. 1281 note 6, and 1286. See also Richard B. Morris, "Primogeniture and Entailed Estates in America," *Columbia Law Review* 27 (1927): 24; Morris, *Studies in the History of American Law* (New York: Columbia University Press, 1930), 102; and Marshall D. Harris, *Origin of the Land Tenure System in the United States* (Ames, Iowa: Iowa State University Press, 1953), 373–375.

29. Jefferson to Adams, Oct. 28, 1813, in Peterson, ed., *Writings*, 1307.

30. Harold Hellenbrand, *The Unfinished Revolution: Education and Politics in the Thought of Thomas Jefferson* (Newark: University of Delaware Press, 1990), 98 (first and second quotes), 100 (third quote), 103 (fourth quote).

31. Jefferson to William Short, January 3, 1793, and Jefferson to William S. Smith, Nov. 13, 1787, widely available online.

32. Jefferson to John Tyler, May 26, 1810, Koch and Peden, eds., *Life and Selected Writings*, 605.

33. For Jefferson's use of the term "selfish minority," see Jefferson to Joseph C. Cabell, Feb. 2, 1816, *Life and Selected Writings*, 661.

34. Jefferson to Joseph C. Cabell, Feb. 2, 1816, in Adrienne Koch and William Peden, eds., *The Life and Selected Writings of Thomas Jefferson* (New York: Modern Library, 1944), 660–662.

35. Jefferson to Joseph C. Cabell, Dec. 25, 1820, Jefferson Papers, Library of Congress.

36. Jefferson to Joseph C. Cabell, 22 Jan. 1820, in *Works of Thomas Jefferson*, ed. Paul L. Ford, 12 vols. (New York: Putnam, 1904–5), 12:155.

37. Peterson, *Jefferson and the New Nation*, 977, 979, 984–985.

38. Jefferson to Lafayette, January 16, 1825, in Lipscomb and Bergh, eds., *Writings of Jefferson*, 19: 281.

39. On Jefferson's preference for New England and British scholars to teach at his university, see Malone, *Sage of Monticello*, chapters 27 and 28, passim.

40. The most convenient source for finding out the colleges that congressional representatives attended is the *Biographical Directory of Congress*.

41. Jefferson to Charles Yancey, January 6, 1816, in Looney, ed., *Jefferson Papers: Retirement Series*, 9: 330–331. I have retained Jefferson's original spelling and punctuation, except for capitalizing the beginning of sentences, which he usually did not capitalize.

42. Jefferson to Charles Yancey, January 6, 1816, in Looney, ed., *Jefferson Papers: Retirement Series*, 9: 331.

43. Jefferson to Joseph Cabell, Dec. 25, 1820, Jefferson Papers, Library of Congress. See also Dumas Malone, *Sage of Monticello*, vol. 6 of *Jefferson and His Time* (Boston: Little, Brown, 1981), 387.

Chapter 18

1. See Leonard L. Richards, *The Slave Power* (New York: Oxford University Press, 2002).

2. Jefferson to William Short, Oct. 19, 1822, Jefferson Papers, Library of Congress. (Punctuation has been modernized.) As president, Jefferson sought to appease New England merchants and attach them to his Democratic-Republican Party. He supported drawbacks of duties on the

re-export of colonial goods and the exemption of domestic shipping from lighthouse fees and other taxes. Brian W. Schoen, "Calculating the Price of Union: Republican Economic Nationalism and the Origins of Southern Sectionalism, 1790–1828," *Journal of the Early Republic* 23 (Summer 2003): 180–83. Moreover, he regarded his Embargo Act as a way to protect the vessels of New Englanders and other Americans from confiscation by the British and French, and their seamen from British impressment. He attempted to overlook their hatred for this policy, which cut into their profits. Burton Spivak, *Jefferson's English Crisis* (Charlottesville: University Press of Virginia, 1979), *passim*.

3. Jefferson to Joseph C. Cabell, Feb. 2, 1816, in Adrienne Koch and William Peden, eds., *Life and Selected Writings of Thomas Jefferson* (New York: Modern Library, 1944), 660–662.

4. Jefferson to Joseph C. Cabell, Feb. 2, 1816, in Peterson, ed., *Thomas Jefferson: Writings*, 1380–81. My italics. There are several typographical errors in this widely-available version of the letter, when compared with the original in Jefferson Papers, Library of Congress.

5. Jefferson to John Taylor of Caroline, Feb. 14, 1821, "Jefferson Papers," *Collections of the Massachusetts Historical Society*, 7th Series, Vol. I [Vol. 61] (1900): 306.

6. Jefferson to Cabell, Feb. 2, 1816, Peterson, ed., *Writings*, 1381.

7. Jefferson to Cabell, Feb. 2, 1816, in Koch and Peden, *Life and Selected Writings*, 662.

8. Jefferson to John Taylor of Caroline, May 28, 1816, *ibid.*, 670.

9. Jefferson to John Taylor of Caroline, May 28, 1816, *ibid.*, 670. Jefferson was also possibly thinking of Pennsylvania, which was in the throes of a Presbyterian religious revival which he found odious. Jefferson to Dr. Thomas Cooper, Nov. 2, 1822, in Peterson, ed., *Writings*, 1464. He blamed "Presbyterian" fanaticism for hindering the deist Thomas Cooper's appointment to the faculty of the University of Virginia and blocking increased state funding to the fledgling institution, warning that the "priests [*sic*] of the different religious sects ... pant to reestablish *by law* that holy inquisition, which they can now only infuse into *public opinion*." Jefferson to William Short, April 13, 1820, in Dickinson W. Adams, ed., *Jefferson's Extracts from the Gospels* (Princeton: Princeton University Press, 1983), 392–93.

10. Jefferson to William H. Crawford, June 20, 1816, in Lipscomb and Bergh, ed., *Writings of Jefferson*, 15: 28.

11. Ibid., 29.

12. David Waldstreicher, *Slavery's Constitution: From Revolution to Ratification* (New York: Hill and Wang, 2009). See Robin Einhorn, *American Taxation, American Slavery* (Chicago, 2006); Bertram Wyatt-Brown, *Southern Honor* (New York, 1982); Eugene D. Genovese, "Yeomen Farmers in a Slaveholders' Democracy," *Agricultural History* 49, no. 2 (Spring 1975): 331–342; and Robert McColley, *Slavery in Jeffersonian Virginia* (Urbana, Ill., 1964), for the prevalence of class consciousness and latent class conflict in the South in the 1790s. McColley notes that during the 1790s, Virginia congressmen supported a direct tax on land and slaves to appease their non-slaveholding constituents. The best discussion of the diverse tax structures and preferences of the Southern, Eastern, and Middle States is probably H. James Henderson, "Taxation and Political Culture: Massachusetts and Virginia, 1760–1800," *William and Mary Quarterly*, 47, no. 1(January 1990): 90–114. Henderson concludes that, because slaveholders were relatively heavily-taxed by state poll taxes on their slaves of both sexes, the wealthy paid a greater proportion of taxes in Virginia than in Massachusetts, where the poor and middle classes were more heavily burdened than in Virginia. See also Robert A. Becker, *Revolution, Reform, and the Politics of American Taxation, 1763–1783* (Baton Rouge: Louisiana State University Press, 1980).

13. The best study of Massachusetts tax system during the 1780s and how it adversely affected the small towns is Van Beck Hall, *Politics Without Parties: Massachusetts, 1780–1791* (Pittsburgh: University of Pittsburgh Press, 1972).

14. Jefferson to Madison, June 7, 1798, in Oberg, ed., *Jefferson Papers*, 30: 394.

15. Jefferson to Pierre Samuel Du Pont de Nemours, April 15, 1811, in J. Jefferson Looney, ed., *Papers of Thomas Jefferson: Retirement Series* (Princeton: Princeton University Press, 2006), 3: 559–60, (quotation). I have modernized Jefferson's spelling and punctuation.

16. Ibid., 560.

17. Jefferson to Du Pont, April 15, 1811, ibid., 560 (quotation). In April 1802, Congress, following a recommendation in Jefferson's First Annual Message to Congress, repealed all the excise laws of the Federalist administrations of Washington and Adams.

18. Jefferson to Du Pont, April 15, 1811, ibid., 560 (quotation).

19. Ibid., 560 (quotation).

20. It is likely that Jefferson was suffering from painful rheumatism when he wrote this letter to Du Pont. This may have contributed to his lapse of memory in forgetting that the salt tax was repealed in 1807. In July 1811, he wrote to William Duane, "The powers of life have declined with me more in the last six months than in as many preceding years. A rheumatic indisposition, under which your letter found me, has caused this delay in acknowledging its receipt, and in the expressions of regret that I had inadvertently said or done anything which had given you uneasiness." Jefferson to William Duane, July 25, 1811, in Lipscomb and Bergh, eds., *Writings of Jefferson*, 13: 67.

21. Salt was taxed at six cents per bushel in the first tariff act, passed July 4, 1789. Richard Peters, ed., *Public Statutes at Large of the United States* (Boston: Little and Brown, 1850), 1: 2S.

22. Henry Adams, *History of the United States during the Administrations of Thomas Jefferson* (1901; reprinted, New York: Library of America, 1986), 729.

23. Jefferson's Sixth Annual Message to Congress, Dec. 2, 1806, in Peterson, *Jefferson: Writings*, 529.

24. The text of the law repealing the salt tax, which passed March 3, 1807, "Repeal of Duties on Salt, duties on Merchandises," is in *U.S. Statutes at Large*, 2: 436. On the debate in Congress over the repeal of the salt tax, in which Federalists seeking to embarrass Jefferson's administration joined Randolph's anti–Administration "Quid" faction of state's rights Republicans, see Adams, *History of the United States during the Administration of Thomas Jefferson*, 729.

25. Jefferson to Du Pont, April 15, 1811, Looney, ed., *Jefferson Papers: Retirement*, 3: 560 (quotation). I have modernized some spelling and punctuation.

26. Jefferson to William H. Crawford, June 20, 1816, in Lipscomb and Bergh, ed., *Writings of Jefferson*, 15: 29.

27. For the common belief that the Union was not inviolable, which persisted until Andrew Jackson's Force Bill in 1832, see Kenneth Stampp, "The Concept of a Perpetual Union," *Journal of American History* 65 (June 1978): 5–33.

28. Jefferson to Crawford, June 20, 1816, Lipscomb and Bergh, ed., *Writings of Jefferson*, 14: 30. Jefferson's conviction that the "direct trade" in domestically produced goods, which served the nation's farmers, was more intrinsically "republican" than the New Englanders' "carrying trade" of

tropical colonial produce to Europe is a major theme of Burton W. Spivak's *Jefferson's English Crisis* (Charlottesville, 1979).

29. Jefferson to John Adams, May 17, 1818, in Ford, ed., *Works of Thomas Jefferson*, 12: 94. On Kentuckians' affinity for revivalism at this time, see Dickson D. Bruce, *And They All Sang Hallelujah: Plain-Folk Camp-Meeting Religion, 1800–1845* (Knoxville: University of Tennessee Press, 1974), and Christine L. Heyrman, *Southern Cross: The Beginnings of the Bible Belt* (New York: Knopf, 1997).

30. Adams to Joseph Hawley, Aug.21, 1776, in Charles Francis Adams, ed., *Works of John Adams* (10 vols., Boston: Little, Brown, 1850–1856), 9: 434, quoted in Andy Trees, "John Adams and the Problem of Virtue," *Journal of the Early Republic*, 21 (Fall 2001): 393–412, 403. On Adams's idealization of New England's colonial charters, especially Connecticut's, and his swift disillusionment after 1776, when he grew increasingly alarmed by the "leveling" propensities of Massachusetts' citizens, see Timothy H. Breen, "John Adams' Fight Against Innovation in the New England Constitution: 1776," *New England Quarterly* 40 (Dec. 1967): 501–520.

31. Jefferson to Taylor, May 28, 1816, in *Life and Selected Writings*, 670.

32. Jefferson to John Cartwright, 5 June 1824, in Bergh, ed., *Writings of Jefferson*, 16: 46. Contrary to Michael P. Zuckert's observation, in this letter to Cartwright Jefferson did not mention the Massachusetts town meeting as a source for his idea of active, participatory local governments. He claimed his inspiration was the old Saxon "hundreds" of medieval England. See Zuckert, "Founder of the Natural Rights Republic," in Thomas S. Engeman, ed., *Thomas Jefferson and the Politics of Nature* (Notre Dame: University of Notre Dame Press, 2000), 11–58, at 49. On Jefferson's desire to emulate the semi-mythical mass meeting of English Saxons during the Middle Ages, the *Witanagemot*, which he considered a prototype for representative democracy, see H. Trevor Colbourn, "Thomas Jefferson's Use of the Past," *William and Mary Quarterly* 15 (1958): 56–70, and Colbourn, *The Lamp of Experience: Whig History and the Intellectual Origins of the American Revolution* (Chapel Hill: University of North Carolina Press, 1965).

33. Jefferson to Cartwright, 5 June 1824, in Bergh, ed., *Writings of Jefferson*, 16: 46. In 1787, while disapproving his friend Madison's proposal that the new Constitution grant Congress the right to veto state laws it found objectionable or "oppressive," Jefferson suggested "appeal from the state judicatures to a federal court, in all cases where the act of Confederation [*sic*] controuled the question." Jefferson to Madison, 20 June 1787, Robert A. Rutland, ed., *Papers of James Madison* 10: 64, quoted in Shlomo Slonim, "Securing States' Interests at the 1787 Constitutional Convention: A Reassessment," *Studies in American Political Development* 14.1 (Spring 2000): 1–14, at 7–8n. See also Malone, *Jefferson and the Ordeal of Liberty*, 397–98.

34. In his *Defence of the Constitutions of Government of the United States*, published in 1787–1788, Adams made clear his belief that corruptible individuals required restraint by "virtuous" institutions. As he put it, "The best republics will be virtuous and have been so; but we may hazard a conjecture, that the virtues have been the effect of the well-ordered constitution, rather than the cause." *Defence*, quoted in Ellis, *Passionate Sage*, 149.

35. Jefferson to Adams, Oct. 28, 1813, in Peterson, *Writings*, 1309. As Jefferson wrote to John Taylor of Caroline in his famous letter of May 28, 1816, he believed that most Virginians were so virtuous and law-abiding that, "I verily believe they would go on well with us under an absolute

monarch, while our present character remains, of order, industry and love of peace."

36. Apparently, Massachusetts farmers owned smaller plots of land, typically only about twenty acres, than Jefferson thought. See Bettye Hobbs Pruitt, "Self-Sufficiency and the Agricultural Economy of Eighteenth-Century Massachusetts," *William and Mary Quarterly*, 3d ser., 41 (July 1984): 333–64; Kenneth Lockridge, "Land, Population, and the Evolution of New England Society," *Past and Present* 39 (April 1968): 62–80; James A. Henretta, "Families and Farms: *Mentalité* in Pre-Industrial America," *William and Mary Quarterly* 35 (Jan. 1978): 3–32; Richard L. Bushman, "Family Security in the Transition from Farm to City, 1750–1850," *Journal of Family History* 6 (Fall 1981): 238–256; and Bushman, "Markets and Composite Farms in Early America," *William and Mary Quarterly* 55 (July 1998): 351–374.

37. Jefferson to John Adams, 24 January 1814, in Cappon, ed., *Adams-Jefferson Letters* (Chapel Hill: University of North Carolina Press, 1988), 424. On the persistence of a blood-related gentry oligarchy in Virginia politics into the 1840s, see Daniel P. Jordan, *Political Leadership in Jefferson's Virginia* (Charlottesville: University Press of Virginia, 1983), 210.

38. Jefferson to Taylor, May 28, 1816, in *Life and Selected Writings*, 672. Jefferson said something similar in his famous letter to John Adams, Oct. 28, 1813, quoted above.

39. Jefferson to Taylor, May 28, 1816, *ibid.* For earlier statements by Jefferson on the tenuity of republican virtue and the temptation to "corruption" among voters and legislators alike, see *Notes on Virginia*, Queries XIII and XV, in Peterson, ed., *Writings*, 246, 287.

40. Jefferson to Samuel Kercheval, July 12, 1816, in Merrill D. Peterson, ed., *The Portable Thomas Jefferson* (New York, 1975), 553–54 (My italics). Thomas Perkins Abernethy, a leading historian of the antebellum South, notes, "In this epistle the former President suggested many changes in the fundamental law of his state, including the introduction of the New England township plan for the administration of local government, equal representation based on white population, liberal suffrage, and the election of the governor, judges, jurors, and sheriffs by popular vote." Thomas P. Abernethy, *The South in the New Nation, 1789–1819* (Baton Rouge: Louisiana State University Press, 1961), 436.

41. Jefferson to Samuel Kercheval, Sept. 5, 1816, in Bergh, ed., *Writings of Jefferson*, 15: 72.

42. Jefferson to Samuel Kercheval, Sept. 5, 1816, in Bergh, ed., *Writings of Jefferson*, 15: 72–73, and Paul L. Ford, ed., *Works of Thomas Jefferson* (12 vols., New York: Putnam, 1904–1905), 12: 15–17n., a more accurate transcription.

43. In *Jefferson's Empire*, Onuf misreads this letter from Jefferson to Kercheval. He contends that Jefferson declared that Connecticut was a "foreign country" which it might be necessary to destroy for its disloyalty to republicanism. Actually, Jefferson was referring to the national government of the United States, and only by way of analogy, as "foreign," in its lack of authority over a state's local concerns. *Jefferson's Empire*, 121. Onuf's student Andy Trees similarly argues that the letter betrayed Jefferson's political intolerance and his conviction that New England constituted a pro-monarchical, "foreign state" that must be subdued. "Jefferson's vision of the coincidence of domestic and political tranquillity left no room for dissent," Trees asserts. "In the face of Federalist opposition, Jefferson's solution was to externalize all opposing voices, to recast the Federalist as foreigners…. At times, he even considered other states within the Union 'foreign.'" Andy Trees, "Private Correspondence for the Public Good: Thomas Jefferson to Elbridge

Gerry, 26 January 1799," *Virginia Magazine of History and Biography* 198 (2000): 217–254, quotation at 241.

44. Jefferson to William Short, Jan. 8, 1825, Thomas Jefferson Papers, Library of Congress. The letter is printed in Ford, ed., *Works of Jefferson*, 12: 394–95, and Bergh, ed., *Writings of Jefferson*, 16: 93. For Jefferson's purchase of *Defence* for his university library a few months before he died, which suggests that he did not consider its ideas dangerous to republicanism, see Jefferson to Cummings, Hilliard & Co., Invoice No. 3, Boston, Oct. 6, 1825, Thurlow-Berkeley Calendar, Thomas Jefferson Papers, University of Virginia, reel 10 (microfilm). Leonard W. Levy's influential study of cases of Jefferson's hostility to intellectual freedom claims that, as in refusing to select David Hume's pro-monarchical *History of England*, Jefferson would not purchase books for the University of Virginia if he disagreed with their contents. Levy, *Jefferson and Civil Liberties: The Darker Side* (Cambridge, Mass., 1963), 142–57. By Levy's logic, Jefferson's purchase of Adams' *Defence* reveals he actually sympathized with at least some of its views.

45. Jefferson's Second Library, Offered for Sale at Public Auction, Feb. 27, 1829, in Jefferson Papers, Library of Congress, Seventh Series, also available in published pamphlet form: *A Catalogue of the Extensive and Valuable Library of the Late President Jefferson … to be sold by Nathaniel Poor at Public Auction, 27 Feb. 1829* (1829; reprinted, Ypsilanti, Mich.: University Lithographers, 1944).

46. William Short to Jefferson, Dec. 18, 1824, Jefferson Papers, Library of Congress (online at American Memory). Robert Goodloe Harper had converted from being a Federalist to an Andrew Jackson supporter. He was author of *Reasons of a Plain Man: for preferring Gen. Jackson to Mr. Adams…*. (Baltimore, 1825).

47. William Short to Jefferson, Dec. 18, 1824, Jefferson Papers, Library of Congress (online at American Memory). Short was referring to Harper's five letters to Robert Walsh, Jr., editor of the Philadelphia *National Gazette*, dated August 1824 but published in December. The letters were widely republished, in such journals as the *New York Advertiser*, the *Salem Gazette*, and the *Trenton Federalist*. See also Livermore, *Twilight of Federalism*, 167. For Monroe and Jackson's views, see Monroe to Jackson, Dec. 14, 1816, in Stanislaus M. Hamilton, ed., *Writings of James Monroe* (7 vols.; New York: Putnam, 1898–1903), 5: 344–346, and Andrew Jackson to James Monroe, 6 Jan. 1817, in Harold D. Moser et al., eds., *The Papers of Andrew Jackson* (Knoxville: University of Tennessee Press, 1980–), 4: 81.

48. Short to Jefferson, Dec. 18, 1824, Jefferson Papers, Library of Congress.

49. Short to Jefferson, Dec. 18, 1824, Jefferson Papers. Spelling and punctuation in the original. "Praise God Barebones," also known as Praise-God Barbon, was a London merchant and a fanatical republican Baptist preacher who participated in the English Civil War. His radical Puritan congregational followers chose him as London's representative to Cromwell's short-lived unicameral parliament, the Nominated Assembly, from July-December 1653. On December 12, 1653, Cromwell's Army dissolved the ultraradical assembly and Cromwell ruled arbitrarily as Lord Protector from 1654–1658. Alluding to Barbon, conservatives and royalists often derisively called the assembly the "Barebones Parliament."

50. William Short to John Hartwell Cocke, Dec. 3, 1833, Cocke Family Papers, University of Virginia, quoted in Shackelford, *Jefferson's Adoptive Son*, 170–171. The details about Short in this paragraph rely on Shackelford, 170–174.

51. Adams, *Defence*, 1: 111. Catalogue of Jefferson's Second Library, Offered for Sale at Public Auction, Feb. 27,

1829, Jefferson Papers, Library of Congress, Series 7, Miscellaneous Bound Volumes ("American Memory Series," online). When they served as ministers abroad in 1787, Adams sent Jefferson one of the first copies of the *Defence*, printed in London. The original work, published by C. Dilly, was part of the collection Jefferson sold to the Library of Congress in 1815. E. Millicent Sowerby, ed., *Catalogue of the Library of Thomas Jefferson* (5 vols., Washington, 1952–1959), 3: 219. Contrary to the claims of several historians, Jefferson was not initially repelled by the ideas in Adams' *Defence* (written in 1786–1787), although he was hostile toward the later, pro-monarchical *Discourses on Davila* (1790–91). The most extreme statement in Adams's *Discourses on Davila* was in No. 32, in [Philadelphia] *Gazette of the United States*, April 27, 1791. He argued that human avarice and ambition made "hereditary succession" a more feasible form of government than those where violently competitive "frequent elections" took place. On *Discourses on Davila*, see John Ferling, *John Adams: A Life* (Knoxville, 1992), 307. Obviously, Jefferson read at least part of volume one of *Defence*, although some recent historians assert he denounced it later without reading it. Comprising part of his personal library when he died, it was sold at auction with the remainder of his last library in 1829. For a general discussion of the political affinities between Jefferson and Adams, see also Arthur Scherr, "John Adams and Thomas Jefferson's Constitutionalism in the 1780s: A Reappraisal," *Mid-America: An Historical Review*, 83 (Fall 2001): 215–282.

52. Recent historical works that emphasize Virginia voters' tendency to elect wealthy planters to office and to abjure political activity include Jordan, *Political Leadership in Jefferson's Virginia*, and especially Brent Tarter, *Grandees of Government: The Origins and Persistence of Undemocratic Government in Virginia* (Charlottesville: University of Virginia Press, 2013).

53. Jefferson to Short, Jan. 8, 1825, Jefferson Papers, Library of Congress. "Monocrat" was one of Jefferson's favorite words for Anglophile Federalists during the 1790s, which according to the *Oxford English Dictionary* was coined by him and which he used mostly during the 1790s.

54. Jean-Jacques Rousseau, *The Social Contract*, Book II, Chapter 4, in G. D. H. Cole, ed., *The Social Contract and Discourses by Jean-Jacques Rousseau* (New York: Dutton, 1950), 29.

Chapter 19

1. David Sehat, *Myth of American Religious Freedom* (New York: Oxford University Press, 2011), 56–57; Sidney E. Mead, *The Lively Experiment* (New York: Harper and Row, 1963), 52–54. For a depiction of Dwight as more rational and less hostile to Jefferson than most other scholars purvey, see Robert J. Imholt, "Timothy Dwight, Federalist Pope of Connecticut," *New England Quarterly*, 73 (Sept. 2000): 386–411.

2. Jonathan A. Wright, *Shapers of the Great Debate on Freedom of Religion* (Westport, 2005), 118; Snyder, "Foundations of Liberty: The Christian Republicanism of Timothy Dwight and Jedidiah Morse," 397 (quotation).

3. Jefferson to Wells and Lilly, April 1, 1818, in Peterson, ed., *Jefferson: Writings*, 1414. I have revised some of the punctuation for clarity.

4. Jefferson to John Adams, Jan. 22, 1821, in Lester J. Cappon, ed., *Adams-Jefferson Letters* (Chapel Hill: University of North Carolina Press, 1988), 569. On Adams's role at the 1820–21 constitutional convention, see Peter Shaw, *The Character of John Adams* (New York: Norton, 1977),

309, John R. Howe, Jr., *The Changing Political Thought of John Adams* (Princeton: Princeton University Press, 1966), 226–27; and Gilbert Chinard, *Honest John Adams* (rev. ed., Boston: Little, Brown, 1964), 341.

5. Adams to Jefferson, June 25, 1813, in Cappon, ed., *Adams-Jefferson Letters*, 334; Daniel Walker Howe, *The Unitarian Conscience: Harvard Moral Philosophy, 1805–1861* (Middletown, Conn.: Wesleyan University Press, 1988), 210. Adams was referring to *The General Repository and Review*. A quarterly founded by Andrews Norton, it was the mouthpiece for Boston Unitarianism from January 1812 to October 1813, when it folded. Frank L. Mott, *History of American Magazines, 1741–1850* (Cambridge, Mass.: Harvard University Press, 1966), 277–78. After Adams' death, Unitarians eulogized him as an example of well-developed human faculties. Howe, *Unitarian Conscience*, 210. Ambivalent toward the Unitarians in his final years, Adams admired some of their religious tenets. He insisted that other denominations tolerate them despite their "hypocritical," aggressive, "Roman catholick" tendencies. See Adams to Jedidiah Morse, May 15, 1815, quoted in Donald H. Stewart and George P. Clark, "Misanthrope or Humanitarian? John Adams in Retirement," *New England Quarterly* 28 (1955): 227, and in general, *ibid.*, 219–29. Despite all the attention that writers have bestowed on Adams lately, there is still no adequate work on his religious views. The best study, within its limited context, is John Witte, Jr., "'A Most Mild and Equitable Establishment of Religion': John Adams and the Massachusetts Experiment," *Journal of Church and State* 41, no. 2 (Spring 1999): 213–252. See also Robert B. Everett, "The Mature Religious Thought of John Adams," *Proceedings of the South Carolina Historical Association* (1966): 49–57, and Constance B. Schulz, "John Adams on 'the Best of All Possible Worlds,'" *Journal of the History of Ideas* 44 (1983): 561–77.

6. Adams to Jefferson, June 25, 1813, in Cappon, ed., *Adams-Jefferson Letters*, 334.

7. Jefferson to P. H. Wendover, March 13, 1815, in Albert E. Bergh, ed., *Writings of Thomas Jefferson*, 14: 283.

8. Jefferson to P. H. Wendover, March 13, 1815, in Albert E. Bergh, ed., *Writings of Thomas Jefferson*, 14: 283. For a fine account of the Congregational clergy of Massachusetts whom Jefferson castigated, see Peter S. Field, *Crisis of the Standing Order: Clerical Intellectuals and Cultural Authority in Massachusetts, 1780–1833* (Amherst: University of Massachusetts Press, 1998), See also Thomas E. Buckley, "The Religious Rhetoric of Thomas Jefferson," in Daniel L. Dreisbach et al., eds., *The Founders on God and Government* (Lanham, Md.: Rowman Lirttelfield, 2004), 53–82, 80 note 43. On Jefferson's conflict with John Holt Rice over Thomas Cooper's appointment to the University of Virginia faculty, see David E. Swift, "Thomas Jefferson, John Holt Rice and Education in Virginia, 1815–25," *Journal of Presbyterian History* 49 (1971): 32–58.

9. Jefferson to Horatio Gates Spafford, Jan. 10, 1816, in Paul L. Ford, ed., *Works of Thomas Jefferson* (New York, 1904–5), 10: 15; Jefferson to Thomas Ritchie, Jan. 21, 1816, Jefferson Papers, Library of Congress. Jefferson was especially alarmed by the program of nationwide missionary activities outlined by Lyman Beecher, chairman of the Presbyterian Committee of Supplies of the Education Society of the Connecticut, in such tracts as *An Address of the Charitable Society for the Education of Indigent Pious Young Men for the Ministry of the Gospel* (New Haven, 1814; Shaw and Shoemaker #30833), which Jefferson denounced in this letter to Spafford. The *Address of the Charitable Society* was also published as Tract No. 70 of the American Tract Society in 1815 by Beecher, bearing the title *On the Importance of*

Assisting Young Men of Piety and Talents in Obtaining an Education for the Gospel Ministry (New York: Dodge & Sayre, 1815; Andover: Flagg & Gould, 1816). See Benjamin Waterhouse's comments in his letter to Jefferson, Dec. 14, 1815, in Looney, ed., *Jefferson Papers: Retirement Series*, 9: 255–257.

10. Jefferson included the diatribe against Beecher and other evangelizing New Englanders, which he struck out of this letter to Spafford, as a passage in the letter to Thomas Ritchie, 21 Jan. 1816, printed by Ritchie anonymously in his newspaper, the *Richmond Enquirer*, 27 Jan. 1816. Dumas Malone, *Sage of Monticello*; vol. 6 of *Jefferson and His Time* (Boston: Little, Brown, 1981), 249n.

11. Jefferson to Dr. Thomas Cooper, 2 Nov. 1822, and Jefferson to the Rev. Jedidiah Morse, 6 March 1822, in Peterson, ed., *Jefferson: Writings*, 1463–65, 1454–58; Jefferson to Charles Clay, 29 Jan. 1815, Jefferson Papers, Library of Congress. Some scholars argue that for Presbyterians, the Second Great Awakening in Virginia was a rational affair. They used "Christian apologetics" in a logical manner to appeal to elite and "genteel" citizens rather than the lower classes. Reverend John Holt Rice, who denounced Thomas Cooper, thwarting Jefferson's desire to implement a pro-deist religious regimen at the University of Virginia, is depicted as a leader of these "rational" Awakeners. See Arthur Dicken Thomas, Jr., "Reasonable Revivalism: Presbyterian Evangelization of Educated Virginians, 1787–1837," *Journal of Presbyterian History* (August 1983): 316–34.

12. Mulder, *Controversial Spirit*, 166.

13. John Holt Rice to William McPheerson, Dec. 27, 1817, William McPheeters Presbyterian Church Collection (USA), Dept. of History, Montreat, North Carolina, cited ibid., 127.

14. Charles R. Keller, *The Second Great Awakening in Connecticut* (New Haven: Yale University Press, 1942), 42–44; Clifford E. Clark, Jr., *Henry Ward Beecher: Spokesman for Middle-Class America* (Urbana: University of Illinois Press, 1978).

15. Clark, *Beecher*, 8; see also James W. Fraser, *Pedagogue for God's Kingdom: Lyman Beecher and the Second Great Awakening* (Lanham, Md.: Rowman Littlefield, 1988).

16. James W. Fraser, "The Beginning of Theological Education at Andover," *Historical Journal of Massachusetts* 13 (June 1985): 101–116, 104.

17. Ibid.

18. Ibid., 105–106.

19. Ibid., 108. For Mason's attack on Jefferson in 1800, see Charles O. Lerche, Jr., "Jefferson and the Election of 1800: A Case Study in the Political Smear," *William and Mary Quarterly* 3rd ser., 5 (Oct. 1948): 467–491, esp. 472–473.

20. Fraser, "Theological Education," 108–109.

21. Ibid., 112.

22. For a list of the Charitable Society's most important officials, see Lyman Beecher, *Address of The Charitable Society for the Education of Indigent Pious Young Men, for the Ministry of the Gospel* (New Haven: n.p., 1814; Shaw and Shoemaker #30833), 27–28.

23. Jefferson to Horatio Gates Spafford, Jan. 10, 1816, Jefferson to Thomas Ritchie, Jan. 21, 1816, in Ford, ed., *Works of Jefferson*, 10: 15 and note; *Richmond Enquirer*, Jan. 27, 1816. See also Malone, *Sage of Monticello*, 249.

24. Lyman Beecher, *Address of The Charitable Society for the Education of Indigent Pious Young Men, for the Ministry of the Gospel* (New Haven, n.p.,1814), 7. Italics in original. The *Address* is available in *Early American Imprints: Second Series* (Shaw and Shoemaker #30833).

25. Ibid., 1–2.

26. Ibid., 3–4.

27. Jefferson to Horatio G. Spafford, January 10, 1816 [not sent], Jefferson Papers, Library of Congress, anonymously printed in *Richmond Enquirer*, January 27, 1816.

28. Jefferson to Horatio Gates Spafford, Jan. 10, 1816, in Ford, ed., *Works*, 9: 15 (unsent paragraph of the letter, which Jefferson mailed to Thomas Ritchie, editor of the *Richmond Enquirer*, which Ritchie published without specifically mentioning Jefferson as the author in the *Richmond Enquirer*, Jan. 27, 1816); Beecher, *Address of The Charitable Society*, 25 (Article 1 of the Constitution of the Charitable Society).

29. Beecher, *Address of The Charitable Society*, 5–6.

30. Ibid.

31. Ibid., 5n.

32. Ibid., 6.

33. Ibid., 6.

34. Ibid., 6.

35. Ibid., 9–10.

36. Ibid., 11.

37. Ibid.

38. Ibid., 25, 21.

39. Ibid., 12–13.

40. Ibid., 14.

41. Ibid., 14–15.

42. Ibid., 15–16. For Tapping Reeve's hostility to Jefferson, see the capsule biographies of Reeve in *American National Biography* and *Dictionary of American Biography*, and Dumas Malone, *Jefferson the President: Second Term* (Boston: Little, Brown, 1974), chap. 21.

43. Beecher, *Address of The Charitable Society*, 16.

44. Ibid., 16–18.

45. Ibid., 20. I am alluding to Nathan Hatch's influential works, *The Sacred Cause of Liberty: Republican Thought and the Millennium in Revolutionary New England* (New Haven: Yale University Press, 1977), and *The Democratization of American Christianity* (New Haven: Yale University Press, 1989).

46. Beecher, *Address*, 20.

47. Beecher, *Address of The Charitable Society*, 20. For Rush, see his "Thoughts Upon the Mode of Education Proper in a Republic" (1786), in Frederick Rudolph, ed., *Essays on Education in the Early Republic* (Cambridge, Mass.: Harvard University Press, 1965), 9–23.

48. Beecher, *Address*, 19.

49. Ibid., 19. For a recent discussion of Jefferson's liberal religious views and their reflection in his plans for the University of Virginia, see Arthur Scherr, "Thomas Jefferson versus the Historians: Christianity, Atheistic Morality, and the Afterlife," *Church History* 83, no. 1 (March 2014): 60–109.

50. Ibid., 19. In 1885, the U.S. population was about 60 million. Richard N. Current, et al., *American History : A Survey* (New York, 1961), Appendix, 905.

51. Beecher, *Address of The Charitable Society*, 19.

52. Ibid., 20.

53. Ibid., 21.

54. Ibid., 22.

55. Beecher, *Address of The Charitable Society*, 23.

56. Ibid., 24–25. See also Fred J. Hood, *Reformed America: The Middle and Southern States, 1783–1837* (Tuscaloosa: University of Alabama Press, 1980); Christopher Grasso, *A Speaking Aristocracy: Transforming Public Discourse in Eighteenth-Century Connecticut* (Chapel Hill: University of North Carolina Press, 1999).

57. Jefferson to Benjamin Waterhouse, Oct. 13, 1815, in Ford, ed., *Writings of Jefferson*, 9: 532.

58. Benjamin Waterhouse to Jefferson, Sept. 1, 1815, Looney, ed., *Jefferson Papers: Retirement Series*, 9: 4.

59. Ibid.

60. Jefferson to Benjamin, Waterhouse, Oct. 13, 1815, in Ford, ed., *Writings of Jefferson*, 9: 532, and J. Jefferson Looney, ed., *Jefferson Papers: Retirement Series*, 9: 78–79. "Cossac priests" was Cobbett's term for the Massachusetts clergy who praised Russian troops' occupation of Paris in 1814. Although "Brother Jonathan" later became a universal symbol for the United States, anticipating "Uncle Sam" later, Jefferson was probably referring to Cobbett's pseudonym, "Jonathan," in his *Address to the Clergy*. Ibid., 9: 6n. James T. Austin (1784–1870), author of a still-useful *Life of Elbridge Gerry* (1829), delivered *An Oration pronounced at Lexington, Mass., in commemoration of the independence of the United States of America and the Restoration of Peace* on July 4, 1815. John Holmes' speech was *An oration pronounced at Alfred [Maine], on the 4th of July 1815* (Boston, 1815).

61. Jefferson to Benjamin, Waterhouse, Oct. 13, 1815, in Ford, ed., *Writings of Jefferson*, 9: 532–533.

62. For Jefferson's admiration of the Indians' style of (non) government, see Jefferson to Francis W. Gilmer, June 7, 1816, in Ford, ed., *Works of Jefferson*, 11: 535.

63. Jefferson to George Logan, Oct. 15, 1815, in Lipscomb and Bergh, *Writings*, 14: 354; and Looney, ed., *Jefferson Papers: Retirement Series*, 9: 90–91. Logan believed that the U.S.' aggressive, expansionist acts (he probably had its policies toward Spain in mind) had aroused the hostility of the European monarchs and proved that republics could be as warlike as monarchies. He argued that, for purposes of self-defense, the U.S. should form alliances with Russia and Great Britain, whose peoples and leaders in varying degrees shared its ideals of freedom and representative government. Although many Republicans anticipated a renewed war with Great Britain, Logan said, "From [the British] we have not much of real injury to apprehend. For however blind and corrupt the ministry, the spirit of liberty diffused among the people; supported by many of the most enlightened men in that nation; will secure us from any wanton attack." George Logan to Jefferson, Aug. 16 and Oct. 21, 1815 (quotation), in Jefferson Papers, Library of Congress; and in Looney, ed., *Jefferson Papers: Retirement Series*, 8: 671, and 9: 109–111.

64. Jefferson to William Bentley, Dec. 28, 1815, in Lipscomb and Bergh, *Writings*, 14: 363.

65. Jedidiah Morse, *American Geography* (revised edition; London: John Stockdale, 1794), 497–498. Fortuitously, I discovered that Ebenezer Hazard's journal had earlier used the same words in criticizing Virginia by randomly searching the Internet. See Hugh Buckner Johnston, ed., "Journal of Ebenezer Hazard, 1777–1778," *North Carolina Historical Review* 36, no. 3 (July 1959): 358–381, 362 (quotation) and Ralph H. Brown, "The American Geographies of Jedidiah Morse," *Annals of the Association of American Geographers*, 31, no. 3 (Sept. 1941): 158–159, 161.

66. Jedidiah Morse, *American Geography* (revised edition; London: John Stockdale, 1794), 497–498.

67. Jedidiah Morse, *American Geography* (revised edition; London: John Stockdale, 1794), 497–498.

68. Jefferson to Benjamin Waterhouse, Oct. 13, 1815, in Ford, ed., *Writings of Jefferson*, 9: 533, and Looney, ed., *Jefferson Papers: Retirement Series*, 9: 78.

69. For Jefferson's later pessimism, describing women's proclivities toward religious fanaticism, see his famous letter to Thomas Cooper, Nov. 2, 1822, in Peterson, ed., *Jefferson: Writings*, 1463–64, further discussed below.

70. Jefferson to Horatio G. Spafford, January 10, 1816 [not sent], Jefferson Papers, Library of Congress, anonymously printed in *Richmond Enquirer*, January 27, 1816.

71. Jefferson's Introduction to *The Anas, 1791–1808*,

reprinted in Peterson, ed., *Jefferson: Writings*, 672. Jefferson's strange phrases were allusions to various pamphlets, rumors, and events that were taking place during the late 1790s, most of which concerned Federalist accusations that Republicans were violent Jacobins conspiring with the radical French revolutionary government to overthrow the republican regime in the United States. For instance, the term "bloody buoy" refers to the anti–French Revolutionary journalist William Cobbett's pamphlet, *The Bloody Buoy Thrown Out as a Warning to the Political Parties of all Nations*, (Philadelphia, 1796).

72. Jefferson to Benjamin Waterhouse, Oct. 13, 1815, in Ford, ed., *Writings of Jefferson*, 9: 532–533.

73. Jefferson to Dr. Benjamin Waterhouse, June 26, 1822, in Dickinson W. Adams, ed., *Jefferson's Extracts from the Gospels* (Princeton: Princeton University Press, 1983), 406.

74. Jefferson to Dr. Benjamin Waterhouse, June 26, 1822, in Dickinson W. Adams, ed., *Jefferson's Extracts from the Gospels* (Princeton: Princeton University Press, 1983), 406. In the Bible, "Aceldama" was a potter's field or burial-ground for foreigners, on land bought by the Jewish priests with the thirty pieces of silver they gave to Judas for betraying Jesus, after he returned it to them. Some transcriptions of Jefferson's letter to Waterhouse replace the obscure Aramaic term, "Aceldama," with the more readily understandable word, "slaughterhouse," although Jefferson did not use it here to refer to Christendom. In any case, Jefferson was implying that he considered Christianity responsible for the death of millions through its persecutions and religious wars. On the *Baker v. Fales* decision, see Conrad Edick Wright, "The Dedham Case Revisited," Massachusetts Historical Society, *Proceedings* 100 (1988): 15–39. For the declining number of Unitarians, see Richard E. Sykes, "The Changing Class Structure of Unitarian Parishes in Massachusetts, 1780–1880," *Review of Religious Research* 12 (Fall 1970): 26–34.

75. Jefferson to Waterhouse, June 26, 1822, in Adams, ed., *Jefferson's Extracts*, 406. During the quasi-war with France in 1798, for instance, Jefferson expressed suspicion of Pennsylvania Quakers' patriotism. He charged that the Quakers favored war with France despite their reputation for pacifism because they thought that it would help their Mother Country, England. "It seems to be well understood that their attachment to England is stronger than to their principles and their country," he asserted. "The revolution[ary] war was a first proof of this." Jefferson to Madison, March 29, 1798, Jefferson Papers, Library of Congress, and Oberg, ed., *Jefferson Papers*, 30: 228. Jefferson believed that the Quakers, obeying the dictates of their "Mother-society" in England, were Loyalists during the American Revolution. He thought that they supported Adams and the Federalists (the Anglophile Party) during the Wars of the French Revolution. See Jefferson to Madison, March 29, 1798, in Barbara B. Oberg, ed., *Papers of Thomas Jefferson*, 39 vols., in progress, Princeton, 1950–), 30: 228; Jefferson to William Baldwin, Jan. 19, 1810, in Dickinson W. Adams, ed., *Jefferson's Extracts from the Gospels* (Princeton, 1983), 345- 346 (quotation); and Jefferson to Marquis de Lafayette, May 14, 1817, in Peterson, ed., *Thomas Jefferson: Writings*, 1408. See also Kenneth W. Keller, *Rural Politics and the Collapse of Pennsylvania Federalism* (Philadelphia: American Philosophical Society, 1982) [*Transactions of the American Philosophical Society*, Vol. 72, Pt. 6].

Chapter 20

1. Jefferson to Benjamin Waterhouse, July 19, 1822, in Adams, ed., *Jefferson's Extracts from the Gospels*, 407. Spelling

and punctuation in the original. "Inestimable" means outstanding, priceless; excellent beyond measure. *Oxford English Dictionary*.

2. Jefferson to Timothy Pickering, Feb. 27, 1821, and Jefferson to George Thacher, January 26, 1824, Adams, ed., *Jefferson's Extracts*, 402–204, 414–415.

3. Jefferson to Horatio G. Spafford, January 10, 1816 [not sent], Jefferson Papers, Library of Congress, anonymously printed in *Richmond Enquirer*, January 27, 1816.

4. Jefferson to Dr. Thomas Cooper, Nov. 2, 1822, in Peterson, ed., *Jefferson: Writings*, 1463–64.

5. Ibid.

6. Jefferson to Thomas Cooper, Nov. 2, 1822, in Peterson, *Writings*, 1464, and in Thomas Jefferson Papers, Library of Congress (American Memory online). A careful examination of the manuscript reveals that Jefferson evidently wrote "mere earthly lover," although most transcriptions convey the text as "more earthly lover."

7. Jefferson to Jedediah Morse, March 6, 1822, Ford, ed., *Jefferson's Works*, 12: 222–227, 223 (quotation).

8. Jefferson to Madison, Feb. 25, 1822, in Ford, ed., *Jefferson's Works*, 12: 227n. Spelling in original.

9. Jefferson to Monroe, March 19, 1822, ibid., 228n.

10. Jefferson to John Adams, Jan. 22, 1821, in Cappon, ed., *Adams-Jefferson Letters*, 569. Jefferson was fond of neologisms, new words not yet incorporated into the dictionary. Jefferson to John Waldo, Aug. 16, 1813, and Jefferson to John Adams, Aug. 15, 1820, in Peterson, *Writings*, 1295–1300, 1442–1443. In 1821, "liberalism," in the sense of "the holding of liberal opinions in politics or theology," rather than a display of personal kindness ("liberality") or generosity, was such a neologism. The *OED* dates it from 1819. *Oxford English Dictionary*, 2nd edition, 8: 882.

11. On the Massachusetts constitution of 1821 and its expansion of the suffrage, see Chilton Williamson, *American Suffrage: From Property to Democracy, 1760–1860* (Princeton: Princeton University Press, 1960), 191–95. As Quincy's delegate to the convention of 1820–21, Adams persisted in his lifetime opposition to an expanded suffrage. *Ibid*. See also Ronald P. Formisano, *The Transformation of Political Culture: Massachusetts Parties, 1790s-1840s* (New York: Oxford University Press, 1983), 137, 141, 299; Harlow W. Sheidley, *Sectional Nationalism: Massachusetts Conservative Leaders and the Transformation of America, 1815–1836* (Boston: 1998), 35–36; and Alexander Keyssar, *The Right to Vote: The Contested History of Democracy in the United States* (New York, 2000), 1, 13, 407 n.38.

12. Jefferson to John Adams, Jan. 22, 1821, Jefferson Papers, Library of Congress. Richard K. Matthews, *The Radical Politics of Thomas Jefferson: A Revisionist View* (Lawrence, 1984); Joseph J. Ellis, *American Sphinx: The Character of Thomas Jefferson* (New York, 1997); Conor Cruise O'Brien, *The Long Affair: Thomas Jefferson and the French Revolution, 1785–1800* (Chicago, 1996).

13. Jefferson to Adams, May 5, 1817 (on Connecticut), and Jefferson to Adams, Nov. 25, 1816 (on the inevitability of a republican revolution in Britain), in Cappon, ed., *Adams-Jefferson Letters*, 517, 496. For Jefferson's enthusiasm for revolution in England as early as 1794, see Jefferson to Tench Coxe, 1 May 1794, in Boyd et al., ed., *Jefferson Papers*, 28: 67; Jefferson to Coxe, 1 June 1795, and Jefferson to William Branch Giles, 27 April 1795, in Boyd et al., ed., *Jefferson Papers*, 28: 373–74, 337. He said he would not strongly object even if the French Armies imposed republicanism on the British by conquest. See Jefferson to Peregrine Fitzhugh, Feb. 23, 1798, in Ford, ed., *Works of Jefferson*, 8: 378.

Chapter 21

1. Jefferson to John Holmes, April 22, 1820, Jefferson Papers, Library of Congress.

2. For this thesis, see Fehrenbacher, *Slaveholding Republic*, 264–265. For a recent article on Missourians' resentment of the attempts of Congress to prohibit slavery, depicting the residents of the "Show Me State" as rugged individualists intent on protecting their "natural right" to property, including property in slaves, see John Korasick, "The Concept of Liberty in Territorial Missouri, 1819," *Missouri Historical Review* 109, no. 3 (April 2015): 179–197.

3. Jefferson to John Holmes, April 22, 1820, Jefferson Papers, Library of Congress. In New England towns, freemanship meant the right of a town or city dweller to practice a particular trade or profession by gaining a license to do so, making him a "freeman of the town." Freemen of a town corporation were those who could practice various arts, trades, and other occupations, such as skilled mechanics, merchants, and shopkeepers. It is the second definition of "freeman" in *Oxford English Dictionary*: "a person (esp. a man) who possessed the freedom of a city, borough, company, guild, etc." See also, e.g., B. Katherine Brown, "Freemanship in Puritan Massachusetts," *American Historical Review* 59, no. 4 (July 1954): 865–883, and Bruce P. Stark, "Freemanship in Lebanon, Connecticut: A Case Study," *Connecticut History* 16 (Sept. 1975): 27–48. Unfortunately, the knowledge of American history has become so diluted that even some professional historians assume that Jefferson is referring to a freed slave ("freedman"), rather than a "Connecticut freeman," as, seeking to particularize the issue of states' rights, he specifically said.

4. Jefferson to John Holmes, April 22, 1820, Jefferson Papers, Library of Congress. At Maine's constitutional convention in 1819, Holmes successfully demanded the vote for free blacks in the new state. Matthew Mason, "The Maine and Missouri Crisis: Competing Priorities and Northern Slavery Politics in the Early Republic," *Journal of the Early Republic* 33 (Winter 2013): 680.

5. Jefferson to John Holmes, April 22, 1820, Jefferson Papers, Library of Congress.

6. Jefferson to John Holmes, April 22, 1820, Jefferson Papers, Library of Congress.

7. Glover Moore, *The Missouri Controversy, 1819–1821* (Lexington: University of Kentucky Press, 1953), 35.

8. See the entry, "Tallmadge, James," in *Dictionary of American Biography*.

9. Glyndon G. Van Deusen, *Thurlow Weed: Wizard of the Lobby* (Boston: Little, Brown, 1947), 27.

10. Paul J. Polgar, "'Whenever They Judge it Expedient': The Politics of Partisanship and Free Black Voting Rights in Early National New York," *American Nineteenth Century History* 12, no. 1 (March 2001): 1–23, 12. According to Robert Pierce Forbes, *The Missouri Compromise and its Aftermath: Slavery and the Meaning of America* (Chapel Hill, 2006), 72, on Jan. 17, 1820, the New York legislature unanimously instructed its congressmen to vote against the admission of any new slave states into the Union.

11. For black and white suffrage requirements, see New York State Constitution (1821), Article Two, Section One. In an effort to reduce the black electorate, Van Burenite Democrats in the convention, aware that blacks voted for Clintonians, imposed restrictions on black voters that did not apply to white males. Black men were required to own a substantial freehold estate in order to vote, but were exempt from taxation if they did not own this amount of real property: "No man of colour, unless he shall have been for three years a citizen of this state, and for one year next preceding any election, shall be seized and possessed of a freehold estate of the value of 250 dollars, and shall have paid tax thereon, shall be entitled to vote. And no person of colour shall be subject to direct taxation unless he shall be seized and possessed of such real estate as aforesaid." See also Polgar, 'The Politics of Partisanship and Free Black Voting Rights," *American Nineteenth Century History* 12, no. 1 (March 2001): 1–23; Dixon Ryan Fox, "The Negro Vote in Old New York," *Political Science Quarterly* 32, no. 2 (June 19197): 252–275; David N. Gellman, *Emancipating New York: The Politics of Slavery and Freedom, 1777–1827* (Baton Rouge: Louisiana State University Press, 2006), 207–214. Merrill D. Peterson, ed., *Democracy, Liberty, Property: The State Constitutional Conventions of the 1820s* (Indianapolis: Boobs-Merrill, 1965), 214–233, contains selections on the African American suffrage debate, but Tallmadge is not mentioned. For Tallmadge's antislavery speech, see *Proceedings of the New York Constitutional Convention of 1821* (New York, 1822), 167. New York's emancipation laws are confusing. The 1799 law freed all slave children born after July 4, 1799, but males would have to wait until they turned twenty-eight and females until they turned twenty-five. Those slaves in servitude before 1799 remained enslaved for life. In 1817, the law was changed to emancipate all slaves born before 1799 on July 4, 1827. Governor Daniel D. Tompkins proposed this law, reasoning that these slaves would be so old that they would have been a burden to their owners. (It is not clear whether, as in Virginia, former masters would be responsible for the well-being of elderly emancipated slaves.)

12. Glover Moore, *The Missouri Controversy, 1819–1821* (Lexington: University of Kentucky Press, 1953), remains the best account. A more recent, less detailed, sometimes humorously speculative study, Forbes, *The Missouri Compromise and its Aftermath*, is also useful. See also Don Fehrenbacher's insightful work, *The Slaveholding Republic: An Account of the United States Government's Relations to Slavery* (New York: Oxford University Press, 2001), 263–264.

13. John Adams to Jefferson, Nov. 23, 1819, Cappon, ed., *Adams-Jefferson Letters*, 548.

14. Jefferson to John Adams, Dec. 10, 1819, in Cappon, ed., *Adams-Jefferson Letters*, 548–549; and Lipscomb and Bergh, eds., *Writings*, 15: 232–233.

15. Jefferson to John Adams, Dec. 10, 1819, in Cappon, ed., *Adams-Jefferson Letters*, 548–549; Lipscomb and Bergh, eds., *Writings*, 15: 232–233. In a work often marred by inaccuracy, the popular author Joseph J. Ellis wrote misleadingly concerning this letter, "In his correspondence with Adams, Jefferson's initial reaction to what was being called the Missouri question was calm and assured. He expressed the hope that the issue would pass 'like waves in a storm pass under the ship.'" Ellis, *American Sphinx* (New York, 1997), 264, citing Cappon, *Adams-Jefferson Letters*, 2: 548–49. (Sadly, Ellis is quoting Adams's remarks in a letter of Dec. 21, 1819, not Jefferson's.) Peter Onuf similarly misreads Jefferson's reaction to Congressional rejection of Missouri's admission to the Union. He writes that, during the Missouri crisis, Jefferson never entertained the possibility that Missouri or Massachusetts might secede from the Union; that his only fear was of "consolidated," nationalist government spearheaded by Marshall's allegedly hyper-nationalist Supreme Court decisions. Onuf, *Jefferson's Empire*, 212 note 8.

16. Jefferson to John Adams, Dec. 10, 1819, in Cappon, ed., *Adams-Jefferson Letters*, 548–549; Lipscomb and Bergh, eds., *Writings*, 15: 232–233. Rufus King's speeches against slavery in Missouri began as a legalistic argument that the perpetuation of slavery would reduce the Union's ability to

defend itself against external aggressors and domestic rebellions, and ended as a crusade against the evils and immorality of slavery. Robert Ernst, *Rufus King: American Federalist* (Chapel Hill: University of North Carolina Press, 1967), 369–375; Robert Ernst, "Rufus King, Slavery, and the Missouri Crisis," *New-York Historical Society Quarterly* 46 (1962): 357–382; and Joseph L. Arbena, "Politics or Principle? Rufus King and the Opposition to Slavery, 1785–1825," *Essex Institute Historical Collections* 101 (1965): 56–77.

17. Jefferson to James Monroe, March 3, 1820, James Monroe Papers, Library of Congress, reel 7. For a brief biography of Ellery, see the *Biographical Directory of the American Congress,* available online. A more detailed account of the altercation between Rutledge and Ellery is in Elizabeth Cometti, "John Rutledge, Jr., Federalist," *Journal of Southern History* 13, no. 2 (May 1947): 186–219.

18. Jefferson to James Monroe, March 3, 1820, James Monroe Papers, Library of Congress, reel 7.

19. King's speeches in the Senate on the Missouri bill during Feb. 1819 are discussed in Ernst, *King,* 371. For King's defense of slavery (and Robert Morris of Pennsylvania's silence) in 1790, when only Democratic-Republican Pennsylvania Senator William Maclay supported an antislavery petition presented under Pennsylvania Abolition Society President Benjamin Franklin's signature, see Edgar S. Maclay, ed., *Journal of William Maclay, United States Senator from Pennsylvania, 1789–1791* (New York: Appleton, 1890), 196–97 (Maclay's Journal, Feb. 15, 1790). See also William C. di Giacomantonio, "'For the Grateful of a Volunteering Society': Antislavery and Pressure Group Politics in the First Federal Congress," *Journal of the Early Republic* 15, no. 2 (Summer 1995): 169–197.

20. Adams to Jefferson, Dec. 21, 1819, in Cappon, ed., *Adams-Jefferson Letters,* 551, and Adams, ed., *Works,* 10: 386, where it is dated Dec. 18, 1819. A letter with this precise date is not listed in Jefferson's "Summary Journal of Letters," although he perhaps mistakenly noted one dated Dec. 23, 1819. Jefferson Papers, Library of Congress (online at American Memory). Image 396.

21. Adams to Jefferson, Feb. 21, 1820, in Cappon, ed., *Adams-Jefferson Letters,* 561.

22. Jefferson to Hugh Nelson, Feb. 7, 1820, Jefferson Papers, Library of Congress.

23. Jefferson to Hugh Nelson, March 12, 1820, Jefferson Papers, Library of Congress.

24. Jefferson to Hugh Nelson, Feb 7, 1820, Jefferson Papers, Library of Congress. For Jefferson's other uses of the "cannibals" metaphor, see Arthur Scherr, "Jefferson's 'Cannibals' Revisited: A Closer Look at his Notorious Phrase," *Journal of Southern History* 77, no. 2 (May 2011): 251–282. For a general study of the pervasiveness of the "cannibals" theme in modern Western culture, see Priscilla L. Walton, *Our Cannibals, Ourselves* (Urbana: University of Illinois Press, 2004).

25. Jefferson to John Holmes, April 22, 1820 (first quotation), Jefferson to Mark Langdon Hill, April 5, 1820 (second quotation), Jefferson to William Short, April 13, 1820 (third quotation), Lipscomb and Bergh, eds., *Writings of Jefferson,* 15: 249, 242–243, 246–248; Jefferson to David Bailie Warden, Dec. 26, 1820, Ford, ed., *Works,* 12: 180 (fourth quotation); Jefferson to James Monroe, March 3, 1820, James Monroe Papers, Library of Congress, reel #7 (fifth quotation); Jefferson to Richard Rush, Oct. 20, 1820, Lipscomb and Bergh, eds., *Writings of Jefferson,* 15: 283–284 (sixth quotation). See also Glover Moore, *The Missouri Controversy, 1819–1821* (Lexington: University Press of Kentucky, 1953), 140, 203, 216–217, 277–278; Robert P. Forbes,

"Slavery and the Meaning of America, 1819–1837" (Ph.D. dissertation, Yale University, 1994), 178.

26. Fehrenbacher, *Slaveholding Republic,* 263, explained that the Missouri controversy "put antislavery elements at a serious disadvantage because any effort to introduce a prohibition or restriction at the state-making stage was likely to be, in practical terms, too late, and in constitutional terms, highly questionable."

27. Jefferson to John Holmes, April 22, 1820, in Peterson, ed., *Jefferson: Writings,* 1433–1435; Noble E. Cunningham, Jr., *Presidency of James Monroe* (Lawrence: University Press of Kansas, 1996), 98–104.

28. Jefferson to Richard Rush, Oct. 20, 1820, in Bergh, ed., *Writings of Jefferson* 15: 283–84. William W. Freehling is a prominent modern historian who agrees with Jefferson. He argues that Jefferson hoped that the original slaveholding Southern states would eventually become as independent of slavery as the Northern states and voluntarily abolish it, once slaves were diffused (i.e., sold) to different parts of the country. William W. Freehling, "The Louisiana Purchase and the Coming of the Civil War," chap. 3 of Sanford Levinson and Bartholomew H. Sparrow, eds., *The Louisiana Purchase and American Expansion, 1803–1898* (Lanham, Md.: Rowman Littlefield, 2005), 69–82. Calculating that eleven "free" states and three slave states (Louisiana, Missouri, and Arkansas) were formed from the acquisition, Freehling asserts that the Purchase constituted a "nontropical landed feast that would eventually curdle in the slaveholders' stomachs" (70), with 85 percent of the territory unsuitable for slavery (73).

29. Jefferson to Richard Rush, Oct. 20, 1820, in Bergh, ed., *Writings of Jefferson* 15: 283.

30. Jefferson to Rush, Oct. 20, 1820, ibid., 284. My reference to "refresh" refers to Jefferson's controversial letter to William S. Smith about Shays' Rebellion, Nov. 13, 1787, with the famous words: "The tree of liberty must be refreshed from time to time with the blood of patriots and tyrants. It is its natural manure." On Jefferson's respect for revolution, see also Harris G. Mirkin, "Rebellion, Revolution, and the Constitution: Thomas Jefferson's Theory of Civil Disobedience," *American Studies* 13 (Fall 1972): 61–74.

31. Jefferson to Rush, Oct. 20, 1820, Bergh, ed., *Writings,* 15: 284. For a different interpretation, based on an incomplete reading of this letter, see Andrew Trees, *The Founding Fathers and the Politics of Character* (Princeton: Princeton University Press, 2004), 144. Trees unwarrantedly observes that the letter to Rush showed that Jefferson "preferred to see the Union broken" rather than force Missouri to enter the Union as a free state. Adopting a strained interpretation of Peter Onuf's language concerning Jefferson's obsession with the "affections," he concludes that Jefferson felt politically and personally rejected by the antislavery, Federalist East, which had been insufficiently "affectionate" toward him because it insisted on prohibiting slavery in the new states. In retaliation, Jefferson vengefully desired the Union's destruction. As our extended analysis of the letter has shown, Jefferson's sentiments were actually the opposite. He lent his voice to the preservation of the Union, and was hopeful that the East and the South would recognize their mutual dependence and reconcile. He thought this was essential to their happiness and to humankind's well-being.

32. For Ohio's laws hindering free black residence in the state as early as 1804, see Leon F. Litwack, *North of Slavery* (Chicago: University of Chicago Press, 1961), 72.

33. Jefferson to Albert Gallatin, Dec. 26, 1820, in Peterson, ed., *Writings,* 1449–50. States carved out of the Old Northwest barred free blacks or placed difficult conditions

for their entry into the state, such as posting large monetary bonds of from five hundred to one thousand dollars guaranteeing their good behavior and presenting their court certificates of freedom. Ohio, the first state to emerge from the Northwest Ordinance, passed such laws in 1804, 1807, and 1809. Litwack, *North of Slavery*, 70, 72–74.

34. Jefferson to Henry Dearborn, August 17, 1821, in Ford, ed., *Works of Jefferson*, 12: 205–206, 206 (quotation).

35. Jefferson to Dearborn, Aug. 17, 1821, Ford, ed., *Works*, 12: 206.

36. My thoughts on this topic have been influenced by Stuart Leibiger, "Thomas Jefferson and the Missouri Crisis: An Alternative Interpretation," *Journal of the Early Republic* 17 (Spring 1997): 121–30, although my conclusions differ.

37. On Jefferson's desire to end political parties after he became president, see Noble E. Cunningham, Jr., *The Jeffersonian Republicans in Power: Party Operations, 1801–1809* (Chapel Hill: University of North Carolina Press, 1963), chapter 2. Despite the value of Leibiger's brief article, he engages in tunnel vision rooted in the anti–Jefferson views of the historians' Establishment. For example, he claims that Jefferson feigned anxiety over the Missouri crisis in order to gain Northern concessions to the South by frightening Northern politicians; and that his attitudes were "ideologically bankrupt." In fact, Jefferson exerted little political influence at this time. His reaction to the crisis led him to seek more creative solutions than other, more active politicians, although they ignored his ideas. The Missouri crisis disturbed Jefferson so much that it spurred him to formulate plans for the emancipation of the slaves and their emigration to the black nation-state of Haiti. In addition, as Leibiger implies, Jefferson's dread of disunion following the Missouri debates reconciled him to dealing with the Old School Hamiltonian Federalist Party that preferred government centralization (what he sometimes hyperbolically called "monarchism" for short) but was relatively apathetic on the issue of slavery. He feared that organization, which he undoubtedly thought had been routed by Republicans in the election of 1800 and had never recovered its power, less than what he considered the new Federalist strategy of "humanitarian" abolitionism to attract Northern Republicans to a new sectional antislavery party.

38. Jefferson to William Short, April 13, 1820, in Bergh, ed., *Writings*, 15: 247.

39. Jefferson to William Short, April 13, 1820, ibid., 248. In 1820, the present state of West Virginia was part of the State of Virginia. West Virginia did not become a separate state until 1863, during the Civil War.

40. Jefferson to William Short, April 13, 1820, ibid., 248.

41. Moore, *Missouri Controversy*, 255, citing Nathaniel F. Cabell, ed., *Early History of the University of Virginia*, (Richmond: J.W. Randolph, 1856), 239.

42. Moore, *Missouri Controversy*, 256.

43. Jefferson to Joseph C. Cabell, January 31, 1821, in Cabell, ed., *Early History of the University of Virginia*, 201–202.

44. Jefferson to Joseph C. Cabell, January 25, 1822, ibid., 239–240.

45. Malone, *Sage of Monticello*, 473–475.

46. "Thoughts on Lotteries," in Lipscomb and Bergh, eds., *Writings of Jefferson*, 17: 462–63.

47. Ibid., 462.

48. Ibid. Jefferson may have also had in mind the political diversity that he intended to encourage at his institution. The required reading at his law school would include such documents associated with his former political opponents as the classic *Federalist Papers*, one of his favorite books, even though the main author was Hamilton; and Washington's Farewell Address, a virtual Federalist Party manifesto of the 1790s. Jefferson proposed that the University not purchase David Hume's *History of England Under the Stuarts*, which he considered a "seductively" brilliant exposition of the virtues of monarchy, particularly the near-absolute monarchy of Charles I, inappropriate for republican scholars. However, Jefferson's suggestion hardly justifies accusations by historians such as Leonard W. Levy in *Jefferson and Civil Liberties* that Jefferson thereby revealed his intolerance of dissent and desire to blot out Federalist works; Hume's *History* was in no sense a Federalist document. Charles H. Moffat foreshadowed Levy's criticisms. Relying on early twentieth-century Harvard Professor Herbert Baxter Adams' work, he wrote, "By careful selection of the instructors and by prescribing a rigid curriculum in conformity with his political principles, Jefferson was able to lay the groundwork for an articulate and effective school of Southern nationalism." Moffat further argued that Jefferson intended to employ his university to indoctrinate students with Jeffersonian ideology as a virtual "party platform." Charles H. Moffat, "Jefferson's Sectional Motives in Founding the University of Virginia," *West Virginia History* 12 (1950): 61–69, quotations at 64–65. For Jefferson's recommendation of the *Federalist Papers* and Washington's Farewell Address as part of the University of Virginia's law curriculum, see University of Virginia, "Regulations, Political Science," March 4, 1825, in Padover, ed., *Complete Jefferson*, 1112.

49. "Thoughts on Lotteries," in Lipscomb and Berg, eds., *Writings of Jefferson*, 17: 462–63.

50. Ibid., 463.

51. Jefferson to William Branch Giles, Dec. 26, 1825, in ibid., 16: 150–151, and Peterson, ed., *Jefferson: Writings*, 1512. For Jefferson's most comprehensive statement of constitutional principles in old age, see Jefferson to Samuel Kercheval, July 12, 1816, ibid., 1395–1403, esp. 1400. In his letter to Kercheval, Jefferson rejected the "three-fifths clause" in Virginia's legislative apportionment, and in other ways showed hostility to slavery and slaveholders. For Jefferson's early recommendation of including judicial review and the Supreme Court's power to veto congressional laws in the U.S. Constitution, see Jefferson to Madison, Dec. 20, 1787, ibid., 915.

52. Jefferson to Short, Jan. 8, 1825, Jefferson Papers, Library of Congress.

53. Jefferson to Short, Jan. 8, 1825, Jefferson Papers, Library of Congress.

54. Jefferson to William Short, January 8, 1825, Berg, ed., *Writings*, 16: 94–95.

55. Jefferson to William Short, January 8, 1825, ibid., 16: 94–95.

56. Jefferson to William Short, January 8, 1825, ibid., 95.

57. The great anti–Jefferson writer Henry Adams' *History of the United States during the Administrations of Jefferson and Madison* long ago belabored the idea that Jefferson's protests against national executive power contradicted many of his actions as president. That Jefferson did not seriously fear presidential power when it was in the right hands, those of someone who acknowledged being the servant rather than the master of the people (in other words, himself and his friends) is obvious. For a well-done scholarly, book-length development of this topic, see Jeremy D. Bailey, *Thomas Jefferson and Executive Power* (Cambridge: Cambridge University Press, 2007).

58. Jefferson to William Short, January 8, 1825, Bergh, ed., *Writings*, 16: 96.

59. Jefferson to William Short, January 8, 1825, ibid., 96.

60. Ibid., 96.

61. Jefferson to Henry Lee, Jr., Aug. 10, 1824, in Ford, ed., *Writings*, 10: 317.

62. Jefferson to William Short, 8 Sept. 1823, Jefferson Papers, Library of Congress. Spelling in original.

63. John Holmes, "Letter to the People of Maine," dated Washington, D.C., April 10, 1820, enclosed in John Holmes to Jefferson, April 12, 1820, Jefferson Papers, Library of Congress. [Maine] *American Advocate and Kennebec Advertiser*, Saturday, April 29, 1820, printed the "Circular Letter from Mark Langdon Hill to the Citizens of Maine, Concerning his Vote on the Missouri Question, dated March 31, 1820, and Mr. Holmes' Letter to the People of Maine, April 10, 1820." Holmes' circular letter is conveniently reprinted in Noble E. Cunningham, Jr.'s indispensable collection, *Circular Letters of Congressmen to their Constituents, 1789–1829* (13 vols.; Chapel Hill, 1978), 3: 1109–1115. For a detailed study of Holmes' activities advocating free black suffrage in Maine while upholding slavery in Missouri during the crisis, which unfortunately overlooks Holmes' lengthy theoretical endorsement of "diffusion," see Matthew Mason, "The Maine and Missouri Crisis: Competing Priorities and Northern Slavery Politics in the Early Republic," *Journal of the Early Republic* 33 (Winter 2013): 675–700.

Chapter 22

1. Wendell G. Schaeffer, "The Delayed Cession of Spanish Santo Domingo to France, 1795–1801," *Hispanic-American Historical Review*, 29 (1949): 67–8; Arthur Scherr, "Arms and Men: The Diplomacy of US Weapons Traffic with Saint-Domingue under Adams and Jefferson," *International History Revview* 35, no. 3 (2013): 600–648, esp. 606–607. For Jefferson's acceptance of black rule over St. Domingo (Haiti), see Jefferson to William Short, Nov. 24, 1791, in Boyd, ed., *Jefferson Papers*, 22: 330–331.

2. On President Washington's Administration's support for crushing the slave rebellion in Haiti (called Saint-Domingue or St. Domingo by contemporaries), see Timothy M. Matthewson, "George Washington's Policy toward the Haitian Revolution," *Diplomatic History* 3 (Summer 1979), 321–36; For Jefferson's recommendation that Virginia deport its rebellious slaves to Haiti, see Jefferson to the Governor of Virginia (James Monroe), Nov. 24, 1801, in Peterson, ed., *Jefferson: Writings*, 1097. For Jefferson's support of trade with Haiti as president, see Arthur Scherr, "Arms and Men: The Diplomacy of US Weapons Traffic with Saint-Domingue under Adams and Jefferson," *International History Review* 35, no. 3 (2013): 600–648. A provocative revisionist study, Arthur Scherr, *Thomas Jefferson's Haitian Policy*, argues that Jefferson favored Haitian independence as a means to preserve a hemispheric balance of power and because he wanted to send the South's emancipated slaves there, something he would be unable to do if Napoleon regained control of Saint-Domingue (Haiti).

3. Jefferson to Joel Barlow, Oct. 8, 1809, in Ford, ed., *Works of Jefferson*, XI, 121; and in Looney, ed., *Papers of Thomas Jefferson: Retirement Series*, 1: 589. My italics.

4. On John Quincy Adams' opposition to recognizing Haiti's independence, see Rayford W. Logan, *Diplomatic Relations of the United States with Haiti, 1776–1891* (Chapel Hill: University of North Carolina Press, 1941), 227. For Jefferson's support for Haiti, see Arthur Scherr's brief article, "Light at the End of the Road: Thomas Jefferson's Endorsement of Free Haiti in His Final Years," *Journal of Haitian Studies* 15 (2009): 203–216.

5. Jefferson to Jared Sparks, Feb. 4, 1824, in Ford, ed., *Works of Jefferson*, 12: 337–38. In his farewell address to the U.S. Senate on February 18, 1825, Rufus King proposed that, after paying off the public debt, the U.S. Government use

receipts from public land sales to finance individual state laws permitting the manumission and deportation of slaves and free blacks. Betty L. Fladeland, "Compensated Emancipation: A Rejected Alternative," *Journal of Southern History* 42 (May 1976): 176. For other, similar proposals during this period, see Fladeland, "Compensated Emancipation," 169–186, and Eric Burin, *Slavery and the Peculiar Solution: A History of the American Colonization Society* (Gainesville: University Press of Florida, 2005), chapter one. Adam Rothman denounces Jefferson's ostensibly myopic view of the possibilities of black and white coexistence. "Jefferson and Slavery," in *Seeing Jefferson Anew*, ed. John B. Boles and Randal L. Hall (Charlottesville: University of Virginia Press, 2010), 103–125.

6. *Notes*, Query XIV, in Peterson, ed., *Jefferson: Writings*, 264, 270; Jefferson to Jared Sparks, February 4, 1824, in Ford, ed., *Works of Jefferson*, 12: 337–38; Steven Hahn, *Political Worlds of Slavery and Freedom* (Cambridge, Mass.: Harvard University Press, 2009). See also Peter S. Onuf, "To Declare them a Free and Independant People': Race, Slavery, and National Identity in Jefferson's Thought," *Journal of the Early Republic* 18, no. 1 (Spring 1998): 1–46.

7. Jefferson to Albert Gallatin, Dec. 26, 1820, in Peterson, ed., *Writings*, 1450. For Randolph's plan to gradually emancipate all of Virginia's slaves and force them to emigrate to Haiti, see William H. Gaines, Jr., *Thomas Mann Randolph, Jr.: Jefferson's Son-in-Law* (Baton Rouge, 1966), 124–126; Charles S. Sydnor, *Development of Southern Sectionalism, 1819–1848* (Baton Rouge, 1948), 96; Randolph to Speaker of the Va. House of Delegates, Dec. 4, 1820, in *Richmond Enquirer*, Dec. 5, 1820.

8. Jefferson had subscribed to *Niles Weekly Register*, edited by the antislavery Baltimore Jeffersonian Hezekiah Niles, since at least 1811, and continued to read it until the month of his death. For Jefferson's payments for his subscriptions for1826 and preceding years, see James A. Bear and Lucia C. Stanton, eds., *Jefferson's Memorandum Books* (2 vols., Princeton, 1997), 2: 1307, 1417, passim. *Niles' Weekly Register* is listed in the catalogue of his final library, sold by his family to pay his creditors in 1829, three years after his death. Catalogue of Jefferson's Second Library, Offered for Sale at Public Auction, Feb. 27, 1829, Jefferson Papers, Library of Congress, Series 7, Miscellaneous Bound Volumes ("American Memory" Series, online). See the proclamation of Haiti's foreign minister, Joseph Balthazar Inginac, in 1817, offering to pay the transportation of black and Native American immigrants to Haiti, printed in "People of Color," *Niles' Weekly Register*, 15 (Sept. 1818-Feb. 1819): 117–18 (weekly edition of Oct. 17, 1818).

9. Jefferson to Albert Gallatin, Dec. 26, 1820, in Peterson, ed., *Writings*, 1450.

10. For a brief, somewhat misleading discussion of Jefferson's views on slavery and "colonization" at the time of the Missouri crisis, see Peter S. Onuf, "Domesticating the Captive Nation: Thomas Jefferson and the Problem of Slavery," in John Milton Cooper, Jr., and Thomas J. Knock, eds., *Jefferson, Lincoln, and Wilson: The American Dilemma of Race and Democracy* (Charlottesville: University of Virginia Press, 2010), 34–60, esp. 43–49.

11. Jefferson to Doctor Thomas Humphreys, Feb. 8, 1817, Ford, ed., *Works of Jefferson*, 12: 53–54, and Lipscomb and Bergh, eds., *Writings of Jefferson*, 15: 102–103.

12. Jefferson to John Holmes, April 22, 1820, in Lipscomb and Bergh, eds., *Writings of Jefferson*, 15: 249. Lawyer-turned-historian Paul Finkelman, in an article in *Federalists Reconsidered*, invented a non-existent letter that Holmes wrote Jefferson asking his support for a plan he devised to abolish slavery in Missouri; and Jefferson rejected him. Paul

Finkelman, "The Problem of Slavery in the Age of Federalism," in Barbara B. Oberg and Doron Ben-Atar, eds., *Federalists Reconsidered* (Charlottesville, 1998), 142. For a detailed study of Holmes' activities upholding slavery in Missouri during the Missouri crisis, see Matthew Mason, "The Maine and Missouri Crisis: Competing Priorities and Northern Slavery Politics in the Early Republic," *Journal of the Early Republic* 33 (Winter 2013): 675–700. For Missourians' insistence, as frontier individualist entrepreneurs of lower-class origin, that congressional prohibition of slavery violated their "natural right" to property, especially property in slaves, see John Korasick, "The Concept of Liberty in Territorial Missouri, 1819," *Missouri Historical Review* 109, no. 3 (April 2015): 179–197.

13. Jefferson to John Holmes, April 22, 1820, Jefferson Papers, Library of Congress, and numerous online sites. For Holmes' Circular Letter to his constituents, which he sent to Jefferson, inspiring Jefferson to write this letter, see Noble E. Cunningham, Jr., ed., *Circular Letters of Congressmen to their Constituents* (3 vols.; Chapel Hill, 1978), 3: 1109–1115. Paul Finkelman composed a ludicrously funny Op-Ed piece in the *New York Times*, replete with erroneous statements about Jefferson's attitudes toward the Missouri Compromise and slavery. Paul Finkelman, "The Monster of Monticello," *New York Times*, Nov. 30, 2012.

14. See Arthur Scherr, "Thomas Jefferson's Nationalist Vision of New England and the War of 1812," *Historian*, 69, no. 1 (Spring 2007): 1–35.

15. Jefferson to John Adams, January 22, 1821, Lipscomb and Bergh, eds., *Writings of Jefferson*, 15: 308–309. For Adams' attitude toward slavery, see John R. Howe, Jr., "John Adams' Views of Slavery," *Journal of Negro History* 49 (July 1964): 201–205.

16. Jefferson to John Adams, January 22, 1821, Lipscomb and Bergh, eds., *Writings of Jefferson*, 15: 309. A "Bedlamite" is an inmate of a mental institution or lunatic asylum.

17. For an older, brief, insightful depiction of Jefferson's nationalist views, see Harris G. Mirkin, "Rebellion, Revolution, and the Constitution: Thomas Jefferson's Theory of Civil Disobedience," *American Studies* 13 (Fall 1972): 61–74. More recent studies stressing Jefferson's nationalism include: Joseph H. Harrison, "*Sic et Non*: Thomas Jefferson and Internal Improvement," *Journal of the Early Republic* 7 (Winter 1987): 335–349, esp. 344; James R. Sofka, "The Jeffersonian Idea of National Security: Commerce, the Atlantic Balance of Power, and the Barbary War, 1786–1805," *Diplomatic History* 21 (Fall 1997): 519–544; Stephen H. Browne, *Jefferson's Call for Nationhood: The First Inaugural Address* (College Station, Tex.: Texas A & M Press, 2003); Brian D. Steele, "Thomas Jefferson and the Making of an American Nationalism" (Ph.D. dissertation, University of North Carolina at Chapel Hill, 2003); Steele, *Thomas Jefferson and American Nationhood* (Cambridge: Cambridge University Press, 2012); Bernard Bailyn, *To Begin the World Anew: The Genius and Ambiguities of the American Founders* (New York: Knopf, 2004), 37–59; and Jeremy David Bailey, "Executive Prerogative and the 'Good Officer' in Thomas Jefferson's Letter to John B. Colvin," *Presidential Studies Quarterly* 34 (Dec. 2004): 732–754.

18. Years earlier, Jefferson had shown a resigned, almost tolerant attitude to the possibility that the western territories would secede if the United States surrendered its right to free navigation of the Mississippi River. See Jefferson to Madison, Jan. 30, 1787 and June 20, 1787, in Boyd et al., eds., *Jefferson Papers*, 11: 93–94, 481. For Adams' view, see Adams to Jefferson, Dec. 21, 1819, Cappon, ed., *Adams-Jefferson Letters*, 2: 551. On the general topic of secession's legality, see Stampp, "The Concept of a Perpetual Union."

19. Stuart Leibiger, "Thomas Jefferson and the Missouri Crisis: An Alternative Interpretation," *Journal of the Early Republic* 17 (Spring 1997): 121–30. As Leibiger observes, Jefferson had seen the Republican Party as a temporary vehicle to unite the nation against the "monarchical" threat of the Federalists. But after the Missouri Crisis, he viewed permanent national parties of "aristocrats" versus "democrats" as positive forces that would dilute sectionalism and prevent it from fracturing the Union. He preferred conflicts over the comparatively empty question of "aristocracy" to fights over slavery, which might easily spread from the House floor to the battlefield.

20. See Jefferson to Madison, April 27, 1809, in Lipscomb and Bergh, eds., *Writings of Jefferson*, 12: 277.

21. Jefferson to Charles Pinckney, Sept. 30, 1820, in Ford, ed., *Works of Jefferson*, 12: 165–66. For Pinckney's proslavery attitude during the Missouri debates, see Moore, *Missouri Controversy, 1819–1821*, 114–15, 122, 125–26.

22. Jefferson to Charles Pinckney, Sept. 30, 1820, in Lipscomb and Bergh, eds., *Writings of Jefferson*, 15: 279–80, and Ford, ed., *Works*, 12: 165–66; Charles Pinckney to Jefferson, Sept. 6, 1820, Jefferson Papers, Library of Congress. On Jefferson's lack of influence on Madison, his closest friend and erstwhile political ally, see Roy J. Honeywell, "President Jefferson and his Successor," *American Historical Review*, 46 (1940): 64–75.

23. On Northern objections to the Missouri Compromise, see Moore, *Missouri Controversy*, 170–217, and the revealing Congressional roll calls that show Massachusetts' and Vermont's consistent hostility to compromise, ibid., 61, 108, 109, 110, 144, 145, 149, 156, 158. For Virginia's vote in February 1820, 4 to 18 against the Thomas Proviso, see ibid., 111.

24. Jefferson to Pinckney, Sept. 30, 1820, in Lipscomb and Bergh, eds., *Writings of Jefferson*, 15: 280–281.

25. Jefferson to Pinckney, Sept. 30, 1820, in Lipscomb and Bergh, eds., *Writings of Jefferson*, 15: 280–281.

26. Jefferson to Charles Pinckney, Sept. 30, 1820, in Ford, ed., *Works of Jefferson*, 12: 166.

27. Isaac Briggs described his visit with Jefferson in a letter to his wife and children, Nov. 21, 1820, printed in Merrill D. Peterson, ed., *Visitors to Monticello* (Charlottesville: University Press of Virginia, 1989), 81, 90–92, 90 (quotation). Peterson's commentary misreads Jefferson's statements as being opposed to the Missouri Compromise. But Jefferson actually *favored* the compromise, which permitted slavery in Missouri but barred it from the portions of the Louisiana Purchase where it did not exist. He only feared that Congress would resume its efforts to abolish slavery in Missouri, which might be followed by legislative attempts to eliminate it from the original thirteen states, including Virginia. Article Three of the Louisiana Purchase Treaty with Napoleon stated: "The inhabitants … shall be incorporated into the Union of the United States and admitted as soon as possible, according to the principles of the federal Constitution to the enjoyment of all these rights, advantages and immunities of citizens of the United States, and in the mean time they shall be maintained in the free enjoyment of their liberty, property and the Religion which they profess." The Louisiana Purchase Treaty, April 30, 1803, is available online at Yale Law School's *Avalon Project*.

Chapter 23

1. Jefferson called William Short his "adoptive son" in a letter to John Trumbull, June 1, 1789, in Julian P. Boyd et al., eds., *Papers of Thomas Jefferson* (43 vols., in progress;

Princeton, 1950–), 15: 164. He offered his opinion of New York in a letter to William Short, Sept. 8, 1823, Jefferson Papers, Library of Congress. For Jefferson's remarks on Jay's opposition to the Declaration of Independence, see Jefferson to John Adams, Sept. 4, 1823, and Jefferson to Samuel Adams Wells, May 12, 1819, in Peterson, *Writings*, 1478–79, 1421.

2. Jefferson to George A. Otis, Feb. 15, 1821, in Paul L. Ford, ed., *The Writings of Thomas Jefferson* (10 vols.; New York: Putnam, 1892–1899), 10: 187–88. Carlo Botta's (1766–1837) four-volume *History of the War of Independence of the United States of America* first appeared in Italian in 1809. He was an Italian who went to France and supported the French Revolution and Napoleon, although he finally turned against his dictatorship. Much of his book is apocryphal, although some of it rested on contemporary documents and material supplied by the Marquis de Lafayette. It was translated into English and published in Philadelphia in 1820–1821. With regard to the history of Virginia, Jefferson is probably referring to a recently written, four-volume work, by John Daly Burk, Skelton Jones, and Louis Hue Girardin, entitled, *The History of Virginia, From its First Settlement to the Present Day* (Petersburg, Va., 1804–1816). Girardin wrote part of volume four.

3. Jefferson to John Randolph, Aug. 25, 1775, in Peterson, *Writings*, 750. For Sam Adams' views, see Pauline Maier, *The Old Revolutionaries: Political Lives in the Age of Samuel Adams* (New York: Knopf, 1980), 23–26.

4. See the accounts of Adams's retirement in Joseph J. Ellis, *Passionate Sage* (New York: Knopf, 1993) and Peter Shaw, *The Character of John Adams* (Chapel Hill: University of North Carolina Press, 1976), as well as James H. Hutson, *John Adams and the Diplomacy of the American Revolution* (Lexington: University Press of Kentucky, 1980). Gordon S. Wood, *The Americanization of Benjamin Franklin* (New York: Penguin Press, 2004) emphasizes Adams's long-standing hatred and envy of Franklin.

5. Jefferson to George A. Otis, 25 Dec. 1820, in "The Jefferson Papers," *Collections of the Massachusetts Historical Society*, 7th Series, Vol. I (1900) [Vol. 61 of the *Collections*]: 301.

6. On this topic, see in general, William Rogers Taylor, *Cavalier and Yankee* (New York: George Braziller, 1961). Unfortunately, Taylor's lengthy analysis (25–33) of the Adams/Jefferson dialogue on "natural aristocracy" from a Massachusetts vs. Virginia perspective is seriously flawed, even attributing Adams's words to Jefferson. One example is particularly relevant to the topic of Jefferson's attitude toward New England. Taylor mistakenly attributes Adams' statement in a letter to Jefferson, dated June 30, 1813, in which he predicted a "civil war between the U.S. and Massachusetts," and deplored "the damnable rivalry between Virginia and Massachusetts," as a statement from *Jefferson to Adams*, dated June 30, 1813. Unlike some other historians, I caught Taylor's mistake because, after years of studying Jefferson's opinion of New England, I understood that Jefferson was too conciliatory to say something as blunt as that to Adams, whom he was trying to pacify through their renewed correspondence. Taylor, *Cavalier and Yankee*, 26. For the letter's text, see Cappon, ed., *Adams-Jefferson Letters*, 2: 348.

7. Jefferson to Joshua Dodge, Aug. 3, 1823, in Lipscomb and Bergh, eds., *Writings of Jefferson*, 18: 322.

8. Jefferson to Joshua Dodge, Aug. 3, 1823, in Lipscomb and Bergh, eds., *Writings of Jefferson*, 18: 322.

9. Ibid.

10. Jefferson to Joshua Dodge, Aug. 3, 1823, ibid. See also Walter Muir Whitehill, "The Union of New England

and Virginia," *Virginia Quarterly Review* 40, number 4 (Autumn, 1964): 516–530.

11. Charles Sellers, *The Market Revolution: Jacksonian America, 1815–1846* (New York: Oxford University Press, 1991), 269. Sellers' source for Jefferson's comments to Webster is Paul Leicester Ford's *Writings of Thomas Jefferson* (10 vols.; New York: Putnam, 1892–1899), which in turn quoted the *Private Correspondence of Daniel Webster*, 1: 364, which was published in 1857, after Webster died.

12. James Parton, *Life of Andrew Jackson* (3 vols.; New York, 1860), I, 219; Arthur M. Schlesinger, Jr., *Age of Jackson* (Boston, 1945), 37, citing John Quincy Adams, *Memoirs*, ed. Charles Francis Adams, IV, 76. See also the one-volume summary of Adams' *Memoirs* edited by Allan Nevins, *Diary of John Quincy Adams, 1794–1845* (New York, 1929), 195.

13. Randall, *Jefferson*, 3: 504, 509 (quotation).

14. Jefferson to James Monroe, Dec. 15, 1824, in Paul L. Ford, ed., *Works of Thomas Jefferson* (12 vols.; New York: Putnam, 1904–1905), 12: 387.

15. There is no record of any correspondence between Jefferson and Webster in Jefferson's papers.

16. Sean Wilentz, *The Rise of American Democracy: From Jefferson to Lincoln* (New York: Norton, 2005), 865 note 23. (first quotation), 851 note 59 (second quotation). Wilentz's source is Webster's "Notes of Mr. Jefferson's Conversation 1824 at Monticello," from Charles M .Wiltse, ed., *Papers of Daniel Webster* (Hanover, N.H.: University Press of New England, 1974–1988), 1: 375–76. (However, the notes were in Mrs. Ticknor's handwriting, not George's.) John Buchanan, *Jackson's Way: Andrew Jackson and the People of the Western Waters* (New York: Wiley, 2001), 161–162, takes Jefferson's alleged comments about Jackson's inept Senatorial performance seriously. Probably alluding to Webster and Ticknor's trip to Monticello in 1824, Merrill D. Peterson merely writes, "Jefferson had reservations about Jackson," but he cast them aside in his dismay at John Quincy Adams' ultra-nationalistic annual message to Congress in December 1825. Moreover, most Democratic-Republicans considered Jackson the heir to Jefferson's "Revolution of 1800." Merrill D. Peterson, *Thomas Jefferson and the New Nation* (New York: Oxford University Press, 1970), 1002–1003.

17. James P. Ronda, "Jefferson and the Imperial West," *Journal of the West* 31 (July 1992): 13–19, at 18. Ronda cites Daniel Webster's Memorandum of December 24, 1824, from Charles M. Wiltse, ed., *Papers of Daniel Webster* (Hanover, N.H., 1974), 1: 371.

18. Celia Morris Eckhardt, *Fanny Wright: Rebel in America* (Cambridge, Mass.: Harvard University Press, 1984), 86.

19. Amy S. Greenberg, *A Wicked War: Polk, Clay, Lincoln, and the 1846 U.S. Invasion of Mexico* (New York: Knopf, 2012), 92–93.

20. Daniel Walker Howe, *Political Culture of the American Whigs* (Chicago, 1979), 24 (first quotation), 91 (second quotation). More recently, Howe's Pulitzer Prize-winning, *What Hath God Wrought? The Transformation of America, 1815–1848* (New York, 2007), 205, quotes Jefferson as saying to Webster about Jackson, "He is one of the most unfit men I know of" for the presidency. (Howe's source is Michael G. Heale, *The Presidential Quest* (London: Longmans, 1982), 55.

21. Raymond Walters, Jr., *Albert Gallatin: Jeffersonian Financier and Diplomat* (New York: Macmillan, 1957), 361–62.

22. Robert M. S. McDonald, "West Point's Lost Founder: Jefferson Remembered, Forgotten, and Reconsidered," in Robert M. S. McDonald, ed., *Thomas Jefferson's Military Academy: Founding West Point* (Charlottesville: University Press of Virginia, 2004), 186 (quotation).

23. David Brown, "Jeffersonian Ideology and the Second Party System," *The Historian* 62, no. 1 (Sept. 1999): 17–30, at 22. "During Jackson's presidency (1829–1837), Monroe openly criticized the General." Ibid. [Monroe died on July 4, 1831, so he did not have much time to criticize Jackson in any case.] James Monroe to T. Ringgold, May 8, 1826, in Stanislaus M. Hamilton, ed., *Writings of James Monroe* (7 vols.; New York: Putnam, 1898–1903), 7: 82 (first quotation); Monroe to John C. Calhoun (?), 1827, ibid., 7: 141 (second quotation). For Monroe and Madison's refusal to endorse John Quincy Adams or denounce Jackson in the presidential election of 1828, see John Sullivan, "Indecorous Argument: The Use of Madison and Monroe in the Election of 1828," *Southern Speech Communication Journal*, 45, no. 4 (1980): 378–393.

24. Augustus C. Buell, *History of Andrew Jackson* (2 vols.; New York: Scribner, 1904), 1: 204–205.

25. Milton W. Hamilton, "Augustus C. Buell: Fraudulent Historian," *Pennsylvania Magazine of History and Biography* 80, no. 4 (Oct. 1956): 478–93. Unfortunately, a few popular writers, such as Alan Pell Crawford, unquestioningly accept Buell's story. See Alan Pell Crawford, *Twilight at Monticello: The Final Years of Thomas Jefferson* (New York: Random House, 2008), 128, who cites Burke Davis, *Old Hickory: A Life of Andrew Jackson* (New York: Dial Press, 1977), 57. As one might expect, Davis's "source" (listed in his loosely-arranged "Notes," 391) is Buell, who he claims cites a letter from Jackson to Francis P. Blair.

26. Harold D. Moser, ed., *Papers of Andrew Jackson* (Knoxville: University of Tennessee Press, 1984), 2: 165.

27. I attempted to locate Jackson's abusive speech by using the online database, "America's Historical Newspapers," to search the *Richmond Enquirer* for 1824, but found nothing.

28. For Webster's disappointment at Jefferson's election, see Daniel Webster to Charles Herbert, January 7, 1801, in Wiltse, ed., *Papers of Daniel Webster*, 1: 31.

29. "Notes of Mr. Jefferson's Conversation 1824 at Monticello: 1825," in Wiltse, ed., *Papers of Daniel Webster*, 1: 375–76. According to Arthur M. Schlesinger, Jr., Webster's Notes first appeared in Fletcher Webster, ed., *Private Correspondence of Daniel Webster* (2 vols.; Boston: Little, Brown, 1857), 1: 371, from which they are quoted in Schlesinger, *Age of Jackson* (Boston: Houghton Mifflin, 1945), 37n. For Webster as an opponent of Congressional purchase of Jefferson's library in 1815, see Dumas Malone, *Sage of Monticello* (Boston: Little, Brown, 1981), 178. Although New England congressional representatives like Webster, Pickering, and Cyrus King were the foremost opponents of purchasing Jefferson's library, even some excessively frugal Southern Democratic-Republicans like Jefferson's old friend, North Carolinian Nathaniel Macon, opposed incurring the additional expense in wartime. Ibid., 177–179.

30. Cynthia A. Kierner, *Martha Jefferson Randolph: Daughter of Monticello* (Chapel Hill: University of North Carolina Press, 2012), 214.

31. Matthew Warshauer, *Andrew Jackson and the Politics of Martial Law* (Knoxville: University of Tennessee Press, 2006), 122. Warshauer cites as his source Paul L. Ford, ed., *Writings of Thomas Jefferson* (10 vols.; New York: Putnam, 1892–1899), 10: 331. He actually means p. 331n., which consists of a footnote in which Ford explicitly stated that he was printing Webster's memo about Jefferson, *not a letter* from Jefferson to Webster. However, since Ford relegated the memo to a footnote and the print is rather small, Warshauer's error is understandable. See also Matthew Warshauer, "Andrew Jackson as a 'Military Chieftain' in the 1824 and 1828 Presidential Elections: The Ramifications of Mar-

tial Law on American Republicanism," *Tennessee Historical Quarterly* 57, no. 1 (March 1998): 4–23.

32. "Notes of Mr. Jefferson's Conversation 1824 at Monticello: 1825," in Webster, ed., *Private Correspondence*, I, 375, quoted in Brown, "Jeffersonian Ideology," 23; and Warshauer, *Andrew Jackson and the Politics of Martial Law*, 122.

33. Henry Clay to Francis T. Brooke, January 28, 1825, quoted in Harry L. Watson, ed., *Andrew Jackson vs. Henry Clay: Democracy and Development in Antebellum America* (Boston: Bedford/St. Martin's, 1998), 158. See also Kristofer Ray, "The Corrupt Bargain and the Rise of the Jacksonian Movement, 1825–1828," in Brian D. McKnight and James S. Humphreys, eds., *Age of Andrew Jackson* (Kent, Ohio: Kent State University Press, 2011), 22–35; and Wilentz, *Rise of American Democracy*, 255–256.

34. Jackson to Samuel Swartwout, Feb. 22, 1825, in Watson, ed., *Andrew Jackson*, 159.

35. *Washington Gazette*, Feb. 11, 1825 ("Mr. Clay and his Conscience"), in ibid., 161.

36. Editorial note, in Wiltse, ed., *Papers of Daniel Webster*, 1: 368.

37. Robert V. Remini, *Daniel Webster: The Man and his Time* (New York: Norton, 1997), 233. On December 19, 1824, the day of their departure, Webster's three-year-old son died, causing him great sorrow when he found out about it a few days later. Ibid., 235.

38. Fletcher Webster, ed., *Private Correspondence of Daniel Webster* (2 vols.; Boston: Little, Brown, 1857), 1: 364–373.

39. Papers of Daniel Webster, microfilm edition, Dartmouth College Library, reel four, frames 4495–4497, original in George F. Hoar Papers, Massachusetts Historical Society. For a description of Jefferson's physical appearance, see also *National Edition of Webster's Writings* (18 vols.; Boston: Little, Brown, 1903), 17: 364–373.

40. James Monroe to Jefferson, Dec. 9, 1824, Jefferson Papers, Library of Congress. I have modernized spelling and punctuation.

41. Jefferson to George Ticknor, Nov. 8, 1824, Thomas Jefferson Papers, Library of Congress, available at American Memory online; also quoted in George Ticknor Curtis, *Life of Daniel Webster* (2 vols.; New York: Appleton, 1870), 1: 222–23, and in Remini, *Daniel Webster: The Man and his Time*, 232.

42. Daniel Webster to Jeremiah Mason, Dec. 29, 1824, in Wiltse, ed., *Papers of Daniel Webster*, 1: 379.

43. Remini, *Webster*, 234; Curtis, *Life of Daniel Webster*, 1: 235.

44. Daniel Webster to William Plumer, Jr., Monticello, Dec. 18, 1824, Plumer Papers, New Hampshire State Library, on microfilm in Daniel Webster Papers, compiled by Dartmouth College, reel four; and in Wiltse, ed., *Webster Papers*, 1: 368–369.

45. Curtis, *Life of Webster*, 1:222–223; Remini, *Daniel Webster: The Man and his Time*, 232.

46. Wiltse, ed., *Papers of Daniel Webster*, 1: 380. Webster's italics.

47. Webster to Joseph Hopkinson, Dec. 31, 1824, Wiltse, ed., *Papers of Daniel Webster*, 1: 381–382. A prominent Adams Federalist, Joseph Hopkinson was a Philadelphia congressman and an influential attorney. He represented Dr. Benjamin Rush in his libel suit against Federalist journalist William Cobbett and defended Justice Samuel Chase at his impeachment trial by the Senate in 1804, winning both cases. In 1828, President John Quincy Adams commissioned him judge of the federal district court for the eastern district of Pennsylvania, a position he held until his death in 1842. A foe of democracy, as a delegate to the Pennsyl-

vania constitutional convention in 1837–1838 he opposed democratic innovations such as the popular election of judges and their service for a limited tenure. See *Dictionary of American Biography*, s.v., "Hopkinson, Joseph."

48. Ibid. On American attitudes toward the death of children during the 1820s, see David E. Stannard, *The Puritan Way of Death: Study in Religion, Culture, and Social Change* (New York: Oxford University Press, 1977).

49. See *Dictionary of American Biography*, s.v., "Curtis, George Ticknor."

50. George Ticknor Curtis, *Life of Daniel Webster* (2 vols.; New York: Appleton, 1870), 1: 581–89, "Appendix." Remini discusses Webster and Ticknor's visit to Madison and Jefferson in *Webster*, 232–235. Disappointingly, Merrill D. Peterson, *Jefferson Image in the American Mind* (New York: Oxford University Press, 1960), 26, hardly mentions what he calls Webster's "report."

51. George S. Hilliard, "Preface to [the] Original Edition," Boston, December 1875, in G.S. Hilliard and Anna Eliot Ticknor, ed., *Life, Letters, and Journals of George Ticknor* (2 vols.; Boston: James R. Osgood, 1876), 1: xiii.

52. Curtis, *Life of Daniel Webster*, I, 224.

53. Ibid., I, 222.

54. Remini, *Daniel Webster: The Man and his Time* (New York: Norton, 1997), 277.

55. Ibid., 223.

56. George Ticknor to W. H. Prescott, Dec. 16, 1824, in Ferris Greenslet, ed., *Life, Letters, and Journals of George Ticknor* (2 vols.; Boston: Houghton Mifflin, 1909), 1: 347.

57. George Ticknor Curtis, *Life of Daniel Webster* (2 vols.; New York: Appleton, 1870), 1: 223.

58. Ibid., 1: 224. According to Remini, Clay considered Madison a great man, too. Remini, *Webster*, 232; Robert V. Remini, *Henry Clay: Spokesman for the Union* (New York: Norton, 1991), 524.

59. See Irving H. Bartlett, *Daniel Webster* (New York: Norton, 1978), 60–66, for a good summary of Webster's anti-war activities in Congress, his support of nullification during the war, and the above quotation.

60. George Ticknor to William H. Prescott, Dec. 16, 1824, in *Life, Letters, and Journals of George Ticknor*, 1: 347–349.

61. George Ticknor to C. S. Daveis, Sept. 28, 1824, in G.S. Hilliard and Anna Eliot Ticknor, ed., *Life, Letters, and Journals of George Ticknor* (2 vols.; Boston: James R. Osgood, 1876), 1: 345.

62. Wiltse, ed., *Papers of Daniel Webster*, 1: 371.

63. Curtis, *Daniel Webster*, 1: 581–89 (quotation at 581). Jefferson's insulting remarks about Jackson appear on 589. The Ticknor reminiscences are dated May 1, 1869. Ibid., 581.

64. Memo of Conversation with Thomas Jefferson, Dec. 19, 1824, in Papers of Daniel Webster, Dartmouth College Library, frames 4495–4498, reel four (microfilm). Italics in original.

65. Jefferson to George Washington, Sept. 9, 1792, in Merrill D. Peterson, ed., *Portable Thomas Jefferson* (New York, 1975), 463–64.

66. William Plumer to William Plumer, Sr., Dec. 3, 1823, in Everett S. Brown, ed., *The Missouri Compromise and Presidential Politics, 1820–1825* (St. Louis: Missouri Historical Society, 1926), 85.

67. Sydney Nathans, *Daniel Webster and Jacksonian Democracy* (Baltimore: Johns Hopkins University Press, 1973), 23.

68. For the Eliot family's anti-populist attitudes, see David B. Tyack, *George Ticknor and the Boston Brahmins* (Cambridge, Mass.: Harvard University Press, 1967), 17–18, 216–218.

69. Webster's "Notes," in Wiltse, ed., *Papers of Daniel Webster*, 1: 371.

70. Daniel Webster to Ezekiel Webster, Feb. 22, 1824, in Webster, *Private Correspondence*, 1: 346.

71. Nathans, *Webster and Jacksonian Democracy*, 13–14; Michael E. Chapman, "Pragmatic, *ad hoc* Foreign-Policy Making of the Early Republic: Thomas H. Perkins' Boston-Smyrna-Canton Opium Model and Congressional Rejection of Aid for Greek Independence," *International History Review* 35, no. 3 (2013): 449–464.

72. For Webster's efforts to present himself as a "public man," the member of an elite vital to the republic's survival, who surmounted blind party loyalties and dispassionately guided the masses, see Sydney Nathans, *Daniel Webster and Jacksonian Democracy* (Baltimore: Johns Hopkins University Press, 1973), 13 (Webster as Federalist congressman), 6 (quotation). In general, see ibid., 29–73. See also Lynn Marshall, "The Strange Stillbirth of the Whig Party," *American Historical Review* 72 (January 1967): 448–468; and John B. Kirby, "Early American Politics: The Search for Ideology: An Historiographical Analysis and Critique of the Concept of Deference," *Journal of Politics* 32 (Nov. 1970): 808–838.

73. Nathans, *Webster and Jacksonian Democracy*, chapters 1 and 2. See also Norman D. Brown, "The Webster-Jackson Movement for a Constitution and Union Party in 1833," *Mid-America: A Historical Review* 46 (July 1964): 147–171.

74. Parton, *Life of Andrew Jackson*, I, 219; Schlesinger, *Age of Jackson*, 37; John Spencer Bassett, *Life of Andrew Jackson* (1911; 2 vols. in one, New York: Macmillan, 1928), 329.

75. "Notes of Mr. Jefferson's Conversation 1824 at Monticello: 1825," in Wiltse, ed., *Papers of Daniel Webster*, 1: 373.

76. "Notes of Mr. Jefferson's Conversation 1824 at Monticello: 1825," in Wiltse, ed., *Papers of Daniel Webster*, 1: 373.

77. Bernard Mayo, *Myths and Men: Patrick Henry, George Washington, Thomas Jefferson* (Athens: University of Georgia Press, 1959), 8–23.

78. On Wirt and Jefferson, see Andrew Burstein, *Jefferson's Secrets: Death and Desire at Monticello* (New York: Basic Books, 2005), 217–18, 278.

79. "Notes of Mr. Jefferson's Conversation 1824 at Monticello: 1825," in *Papers of Webster*, I, 370–78. 375 (quotation).

80. In order by age, the following were the members of the Virginia delegation to the Second Continental Congress who signed the Declaration of Independence, and their birth and death dates: George Wythe (1726–1806); Benjamin Harrison (1726–1791); Richard Henry Lee (1732–1794); Francis Lightfoot Lee (1734–1797); Carter Braxton (1736–1797); Thomas Nelson, Jr. (1738–1789); and Thomas Jefferson (1743–1826). For their birth and death dates, see *Concise Dictionary of American Biography*.

81. Pauline Maier, *American Scripture: Making the Declaration of Independence* (New York: Knopf, 1997), 42, 48,103.

82. Jefferson to John Sanderson, August 31, 1820, Jefferson Papers, Library of Congress (online at American Memory).

83. Jefferson's *Autobiography*, January 1821, printed in Peterson, ed., *Jefferson: Writings* (New York, 1984), 36 (first quotation), 5n. (second quotation).

84. Dumas Malone, *Jefferson the Virginian* (Boston: Little, Brown, 1948), 65. Malone spells Sanderson's name "Saunderson," following Jefferson's orthography.

85. Allan Nevins, *Diary of John Quincy Adams, 1794–1845* (New York: Ungar, 1951), 233 (March 14, 1820).

86. See Jefferson to Colonel Edward Carrington, May 27, 1788, in *Life and Selected Writings of Thomas Jefferson*, 447.

87. Jefferson to Charles Clay, Feb. 21, 1815, Jefferson Papers, University of Virginia, reel 7. In November 1815, Jackson visited Jefferson at Poplar Forest, his Bedford County estate. Edwin M. Betts and James A. Bear, Jr., eds., *Family Letters of Thomas Jefferson* (Columbia, Mo., 1966), 411–12.

Chapter 24

1. Jefferson to William Branch Giles, Dec. 26, 1825, in Ford, ed., *Writings*, 10: 355–56.
2. Jefferson to William Branch Giles, Dec. 26, 1825, in Ford, ed., *Writings*, 10: 355–56. For a brief survey of Jefferson's generally favorable attitude toward internal improvements on both state and national levels, see Joseph H. Harrison, Jr., "*Sic et Non*: Thomas Jefferson and Internal Improvement," *Journal of the Early Republic* 7 (Winter 1987): 335–349. According to Harrison, Jefferson's language at least till 1813 was "that of a decided nationalist, and if Jefferson had died at seventy he would have been so considered, at least by those unable to write him off as an opportunist" (ibid., 344).
3. Jefferson to William F. Gordon, Jan. 1, 1826, Ford, ed., *Writings*, 10: 359.
4. Jefferson to William F. Gordon, Jan. 1, 1826, Ford, *Writings*, 10: 359. Shalhope, "Thomas Jefferson's Republicanism and Antebellum Southern Thought," 553–54, depicts Jefferson as a would-be secessionist in this instance, but Malone, *Sage of Monticello* (Boston: Little, Brown, 1981), 438–39, has a more detailed and balanced account.
5. Jefferson to Robert Selden Garnett, Feb. 14, 1824, in Lipscomb and Bergh, eds., *Writings*, 16: 14.
6. Jefferson to Robert Selden Garnett, Feb. 14, 1824, in Lipscomb and Bergh, eds., *Writings*, 16: 15.
7. Jefferson to Robert Selden Garnett, Feb. 14, 1824, in Lipscomb and Bergh, eds., *Writings*, 16: 15.
8. Ibid., 15–16.
9. Jackson Turner Main, "Distribution of Property in Post-Revolutionary Virginia," *Mississippi Valley Historical Review* 41, no. 2 (Sept. 1954): 241–258, esp. 243–245. On the prevalence of slaveholding whites in South Carolina and elsewhere, see Kenneth Stampp, *Peculiar Institution: Slavery in the Ante-Bellum South* (1956; reprinted, New York: Knopf, 1975), 29–31; and Otto H. Olsen, "Historians and the Extent of Slave Ownership in the United States," *Civil War History* 50, no. 4 (Dec. 2004): 401–17 (originally published in July 1972). On the small size of Massachusetts farms, often consisting of only eight to ten improved acres, see Pruitt, "Self-Sufficiency and the Agricultural Economy of Eighteenth-Century Massachusetts," *William and Mary Quarterly*, 3d ser., 41 (July 1984): 333–64.
10. Jackson T. Main, "The One Hundred," *William and Mary Quarterly*, 3d ser., 11, no. 3 (July 1954): 355–384. In Virginia as a whole, more slaves per acre worked the Piedmont plantations than the more fertile Northern Neck.
11. Jefferson to Robert Selden Garnett, Feb. 14, 1824, in Lipscomb and Bergh, eds., *Writings*, 16: 16.
12. Jefferson to Robert Selden Garnett, Feb. 14, 1824, in Lipscomb and Bergh, eds., *Writings*, 16: 14–16 (Garnett is incorrectly identified there). *Annals of Congress*, 18th Congress, 1st Sess., Jan. 24, 1824: 1179–1180. The Senate passed a similar presidential election amendment on Jan. 30, 1824, and sent it to the House, which failed to act. *Annals*, Jan. 30, 1824: 1292.
13. Jefferson to Garnett, Feb. 14, 1824, Lipscomb and Bergh, eds., *Writings*, 16: 14–16 .
14. See Jefferson to John Taylor, Jan. 5, 1805, in Peterson,

ed., *Jefferson: Writings*, 1153–54. The resolutions of the Hartford Convention, Jan. 4, 1815, may be found in Henry Steele Commager, ed., *Documents of American History* (2 vols.; Englewood Cliffs: Prentice-Hall, 1973), 1: 211. It proposed the constitutional amendment, "That the same person shall not be elected president of the United States a second time."
15. For Jefferson's abolitionist proposal, see Jefferson to Jared Sparks, Feb. 4, 1824, Lipscomb and Bergh, eds., Writings, 16: 8–14. For illuminating accounts of Sparks' travels in the South from 1819–21, including excerpts from his journals, see John Hammond Moore, "Jared Sparks in South Carolina," *South Carolina Historical Magazine* 72 (1971): 150–60; "Jared Sparks in North Carolina." *North Carolina Historical Review* 40 (1963): 283–94; and "Jared Sparks in Georgia," *Georgia Historical Quarterly* 47 (1963): 425–35.
16. Jefferson to Garnett, Feb. 14, 1824, in *Writings*, 16: 14–16. He often expressed his desire for a two-term limit for the president, notably in Jefferson to John Taylor of Caroline, Jan. 6, 1805, Peterson, ed., *Writings*, 1153–54. For the ubiquitous concept of inevitable republican decline as the economy matured and wealth became concentrated in fewer hands expressed by American eighteenth- and nineteenth-century thinkers, see, e.g., Drew McCoy, *The Elusive Republic: Political Economy in Jeffersonian America* (Chapel Hill: University of North Carolina Press, 1980); Michael Lienesch, *New Order of the Ages: Time, the Constitution, and the Making of Modern American Political Thought* (Princeton: Princeton University Press, 1988); and Thomas M. Allen, *A Republic in Time: Temporality and Social Imagination in Nineteenth-Century America* (Chapel Hill: University of North Carolina Press, 2006).
17. For McDuffie's amendment, see *Register of Congressional Debates*, House of Representatives, Feb. 15, 1826, 1365.
18. Edward Everett to Jefferson, Feb. 14, 1822; Jefferson to Edward Everett, March 2, 1822, Jefferson Papers, Library of Congress.
19. Everett's March 1826 speech defending slavery is printed in the *Register of Congressional Debates*, 2, pt. 1: 1579–1580.
20. Jefferson to Edward Everett, April 8, 1826, in Ford, ed., *Works of Thomas Jefferson*, 12: 469.
21. Ibid.
22. For a typical example of how otherwise competent historians ignore Jefferson's progressive political ideas during his retirement, see Robert M. S. McDonald, "Thomas Jefferson and Historical Self-Construction: The Earth Belongs to the Living?" *The Historian* 61 (Winter, 1999): 289–310.
23. On Jefferson's expansive vision of the republic, see Jefferson to Madison, April 27, 1809, in Lipscomb and Bergh, eds., *Writings of Jefferson*, 12: 277. See also Douglass G. Adair, *Intellectual Origins of Jeffersonian Democracy: Republicanism, The Class Struggle, and the Virtuous Farmer* (Lanham, Md.: Lexington Books, 2001); Julian P. Boyd, "Thomas Jefferson's 'Empire for Liberty,'" *Virginia Quarterly Review* 24 (Autumn 1948): 538–54, and McCoy, *The Elusive Republic*, 248–56.
24. Jefferson's first inaugural address, March 4, 1801, in Peterson, ed., *Writings*, 493 (first quotation); Jefferson to Colonel William Duane, March 28, 1811, Jefferson Papers, Library of Congress (second quotation). Jefferson's pessimism about the future of the South American governments arose from fear that "despotism may come upon them before they are qualified to save the ground they will have gained." Jefferson to Alexander Von Humboldt, April 14, 1811, in Peterson, ed., *Writings*, 1248 (quotation), and Jefferson to Humboldt, Dec. 6, 1813, Jefferson to Lafayette, May 14, 1817, and to John Adams, Sept. 4, 1823, *ibid.*, 1311–12, 1408–9, 1477–78.

25. For Jefferson and Crawford, see Chase C. Mooney, *William H. Crawford, 1772–1834* (Lexington: University Press of Kentucky, 1974), 256, 276, 289, 297. The nationalist Gallatin, who favored active government intervention in the economy, also supported Crawford in 1824. He feared Jackson as a potential militarist. Ibid., 26, 256, 276n. Mooney's biography is the best study of Crawford.

26. Jefferson to Marquis de La Fayette, Nov. 4, 1823, in Lipscomb and Bergh, eds., *Writings of Jefferson*, 15: 491.

27. Ibid. Among numerous studies of the frustration of Jefferson's impractical hope, shared with most of the Founding Fathers, that under a republican government political parties would not exist because all politicians would be devoted to the "public good," see Cunningham, *Jeffersonian Republicans in Power*; Hofstadter, *Idea of a Party System, 1780–1840*, 151–156, 166–168, 183, 193; David Hackett Fischer, *The Revolution of American Conservatism: The Federalist Party in the Era of Jeffersonian Democracy* (New York: Harper and Row, 1965); and Ralph Ketcham, *Presidents Above Party: The First American Presidency, 1789–1829* (Chapel Hill: University of North Carolina Press, 1984).

28. Jefferson to Marquis de La Fayette, Nov. 4, 1823, in Lipscomb and Bergh, eds., *Writings of Jefferson*, 15: 492.

29. See Paul L. Ford, ed., *Jefferson's Works*, 8: 1.

30. See Thomas N. Baker, "'An Attack Well Directed': Aaron Burr Intrigues for the Presidency," *Journal of the Early Republic* 31, no. 4 (Winter 2011): 553–598.

31. See John A. Ragosta, *Religious Freedom* (Charlottesville: University of Virginia Press, 2013), chapter one.

32. Jefferson to Marquis de La Fayette, Nov. 4, 1823, in Lipscomb and Bergh, eds., *Writings of Jefferson*, 15: 492.

33. Jefferson to Joel Barlow, May 3, 1802, Jefferson Papers, Library of Congress.

34. Jefferson to Marquis de La Fayette, Nov. 4, 1823, in Lipscomb and Bergh, eds., *Writings of Jefferson*, 15: 492. Indirectly, events in Virginia after the Revolution may have inspired Jefferson's concept of the "diffusion" of slavery. The state's poorer, non-slaveholding citizens went west. They moved to Kentucky, in part to escape paying back taxes. The richer, slaveholding Virginians who remained in the Piedmont's Caroline County, for example, in 1784 complained about this to the state legislature. They became more insistent on retaining slavery in the state. Consequently, they increased their political power when many non-slaveholders left for Kentucky and points west. See Michael A. McDonnell, *The Politics of War* (Chapel Hill: University of North Carolina Press, 2007), 485.

35. See William W. Freehling, *Road to Disunion: Volume 1: Secessionists at Bay, 1776–1854* (New York: Oxford University Press, 1990); and Ari Helo, *Thomas Jefferson's Ethics and the Politics of Human Progress: the Morality of a Slaveholder* (New York: Cambridge University Press, 2014).

36. Jefferson to Marquis de La Fayette, Nov. 4, 1823, in Lipscomb and Bergh, eds., *Writings of Jefferson*, 15: 492–493.

37. See Dunbar, *A Study of 'Monarchical Tendencies' in the United States*.

38. Jefferson to Martin Van Buren, June 29, 1824, in Lipscomb and Bergh, eds., *Writings of Jefferson*, 16: 66. In several works, Professor of Government Mark A. Graber has compellingly argued that, rather than being provocatively hypernationalist, Marshall's Supreme Court decisions were actually designed to appease the Democratic-Republican presidents. Indeed, Monroe's opinions were akin to those of Marshall, and they remained close friends. In other words, Marshall's nationalist bark was worse than his bite. See, e.g., Mark A. Graber, "Federalist or Friends of Adams: The Marshall Court and Party Politics," *Studies in American Political Development* 12, no. 2 (Oct. 1998): 229–266.

39. Jefferson to Martin Van Buren, June 29, 1824, in Lipscomb and Bergh, eds., *Writings of Jefferson*, 16: 61.

40. Ibid., 69.

41. Jefferson to Marquis de La Fayette, Nov. 4, 1823, in Lipscomb and Bergh, eds., *Writings of Jefferson*, 15: 493.

42. On Jefferson's conception of slaves as human property, see Arthur Scherr, "Thomas Jefferson's 'Poor Woman': A Symbol of Sentiment or Social Inequality?" *Midwest Quarterly* 39, no. 3 (Spring 1998): 329–346.

43. Jefferson to Henry Lee, Jr., Aug. 10, 1824, in Paul L. Ford, ed., *Writings of Thomas Jefferson* (10 vols.; New York, 1892–1899), 10: 317–318.

44. Jefferson to Henry Lee, Jr., Aug. 10, 1824, in Paul L. Ford, ed., *Writings of Thomas Jefferson* (10 vols.; New York, 1892–1899), 10: 317–318. Henry Lee, Jr., was the son of Henry Lee, one of Jefferson's old Virginia Federalist enemies, a Revolutionary War general (also father of the more famous Robert E. Lee) who bore a personal grudge against Jefferson arising from distaste for his democratic views. Lee had attempted to turn George Washington against Jefferson during the late 1790s. See Malone, *Jefferson and the Ordeal of Liberty*, 269–270; and, in general, Charles Royster, *Light Horse Harry Lee and the Legacy of the American Revolution* (New York: Knopf, 1981).

45. Jefferson to Henry Lee, Jr., Aug. 10, 1824, in Ford, ed., *Writings*, 10: 317.

Conclusion

1. Thomas Cooper to Jefferson, April 19, 1818, in "Jefferson Papers," *Massachusetts Historical Society Collections* 61 (1900): 271–272. Lawrence S. Kaplan, "Jefferson as Anglophile: Sagacity or Senility in the Era of Good Feelings," *Diplomatic History* 16, no. 3 (July 1992): 487–494, partially corrects this historiographical misunderstanding.

2. Jefferson to William Clark, Sept. 12, 1825, Jefferson Papers, Library of Congress.

3. Dumas Malone, *Sage of Monticello* (Boston: Little, Brown, 1981), 464. This was the situation in September 1825, the time of Jefferson's letter to William Clark.

4. Jefferson to William Short, Aug. 9, 1825, Jefferson Papers, Massachusetts Historical Society; and Jefferson to Ellen Randolph, Aug. 27, 1825, in Edwin Betts and James A. Bear, eds., *Family Letters of Thomas Jefferson* (Columbia: University of Missouri Press, 1966), 458.

5. Nicholas Trist to Jefferson, Sept. 18, 1825, Nicholas Trist Papers, Library of Congress.

6. Malone, *Sage of Monticello*, 464–466.

7. Ibid., 467.

8. Jefferson to Joseph Coolidge, Jr., Oct. 13, 1825, in *Thomas Jefferson Papers: Massachusetts Historical Society Collections* (1900), 356; Jefferson to William Short, Oct. 14, 1825, Jefferson Papers, Library of Congress; Malone, *Sage of Monticello*, 468–469; John M. Dorsey, ed., *Jefferson-Duglison Letters* (Charlottesville: University of Virginia Press, 1960).

9. Malone, *Sage of Monticello*, 483–84.

10. Jefferson to Coolidge, June 4, 1826, quoted ibid., 483–84.

11. Malone, *Sage of Monticello*, 484.

12. For Jefferson's meeting with Joseph Coolidge, who favorably impressed him, see Malone, *Sage of Monticello*, 458. On Thomas Jefferson Coolidge, see the entry, "Coolidge, Thomas Jefferson," in *American National Biography*.

13. Ellen Randolph Coolidge to Jefferson, Aug. 1, 1825, in Edwin M. Betts and James A. Bear, Jr., eds., *Family Letters*

of *Thomas Jefferson* (Columbia: University of Missouri Press, 1966), 454–455.

14. Ibid., 455.

15. Ibid., 456. For an account of Ellen W. Coolidge's protectiveness of her grandfather's reputation in later life and her defensiveness during the late 1850s regarding charges that he fathered several children with his slave Sally Hemings, see Dumas Malone, "Mr. Jefferson's Private Life," *Proceedings of the American Antiquarian Society* 84 (1974): 65–72.

16. Jefferson to Ellen W. Coolidge, Aug. 27, 1825, in Koch and Peden, *Life and Selected Writings*, 720–721.

17. Jefferson to Jared Sparks, Feb. 4, 1824, in Ford, ed., *Works of Jefferson*, 12: 336–37. For Jefferson's advocacy of Haiti as the site of settlement for emancipated U.S. slaves, see Jefferson to James Monroe, Nov. 24, 1801, in Lipscomb and Bergh, ed., *Writings*, 10: 296–298; Jefferson to David B. Warden, Dec. 26, 1820, Ford, ed., *Works*, 12: 181; Jefferson to Gallatin, Dec. 26, 1820, Peterson, ed., *Writings*, 1450; Jefferson to Jared Sparks, Feb. 4, 1824, in Ford, ed., *Works*, 12: 337–338; Ford, ed., *Writings*,10: 289–293, and Lipscomb and Bergh, eds., *Writings*, 16: 9–12; Jefferson to William Short, Sept. 8, 1823, in Jefferson Papers, Library of Congress; Jefferson to William Short, Jan. 18, 1826, in Ford, ed., *Works*, 12: 434; and Jefferson to Joel Barlow, Oct. 8, 1809, in Ford, ed., *Works of Jefferson*, XI, 121; and in Looney, ed., *Papers of Thomas Jefferson: Retirement Series*, 1: 589.

18. Jefferson's "Draft Declaration and Protest of the Commonwealth of Virginia, on the Principles of the Constitution of the United States of America, and on the Violations of them," December 1825, in Peterson, ed., *Writings*, 482–486. Embittered because he had failed to achieve greater political success, Giles may have written newspaper articles in 1822 under the pseudonym, "A Native of Virginia." The author of these obscure and vituperative essays, which accused Jefferson of stealing money from the Treasury as minister to France in the 1780s, has not been definitely determined.

19. Jefferson's "Draft Declaration and Protest of the Commonwealth of Virginia, on the Principles of the Constitution of the United States of America, and on the Violations of them," December 1825, in Peterson, ed., *Writings*, 482–486, quote at 484.

20. Jefferson's "Draft Declaration and Protest of the Commonwealth of Virginia, on the Principles of the Constitution of the United States of America, and on the Violations of them," December 1825, in Peterson, ed., *Writings*, 482–486, quotes at 484, 485–86. On the advice of Madison, Jefferson never returned this document to Giles. Jefferson to Madison, Dec. 24, 1825, Jefferson to Giles, Dec. 26, 1825, Ford, ed., *Works of Jefferson*, 12: 417, 425; Madison to Jefferson, Dec. 28, 1825, in Gaillard Hunt, ed., *Writings of James Madison*, 9 vols. (New York: Putnam, 1900–1901), 9: 236–240. See also Harrison, "Jefferson and Internal Improvement," 347.

21. Jefferson to Madison, Dec. 24, 1825, in Ford, ed., *Works of Jefferson*, 12: 416.

22. Jefferson's "Solemn Declaration and Protest" of the Virginia General Assembly, in Ford, ed., *Works of Jefferson*, 12: 420n.

23. Ibid.

24. Ibid., 420n.

25. Jefferson's "Solemn Declaration and Protest," ibid., 421n.

26. John Quincy Adams, first annual message to Congress, December 6, 1825, in James D. Richardson, ed., *Compilation of the Messages and Papers of the Presidents* (10 vols.; Washington, D.C.: Government Printing Office, 1900), 2: 316; also available online.

27. Jefferson's "Solemn Declaration and Protest," Ford, ed., *Works of Jefferson*, 12: 421n.

28. See Michael P. Zuckert, *The Natural Rights Republic* (Notre Dame: University of Notre Dame Press, 1996), 87–89, and Robert B. Fowler, "Mythologizing of a Founder," in Thomas S. Engeman, ed., *Thomas Jefferson and the Politics of Nature* (Notre Dame: University of Notre Dame Press, 2000), 129.

29. Jefferson to William B. Giles, Dec. 26, 1825, in Peterson, ed., *Writings*, 1510–1511.

30. Jefferson to William B. Giles, Dec. 26, 1825, ibid., 1511–1512; Giles to Jefferson, Dec. 15, 1825 (two letters), Jefferson Papers, Library of Congress. See also Samuel F. Bemis, *John Quincy Adams and the Union* (New York: Knopf, 1956), 161–165, and Bemis, *John Quincy Adams and the Foundations of American Foreign Policy* (New York: Knopf, 1949), 142–147.

31. Jefferson to Giles, Dec. 26, 1825, in Peterson, ed., *Writings*, 1511. For Jefferson's relief that the Missouri crisis had subsided, and that the old aristocrat/democrat dichotomy between the Republicans and Federalists would replace the abortive Federalist project, suspected by him and other Republicans, to erect a sectionally based antislavery party, see Robert Pierce Forbes, "Slavery and the Meaning of America, 1819–1837" (Ph.D. dissertation, Yale University, 1994), 263–66, and Stuart Leibiger, "Thomas Jefferson and the Missouri Crisis: An Alternative Interpretation," *Journal of the Early Republic* 17 (Spring 1997): 121–130.

32. Jefferson to Giles, Dec. 26, 1825, in Ford, ed., *Works of Jefferson*, 12: 427–428. For Jefferson's earlier recommendation that his nephew study French and Spanish rather than Greek, Latin, or even mellifluous (as he thought it) modern Italian, see Jefferson to Peter Carr, Aug. 19,1785, and Jefferson to Peter Carr, Aug. 10, 1787, in Peterson, ed., *Jefferson: Writings*, 816–818, 901. On Jefferson's opposition to teaching the "dead" classical languages at the College of William and Mary, see Meyer Reinhold, *Classica Americana* (Detroit: Wayne State University Press, 1984), 124–25. For Jefferson's belief that only a select elite should be exposed to classical education, see also Carl J. Richard, *The Founders and the Classics* (Cambridge, Mass.: Harvard University Press, 1994), 34–35, and Daniel J. Boorstin, *The Lost World of Thomas Jefferson* (New York: Holt, 1948), 220–221, 289n. Nonetheless, Jefferson was always proud of his knowledge of classical Greek and Latin and grateful to his father for exposing him to it. He also believed, "that the classical languages are a solid basis for most, and an ornament to all the sciences." Jefferson to John Brazier, Aug. 24, 1819, Peterson, ed., *Jefferson: Writings*, 1425.

33. Jefferson to Giles, Dec. 26, 1825, in Ford, ed., *Works of Jefferson*, 12: 428.

34. See Jennings L. Wagoner, Jr., "Honor and Dishonor at Mr. Jefferson's University: The Antebellum Years," *History of Education Quarterly* 26 (Summer 1986): 155–179.

35. Jefferson to Adams, March 25, 1826, Cappon, ed., *Adams-Jefferson Letters*, 613–614.

36. Adams to Jefferson, April 17, 1826, *ibid.*, 614.

37. Jefferson's "Notes on Locke (1776)," in Boyd, ed., *Papers of Thomas Jefferson* (Princeton, 1950–), 1: 548.

38. See the contrasting viewpoints of Jan Lewis and Peter S. Onuf, "American Synecdoche: Thomas Jefferson as Image, Icon, Character, and Self," *American Historical Review* 103 (Feb.1998): 125–136, and Jeffrey L. Pasley, "Politics and the Misadventures of Thomas Jefferson's Modern Reputation: A Review Essay," *Journal of Southern History* 72 (Nov. 2006): 871–908.

Bibliography

Primary Sources

Adams, John. *Adams-Jefferson Letters.* Ed. Lester J. Cappon. 2 vols. Chapel Hill: University of North Carolina Press, 1959. Published in one-volume edition in 1988.

_____. *The Political Writings of John Adams: Representative Selections.* Ed. George A. Peak. Indianapolis: Bobbs-Merrill, 1954.

_____. *Works of John Adams.* Ed. Charles Francis Adams. 10 vols. Boston: Little, Brown, 1850–1856.

Adams, John Quincy. *Diary of John Quincy Adams, 1794–1845.* Ed. Allan Nevins. New York: Frederick Ungar, 1951.

America's Historical Newspapers. READEX Database.

Austin, James T. *An Oration pronounced at Lexington, Mass., July 4th, 1815, in commemoration of the independence of the United States of America and the Restoration of Peace.* Boston: Rowe and Hooper, 1815.

Bache, Benjamin Franklin. Bache Family Papers, Castle Collection, American Philosophical Society (microfilm).

Beecher, Lyman. *An Address of the Charitable Society for the Education of Indigent Pious Young Men for the Ministry of the Gospel.* New Haven, 1814. Shaw and Shoemaker #30833.

Brookes, Joshua. "A Dinner at Mt. Vernon: From the Unpublished Journal of Joshua Brookes (1773–1859)." Ed. R. W. G. Vail. *New-York Historical Society Quarterly* 31, no. 4 (April 1947): 72–85.

Brown, Everett S., ed., *The Missouri Compromise and Presidential Politics, 1820–1825.* St. Louis: Missouri Historical Society, 1926.

Brown, Roger H. *The Republic in Peril: 1812.* New York: Columbia University Press, 1964.

Burr, Aaron. *Political Correspondence and Public Papers of Aaron Burr.* Ed. Mary-Jo Kline. 2 vols. Princeton: Princeton University Press, 1983.

Commager, Henry Steele, ed. *Documents of American History.* 2 vols. Englewood Cliffs: Prentice-Hall, 1973.

Connecticut Courant [Hartford].

Cutler, William P. and Julia P. Cutler, *Life, Journals, and Correspondence of Reverend Manasseh Cutler.* 2 vols. Cincinnati: Robert Clarke, 1888.

Daily National Intelligencer [Washington].

Farmer's Weekly Museum [Walpole, N.H.].

The Federalist; or, the New Constitution. Ed. W. R. Brock. 1788; London: J. M. Dent, 1961.

General Advertiser: Aurora [Philadelphia].

Greensleet, Ferris, ed., *Life, Letters, and Journals of George Ticknor.* 2 vols. Boston: Houghton Mifflin, 1909.

Hamilton, Alexander. *Papers of Alexander Hamilton.* Ed. Harold C. Syrett. 27 vols. New York: Columbia University Press, 1961–87.

Hampden. *Letter to the President of the United States, Touching the Prosecutions Under his Patronage, Before the Circuit Court of the District of Connecticut.* New Haven: Oliver Steele, 1808. Shaw and Shoemaker #15422.

Harper, Robert Goodloe. *Correspondence Respecting Russia between Robert Goodloe Harper and Robert Walsh, Jr.* Philadelphia: William Fry, 1813. Shaw and Shoemaker #30439.

_____. *Plain Reasons of a Plain Man: for preferring Gen. Jackson to Mr. Adams.* Baltimore: Benjamin Edes, 1825.

Hayes, Kevin P. ed., *Jefferson in His Own Time.* Iowa City: University of Iowa Press, 2012.

Hillard, G.S. and Anna Eliot Ticknor, ed., *Life, Letters, and Journals of George Ticknor.* 2 vols.: Boston: James R. Osgood, 1876.

Holmes, John. *An oration pronounced at Alfred* [Maine], *on the 4th of July, 1815.* Boston: Rowe and Hooper, 1815.

Hunt, Gaillard ed., *Disunion Sentiment in Congress in 1794.* Washington: W. H. Lowdermilk, 1905.

Independent Chronicle [Boston].

Jackson, Andrew. *The Papers of Andrew Jackson.* Ed. Harold D. Moser, et al. Knoxville: University of Tennessee Press, 1980– .

Jefferson, Thomas. Catalogue of Jefferson's Second Library, Offered for Sale at Public Auction, Feb. 27, 1829, Jefferson Papers, Library of Congress, Series 7. Miscellaneous Bound Volumes. "American Memory" Series, online.

_____. *A Catalogue of the Extensive and Valuable Library of the Late President Jefferson… to be sold by Nathaniel Poor at Public Auction, 27 Feb. 1829.* 1829; reprinted, Ypsilanti, Mich.: University Lithographers, 1944

_____. *Complete Anas of Thomas Jefferson.* Ed. Franklin B. Sawvel. 1903; reprinted, New York: DaCapo Press, 1970.

_____. *Complete Jefferson.* Ed. Saul K. Padover. New York: Duell, Sloan, and Pearce, 1943.

_____. *Family Letters of Thomas Jefferson.* Ed. Edwin Betts and James A. Bear. Columbia: University of Missouri Press, 1966.

_____. *Jefferson-Duglison Letters.* Ed. John M. Dorsey. Charlottesville: University of Virginia Press, 1960.

_____. "Jefferson Papers." *Collections of the Massachusetts Historical Society,* 7th Series, Vol. I [Vol. 61] (1900).

_____. *Jefferson's Extracts from the Gospels.* Ed. Dickinson W. Adams. Princeton: Princeton University Press, 1983.

_____. *Jefferson's Memorandum Books.* Ed. James A. Bear and Lucia C. Stanton. 2 vols. Princeton: Princeton University Press, 1997.

_____. *Life and Selected Writings of Thomas Jefferson.* Ed. Adrienne Koch and William Peden. New York: Modern Library, 1944.

_____. Papers. University of Virginia (microfilm).

_____. Papers, Library of Congress. Available on microfilm and online in Library of Congress "American Memory" series.

_____. *Papers of Thomas Jefferson.* Ed. Julian P. Boyd, Barbara B. Oberg, et al. 41 vols., in progress, Princeton: Princeton University Press, 1950– .

_____. *Papers of Thomas Jefferson: Retirement Series.* Ed. J. Jefferson Looney. 11 vols., in progress. Princeton: Princeton University Press, 2004–.

_____. *The Portable Thomas Jefferson.* Ed. Merrill D. Peterson New York: Knopf, 1975.

_____. *Republic of Letters: The Correspondence between Thomas Jefferson and James Madison, 1776–1826.* Ed. James Morton Smith. 3 vols. New York: Norton, 1995.

_____. "Some Jefferson Letters." Ed. Sigmund Diamond. *Mississippi Valley Historical Review* 28, no. 2 (Sept. 1941): 225–242.

_____. *Thomas Jefferson: Writings.* Ed. Merrill D. Peterson. New York: Library of America, 1984.

_____. *Works of Thomas Jefferson.* Ed. Paul L. Ford. 12 vols. New York: Putnam, 1904–5.

_____. *Writings of Thomas Jefferson.* Ed. Albert Ellery Bergh. 20 vols. Washington, D. C.: Thomas Jefferson Memorial Foundation, 1907.

_____. *Writings of Thomas Jefferson.* Ed. Andrew A. Lipscomb and Albert E. Bergh. 20 vols. Washington, D.C.: Thomas Jefferson Memorial Foundation, 1903.

_____. *Writings of Thomas Jefferson.* Ed. Paul Leicester Ford. 10 vols. New York: Putnam, 1892–1899.

Johnston, Hugh Buckner, ed. "Journal of Ebenezer Hazard, 1777–1778." *North Carolina Historical Review* 36, no. 3 (July 1959): 358–381.

Lee, Richard Henry. *The Letters of Richard Henry Lee.* Ed. James C. Ballagh. 2 vols. New York, 1911–1914.

Linn, William. *Serious Considerations on the Election of a President, Addressed to the Citizens of the United States.* New York: J. Furman, 1800.

Madison, James. *Papers of James Madison.* Ed. J.C.A. Stagg; Robert A. Rutland; William T. Hutchinson; W. M. E. Rachal, et al. Chicago and Charlottesville: University of Chicago Press and University of Virginia Press, 1962

_____. *Writings of James Madison.* Ed. Gaillard Hunt. 9 vols. New York: Putnam, 1900–1910.

Mason, John M. *The Voice of Warning to Christians, on the Ensuing Election of a President of the United States.* New York: G. F. Hopkins, 1800.

Monroe, James. Papers, New York Public Library.

_____. *Writings of James Monroe.* Ed. Stanislaus M. Hamilton. 7 vols. New York: Putnam, 1898–1903.

Montesquieu, Charles Secondat, Baron de. *The Spirit of the Laws.* Trans. Thomas Nugent. 1748. New York: Hafner, 1949.

Morse, Jedidiah. *American Geography.* Revised edition. London: John Stockdale, 1794.

Niles Weekly Register.

Oxford English Dictionary. Available online.

Peterson, Merrill D., ed., *Visitors to Monticello.* Charlottesville: University Press of Virginia, 1989.

Pickering, Timothy. Papers. Massachusetts Historical Society. (Index at Vol. 51).

Port Folio [Philadelphia].

Public Statutes at Large of the United States. Ed. Richard Peters. Boston: Little and Brown, 1850.

Register of Congressional Debates. House of Representatives.

Richardson, James D., ed. *Compilation of the Messages and Papers of the Presidents.* 10 vols. Washington, D.C.: Government Printing Office, 1900.

Richmond Enquirer

Rousseau, Jean-Jacques. *The Social Contract and Discourses by Jean-Jacques Rousseau.* Ed. G. D. H. Cole. New York: Dutton, 1950.

Rush, Benjamin. "Thoughts Upon the Mode of Education Proper in a Republic" (1786). In Frederick Rudolph, ed., *Essays on Education in the Early Republic.* Cambridge: Harvard University Press, 1965, 9–23.

Sowerby, E. Millicent, ed. *Catalogue of the Library of Thomas Jefferson.* 5 vols. Washington: Library of Congress, 1952–1959.

Thorpe, Francis Newton, ed. *Federal and State Constitutions.* 7 vols. Washington: Government Printing Office, 1909.

Tocqueville, Alexis de. *Democracy in America.* Ed. J. P. Mayer and Max Lerner. Translated by George Lawrence 1835. 2 vols. in one, New York: Harper & Row, 1966.

Watson, Harry L., ed., *Andrew Jackson vs. Henry Clay: Democracy and Development in Antebellum America.* Boston: Bedford/St. Martin's, 1998.

Webster, Daniel. Papers of Daniel Webster. Microfilm edition. Dartmouth College Library

_____. *Papers of Daniel Webster,* Series One. Ed. Charles M .Wiltse. 7 vols. Hanover, N.H.: University Press of New England, 1974–1988.

_____. *Private Correspondence of Daniel Webster.* Ed. Fletcher Webster. 2 vols. Boston: Little, Brown, 1857.

_____. *National Edition of Webster's Writings.* 18 vols. Boston: Little, Brown, 1903.

United States Congress. *Debates and Proceedings.* 42 vols. Washington, D.C.: Gales and Seaton, 1834–1856. Often referred to as *Annals of Congress.*

Yale University Law School. *Avalon Project.* Online database of historical sources.

Secondary Sources

Abernethy, Thomas P. *The South in the New Nation, 1789–1819.* Baton Rouge: Louisiana State University Press, 1961.

Adair, Douglass G. *Intellectual Origins of Jeffersonian Democracy: Republicanism, The Class Struggle, and the Virtuous Farmer.* Lanham, Md.: Lexington Books, 2001.

Adams, Henry. *History of the United States during the Administrations of Thomas Jefferson.* 1901; reprinted, New York: Literary Classics of the United States, 1986.

_____. *History of the United States of America during the Administrations of Thomas Jefferson and James Madison,* 9 vols. 1891–1896; reprinted, New York: Antiquarian Press, 1962.

Allen, Thomas M. *A Republic in Time: Temporality and Social Imagination in Nineteenth-Century America.* Chapel Hill: University of North Carolina Press, 2006.

Anderson, Philip J. "William Linn, 1752–1808: American Revolutionary and Anti-Jeffersonian." *Journal of Presbyterian History* 55, no. 4 (Nov. 1977): 381–394.

Appleby, Joyce. *Inheriting the Revolution: The First Generation of Americans.* Cambridge: Harvard University Press, 2000.

_____. "What Is Still American in the Political Philosophy of Thomas Jefferson?" *William and Mary Quarterly,* 3d ser., 39, no. 2 (April 1982): 287–309.

Arbena, Joseph L. "Politics or Principle? Rufus King and the Opposition to Slavery, 1785–1825." *Essex Institute Historical Collections* 101 (1965): 56–77.

Aronson, Sidney H. *Status and Kinship in the Higher Civil Service.* Cambridge: Harvard University Press, 1964.

Bailey, Jeremy D. "Constitutionalism, Conflict, and Consent: Jefferson on the Impeachment Power." *Review of Politics* 70, no. 4 (Fall 2008): 572–594.

_____. "Executive Prerogative and the 'Good Officer' in Thomas Jefferson's Letter to John B. Colvin." *Presidential Studies Quarterly* 34 (Dec. 2004): 732–754.

_____. *Thomas Jefferson and Executive Power.* Cambridge: Cambridge University Press, 2007.

Bailyn, Bernard. *To Begin the World Anew: The Genius and Ambiguities of the American Founders.* New York: Knopf, 2004.

Baker, Thomas N. "'An Attack Well Directed': Aaron Burr Intrigues for the Presidency." *Journal of the Early Republic* 31, no. 4 (Winter 2011): 553–598.

Banner, James M. "A Shadow of Secession? The Hartford Convention." *History Today* 38, no. 9 (Sept. 1988): 24–30.

_____. *To the Hartford Convention: The Federalists and the Origins of Party Politics in Massachusetts, 1789–1815.* New York: Knopf, 1970.

Banning, Lance. *The Jeffersonian Persuasion: Evolution of a Party Ideology.* Ithaca: Cornell University Press, 1978.

_____. *The Sacred Fire of Liberty: James Madison and The Founding of the Federal Republic.* Ithaca: Cornell University Press, 1995.

Bartlett, Irving H. *Daniel Webster.* New York: Norton, 1978.

Bassett, John Spencer. *Life of Andrew Jackson.* 1911; 2 vols. in one. New York: Macmillan, 1928.

Baumann, Roland M. "John Swanwick: Spokesman for 'Merchant-Republicanism' in Philadelphia, 1790–1798." *Pennsylvania Magazine of History and Biography,* 97 (April 1973): 131–182.

Becker, Robert A. *Revolution, Reform, and the Politics of American Taxation, 1763–1783.* Baton Rouge: Louisiana State University Press, 1980.

Billias, George Athan. *Elbridge Gerry: Founding Father and Republican Statesman.* New York: McGraw-Hill, 1976.

Binger, Carl A. *Thomas Jefferson: A Well-Tempered Mind*. New York: Norton, 1970.

Bloch, Ruth. *Visionary Republic: Millennial Themes in American Thought, 1756–1800*. Cambridge: Cambridge University Press, 1985.

Bolster, William Jeffrey. "The Impact of Jefferson's Embargo on Coastal Commerce." *Log of Mystic Seaport* 37 (January 1986): 111–123.

Boorstin, Daniel J. *The Lost World of Thomas Jefferson*. New York: Henry Holt, 1948.

Boyd, Julian P. "Horatio Gates Spafford." *Proceedings of the American Antiquarian Society* 51, no. 2 (Oct. 1941): 279–350.

_____. "Thomas Jefferson's 'Empire for Liberty.'" *Virginia Quarterly Review* 24 (Autumn 1948): 538–54.

Breen, Timothy H. "John Adams' Fight Against Innovation in the New England Constitution: 1776." *New England Quarterly* 40 (Dec. 1967): 501–520.

Brewer, Holly. "Entailing Aristocracy in Colonial Virginia: 'Ancient Feudal Restraints' and Revolutionary Reform." *William and Mary Quarterly*, 3rd ser., 54, no. 2 (April 1997), 307–346.

Brigham, Clarence S. *History and Bibliography of American Newspapers, 1690–1820*. 2 vols. Worcester: American Antiquarian Society, 1947.

Brown, David. "Jeffersonian Ideology and the Second Party System." *The Historian* 62, no. 1 (Sept. 1999): 17–30.

Brown, Norman D. "The Webster-Jackson Movement for a Constitution and Union Party in 1833." *Mid-America: A Historical Review* 46 (July 1964): 147–171.

Brown, Robert E. *Middle-Class Democracy and the Revolution in Massachusetts*. East Lansing: Michigan State University Press, 1955.

Browne, C. A. "Leland and the Mammoth Cheshire Cheese." *Agricultural History* 18 (1944): 145–153.

Browne, Stephen H. *Jefferson's Call for Nationhood: The First Inaugural Address*. College Station, Tex.: Texas A & M Press, 2003.

Bruce, Dickson D. *And They All Sang Hallelujah: Plain-Folk Camp-Meeting Religion, 1800–1845*. Knoxville: University of Tennessee Press, 1974.

Buchanan, John. *Jackson's Way: Andrew Jackson and the People of the Western Waters*. New York: Wiley, 2001.

Buckley, Thomas E. "The Religious Rhetoric of Thomas Jefferson," in *The Founders on God and Government*. Ed. Daniel L. Dreisbach et al. Lanham, Md.: Rowman Littlefield, 2004, pp. 53–82.

Buel, Richard, Jr. *America on the Brink: How the Political Struggle over the War of 1812 Almost Destroyed the Republic*. New York: Palgrave Macmillan, 2005.

_____. *Securing the Revolution: Ideology in American Politics, 1789–1815*. Ithaca: Cornell University Press, 1972.

Buell, Augustus C. *History of Andrew Jackson*. 2 vols. New York: Scribner, 1904.

Burin, Eric. *Slavery and the Peculiar Solution: A History of the American Colonization Society*. Gainesville: University Press of Florida, 2005.

Burns, Edward M. "The Philosophy of History of the Founding Fathers." *The Historian* 16 (Spring 1954): 142–168.

Burstein, Andrew. *Jefferson's Secrets: Death and Desire at Monticello*. New York: Basic Books, 2005.

Bushman, Richard L. "Family Security in the Transition from Farm to City, 1750–1850." *Journal of Family History* 6 (Fall 1981): 238–256.

_____. "Markets and Composite Farms in Early America." *William and Mary Quarterly* 55 (July 1998): 351–374.

Butterfield, Lyman H. "Elder John Leland, Jeffersonian Itinerant." *American Antiquarian Society, Proceedings* 62, no. 2 (Oct. 1952): 155–242.

Carrithers, David W. "Montesquieu, Jefferson, and the Fundamentals of Eighteenth Century Republican Theory." *French-American Review* 6, no. 2 (Fall 1982): 160–88.

Cary, John. "Statistical Method and the Brown Thesis on Colonial Democracy." *William and Mary Quarterly*, 3d ser., 20, no. 2 (April 1963): 251–264.

Chambers, William Nisbet. "Party Development and Party Action: The American Origins." *History and Theory*, 3 (Feb. 1963): 91–120.

Chapman, Michael E. "Pragmatic, *ad hoc* Foreign-Policy Making of the Early Republic: Thomas H. Perkins' Boston-Smyrna-Canton Opium Model and Congressional Rejection of Aid for Greek Independence." *International History Review* 35, no. 3 (2013): 449–464.

Chinard, Gilbert. *Honest John Adams*. Rev. ed. Boston: Little, Brown, 1964.

_____. *Volney et l'Amérique*. Baltimore: Johns Hopkins University Press, 1923.

Clark, Clifford E., Jr., *Henry Ward Beecher: Spokesman for Middle-Class America*. Urbana: University of Illinois Press, 1978.

Cogliano, Francis. *Emperor of Liberty: Thomas Jefferson's Foreign Policy*. New Haven: Yale University Press, 2014.

_____. *Thomas Jefferson: Reputation and Legacy*. Edinburgh, 2006.

Colbourn, H. Trevor. *The Lamp of Experience: Whig History and the Intellectual Origins of the American Revolution*. Chapel Hill: University of North Carolina Press, 1965.

_____. "Thomas Jefferson's Use of the Past." *William and Mary Quarterly*, 3d ser., 15, no. 1 (January 1958): 56–70.

Coleman, Peter J. *The Transformation of Rhode Island, 1790–1860*. Providence: Brown University Press, 1963.

Cook, Edmund. *The Fathers of the Towns: Leadership and Community Structure in Eighteenth-Century New England*. Baltimore: Johns Hopkins University Press, 1976.

Crawford, Alan Pell. *Twilight at Monticello: The Final Years of Thomas Jefferson*. New York: Random House, 2008.

Cunningham, Noble E., Jr. *Jeffersonian Republicans: The Formation of Party Organization, 1789–1801*. Chapel Hill: University of North Carolina Press, 1957.

_____. *The Jeffersonian Republicans in Power: Party Operations, 1801–1809*. Chapel Hill: University of North Carolina Press, 1963.Current, Richard N., et al. *American History: A Survey*. New York: Knopf, 1961.

Curtis, George Ticknor. *Life of Daniel Webster*. 2 vols. New York: Appleton, 1870.

Dauer, Manning J. *The Adams Federalists*. Baltimore: Johns Hopkins University Press, 1953.

Davis, Burke. *Old Hickory: A Life of Andrew Jackson*. New York: Dial Press, 1977.

Davis, David B. "American Equality and Foreign Revolutions," *Journal of American History*, 76, no. 3 (Dec. 1989): 729–752.

_____. *The Problem of Slavery in the Age of Revolution, 1770–1823*. Ithaca: Cornell University Press, 1975.

Davis, Thomas Lawrence. "Aristocrats & Jacobins in Country Towns: Party Formation in Berkshire Country, Massachusetts (1775–1816)." Ph.D. dissertation, Boston University, 1975.

Dennis, Everette E. "Stolen Peace Treaties and the Press: Two Case Studies," *Journalism History*, 2 (1975): 6–14.

Dreisbach, Daniel L. "The Constitution's Forgotten Religion Clause: Reflections on the Article VI Religious Test Ban." *Journal of Church and State* 38 (Spring 1996): 261–295.

_____. *Thomas Jefferson and the 'Wall of Separation' Between Church and State*. New York: New York University Press, 2002.

Dubin, Michael J. *United States Presidential Elections, 1788–1860: The Official Records by County and State*. Jefferson, N.C.: McFarland, 2002.

Dumbauld, Edward. *Thomas Jefferson: American Tourist*. Norman: University of Oklahoma Press, 1946.

Dunbar, Louise B. *A Study of 'Monarchical Tendencies' in the United States from 1776–1801*. Urbana: University of Illinois Press, 1922.

Durey, Michael. *Transatlantic Radicals and the Early American Republic*. Lawrence: University Press of Kansas, 1997.

Eckhardt, Celia Morris. *Fanny Wright: Rebel in America*. Cambridge: Harvard University Press, 1984.

Einhorn, Robin. *American Taxation, American Slavery*. Chicago: University of Chicago Press, 2006.

Elkins, Stanley, and Eric McKitrick. *The Age of Federalism*. New York: Oxford University Press, 1993.

Ellis, Joseph J. *American Sphinx: The Character of Thomas Jefferson*. New York: Knopf, 1997.

_____. *Passionate Sage: The Character and Legacy of John Adams*. New York: Norton, 1993.

Ernst, Robert. *Rufus King: American Federalist*. Chapel Hill: University of North Carolina Press, 1967.

_____. "Rufus King, Slavery, and the Missouri Crisis." *New-York Historical Society Quarterly* 46 (1962): 357–382.

Essig, James David. *The Bonds of Wickedness: American Evangelicals Against Slavery, 1770–1808*. Philadelphia: Temple University Press, 1982.

_____. "'A Very Wintry Season': Virginia Baptists and Slavery, 1785–1797." *Virginia Magazine of History and Biography* 88, no. 2 (April 1980): 170–185.

Everett, Robert B. "The Mature Religious Thought of John Adams." *Proceedings of the South Carolina Historical Association* (1966): 49–57.

Fabel, Robin F.A. "Self-Help in Dartmoor: Black and White Prisoners in the War of 1812." *Journal of the Early Republic* 9, no. 2 (Summer 1989): 165–190.

Ferling, John. *John Adams: A Life*. Knoxville: University of Tennessee Press, 1992.

_____. *Setting the World Ablaze: Washington, Adams, Jefferson, and the American Revolution*. New York: Oxford University Press, 2000.

Field, Peter S. *Crisis of the Standing Order: Clerical Intellectuals and Cultural Authority in Massachusetts, 1780–1833*. Amherst: University of Massachusetts Press, 1998.

Fink, Zera S. *The Classical Republicans*. Evanston: Northwestern University Press, 1945.

Finkelman, Paul. "The Founding Fathers and Slavery: Making A Covenant With Death," *Beyond Confederation*. Ed. Richard R. Beeman et al. Chapel Hill: University of North Carolina Press, 1986, pp. 188–225.

Fischer, David Hackett. "The Myth of the Essex Junto." *William and Mary Quarterly*, 3d ser., 21 (April 1964): 191–235.

_____. *The Revolution of American Conservatism: The Federalist Party in the Era of Jeffersonian Democracy*. New York: Harper and Row, 1965.

Fladeland, Betty L. "Compensated Emancipation: A Rejected Alternative." *Journal of Southern History* 42 (May 1976): 169–186.

Forbes, Robert P. *The Missouri Compromise and its Aftermath: Slavery and the Meaning of America*. Chapel Hill: University of North Carolina Press, 2006.

_____. "Slavery and the Meaning of America, 1819–1837." Ph.D. dissertation, Yale University, 1994.

Formisano, Ronald P. *The Transformation of Political Culture: Massachusetts Parties, 1790s-1840s*. New York: Oxford University Press, 1983.

Fortenbaugh, William W. *Aristotle on Emotions* (New York: Barnes & Noble, 1975).

Fowler, Robert B. "Mythologizing of a Founder," in *Thomas Jefferson and the Politics of Nature*. Ed. Thomas S. Engeman. Notre Dame: University of Notre Dame Press, 2000.

Frankel, Jeffrey A. "The 1807–1809 Embargo Against Great Britain." *Journal of Economic History* 42, no. 2 (1982): 291–308.

Fraser, James W. "The Beginning of Theological Education at Andover." *Historical Journal of Massachusetts* 13 (June 1985): 101–116.

_____. *Pedagogue for God's Kingdom: Lyman Beecher and the Second Great Awakening*. Lanham, Md.: Rowman Littlefield, 1988.

Freehling, William W. "The Louisiana Purchase and the Coming of the Civil War." Chap. 3 of *The Louisiana Purchase and American Expansion, 1803–1898*. Ed. Sanford Levinson and Bartholomew H. Sparrow. Lanham, Md.: Rowman Littlefield, 2005, pp. 69–82.

_____. *Road to Disunion: Volume 1: Secessionists at Bay, 1776–1854*. New York: Oxford University Press, 1990.

Fry, Joseph A. *Dixie Looks Abroad: The South and U.S. Foreign Relations, 1789–1973*. Baton Rouge: Louisiana State University Press, 2002.

Gaines, William H. Jr., *Thomas Mann Randolph, Jr.: Jefferson's Son-in-Law*. Baton Rouge: Louisiana State University Press, 1966.

Gannon, Kevin M. "Escaping 'Mr. Jefferson's Plan of Destruction': New England Federalists and the Idea of a Northern Confederacy, 1803–1804." *Journal of the Early Republic* 21, no. 3 (Fall 2001): 413–443.

Garraty, John A., ed. *American National Biography*. 24 vols. New York: Oxford University Press, 1999.

Gellman, David N. *Emancipating New York: The Politics of Slavery and Freedom, 1777–1827*. Baton Rouge: Louisiana State University Press, 2006.

Genovese, Eugene D. "Yeomen Farmers in a Slaveholders' Democracy." *Agricultural History* 49, no. 2 (Spring 1975): 331–342.

Gilbert, Felix. *To the Farewell Address: Ideas of Early American Foreign Policy*. Princeton: Princeton University Press, 1961.

Goodman, Paul. *The Democratic-Republicans of Massachusetts: Politics in a Young Republic*. Cambridge: Harvard University Press, 1964.

Graffagnino, J. Kevin s.v., "Robinson, Moses," in *American National Biography*.

Graber, Mark A. "Federalist or Friends of Adams: The Marshall Court and Party Politics." *Studies in American Political Development* 12, no. 2 (Oct. 1998): 229–266.

Grasso, Christopher. *A Speaking Aristocracy: Transforming Public Discourse in Eighteenth-Century Connecticut*. Chapel Hill: University of North Carolina Press, 1999.

Greenberg, Amy S. *A Wicked War: Polk, Clay, Lincoln, and the 1846 U.S. Invasion of Mexico*. New York: Knopf, 2012.

Gummere, Richard M. "The Classical Ancestry of the United States Constitution." *American Quarterly* 14 (Spring 1962): 3–18.

Gutzman, K. R. Constantine. "The Virginia and Kentucky Resolutions Reconsidered: An Appeal to the 'Real Laws' of Our Country." *Journal of Southern History* 66 (Aug. 2000): 473–96.

Hahn, Steven. *Political Worlds of Slavery and Freedom*. Cambridge: Harvard University Press, 2009.

Hall, Van Beck. *Politics Without Parties: Massachusetts, 1780–1791*. Pittsburgh: University of Pittsburgh Press, 1972.

Hamilton, Milton W. "Augustus C. Buell: Fraudulent Historian." *Pennsylvania Magazine of History and Biography* 80, no. 4 (Oct. 1956): 478–93.

Hanyan, Craig R. "DeWitt Clinton and Partisanship: The Development of Clintonianism from 1812 to 1820." *New-York Historical Society Quarterly* 56, no. 2 (1972): 108–131.

Harris, Marshall D. *Origin of the Land Tenure System in the United States*. Ames: Iowa State University Press, 1953.

Harrison, Joseph H., Jr., "*Sic et Non*: Thomas Jefferson and Internal Improvement," *Journal of the Early Republic* 7 (Winter 1987): 335–349.

Haskins, George Lee. "The Beginnings of Partible Inheritance in the American Colonies," *Yale Law Journal* 51, no. 8 (June 1942): 1280–1315.

Hatch, Nathan. *The Democratization of American Christianity*. New Haven: Yale University Press, 1989.

_____. *The Sacred Cause of Liberty: Republican Thought and the Millennium in Revolutionary New England*. New Haven: Yale University Press, 1977.

Hatzenbuehler, Ronald L. "Growing Weary in Well-Doing: Thomas Jefferson's Life Among the Virginia Gentry," *Virginia Magazine of History and Biography* 101 (Jan. 1993): 5–36;

_____. "'Refreshing the Tree of Liberty with the Blood of Patriots and Tyrants': Thomas Jefferson and the Origins of the U.S. Constitution," in *Essays on Liberty and Federalism: The Shaping of the U.S. Constitution*. Ed. John M. Murrin and David E. Narrett. College Station: Texas A & M University, 1988, 88–104.

Heale, M. J. *The Presidential Quest: Candidates and Images in American Political Culture, 1787–1852*. London: Longman, 1982.

Hellenbrand, Harold. *The Unfinished Revolution: Education and Politics in the Thought of Thomas Jefferson*. Newark: University of Delaware Press, 1990.

Helo, Ari. *Thomas Jefferson's Ethics and the Politics of Human Progress: the Morality of a Slaveholder*. New York: Cambridge University Press, 2014.

Henderson, Herbert James. *Party Politics in the Continental Congress*. New York: McGraw-Hill, 1974.

_____. "Taxation and Political Culture: Massachusetts and Virginia, 1760–1800." *William and Mary Quarterly*, 3rd ser., 47, no. 1(January 1990): 90–114.

Henretta, James A. "Families and Farms: *Mentalité* in Pre-Industrial America." *William and Mary Quarterly* 3rd ser., 35 (Jan. 1978): 3–32.

Heyrman, Christine L. *Southern Cross: The Beginnings of the Bible Belt*. New York: Knopf, 1997.

Hickey, Donald R. "American Trade Restrictions during the War of 1812." *Journal of American History* 68, no. 3 (Dec. 1981): 517–538.

_____. "New England's Defense Problem and the Genesis of the Hartford Convention." *New England Quarterly* 50 (Dec. 1977): 587–604.

_____. *The War of 1812: A Forgotten Conflict*. Urbana: University of Illinois Press, 1989.

Higham, Robin D. S. "The Port of Boston and the Embargo, 1807–1809." *American Neptune* 16, no. 3 (1956): 189–210.

Hofstadter, Richard. *The Idea of a Party System: The Rise of Legitimate Opposition in the United States, 1780–1840*. Berkeley: University of California Press, 1969.

Hogue, William M. "The Civil Disability of Ministers of Religion in State Constitutions." *Journal of Church and State* 36 (Spring 1994): 329–55.

Honeywell, Roy J. "President Jefferson and his Successor." *American Historical Review*, 46 (1940): 64–75.

Hood, Fred J. *Reformed America: The Middle and Southern States, 1783–1837*. Tuscaloosa: University of Alabama Press, 1980.

Hopkins, Joseph G. E., ed. *Concise Dictionary of American Biography*. 2d edition. New York: Scribner, 1977.

Horsman, Reginald *The War of 1812*. New York: Knopf, 1969.

Howe, Daniel Walker. *Political Culture of the American Whigs*. Chicago: University of Chicago Press, 1979.

_____. *The Unitarian Conscience: Harvard Moral Philosophy, 1805–1861*. Middletown, Conn.: Wesleyan University Press, 1988.

_____. *What Hath God Wrought? The Transformation of America, 1815–1848*. New York: Oxford University Press, 2007.

Howe, John R., Jr. *The Changing Political Thought of John Adams*. Princeton: Princeton University Press, 1966.

_____. "John Adams's Views of Slavery." *Journal of Negro History* 49 (July 1964): 201–206.

Hutson, James H. *Church and State in America: The First Two Centuries*. Cambridge: Cambridge University Press, 2008.

_____. *Forgotten Features of the Founding*. Lanham, Md.: Rowman and Littlefield, 2003.

_____. *John Adams and the Diplomacy of the American Revolution*. Lexington: University Press of Kentucky, 1980.

_____. "The Origins of 'The Paranoid Style in American Politics': Public Jealousy from the Age of Walpole to the Age of Jackson," in *Saints and Revolutionaries: Essays on Early American History*. Ed. David D. Hall et al. New York: Norton, 1984, 332–372.

_____. "Thomas Jefferson's Letter to the Danbury Baptists: A Controversy Rejoined." *William and Mary Quarterly* 56, no. 4 (Oct. 1999): 775–790.

Imholt, Robert J. "Timothy Dwight, Federalist Pope of Connecticut." *New England Quarterly*, 73 (Sept. 2000): 386–411.

Isenberg, Nancy. *Fallen Founder: The Life of Aaron Burr*. New York: Viking, 2007.

Jensen, Merrill. *The New Nation: A History of the United States during the Confederation, 1781–1789*. New York: Knopf, 1950.

Johnson, Allen, and Dumas Malone. *Dictionary of American Biography*. 20 vols. New York: Scribner, 1928–1936.

Jones, Douglas Lamar. "'The Caprice of Juries': The Enforcement of the Jeffersonian Embargo in Massachusetts." *American Journal of Legal History* 24, no. 4 (Oct. 1980): 307–330.

Jordan, Daniel P. *Political Leadership in Jefferson's Virginia*. Charlottesville: University Press of Virginia, 1983.

Kaplan, Lawrence S. "France and Madison's Decision for War, 1812." *Mississippi Valley Historical Review* 50, no. 4 (March 1964): 652–671.

_____. "Jefferson as Anglophile: Sagacity or Senility in the Era of Good Feelings." *Diplomatic History* 16, no. 3 (July 1992): 487–494.

_____. "Toward Isolationism: The Rise and Fall of the Franco-American Alliance, 1775–1801," in Kaplan, *Entangling Alliances With None: American Foreign Policy in the Age of Jefferson*. Kent, Ohio: Kent State University Press, 1987, pp. 79–95.

Keller, Charles R. *The Second Great Awakening in Connecticut*. New Haven: Yale University Press, 1942.

Keller, Kenneth W. *Rural Politics and the Collapse of Pennsylvania Federalism*. Philadelphia: American Philosophical Society, 1982. [*Transactions of the American Philosophical Society*, Vol. 72, Pt. 6].

Ketcham, Ralph. "James Madison and the Nature of Man." *Journal of the History of Ideas* 19, no. 1 (Jan. 1958): 62–76.

_____. *Presidents Above Party: The First American Presidency, 1789–1829*. Chapel Hill: University of North Carolina Press, 1984.

Keyssar, Alexander. *The Right to Vote: The Contested History of Democracy in the United States*. New York: Basic Books, 2000.

Kirby, John B. "Early American Politics: The Search for Ideology: An Historiographical Analysis and Critique of the Concept of Deference." *Journal of Politics* 32 (Nov. 1970): 808–838.

Koch, Adrienne. *Jefferson and Madison: The Great Collaboration.* New York: Knopf, 1950.

———. *Philosophy of Thomas Jefferson.* New York: Columbia University Press, 1943.

Kramnick, Isaac. *Bolingbroke and his Circle: The Politics of Nostalgia in the Age of Walpole.* Cambridge: Harvard University Press, 1968

Kurtz, Stephen G. *The Presidency of John Adams: The Collapse of Federalism, 1795–1800.* Philadelphia: University of Pennsylvania Press, 1957.

LaCroix, Alison L. "'A Singular and Awkward War': The Transatlantic Context of the Hartford Convention." *American Nineteenth-Century History* 6 (March 2005): 3–32.

Latimer, Margaret K. "South Carolina: A Protagonist of the War of 1812." *American Historical Review* 61, no. 4 (June 1956): 914–929.

Leibiger, Stuart. "Thomas Jefferson and the Missouri Crisis: An Alternative Interpretation." *Journal of the Early Republic* 17 (Spring 1997): 121–30.

Lerche, Charles O. Jr., "Jefferson and the Election of 1800: A Case Study in the Political Smear." *William and Mary Quarterly* 3rd ser., 5 (Oct. 1948): 467–491,

Levy, Leonard W. *Jefferson and Civil Liberties: The Darker Side.* Cambridge: Harvard University Press, 1963.

Lewis, Jan, and Peter S. Onuf. "American Synecdoche: Thomas Jefferson as Image, Icon, Character, and Self." *American Historical Review* 103 (Feb.1998): 125–136.

Lewis, Robert E. "Ashbel Green, 1762–1848: Preacher, Educator, Editor." *Journal of the Presbyterian Historical Society* 36, no. 3 (1957): 141–156.

Lienesch, Michael. *New Order of the Ages: Time, the Constitution, and the Making of Modern American Political Thought.* Princeton: Princeton University Press, 1988.

Litwack, Leon F. *North of Slavery: The Negro in the Free States, 1790–1860.* Chicago: University of Chicago Press, 1961.

Livermore, Shaw, Jr., *The Twilight of Federalism: The Disintegration of the Federalist Party, 1815–1830.* Princeton: Princeton University Press, 1962.

Lockridge, Kenneth. "Land, Population, and the Evolution of New England Society." *Past and Present* 39 (April 1968): 62–80.

Logan, Rayford W. *Diplomatic Relations of the United States with Haiti, 1776–1891.* Chapel Hill: University of North Carolina Press, 1941.

Long, Orie W. *Thomas Jefferson and George Ticknor: A Chapter in American Scholarship.* Williamstown, Mass.: McClelland Press, 1933.

Lynd, Staughton. *Class Conflict, Slavery, and the U.S. Constitution: Ten Essays.* Indianapolis: Bobbs-Merrill, 1967.

Maier, Pauline. *American Scripture: Making the Declaration of Independence.* New York: Knopf, 1997.

———. *The Old Revolutionaries: Political Lives in the Age of Samuel Adams.* New York: Knopf, 1980.

Main, Gloria L. "Inequality in Early America: The Evidence from Probate Records in Massachusetts and Maryland." *Journal of Interdisciplinary History* 7, no. 4 (April 1977): 559–581.

Main, Jackson Turner. *The Antifederalists: Critics of the Constitution, 1781–1788.* Chapel Hill: University of North Carolina Press, 1961.

———. "Distribution of Property in Post-Revolutionary Virginia." *Mississippi Valley Historical Review* 41, no. 2 (Sept. 1954): 241–258.

———. "The One Hundred." *William and Mary Quarterly*, 3d ser., 11, no. 3 (July 1954): 355–384.

———. *Society and the Economy in Colonial Connecticut.* Princeton: Princeton University Press, 1985.

———. *The Sovereign States, 1775–1783.* New York: Franklin Watts, 1973.

Malanson, Jeffrey J. "'If I Had it in His Hand Writing I Would Burn It': Federalists and the Authorship Controversy over George Washington's Farewell Address, 1808–1809." *Journal of the Early Republic* 34, no. 2 (Summer 2014): 219–242.

Malone, Dumas. *Jefferson and the Ordeal of Liberty.* Boston: Little, Brown, 1962.

———. *Jefferson and the Rights of Man.* Boston: Little, Brown, 1951.

———. *Jefferson the President: First Term, 1801–1805.* Boston: Little, Brown, 1970.

———. *Jefferson the Virginian.* Boston: Little, Brown, 1948.

———. "Mr. Jefferson's Private Life." *Proceedings of the American Antiquarian Society* 84 (1974): 65–72.

———. *Sage of Monticello;* vol. 6 of *Jefferson and His Time.* Boston: Little, Brown, 1981.

Marshall, Lynn. "The Strange Stillbirth of the Whig Party." *American Historical Review* 72, no. 2 (January 1967): 445–468.

Martell, J.S. "A Sidelight on Federalist Strategy during the War of 1812." *American Historical Review* 43, no. 3 (April 1938): 553–566.

Marvick, Elizabeth W. "Jefferson's Personality and his Politics," *Psychohistory Review*, 25, no. 2 (1997), 127–163.

Matthews, Richard K. *If Men Were Angels: James Madison and the Heartless Empire of Reason.* Lawrence: University Press of Kansas, 1995.

_____. *The Radical Politics of Thomas Jefferson: A Revisionist View* Lawrence: University Press of Kansas, 1984.

Matthewson, Timothy M. "George Washington's Policy toward the Haitian Revolution." *Diplomatic History* 3 (Summer 1979): 321–36.

May, Henry F. *The Enlightenment in America*. New York: Oxford University Press, 1976.

Mayo, Bernard. *Myths and Men: Patrick Henry, George Washington, Thomas Jefferson*. Athens: University of Georgia Press, 1959.

McColley, Robert. *Slavery and Jeffersonian Virginia*. Urbana: University of Illinois Press, 1964.

McCormick, Richard P. *The Second American Party System*. Chapel Hill: University of North Carolina Press, 1966.

McCoy, Drew. *The Elusive Republic: Political Economy in Jeffersonian America*. Chapel Hill: University of North Carolina Press, 1980.

McCullough, David. *John Adams*. New York: Simon & Schuster, 2001.

McDonald, Robert M. S. "Thomas Jefferson and Historical Self-Construction: The Earth Belongs to the Living?" *The Historian* 61, no. 2 (Winter 1999): 289–310.

_____. "West Point's Lost Founder: Jefferson Remembered, Forgotten, and Reconsidered." In *Thomas Jefferson's Military Academy: Founding West Point*. Ed. Robert M. S. McDonald. Charlottesville: University of Virginia Press, 2004.

McDonnell, Michael A. *The Politics of War*. Chapel Hill: University of North Carolina Press, 2007.

McGlone, Robert E. "Deciphering Memory: John Adams and the Authorship of the Declaration of Independence." *Journal of American History*, 85, no. 2 (Sept. 1998): 411–438.

McLachlan, James. *Princetonians, 1748–1768: A Biographical Dictionary*. Princeton: Princeton University Press, 1976.

Mead, Sidney E. *The Lively Experiment*. New York: Harper and Row, 1963.

Miller, Charles A. *Jefferson and Nature: An Interpretation*. Baltimore: Johns Hopkins Press, 1988.

Mirkin, Harris G. "Rebellion, Revolution, and the Constitution: Thomas Jefferson's Theory of Civil Disobedience." *American Studies* 13 (Fall 1972): 61–74.

Mooney, Chase C. *William H. Crawford, 1772–1834*. Lexington: University Press of Kentucky, 1974.

Moore, Glover. *The Missouri Controversy, 1819–1821*. Lexington: University Press of Kentucky, 1953.

Moore, John Hammond. "Jared Sparks in Georgia." *Georgia Historical Quarterly* 47 (1963): 425–35.

_____. "Jared Sparks in North Carolina." *North Carolina Historical Review* 40 (1963): 283–94

_____. "Jared Sparks in South Carolina." *South Carolina Historical Magazine* 72 (1971): 150–60.

Morris, Richard B. "Primogeniture and Entailed Estates in America." *Columbia Law Review* 27 (January 1927): 24–51.

_____. *Studies in the History of American Law*. New York: Columbia University Press, 1930.

Mott, Frank L. *History of American Magazines, 1741–1850*. Cambridge: Harvard University Press, 1966.

Mulder, Philip N. *A Controversial Spirit: Evangelical Awakenings in the South*. New York: Oxford University Press, 2002.

Murray, Craig C. *Benjamin Vaughan (1751–1835): The Life of an Anglo-American Intellectual*. New York: Arno Press, 1982.

Murray, Craig Compton. "Benjamin Vaughan (1751–1835): The Life of an Anglo-American Intellectual." Ph.D. diss., Columbia University, 1989

Nash, Gary B. "The American Clergy and the French Revolution." *William and Mary Quarterly*, 3rd ser., 22 (July 1965): 392–412.

Nathans, Sydney. *Daniel Webster and Jacksonian Democracy*. Baltimore: Johns Hopkins University Press, 1973.

Neem, Johann N. "Beyond the Wall: Reinterpreting Jefferson's Danbury Address." *Journal of the Early Republic* 27 (Spring 2007): 139–154

Newman, Richard S. *Transformation of American Abolitionism*. Chapel Hill: University of North Carolina Press, 2002.

O'Brien, Conor Cruise. *The Long Affair: Thomas Jefferson and the French Revolution, 1785–1800*. Chicago: University of Chicago Press, 1996.

Olsen, Otto H. "Historians and the Extent of Slave Ownership in the United States." *Civil War History* 50, no. 4 (Dec. 2004): 401–17.

Onuf, Peter S. "Domesticating the Captive Nation: Thomas Jefferson and the Problem of Slavery," in *Jefferson, Lincoln, and Wilson: The American Dilemma of Race and Democracy*. Ed. John Milton Cooper, Jr. and Thomas J. Knock. Charlottesville: University of Virginia Press, 2010.

_____. *Jefferson's Empire: The Language of American Nationhood*. Charlottesville: University Press of Virginia, 2000.

_____. "Thomas Jefferson, Missouri, and the 'Empire of Liberty,'" in *Thomas Jefferson and the Changing West: From Conquest to Conservation*. Ed. James P. Ronda. Albuquerque and St. Louis: University of New Mexico Press and Missouri Historical Society, 1997), pp. 111–53.

_____. "To Declare them a Free and Independant People': Race, Slavery, and National Identity in Jefferson's Thought." *Journal of the Early Republic* 18, no. 1 (Spring 1998): 1–46.

Onuf, Nicholas G., and Peter S. *Nations, Markets, and War: Modern History and the American Civil War*. Charlottesville: University of Virginia Press, 2007.

Page, Anthony. "'A Species of Slavery': Richard Price's Rational Dissent and Antislavery," *Slavery and Abolition* 32 (March 2011): 53–73.

Palmer, Robert R. *Age of the Democratic Revolution.* 2 vols. Princeton: Princeton University Press, 1959–64.

Parkinson, Robert G. "First From the Right: Massive Resistance and the Image of Thomas Jefferson in the 1950s." *Virginia Magazine of History and Biography* 112 (2004): 2–35.

Parton, James. *Life of Andrew Jackson.* 3 vols. New York: Mason Brothers, 1860.

Pasley, Jeffrey L. "The Cheese and the Words: Popular Political Culture and Participatory Democracy in the Early American Republic," in *Beyond the Founders: New Approaches to the Political History of the Early American Republic.* Ed. Jeffrey L. Pasley, Andrew W. Robertson, and David Waldstreicher. Chapel Hill: University of North Carolina Press, 2004, pp. 31–56.

_____. "Politics and the Misadventures of Thomas Jefferson's Modern Reputation: A Review Essay." *Journal of Southern History* 72 (Nov. 2006): 871–908.

_____. *'The Tyranny of Printers': Newspaper Politics in the Early American Republic.* Charlottesville: University Press of Virginia, 2001.

Patterson, Stephen E. "The Federalist Reaction to Shays' Rebellion," in *In Debt to Shays: The Bicentennial of an Agrarian Insurrection.* Ed. Robert A. Gross. Charlottesville: University of Virginia Press, 1993.

Perkins, Bradford. *Castlereagh and Adams: England and the United States, 1812–1823.* Berkeley and Los Angeles: University of California Press, 1964.

Peterson, Merrill D. *Jefferson Image in the American Mind.* New York: Oxford University Press, 1960.

_____. *Thomas Jefferson and the New Nation: A Biography.* New York: Oxford University Press, 1970.

Pocock, J. G. A. *The Machiavellian Moment: Florentine Political Thought and the Atlantic Republican Tradition.* Princeton: Princeton University Press, 1975.

Pole, J. R. "Historians and the Problem of Early American Democracy." *American Historical Review* 67, no. 3 (April 1962): 626–646.

Polgar, Paul J. "'Whenever They Judge it Expedient': The Politics of Partisanship and Free Black Voting Rights in Early National New York." *American Nineteenth Century History* 12, no. 1 (March 2001): 1–23.

Polishook, Irving. *Rhode Island and the Union, 1774–1795.* Evanston: Northwestern University Press, 1969.

Potts, Louis W. "Manasseh Cutler, Lobbyist." *Ohio History* 96 (Summer/Autumn 1987): 101–123.

Prince, Carl E. *The Federalists and the Origins of the U.S. Civil Service.* New York: New York University Press, 1977.

_____. "The Passing of the Aristocracy: Jefferson's Removal of the Federalists, 1801–1805." *Journal of American History* 57, no. 3 (Dec. 1970): 563–575.

Pruitt, Bettye Hobbs. "Self-Sufficiency and the Agricultural Economy of Eighteenth-Century Massachusetts." *William and Mary Quarterly* 3rd ser., 32, no. 3 (July 1984): 333–364.

Pybus, Cassandra. "Jefferson and Slavery." In *Wiley-Blackwell Companion to Thomas Jefferson.* Ed. Francis D. Cogliano. Malden, Mass.: Wiley-Blackwell, 2012, pp. 271–283.

Ragosta, John A. *Religious Freedom: Jefferson's Legacy, America's Creed.* Charlottesville: University of Virginia Press, 2013.

Ray, Kristofer. "The Corrupt Bargain and the Rise of the Jacksonian Movement, 1825–1828," in *Age of Andrew Jackson.* Ed. Brian D. McKnight and James S. Humphreys. Kent, Ohio: Kent State University Press, 2011, pp. 22–35.

Reinhold, Meyer. "Classical Influences and Eighteenth-Century American Political Thought," in Reinhold, *Classica Americana.* Detroit: Wayne State University Press, 1984, pp. 94–115.

Remini, Robert V. *Daniel Webster: The Man and his Time.* New York: Norton, 1997.

_____. *Henry Clay: Spokesman for the Union.* New York: Norton, 1991.

Richard, Carl J. *The Founders and the Classics.* Cambridge: Harvard University Press, 1994.

Richards, Leonard L. *The Slave Power: The Free North and Southern Domination, 1780–1860.* New York: Oxford University Press, 2000.

Riley, Padraig G. "Northern Republicans and Southern Slavery: Democracy in the Age of Jefferson, 1800–1819." Ph.D. dissertation, University of California, Berkeley, 2007.

Robbins, Caroline. "'Discordant Parties': A Study of the Acceptance of Party Among Englishmen." *Political Science Quarterly* 73 (Dec. 1958): 505–529.

Robinson, William Alexander. *Jeffersonian Democracy in New England.* New Haven: Yale University Press, 1916.

Roeber, Anthony G. *Faithful Magistrates and Republican Lawyers: Creators of Virginia Legal Culture, 1680–1810.* Chapel Hill: University of North Carolina Press, 1981.

Rogers, Pat. "Swift and Bolingbroke on Faction." *Journal of British Studies* 9 (May 1970): 71–101.

Ronda, James P. "Jefferson and the Imperial West." *Journal of the West* 31 (July 1992): 13–19.

Rosenthal, Bernard "Puritan Conscience and New England Slavery." *New England Quarterly* 46 (1973): 62–81.

Royster, Charles. *Light Horse Harry Lee and the Legacy of the American Revolution.* New York: Knopf, 1981.

Rutland, Robert A. *The Presidency of James Madison.* Lawrence: University Press of Kansas, 1990.

Salter, Mary Ann. "George Flower Comes to the Illinois Country: A New Look at Motivations." *Journal of the Illinois Historical Society,* 69, no. 3 (August 1976): 213–223.

Sassi, Jonathan D. "The First Party Competition and Southern New England's Public Christianity." *Journal of the Early Republic* 21, no. 2 (Summer 2001): 261–299.

Scherr, Arthur. "Arms and Men: The Diplomacy of US Weapons Traffic with Saint-Domingue under Adams and Jefferson." *International History Review* 35, no. 3 (2013): 600–648.

_____. "Inventing the Patriot President: Bache's *Aurora* and John Adams." *Pennsylvania Magazine of History and Biography* 119 (Oct. 1995): 369–399.

_____. "James Monroe on the Presidency and 'Foreign Influence': From the Virginia Ratifying Convention (1788) to Jefferson's Election (1801)." *Mid-America: An Historical Review* 84 (2002): 145–206.

_____. "Jefferson's 'Cannibals' Revisited: A Closer Look at his Notorious Phrase." *Journal of Southern History* 77, no. 2 (May 2011): 251–282.

_____. "John Adams and Thomas Jefferson's Constitutionalism in the 1780s: A Reappraisal." *Mid-America: An Historical Review*, 83 (Fall 2001): 215–282.

_____. "John Adams, Providential Rhetoric and Party Warfare: A Note on Massachusetts Politics in the Late 1790s." *Mid-America: An Historical Review*, 73 (Jan. 1991): 7–27.

_____. "Light at the End of the Road: Thomas Jefferson's Endorsement of Free Haiti in His Final Years." *Journal of Haitian Studies* 15 (2009): 203–216.

_____. "The Limits of Republican Ideology: James Monroe in Thermidorian Paris, 1794–1796." *Mid-America: An Historical Review* 79 (Winter 1997): 5–45.

_____. "'The Most Agreeable Country': New Light on Democratic-Republican Opinion of Massachusetts in the 1790s." *Historical Journal of Massachusetts* 35, no. 2 (Summer 2007): 148–166.

_____. "Thomas Jefferson versus the Historians: Christianity, Atheistic Morality, and the Afterlife." *Church History* 83, no. 1 (March 2014): 60–109.

_____. *Thomas Jefferson's Haitian Policy: Myths and Realities*. Lanham, Md.: Lexington Books, 2011.

_____. "Thomas Jefferson's Nationalist Vision of New England and the War of 1812." *Historian*, 69, no. 1 (Spring 2007): 1–35.

_____. "Thomas Jefferson's 'Poor Woman': A Symbol of Sentiment or Social Inequality?" *Midwest Quarterly* 39, no. 3 (Spring 1998): 329–346.

Schlesinger, Arthur M., Jr., *Age of Jackson*. Boston: Houghton Mifflin, 1945.

Schulz, Constance B. "John Adams on 'the Best of All Possible Worlds.'" *Journal of the History of Ideas* 44, no. 4 (Oct.-Dec.1983): 561–77.

_____. "'Of Bigotry in Politics and Religion': Jefferson's Religion, the Federalist Press, and the *Syllabus*." *Virginia Magazine of History and Biography* 91, no. 1 (January 1983): 73–91.

Schoen, Brian W. "Calculating the Price of Union: Republican Economic Nationalism and the Origins of Southern Sectionalism, 1790–1828." *Journal of the Early Republic* 23, no. 2 (Summer 2003): 173–206.

Scofield, Merry Ellen. "The Fatigues of His Table: The Politics of Presidential Dining During the Jefferson Administration." *Journal of the Early Republic* 26, no. 3 (Fall 2006): 449–469.

Sears, Louis Martin. *Jefferson and the Embargo*. Durham: Duke University Press, 1927.

_____. "The South and the Embargo." *South Atlantic Quarterly* 20 (July 1921): 254–275.

Sehat, David. *Myth of American Religious Freedom*. New York: Oxford University Press, 2011.

Sellers, Charles G. *The Market Revolution: Jacksonian America, 1815–1846*. New York: Oxford University Press, 1991.

Shackelford, George Green. *Jefferson's Adoptive Son: The Life of William Short, 1759–1848*. Lexington: University Press of Kentucky, 1993.

Shalhope, Robert E. *John Taylor of Caroline: Pastoral Republican*. Columbia: University of South Carolina Press, 1980.

Shalhope, Robert E. "Thomas Jefferson's Republicanism and Antebellum Southern Thought." *Journal of Southern History* 42 (Nov. 1976): 529–56.

Sharp, James Roger. *American Politics in the Early Republic: The New Nation in Crisis*. New Haven: Yale University Press, 1993.

_____. "Unraveling the Mystery of Jefferson's Letter of April 27, 1795." *Journal of the Early Republic* 6 (Winter 1986): 411–18;

Shaw, Peter. *The Character of John Adams*. Chapel Hill: University of North Carolina Press, 1976.

Sheidley, Harlow W. *Sectional Nationalism: Massachusetts Conservative Leaders and the Transformation of America, 1815–1836*. Boston: Northeastern University Press, 1998.

Sheldon, Garrett Ward. *The Political Philosophy of Thomas Jefferson*. Baltimore: Johns Hopkins University Press, 1991.

Sheridan, Eugene R. "Thomas Jefferson and the Giles Resolutions." *William and Mary Quarterly*, 3rd ser., 49 (Oct. 1992): 589–608.

Siry, Steven Edwin. "The Sectional Politics of 'Practical Republicanism': DeWitt Clinton's Presidential Bid, 1810–1812." *Journal of the Early Republic* 5, no. 4 (Winter 1985): 441–462.

Skeen, C. Edward. *Citizen Soldiers of the War of 1812*. Lexington: University Press of Kentucky, 1999.

Slonim, Shlomo. "The Founders' Fears of Foreign Influence." *Mid-America: An Historical Review* 81 (Summer 1999): 125–146.

_____. "Securing States' Interests at the 1787 Constitutional Convention: A Reassessment." *Studies in American Political Development* 14, no.1 (Spring 2000): 1–14,

Smelser, Marshall. "George Washington and the Alien and Sedition Acts." *American Historical Review* 59, no. 2 (Feb. 1954): 322–334.

Smith, Gene Allen. *For the Purposes of Defense: The Politics of the Jeffersonian Gunboat Program.* Newark: University of Delaware Press, 1996.

Smith, James Morton. *Freedom's Fetters.* Ithaca: Cornell University Press, 1956.

Smith, Jeffery A. *Franklin and Bache: Envisioning the Enlightened Republic.* New York: Oxford University Press, 1991.

Snyder, Kim Alan. "Foundations of Liberty: The Christian Republicanism of Timothy Dwight and Jedidiah Morse." *New England Quarterly* 56, no. 3 (Sept. 1983): 382–397.

Sofka, James R. "The Jeffersonian Idea of National Security: Commerce, the Atlantic Balance of Power, and the Barbary War, 1786–1805." *Diplomatic History* 21 (Fall 1997): 519–544.

Spivak, Burton W. *Jefferson's English Crisis.* Charlottesville: University Press of Virginia, 1979.

Stagg, J. C. A. *Mr. Madison's War: Politics, Warfare, and Diplomacy in the Early American Republic, 1783–1830.* Princeton: Princeton University Press, 1983.

Stampp, Kenneth. "The Concept of a Perpetual Union." *Journal of American History* 65, no. 1 (June 1978): 5–33.

_____. *Peculiar Institution: Slavery in the Ante-Bellum South.* 1956; reprinted, New York: Knopf, 1975.

Stannard, David E. *The Puritan Way of Death: Study in Religion, Culture, and Social Change.* New York: Oxford University Press, 1977.

Steele, Brian D. *Thomas Jefferson and American Nationhood.* Cambridge: Cambridge University Press, 2012.

_____. "Thomas Jefferson and the Making of an American Nationalism." Ph.D. dissertation, University of North Carolina at Chapel Hill, 2003.

_____. "Thomas Jefferson, Coercion, and the Limits of Harmonious Union." *Journal of Southern History* 74 (Nov. 2008): 823–854.

Stewart, Donald H. *The Opposition Press of the Federalist Period.* Albany: State University of New York Press, 1969.

_____, and George P. Clark. "Misanthrope or Humanitarian? John Adams in Retirement." *New England Quarterly* 28, no. 2 (June 1955): 216–236.

Striner, Richard. "Political Newtonianism: The Cosmic Model of Politics in Europe and America." *William and Mary Quarterly*, 3d ser., 52 (Oct.1995): 583–604.

Swift, David E. "Thomas Jefferson, John Holt Rice and Education in Virginia, 1815–25." *Journal of Presbyterian History* 49 (1971): 32–58.

Sydnor, Charles S. *Development of Southern Sectionalism, 1819–1848.* Baton Rouge: Louisiana State University Press, 1948.

Sykes, Richard E. "The Changing Class Structure of Unitarian Parishes in Massachusetts, 1780–1880." *Review of Religious Research* 12 (Fall 1970): 26–34.

Tagg, James. *Benjamin Franklin Bache and the Philadelphia Aurora.* Philadelphia: University of Pennsylvania Press, 1991.

Taylor, William Rogers. *Cavalier and Yankee.* New York: George Braziller, 1961.

Thomas, Arthur Dicken, Jr., "Reasonable Revivalism: Presbyterian Evangelization of Educated Virginians, 1787–1837." *Journal of Presbyterian History* 61, no. 3 (Fall 1983): 316–34.

Thomas Jefferson Encyclopedia, s.v., "Rebellion to tyrants is obedience to God." Online.

Thompson, Ernest T. *Presbyterians in the South.* 3 vols. Richmond: John Knox Press, 1963–1973.

Thompson, J. M. *Robespierre.* 2 vols. New York: Appleton-Century, 1936.

Tillson, Albert. "Friendship and Commerce: The Conflict and Coexistence of Values on Virginia's Northern Neck in the Revolutionary Era." *Virginia Magazine of History and Biography* 111(2003): 221–262.

Trees, Andy. *The Founding Fathers and the Politics of Character.* Princeton: Princeton University Press, 2004.

_____. "Private Correspondence for the Public Good: Thomas Jefferson to Elbridge Gerry, 26 January 1799." *Virginia Magazine of History and Biography* 108 (2000): 217–254.

Turner, Lynn W. *William Plumer of New Hampshire.* Chapel Hill: University of North Carolina Press, 1962.

Tyack, David B. *George Ticknor and the Boston Brahmins.* Cambridge: Harvard University Press, 1967.

Van Deusen, Glyndon G. *Thurlow Weed: Wizard of the Lobby.* Boston: Little, Brown, 1947.

Van Fenstermaker, J. and John E. Filer. "The U.S. Embargo Act of 1807: Its Impact on New England Money, Banking, and Economic Activity." *Economic Inquiry,* 28, no. 1 (1990): 163–84.

Varg, Paul A. *New England and Foreign Relations, 1789–1850.* Hanover, N.H.: University Press of New England, 1980.

Wagoner, Jennings L. Jr. "Honor and Dishonor at Mr. Jefferson's University: The Antebellum Years." *History of Education Quarterly* 26 (Summer 1986): 155–179.

Waldstreicher, David. *Slavery's Constitution: From Revolution to Ratification.* New York: Hill and Wang, 2009.

Walters, Raymond, Jr. *Albert Gallatin: Jeffersonian Financier and Diplomat.* New York: Macmillan, 1957.

Walton, Craig. "Hume and Jefferson on the Uses of History," in *Hume: A Re-evaluation.* Ed. Donald W. Livingston. New York: Fordham University Press, 1976, pp. 389–403.

Walton, Priscilla L. *Our Cannibals, Ourselves.* Urbana: University of Illinois Press, 2004.

Warshauer, Matthew. *Andrew Jackson and the Politics of Martial Law.* Knoxville: University of Tennessee Press, 2006.

_____. "Andrew Jackson as a 'Military Chieftain' in the 1824 and 1828 Presidential Elections: The Ramifications of Martial Law on American Republicanism." *Tennessee Historical Quarterly* 57, no. 1 (March 1998): 4–23.

Watts, Steven. *The Republic Reborn: War and the Making of Liberal America, 1790–1820.* Baltimore: Johns Hopkins University Press, 1987.

Wheeler, William Bruce. "Urban Politics in Nature's Republic: The Seaport Cities in the Federalist Era, 1789–1801." Ph.D. dissertation, University of Virginia, 1967.

White, Leonard D. *The Jeffersonians: A Study in Administrative History, 1801–1829.* New York: Macmillan, 1951.

Whitehill, Walter Muir. "The Union of New England and Virginia." *Virginia Quarterly Review* 40, number 4 (Autumn 1964): 516–530.

Wiebe, Robert H. *The Opening of American Society: From the Adoption of the Constitution to the Eve of Disunion.* New York: Knopf, 1984.

Wilentz, Sean. *The Rise of American Democracy: Jefferson to Lincoln.* New York: Norton, 2005.

Williamson, Chilton. *American Suffrage: From Property to Democracy, 1760–1860.* Princeton: Princeton University Press, 1960.

Wills, Garry. *A 'Negro President': Jefferson and the Slave Power.* Boston: Houghton Mifflin, 2003.

Wilson, Douglas L. "Jefferson vs. Hume." *William and Mary Quarterly*, 3rd ser., 46, no. 1 (January 1989): 49–70.

Witte, John. Jr. "A Most Mild and Equitable Establishment of Religion': John Adams and the Massachusetts Experiment." *Journal of Church and State* 41, no. 2 (Spring 1999): 213–252.

Wolf, Joshua. "'To Be Enslaved or Thus Deprived': British Impressment, American Discontent, and the Making of the *Chesapeake-Leopard* Affair, 1803–1807." *War & Society* 29, no. 1 (May 2010): 1–19.

Wood, Gordon S. *The Americanization of Benjamin Franklin.* New York: Penguin Books, 2004.

_____. "Conspiracy and the Paranoid Style: Causality and Deceit in the Eighteenth Century." *William and Mary Quarterly* 39, no. 3 (July, 1982): 401–441.

Wright, Conrad Edick. "The Dedham Case Revisited." Massachusetts Historical Society, *Proceedings* 100 (1988): 15–39.

Wright, Jonathan A. *Shapers of the Great Debate on the Freedom of Religion.* Westport: Greenwood Press, 2005.

Wyatt-Brown, Bertram. *Southern Honor: Ethics and Behavior in the Old South.* New York: Oxford University Press, 1982.

Yarbrough, Jean M. *American Virtues: Thomas Jefferson on the Character of a Free People.* Lawrence: University Press of Kansas, 1998.

_____. "Republicanism Reconsidered: Thoughts on the Foundation and Preservation of the American Republic." *Review of Politics* 41 (Jan. 1979): 61–95.

Young, Alfred F. *The Democratic-Republicans of New York: The Origins, 1763–1797.* Chapel Hill: University of North Carolina Press, 1967.

Zuckerman, Michael. *Peaceable Kingdoms.* New York: Knopf, 1970.

Zuckert, Michael P. "Founder of the Natural Rights Republic," in *Thomas Jefferson and the Politics of Nature.* Ed. Thomas S. Engeman. Notre Dame: University of Notre Dame Press, 2000, pp. 11–58.

_____. *The Natural Rights Republic.* Notre Dame: University of Notre Dame Press, 1996.

Index